ON THE NATURE OF PREJUDICE

This book is dedicated to:

Florence Langone Dovidio
Karen Carr Glick
Robert B. Jorissen

and to Gordon W. Allport

On the Nature of Prejudice

Fifty Years after Allport

Edited by

John F. Dovidio, Peter Glick,
and Laurie A. Rudman

Blackwell
Publishing

BLACKWELL PUBLISHING
350 Main Street, Malden, MA 02148-5020, USA
9600 Garsington Road, Oxford OX4 2DQ, UK
550 Swanston Street, Carlton, Victoria 3053, Australia

First published 2005 by Blackwell Publishing Ltd

1   2005

Library of Congress Cataloging-in-Publication Data

On the nature of prejudice : fifty years after Allport / edited by John F. Dovidio,
Peter Glick, and Laurie A. Rudman.
p. cm.
Includes bibliographical references and indexes.
ISBN-13: 978-1-4051-2750-9 (hardcover : alk. paper)
ISBN-10: 1-4051-2750-3 (hardcover : alk. paper)
ISBN-13: 978-1-4051-2751-6 (pbk. : alk. paper)
ISBN-10: 1-4051-2751-1 (pbk. : alk. paper)
1. Prejudices.   2. Allport, Gordon W. (Gordon Willard), 1897–1967. Nature of
prejudice.   I. Dovidio, John F.   II. Glick, Peter Samuel.   III. Rudman, Laurie A.

BF575.P9062 2005
303.3'85—dc22
2004029764

A catalogue record for this title is available from the British Library.

Set in 10.5/12.5pt Bembo
by Graphicraft Limited, Hong Kong
Printed and bound in Great Britain by TJ International, Padstow, Cornwall

The publisher's policy is to use permanent paper from mills that operate a
sustainable forestry policy, and which has been manufactured from pulp
processed using acid-free and elementary chlorine-free practices. Furthermore,
the publisher ensures that the text paper and cover board used have met acceptable
environmental accreditation standards.

For further information on
Blackwell Publishing, visit our website:
www.blackwellpublishing.com

Contents

Contributors

Frances E. Aboud, Department of Psychology, McGill University, Montréal, Canada.

C. Daniel Batson, Department of Psychology, University of Kansas, Lawrence, USA.

Rupert Brown, Department of Psychology, University of Sussex, UK.

Tracy L. Caldwell, Department of Psychology, University of Illinois, Chicago, USA.

Olivier Corneille, Department of Psychology, Catholic University of Louvain at Louvain-la-Neuve, Belgium.

Christian S. Crandall, Department of Psychology, University of Kansas, Lawrence, USA.

Patricia G. Devine, Department of Psychology, University of Wisconsin, Madison, USA.

Amanda B. Diekman, Department of Psychology, Miami University, Oxford, Ohio, USA.

John F. Dovidio, Department of Psychology, University of Connecticut, Storrs, USA.

John Duckitt, Psychology Department, University of Auckland, New Zealand.

Alice H. Eagly, Department of Psychology, Northwestern University, Evanston, USA.

Victoria M. Esses, Department of Psychology, University of Western Ontario, London, Canada.

Susan T. Fiske, Department of Psychology, Princeton University, USA.

Samuel L. Gaertner, Department of Psychology, University of Delaware, Newark, USA.

Peter Glick, Department of Psychology, Lawrence University, Appleton, USA.

David L. Hamilton, Department of Psychology, University of California, Santa Barbara, USA.

Miles Hewstone, Department of Experimental Psychology, University of Oxford, UK.

Gordon Hodson, Department of Psychology, Brock University, St. Catharine's, Canada.

Mary R. Jackman, Department of Sociology, University of California, Davis, USA.

Lynne M. Jackson, Department of Psychology, King's University College, the University of Western Ontario, London, Canada.

James M. Jones, Department of Psychology, University of Delaware, Newark, USA.

John T. Jost, Department of Psychology, New York University, USA.

Charles M. Judd, Department of Psychology, University of Colorado, Boulder, USA.

Jared B. Kenworthy, Department of Experimental Psychology, University of Oxford, UK.

Tirza Leader, Department of Psychology, Syracuse University, USA.

Diane M. Mackie, Department of Psychology, University of California, Santa Barbara, USA.

Brenda Major, Department of Psychology, University of California, Santa Barbara, USA.

Brian Mullen, Department of Psychology, Syracuse University, USA.

Leonard S. Newman, Department of Psychology, University of Illinois, Chicago, USA.

Bernadette Park, Department of Psychology, University of Colorado, Boulder, USA.

Thomas F. Pettigrew, Department of Psychology, University of California, Santa Cruz, USA.

Laurie A. Rudman, Department of Psychology, Rutgers University, New Brunswick, USA.

David O. Sears, Department of Psychology, University of California, Los Angeles, USA.

Eliot R. Smith, Department of Psychology, Indiana University, Bloomington, USA.

Charles Stangor, Department of Psychology, University of Maryland, College Park, USA.

Cookie White Stephan, Department of Sociology and Anthropology, New Mexico State University, Las Cruces, USA.

Walter G. Stephan, Department of Psychology, New Mexico State University, Las Cruces, USA.

E. L. Stocks, Department of Psychology, University of Kansas, Lawrence, USA.

Linda R. Tropp, Department of Psychology, Boston College, USA.

Rhiannon N. Turner, Department of Experimental Psychology, University of Oxford, UK.

S. Brooke Vick, Department of Psychology, University of California, Santa Barbara, USA.

Alberto Voci, Department of Psychology, University of Padova, Italy.

Vincent Yzerbyt, Department of Psychology, Catholic University of Louvain at Louvain-la-Neuve, Belgium.

Hanna Zagefka, Department of Psychology, University of Sussex, UK.

Foreword

The Society for the Psychological Study of Social Issues (SPSSI) is very pleased to sponsor *On the Nature of Prejudice*. This book is very timely, marking the 50th anniversary of Allport's *The Nature of Prejudice*, first published in 1954. Allport's *The Nature of Prejudice* has been extremely influential in defining the direction that the field of psychology has taken over the course of the last 50 years. Not only does the current volume update Allport's work, but it reexamines fundamental concepts and themes that were central to *The Nature of Prejudice* and are of enduring importance. The editors and authors are respected leaders in the field, and in this volume have constructed comprehensive theories that clarify concepts, synthesize complex research results, and generate new directions for future research. Thus, just as *The Nature of Prejudice* provided a framework for examining prejudice in the last 50 years, the current volume is likely to guide theorizing and research in prejudice for decades to come. The authors of individual chapters, and especially the editors, have invested time, energy, and expertise in this book. Yet the royalties from sales will go to SPSSI to further the Society's educational and scientific endeavors. We are deeply grateful to them for allowing SPSSI to be the official sponsor of this unique and valuable book.

It is very apt that SPSSI be the official sponsor of this book. Gordon Allport played a major role in the history of SPSSI, as a founding member of the organization, a council member in 1936–40 and 1946–7, and president in 1943–4. One of SPSSI's major awards is named in honor of Gordon Allport, and a number of the contributors to the volume have received this prestigious award. In addition, SPSSI's mission is to bring theory and practice into focus on human problems of the group, the community, and nations, as well as the increasingly important problems that have no national boundaries. Prejudice is an enduring problem that continues to be of national and international importance, and psychological research makes important contributions in understanding and seeking to combat this human problem. Thus, the topic of prejudice has historically been and continues to be a major focus of SPSSI.

We invite psychologists and other social scientists who are interested in social issues to learn more about SPSSI. We have over 3,000 members from all over the world, and we publish print and electronic journals, hold a biennial conference, and provide grants and awards for research on social issues. More information about joining SPSSI can be found at www.spssi.org.

Victoria M. Esses
University of Western Ontario
Canada

Preface

The year 2004 marked the 50th anniversary of the publication of Gordon Allport's *The Nature of Prejudice*. Few works have had such a significant and lasting impact on psychology. Allport's ideas foreshadowed many of the "new" developments in the field, and his book has provided a scholarly foundation for generations of students, teachers, and scholars in this area. In the 25th anniversary edition of the book (1954/1979), Kenneth Clark wrote in the preface, "As is generally recognized, *The Nature of Prejudice* is a classic. Its table of contents establishes the parameters for a scholarly social science approach to the discussion and understanding of this complex human problem" (p. ix). In the introduction to the same volume, Thomas Pettigrew concurred, "The table of contents . . . has in fact organized the scholarly study of the important concept of prejudice. *The Nature of Prejudice* delineated the area of study, set up its basic categories and problems, and cast it in a broad, eclectic framework that remains today" (p. xiii). As you will see from the chapters in this volume, *The Nature of Prejudice* remains a classic at its 50th anniversary, and Allport's ideas have influenced scholars in the field as much over the past 25 years as they did in the book's first 25 years.

Given the contemporary prominence of *The Nature of Prejudice*, as well as its historical significance, the idea for this volume should have seemed obvious to us. It was not. The inspiration for this book evolved out of a conference, sponsored by the Fetzer Institute, designed to provide a forum for experienced scientists to collectively think about prejudice research – where it has been, where it is going – and to provide their own unique perspective on how the field's approach to studying intergroup relations might be improved. This necessarily involved thinking critically about how prejudice has historically been defined, operationalized, and investigated, with an eye toward expanding the field's approach.

The conference attracted a distinguished group of participants. A volume on the proceedings was proposed, but initially met with limited enthusiasm. Some of the participants felt that another volume with chapters on "What have I done lately?" could not compete with other professional demands on their time. However, when an alternative was proposed – the present volume commemorating the 50th anniversary of *The Nature of Prejudice* – the response was immediately supportive. People recognized the monumental contribution of Allport's book and welcomed the opportunity to reflect on its historical contribution while evaluating the present state of research and projecting important future directions.

The current volume is thus designed as a companion to *The Nature of Prejudice*. Our goal is to build on and to reexamine the groundbreaking insights of Gordon Allport in his classic book, providing up-to-date coverage of critical contemporary issues in the social-psychological study of prejudice, stereotyping, and discrimination. The contributions are linked to specific chapters and topics in the classic book. As both Clark and Pettigrew acknowledged, the table of contents of *The Nature of Prejudice* has defined the field over the past 50 years.

The chapters follow a fixed format. They briefly summarize Allport's position on a topic, examine developments in the area since Allport published his book, introduce new conceptual frameworks for understanding the topic, assess how Allport's ideas have been supported, and identify promising new directions of inquiry. Quotes from Allport correspond to the 1954/1979 25th anniversary republication of *The Nature of Prejudice*, the edition that is most readily available to students and scholars at this time. Although the chapters all recognize Allport's significant contributions and honor his work, in the tradition of scholarly exchange that Allport valued so deeply, the authors also offer critical appraisals of his ideas in light of current evidence, discuss where and how some of his ideas were limited, and reveal new insights and phenomena that Allport did not consider.

This book should be valuable to advanced undergraduates, graduate students, and professionals who are interested in the areas of prejudice, stereotyping, and discrimination, but it should also be accessible to a general lay audience. The orientation of the book is social psychological, but the volume is also intended to appeal to students and scholars in sociology, political science, and education, as well as to academics and practitioners interested in antibias education and prejudice reduction techniques and strategies.

The contributors to the volume are highly respected and prolific prejudice theorists and researchers, all of whom have proven their ability to construct influential theories that clarify concepts and synthesize complex research results. Given their stature and the currently dynamic state of the field, we believe that this volume will provide a framework to guide theorizing and research in prejudice and stereotypes for decades to come and continue to remind the field of Gordon Allport's critical role in shaping it. We did not know Gordon Allport personally, but we are well aware of his significant intellectual legacy. This book honors that legacy.

The editors are very grateful to the Fetzer Institute for sponsoring the conference "Revisiting *The Nature of Prejudice*" in September 2002, which stimulated the idea for the book. Special thanks are due to Lynn Underwood, Heidi Matteo, and Wayne Ramsey. We also express our sincere appreciation for the skillful and patient administrative assistance provided by Kathy Langworthy throughout the process. Finally, we acknowledge the support of NIMH Grant MH 48721 (to Jack Dovidio) and National Science Foundation Grant BCS-0109997 (to Laurie Rudman) during the preparation of the volume.

Chapter One

Introduction: Reflecting on *The Nature of Prejudice*: Fifty Years after Allport

John F. Dovidio, Peter Glick,
and Laurie A. Rudman

There is no debate that Gordon W. Allport's (1954/1979) *The Nature of Prejudice* is the foundational work for the social psychology of prejudice. Contemporary prejudice researchers and scholars regularly refer back to this work not only for apt quotations but also for inspiration. Social science instructors often pair Allport's book with recent articles. Indeed, any student of prejudice ignorant of Allport would be rightly considered illiterate. Social science is all too often subject to fleeting fads and fashions. Books written a decade ago are typically considered to be outdated. Yet half a century after its publication, *The Nature of Prejudice* remains the most widely cited work on prejudice. The scope and endurance of its influence has been nothing short of remarkable.

Why has this been so? Allport's profound insights, which have had lasting impact on the field, represent the obvious reason. Allport defined the core issues that the field continues to explore, struggle with, and reconsider. But there are others reasons, including Allport's inclusiveness and rich use of examples. Allport did not advocate a single pet theory of prejudice but chose instead to identify and illustrate a variety of perspectives, ranging from macro, or social-structural causes, to micro, or individual causes. He included provocative examples that, even when he chose not to interpret them in depth, could be used and exploited by others. In short, he was a synthetic and generous thinker.

The flip side of this breadth, generosity, and intellectual dexterity is that Allport embraced seemingly contradictory views at different points in *The Nature of Prejudice*. Thus, he has been many things to many thinkers. For example, Allport is the founder of the cognitive approach to prejudice, which views stereotyping and categorization as normal and inevitable byproducts of how people think. Yet he also viewed prejudice as a fundamentally irrational hatred, born of ignorance and the ego-defensive maneuvers of people with weak personality structures. Thus, from the standpoint of logical consistency, Allport often left much to be desired, but from the standpoint of generating ideas, he could hardly have been more successful; his book has been, and will likely continue to be, mined productively by generations of theorists and researchers.

The apparent inconsistencies in Allport's thinking, however, stem in part from the complexity of the phenomenon. A prominent example concerns the role of stereotyping in prejudice. Early on in *The Nature of Prejudice*, in chapter 2, he implicated stereotypic thinking as a foundation for prejudice. He observed, "The category saturates all that it contains with the same ideational and emotional flavor" (1954/1979, p. 21). Later, in chapter 12, he wrote that stereotypes are "primarily rationalizers. They adapt to the prevailing temper of prejudice or the needs of the situation. While it does no harm (and may do some good) to combat them . . . it must not be thought that this attack alone will eradicate the roots of prejudice" (p. 204). Allport explicitly addressed the apparent contradiction in these statements, embracing stereotypes as both causes and consequences of prejudice: "The stereotype acts as both a justificatory device for categorical acceptance or rejection of a group, and as a screening or selective device to maintain simplicity in perception and thinking" (p. 192). Fifty years later, after thousands of studies on stereotyping, the extent to which stereotypes are cause or consequence of prejudice remains a subject of lively debate.

This volume honors Allport in the way he would like best – by offering critical reflections on his seminal tract that reveal where he blazed important new paths and where he missed critical turns, where he led the field forward and where he led it astray. We have come neither uncritically to praise nor to bury Allport, but to engage in a conversation with him, to give our response to his call. Like *The Nature of Prejudice*, this book approaches prejudice from multiple angles and embraces many views, which we hope will stimulate decades of new research and theoretical advances in the study of prejudice. However, unlike Allport's monograph, our book has taken 44 people (to his one) to do it – which is both a testament to Allport's achievement and an indication of how the field has grown.

The fact that growth in prejudice research has often followed the contours outlined in *The Nature of Prejudice* also signifies the depth of its impact on the field. Allport himself believed that the book's thematic organization was his greatest and most lasting contribution, and we concur. Although we did not strive for one-to-one correspondence between the two volumes' chapters, we intended our book to serve as a companion piece to the original, and so we followed its structure. Additionally, the chapters in the current volume follow a common organization. Each chapter summarizes Allport's views on the topic, reviews developments since the publication of *The Nature of Prejudice*, presents at least one new framework, assesses current support for Allport's position, and identifies promising directions for future research.

Instead of summarizing each of the chapters contained in this edited volume, as is common practice, this Introduction reviews the volume's overarching themes. To do so, we focus on Allport's enduring contributions, identify seemingly contradictory strands of arguments, and, with the benefit of 50 years of additional research (i.e., informed hindsight), highlight the limitations of Allport's analysis.

Allport's Enduring Insights

Gordon Allport is widely recognized for his significant insights into prejudice. His expertise on the topic was clearly deep and broad, but he also had a unique capacity for integration. He organized many disparate views on prejudice and synthesized them around three basic themes, concerning cognitive, motivational, and sociocultural processes. These processes are frequently intertwined in practice, and each chapter in this volume typically addresses all three types. Allport himself acknowledged that "[intergroup] conflict is like a note on an organ. It sets all prejudices that are attuned to it in simultaneous vibration" (1954/1979, p. 233). However, as will be outlined below, each of these components involves some conceptually distinct processes.

Social Cognitive Processes

Allport emphasized the importance of social categorization in prejudice in a manner that was unprecedented in his day. Although ingroup–outgroup distinctions had been previously recognized as a source of bias (Sumner, 1906), Allport focused on the normality and inevitability of categorizing social groups. Allport noted, "The human mind must think with the aid of categories. . . . Once formed, categories are the basis for normal prejudgment. We cannot possibly avoid this process. Orderly living depends upon it" (p. 20). The role of social categorization is now widely acknowledged as a fundamental process in the development and maintenance of prejudice in such diverse approaches as Social Identity Theory (Tajfel & Turner, 1979), social cognition (Hamilton & Trolier, 1986), and Self-Categorization Theory (Turner, Hogg, Oakes, Reicher, & Wetherell, 1987).

In the present volume, cognitive processes that originate with social categorization and influence the way people perceive and think about others are central to chapters by Fiske (chapter 3: Social Cognition and the Normality of Prejudgment), Yzerbyt and Corneille (chapter 11: Cognitive Processes: Reality Constraints and Integrity Concerns in Social Perception), Brown and Zagefka (chapter 4: Ingroup Affiliations and Prejudice), Gaertner and Dovidio (chapter 5: Categorization, Recategorization, and Intergroup Bias), Judd and Park (chapter 8: Group Differences and Stereotype Accuracy), and Jost and Hamilton (chapter 13, Stereotypes in Our Culture).

Each of these chapters notes how developments since Allport have borrowed from and built upon his insights concerning cognitive functioning. Fifty years ago, he explained how social categorization "dominates our entire mental life. . . . A new experience must be redacted into old categories" (p. 20), and that "it selects, accentuates, and interprets the sensory data" (p. 166), thereby guiding subsequent perception and evaluation (Fiske). Because, as Allport observed, the cognitive processes involved in prejudice are part of normal functioning, they operate within the general constraints of "reality" and are influenced by people's salient goals and motivations (Yzerbyt & Corneille).

Allport also clearly recognized how group affiliation affects the ways in which people value others and how individuals differ in their identification with their group (Brown & Zagefka). He remarked that "the sense of belonging is a highly personal matter. Even two members of the same actual in-group may view its composition in widely divergent ways" (p. 36). Moreover, he illustrated how the salience of group identity is alterable – how categorization can become recategorization – and how people can be members of multiple categories and possess multiple identities (Gaertner & Dovidio). For example, he wrote that "in-group memberships are not permanently fixed. For certain purposes an individual may affirm one category of membership, for other purposes a slightly larger category" (p. 35).

One of Allport's strongest legacies is that he focused social psychologists' attention on the role of stereotypes, not merely as group descriptions (Lippmann, 1922), but also as cognitive structures that shape thoughts, feelings, and action. He observed that "categorization assimilates as much as it can to the cluster" (p. 20), and he considered the role of categorization on perceptions of both typicality and variability within groups, as well as in terms of between-group differences (Judd & Park). In addition,

Allport argued that racial and ethnic categories reflect a pernicious kind of essentialism that shapes the nature of stereotypes (Jost & Hamilton). These beliefs develop because categories often stem from differences in physical appearance that are visibly salient. Allport noted, "Even a fragment of visibility . . . focuses people's minds on the possibility that everything may be related to this fragment" (p. 109); and he observed, "Where visibility does exist, it is almost always thought to be linked with deeper lying traits than is in fact the case" (p. 132). The chapters in this volume cited above speak directly to each of these points. Along with Allport's text, they highlight the central role of social categorization and other social cognitive processes in prejudice.

Although the field subsequently emphasized a cognitive approach to prejudice consistent with Allport's views, Allport was remarkably comfortable integrating motivational and cognitive influences. Allport maintained a balance in his consideration of these two important sources of prejudice that psychologists since have had difficulty achieving (see Tetlock & Levi, 1982), but which authors in this volume have striven to recapture.

Motivational Influences

Allport acknowledged the functional nature of prejudice and identified both material gain and self-enhancement as basic motivational processes underlying prejudice. In terms of material gain, he noted, "Outright greed is certainly a cause of prejudice" (p. 370). With respect to psychological needs, Allport suggested that self-esteem can often be a goal in itself: "most people want to be higher on the status ladder than they are" (p. 371). However, self-enhancement can be based in avoidance as well as approach motives. Insecurity, fear, and anxiety can stimulate a need for self-enhancement, which, in some cases, creates or exacerbates prejudice. Allport believed that the "hunger for status is matched by a haunting fear that one's status may not be secure. The effort to maintain a precarious position can bring with it an almost reflex disparagement of others" (p. 371).

The fundamental motives to maintain power, status, and control and to meet one's ideals and aspirations, both materially and symbolically, are a central focus of much of Allport's classic book and at the heart of several chapters in the current volume: Jackman (chapter 6: Rejection or Inclusion of Outgroups?), Eagly and Diekman (chapter 2: What is the Problem? Prejudice as Attitude-in-Context), Rudman (chapter 7: Rejection of Women? Beyond Prejudice as Antipathy), Esses, Jackson, Dovidio, and

Hodson (chapter 14: Instrumental Relations among Groups: Group Competition, Conflict, and Prejudice); Smith and Mackie (chapter 22: Aggression, Hatred, and Other Emotions); Kenworthy, Turner, Hewstone, and Voci (chapter 17, Intergroup Contact: When Does It Work, and Why?); Devine (chapter 20: Breaking the Prejudice Habit: Allport's "Inner Conflict" Revisited); Duckitt (chapter 24: Personality and Prejudice); Newman and Caldwell (chapter 23: Allport's "Living Inkblots": The Role of Defensive Projection in Stereotyping and Prejudice); Glick (chapter 15: Choice of Scapegoats); Major & Vick (chapter 9: The Psychological Impact of Prejudice); and Jones (chapter 10: Mechanisms for Coping with Victimization: Self-Protection *Plus* Self-Enhancement).

Adopting a broad perspective, Allport observed that "there lies at the heart of any diversified and stratified social system the tempting possibility that economic, sexual, political, and status gains may result from the deliberate (and even from unconscious) exploitation of minorities. To achieve these gains prejudice is propagated by those who stand to win the most advantage" (p. 234). Although his own definition of prejudice was restricted to prejudice as antipathy, this functional view of prejudice – prejudice as "rationalized exploitation" (p. 209) – is compatible with social-structural conceptions of prejudice, which suggest that prejudice has mutated in the wake of changing social mores to involve a blend of negative affect and individualistic values (Sears), can manifest itself as an ostensibly benevolent paternalism that perpetuates inequality and exploitation (Jackman), and reflects negative responses to deviations from traditional stereotypic roles and characteristics that serve to reinforce the status quo (Eagly & Diekman; Rudman).

Competition and conflict over material resources and symbolic issues had an important place in Allport's analysis of the nature of prejudice (Esses, Jackson, Dovidio, & Hodson). In reference to realistic group conflict, he noted that "there are many economic, international, and ideological conflicts that represent a genuine clash of interests" (p. 233); with respect to symbolic conflict, he observed, "Differences are numerous and visible. The resulting clash of customs, tastes, ideologies cannot help but engender friction" (p. 222).

Because Allport defined prejudice as an antipathy, he emphasized negative emotions as a critical element of intergroup relations. Allport devoted three chapters to these emotions: chapter 21, "Frustration"; chapter 22, "Aggression and Hatred"; chapter 23, "Anxiety, Sex, Guilt." Contemporary prejudice research has recently "rediscovered" emotions and how different emotions may reflect different types of prejudice and precipitate different kinds of responses (Smith & Mackie). Intergroup contact that arouses identity or realistic threat increases bias, whereas appropriately structured, cooperative contact can reduce prejudice, at least in part by reducing intergroup anxiety and threat (Kenworthy, Turner, Hewstone, & Voci). Certain negative emotions, such as guilt and compunction, when appropriately aroused can motivate efforts to become less prejudiced (Devine). Allport argued that although "self-insight . . . does not automatically cure prejudice" (p. 328), many people who come to recognize discrepancies between their actual behavior and their egalitarian ideals will experience compunction, which motivates change. Allport explained, "They wish to face the whole issue and get it settled so that their daily conduct will be under the dominance of a wholly consistent philosophy of human relationships" (p. 338).

Needs for group status or personal esteem, which may be rooted in feelings of anxiety and threat, motivate individuals, according to Allport, to seek a "crutch": "The crutch he needs must perform several functions. It must give reassurance for past failures, safe guidance for present conduct, and ensure confidence in facing the future. While prejudice by itself does not do all of these things, it develops as an important incident in the total protective adjustment" (p. 396). These needs may be related to personality structure (Duckitt), social circumstances, or social institutions, such as religion (Batson & Stocks). For example, Allport observed that religion can be positively or negatively related to prejudice, and remarked, "Its functional significance may range from its crutch-like ability to bolster infantile and magical forms of thinking to its support for a guiding and comprehensive view of life that turns the individual from his self-centeredness towards genuine love for his neighbor" (pp. 451–2).

Needs for status and esteem can also result in projection (Newman & Caldwell) or more extreme psychological responses, such as scapegoating (Glick). According to Allport, "Projection may be defined as the tendency to attribute falsely to other people motives or traits that are our own, or in some way explain or justify our own" (p. 382). With respect to scapegoating, he added, "The nearest to an all-duty scapegoat then is a religious, ethnic, or racial group. Having permanence and stability, they can be given a definite status and stereotyped as a group" (p. 246).

Allport also considered self-protective strategies from the standpoint of the targets of prejudice. Contrary to prevailing views arguing for targets' inevitable self-hatred, Allport realized that active motivations to cope with prejudice, which could be directed inwardly or outwardly, could be critical factors in the psychology of stigmatized group members (e.g., ethnic minorities). He commented that "since no one can be indifferent to the abuse and expectations of others, we must anticipate that ego defensiveness will frequently be found among members of groups that are set off for ridicule, disparagement, and discrimination" (p. 143). These ego defenses can be viewed as part of more general processes involved in coping with stress (Major & Vick) and may reflect not only reactive responses to oppression but also active attempts for self-enhancement shaped by a minority group's cultural traditions and beliefs (Jones).

In sum, Allport characterized intergroup conflict as stemming from both perceptual and goal-driven causes, which could be rational or irrational. Further, he recognized in *The Nature of Prejudice* that cognitive and motivational precursors to prejudice operate in a context that is influenced by developmental processes and socialization forces.

Sociocultural Processes

Allport devoted three chapters explicitly to the development of prejudice: chapter 17, "Conforming"; chapter 18, "The Young Child"; and chapter 19, "Later Learning." There are two related chapters in our volume, one by Crandall and Stangor (chapter 18: Conformity and Prejudice) and the other by Aboud (chapter 19: The Development of Prejudice in Childhood and Adolescence). Allport identified how both overt pressure and more subtle influences, such as identification, help to transmit prejudice across people and generations. He commented that "parents sometimes deliberately inculcate ethnocentrism, but more often they are unaware of doing so" (p. 292). Allport also recognized the effect of maturation processes on developing "fear of the strange" (p. 300) and the "dawn of racial awareness" (p. 301), as well as social learning, peer influence, and cultural immersion later in life.

Social prejudices, according to Allport, could then become embedded in social mechanisms, such as language, that maintained these biases and transmitted them broadly across space and time. He wrote, "In order to hold a generalization in mind for reflection and recall, for identification and for action, we need to fix it in words." The depth of Allport's insight is examined by Mullen and Leader (chapter 12: Linguistic Factors: Antilocutions, Ethnonyms, Ethnophaulisms, and Other Varieties of Hate Speech).

Allport, however, felt that social interventions, drawing on these same principles, held great promise for reducing prejudice. He proposed, building on the earlier work of Williams (1947), that appropriately structured intergroup contact could effectively decrease bias at the individual level.

He observed that personal acquaintance, residential contact, occupational contact, and pursuit of common goals were often critical for prejudice reduction. At the end of chapter 16, "The Effect of Contact," he outlined what has come to be known as the Contact Hypothesis:

> Prejudice . . . may be reduced by equal status contact between majority and minority groups in the pursuit of common goals. The effect is greatly enhanced if this contact is sanctioned by institutional supports (i.e., by law, custom, or local atmosphere), and provided it is of the sort that leads to the perception of common interests and common humanity between members of the two groups. (p. 281)

Pettigrew and Tropp's contribution to the present volume, chapter 16, "Allport's Intergroup Contact Hypothesis: Its History and Influence," attests to the profound influence and enduring wisdom of Allport's proposal. Kenworthy, Turner, Hewstone, and Voci (chapter 17: Intergroup Contact: When Does it Work, and Why?) further explore developments in contact research, including what is currently known about precisely when and why intergroup contact reduces prejudice.

Allport also described other valuable social interventions, including formal education programs, acquaintance programs, and group retraining programs. These and other, newer approaches are reviewed by Stephan and Stephan (chapter 26: Intergroup Relations Program Evaluation). Allport described the effects of these programs as diverse and complex but still promising, and he suggested that social-psychological research could better inform practice in reducing bias. Stephan and Stephan echo these conclusions today. Finally, Allport recognized laws as a fundamental socializing agent that could have profound influence on attitudes. He argued that attitudes have to be changed to a certain degree to pass legislation, but "when the initial work has been done, then the legislation in turn becomes educative. The masses of people do not become converts in advance; rather they are converted by the *fait accompli*. . . . They allow themselves to be re-educated by the new norm that prevails" (p. 471). Thus Allport believed that sociocultural influences – from parental influence, to peer pressure, to laws – could both create and maintain prejudice and be a fundamental key to eliminating prejudice.

A reverberating theme throughout many of the chapters in this volume concerns Allport's prescience. Yet, no one could have fully anticipated all of the developments in the study of prejudice that have occurred in the past 50 years. Allport's views were limited not only by a restricted empirical base, but also by prevailing social views and values. As a consequence,

Allport missed important aspects of the nature of prejudice. Moreover, because of his profound influence, his blindspots became the field's blindspots for many years.

Moving Beyond Allport

Allport intended to stimulate the study of prejudice, and he did. Since the publication of *The Nature of Prejudice* there have been thousands of contributions, in the form of research articles, reviews, chapters, and books, to the understanding of prejudice. This body of work reinforces many of Allport's conclusions and speculations, but it has also moved beyond his ideas and data, demonstrating tensions and limitations in his thinking. Reflecting on Allport's tensions has often proved to be creative, with the field circling back years later to rediscover (to good effect) a relatively ignored strand of Allport's thought (e.g., the revival of motivated cognition). Discovering what Allport missed has taken longer, which testifies to Allport's impact. Allport, one suspects, would be no less delighted by the convincing disconfirmation of some of his ideas than by the revitalization of others – both have been instrumental to the development of the field.

In this section, we review four topics that have developed most significantly beyond Allport's treatment of prejudice, focusing on the seemingly contradictory strands or premature conclusions that created unresolved tensions in Allport's thought and highlighting what Allport missed. In some cases, Allport's premature conclusions led the field astray (e.g., defining prejudice); in other areas he simply stopped short and did not recognize fertile areas for empirical and conceptual development (e.g., nonconscious prejudice).

Conceptualizing Prejudice

Allport's most fundamental blindspot concerns his definition of prejudice as "an antipathy based upon a faulty and inflexible generalization" (p. 9). Chapters by Eagly and Diekman, Jackman, and Rudman in the current volume explore how this definition has obscured important aspects of prejudice, both pragmatically and theoretically. Allport's emphasis on antipathy directed the field toward types of prejudice that produce exclusion and violence, but it distracted the field from other types of bias involving more subtle types of control and exploitation (e.g., affectionate paternalism).

Perhaps a victim of his time, he overlooked, as Rudman describes it, the "ordinariness of gender prejudice." Only two pages of his book (pp. 33–4) were dedicated to an analysis of sexism. Several chapters in our volume (Eagly & Diekman, Jackman, and Rudman) redress this oversight, drawing attention not only to the issue of sexism, but also to the inadequacy of defining prejudice solely as an antipathy. The consequence of this challenge to conceptions of the nature of prejudice is profound, suggesting that prejudice comes in qualitatively different forms, such as an ostensibly benevolent paternalism that disadvantages groups without apparent antipathy, that Allport and, for many years, the rest of the field, simply missed.

Prejudice as Coercion versus Compliance

Allport recognized that prejudice functioned to maintain the advantaged status of majority groups while rationalizing the exploitation of minority groups. However, he did not consider other, arguably more prevalent mechanisms of control, such as those involving protection and benevolence (e.g., paternalism; Jackman). In this way, he missed the broader dynamics of prejudice that can contribute to systemic inequities by co-opting minority-group members. A focus on the *relations* between groups reveals evidence of seemingly "cooperative" behaviors of victimization by the targets of prejudice and of subtle "backlash" to even positive behaviors, if they deviate from the status quo (see Jackman, Rudman, and Eagly & Diekman).

Furthermore, because of his limited view of prejudice as antipathy, Allport also missed the full impact on victims of prejudice (Major & Vick, Jones, Jost & Hamilton). He noted that targets of prejudice often internalized hostile orientations: "His natural self-love may, under the persistent blows of contempt, turn his spirit to cringing and self-hate" (p. 143). To his credit, he rejected the contemporaneous view that self-hatred was inevitable and, instead, identified diverse responses to victimization, including self-directed (intropunitive) responses, such as denial of group membership, and other-directed (extropunitive) reactions, such as aggression. Nonetheless, he did not integrate these responses into a coherent framework or anticipate the possibility that they reflect different stages of identity development (Jones). He also did not link them to general processes (such as coping with stress; Major & Vick). Finally, he did not consider how the conflict between targets' own and society's evaluations of their group might lead them to have different conscious and nonconscious responses to prejudice (Jost & Hamilton).

The Normality and Consciousness of Prejudice

As the title of chapter 2 in *The Nature of Prejudice*, "The Normality of Prejudgment," proclaims, Allport understood prejudice and discrimination as byproducts of cognitive mechanisms that are typically functional in everyday life (e.g., categorization). His insights led directly to the social-cognitive revolution that continues to make an enormous contribution to the study of prejudice. Still, he wrestled with psychodynamic themes that permeated the field in his day, including the notion that people are instinctually destructive. He was openly critical of the tautology of this approach, noting that "widespread conflict does not mean in itself that instinct underlies it" (p. 214). However, psychodynamics held a place of prominence in *The Nature of Prejudice*.

Allport walked a precarious tightrope with his treatment of the psychodynamic approach to prejudice. He borrowed heavily from the topics it emphasized, but he scrupulously avoided advocating purely psychoanalytic explanations; instead, he incorporated psychodynamic ideas into his own positions. In his section "The Dynamics of Prejudice," Allport noted that while the "major insights [it contained] are in many instances derived from psychoanalytic work," he would occasionally "have to place strictures upon the exuberance of the theorizing . . . Yet this criticalness will not in the least diminish our indebtedness to Freud and to psychoanalysis" (pp. 352–3).

In chapter 25, "The Prejudiced Personality," he considered psychodynamic themes such as ambivalence toward parents, dichotomization (i.e., rigid thinking), and authoritarianism as key influences in the prejudiced personality (Duckitt). He also devoted full chapters to scapegoating (see Glick) and projection (see Newman & Caldwell). Yet throughout, Allport reminded readers of the normality and the seemingly logical nature of prejudgment.

Perhaps because of his unwillingness to fully embrace psychoanalysis, Allport made passing references to unconscious processes, but gave them limited emphasis in his book. When he did, he downplayed their role. For example, with respect to scapegoat theory, he noted that there could be "a large amount of unconscious mental operation in the individual" (p. 352), but he thought people to be more unaware of the source of their orientation than of their attitude toward the group, observing, "Few people know the real reason for their hatred of minority groups" (p. 352). In his "Inner Conflict" chapter, he concluded that there is "a sizable group who totally lack insight. They are filled with prejudices and deny this fact" (p. 329). However, rather than probing more deeply into the different reasons why people may not have insight into, or even awareness of, their biases, he dismissed this group as "genuine bigots."

In contrast, research since the publication of *The Nature of Prejudice* has recognized that people may not only be unaware of the source of their prejudice (Sears) but also may not be conscious that they have prejudiced beliefs and feelings that influence their behavior in significant ways (Fiske, Gaertner & Dovidio, Rudman). Allport did not anticipate nor prepare the field for the significant impact of research on *implicit* social cognition that has occurred over the past decade for understanding prejudice, stereo-typing, and discrimination.

Prejudice as a Group versus Individual Process

As noted earlier, *The Nature of Prejudice* is widely hailed for its theoretical inclusiveness. Allport weaved historical, economic, sociological, and psychological perspectives together into coherent themes and explanations across the book. He emphasized the fundamental nature of social categorization and group identification as a foundation for prejudice (Brown & Zagefka; Gaertner & Dovidio) and the effect it has on perceptions (Jost & Hamilton, Judd & Park; Yzerbyt & Corneille) and emotional reactions to others (Smith & Mackie). He advocated intergroup contact as an important intervention for reducing bias (Kenworthy, Turner, Hewstone, & Voci; Pettigrew & Tropp).

However, his focus throughout remained on the individual's phenomenology of being a group member and how individuals think about, react to, and behave toward members of another group. Allport did acknowledge the possibility of the unique quality of group identity relative to personal identity. For example, on page 40 he quoted Sherif and Sherif (1953), who said, "Ordinarily the factors leading individuals to form attitudes of prejudice are not piecemeal. Rather, their formation is functionally related to becoming a group member – to adopting the group and its values (norms) as the main anchorage in regulating experience and behavior" (p. 218). But Allport was critical of this perspective, commenting that "there is something unnecessarily 'collectivistic' about the theory" (p. 40). He acknowledged that prejudice could be, in part, a "mass phenomenon," but he preferred to emphasize the "individual play of attitudes." Within the next two decades, the work of Tajfel and his colleagues (e.g., Tajfel & Turner, 1979) on Social Identity Theory transformed the field with its emphasis on group-level processes as qualitatively distinct from individual-level processes. Allport did not see it coming.

Thus, Allport overemphasized the role of personality in prejudice, seeing bigots as having weak personalities, as insecure, easily frustrated, and intolerant of ambiguity. A more politically sophisticated psychology now emphasizes individual differences in adherence to group-based ideologies as accounting for individuals' proneness to prejudice. In an often-cited example, Allport (p. 13) provided a hypothetical conversation illustrating how the prejudiced Mr. X's stereotypical beliefs about Jews conveniently shift in response to factual counterevidence offered by the tolerant Mr. Y, but always in ways that maintain and justify his antipathy toward Jewish people. For Allport, such slipperiness was evidence of irrational motivational and emotional needs. Contemporary perspectives on prejudice (e.g., Jackman; Jost & Hamilton) interpret such rationalizations in a different light, as well-rehearsed, internally consistent, and socially validated justifications for group inequality.

As Duckitt notes, neither authoritarianism nor the other most prominent individual difference measure of prejudice, social dominance orientation (Sidanius & Pratto, 1999), are related to indices of psychopathology (as Allport would have predicted); rather they are better conceived as individual differences in people's belief in social and political attitudes or ideologies. Similarly, although Allport recognized the limitations of a scapegoat theory that focused on individuals' lack of tolerance for frustration, he failed to recognize that scapegoat movements are often group-level phenomena, coordinated by adherence to a socially validated ideology (Glick).

Conclusion

Gordon W. Allport died in 1967 at the age of 70. We did not know him personally. We are not his students nor are we students of his students. However, his impact on us, through *The Nature of Prejudice*, has been profound. We are not alone. Thomas Pettigrew, who was one of Allport's students, described *The Nature of Prejudice* as "his most explicit attempt to influence public opinion" (Pettigrew, 1999, p. 415). And the volume did attract significant public attention at the time. In the Foreword to the 25th anniversary edition of *The Nature of Prejudice*, Pettigrew (1979) recounted, "Gordon Allport's book was both a harbinger and a reflection of the thinking that went into the Supreme Court decision [*Brown v. Board of Education*, 1954]. *The Nature of Prejudice* is a remarkable mixture of careful scholarship and humane values" (pp. xii–xiv).

Beyond its appeal to the public and to policymakers, however, *The Nature of Prejudice* has had an even more enduring impact on generations of scholars in a variety of disciplines. We concur with Pettigrew (1999), who noted that the book was "balanced, ahead of its time, and elegantly written. It has organized the study of prejudice over the past half century" (p. 415). We suspect that Allport would be impressed by the advances that have been made in the study of prejudice over the past 50 years, many of which stemmed directly from his ideas, both concrete and speculative. As described earlier in this chapter, the impact of *The Nature of Prejudice* on the field has been not only in terms of insights confirmed but also in ideas proposed, including those that were not quite right or did not go quite far enough. We also believe that he would appreciate the challenges to his analysis of prejudice and be pleased with the new frameworks presented in the chapters in the current volume. Pettigrew (1999) described Gordon Allport "as a great teacher and a fine human being" (p. 424). He has clearly been a great teacher not only to those who knew him and worked with him, but to those of us who have followed, years later, in his footsteps.

REFERENCES

Allport, G. W. (1954/1979). *The nature of prejudice*. Cambridge, MA: Perseus Books.

Hamilton, D. L. & Trolier, T. K. (1986). Stereotypes and stereotyping: An overview of the cognitive approach. In J. F. Dovidio & S. L. Gaertner (eds.), *Prejudice, discrimination, and racism*. Orlando, FL: Academic Press.

Lippmann, W. (1922). *Public opinion*. New York: Harcourt-Brace.

Pettigrew, T. F. (1979). Foreword. In G. W. Allport, *The nature of prejudice* (pp. xiii–xiv). Cambridge, MA: Perseus Books.

Pettigrew, T. F. (1999). Gordon Willard Allport: A tribute. *Journal of Social Issues, 55*, 415–27.

Sherif, M. & Sherif, C. W. (1953). *Groups in harmony and tension*. New York: Harper.

Sidanius, J. & Pratto, F. (1999). *Social dominance: An intergroup theory of social hierarchy and oppression*. Cambridge: Cambridge University Press.

Sumner, W. G. (1906). *Folkways*. Boston, MA: Ginn.

Tajfel, H. & Turner, J. C. (1979). An integrative theory of intergroup conflict. In W. G. Austin & S. Worchel (eds.), *The social psychology of intergroup relations*. Monterey, CA: Brooks/Cole.

Tetlock, P. E. & Levi, A. (1982). Attribution bias: On the inconclusiveness of the cognition-motivation debate. *Journal of Experimental Social Psychology, 18*, 68–88.

Turner, J. C., Hogg, M. A., Oakes, P. J., Reicher, S. D., & Wetherell, M. S. (1987). *Rediscovering the social group: A self-categorization theory*. Oxford, UK: Blackwell.

Williams, R. M., Jr. (1947). *The reduction of intergroup tensions*. New York: Social Science Research Council.

PREFERENTIAL THINKING

Chapter Two

What is the Problem? Prejudice as an Attitude-in-Context

Alice H. Eagly and Amanda B. Diekman

The study of prejudice owes a great debt to Gordon Allport, who insightfully outlined the field's major issues in 1954. Although Allport's definition of prejudice (ch. 1, "What is the Problem?") as "an antipathy based upon a faulty and inflexible generalization" (1954/1979, p. 9) drew attention to troubling social problems, it did not account for the complexities of the prejudices that social scientists have since contemplated. The particular complexity that we analyze first in this chapter is that many groups that experience discrimination are not the targets of generalized negative attitudes – the "antipathy" of Allport's definition. Our second focus is accuracy – the "faulty generalization" of Allport's definition; we propose a dialectical principle whereby the stereotypes that underlie prejudice may typically be accurate at the group level but inaccurate in relation to individuals in the role-incongruent contexts that elicit prejudiced actions. Finally, we will show that prejudices are not necessarily inflexible but depend fundamentally on social context and slowly yield to changes in groups' positioning in the social structure.

Our expanded treatment of prejudice rests upon the simple idea of role incongruity – that prejudice often results from the mismatch between beliefs about the attributes typically possessed by members of a social group (that is, their stereotype) and beliefs about the attributes that facilitate success in valued social roles. In this analysis, a member of a group whose stereotypical attributes are thought to facilitate performance in a role is ordinarily preferred over a member of a group whose stereotypical attributes are thought to impede performance, even in the absence of objective differences between the two individuals. Such incongruity between stereotypical characteristics and social roles does not necessarily lead to a generalized hostile attitude toward the mismatched individual but to a decline in evaluation relative to a matched individual in the context of the particular role.

Allport's Views on "The Nature of Prejudice"

Allport defined the target of prejudice as a social group in general – for example, Jews, African Americans, Latinos, Japanese, and poor people. His emphasis on negativity was in part a byproduct of the extreme prejudices to which he paid the most attention, such as those that produced the Holocaust and lynchings. Allport's (1954/1979) discussion focused on ethnic and religious prejudice, primarily racism and anti-Semitism. Antipathy toward a group as a whole (and its individual members) thus formed the core of Allport's definition of prejudice. In contrast, he ignored (with one brief exception, pp. 33–4) a prejudice that targets about half the population, namely sexism, whose nature poses a critical challenge to defining prejudice as an antipathy.

Allport further included inaccurate perception as one of the defining elements of both prejudice and stereotypes. Although he acknowledged that a "kernel of truth" may exist (1954/1979, p. 190), prejudice in Allport's treatment is based on a "faulty and inflexible generalization" (p. 9). To elaborate this point, he described an anthropologist who studied a tribe of Native Americans but did not allow his children to mingle with the children of the tribe. Because this restriction was based on the anthropologist's accurate perception that many people in the tribal village suffered from tuberculosis, he concluded that the anthropologist was not prejudiced but acted upon "rational and realistic grounds" (p. 4).

Although antipathy became an enduring (if problematic) fixture of definitions of prejudice subsequent to Allport's book, many theorists dropped the requirement that the beliefs about target groups are necessarily inaccurate, paralleling the removal of inaccuracy from most definitions of stereotype (see Ashmore & Del Boca, 1981). The resulting minimalist definition of prejudice as an overall negative attitude toward a group then became widely accepted in social psychology (e.g., Esses, Haddock, & Zanna, 1993). Removal of the accuracy criterion from the definition of prejudice opened the way to a more sophisticated analysis of accuracy and inaccuracy in stereotyping and prejudice (Judd & Park, ch. 8 this volume).

Developments since Allport: Evidence of Prejudice in the Absence of Negativity

Late twentieth-century research made clear that some prejudices are not marked by negative attitudes. Empirical work not only documented subtle, "modern" prejudices toward many racial and ethnic minorities, but also revealed positive attitudes toward women, who are better liked even if less respected than men. These prejudices are ambivalent, not uniformly hostile.

Research on subtle, modern prejudices began with recognition of a change over time in the attitudes that many Whites held toward Blacks in the United States. Representative national surveys documented a dramatic change from endorsement of racial segregation, discrimination, and the innate inferiority of Blacks to rejection of these practices and ideas (see Sears, ch. 21 this volume). However, Whites nonetheless often endorse beliefs denying that Blacks' social and economic problems can be ascribed to external factors such as job discrimination, and ascribe them, implicitly or explicitly, to internal factors such as lack of motivation. Although such ideas have unfavorable implications for disadvantaged groups, they do not necessarily imply a generalized antipathy. This decrease in overall negativity also has appeared in research on various ethnic and national stereotypes held by students in the United States (Madon et al., 2001) and Europe (Meertens & Pettigrew, 1997).

Challenges to Allport's antipathy definition of prejudice also emerged from work on intergroup relations. Brewer (1999) argued that outgroups do not typically elicit strong negative evaluation but merely fail to elicit positive evaluation. In her view, much intergroup discrimination arises not from hostility toward outgroup members, but from identification with one's ingroup, which fosters preferential treatment of ingroup members (Mummendey et al., 1992; see also in this volume ch. 4 by Brown & Zagefka and ch. 5 by Gaertner & Dovidio). Jackman (ch. 6 this volume) goes further, arguing that paternalism, which disguises dominance with an overlay of affection toward subordinates, is the preferred mode by which dominants maintain their advantages and undermine subordinates' resistance.

The clearest challenge to the traditional analysis of prejudice derives from research on sexism, a topic that Allport neglected. Sexism researchers have since documented that women elicit predominantly positive sentiments but are often targets of prejudice. Initial explanations for sex discrimination rested upon the belief that attitudes toward women were negative (see Rudman, ch. 7 this volume), but empirical examination of evaluations of women and men as social groups showed positive attitudes toward women (see review by Eagly & Mladinic, 1994), deriving especially from the communal qualities that people associate with women (e.g., warm, friendly, sensitive). The evaluative edge of women over men appears on standard attitude measures, such as evaluative thermometer ratings or semantic differential ratings of women as a social group, and has been dubbed the *women-are-wonderful effect* (Eagly & Mladinic, 1994). These findings are compatible with Glick and Fiske's (1996) demonstrations that people often hold benevolently sexist beliefs that describe women favorably in the implicit context of the traditional female roles that are inherent in patriarchal arrangements. Even though Allport acknowledged that dictionary definitions recognize positive as well as negative prejudice (p. 6), he disallowed positive sentiments as relevant to his understanding of prejudice and confined his analysis to prejudice as antipathy.

Evidence from nonobvious methodologies dispels concerns that respondents' positive evaluations of women are contaminated by social desirability or political correctness. Implicit attitudinal measures, such as the Implicit Association Test, assess the strength of association between concepts and positive or negative evaluation without participant awareness (Greenwald, McGhee, & Schwartz, 1998). Research using this method has also obtained more positive evaluation of women than men (Rudman, ch. 7 this volume). Another nonobvious method of assessing gender prejudice involves disguising the purpose of participants' evaluations. In the Goldberg Paradigm (1968), participants evaluate a product – such as an article or a résumé – ascribed to a person who is identified by a male or female first name. Participants are unaware that the purpose is to detect gender prejudice because they receive only one set of materials in the typical between-subjects design. In a meta-analysis of 123 such studies, only a very slight bias against women was detected when the findings were summarized across evaluations of many types of materials (Swim, Borgida, Maruyama, & Myers, 1989), and this bias disappears when potential confounding factors (such as associations with specific male and female names; Kasof, 1993) are considered. Although these studies do show systematic biases under certain, specified conditions, which we discuss later, the Goldberg Paradigm has *not* demonstrated any *overall* tendency to devalue women or their work. And, as we have already indicated, other paradigms often reveal a bias in favor of women. Thus, the lack of evidence for overall negative evaluations of women as a social group does not appear to be an artifact of respondents' efforts to appear unprejudiced.

The weakness of contemporary evidence that prejudice toward ethnic minorities or women is predominantly negative does not indicate that prejudice has disappeared. For example, economists continue to document a wage gap between women and men that is in part discriminatory (e.g., Lips, 2003), and psychologists provide evidence that women, more frequently than men, are targets of sexual harassment in the workplace (e.g., Fitzgerald, 1993). Daily diary studies reveal that women report being the targets of sexist incidents much more than men do (Swim, Hyers, Cohen, & Ferguson, 2001). Likewise, African American students report frequent experiences of discriminatory behavior (Swim, Hyers, Cohen, Fitzgerald,

& Bylsma, 2003). Prejudicial phenomena thus appear to be alive and well, despite the lack of evidence that attitudes toward these groups conform to textbook definitions of prejudice.

A New Framework: Prejudice at the Intersection of Stereotypes and Social Roles

The best way to understand the nature of prejudice is to take both the structure of the social environment and the psychological structure of the individual into account. This does not constitute a complete departure from Allport's (1954/1979) views because he allowed for sociocultural conditions as moderators of prejudice. For example, in chapter 14 he considered "sociocultural laws of prejudice" (pp. 211–13), such as how rapid social change fosters prejudice. Despite these insights, Allport did not appreciate the fundamental sense in which prejudice relies on discordance between the qualities ascribed to a group and the qualities believed to be essential for carrying out available social roles.

Our framework thus retains Allport's emphasis on feelings and beliefs about a social group but also emphasizes the social-structural position of targeted groups. We argue that the potential for prejudice exists when social perceivers hold a stereotype about a social group that is inconsistent with the attributes that are believed to be required for success in certain classes of social roles. We reject Allport's (1954/1979) prescription that a stereotype must generally be an "exaggerated belief associated with a category" (p. 191). Regardless of the accuracy of the consensual beliefs held about a social group, prejudice consists of a lowering of the evaluation of members of the stereotyped group as occupants or potential occupants of an incongruent role, compared with the evaluation of members of groups for whom the role is congruent. This evaluative decline can occur regardless of whether or not the targeted *individual* fits the stereotype.

In the face of role incongruity, perceivers may suspect that a group member does not possess the attributes required for success in the role, regardless of his or her actual insufficiency. Even if the group stereotype is accurate on the whole, these beliefs are often misapplied to an individual group member. This result constitutes prejudice in the form of a less favorable attitude-in-context toward persons who are stereotypically mis-matched with the requirements of a role, compared with attitudes toward those who are matched. This approach incorporates Allport's view that prejudice occurs when people are placed at some disadvantage that is not warranted by their individual actions or qualifications – "thinking ill of others without sufficient warrant" (p. 6). However, in contrast to Allport's understanding, this prejudicially lowered evaluation refers not to the overall attitude toward the group, but to attitudes toward individual group members in role-incongruent contexts. This attitude can be expressed through downward shifts in all three of the modes in which attitudes are generally expressed (Eagly & Chaiken, 1993), specifically (a) beliefs, (b) emotions, and (c) discriminatory behaviors.

Incongruities between group members' stereotypic attributes and the requirements of roles are obviously important for workplace evaluations. Heilman's (1983) *lack-of-fit model* suggests that perceived inconsistencies between workplace roles and the attributes ascribed to an individual decrease performance expectations. In Heilman's approach, gender stereotypes affect perceptions of individuals' attributes, producing perceived lack of fit. Eagly and Karau (2002) argue that female leaders often suffer from incongruity between their leadership role and gender role, creating prejudice against them.

The unfavorable attitudinal shift that follows from role incongruity will not necessarily produce a negative attitude-in-context. If a role has high status, the attitude toward the group members as role occupants probably would not be negative but merely less positive than the corresponding attitude toward members of the groups who have historically occupied the role. For example, consider the role incongruity that an African American physician or dentist might encounter, perhaps being thought to have less technical competence than his or her European American counterpart. Attitudes toward such a medical practitioner are unlikely to be negative because such roles have considerable prestige. Rather, African American physicians and dentists might be evaluated favorably, but less favorably than their European American counterparts. Discriminatory behavior (e.g., reluctance to become a patient of an African American) is a likely outcome. It is this lowering of the evaluation of members of the target group because of their group membership that constitutes role-incongruity prejudice.

This decline in evaluation can take place toward members of groups whose overall stereotypes are predominantly negative, positive, or ambivalent. Positive stereotypical attributes – for example, the niceness ascribed to women – become a liability in some social roles. When a generally positive attribute such as niceness is mismatched to role requirements, perceivers suspect that this attribute would foster behavior inappropriate to the role. For example, a female prosecuting attorney may be devalued because her presumed niceness jeopardizes her success as a litigator. Similarly, positive qualities commonly ascribed to men, such as independence and assertiveness, can block their access to caretaking roles requiring inter-personally sensitive and nurturant qualities (see also Jackman, ch. 6 this volume; Rudman, ch. 7 this volume).

Even unfavorably evaluated qualities, such as extremely dominant behavior, can be positively evaluated if they are considered within a specific role context in which they are useful, such as engaging in competitive activity (Diekman, 2001). As these examples show, personal qualities that are positive in the abstract can take on less positive or even negative connotations in the context of incongruent roles, and qualities that are negative in the abstract can take on less negative or even positive connotations.

Prejudice as Contextual

Consistent with this analysis, variations in role requirements frame pre-judices. Allport (1954/1979) recognized the contextual quality of prejudice with examples of the "curious patterns" (p. 55) of discrimination such as allowing "a Negro to work in my kitchen but not a Jew" whereas "a Jew but not a Negro may sit in my parlor" (p. 55). However, he did not provide an abstract analysis of this contextualism or recognize its general-ity. This generality has become fully apparent in contemporary research. For example, in a meta-analysis of Goldberg Paradigm experiments, more substantial bias was present when women were evaluated in a masculine or neutral domain rather than a feminine domain (Swim et al., 1989). Simi-larly, a meta-analysis of Goldberg Paradigm studies of leadership behavior showed that women are more devalued, compared with equivalent men, when occupying male-dominated roles that are presumably incongruent for women (Eagly, Makhijani, & Klonsky, 1992). Organizational research has confirmed that women who enter male-dominated work settings often receive hostile reactions (e.g., Collinson, Knights, & Collinson, 1990), which can include sexual harassment (Fitzgerald, 1993). Also, gay men are particularly at risk for prejudiced reactions in roles to which they are stereotypically mismatched – for example, military service (Segal, Gade, & Johnson, 1993). Gay men's relatively effeminate image is incongruent with the tough, masculine role that military organizations construct for soldiers (Goldstein, 2001).

Because prejudice exists at the intersection of group stereotypes and the requirements of social roles, it is fundamentally responsive to social context (Blair, 2002). Prejudice is nonrandom, however, because it is predictable from the perceived requirements of social roles. Even though perceivers possess overall, abstract evaluations of social groups, evaluations of target group members in particular situations are emergent attitudes that depend upon the perceived congruity versus incongruity of the attributes attached to the individual's group and to the role in question. This approach is consistent with the attitudes-as-constructions position often advocated by attitude researchers (e.g., Schwarz, 2000; Wilson & Hodges, 1992).

Depending on role context, members of advantaged groups (e.g., men, Whites, heterosexuals) can also be targets of prejudice when their stereotypical attributes are mismatched to role requirements. The most extensive meta-analysis of the subset of Goldberg studies presenting job résumés or applications for evaluation showed precisely this effect: Women were preferred over equivalent men for jobs rated as female sex-typed, and men over equivalent women for jobs rated as male sex-typed (Davison & Burke, 2000). Stereotypical mismatch to the requirements of social roles can diminish evaluations of members of advantaged groups. However, dominant group members are unlikely to pursue roles that offer lesser rewards and status. Therefore, few men attempt to enter female-dominated roles and few Whites attempt to enter minority-dominated roles.

Prejudice as Varying in Degree

The intensity of prejudicial reactions depends on the alignment between stereotypes and role requirements. Because both stereotypes of groups and qualities required by social roles typically encompass a set of attributes, stereotype-role inconsistency can range from nonexistent to mild, moderate, and extreme. For example, the physician role is only moderately inconsistent with the female gender role because it requires not only scientific competence but also communal qualities of sensitivity and nurturance (e.g., Fennema, Meyer, & Owen, 1990). Therefore, women match the physician role on communal qualities but are mismatched on many other qualities, resulting in more moderate prejudice against female physicians than female soldiers or firefighters, jobs that entail a more extreme mismatch.

Moderate mismatches may produce subtle prejudice that channels group members into certain role subtypes. Among US physicians, 47 percent of women but only 30 percent of men specialize in primary care, a specialty that requires communal traits (American Medical Association, 2000). The subset of physician roles that emphasize matched qualities lessen the potential for discrimination because they reduce the role incongruity (More & Greer, 2000). In effect, preemptive discrimination may occur because group members are channeled toward roles that appear to be congruous with their group's stereotypical traits. This channeling is unlikely to be recognized as prejudicial because people regard themselves as helping others to seek out roles for which they are most suited.

Prejudice Made Apparent by Socioeconomic Change

When social, political, or economic circumstances change, group members may attempt to gain access to roles they have not previously occupied. For example, the decline of birth rates in industrialized countries (United Nations, 2001) and the mechanization and commercialization of domestic labor has changed the status of women. Similarly, African Americans' status changed when they migrated from the rural South to the urban North in the United States (Lemann, 1991). As large numbers of group members attempt to move into nontraditional roles, prejudice becomes a recognized social issue. Group members are thought to fit their traditional niches – that is, to have special qualities that enable them to do the work their group has always done. For example, 44 percent of survey respondents in the United States believed that it would be "worse for society" if most family providers were women and most of their spouses stayed home to raise children (Roper Center, 2000), presumably because of widely held beliefs that women are better suited to childrearing than men are.

The comfortable perceived fit between people's characteristics and their existing social roles becomes problematic when group members seek to change their roles; they are marked by their old roles, both in how they are perceived but also to some extent in terms of their actual characteristics due to socialization processes that have fit them to their typical roles. It is in this sense that stereotypes gain accuracy (e.g., Hall & Carter, 1999) and thereby possess considerable power to justify the existing social system (Jost & Hamilton, ch. 13 this volume). As Allport (1954/1979, p. 191) emphasized, stereotypes "justify (rationalize) our conduct" in relation to social groups. When group members try to move into different roles, they are thought to be relatively unqualified. These newcomers encounter barriers preventing their entry into nontraditional roles and devaluation of their work in the new context, as demonstrated for women entering male-dominated leadership roles (Eagly & Karau, 2002).

The role-incongruity view of prejudice has a decidedly rational flavor: It is reasonable to think that groups of people who have long fulfilled certain roles and therefore been shaped by them (in terms of socialization and social learning) would tend to be less than prepared for roles with quite different demands. The unfairness derives from social perceivers' weighting of group membership and thus not fully crediting the individual qualifications that individual group members possess for the new roles. This unfairness arises from assimilating individuals to stereotypes, a common psychological process. Nonetheless, irrationality comes to the fore as this basically rational process becomes co-opted by motivations. As Allport (1954/1979, chs. 21–4) argued, persons with personality deficiencies arising from anxiety, guilt, frustration, and similar states may especially seize on arguments that characterize members of outgroups as inadequate and unqualified, weighing group membership especially heavily. Similarly, motivations to defend the privileges of one's own group may fuel especially stringent attention to role newcomers' possible lack of qualifications (Jackman, ch. 6 this volume). However, stereotypes are not invented from whole cloth to defend people from personal inadequacies or protect their own groups' privileges. Instead, the processes of role incongruity provide the basic material that then enables motivated reasoning in defense of oneself or one's group.

Prejudice becomes an acknowledged social problem when a substantial number of group members aspire to incongruent social roles. Both incongruity and entrenched defense of privilege lead attitudes toward the pathbreakers to be more negative than attitudes toward group members who remain in their accustomed roles, as illustrated by the less positive stereotype of feminists compared with housewives (e.g., Haddock & Zanna, 1994) and by national polls showing unfavorable impressions of feminists (Huddy, Neely, & Lafay, 2000). In short, group members who try to move up in a social hierarchy into new roles become targets of prejudice. In contrast, group members who continue to accept their group's traditional roles, such as women in the domestic role and African Americans in service roles, may be generally appreciated, albeit with an approval that is tinged with paternalism (Jackman, ch. 6 this volume; Rudman, ch. 7 this volume).

This insight that prejudice becomes a social problem in the context of group members' attempts to change their social roles is consistent with the specific content of instruments designed to assess modern prejudices. Typical items assess resistance to change. Consider the Modern Racism Scale item, "Blacks are getting too demanding in their push for equal rights" (McConahay et al., 1981, p. 568). Similarly, the Ambivalent Sexism Inventory (Glick & Fiske, 1996), is built around the principle of resistance to change in women's roles. This instrument's negative dimension (*hostile sexism*) assesses unfavorable reactions to women in nontraditional roles, and its positive dimension (*benevolent sexism*) assesses favorable reactions to women in traditional roles.

Has Allport Been Supported?
Prejudice as a Social Problem

The role-incongruity analysis of prejudice encompasses Allport's emphasis on negative attitudes toward groups by acknowledging that the overall evaluative content of a group's stereotype can restrict the social roles for which group members are thought to be qualified. Social roles that offer prestige, status, income, love, and other outcomes will require many positive attributes; consequently, group stereotypes that are especially negative overall hinder access to a wide range of desirable roles because role-relevant positive attributes are absent from the stereotype.

Furthermore, the role-incongruity framework is consistent with Allport's insight that in times of social stability, prejudice is latent in the beliefs and feelings toward social groups in that it is unlikely to become an acknowledged social issue if most group members remain in traditional roles (see Allport's ch. 14). Yet, our approach explains Allport's (1954/1979) insight that "heterogeneity and the urge toward upward mobility thus make for ferment in society and are likely to bring ethnic prejudice in their wake" (p. 224): Group members are perceived to be adapted to their accustomed social roles and therefore seem unqualified for new roles with different demands. The prejudice against these potential role occupants, however, goes unrecognized unless agitation for roles is at least moderately widespread. Therefore, in popular and social-scientific discourse, "gender prejudice" is understood to refer to prejudice against women, many of whom have been striving to attain new roles. Similarly, as Blacks attempt to obtain roles that have been dominated by Whites, "racial prejudice" has come to refer to prejudice against Blacks. In this vein, Allport's focus on racism and omission of sexism ironically illustrate his point that prejudices, though they exist before they are "problematized," become recognized as prejudices only when social movements challenge the status quo. The Civil Rights movement was beginning to present this challenge when Allport was writing his book, whereas the feminist movement became culturally salient only later.

Although Allport recognized the role of social change in prejudice, his general definition of prejudice was tailored to understanding prejudicial reactions to generally devalued groups, whose members suffer from wide-ranging stereotype-role incongruity and have generally reduced access to rewarding roles. However, many, if not most, of the important phenomena of everyday prejudice lie outside of the boundaries of this framing of prejudice. Thus, Allport's definition of prejudice as generalized antipathy has proved to be too restrictive when a fuller range of prejudices is considered.

Future Directions: Accuracy and Change of Stereotypes

Although Allport viewed stereotype accuracy as a central issue, social scientists subsequently placed less emphasis on it (though see Judd & Park, ch. 8 this volume). Stereotype accuracy warrants reconsideration, in part because social change that has the potential to improve the status of a social group raises questions about the accuracy of the stereotypes that have characterized them. Members of groups seeking social change commonly attack their group's stereotype because new roles require non-stereotypical characteristics. For example, the role of business executive is thought to require male-stereotypical attributes, such as being action oriented, decisive, and competitive (e.g., Martell, Parker, Emrich, & Crawford, 1998). Thus, stereotypes that portray women as deficient compared with men in these qualities restrict women's opportunities; the content of such stereotypes is inconsistent with women's aspirations for social and political equality. Therefore, eradicating these ideas became a major focus of the feminist movement. Because activists rail against the stereotypes that have characterized their groups on the basis of their traditional social position, theorists such as Allport have overaccommodated by defining stereotypes as necessarily inaccurate.

The inaccuracy of stereotypes should be understood in the context of the group's changing status. Group members who are in the forefront of desiring access to new roles are ordinarily somewhat atypical of their group. They often have the characteristics needed for these desired roles, but their competence is not acknowledged. In these contexts, Allport's focus on stereotype inaccuracy makes sense. Social perceivers may be skeptical, for example, that a woman is brave or strong enough to be a soldier or that a Mexican American is ambitious or savvy enough to become a Fortune 500 Chief Executive Officer.

When a group's status is rising, considerable tension can derive from group members' efforts to alter their characteristics as they prepare for and occupy new roles. For example, as Blacks move into roles dominated by Whites, they are sometimes accused of having changed to be like Whites and are labeled pejoratively by terms such as "Oreo" (e.g., Willie, 1975). Similarly, in relation to women's entry into managerial roles, debates center on whether managerial women should accommodate to the masculine mode of managing or maintain a more feminine style that some argue is more effective (see Eagly & Karau, 2002).

This misapplication of stereotypes to group members who do not conform to their traditional stereotype has caused social scientists to regard prejudice as involving a rigid, inflexible belief system (e.g., Allport, 1954/1979). However, mounting evidence suggests that beliefs about groups can be quite malleable across different contexts. For example, different components of stereotypes and attitudes are activated when target group members are viewed in different situations (e.g., African American individuals on a street corner versus in a church; Wittenbrink, Judd, & Park, 2001).

The role-incongruity perspective suggests that even apparently inflexible stereotypes eventually change to the extent that change occurs in the roles that group members typically occupy. As new roles become common, the qualities associated with them will be perceived as characteristic of group members. Work on *dynamic stereotypes* (Diekman & Eagly, 2000) has documented that people perceive women as increasing in masculine characteristics from the past to the present; these new beliefs correspond to women's shift into traditionally male-dominated roles. In addition, perceivers project women as continuing to assume masculine characteristics in the future. Moreover, perceivers anticipate that the evaluation of women's male-stereotypical attributes will become more positive over time (Diekman & Goodfriend, 2004). To the extent that newly occupied roles require different characteristics, those characteristics are expected to be valued in the new role occupants. Such beliefs about a group's future change can ease their transition into roles that were previously thought to be incongruous. A promising direction for future research is the systematic study of how stereotypes actually change over time and how this relates to change in groups' social position.

In conclusion, it is insufficient to view prejudice solely as a rigid, generalized negative attitude toward a group. Much everyday prejudice consists of the relative devaluation in specific role contexts of members of a particular group compared to equivalent members of other groups. In this analysis, prejudice remains attitudinal, as in Allport's definition, and therefore can be expressed in beliefs, affects, and behaviors. However, the devaluation − that is, the downward attitudinal shift − does not necessarily produce a negative attitude, nor is the overall context-free attitude toward the target group necessarily negative. The key eliciting condition for prejudice is the potential or actual entry of group members into social roles to which they are stereotypically mismatched. Given this mismatch, even those individuals who actually have the qualities demanded by the new social roles tend to be perceived as deficient in these qualities because they are stereotypically prejudged.

Social forces operate in concert with these psychological processes to perpetuate prejudice. When social hierarchies are stable, with groups occupying their accustomed social roles, the stereotypes that reflect these roles and the structural barriers that shore up these stereotypes crush most all aspirations for roles that are atypical of one's group (see Jackman, this volume). Without noticeable aspirations on the part of members of disadvantaged groups, prejudice is not generally acknowledged as a social problem. However, as subgroups from disadvantaged groups attempt to move upward into more advantaged roles and have at least a modicum of success, prejudice not only becomes more visible but also becomes acknowledged and debated. Prejudice against group members who enter nontraditional roles dissipates only after large numbers of newcomers prove their success in the new roles and thereby change the stereotype through which they are perceived. Nonetheless, consistent with Allport's views about the inflexibility of stereotypes, social perceivers do not relinquish their stereotypes in response to limited exposure to disconfirming information.

Despite this emphasis on inflexibility, Allport (1954/1979) also acknowledged groups' mobility and indeed argued that a social system itself can contribute to social change: "Our very gusto for change may bring it about, if anything can. A social system does not necessarily retard change; sometimes it encourages it" (p. 507). As a society becomes acclimated to new economic, political, social, and technological realities, new qualities are cultivated and valued in its citizens. As we have argued, new realities lead individuals to seek out new roles – often roles for which members of their group are thought to be unsuited. Group members who succeed in their new roles contribute to the redefinition of their group stereotype and a reduction of prejudice.

REFERENCES

Adorno, T. W., Frenkel-Brunswik, E., Levinson, D. J., & Sanford, R. N. (1950). *The authoritarian personality.* New York: Harper & Row.

Allport, G. W. (1954/1979). *The nature of prejudice.* Cambridge, MA: Perseus Books.

American Medical Association (2000). *Physician masterfile: Physician statistics* *now – graph.* Retrieved Jan. 11, 2004 from www.ama-assn.org/ama/pub/category/2687.html.

Ashmore, R. D. & Del Boca, F. K. (1981). Conceptual approaches to stereotypes and stereotyping. In D. L. Hamilton (ed.), *Cognitive processes in stereotyping and intergroup behavior* (pp. 1–35). Hillsdale, NJ: Erlbaum.

Blair, I. V. (2002). The malleability of automatic stereotypes and prejudice. *Personality and Social Psychology Review*, 6, 242–61.

Brewer, M. B. (1999). The psychology of prejudice: Ingroup love or outgroup hate? *Journal of Social Issues, 55*, 429–44.

Collinson, D. L., Knights, D., & Collinson, M. (1990). *Managing to discriminate*. New York: Routledge.

Davison, H. K. & Burke, M. J. (2000). Sex discrimination in simulated employment contexts: A meta-analytic investigation. *Journal of Vocational Behavior, 56*, 225–48.

Diekman, A. B. (2001). Exploring the structure of social norms: Evaluations of dominance in men and women. *Dissertation Abstracts International: Section B: The Sciences and Engineering, 61(11)*, 6185B.

Diekman, A. B. & Eagly, A. H. (2000). Stereotypes as dynamic constructs: Women and men of the past, present, and future. *Personality and Social Psychology Bulletin, 26*, 1171–88.

Diekman, A. B. & Goodfriend, W. (2004). Evaluation in context: A role congruity perspective on injunctive gender norms. Unpublished manuscript, Miami University, Oxford, OH.

Eagly, A. H. & Chaiken, S. (1993). *The psychology of attitudes*. Fort Worth, TX: Harcourt, Brace, Jovanovich.

Eagly, A. H. & Karau, S. J. (2002). Role congruity theory of prejudice toward female leaders. *Psychological Review, 109*, 573–98.

Eagly, A. H., Makhijani, M. G., & Klonsky, B. G. (1992). Gender and the evaluation of leaders: A meta-analysis. *Psychological Bulletin, 111*, 3–22.

Eagly, A. H. & Mladinic, A. (1994). Are people prejudiced against women? Some answers from research on attitudes, gender stereotypes, and judgments of competence. In W. Stroebe & M. Hewstone (eds.), *European review of social psychology* (vol. 5, pp. 1–35). New York: Wiley.

Esses, V. M., Haddock, G., & Zanna, M. P. (1993). Values, stereotypes, and emotions as determinants of intergroup attitudes. In D. M. Mackie & D. L. Hamilton (eds.), *Affect, cognition, and stereotyping: Interactive processes in group perception* (pp. 137–66). San Diego, CA: Academic Press.

Fennema, K., Meyer, D. L., & Owen, N. (1990). Sex of physician: Patient preferences and stereotypes. *Journal of Family Practice, 30*, 441–6.

Fitzgerald, L. F. (1993). Sexual harassment: Violence against women in the workplace. *American Psychologist, 48*, 1070–6.

Fitzgerald, L. F., Drasgow, F., Hulin, C. L., Gelfand, M. J., & Magley, V. J. (1997). Antecedents and consequences of sexual harassment in organizations: A test of an integrated model. *Journal of Applied Psychology, 82*, 578–89.

Glick, P. & Fiske, S. T. (1996). The Ambivalent Sexism Inventory: Differentiating hostile and benevolent sexism. *Journal of Personality and Social Psychology, 70*, 491–512.

Goldberg, P. (1968). Are women prejudiced against women? *Transaction, 5*, 316–22.

Goldstein, J. S. (2001). *War and gender: How gender shapes the war system and vice versa*. Cambridge, UK: Cambridge University Press.

Greenwald, A. G., McGhee, D. E., & Schwartz, J. L. K. (1998). Measuring individual differences in implicit cognition: The Implicit Association Test. *Journal of Personality and Social Psychology*, 74, 1464–80.

Haddock, G. & Zanna, M. P. (1994). Preferring "housewives" to "feminists." *Psychology of Women Quarterly*, 18, 25–52.

Hall, J. A. & Carter, J. D. (1999). Gender-stereotype accuracy as an individual difference. *Journal of Personality and Social Psychology*, 77, 350–9.

Heilman, M. E. (1983). Sex bias in work settings: The Lack of Fit Model. *Research in Organizational Behavior*, 5, 269–98.

Herek, G. M. (1987). Can functions be measured? A new perspective on the functional approach to attitudes. *Social Psychology Quarterly*, 50, 285–303.

Huddy, L., Neely, F. K., & Lafay, M. R. (2000). The polls – trends: Support for the women's movement. *Public Opinion Quarterly*, 64, 309–50.

Jackman, M. R. (1994). *The velvet glove: Paternalism and conflict in gender, class, and race relations*. Berkeley: University of California Press.

Jacobsen, J. P. (1998). *The economics of gender* (2nd ed.). Malden, MA: Blackwell.

Kasof, J. (1993). Sex bias in the naming of stimulus persons. *Psychological Bulletin*, 113, 140–63.

Lemann, N. (1991). *The promised land: The great Black migration and how it changed America*. New York: Knopf.

Lips, H. M. (2003). The gender pay gap: Concrete indicators of women's progress toward equality. *Analyses of Social Issues and Public Policy*, 3, 87–109.

Madon, S. (1997). What do people believe about gay males? A study of stereotype content and strength. *Sex Roles*, 37, 663–85.

Madon, S., Guyll, M., Aboufadel, K., Montiel, E., Smith, A., Palumbo, & Jussim, L. (2001). Ethnic and national stereotypes: The Princeton trilogy revisited and revised. *Personality and Social Psychology Bulletin*, 27, 996–1010.

Martell, R. F., Parker, C., Emrich, C. G., & Crawford, M. S. (1998). Sex stereotyping in the executive suite: "Much ado about something." *Journal of Social Behavior and Personality*, 13, 127–38.

McConahay, J. B. (1986). Modern racism, ambivalence, and the Modern Racism Scale. In G. F. Dovidio & S. L. Gaertner (eds.), *Prejudice, discrimination, and racism* (pp. 91–125). Orlando, FL: Academic Press.

McConahay, J. B., Hardee, B. B., & Batts, V. (1981). Has racism declined in America? It depends on who is asking and what is asked. *Journal of Conflict Resolution*, 25, 563–79.

Meertens, R. W. & Pettigrew, T. F. (1997). Is subtle prejudice really prejudice? *Public Opinion Quarterly*, 61, 54–71.

More, E. S. & Greer, M. J. (2000). American women physicians in 2000: A history in progress. *Journal of the American Medical Women's Association*, 55, 6–9.

Mummendey, A., Simon, B., Dietze, C., Grünert, M., Haeger, G., Kessler, S., Lettgen, S., & Schäferhoff, S. (1992). Categorization is not enough: Intergroup discrimination in negative outcome allocation. *Journal of Experimental Social Psychology*, 28, 125–44.

Roper Center (2000). *Women, equality, work, family, men.* Roper Center at

University of Connecticut Public Opinion Online. Retrieved March 2, 2002 from http://web.lexis-nexis.-com/universe/document?_m-=1483408bb970a78276147e76d331a-609&_docnum=13&wchp=dGLSzV-lSlAl&_md5=ad7bc35675d8d5a-2cc25dbea0cc4714b

Schuman, H., Steeh, C., & Bobo, L. (1985). *Racial attitudes in America: Trends and interpretations.* Cambridge, MA: Harvard University Press.

Schwarz, N. (2000). Social judgment and attitudes: Warmer, more social, and less conscious. *European Journal of Social Psychology, 30,* 149–76.

Segal, D. R., Gade, P. A., & Johnson, E. M. (1993). Homosexuals in Western armed forces. *Society, 31,* 37–42.

Swim, J., Borgida, E., Maruyama, G., & Myers, D. G. (1989). Joan McKay versus John McKay: Do gender stereotypes bias evaluations? *Psychological Bulletin, 105,* 409–29.

Swim, J. K., Hyers, L. L., Cohen, L. L., & Ferguson, M. J. (2001). Every-day sexism: Evidence for its incidence, nature, and psychological impact from three daily diary studies. *Journal of Social Issues, 57,* 31–53.

Swim, J. K., Hyers, L. L., Cohen, L. L., Fitzgerald, D. C., & Bylsma, W. H. (2003). African American college students' experiences with everyday racism: Characteristics of and responses to these incidents. *Journal of Black Psychology, 29,* 38–67.

United Nations. (2001). *World population prospects: The 2000 revision.* New York: United Nations.

Willie, C. V. (1975). *Oreo: A perspective on race and marginal men and women.* Wakefield, MA: Parameter Press.

Wilson, T. D. & Hodges, S. D. (1992). Attitudes as temporary constructions. In A. Tesser & L. Martin (eds.), *The construction of social judgment* (pp. 37–65). Hillsdale, NJ: Erlbaum.

Wittenbrink, B., Judd, C. M., & Park, B. (2001). Spontaneous prejudice in context: Variability in automatically activated attitudes. *Journal of Personality and Social Psychology, 81,* 815–27.

Chapter Three

Social Cognition and the Normality of Prejudgment
Susan T. Fiske

Allport (1954/1979) argued that prejudice can be entirely normal. He also recognized that prejudice can be irrational. But his contentions in chapter 2 ("The Normality of Prejudgment") effectively undermined the intuitive view that prejudice is solely the product of sick motives and anticipated psychology's cognitive revolution by analyzing prejudice as a product of normal categorization processes, merely applied to people.

"The category enables us quickly to identify a related object," Allport wrote; categories' "whole purpose seems to be to facilitate perception and conduct – in other words, to make our adjustment to life speedy, smooth, and consistent" (1954/1979, p. 21). Modern social-cognition work built on Allport's insight by documenting ordinary mechanisms of perception and interpretation that discriminate against outgroups. The latest research emphasizes (a) the unconscious, automatic, implicit, ambiguous nature of prejudgment, which explains why people do not acknowledge their own biases, and (b) the interplay of social motives and cognition, which explains what facilitates and thwarts prejudice. Allport was incredibly prescient and left us an ambitious but wise research agenda.

Allport's Views: The Normality of Prejudgment

In titling his chapter 2 "The Normality of Prejudgment," Allport sparked a revolution; humans have a normal, natural propensity toward prejudgment. Whereas most social-scientific observers had viewed prejudice as the product of complex psychodynamics, Allport provided an alternative. Even now, most lay people believe prejudice is the purview of a disfavored few, those with abnormal impulses. Instead, Allport suggested, all people are subject to prejudices, as a function of the normal human cognitive apparatus.

Allport observed that people universally and spontaneously separate themselves into homogeneous groups, into *us* and *them* categories. Being more comfortable with their own group, people rarely deal with other groups, allowing glib generalizations ("they" are all the same and different from "us") with little risk of contradiction. Yet Allport (1954/1979) believed that categorization is necessary; "orderly living depends on it" (p. 20); "rubrics are essential to mental life" (p. 24), for five reasons:

- *Categories enable people to function in the world.* When people categorize a person as a gas station attendant, they know how to interact. People cannot possibly treat every person (or object) as unique, but must understand them in terms of prior experiences.
- To be efficient and effective, *categories gather as much as they feasibly can into their cluster.* Grosser categories are more pragmatic for most purposes than are fine-grained categories. Least effort is most efficient, as long as it can guide interactions with the environment.
- *Categories aid identification.* When one classifies objects or other people, one knows what they are. The category links relevant associations and concepts, allowing prejudgment. For social groups, stereotypes guide perceptions of and interactions with people, facilitating speedy adjustments.
- *Categories provide affective tags.* "The category saturates all that it contains with the same ideational and emotional flavor" (Allport, 1954/1979, p. 21), linking it to emotional prejudices.
- *Categorization processes reflect significant irrationality.* Irrational categories, Allport argued, are formed more easily, carry intense emotional baggage, and resist evidence, admitting but ignoring exceptions.

Overall, Allport anticipated most of the important themes of social-cognitive approaches to stereotyping, the dominant area of research in social psychology in the 1980s and 1990s, just after the cognitive revolution. Subsequent researchers have explored the central questions Allport defined: How exactly do social categories lump people together, and with what impact on understanding, feelings, and action?

Developments Since Allport: Contributions of the Cognitive Revolution

Social cognition, the processes by which people make sense of other people, swept into social psychology on the slipstream of the general cognitive revolution in psychology (Fiske & Taylor, 1984, 1991). Cognitive information-processing approaches freed social psychology from sovereign motivational theories (e.g., Freudian theories). The new challenge was to push cognitive mechanisms as far as possible, to discover the limits of their potential for explaining social phenomena, including intergroup biases. The resulting focus naturally was stereotypes, the cognitive aspect of intergroup biases. Categorization approaches found a ready inspiration in Allport's precedent for blaming bias on normal human cognition. Advances in cognitive research focused on the flow from initial categorization to later category-consistent interpretations.

Categorization in Initial Perceptions: "Normal" Means Immediate and Pervasive

People efficiently categorize other people, and thereby confuse some with each other, favor some over others, and notice the ones who stand out. Each of these processes occurs rapidly and widely in initial perception (see Fiske, 1998, 2000).

Immediate categorization: confusing who said what

Emblematic of the activated concept with a "close and immediate tie" (p. 21) to what people see is the category-confusion or who-said-what paradigm (Taylor, Fiske, Etcoff, & Ruderman, 1978), an early demonstration of social categories' power. In meetings, people often misattribute one person's suggestion to another person, but the errors systematically confuse speakers within gender and race, as if, for example, all the women or all the blacks are interchangeable. This is the hallmark of categorical perception; when people tag comments by race or gender, they neglect the individual. Category errors are not merely annoying; they reflect prejudice. They increase both when the category reinforces stereotypic roles or attitudes and when people are prejudiced (Fiske, 1998).

Automatic categorization facilitates prejudice: we are good; they are less good

Allport anticipated the rapid, thoughtless, even automatic nature of categorization, and its link to prejudices: "The human mind *must* think with the aid of categories . . . We *cannot possibly avoid* this process . . . [that] results *inevitably* in prejudgments" (Allport, 1954/1979, pp. 20, 24, italics added). Social psychologists and their lay audiences have been shocked by how rapidly categories cue ingroup advantages to *us* and match outgroup stereotypes to *them*. For example (Gaertner & McLaughlin, 1983), white participants, primed with the words "whites" or "blacks," then had to distinguish words from nonwords. Compared to "blacks," the prime "whites" speeded decisions about white stereotypic words (*ambitious, smart, clean*). This result and others like it showed the rapid, apparently unavoidable impact of race, age, gender, and even literal "us–them" categories on prejudgment (for a review, see Fiske, 1998).

A landmark study demonstrated that people make preconscious, automatic stereotypic associations to race categories (Devine, 1989). Whites subliminally primed with black stereotypic words (*black, lazy, athletic*) subsequently rated a race-neutral person, who behaved ambiguously, as more (stereotypically) hostile, *regardless of self-reported prejudice*. The now widely-used Implicit Associations Test complements these results (for a review, see Greenwald et al., 2002). The IAT pairs category-relevant cues (e.g., stereotypically black or white names, black or white faces) with positive and negative terms. People more rapidly associate positive terms with higher-status groups (and sometimes ingroups) but more negative terms with lower-status groups (and sometimes outgroups).

As does the who-said-what paradigm, automatic and implicit techniques show the rapid, subtle, indirect assessment of categories as the basis for normal prejudgment, making adjustments to life "speedy, smooth, and consistent" (Allport, 1954/1979, p. 21).

Salience: who stands out from the majority (ingroup) category.

In initial perception, categories highlight people who do not fit with the majority. Attention rivets on the solo or token member of a group otherwise homogenous on race or gender. The salience of the solo reveals the social importance of the category that makes the individual stand out. In a group with a solo, the group members are especially categorized along that dimension. Solos attract attention and realize it, which sometimes interferes with their concentration (Saenz, 1994). Solos are perceived in exaggerated, stereotypic ways (Taylor, 1981).

Subtypes and subgroups: who doesn't fit the minority (outgroup) category

When people confront individuals whose character disputes their outgroup stereotypes, they readily admit the individual exceptions only to "re-fence" the stereotype (Allport, 1954/1979, p. 23): People create small subtypes to contain the exceptions, thereby protecting their overall categories (for references, see Fiske, 1998). Subtypes are cognitively convenient because they allow people to retain their comfortable categories. And they are socially convenient because they justify the *status quo*.

People find it convenient to retain overgeneralized categories because "it takes less effort, and effort . . . is disagreeable" (Allport, 1954/1979, p. 21). But even convenience has its limits. Allport amended the principle of least effort: "except in the area of our most intense interests" (p. 21). When observers are motivated (and knowledgeable), they move from subtypes to subgroups. That is, they do not merely exclude the few exceptional subtypes but begin to see variety within the category: subsets of similar individuals within the overall group. People learn that the larger category contains subgroup clusters (e.g., within Latinos, subgroups of Cubans, Mexicans, Puerto Ricans). Although Allport did not anticipate the subgroup idea, his subtype idea paved the way for the distinction between them. Because subgroups increase the perceived variability of the category, they limit the tyranny of categories, whereas subtypes (which "fence off" exceptions to the general stereotype) maintain it.

Evident and Elaborate Interpretation: "Normal" Means Integral to Everyday Understanding

After initial perception, "all sorts of psychological elaboration" makes people "easily exaggerate the degree of difference between groups, and readily misunderstand the grounds for it" (Allport, 1954/1979, p. 19).

Group homogeneity: "They" are all alike

Categorization exaggerates between-group differences and minimizes within-group differences (Tajfel, 1970). Minimizing within-group differences especially occurs for outgroups. People typically see outgroups as *less* variable than average (i.e., as "all alike"), and to a lesser extent see ingroups as *more* variable than average (i.e., "we" are varied); this sets the stage for prejudgments of outgroup members (see Judd & Park, ch. 8 this volume). Sometimes ingroup homogeneity also occurs, especially for minorities and on dimensions important to one's identity (e.g., Simon, 1992). Perceived homogeneity on either side sharpens the interpretation of differences between groups.

Attributions: "We" are intrinsically good

Explanations for group outcomes psychologically elaborate the difference between groups and the grounds for it. When one attributes an outgroup failure to their inherent, dispositional features, but their success to a random fluke, one affirms their inferiority. And the opposite logic holds for ingroup outcomes. The "ultimate attribution error" (Pettigrew, 1979) contributes to prejudgment, by viewing favorable group differences as stable and unfavorable ones as mutable. This occurs for gender, primarily with the advantage to men on high-status (masculine) tasks (Swim & Sanna, 1996) as well as for interethnic comparisons (Hewstone, 1990).

The linguistic intergroup bias (Maass, Salvi, Arcuri, & Semin, 1989) carries the same message, only more subtly. Outgroup negative behavior merits abstract descriptions ("aggressive"), suggesting stability, whereas the identical ingroup behavior nets only the specifics of the particular instance ("punched somebody"). And positive behavior elicits the converse communication style.

Thus, various mechanisms of interpretation – namely, group homogeneity and attributions for outcomes – substantially operate in support of categories. After perception and interpretation, the cognitive bases for a memory trace are established.

Memory: dealing with inconsistencies

Memory serves as another mechanism helping categories to be "stubborn and resist change" (Allport, 1954/1979, p. 23). Although people certainly notice (and often re-fence) exceptions to the rule, memory operates with a stereotype-matching advantage under many conditions: when the expectancy is strong and prior, discrepancies are minimal or ambiguous, other tasks interrupt, and the observer operates under cognitive overload (see Rojahn & Pettigrew, 1992; Stangor & McMillan, 1992), all features of daily life.

Comment on Purely Cognitive Perspectives

The long menu of cognitive biases underlying categorization and the normality of prejudgment is an impressive tribute to Allport's perspicacity. Nonetheless, in the enthusiasm to uncover every last cognitive culprit, researchers neglected the more unsavory motivations and emotional prejudices that underlie discriminatory behavior. Fortunately, the tide is turning back to uncover these neglected areas; in the process, new directions in prejudice research are emerging.

New Framework: Social Motives in Prejudgment

Allport (1954/1979, p. 17) admitted that his chapter 2 presented "a somewhat 'cognitive' view of prejudgment. For the time being, many ego-involved, emotional, cultural, and personal factors that are simultaneously operating [were], of necessity, held in suspense" for other chapters. Social-cognitive stereotyping researchers have lately recognized the same neglect, both in their own explanations and in borrowing those of Allport. Lately, researchers have chosen not to go overboard on cognition; after all, Allport clearly believed in motives, too. Motives and emotions matter as the motor that translates cognitions into actions. Cold cognitions may steer behavior, but hot biases energize it. This section focuses on the interplay between cognitions and motivation, which reflects one main direction of prejudice research (e.g., Smith & Mackie, ch. 22 this volume).

But where to begin? One can parse the relevant motives in various ways. One approach (Fiske, 1998, 2004) depends on core social motives repeatedly identified over the last century by social and personality psychologists, including Allport. Starting from the premise that people's primary adaptational niche is other people, five motives arguably facilitate sociality: Belonging, understanding, controlling, enhancing self, and trusting others – each elaborated next. As Allport noted, in adapting to ingroups, people reject outgroups, so the motives fit well with both current and classic thinking about prejudgment.

Belonging: Adapting to Ingroups

People survive and thrive better within an ongoing ingroup that presumably shares their goals, defining the group and setting it apart from other groups that have different and therefore competing goals. Emotional prejudices follow from those presumed outgroup goals (Fiske & Ruscher, 1993), which often mystify, inconvenience, annoy, and frustrate the ingroup.

Hence, arguably, people want to know a first basic fact about other groups: *Friend or foe?* From this determination of intent follows the inference that the other group is friendly, warm, sincere (if not competing), or unfriendly, not warm, insincere (if competing). The second basic fact about the other group is: *Able or unable?* From this determination of capability follows the inference that the other group is competent, intelligent, skillful, or not. The inference of competence stems from the other group's status in society. A two-dimensional warmth by competence space distinguishes among a wide variety of outgroups (Fiske, Cuddy, Glick, & Xu, 2002). Moreover, it holds up across at least a dozen cultures tested so far (Cuddy, Fiske, Kwan, Glick, et al., under review).

Part of what is significant about this mapping of outgroups is that so many of them receive ambivalent reactions. In sample after sample, many or most groups fall into the ambivalently perceived combinations of (a) high warmth, low competence (e.g., older people, disabled people) or (b) low warmth, high competence (e.g., rich people, professionals). The nice but dumb ones are pitied and receive help but also neglect, whereas the smart but cold ones are envied and receive affiliation but also attack. Of course, some groups are simply despised, and these are the (c) low-competence, low warmth ones (e.g., poor people, welfare recipients), who receive disgust and contempt. They also receive both active harm (attack) and passive harm (neglect). At the opposite pole, some groups are simply loved, (d) the allegedly high-warmth, high competence ones (us and our allies, societal reference groups). They inspire pride and admiration, as well as both help and affiliation (Cuddy, Fiske, & Glick, 2004).

Although Allport primarily focused on prejudice as antipathy (the low–low cluster), he also emphasized love prejudice for the ingroup (the high–high cluster). And (despite his equation of prejudice with antipathy) he was aware of the ambivalence toward certain outgroups on competence and warmth dimensions (see his chapter 12): Jews were viewed as intelligent and hard-working, but not socially acceptable, whereas blacks were characterized as lazy and impulsive, but fun-loving and sexual.

Approaches to the content of stereotypes revolve around the tension between *us* with our interests and *them* with their interests. Viewed through the lens of group goals, the content of stereotypes reflects people's core motive of belonging to their ingroup, the attachments that "are essential to life . . . family and friendship circles . . . [help] define the 'out-groups' which are a menace" (Allport, 1954/1979, p. 25). From love prejudice and belonging follow outgroup resentments.

Extremities of love prejudice, however, do not necessarily predict extremities of outgroup prejudice (Brewer & Brown, 1998; Mummendey & Otten, 1998). Also, in collectivist East Asian settings, ingroups are seen more modestly than in Western samples (Cuddy et al., 2004); they are characterized moderately on both warmth and competence, instead of high on both, compared to other groups. Nevertheless, East Asian cultures otherwise demonstrate the same competence/warmth map of outgroups. Thus, outgroup stereotypes do not necessarily require extremes of love prejudice.

Understanding: Socially Shared Cognition

Allport discussed the importance of the ingroup sharing values, beliefs, and practices, which include prejudgments about outgroups. Because people are interdependent within the ingroup, they struggle to find socially shared ways to make sense of outgroups, often to outgroups' detriment. For example, after a negative revelation (e.g., discovering a previously unknown stigma), conversational dyads' shared impressions of another person focus on stereotypes, especially negative, stigma-congruent information. Also, the more people are motivated toward consensus, the more they seek to construct shared stereotypic impressions (see Ruscher, 2001).

Social sharing among ingroup members – gossip, rumor, opinions, stories, media – contribute to consensus in stereotyped beliefs and related prejudices. The most easily communicated traits constitute the core of most stable stereotypes (Schaller & Conway, 2001). The knowledge that their prejudices and stereotypes are shared gives people social permission to express their biases, reinforcing their own and other people's stereotypes and prejudice. These prejudiced communications demonstrate the explicitly social shared understandings that underlie normal prejudice.

Usually, one is less motivated to be accurate about outgroup members and more motivated to share the ingroups' understanding of them. Nevertheless, social understanding can also serve intergroup understanding. When people become interdependent with the outgroup, they focus more on the outgroup member's unique, counterstereotypic attributes. This results from increased motivation to be accurate about someone whose goals one shares (the definition of an ingroup) (for a review, see Fiske, Lin, & Neuberg, 1999). This may explain why expanding the boundaries of *us* to include *them* alters people's views of the outgroup (see chapters by Gaertner & Dovidio and Kenworthy et al., chs. 5 and 17 this volume); people depend on their (expanded) ingroup and need to understand them accurately. A motive to understand accurately also can result from accountability to a third party, the responsibility of holding unique information, or typically feeling uncertain about why things happen as they do.

Cognitive indicators of socially shared understanding have recently revealed themselves to be less automatic and more malleable than psychologists originally thought (Payne, 2001). If the relatively automatic forms of understanding indeed are controllable, then they should correlate with more explicit forms of response, and researchers do sometimes find that the two kinds of responses correlate nicely (e.g., Rudman, Ashmore, & Gary, 2001). Motives can operate even on an unconscious level: Chronically active egalitarian goals can prevent preconscious, automatic activation of stereotypes (Moskowitz, Gollwitzer, Wasel, & Schaal, 1999). Social context also moderates what were thought to be relatively automatic associations; a black man in a church is perceived differently than when he is on a run-down street (Wittenbrink, Judd, & Park, 2001). Social limits on cognitive automaticity result from a variety of changes to the social context, suggesting the fundamentally social nature of understandings that lead to prejudgment.

Controlling Perceived Threats to the Ingroup

A third core social motive, also relevant to prejudgment, entails controlling the ingroup's outcomes by protecting it from dangerous outgroups. A variety of perceived threats to ingroup values and economic status create intergroup anxiety, which fuels prejudice (Duckitt, 2001, ch. 24 this volume; Stephan & Stephan, 2000).

Tangible or symbolic threats create prejudice against people who are different (see Crandall & Stangor, ch. 18 this volume). These include (a) resource conflict (with outgroups or with ingroup traitors), (b) dangers to physical health (from someone who is contagious), (c) symbolic threat to bodily integrity or mortality (from someone physically deformed or dying), (d) violations of a just world (from apparent innocents who suffer), and (e) moral undermining (from deviants). Tangible or symbolic threat stigmatizes people with leprosy, facial damage, terminal illness, accidental disability, and homosexual orientation (see also Blascovich et al., 2001). These new lines of work characterize the evolution of social cognitions about stigma as a form of social control over the ingroup's outcomes (see also Neuberg, Smith, & Asher, 2000).

Ingroup control is fundamental in that threats to the ingroup operate as threats to self. People treat the ingroup as an extension of self, protecting it as they do the self. Vicarious dissonance, the finding that individuals change their attitudes when ingroup members engage in inconsistent behavior, is a clear example (Norton, Monin, Cooper, & Hogg, 2003). Just as with individual dissonance, vicarious dissonance appears to be mediated by vicarious discomfort (in this case resulting from the ingroup member's dissonant behavior). Thus, protecting the integrity of the ingroup operates by way of emotional discomfort.

The link between intergroup threat and emotion is even more explicit in other recent theories. Individuals appraise environmental threats to self, resulting in predictable emotions and action tendencies. Similarly, intergroup emotions follow from appraisal of threats to the ingroup, based in the perceiver's social identity. For example, intergroup anger and fear represent distinct emotions, respectively triggering inclination to act against or move away from the outgroup, as a function of ingroup strength (Smith & Mackie, ch. 22 this volume).

A final recent analysis defends the appropriateness of viewing the group as an extension of self, and therefore ingroup threat as a basis for prejudgment. The self, ingroup, and outgroup overlap to varying degrees, depending on self-categorization. People define their ingroups by a process of self-anchoring, viewing the group as similar to the self. Consequently, self-evaluations predict ingroup evaluations, especially for people have a strong need for cognitive structure (Otten & Bar-Tal, 2002). This kind of self-anchoring plausibly underlies ingroup favoritism. Self-ratings predict ingroup favoritism better than does the positivity of the trait, suggesting that generalization from self to ingroup (i.e., self-anchoring), rather than a striving for positive ingroup distinctiveness, might underlie ingroup favoritism (Otten & Wentura, 2001). The intimate connection between self and ingroup links prejudgment to emotions and evaluations (Greenwald et al., 2002).

The self-inspired role of emotions may be even more powerful than the role of simple cold cognitions, which do not necessarily implicate the self. Meta-analyses linking stereotypes, prejudice, and discrimination find prejudice better predicts discrimination than stereotypes do (e.g., Dovidio, Brigham, Johnson, & Gaertner, 1996). Specifically, emotional prejudices predict discriminatory behavior as well as behavioral intentions do, equivalent to $r = 0.38$. Cognitive beliefs and stereotypes predict behavior at only $r = 0.15$ (Talaska, Fiske, & Chaiken, 2004). As the next section shows, many of these intergroup emotions result from perceived threat to the ingroup as an extension of self.

Enhancing Self and Favoring Ingroup

Protecting self from threat and enhancing self constitute related but distinct phenomena. The first one maintains integrity of self and ingroup under threat; the second makes oneself and one's group seem better than others. Allport certainly endorsed this latter kind of self-enhancement motive, noting, "The very act of affirming our way of life often leads us to the brink of prejudice" (1954/1979, p. 25). Antipathy toward outgroups thus allegedly expresses self-love. This hypothesis has had a rocky history. It seems obvious that people would derogate outgroups in order to enhance the self. But recent research on self-esteem and prejudgment suggests that this holds for state (short-term) more than trait (long-term) self-esteem. One direction (from ingroup favoritism to self-esteem) shows that ingroup favoritism may make people feel better temporarily (Rubin & Hewstone, 1998), but not in the long run (Brown, 1995).

The reverse (from threatened self-esteem to ingroup favoritism) also fares better in the short run. When people's self-esteem is specifically threatened – particularly if they have high self-esteem – they increase ingroup favoritism (Crocker, Major, & Steele, 1998). Being insecure or anxious increases stereotyping (Wilder & Shapiro, 1989) and outgroup derogation (Wills, 1981). Self-esteem threat also facilitates the automatic activation of stereotypes (Spencer et al., 1998). However, chronically low self-esteem does not motivate ingroup favoritism (Hewstone et al., 2002).

The ultimate threat to self-esteem might be reminders of one's own mortality. One can counter such existential anxiety by endorsing cultural perspectives that will outlast the self (Solomon, Greenberg, & Pyszczynski, 1991). Social hierarchies, in which some groups dominate other groups, can serve this function. Mortality salience indeed intensifies both ingroup favoritism and outgroup derogation, although this wish to enhance self-esteem may fail in the long-term.

In a related perspective, people may justify their current place in the social system by prejudice toward outgroups (see Jost & Hamilton, ch. 13 this volume). This protects the self-esteem of dominant groups, not subordinate ones, unless subordinate groups are allowed positive stereotypes on some unimportant dimension. For example, ambivalent sexism consists of hostility toward women who violate traditional gender roles and benevolent (paternalistic) appreciation of women who adhere to them (Glick & Fiske, 2001).

Trusting Ingroup Others

According to Allport, people generally feel that "most of the business of life can go with less effort if we stick together with our own kind" (p. 18). We trust ingroupers because they are convenient, and outgroup members are a strain. Recent research documents exactly how true this is. For example, prejudiced whites dealing with a black person are distracted by the burden of regulating their own behavior (Richeson & Shelton, 2003).

Majority groups prejudge minorities as likely to be prejudiced against them, which decreases self-esteem and makes the interaction feel unpleasant as people become narcissistically preoccupied with how they themselves are viewed (Vorauer & Kumhyr, 2001). Nevertheless, this can improve the interaction. Whites often go into interracial interactions with concerns about appearing prejudiced, and the more they do so, the more anxiety they feel and the less they enjoy the interaction. Ironically, their black partner may like them more under precisely those circumstances (Shelton, 2003).

Conversely, if their black partner does indeed expect them to be prejudiced, the black partner apparently tries harder and makes the interaction more enjoyable for the white partner. Trust, like the other core social motives, affects intergroup interactions via our motives to adapt to ingroup others.

Has Allport Been Supported?

Probably the most common word in this book is "Allport," and after that, "prejudice." I would expect that a not-too-distant runner-up would be "prescient." He was so incredibly insightful and accessible that many of us still use Allport's book (accompanied by suitable updates) as a classroom text. And of course, many of us as researchers have thought we had invented a new idea, only to discover that Allport was there first. Never mind. He is eminently quotable, and we have learned a lot by riding on his shoulders, as this book attests.

Researchers can profit by continuing to mine Allport with new methods and insights. Go back to Allport's five principles, listed earlier, and see how many issues are still unresolved or just beginning to be explored. Exactly how do categories function to guide actual behavior? How are prejudiced attitudes and behavior linked? What constitutes a good-enough social category for daily adjustments? Which of many possible categories will people will use? How exactly do categories generalize to individuals? What is the role of differentiated emotions? How irrational, exactly, are social categories?

Future Directions

The potentially irrational, emotional bases for categories seem particularly neglected. As Allport noted, emotions act "like sponges. Ideas, engulfed by an overpowering emotion, are more likely to conform to the emotion than to objective evidence" (1954/1979, p. 22). Category-based emotions adhere to outgroups at fundamental, primitive levels in our brains. Recent brain-imaging studies show a social basis of irrational prejudgment, such as activation of the brain's amygdala (vigilance alarm) during presentation of pictures of unfamiliar faces from a racial outgroup, in comparison to faces from the observers' own group (Hart et al., 2000). In effect, the brain's burglar alarm habituates faster to members of the ingroup. This differential amygdala response correlates with implicit evaluation of racial groups (Phelps et al., 2000). Most relevant here, this apparently automatic response to outgroups itself depends on the social context in which they are encountered (Harris & Fiske, 2003; Wheeler & Fiske, 2005). When people treat the other person categorically on one dimension (age), the amygdala also responds categorically on other dimensions (race). But when people treat the other as a unique individual, the amygdala relaxes its vigilance. This exemplifies how new methods can revive old insights.

What is the forecast? Allport's legacy will continue to attract research attention because the problems are so urgent, though it may not have the continuing hegemony that it has had in the last decade. Elsewhere (Fiske, 2000), I have predicted more use of neuroimaging and, at the opposite extreme, more focus on actual discriminatory behavior, both of which require understanding prejudiced emotions. The apparent tension between studying the brain and studying social behavior may be illusory as each level of analysis complements the other. Similarly, I have predicted a continuing interest in evolutionary and cultural approaches, both efforts to understand prejudgment from a big-picture perspective. Again, these need not be mutually exclusive; people are adapted to absorb culture, and with culture, its prejudgments and social motives. Allport's legacy and variations on his cognitive themes will keep us occupied for decades to come.

REFERENCES

Allport, G. W. (1954/1979). *The nature of prejudice*. Cambridge, MA: Perseus Books.

Blascovich, J., Mendes, W. B., Hunter, S. B., Lickel, B., & Kowai-Bell, N. (2001). Perceiver threat in social interactions with stigmatized others. *Journal of Personality and Social Psychology, 80*, 253–67.

Brewer, M. B. & Brown, R. J. (1998). Intergroup relations. In D. T. Gilbert, S. T. Fiske, & G. Lindzey (eds.), *Handbook of social psychology* (4th ed., vol. 2, pp. 554–94). New York: McGraw-Hill.

Brown, R. (1995). *Prejudice: Its social psychology*. Oxford, UK: Blackwell.

Crocker, J., Major, B., & Steele, C. (1998). Social stigma. In D. T. Gilbert, S. T. Fiske, & G. Lindzey (eds.), *Handbook of social psychology* (4th ed., vol. 2, pp. 504–53). New York: McGraw-Hill.

Cuddy, A. J. C., Fiske, S. T., & Glick, P. (under review). The BIAS map: Behaviors from intergroup affect and stereotypes.

Cuddy, A. J. C., Fiske, S. T., Kwan, V. S. Y., Glick, P., et al. (under review). Toward pancultural principles of stereotyping.

Deaux, K. (1984). From individual differences to social categories: Analysis of a decade's research on gender. *American Psychologist, 39*, 105–16.

Devine, P. G. (1989). Stereotypes and prejudice: Their automatic and controlled components. *Journal of Personality and Social Psychology, 56*, 5–18.

Dovidio, J. F., Brigham, J. C., Johnson, B. T., & Gaertner, S. L. (1996). Stereotyping, prejudice, and discrimination: Another look. In C. N. Macrae, C. Stangor, & M. Hewstone (eds.), *Stereotypes and stereotyping*. New York: Guilford.

Duckitt, J. (2001). A dual-process cognitive-motivational theory of ideology and prejudice. In M. P. Zanna (ed.), *Advances in experimental social psychology* (vol. 33, pp. 41–113). New York: Academic Press.

Fiske, S. T. (1998). Stereotyping, prejudice, and discrimination. In D. T. Gilbert, S. T. Fiske, & G. Lindzey (eds.), *Handbook of social psychology* (4th ed., vol. 2, pp. 357–411). New York: McGraw-Hill.

Fiske, S. T. (2000). Interdependence and the reduction of prejudice. In S. Oskamp (ed.), *Reducing prejudice and discrimination* (pp. 115–35). Mahwah, NJ: Erlbaum.

Fiske, S. T. (2004). *Social beings: A core motives approach to social psychology*. New York: Wiley.

Fiske, S. T., Cuddy, A. J., Glick, P., & Xu, J. (2002). A model of (often mixed) stereotype content: Competence and warmth respectively follow from perceived status and competition. *Journal of Personality and Social Psychology, 82*, 878–902.

Fiske, S. T., Lin, M. H., & Neuberg, S. L. (1999). The Continuum Model: Ten years later. In S. Chaiken & Y. Trope (eds.), *Dual process theories in social psychology* (pp. 231–54). New York: Guilford.

Fiske, S. T. & Ruscher, J. B. (1993). Negative interdependence and prejudice: Whence the affect? In D. M. Mackie & D. L. Hamilton (eds.), *Affect, cognition, and stereotyping: Interactive processes in group perception* (pp. 239–68). San Diego, CA: Academic Press.

Fiske, S. T. & Taylor, S. E. (1984). *Social cognition*. New York: Random House.

Fiske, S. T. & Taylor, S. E. (1991). *Social cognition* (2nd ed.). New York: McGraw-Hill.

Fiske, S. T., Xu, J., Cuddy, A. C., & Glick, P. (1999). (Dis)respecting versus (dis)liking: Status and interdependence predict ambivalent stereotypes of competence and warmth. *Journal of Social Issues, 55*, 473–91.

Gaertner, S. L. & McLaughlin, J. P. (1983). Racial stereotypes: Associations and ascriptions of positive and negative characteristics. *Social Psychology Quarterly, 46*, 23–30.

Glick, P. & Fiske, S. T. (2001). Ambivalent sexism. In M. P. Zanna (ed.), *Advances in experimental social psychology* (vol. 33, pp. 115–88). New York: Academic Press.

Greenwald, A. G., Banaji, M. R., Rudman, L. A., Farnham, S. D., Nosek, B. A., & Mellott, D. S. (2002). A unified theory of implicit attitudes, stereotypes, self-esteem, and self-concept. *Psychological Review, 109*, 3–25.

Harris, L. T. & Fiske, S. T. (2003). Unpublished data, Princeton University.

Hart, A. J., Whalen, P. J., Shin, L. M., McInerney, S. C., Fischer, H., & Rauch, S. L. (2000). Differential response in the human amygdala to racial outgroup vs. ingroup face stimuli. *Neuroreport: For Rapid Communication of Neuroscience Research, 11*, 2351–5.

Hewstone, M. (1990). The "ultimate attribution error"? A review of the literature on intergroup causal attribution. *European Journal of Social Psychology, 20,* 311–35.

Maass, A., Salvi, D., Arcuri, L., & Semin, G. R. (1989). Language use in intergroup contexts: The linguistic intergroup bias. *Journal of Personality and Social Psychology, 57,* 981–93.

Mackie, D. M., Devos, T., & Smith, E. R. (2000). Intergroup emotions: Explaining offensive action tendencies in an intergroup context. *Journal of Personality and Social Psychology, 79,* 602–16.

Moskowitz, G. B., Gollwitzer, P. M., Wasel, W., & Schaal, B. (1999). Preconscious control of stereotype activation through chronic egalitarian goals. *Journal of Personality and Social Psychology, 77,* 167–84.

Mummendey, A. & Otten, S. (1998). Positive–negative asymmetry in social discrimination. In W. Stroebe & M. Hewstone (eds.) *European Review of Social Psychology* (vol. 9, pp. 108–43). New York: Wiley.

Neuberg, S. L., Smith, D. M., & Asher, T. (2000). Why people stigmatize: Toward a biocultural framework. In T. F. Heatherton, R. E. Kleck, M. R. Hebl, & J. G. Hull (eds.), *The social psychology of stigma* (pp. 31–61). New York: Guilford.

Norton, M. I., Monin, B., Cooper, J., & Hogg, M. A. (2003). Vicarious dissonance: Attitude change from the inconsistency of others. *Journal of Personality and Social Psychology, 85,* 47–62.

Otten, S. & Bar-Tal, Y. (2002). Self-anchoring in the minimal group paradigm: The impact of need and ability to achieve cognitive structure. *Group Processes and Intergroup Relations, 5,* 267–84.

Otten, S. & Wentura, D. (2001). Self-anchoring and in-group favoritism: An individual profiles analysis. *Journal of Experimental Social Psychology, 37,* 525–32.

Payne, B. K. (2001). Prejudice and perception: The role of automatic and controlled processes in misperceiving a weapon. *Journal of Personality and Social Psychology, 81,* 181–92.

Pettigrew, T. F. (1979). The ultimate attribution error: Extending Allport's cognitive analysis of prejudice. *Personality and Social Psychology Bulletin, 5,* 461–76.

Phelps, E. A., O'Connor, K. J., Cunningham, W. A., Funayama, E. S., Gatenby, J. C., Gore, J. C., & Banaji, M. R. (2000). Performance on indirect measures of race evaluation predicts amygdala activation. *Journal of Cognitive Neuroscience, 12,* 729–38.

Richeson, J. A. & Shelton, J. N. (2003). When prejudice does not pay: Effects of interracial contact on executive function. *Psychological Science, 14,* 287–90.

Rojahn, K. & Pettigrew, T. F. (1992). Memory for schema-relevant information: A meta-analytic resolution. *British Journal of Social Psychology, 31,* 81–109.

Rudman, L. A., Ashmore, R. D., & Gary, M. L. (2001). "Unlearning" automatic biases: The malleability of implicit prejudice and stereotypes. *Journal of Personality and Social Psychology, 81,* 856–68.

Ruscher, J. B. (2001). *Prejudiced communication: A social psychological perspective.* New York: Guilford Press.

Saenz, D. S. (1994). Token status and problem-solving deficits: Detrimental effects of distinctiveness and performance monitoring. *Social Cognition, 12*, 61–74.

Schaller, M. & Conway, L. G. (2001). From cognition to culture: The origins of stereotypes that really matter. In G. B. Moskowitz (ed.), *Cognitive social psychology: The Princeton symposium on the legacy and future of social cognition* (pp. 163–76). Mahwah, NJ: Erlbaum.

Shelton, J. N. (2003). Interpersonal concerns in social encounters between majority and minority group members. *Group Processes and Intergroup Relations, 6*, 171–85.

Simon, B. (1992). Intragroup differentiation in terms of ingroup and outgroup attributes. *European Journal of Social Psychology, 22*, 407–13.

Smith, R. H. (2000). Assimilative and contrastive emotional reactions to upward and downward social comparisons. In J. Suls & L. Wheeler (eds.), *Handbook of social comparison: Theory and research*. Plenum series in social/clinical psychology (pp. 173–200). Dordrecht, NL: Kluwer.

Solomon, S., Greenberg, J., & Pyszczynski, T. (1991). A terror management theory of social behavior: The psychological functions of self-esteem and cultural world views. In M. P. Zanna (ed.), *Advances in experimental social psychology* (vol. 24, pp. 93–159). San Diego, CA: Academic Press.

Spencer, S. J., Fein, S., Wolfe, C. T., Fong, C., & Dunn, M. A. (1998). Automatic activation of stereotypes: The role of self-image threat. *Person-*

ality and Social Psychology Bulletin, 24, 1139–52.

Stangor, C. & Crandall, C. S. (2000). Threat and the social construction of stigma. In T. F. Heatherton, R. E. Kleck, M. R. Hebl, & J. G. Hull (eds.), *The social psychology of stigma*. New York: Guilford.

Stangor, C. & McMillan, D. (1992). Memory for expectancy-congruent and expectancy-incongruent social information: A meta-analytic review of the social psychological and social developmental literatures. *Psychological Bulletin, 111*, 42–61.

Stephan, W. G. & Stephan, C. W. (2000). An integrated threat theory of prejudice. In S. Oskamp (ed.), *Reducing prejudice and discrimination* (pp. 23–45). Mahwah, NJ: Erlbaum.

Swim, J. K. & Sanna, L. J. (1996). He's skilled, she's lucky: A meta-analysis of observers' attributions for women's and men's successes and failures. *Personality and Social Psychology Bulletin, 22*, 507–19.

Tajfel, H. (1970). Experiments in intergroup discrimination. *Scientific American, 223(2)*, 96–102.

Talaska, C. A., Fiske, S. T., & Chaiken, S. (2004). Predicting discrimination: A meta-analysis of the racial attitudes-behavior literature. Unpublished manuscript, Princeton University.

Taylor, S. E. (1981). A categorization approach to stereotyping. In D. L. Hamilton (ed.), *Cognitive processes in stereotyping and intergroup behavior* (pp. 83–114). Mahwah, NJ: Erlbaum.

Taylor, S. E., Fiske, S. T., Etcoff, N. L., & Ruderman, A. J. (1978). Categorical and contextual bases of person memory and stereotyping. *Journal of*

Personality and Social Psychology, 36, 778–93.

Vorauer, J. & Kumhyr, S. M. (2001). Is this about you or me? Self- versus other-directed judgments and feelings in response to intergroup interaction. *Personality and Social Psychology Bulletin, 27,* 706–19.

Wheeler, M. E. & Fiske, S. T. (2005). Controlling racial prejudice: Social-cognitive goals affect amygdala and stereotype activation. *Psychological Science, 16,* 56–63.

Wilder, D. A. & Shapiro, P. (1989). The role of competition-induced anxiety in limiting the beneficial impact of positive behavior by an out-group member. *Journal of Personality and Social Psychology, 56,* 60–9.

Wills, T. A. (1981). Downward comparison principles in social psychology. *Psychological Bulletin, 90,* 245–71.

Wittenbrink, B., Judd, C. M., & Park, B. (2001). Spontaneous prejudice in context: Variability in automatically activated attitudes. *Journal of Personality and Social Psychology, 81,* 815–27.

Chapter Four

Ingroup Affiliations and Prejudice

Rupert Brown and Hanna Zagefka

". . . one of the most frequent sources, perhaps the most frequent source, of prejudice lies in the needs and habits that reflect the influence of ingroup memberships upon the development of the individual personality"

–Allport, 1954/1979, p. 41

Whatever definition of prejudice one endorses – and in this volume some diversity in this regard is plainly evident (see Eagly & Diekman's ch. 2) – there is some agreement on two points. First, prejudice is ultimately an *intergroup* phenomenon. That is, it involves relations between a person's (or people's) ingroup and some outgroup(s). Second, prejudice carries with it an implication that the ingroup should be regarded or treated in some more favorable way than the outgroup. Thus, an understanding of what constitutes an "ingroup" psychologically speaking, and the consequences of such ingroup affiliations, are fundamental to the study of prejudice.

In this chapter we address these issues first by reminding readers of Allport's own thinking in the formation of ingroups. We then briefly consider Social Identity and Optimal Distinctiveness Theories (see also Gaertner & Dovidio's ch. 5 below), arguably two of the major intellectual descendants of Allport's ideas about ingroups because of their emphasis on ingroup identity as a central explanatory concept. Then, in the heart of the chapter, we review several lines of contemporary research enquiry that have attempted to link social identity to intergroup attitudes and prejudice.

Allport's Conception of Ingroups

As is clear from our opening quotation, Allport himself was in no doubt about the importance of ingroup affiliations in the genesis and manifestation of prejudice. The chapter, "Formation of In-Groups," appears early on in the *The Nature of Prejudice* (Allport, 1954/1979, ch. 3) and lays the foundations for much of his subsequent theorizing about stereotyping, prejudice, and prejudice reduction. Allport begins by considering what ingroups are. Anticipating some later theoretical developments (see below), he suggested that an ingroup exists when "members [of it] all use the term *we* with the same essential significance" (p. 31). Thus, at the outset Allport opts for a subjective conception of the ingroup rather than one based purely on objective criteria, emphasizing that ingroup attachment is a shifting and elastic process, dependent on the particular context in which one finds oneself. He explains that "ingroup memberships are not permanently fixed. For certain purposes an individual may affirm one category of membership, for other purposes a slightly larger category. It depends on his need for self-enhancement" (p. 35).

This linking of category self-definitions to an enhancement motivation is another striking precursor of later thinking on the nature of social identity, as will become apparent. Three other aspects of Allport's treatment of ingroups are worth mentioning. One is that Allport wanted to stress that the *content* of people's ingroup identifications matters. In one example he argues that two people identifying with the same national ingroup could have very different conceptions of what that ingroup signifies, one adopting a much more inclusive and heterogeneous categorization than the other. The second aspect concerns Allport's distinction between ingroups and reference groups. In common with two other social psychologists of that era (Sherif & Sherif, 1964), Allport observed that people's awareness of their group membership(s) (ingroups) does not always coincide with their desire for those group memberships (reference groups). In other words, it is possible to know that one belongs to a group and yet to feel more or less attached to that group. Finally, Allport suggested that ingroup significance – or "potency," as he called it – tended to decline with increasing size and inclusiveness of category memberships. He showed a figure consisting of a series of concentric circles with the "family" at the center and "mankind" as the outermost ring (see figure 5.1 of Gaertner & Dovidio's ch. 5, below). However, he also acknowledged that this need not always be the case and that particular situational contingencies could bring even some very large category memberships to the forefront of people's priorities. Once again, this chimes well with much current thinking on the contextual variability of people's identifications.

What implications did Allport believe ingroup membership holds for people's intergroup attitudes? In a section entitled "Can there be an ingroup without an out-group?," Allport (1954/1979, pp. 41–3) discussed whether ingroup loyalty inevitably implies a corresponding negative attitude towards outgroups. Contrary to earlier wisdom (e.g. Sumner, 1906), Allport suggested that, while the presence of another group, especially in conflictual situations, can increase ingroup cohesion, such cohesion need not lead to prejudice and outgroup hostilities (p. 42). In fact, he proposed that ingroup attachment and preference are psychologically more primary motives and that outgroup hostility usually stems from other sources, an argument that has been resurrected in recent years (Brewer, 1999). Although Allport acknowledged that, in strict logic, an ingroup always requires the existence of some outgroup, he argued that this does not mean that the ingroup necessarily needs to be defined in relation or opposition to this outgroup. In a later section we will discuss some recent evidence that, indeed, people's group identities are not always sustained in relation to other groups.

Developments Since Allport: Two Contemporary Theories of Ingroup Loyalty

As we have seen, in developing his theory of prejudice Allport placed much emphasis on people's attachments to various ingroups. Two decades later this idea was taken up by Tajfel and Turner in their Social Identity Theory (Tajfel & Turner, 1986). Arguably, this theory has developed into the most influential account of intergroup behavior of the past three decades, at least to judge from the plethora of research devoted to it in recent years (Brown, 2000; Capozza & Brown, 2000).

The starting point for this theory was the discovery that the mere fact of being categorized as a group member, however "minimal" that group might be, is sufficient to trigger some elementary intergroup differentiation and discrimination (Tajfel, Flament, Billig, & Bundy, 1971). These findings occasioned many researchers to conclude that simply belonging to a group – providing someone with a primitive form of social identity – can lay the foundations of prejudice towards outgroups.

Social Identity Theory assumes that people's social identities are derived primarily from their membership in various groups: Social identity consists of "those aspects of an individual's self-image that derive from the social categories to which he perceives himself as belonging" (Tajfel & Turner, 1986, p. 16). A second key assumption is that people are generally motivated to achieve and maintain a positive social identity, thereby boosting their self-esteem. Tajfel and Turner (1986) propose that this positive identity derives mainly from comparisons between the ingroup and available or relevant outgroups. The motivation to positivity implies that there will be a preference – in some cases, a group-serving bias – for favorable rather than unfavorable intergroup comparisons. In other words, people look for ways (or outgroups) that will enable the ingroup to be seen as positively distinctive. Fundamentally, then, Social Identity Theory posits that many instances of ingroup favoring perceptual and judgmental biases and intergroup discrimination can be traced to a need for a positive social identity. Supplementing these core ideas, Tajfel and Turner (1986) also proposed three types of variables that would be likely to affect intergroup differentiation: people should be identified with the ingroup; the situation should permit intergroup comparisons to be made; and outgroups should be comparable (i.e. similar or proximal). Generally, pressures for distinctiveness and subsequently enhanced levels of ingroup bias should increase with outgroup comparability.

Another approach has been to extend the concept of identification beyond the "enhancement" motive that is central to the Social Identity Theory formulation. Brewer's (1991) Optimal Distinctiveness Theory, for example, has proposed that social identification should be considered as deriving from two opposed psychological needs: differentiation and assimilation. According to this account, identification with a group will be "optimal" when these two needs balance each other out, and this is most likely to occur in groups of intermediate size – neither so large as to threaten the need to see oneself as "different," nor so small as to challenge the need to see oneself as connected to others. Thus, depending on contextual factors – particularly the relative size of the "ingroup" relative to other possible identity categories – one might not always observe much intergroup differentiation (Leonardelli & Brewer, 2001).

From these thumbnail sketches, three points are apparent. First, Tajfel and Turner (1986), like Allport before them, place the concept of social identification at the center of their analysis of intergroup relations. Although neither theory posits identification to be the exclusive determinant of biased intergroup attitudes – for example, both accept that real conflicts are also important causes of prejudice – an assumption common to both is that some minimal level of ingroup identification is necessary for such favoritism. A second commonality is that ingroups can vary in their psychological significance for their members, either across individuals or across situations. This is most explicit in Brewer's model which strongly echoes Allport's emphasis on variations in group importance with differences in size and inclusiveness. In other words, these theories consider identity to be contextually specific. A third implication is that such differences in strength of identification should be linked to variations in intergroup attitudes: Both Allport and Social Identity Theory imply that groups that are temporarily or chronically more important for their members should evince more evidence of ingroup favoring biases than those which are less subjectively important. This stems from the positivity or group (and self) enhancement assumption common to both theories: Those who are more identified should care more about their group membership and should hence be more motivated to feel good about their ingroups.

However, the two approaches differ somewhat in how much they see this ingroup positivity or positive distinctiveness as a product of biased and self-enhancing intergroup comparisons. Social Identity Theory places intergroup comparisons with relevant reference groups center stage, positing that they are the main means by which positive distinctiveness and positive ingroup identity are achieved. In contrast, Allport emphasizes the primacy of the ingroup, and argues that that ingroups are not necessarily defined in relation or opposition to outgroups. Similarly, as we have just seen, findings from the "minimal group paradigm" have led Social Identity Theory researchers to emphasize that any kind of social categorization – even if very trivial – may suffice to sow the seeds of prejudice. Conversely, Allport surmised that there are many constraints and limiting conditions, which means that these seeds do not always germinate: "while a certain amount of predilection is inevitable in all in-group memberships, the reciprocal attitude toward out-groups may range widely" (1954/1979, p. 42).

New Frameworks: Emerging Issues in Ingroup Identity and Prejudice

In this section we focus on several lines of research that have in common a concern with ingroup identification and its psychological and behavioral correlates, and which directly build on Allport's thinking on ingroups and prejudice.

Identification, Negative Intergroup Attitudes, and Ingroup Bias

As noted above, Social Identity Theory has acquired a preeminent position as an orienting theoretical perspective in research on intergroup relations. Social-identity concepts are frequently invoked as explanations for various manifestations of ingroup favoritism and discrimination. However, at the outset it is of theoretical and practical importance to distinguish between ingroup bias (the ingroup being evaluated more positively than the outgroup) and negative intergroup attitudes (where the outgroup is evaluated negatively or disliked). We will come back to this distinction shortly, after discussing some of the work that came out of the Social Identity Theory tradition in which the focus is typically on ingroup bias (rather than outgroup derogation).

In fact, the vast corpus of work demonstrating the near universal prevalence of ingroup bias in intergroup attitudes and behavior (Brewer & Brown, 1998; Hewstone, Rubin, & Willis, 2002) can be taken as support for the core proposition of Social Identity Theory that ingroup members are strongly motivated to seek some positive distinctiveness for their ingroups in relation to outgroups. Nevertheless, attempts to test another central hypothesis of Social Identity Theory – that these manifestations of ingroup bias should be correlated with strength or importance of group identification – have met with mixed success. One early review of studies investigating the identification–bias relationship concluded that the overall correlation was close to zero with considerable variation among studies (Hinkle & Brown, 1990).

How should we make sense of this heterogeneity? One solution favored by Hinkle and Brown (1990) was to propose two variables that might moderate the identification–bias relationship and hence delineate the conditions under which the identity processes specified by Social Identity Theory would and would not apply. They suggested that individualism–collectivism and autonomous–relational orientation could help to distinguish among group contexts, groups, and even group members. The individualism–collectivism dimension is well known (Triandis, 1995). The autonomous–relational dimension refers to a tendency to evaluate ingroups and their achievements autonomously (i.e. against some absolute or temporal standard), *or* in relation to other groups and their achievements. Hinkle and Brown (1990) predicted that the strongest correlations between identification and bias might be expected in collectivist–relational combinations and the weakest in the individualist–autonomous one. Some support for this model has been found (Brown et al., 1992), although there have also been some striking disconfirmations (Capozza, Voci, & Licciardello, 2000).

Other researchers have taken a different line, speculating that not all social identities are primarily driven by esteem enhancement motives. Among the other identity functions that have been suggested are self insight/understanding and ingroup cooperation and cohesion (Aharpour & Brown, 2002; Deaux, Reid, Mizrahi, & Cotting, 1999), social interaction

(Deaux et al., 1999), uncertainty reduction and meaning (Hogg, 2000; Vignoles, Chryssochoou, & Breakwell, 2002), and continuity (Vignoles et al., 2002). Aharpour and Brown (2002) found that different groups (e.g. trade unionists, football fans, students) differentially privileged some of these identity functions and, moreover, the functions themselves were correlated differently with both identification and ingroup bias in the different groups. It is possible, then, that some of the variance in the identification–bias correlations could be accounted for by the operation of different identity functions in different groups and group contexts. Such a conclusion would certainly be consistent with Allport's contention that the "content" of social identities can play a critical role in how they are expressed in intergroup situations.

Let us conclude this section by returning to the distinction between negative intergroup attitudes and ingroup bias. Consistent with the "positive distinctiveness" postulate of Social Identity Theory, most of the research reviewed above focused on "bias" as a dependent variable, which only demands that the ingroup be seen or treated better than the outgroup. However, such measures may only speak indirectly to those manifestations of prejudice which involve some explicit derogation of or hostility toward an outgroup. As Brewer (1979) pointed out some years ago, most ingroup bias phenomena involve a relative *over*evaluation of the ingroup (or its products) and not a devaluation of the outgroup (and its products). Allport himself also underlined the importance of this distinction: "what is alien is regarded as somehow inferior, less "good," but there is not necessarily hostility against it" (1954/1979, p. 42).

This issue was the subject of a detailed analysis by Brewer (1999) when she asked the question: When does ingroup love turn to outgroup hate? She identified a number of factors that may help to translate an (over)-attachment to the ingroup into a detachment from or dislike of outgroups. These include societal complexity, since simple or hierarchically segmented societies may be more prone to intergroup antagonism than societies with many cross-cutting categories (Gluckman, 1956); ideologies of moral superiority and exclusion which justify mistreatment of outgroups and minorities (Staub, 1990); the existence of clear conflicting interests between groups or material threats to the groups' existence (Sherif, 1966); the presence of superordinate goals without a strong superordinate identity since groups may react against the loss of subgroup identity implied by the cooperative endeavor (Gaertner & Dovidio, 2000); and the endorsement of common values by different groups which may provoke mutually threatening claims for distinctiveness (Mummendey & Wenzel, 1999).

One of the few empirical attempts to examine the effects of identification on outgroup derogation was by Mummendey, Klink, and Brown (2001). Drawing on Hinkle and Brown's (1990) autonomous–relational distinction, Mummendey and colleagues proposed that one important factor would be whether the prevailing social or ideological conditions are such as to define ingroup identity comparatively, in relation to other groups. In contrast, there will be situations in which ingroup identities may be just as strongly endorsed but carry with them less of that socially comparative baggage because they are defined more autonomously, either relative to the ingroup's past or in relation to some absolute standards. When referring to identification with national categories this distinction has been labeled nationalism versus patriotism (Kosterman & Feshbach, 1989). Mummendey et al. (2001) operationalized this distinction experimentally and found that there was only ever a correlation between national identification and xenophobia when people had first conceived of their country *in relation to* other countries; those viewing their country in a temporal perspective or in neutral "control" conditions showed no such link.

In sum, although there is evidence that ingroup identification can sometimes be systematically related to ingroup bias, the picture is somewhat more complicated than anticipated by either Allport or subsequent theorists. Whether significant associations can be observed depends on such moderating factors as whether the ingroup is defined autonomously or relationally, or what the prevailing motives for ingroup identification are.

Identification and Comparisons

As we saw above, while Allport argued for the psychological primacy of ingroups and thus only accorded minor importance to the role of intergroup comparisons, some later theories such as Social Identity Theory put such comparison processes center stage, claiming that a positive social identity crucially depends on their favorability. To date, neither of these two claims has been given much empirical attention. While intra- and interpersonal comparison research flourished after Festinger's (1954) original formulation of Social Comparison Theory, similar research in intergroup relations has been sparse.

On the basis of the "primacy of the ingroup" hypothesis, one would expect intragroup comparisons, such as comparing the ingroup to itself at other points in time (Albert, 1977) or comparing the self to other ingroup members (Crocker & Major, 1989), to be frequent. One might further expect identification to be positively related to interest in comparing with these intragroup or temporal objects, because these tendencies should be exacerbated for those who particularly care about their ingroup. In contrast, from Social Identity Theory one would expect *intergroup* comparisons to be frequent and identification to be positively related to intergroup comparison interest, because more identified people should be more concerned to distinguish their ingroup from other groups.

To test these ideas, we have been engaged in a program of field and experimental work investigating the antecedents of comparison choices in intergroup settings. A clear conclusion from this work is that intragroup and temporal comparisons are at least as prevalent as intergroup comparisons and, moreover, group identification tends to more strongly related to the former kinds of comparisons than the latter. For example, in a longitudinal study of ethnic minority adolescents in the United Kingdom, participants were significantly more interested to compare with ingroup and temporal targets (intragroup, temporal, country of origin) than with all intergroup targets (other minorities, white British, North Americans, people in the developing world) (Zagefka, 2004). Moreover, the cross-sectional data revealed that identification was *positively* correlated with interest in temporal and intragroup comparisons (with other ingroup members), but not with interest in comparing with any of the intergroup objects. Over time, identification *negatively* and causally predicted interest in several of the intergroup objects, namely "Americans," the "developing world," and members of "other minorities." Similar findings have been obtained with other ethnic minority samples in Britain and Germany (Zagefka & Brown, in press). These results seem to support Allport rather than Social Identity Theory.

Experimental work confirmed these findings. In one study, classes of university students were randomly subdivided into groups. In these groups, they completed two tasks, and were given (false) feedback on their performance/score on one of the tasks. They were then given the opportunity to compare their outcome with one other outcome (e.g., another group's scores, temporal comparison). Generally, participants were more interested in temporal comparison options than in the various intergroup options. Further, ingroup identification was positively correlated with interest in temporal comparison, but was unrelated to intergroup comparison interest. Similar results were obtained with university employees when comparing their institution to others (Brown & Zagefka, 2003). Although these preliminary results should certainly be followed up, they nonetheless support Allport's original hypothesis: Outgroups often do not seem to be salient and prominent in people's minds when they think about their ingroup.

Acculturation as Identity Management, and Minority–Majority Attitudes

Allport differentiated "ingroups" from "reference groups," the latter being "groups to which the individual relates himself as a part, or to which he aspires to relate himself psychologically" (Sherif & Sherif, 1964, as quoted by Allport, 1954/1979, p. 37). He gave the example of a Black person who wishes to relate himself or herself to the White majority. The possibility of nominally belonging to one group while wanting to affiliate with another has been a recurrent theme of acculturation research (Berry, 1997). Berry's model identifies four acculturation strategies that minority groups might pursue, formed from the combination of two orientations: a desire to maintain (or relinquish) ethnic identity and a desire to engage with other groups (or not).

Group members can be classified as "high" or "low" on each of these dimensions resulting in the strategies of "integration" (high on both), "assimilation" (low, high), "separation" (high, low), and "marginalization" (low, low). Thus, while incorporating the notion of "reference groups," acculturation research goes beyond this concept by acknowledging the possibility of multiple group memberships, and that people can simultaneously have a positive orientation toward more than one group (integration), or toward neither the minority nor majority group (marginalization). Focusing on outcome variables like stress, self-esteem, and psychosomatic indices, there is now converging evidence that integration is usually the strategy with the most beneficial outcomes for minority members, and marginalization has the worst outcomes (Berry, 1997; Liebkind, 2001).

However, acculturation research is not only concerned with the preferences of minority group members; *majority* group members also have views about the place of minority members in society (Bourhis, Moise, Perreault, & Senecal, 1997). Majority group members, too, might want minority members to integrate, segregate, assimilate, or be marginalized (Gonzalez, Brown, & Zagefka, 2003; Zagefka, Brown, Broquard, & Leventoglu Martin, 2004).

Acculturation researchers have also investigated how the preferences of minorities and majorities "fit" together. For instance, in their Interactive Acculturation Model, Bourhis et al. (1997) argue that a situation of good fit exists when – among other combinations – both minority and majority prefer assimilation. Although, when taken singly, integration has been demonstrated to lead to more favorable acculturative outcomes than assimilation, this more recent research suggests that a preference for assimilation might be similarly advantageous *if* there is concordance between the two groups about the strategy of choice.

A further innovation in acculturation research has been a shift away from a focus on individual acculturative outcomes to the effects of acculturation preferences on the positivity (or otherwise) of intergroup relations (e.g. Zick, Wagner, van Dick, & Petzel, 2001). Generally, this research has replicated patterns previously found for individual outcomes: Integration is the most beneficial strategy, and marginalization the least (Zagefka & Brown, 2002). Furthermore, this research has also shown that "fit" does indeed significantly predict intergroup outcomes. A good "fit" – that is, a good correspondence between minority and majority preferences – results in less conflictual intergroup relations (Zagefka & Brown, 2002; Zagefka et al., 2004).

In sum, focusing on the particular case of immigrants and ethnic minorities, acculturation research has added considerably to psychology's understanding of how ingroups are formed, and how identities are maintained and changed. While some of the issues that emerge in this line of research are reminiscent of some of Allport's original concepts, others are new. The simultaneous focus on several potential ingroups, and the notion of attitude "fit" of how different groups like to define and conduct their interrelations, are valuable new additions.

Identification, Deprivation, and Prejudice

When thinking about the consequences of ingroup identification for prejudice, one further variable of relevance might be deprivation, the "feeling that one has been unjustly deprived of some desired thing" (Crosby, 1976, p. 88). Here we consider two possibilities of how the three variables – identification, deprivation, and prejudice – might be linked. One option proposes identification to *moderate* the effect of deprivation on prejudice. In other words, something different happens among high and low identifiers because of the differential importance of their group memberships to them (Ellemers, Spears, & Doosje, 2002). Another option proposes identification to be the linking process (a *mediator*) between systematic discrimination or deprivation and intergroup outcomes such as outgroup derogation and prejudice (Mummendey, Kessler, Klink, & Mielke, 1999).

There is evidence that feelings of deprivation often lead directly to prejudice (Olson & Hafer, 1996; Pettigrew et al., 1998). According to the "moderation hypothesis" outlined above, one could expect this effect to differ between high and low identifiers. Some empirical evidence for such moderation was found by Struch and Schwartz (1989) in an Israeli interreligious context. They observed that perceptions of conflicting goals (a variable related to deprivation) were correlated with aggressive intentions towards the outgroup, but that the correlation was noticeably stronger amongst those participants who identified strongly with their ingroup. A similar interaction between a group conflict variable – this time between the actual experience (or not) of a particular intergroup dispute – and identification was observed by Brown et al. (2001) in a study of British visitors to France. The effects of the conflict on negative evaluations of French people were more marked amongst more strongly identified respondents. These results suggest that identification might indeed qualify the effects of deprivation on prejudice.

When one considers whether identification can explain (or *mediate*) the effects of deprivation, the picture is more complicated. It is true that some studies have found identification and deprivation to be positively correlated (consistent with the "mediation hypothesis") (Kessler & Mummendey, 2002; Mummendey, Kessler, Klink, & Mielke, 1999; Tropp & Wright, 1999). However, less consistent with the mediation idea, others have found the variables to be unrelated (Tougas & Veilleux, 1988; Guimond & Dube-Simard, 1983) or even negatively related (Zagefka & Brown, in press). Furthermore, the direction of causality here is ambiguous. Does identification increase perceived deprivation because more highly identified group members desire more for their group (Tropp & Wright, 1999)? Or do deprivation and discrimination increase identification because of a greater sense of shared fate and perceived threat (Branscombe, Schmitt, & Harvey, 1999)? Most likely, future research will reveal that some element of bi-causality will be closer to the mark (Tougas & Beaton, 2002).

Has Allport Been Supported?

What have been the major insights gained in the 50 years since the publication of Allport's *The Nature of Prejudice*, and how have Allport's observations and ideas stood the test of time? It is striking that Allport anticipated many of the research issues that proved to be important later: for example the importance of the self-enhancement motive, the "content" of social identities, and identity strength. Further, the concept of "reference groups" is reflected in some of the thinking in acculturation research, and the distinction between ingroup bias and outgroup derogation has proved useful. Finally, Allport may well have been correct in suggesting that strong ingroup identification does not necessarily go hand in hand with heightened competitiveness and outgroup derogation. Some evidence has been obtained that strong identification might instead lead to a heightened *intragroup* focus. However, naturally, not all of Allport's predictions have yielded straightforward support.

Neither he nor subsequent theories (e.g. Social Identity Theory) were completely right about the effects of ingroup identification on prejudice, and research has ascertained that the picture is more complex than initially anticipated. Several issues have emerged: The precise effects on both ingroup bias and outgroup derogation probably depend on a number of influential moderating factors (e.g. autonomous vs. relational definitions of the ingroup, "motives," etc.). Thus, despite Allport's seemingly timeless insights and the significant developments on this topic since the publication of *The Nature of Prejudice*, important issues are still not fully addressed or understood.

Future Directions

In considering the most important and promising directions for future research, several issues suggest themselves. One concerns the still ambiguous relationship between ingroup identification and outgroup rejection. One area where this question has particular topical relevance is identification with the nation. In an era when new nation states are frequently asserting their right to independence, or having their autonomy threatened by other nations, it is a matter of pressing concern to establish whether relatively benign "patriotic" sentiments (i.e., a positive yet critical regard for own country) can be fostered without them degenerating into the destructive chauvinism that is the hallmark of "nationalism" (i.e., an uncritical love of own country coupled with a derogation of other countries). In this regard, further research could usefully address itself to clarifying the conditions under which comparisons with outgroups come to assume lesser significance in ingroup evaluations than other kinds of comparisons (e.g., within the group or over time).

Another priority for future research involves the need for researchers to focus on multiple identities, such as already practiced in the acculturation research tradition. Recent findings emerging from there suggest that multiple identity management strategies are clearly related to intergroup attitudes in ethnic minority–majority settings. Of special interest will be to understand better the processes that underlie the adoption of two (or more) identities simultaneously (e.g., the joint endorsement of ethnic, national, or supranational identifications). In today's "globalized" yet increasingly "multicultural" societies, such hybrid identities seem set to become an increasingly prevalent phenomenon. Finally, since many of the groups that comprise these combined identities may well feel themselves to be deprived relative to other, apparently higher status, groups, the psychological processes that link identification, perceived deprivation, and subsequent collective action remain to be properly clarified. An obvious, though costly, research strategy to tackle such questions involves the use of longitudinal research programs, since they permit an assessment of the likely direction and valence of the underlying causal processes. Broadening the scope of research in this manner is probably necessary for the building of broad, rather than compartmentalized micro-, theories. And, after all, the building of broad and powerful theories with applied value was a project close to Allport's heart.

REFERENCES

Aharpour, S. & Brown, R. (2002). Functions of group identification: An exploratory analysis. *Revue Internationale de Psychologie Sociale, 15(2–3)*, 157–86.

Albert, S. (1977). Temporal comparison theory. *Psychological Review, 84*, 485–503.

Allport, G. W. (1954/1979). *The nature of prejudice*. Cambridge, MA: Perseus Books.

Berry, J. W. (1997). Immigration, acculturation, and adaptation. *Applied Psychology: An International Review, 46(1)*, 5–68.

Bourhis, R. Y., Moise, L. C., Perreault, S., & Senecal, S. (1997). Towards an interactive acculturation model: A social psychological approach. *International Journal of Psychology, 32(6)*, 369–89.

Branscombe, N. R., Schmitt, M. T., & Harvey, R. D. (1999). Perceiving pervasive discrimination among African Americans: implications for group identification and well-being. *Journal of Personality and Social Psychology, 77(1)*, 135–49.

Brewer, M. B. (1979). In-group bias in the minimal intergroup situation: A cognitive-motivational analysis. *Psychological Bulletin, 86*, 307–24.

Brewer, M. B. (1991). The social self: On being the same and different at the same time. *Personality and Social Psychology Bulletin, 17*, 475–82.

Brewer, M. B. (1999). The psychology of prejudice: ingroup love or outgroup hate? *Journal of Social Issues, 55(3)*, 429–44.

Brewer, M. B. & Brown, R. J. (1998). Intergroup relations. In D. T. Gilbert, S. T. Fiske, & G. Lindzey (eds.), *The handbook of social psychology* (4 ed.). New York: McGraw-Hill.

Brown, R. (2000). Social Identity Theory: Past achievements, current problems and future challenges. *European Journal of Social Psychology, 30(6)*, 745–78.

Brown, R. J., Hinkle, S., Ely, P. G., Fox-Cardamone, L., Maras, P., & Taylor, L. A. (1992). Recognising group diversity: Individualist–collectivist and autonomous–relational social orientations and their implications for intergroup process. *British Journal of Social Psychology*, *31*, 327–42.

Brown, R., Maras, P., Masser, B., Vivian, J., & Hewstone, M. (2001). Life on the ocean wave: Testing some intergroup hypotheses in a naturalistic setting. *Group Processes and Intergroup Relations*, *4(2)*, 81–97.

Brown, R. & Zagefka, H. (under review). Choice of comparisons in intergroup settings: Temporal information, comparison motives, and group identification.

Capozza, D. & Brown, R. (eds.) (2000). *Social identity processes: Trends in theory and research*. London: Sage.

Capozza, D., Voci, A., & Licciardello, O. (2000). Individualism, collectivism and social identity theory. In D. Capozza & R. Brown (eds.), *Social identity processes*. London: Sage.

Crocker, J. & Major, B. (1989). Social stigma and self-esteem: The self-protective properties of stigma. *Psychological Review*, *96(4)*, 608–30.

Crosby, F. (1976). A model of egoistical relative deprivation. *Psychological Review*, *83*, 85–113.

Deaux, K., Reid, A., Mizrahi, K., & Cotting, D. (1999). Connecting the person to the social: The functions of social identification. In T. R. Tyler & R. Kramer John (eds.), *The psychology of the social self*. Mahwah, NJ: Lawrence Erlbaum.

Ellemers, N., Spears, R., & Doosje, B. (2002). Self and social identity. *Annual Review of Psychology*, *53*, 161–86.

Festinger, L. (1954). A theory of social comparison processes. *Human Relations*, *7*, 117–40.

Gaertner, S. L. & Dovidio, J. (2000). *Reducing intergroup bias: The common ingroup identity*. New York: Hove.

Gluckman, M. (1956). *Custom and conflict in Africa*. Oxford: Blackwell.

Gonzalez, R., Brown, R., & Zagefka, H. (2003). Interethnic relations in Chile: The case of the indigenous Mapuche. Unpublished MS, Santiago de Chile.

Guimond, S. & Dube-Simard, L. (1983). Relative deprivation theory and the Quebec nationalist movement: The cognition–emotion distinction and the person group deprivation issue. *Journal of Personality and Social Psychology*, *44*, 527–35.

Hewstone, M., Rubin, M., & Willis, H. (2002). Intergroup bias. *Annual Review of Psychology*, *53(1)*, 575–604.

Hinkle, S. & Brown, R. (1990). Intergroup comparisons and social identity: Some links and lacunae. In D. H. Abrams & M. Hogg (eds.), *Social identity theory: constructive and critical advances* (pp. 48–70). Brighton: Harvester Wheatsheaf.

Hogg, M. A. (2000). Subjective uncertainty reduction through self-categorization: A motivational theory of social identity processes. *European Review of Social Psychology*, *11*, 223–55.

Kessler, T. & Mummendey, A. (2002). Sequential or parallel processes? A longitudinal field study concerning determinants of identity management strategies. *Journal of Personality and Social Psychology*, *82*, 75–88.

Kosterman, R. & Feshbach, S. (1989). Towards a measure of patriotic and nationalistic attitudes. *Political Psychology*, *10*, 257–74.

Leonardelli, G. J. & Brewer, M. B. (2001). Minority and majority discrimination: When and why. *Journal of Experimental Social Psychology*, *37*, 468–85.

Liebkind, K. (2001). Acculturation. In R. Brown & S. Gaertner (eds.), *The Blackwell handbook of social psychology* (vol. 4, pp. 387–405). Oxford: Blackwell.

Mummendey, A., Kessler, T., Klink, A., & Mielke, R. (1999). Strategies to cope with negative social identity: Predictions by social identity theory and relative deprivation theory. *Journal of Personality and Social Psychology*, *76(2)*, 229–45.

Mummendey, A., Klink, A., & Brown, R. (2001). Nationalism and patriotism: National identification and outgroup rejection. *British Journal of Social Psychology*, *40(2)*, 159–71.

Mummendey, A. & Wenzel, M. (1999). Social discrimination and tolerance in intergroup relations: Reactions to intergroup difference. *Personality and Social Psychology Review*, *3*, 158–74.

Olson, J. M. & Hafer, C. L. (1996). Affect, motivation, and cognition in relative deprivation research. In R. M. Sorrentino & E. T. Higgins (eds.), *Handbook of motivation and cognition* (vol. 3, pp. 85–117). New York, NY: Guilford Press.

Pettigrew, T. F., Jackson, J. S., Brika, J. B., Lemaine, G., Meertens, R. W., Wagner, U., & Zick, A. (1998). Outgroup prejudice in Western Europe. In W. Stroebe & M. Hewstone (eds.), *European review of social psychology* (vol. 8). Chichester: John Wiley.

Sherif, M. (1966). *Group conflict and cooperation*. London: Routledge and Kegan Paul.

Sherif, M. & Sherif, C. W. (1964). *Reference groups*. New York: Harper & Row.

Staub, E. (1990). Moral exclusion, personal goal theory and extreme destructiveness. *Journal of Social Issues*, *46*, 47–64.

Struch, N. & Schwartz, S. H. (1989). Intergroup aggression: Its predictors and distinctness from ingroup bias. *Journal of Personality and Social Psychology*, *56*, 364–73.

Sumner, W. G. (1906). *Folkways*. New York: Ginn.

Tajfel, H., Flament, C., Billig, M., & Bundy, R. P. (1971). Social categorisation and intergroup behaviour. *European Journal of Social Psychology*, *1*, 149–78.

Tajfel, H. & Turner, J. C. (1986). The social identity theory of intergroup behavior. In S. Worchel & W. G. Austin (eds.), *Psychology of intergroup relations* (pp. 7–24). Chicago: Nelson Hall.

Tougas, F. & Beaton, A. M. (2002). Personal and group relative deprivation: Connecting the "I" to the "we." In I. Walker & H. Smith (eds.), *Relative deprivation: Specification, development, integration* (pp. 119–35). Cambridge: Cambridge University Press.

Tougas, F. & Veilleux, F. (1988). The influence of identification, collective relative deprivation, and procedure of implementation on women's response to affirmative action: A causal modelling approach. *Canadian Journal of Behavioural Science*, *20*, 15–28.

Triandis, H. (1995). *Individualism and collectivism*. Boulder, CO: Westview Press.

Tropp, L. R. & Wright, S. C. (1999). Ingroup identification and relative deprivation: An examination across multiple social comparisons. *European Journal of Social Psychology, 29*, 707–24.

Vignoles, V., Chryssochoou, X., & Breakwell, G. (2002). Evaluating models of identity motivation: Self-esteem is not the whole story. *Self and Identity, 1*, 210–18.

Zagefka, H. (2004). Comparisons and deprivation in ethnic minority settings. Unpublished Ph.D. dissertation, University of Kent.

Zagefka, H. & Brown, R. (2002). The relationship between acculturation strategies, relative fit and intergroup relations: Immigrant–majority relations in Germany. *European Journal of Social Psychology, 32*, 171–88.

Zagefka, H. & Brown, R. (in press). Comparisons and perceived deprivation in ethnic minority settings. *Personality and Social Psychology Bulletin.*

Zagefka, H., Brown, R., Broquard, M., & Leventoglu Martin, S. (2004). Acculturation preferences, fit, intergroup attitudes and economic competition. Unpublished manuscript.

Zick, A., Wagner, U., van Dick, R., & Petzel, T. (2001). Acculturation and prejudice in Germany: Majority and minority perspectives. *Journal of Social Issues, 57(3)*, 541–58.

Chapter Five

Categorization, Recategorization, and Intergroup Bias

Samuel L. Gaertner and John F. Dovidio

The current volume celebrates the 50th anniversary of Allport's *The Nature of Prejudice*, and describes how this classic work anticipated and shaped contemporary research on intergroup relations. Our chapter tracks the development of three themes involving categorization, recategorization, and their relation to Allport's belief that intergroup contact can reduce prejudice (the "Contact Hypothesis"). These themes branch across different chapters in the original text, primarily chapter 2, "The Normality of Prejudgment"; chapter 3, "Formation of In-Groups"; and chapter 16, "The Effect of Contact."

Allport's Views on Categorization, Recategorization, and Intergroup Contact

Allport provided a unique insight into the psychology of prejudice – how fundamental and adaptive cognitive and motivational processes can often contribute to the development and maintenance of prejudice. One of the most basic processes is social categorization. Allport (1954/1979) wrote: "The human mind must think with the aid of categories. . . . Categories are the basis for normal prejudgment. We cannot possibly avoid this process" (p. 20).

According to Allport, this tendency to think in terms of category membership makes group-based distinctions of primary importance to people, and these distinctions guide perceptions, beliefs, and reactions in important ways. Allport (1954/1979) observed that "the category saturates all that it contains with the same ideational and emotional flavor" (p. 21). Moreover, the distinction between groups containing the self (ingroups) and all other groups (outgroups) is of great relevance and consequence. Allport proposed that this differentiation represents the foundation for the development of prejudice. He noted that "in-groups are psychologically primary. We live in them, and sometimes, for them. Hostility toward out-groups helps strengthen our sense of belonging, but it is not required" (p. 42).

Allport (1954/1979) also pin-pointed the function of ingroup and outgroup categorization, observing that "the category enables us quickly to identify a related object" (p. 21). With respect to the importance of ingroup identification and how it may be more fundamental to intergroup bias than even outgroup antipathy, Allport remarked that "there is good reason to believe that this love-prejudice is far more basic to human life than is . . . hate-prejudice. When a person is defending a categorical value of his own, he may do so at the expense of other people's interests or safety. Hate prejudice springs from a reciprocal love prejudice underneath" (pp. 25–6).

Because categorization is the basis of prejudice, Allport argued that changing the way people conceived of category memberships held great promise for reducing prejudice. In particular, he proposed that shifting the focus from membership at a more differentiated level, such as racial groups, to a more inclusive level, such as national or human identity, could undermine the type of categorization that leads to prejudice between racial or ethnic groups. Allport (1954/1979) observed:

> In fact, race itself has become the dominant loyalty among many people . . . It seems today that the clash between the idea of race and of One World . . . is shaping into an issue that may well be the most decisive in human history . . . Can loyalty to mankind [sic] be fashioned before interracial warfare breaks out? (p. 44)

In addition, Allport, building on the work of contemporary scholars, suggested the value of structured intergroup contact for improving intergroup relations. Although Allport's list of prerequisite conditions for successful intergroup contact has received substantial recognition over the past 50 years and stimulated a significant amount of research (see Pettigrew & Tropp, ch. 16 this volume), his point that social categorization may represent a key mechanism in this process has only recently captured the attention of researchers. Allport (1954/1979) stated:

> To be maximally effective, contact . . . should lead to a sense of equality in social status, should occur in ordinary purposeful pursuits . . . and enjoy the sanction of the community in which they occur. While it may help somewhat to place members of different ethnic groups side by side on a job, the

gain is greater if these members regard themselves as part of a *team.* (italics original, p. 489)

These quotations from Allport, separated by over 450 pages in his book, represent the themes that serve as an organizing framework for this chapter. Together, these ideas acknowledge that social categorization as "us" and "them" is not only a fundamental factor that contributes to prejudice, but also one that could be used to establish more harmonious intergroup relations. They also explain, in part, *how* the features that he proposed would facilitate successful intergroup contact (e.g., equality of status during contact) may improve intergroup attitudes.

Developments Since Allport: Social Categorization

Allport's ideas about social categorization and recategorization at higher levels of inclusiveness foreshadowed many of the theoretical and empirical developments of importance to contemporary thinking about prejudice and prejudice reduction. Indeed, social categorization is as central to contemporary work in intergroup relations (see also Brewer & Gaertner, 2001) as it was to Allport's thinking about nature of prejudice. Although Allport's analysis focused primarily on personality dynamics, he identified the central role of categorization, particularly in terms of the distinction between ingroups and outgroups. This distinction became the cornerstone for social-cognitive (Hamilton & Trolier, 1986), social–identity (Tajfel & Turner, 1979), and self-categorization (Turner, 1985) approaches to prejudice.

In the process of categorizing people into groups, people typically classify themselves *into* one of the social categories and *out of* the others. Because of the centrality of the self in social perception, this distinction has a profound influence on evaluations, cognitions, and behavior. Perhaps one reason why ethnocentrism is so prevalent is because these biases operate even when the basis for the categorization is quite trivial, as when group identity is assigned randomly in laboratory experiments.

Tajfel and Turner's (1979) Social Identity Theory (see Brown & Zagefka, ch. 4 this volume; see also the Self-Categorization Theory of Turner et al., 1987) emphasized the motivational and functional aspects of social categorization (see also Yzerbyt & Corneille, ch. 11 this volume). Tajfel and Turner proposed that a person's need for positive self-identity may be satisfied by membership in prestigious social groups. This need motivates social comparisons that favorably differentiate ingroup from outgroup members, thereby providing a basis for restored or enhanced feelings of status and esteem.

Social Identity Theory also recognizes the fundamental distinction between collective and personal identity. That is, a person can define or categorize himself or herself alternatively as the embodiment of a social collective or as a unique individual with personal motives, goals, and achievements. At the group level, the goals and achievements of the group are merged with one's own, and the group's welfare is paramount. At the individual level, one's personal welfare and goals are most salient and important. Intergroup relations begin when people in different groups think about themselves as group members rather than as distinct individuals.

Although the categorization process may place the person at either extreme end of the continuum from social identity to personal identity, Brewer's (1991) Theory of Optimal Distinctiveness suggests that there is an intermediate point along this continuum that optimally satisfies a person's needs for identity. At this point, an individual's need to be different from others (i.e., to be unique) and need to belong (i.e., to share a sense of similarity to others) are balanced. Optimally, perceiving one's group as especially positive and distinctive relative to other groups satisfies both needs for belonging and distinctiveness simultaneously. Unfortunately, one consequence of this process can be intergroup bias. Thus, what these theories have in common is the Allportian view that social categorization into ingroups and outgroups may lay a foundation for intergroup bias or ethnocentrism to develop.

As Allport cautioned, social categorization is not a simple, static process. When people or objects are categorized into groups, actual differences between members of the same category tend to be perceptually minimized (Tajfel, 1969) and often ignored in making decisions or forming impressions. Members of the same category seem to be more similar than they actually are, and more similar than they were before they were categorized together (see Judd & Park, ch. 8 this volume). In addition, although members of a social category may be different in some ways from members of other categories, these differences tend to become exaggerated and overgeneralized. For social categorization, this process becomes more ominous because these within- and between-group distortions, as Allport noted, have a tendency to generalize to additional dimensions (e.g., character traits) beyond those that differentiated the categories originally.

Additional research reveals that, upon social categorization, people favor ingroup members in reward allocations, in attitudes, and in the evaluation of the products of their labor (see Gaertner & Dovidio, 2000). Also, ingroup membership decreases psychological distance and facilitates the arousal of empathy, and, as a consequence, prosocial behavior is offered more readily to ingroup than to outgroup members. Moreover, people are more likely to be cooperative and exercise more personal restraint when using endangered common resources when these are shared with ingroup members than with others (Schroeder, Penner, Dovidio, & Piliavin, 1995).

In terms of information processing, people retain more information in a more detailed fashion for ingroup members than for outgroup members (Park & Rothbart, 1982). In addition, people are more generous and forgiving in their explanations for the behaviors of ingroup relative to outgroup members. Positive outcomes and behaviors are more likely to be attributed to internal, stable characteristics (the personality) of ingroup than outgroup members, whereas negative outcomes and behaviors are more likely to be ascribed to the personalities of outgroup than ingroup members (Hewstone, 1990). Relatedly, observed behaviors of ingroup and outgroup members are encoded in memory at different levels of abstraction (Maass, Ceccarelli, & Rudin, 1996). Undesirable actions of outgroup members are encoded at more abstract levels that presume intentionality and dispositional origin (e.g., she is hostile) than identical behaviors of ingroup members (e.g., she slapped the girl). Desirable actions of outgroup members, however, are encoded at more concrete levels (e.g., she walked across the street holding the old man's hand) relative to the same behaviors of ingroup members (e.g., she is helpful). These cognitive biases help to perpetuate social biases and stereotypes even in the face of countervailing evidence.

Whereas social categorization can initiate intergroup biases, the type of bias due largely to categorization alone primarily represents a pro-ingroup orientation (i.e., preference for ingroup members, or love-prejudice in Allport's words, rather than an anti-outgroup orientation, i.e., hate-prejudice) usually associated with hostility or aggression. Nevertheless, disadvantaged status due to preferential treatment of one group over another can be as pernicious as discrimination based on anti-outgroup orientations. As Allport suggested, love-prejudice can provide a foundation for generating hostility and conflict that can result from intergroup competition for economic resources and political power (see also Esses, Jackson, Dovidio, & Hodson, ch. 14 this volume).

Because categorization is a basic process that is fundamental to intergroup bias, some social psychologists have targeted this process as a place to begin to improve intergroup relations. Thus, in addition to the developments since Allport demonstrating the critical importance of social identity and self-categorization, new frameworks have emerged examining how strategies aimed at altering the nature of ingroup–outgroup social categorization can be effective in reducing intergroup bias and prejudice.

New Frameworks: Category-Based Models for Reducing Prejudice

Strategies for reducing intergroup bias have been directed at eliminating social categorization (decategorization), redefining the context in which categorization occurs (intergroup differentiation), or fostering superordinate group categorizations that can replace original ingroup–outgroup categorizations (recategorization).

Decategorization

In *decategorization* strategies to reduce bias, for example when people are instructed to have an interpersonal rather than a task focus during intergroup interaction, members of different social groups are induced to perceive themselves and others as separate individuals (Wilder, 1981) or to have more personalized interactions (Brewer & Miller, 1984). Reducing the salience of ingroup identity degrades ingroup biases (for example, in terms of evaluations and attributions), which interferes with the use of outgroup stereotypes and, through more personalized contact, undermines the validity of these stereotypes. However, because of the predisposition to categorize elements of the environment, decategorized orientations are unstable and difficult to maintain. Moreover, unless some recognition of group membership is maintained during interactions, the more positive feelings that develop toward someone formerly perceived as an outgroup member but now viewed as a unique individual are unlikely to generalize to other members of the group because the associative links between person and group are severed (Miller, 2002).

Mutual Intergroup Differentiation

Although it may be impossible to short-circuit the categorization process in a way that affords generalizability to the group as a whole, a second strategy, reflected in Hewstone and Brown's (1986) Mutual Intergroup Differentiation Model, suggests that it may be possible to change the tone of the original categorical scheme from mutually threatening to trustful. According to this perspective, intergroup biases can be reduced by encouraging groups to emphasize their mutual distinctiveness, for example by highlighting the different and potentially complementary skills and resources of the groups (e.g., production and marketing groups), in the context of cooperative interdependence (see Kenworthy, Hewstone, Turner, & Voci, ch. 17 this volume). For example, Hewstone and Brown (1986) further propose that interactions that maintain (rather than reduce) the salience of the separate group identities are more likely to generalize to outgroup members beyond the immediate contact situation because the association with other group members not directly involved in the interaction is maintained.

Recategorization

Recategorization approaches, a third general strategy, are designed to alter the salient basis for categorization, thereby changing the boundaries so that the ingroup is more generous, or broadly defined. Recategorization can occur by making people aware that outgroup members are also members of one's own group on a different dimension (e.g., by having one dimension, such as sex, cross-cut another dimension, such as arts and science majors; Urban & Miller, 1998). Alternatively, recategorization may be accomplished by restructuring categorization at a higher level of inclusiveness (e.g., by creating a new group membership or emphasizing an existing common group membership, such as corporate or national identity, that encompasses previous group memberships, such as race), thereby reducing the salience of the original ingroup–outgroup distinction (Gaertner & Dovidio, 2000). The newly recategorized ingroup members (formerly regarded as outsiders) become the beneficiaries of more positive personal evaluations (see Gaertner, Mann, Murrell, & Dovidio, 1989), more empathic, helpful, cooperative, and self-revealing behaviors (see Dovidio et al., 1997), more forgiving situational attributions to explain failure (and more dispositional attributions to explain success), and more positively biased information processing.

One recategorization strategy, represented by our own work on the Common Ingroup Identity Model, involves interventions to change people's conceptions of distinct group memberships to either a single, more inclusive group, or to subgroups within a more inclusive superordinate group (Gaertner & Dovidio, 2000). Allport's (1954/1979, p. 43) "circles of inclusion" diagram nicely depicts the idea that a person's potential ingroups can vary hierarchically in inclusiveness, for example from one's family to one's neighborhood, to one's city, to one's nation, to all of humankind. With recategorization, perceptions of group boundaries of "us" and "them" are transformed into a more inclusive "we."

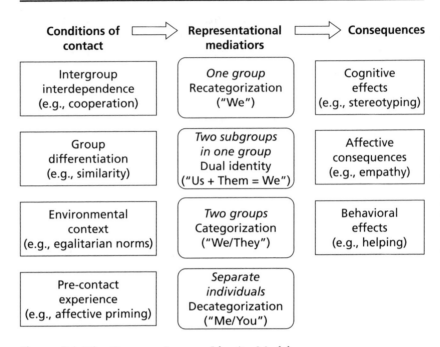

Figure 5.1 The Common Ingroup Identity Model

Common Ingroup Identity Model

The Common Ingroup Identity Model identifies potential antecedents and outcomes of recategorization, as well as mediating processes. Figure 5.1 summarizes the general framework and specifies the causes and consequences of a common ingroup identity. Specifically, it is hypothesized that the different types of intergroup interdependence and cognitive, perceptual, linguistic, affective, and environmental factors can either independently or in concert alter individuals' cognitive representations of the aggregate. These resulting cognitive representations (i.e., one group, two subgroups within one group, two groups, or separate individuals) are then proposed to result in the specific cognitive, affective, and overt behavioral consequences. Thus, the antecedent factors are proposed to influence members' cognitive representations of the memberships that in turn mediate the relationship, at least in part, between the antecedent factors and the cognitive, affective, and behavioral consequences. In addition, we proposed that common ingroup identity may be achieved by increasing the salience of existing common superordinate memberships (e.g., a school, a company, a nation) or by introducing factors (e.g., common goals or fate) that are perceived to be shared by the memberships.

In general, there is strong and consistent support for the basic hypothesis that, as a consequence of recategorization, the cognitive and motivational processes that initially produced ingroup favoritism can be harnessed to reduce intergroup bias and prejudice toward former outgroup members who now share the common, superordinate group identity (see Gaertner & Dovidio, 2000). These findings are consistent with, and extend both conceptually and empirically, Allport's idea that group memberships vary in inclusiveness and intergroup relations can be improved by shifting from difference at one level (e.g., race) to commonality at another level (e.g., humankind).

In one test of our hypothesis, we conducted an experiment that brought two three-person laboratory groups together under conditions designed to foster or reduce intergroup cooperative interaction (Gaertner et al., 1990). As expected, cooperative interaction increased one-group representations (and reduced separate-group representations) and produced more favorable attitudes toward original outgroup members and lower levels of bias. Furthermore, consistent with the Common Ingroup Identity Model, more inclusive, one-group representations *mediated* (i.e., accounted for) the relationship between the interventions and the reduction of bias. This basic finding has been conceptually replicated in a number of laboratory experiments and field studies involving, for example, banking executives who experienced a merger or college students in blended families (see Gaertner & Dovidio, 2000). Thus, developing a common group identity is a key step in the process by which intergroup contact reduces bias, not simply a facilitating factor as suggested by Allport.

Nevertheless, as Allport recognized, one major reason why the positive benefits of intergroup contact may fail to generalize to the outgroup as a whole is that the specific outgroup members present are favorably regarded as exceptions and not necessarily typical of their group as a whole (see also Wilder, 1984). Allport (1954/1979) proposed: "When a fact can not fit into a mental field, the exception is acknowledged, but the field is hastily fenced in again" (p. 23). In this respect, a dual identity (e.g., African American) that involves the recognition of both connection (superordinate group identity) and difference (original subgroup identity) may be a particularly promising mechanism for generalization to occur (see also Turner, 1981).

Dual Identity

With a dual identity relative to the pure one-group representation, the benefits of intergroup contact may more easily generalize to additional outgroup members because the associative link to their original group identity remains intact, as in Hewstone and Brown's (1986) Mutual Intergroup Differentiation Model. Although the convergence of several of Allport's ideas suggests the potential value of a dual identity, this particular concept was not articulated in *The Nature of Prejudice*.

Within the context of the Common Ingroup Identity Model, the development of a common ingroup identity does not necessarily require each group to forsake its less inclusive group identity. As Allport (1954/ 1979) noted, every individual belongs to multiple groups and "concentric loyalties need not clash. To be devoted to a large circle does not imply the destruction of one's attachment to a smaller circle. *The loyalties that clash are almost invariably of identical scope*" (p. 44). Similarly, as denoted by the "subgroups within one group" (i.e., a dual identity) representation (see figure 5.1), we believe that it is possible for people to conceive two groups as distinct units within the context of a common superordinate identity (for example, as citizens of a city within a state, parents and children within a family, or marketers and accountants within a company).

When group identities and their associated cultural values are adaptive, or when they are associated with high status or highly visible cues to group membership, it would be undesirable or impossible for people to relinquish these group identities completely or, as perceivers, to be "colorblind." Indeed, demands to forsake these group identities or to adopt a "colorblind" ideology would likely arouse strong reactance and result in especially poor intergroup relations (see Judd & Park, ch. 8 this volume). If, however, people continued to regard themselves as members of different groups, but all playing on the same team, intergroup relations between these "subgroups" would usually become more positive than if members only considered themselves as "separate groups." Nevertheless, Allport (1954/1979) claimed that these superordinate or "concentric loyalties take time to develop, and often of course they fail completely to do so" (pp. 44–5). However, under conditions in which subgroup identities are recognized and valued and linked positively to the superordinate group identity, a dual identity may be effective for reducing intergroup bias and maintaining harmonious relations between groups.

The consideration of a dual identity within the Common Ingroup Identity Model is, in fact, consistent with other models of cultural identity and well-being. For instance, the alternation model of second-culture acquisition (LaFromboise, Coleman, & Gerton, 1993) suggests that it is possible for an individual to know two cultures, identify with both, and draw on these identities at different times. The multicultural model suggests that an individual can maintain a positive identity while simultaneously participating in and identifying with a larger entity composed of many other racial and ethnic groups (Berry, 1984). Indeed, the development of a bicultural or multicultural identity is not only possible but can contribute to the social adjustment, psychological adaptation, and overall well-being of minority group members (Crocker & Quinn, 2001; LaFromboise et al., 1993) in ways superior to full assimilation or acculturation.

Has Allport Been Supported?

As we noted earlier, Allport identified social categorization as a fundamental process, with general adaptive value, that predisposes people to be prejudiced. In addition, he recognized the primacy of ingroups and the contribution of "love-prejudice" as a fundamental contributor to intergroup bias, often as important and influential as "hate-prejudice" directed toward outgroup members. These ideas and observations have received strong empirical support over the past 50 years, and have been incorporated in new, elaborated frameworks, such as Social Identity Theory, Self-Categorization Theory, and Optimal Distinctiveness Theory, that have evolved to provide more comprehensive and sophisticated perspectives on these issues.

In addition to the detailed treatment of social categorization processes, recent strategies for reducing intergroup bias have capitalized on Allport's insights about the malleability of social categorization and the opportunity to shift emphasis to more inclusive levels of categorization. For example, Allport's brief reference, cited earlier in this chapter, that the gains from intergroup contact are greater if the participating members have a team mentality, has been the focus of contemporary research on this topic. In particular, among the antecedent factors proposed by the Common Ingroup Identity Model (see figure 5.1) are the features of contact situations that Allport proposed would facilitate successful intergroup contact (e.g., interdependence between groups, equal status, egalitarian norms; see Pettigrew and Tropp, ch. 16 this volume). From this perspective, cooperative interaction may enhance positive evaluations of outgroup members and reduce intergroup bias, at least in part, by transforming a person's representations of the memberships from two groups to a more inclusive group (see also Kenworthy et al., ch. 17 this volume).

Although inclusive categorization is recognized by both Allport and the Common Ingroup Identity Model, Allport may have underestimated the important mediating role of perceived common group membership. Allport was aware of the benefits of common group membership, but he seemed to regard it as a catalyst rather than as a consequence of favorable contact conditions. While team membership may indeed facilitate the beneficial effects of contact, our model also suggests that unifying perceptions may be a consequence of cooperative, self-revealing interactions. Indeed, we propose that the perception of common ingroup identity is psychologically instrumental to bringing outgroup members closer to the self, thereby increasing positive orientations toward them.

In terms of developing a common, more inclusive ingroup identity, Allport did not fully anticipate the importance of majority–minority group distinctions and preferences for full assimilation or multicultural acculturation strategies. Whereas majority group members (e.g., White students in the United States or Dutch citizens in the Netherlands) value an assimilation model, members of minority groups (e.g., Black and Latino college students in the United States or immigrants in the Netherlands) prefer a dual identity (an integration-pluralistic model; see Berry, 1984; Dovidio, Gaertner, & Kafati, 2000; van Oudenhoven, Prins, & Buunk, 1998). Thus, interventions designed to improve the intergroup attitudes of one group may not be effective, and may be counterproductive, for improving the attitudes of the other group. Current research thus emphasizes the importance of the reciprocal group responses for understanding and addressing intergroup relations more so than Allport did in *The Nature of Prejudice*. Allport was correct in identifying many of the key elements, but psychologists have made significant progress in integrating these into more comprehensive and dynamic models of intergroup relations.

Future Directions

Research on the role of social categorization is, on the one hand, a mature area of inquiry, while on the other hand, its application to understanding the dynamics of how intergroup contact can reduce intergroup bias is a relatively recent development in the field. Although substantial research on the Contact Hypothesis has been conducted over the past 50 years (see Pettigrew & Tropp, ch. 16 this volume), the concerted focus on the cognitive representation of groups as moderators and mediators of the effect of contact represents a more recent development. This perspective, however, has significant potential for promoting integration of diverse, and previously separate, perspectives on intergroup relations. Thus, we see the pursuit of integration as the direction and promise of future research in this area. The emphases of these efforts we believe will occur in at least three ways: (a) exploring the complementarity of different category-based approaches; (b) understanding the dynamics of multiple identities, considering both majority- and minority-group perspectives; and (c) bridging theory and application in antibias education.

With respect to the first direction, although decategorization or personalization, mutual intergroup differentiation, and recategorization through cross-cutting group memberships or superordinate group identities represent different perspectives for reducing prejudice, rather than viewing these as competing positions and arguing *which* one is correct, future research will likely consider these as complementary rather than as competing frameworks. This research will move from earlier work demonstrating the validity of each position beyond arguments of which is stronger or more influential, to consider *when* each strategy is most effective. Indeed, it is possible that these different processes may operate sequentially to reduce bias (Hewstone, 1996; Pettigrew, 1998). For instance, success in cooperative activities in which groups maintain their separate identities (mutual intergroup differentiation) may facilitate the groups' subsequent acceptance of a common superordinate identity. The development of a common ingroup identity, in turn, may not only produce more positive attitudes toward people formerly perceived only as outgroup members but also may lead to more individuated perceptions of them, and encourage more self-disclosing interactions. Even though the salience of a common ingroup identity may be relatively unstable because of contextual pressures or historical relations between the original groups (Hewstone, 1996), these personalized interactions may then create more enduring positive attitudes, orientations, and social networks between members of the groups, as well as the recognition and development of cross-cutting group identities. Thus the challenge for future research is to discover how and when these processes can operate sequentially over time, recognizing the dynamic and evolving nature of intergroup relations and the psychological processes that underlie them.

A second general direction for future research involves the acknowledgment that people have multiple group identities that can become activated sequentially, alternatively, or simultaneously. Whereas considerable study in the traditions of Social Identity Theory and Self-Categorization Theory has focused on the activation of alternative identities, such as personal and collective identities, we believe that more attention will be devoted to simultaneously activated alternative collective identities, such as a dual identity (e.g., two subgroups within a superordinate group identity).

The impact of a dual identity on prejudice is presently not well understood. Current research indicates that a dual identity can sometimes lead to reduced bias, as hypothesized in the Common Ingroup Identity Model, but other times it can increase prejudice. For example, in the multiethnic high-school setting, a strong dual identity, in which groups recognized their own cultural identity as well as their superordinate national connection (e.g., African American) was related to both positive conditions of contact and to more positive intergroup relations (Gaertner et al., 1996). However, among East Germans, a strong superordinate German identity, together with a strong East German identity, predicted increased bias toward West Germans (Waldzus, Mummendey, Wenzel, & Weber, 2003). Thus, future work should attempt to reconcile these inconsistent findings conceptually.

To that end, a key element determining the impact of a dual identity on intergroup relations is likely what a dual identity signals – whether it is perceived as a sign of progress toward a desired goal or as a cue of threat. In terms of the former, as noted earlier, we found that minority college students value multiculturalism and hold it as an ideal for their institution (Dovidio, Gaertner, & Kafati, 2000). In this context, we found that a dual identity for minority students, one that reaffirmed their cultural heritage while recognizing their common university identity, predicted positive intergroup attitudes and institutional commitment. An assimilationist, university-only identity did not predict these positive orientations.

In contrast, as national crises in Ireland and the former Yugoslavia suggest, in times of unusual competition or threat within a country or of political instability, the existence of a dual identity may intensify the salience of the separate group identities and thus may refuel intergroup conflict compared to a purely one-group or separate-individuals representation. Under these conditions, as Social Identity Theory posits, the tension created between the two incompatible identities may trigger greater intergroup conflict, in part because each subgroup projects its beliefs and values as the standard by which all other groups within the overarching identity should be judged (Mummendey & Wenzel, 1999). This projection increases the likelihood that one's own group will be perceived as superior (increasing "love-prejudice") and that the other group will be viewed as inferior (increasing "hate-prejudice"). Addressing this issue of when and how simultaneously activated dual or multiple identities influence bias will also help to inform current policy debates about the impact of colorblind and multicultural models of social integration (e.g., Wolsko, Park, Judd, & Wittenbrink, 2000).

In terms of the third direction, bridging theory and application, we note that science and practice play important roles that can support and reinforce each other. Integration of these approaches will benefit both basic research and the practical effectiveness of antibias education programs. Through experience, educators can develop tools that are effective at reducing bias. Informed by this effectiveness, researchers can investigate how and why these tools work as they do. In addition, research under highly controlled conditions can shed light on the basic causes of bias, on the types of underlying processes that can most effectively eliminate this bias, and on the conditions under which different processes operate best. Once these processes have been identified and tested, they can be incorporated directly into interventions to address bias under more complex and naturalistic circumstances. Thus, we see practice and theory as complementary enterprises.

If appreciated and managed appropriately, the partnership between researchers and educators will contribute more important and lasting benefits to society than either approach could accomplish alone. This partnership will also help to achieve Allport's fundamental goal of the socially responsible and effective use of social science. Kenneth B. Clark wrote in his introduction to the reissued version of *The Nature of Prejudice*, published on the 25th anniversary of the first edition, "Allport . . . remains an outstanding model of a major social scientist who was not at all apologetic in his insistence that . . . thoughtful, moral, rationalistic social scientists must be the temporary custodians of such enduring values as justice – and that trained human intelligence is an important weapon in the ongoing struggle against ignorance, superstition, and injustice" (Clark, 1979, pp. ix–x). We believe that future research will continue in the direction advocated by Allport: understanding the nature of prejudice with the ultimate goal of eradicating it.

NOTES

Preparation of this chapter was facilitated by NIMH Grant MH 48721.

REFERENCES

Allport, G. W. (1954/1979). *The nature of prejudice*. Cambridge, MA: Perseus Books.

Berry, J. W. (1984). Cultural relations in plural societies. In N. Miller & M. B. Brewer (eds.), *Groups in contact: The psychology of desegregation* (pp. 11–27). Orlando, FL: Academic Press.

Brewer, M. B. (1991). The social self: On being the same and different at the same time. *Personality and Social Psychology Bulletin, 17,* 475–82.

Brewer, M. B. & Gaertner, S. L. (2001). Toward reduction of prejudice: Intergroup contact and social categorization. In R. J. Brown & S. L. Gaertner (eds.), *The Blackwell handbook of social psychology: Intergroup processes* (pp. 451–72). Malden, MA: Blackwell.

Brewer, M. B. & Miller, N. (1984). Beyond the contact hypothesis: Theoretical perspectives on desegregation. In N. Miller & M. B. Brewer (eds.), *Groups in contact: The psychology of desegregation* (pp. 281–302). Orlando FL: Academic Press.

Clark, K. B. (1979). Introduction. In G. W. Allport, *The nature of prejudice: 25th anniversary edition* (pp. ix–xi). Cambridge, MA: Perseus Books.

Crocker, J. & Quinn, D. M. (2001). Psychological consequences of devalued identities. In R. J. Brown & S. L. Gaertner (eds.), *The Blackwell handbook of social psychology: Intergroup processes* (pp. 238–57). Oxford, UK: Blackwell.

Dovidio, J. F., Gaertner, S. L., & Kafati, G. (2000). Group identity and intergroup relations: The Common Ingroup Identity Model. In S. R. Thye, E. J. Lawler, M. W. Macy, & H. A. Walker (eds.), *Advances in group processes* (vol. 17, pp. 1–34). Stamford, CT: JAI Press.

Dovidio, J. F., Gaertner, S. L., Validzic, A., Matoka, K., Johnson, B., & Frazier, S. (1997). Extending the benefits of re-categorization: Evaluations, self-disclosure and helping. *Journal of Experimental Social Psychology, 33,* 401–20.

Gaertner, S. L. & Dovidio, J. F. (2000). *Reducing intergroup bias: The Common Ingroup Identity Model.* Philadelphia, PA: The Psychology Press.

Gaertner, S. L., Mann, J. A., Dovidio, J. F., Murrell, A. J., & Pomare, M. (1990). How does cooperation reduce intergroup bias? *Journal of Personality and Social Psychology, 59,* 692–704.

Gaertner, S. L., Mann, J., Murrell, A., & Dovidio, J. F. (1989). Reducing intergroup bias: The benefits of recategorization. *Journal of Personality and Social Psychology, 57,* 239–49.

Gaertner, S. L., Rust, M. C., Dovidio, J. F., Bachman, B. A., & Anastasio, P. A. (1996). The Contact Hypothesis: The role of a common ingroup identity on reducing intergroup bias among majority and minority group members. In J. L. Nye & A. M. Brower (eds.), *What's social about social cognition?* (pp. 230–360). Newbury Park, CA: Sage.

Hamilton, D. L. & Trolier, T. K. (1986). Stereotypes and stereotyping: An overview of the cognitive approach. In J. F. Dovidio & S. L. Gaertner (eds.), *Prejudice, discrimination and racism.* Orlando, FL: Academic Press.

Hewstone, M. (1990). The "ultimate attribution error"? A review of the literature on intergroup attributions. *European Journal of Social Psychology, 20,* 311–35.

Hewstone, M. (1996). Contact and categorization: Social psychological interventions to change intergroup relations. In C. N. Macrae, M. Hewstone, & C. Stangor (eds.), *Foundations of stereotypes and stereotyping* (pp. 323–68). New York: Guilford.

Hewstone, M. & Brown, R. J. (1986). Contact is not enough: An intergroup perspective on the "Contact Hypothesis." In M. Hewstone &

R. J. Brown (eds.), *Contact and conflict in intergroup encounters* (pp. 1–44). Oxford: Blackwell.

LaFromboise, T., Coleman, H. L. K., & Gerton, J. (1993). Psychological impact of biculturalism: Evidence and theory. *Psychological Bulletin, 114,* 395–412.

Maass, A., Ceccarelli, R., & Rudin, S. (1996). Linguistic intergroup bias: Evidence for in-group-protective motivation. *Journal of Personality and Social Psychology, 71,* 512–26.

Miller, N. (2002). Personalization and the promise of contact theory. *Journal of Social Issues, 58,* 387–410.

Mummendey, A. & Wenzel, M. (1999). Social discrimination and tolerance in intergroup relations: Reactions to intergroup difference. *Personality and Social Psychology Review, 3,* 158–74.

Park, B. & Rothbart, M. (1982). Perception of out-group homogeneity and levels of social categorization: Memory for the subordinate attributes of in-group and out-group members. *Journal of Personality and Social Psychology, 42,* 1051–68.

Pettigrew, T. F. (1998). Intergroup Contact Theory. *Annual Review of Psychology, 49,* 65–85.

Schroeder, D. A., Penner, L. A., Dovidio, J. F., & Piliavin, J. A. (1995). *Psychology of helping and altruism: Problems and puzzles.* New York: McGraw-Hill.

Tajfel, H. (1969). Cognitive aspects of prejudice. *Journal of Social Issues, 25(4),* 79–97.

Tajfel, H. & Turner, J. C. (1979). An integrative theory of intergroup conflict. In W. G. Austin & S. Worchel (eds.), *The social psychology of intergroup*

relations (pp. 33–48). Monterey, CA: Brooks/Cole.

Turner, J. C. (1981). The experimental social psychology of intergroup behavior. In J. C. Turner & H. Giles (eds.), *Intergroup behavior* (pp. 66–101). Chicago, IL: University of Chicago Press.

Turner, J. C. (1985). Social categorization and the self-concept: A social cognitive theory of group behavior. In E. J. Lawler (ed.), *Advances in group processes* (vol. 2, pp. 77–122). Greenwich, CT: JAI Press.

Turner, J. C., Hogg, M. A., Oakes, P. J., Reicher, S. D., & Wetherell, M. S. (1987). *Rediscovering the social group: A self-categorization theory.* Oxford: Blackwell.

Urban, L. M. & Miller, N. (1998). A theoretical analysis of crossed categorization effects: A meta-analysis. *Journal of Personality and Social Psychology, 74,* 894–908.

van Oudenhoven, J. P., Prins, K. S., & Buunk, B. (1998). Attitudes of minority and majority members towards adaptation of immigrants. *European Journal of Social Psychology, 28,* 995–1013.

Verkuyten, M. & Hagendoorn, L. (1998). Prejudice and self-categorization: The variable role of authoritarianism and in-group stereotypes. *Personality and Social Psychology Bulletin, 24,* 99–110.

Waldzus, S., Mummendey, A., Wenzel, M., & Weber, U. (2003). Towards tolerance: Representations of superordinate categories and perceived ingroup prototypicality. *Journal of Experimental Social Psychology, 39,* 31–47.

Wilder, D. A. (1981). Perceiving persons as a group: Categorization and intergroup relations. In D. L. Hamilton (ed.), *Cognitive processes in stereotyping and intergroup behavior* (pp. 213–57). Hillsdale, NJ: Erlbaum.

Wilder, D. A. (1984). Predictions of belief homogeneity and similarity following social categorization. *British Journal of Social Psychology, 23,* 323–33.

Wolsko, C., Park, B., Judd, C. M., & Wittenbrink, B. (2000). Framing interethnic ideology: Effects of multicultural and color-blind perspectives on judgments of groups and individuals. *Journal of Personality and Social Psychology, 78,* 635–54.

Chapter Six

Rejection or Inclusion of Outgroups?
Mary R. Jackman

In his chapter, "Rejection of Out-Groups" (chapter 4), Allport addressed the problem of intergroup discrimination and violence. His treatment was framed by his seminal definition of prejudice as "an antipathy based on a faulty and inflexible generalization" that "may be felt or expressed. . . . toward a group . . . or toward an individual . . . member of that group" (Allport, 1954/1979, p. 9). In that view, discrimination and violence are the spontaneous expressions of prejudice, and the engine that drives prejudice is a person-based, irrational hostility. Fueled by categorical beliefs about social groups that are ignorant, parochial, and rigid, that hostility is discharged without restraint in verbal invectives, discriminatory behaviors, and physical violence. The bad news was that many individuals in privileged groups harbored a destructive hostility toward outgroups. The good news was that the hostility was innocent of political motivation, in both its genesis and expression. In a later chapter, Allport (p. 265) illustrated his thesis with a homily: "*See that man over there? Yes. Well, I hate him. But you don't know him. That's why I hate him.*" Intergroup hostility had no rational basis: it bubbled forth naively from ignorant and misguided individuals to be inflicted unilaterally and without artifice on subordinate victims. The more intense the hostility, the more extreme the negative behavioral manifestations. It would thus be easy to observe, and the ignorance on which it was founded was regrettable but subject to correction.

I begin with a brief outline of Allport's views on prejudice and the rejection of outgroups. I then consider research developments since the publication of his book, noting his hegemonic impact on the main trajectory of research, before outlining the gradual accumulation of theory and data that contradict his position. Following that, I outline a new framework that dethrones hostility as the catalyst for intergroup discrimination and violence. I propose instead that discrimination and violence are driven by self-interested, rational, political motives. The central motivator for dominant groups in unequal social relations is not hatred, but the desire to control. As they seek to lock in the social, economic, and political benefits of long-term relations of inequality, indiscriminate hostility is too incendiary to be effective. By contrast, _positive_ beliefs and feelings – when offered on a conditional basis – have an unrivaled potency. Contrary to Allport's model, privileged groups thus strive to maintain amicable relations with subordinates. The dominant group's success in this endeavor is constrained by the institutional structure of their relations with subordinates. To understand the form that discrimination and violence take and the attitudes that unfold between unequal groups, it is thus critical to assess the structure of their mutual relations. I conclude by assessing support for Allport's views and identifying directions for future research.

Allport's Views on Prejudice and the Rejection of Outgroups

Allport delineated three incremental stages of "rejecting" behaviors toward outgroups: verbal rejection (or "antilocution"), discrimination (including segregation), and physical attack (including lynching, riots, and genocide), arranged in a continuum of increasing severity and animosity but decreasing incidence. He argued that "people's bark (antilocution) is often sharper than their bite (actual discrimination)" (Allport, 1954/1979, pp. 55–6), but each successive stage was dependent on the previous one for its genesis. He saw purely verbal expressions of hostility and rejection as the most common, and in themselves the least harmful, although these too were graded from mild to severe expressions of animosity, with jokes and derision seen as less serious, and name-calling and persistent invectives as more serious (see also Mullen & Leader, ch. 12 this volume). Such verbal negativity provided the breeding ground for some individuals – those with higher levels of animosity – to discriminate against the target group.

Allport defined discrimination as the denial of equal treatment on the basis of group membership. His examples centered heavily on race and reflected the historical era in which he was writing, focusing on "restrictive covenants, boycotts, neighborhood pressure, legal segregation, 'gentlemen's agreements'" as "devices for discrimination" (Allport, 1954/1979, p. 51). Oddly, he did not consider avoidance to be discrimination or even to be especially harmful (a sadly outdated view in light of the bitter ramifications of "White flight" subsequently experienced in American neighborhoods and schools). Allport argued that discrimination in turn provided for the outgrowth of physical violence, the rarest and most vitriolic expression of intergroup animosity. Intergroup violence erupted from the gradual build-up of animosity, the first key step of which was the categorical prejudgment of a group.

Allport made two key arguments about these behaviors. First, they were driven by animosity, and the extremity of the behavior was a direct indicator of the degree of hatred felt by the perpetrator. Second, he was emphatic that there was no rational or economic basis to these behaviors – even discrimination (which does bestow social and economic advantages on one's own group) was motivated solely by irrationally founded, individually generated hatred for the target group. Although he acknowledged the role of "facilitating" factors in the social environment, their effect was to reinforce individual animosity and/or to release individuals from inhibitions about expressing their hatred. The most egregious examples of intergroup violence represented explosions of hatred too intense to be restrained by normal social inhibitions against aggressive behaviors.

Developments since Allport

Allport's analysis of prejudice and its behavioral manifestations did not shock his contemporaries. Indeed, it was consistent with the emphasis of those who preceded him (e.g., Deutsch & Collins, 1951; Myrdal, 1944; Williams, 1947), and *The Nature of Prejudice* loosely synthesized extant research. His homey, lucid exposition quickly became the reigning view (e.g., Duckitt, 2003; Stephan, 1985). Numerous revisions have been proffered to accommodate changes in racial attitudes since 1954 (Krysan, 2000; Gaertner & Dovidio, ch. 5 this volume), but Allport's emphasis on a naively founded, irrational, individual-level hostility as the essential core of the problem has continued to hold sway among prejudice scholars. Consistent with Myrdal's (1944) earlier lament that prejudice was a painful anachronism that clashed with the democratic principles undergirding other facets of American life, scholars hoped to facilitate social progress by finding the cure for democracy's anomalous, festering sore – intergroup animosity based on ignorant, derogatory stereotypes. A vast literature on stereotypes was spawned (e.g., Hamilton, 1981; Tajfel, 1969). Whites' attitudes toward African Americans were the focal concern, and theories concentrated on individual-level factors such as personality, upbringing, or experiences such as education and intergroup contact that were hypothesized to break down ignorance and/or socialize individuals into enlightened, democratic norms (e.g., Adorno, Frenkel-Brunswik, Levinson, & Sanford, 1950; Lipset, 1960; Wilner, Walkley, & Cook, 1955; see also Pettigrew & Tropp, ch. 16 this volume).

Allport's position that intergroup violence was caused by eruptions of intense hostility was also widely shared. For example, feminist scholars linked violence against women (such as spousal assault, rape, and the persecution of women as witches in early modern Europe) with pervasive misogyny (e.g., Barstow, 1995; French, 1992; see also Rudman, ch. 7 this volume), and Goldhagen (1996) alleged in his bestselling book, *Hitler's Willing Executioners*, that the Germans' participation in the mass extermination of Jews during the Second World War could only be explained by their deep-seated anti-Semitism.

At the same time, scattered research has accumulated that throws doubt on Allport's paradigm and points to a more textured, political interpretation of intergroup attitudes, discrimination, and violence. Disparate scholars have directed attention to the importance of organizational and political factors, rather than animosity, for establishing and maintaining group status and advantage (see also Esses, Jackson, Dovidio, & Hodson, ch. 14 this volume). Other research has revealed a complexity to intergroup attitudes and discrimination that cannot be accommodated within Allport's hostility-driven paradigm.

Organizational and Political Constraints

Early on, the Robbers' Cave experiments at a boys' summer camp (Sherif & Sherif, 1953) had demonstrated that people's intergroup attitudes were a product of their group's interests in a specifically structured, intergroup relationship. When relations between the Eagles and Rattlers were structured with repeated zero-sum, win-or-lose contests between groups, reciprocated hostilities quickly developed in the groups' behaviors and attitudes. Hostilities were dispelled by introducing "superordinate goals" that required cooperation and changed the interests of the two groups from mutually opposed to shared and interdependent (see also Gaertner & Dovidio, ch. 5 this volume). Although the Sherifs' field experiments were restricted to a rudimentary dichotomy in intergroup structure (mutually opposed interests with frequent competitive interactions versus shared interests with cooperative interactions), their results pointed to the significance of structural constraints and self-interest in shaping intergroup attitudes and behaviors. Unfortunately, scholars were largely blinded to this implication in the Allportian afterglow that suffused the subject-matter, and instead the Sherifs' results were widely interpreted as affirming the significance of hostility in all intergroup relations.

In 1958, Blumer sketched out a tentatively political argument about prejudice – that it was driven by dominant groups' feelings of threat and sustained by powerful, group-level cultural depictions of subordinates that were designed to protect the dominant group's "sense of group position" (p. 3). Blumer still emphasized hostility as an intrinsic element of prejudice and the importance of stereotypes in feeding that hostility (albeit at the societal/cultural level rather than at the individual level), and he fell short of an unambiguous political argument (see Jackman, 1994), but he vehemently made the case that prejudice was not the product of individual hostility but a cultural, group-level phenomenon designed to protect the dominant group's claims to privileged status. His argument was out of step with the Allport paradigm. It was a sleeper.

In 1960, van den Berghe published an influential paper in sociology on "Distance Mechanisms of Stratification," in which he argued that all systems of stratification devise mechanisms to differentiate subordinates from dominants and to maintain status boundaries between them. Instead of depicting segregation as an intermediate step in the expression of intergroup hostility, he saw it as one of two possible types of distance mechanisms that would necessarily be employed by dominant groups to serve their unequal relations with subordinates. To create an impermeable status barrier between themselves and subordinates, he argued that dominants rely primarily on either *social distance mechanisms* that dictate group-specific social roles (e.g., restricting the occupations subordinates can pursue) and an intergroup etiquette of dominance and deference, or *spatial distance mechanisms* (such as de jure or de facto segregation) that separate the two groups in their use of physical space.

Other researchers have demonstrated that, contrary to Allport's argument, violence does not require a history of animosity at either the group or individual level. Weingast (1997) has shown that social groups can become poised for armed conflict, even when they have a history of good relations and a preference for peace, if political institutions fail to safeguard each group's interests and mutual trust is undermined. At the individual level, experimental research has shown that organizational factors alone transform ordinary people with no personal pathologies or prior hostility into demons who torture and punish their victims for minor infractions or for no reason at all (e.g., Milgram, 1974; Zimbardo, 2004). Such organizational factors include instructions that permit or legitimize the use of violence, a chain of command that relieves perpetrators of responsibility for their acts, the assignment of anonymous identities to perpetrators, and granting pervasive powers to perpetrators without threat of retaliation or sanctions. Experimental results were validated by the revelations in 2004 of widespread torture, abuse, and humiliation of detainees in Iraqi prisons under the supervision of ordinary young American men and women during the American occupation of Iraq.

Even more puzzling for the Allportian argument, much violence against subordinates in unequal social relations is carried out by subordinates themselves (Jackman, 2001), either as the delegated henchmen for punitive actions initiated by dominants or as the self-appointed agents of injuries inflicted against themselves or their children. Chains of command in the workplace or in genocidal actions commonly turn over the dirty work of carrying out punitive or malevolent acts of violence to selected members of the targeted group itself. For example, it was generally slave drivers (who were themselves slaves) who were responsible for whippings and other punishments in antebellum Southern plantations (Van Deburg, 1979), factory foremen are recruited from among the line workers they oversee, and the rounding up of Jews in Polish ghettos to meet Nazi deportation quotas for Holocaust concentration camps was often deputized to the Jewish ghetto police. Examples of self-inflicted injuries committed by subordinates without any direct intervention by dominants include women's zealous participation in many Western beauty practices from nineteenth-century corsets to contemporary liposuction and starvation dieting, the crippling practice of Chinese foot-binding (which women perpetuated devotedly for about 10 centuries until the early twentieth century), female genital mutilation imposed on over 130 million daughters by their mothers in about two dozen African countries today, and the exposure of children to harsh, life-threatening work by their low-income parents throughout history and in many countries today (Jackman, 2001). The Allportian link between hatred and violence cannot make sense of such behaviors.

Complex Intergroup Attitudes

Over the second half of the twentieth century, Whites' racial attitudes evolved in puzzling ways that were not anticipated by Allport's model. From the 1970s, analysts began observing a steady increase in support among Whites for general principles of racial equality, and there was also evidence that categorical stereotypes about Blacks were declining. Racial prejudice, as Allport had conceived it, was eroding – and yet there was also persistent evidence that Whites continued to draw invidious distinctions between the attributes of Whites and Blacks (Bobo & Johnson, 2000; Jackman, 1994) and remained staunchly opposed to specific affirmative racial policies (e.g., Jackman, 1978; Schuman, Steeh, & Bobo, 1985). Further, during the same period that Allportian racial prejudice was declining, research by demographers showed that residential segregation of African Americans was hardening and deepening (Massey & Denton, 1993). Clearly, segregation is not a simple barometer of racial hostility.

An intense debate ensued about the meaning of these puzzling trends (e.g., Krysan, 2000), and scholars began to differentiate "old-fashioned racism" from various newly offered concepts that tinkered with – but did not abandon – Allport's simple, unitary conception. Increasingly, prejudice was seen as something more subtle, more socially sensitive, and more multifaceted and complex (Devine, ch. 20 this volume; Gaertner & Dovidio, ch. 5 this volume). Individually generated hostility remained a key ingredient, but some scholars began to argue that prejudice was affected by political considerations, whether conservatism (e.g., Sniderman & Carmines, 1997), a sense of group threat (e.g., Bobo, 1999), racial resentment (Kinder & Sanders, 1996), social dominance orientation (Sidanius & Pratto, 1999), or group interests (e.g., Jackman & Muha, 1984). Blumer's 1958 paper enjoyed a revival, as some scholars began to search for a more political approach to racial attitudes.

Research on gender attitudes and discrimination has also challenged Allportian assumptions. It has increasingly been shown that while women experience persistent occupational and income discrimination, women in general are liked as much as or more than men (Eagly & Diekman, ch. 2 this volume; Jackman, 1994; Rudman, ch. 7 this volume). In a more generic vein, experiments by Ridgeway (2001) found that, while the resource-rich are more likely to be seen as competent and agentic, the resource-poor are more likely to been seen positively as likeable, considerate, and cooperative (see also Fiske, ch. 3 this volume). Glick and Fiske's (2001) research on "ambivalent sexism" has shown that attitudes toward women bifurcate into "benevolent" and "hostile" types of sexism, depending on whether the female target follows the traditional, deferential (communal) model or the career-oriented, feminist (agentic) model. Hostility is thus reserved only for those women who defy traditional, discriminatory injunctions (Rudman, ch. 7 this volume).

What accounts for these various forms of intergroup attitudes? A comparative analysis of race, class, and gender relations in the US found that the specific configuration of intergroup attitudes varies according to the structure of the relationship (Jackman, 1994). For example, in race relations, marked by pervasive *spatial* distance mechanisms and limited opportunities for personal intergroup contact, the groups manifest a deep ideological rift, substantial own-group preference, and assertions of negative but probabilistically attributed stereotypes about Blacks by a substantial proportion of Whites. In gender relations, marked by pervasive *social* distance mechanisms and dense personal contacts across group lines, there is barely any ideological rift or own-group preference between groups, and women are categorically stereotyped by both groups with positive, communal traits. None of the intergroup relations (race, gender, or class) corresponds to the expectations of Allport's prejudice model, i.e., free-ranging, hostile feelings or unmitigated, derogatory stereotypes. And yet all three intergroup relations have marked inequalities between groups in economic outcomes, status, and power, and pronounced tendencies among dominant group members to maintain these inequalities.

These scattered theoretical and empirical developments raise puzzles that cannot be resolved within Allport's framework. In one way or another, they suggest that the key to the attitudes and behaviors attending intergroup relationships is to be found in their social organization and the constraints and opportunities that are thus created.

A New Framework: Love and Reason in Intergroup Relations

Analysts of social class relations have worked on the premise that unequal groups (socioeconomic classes) are made up of political actors who respond strategically to structural constraints and opportunities as they attempt to maximize their control over societal resources (e.g., Centers, 1949; Gramsci, 1971; Marx & Engels, 1888/1959). In a similar vein, some students of political institutions and behavior borrowed ideas developed by economists (Arrow, 1951) to postulate that political systems are made up of individual strategists who rationally seek to maximize their outcomes for the minimum expenditure of personal resources. In a world vexed by uncertainty and a chronic scarcity of information, people pursue their self-interested goals within the constraints imposed by the structure of political institutions (e.g., Downs, 1957; Grofman, 1995; Jackman & Miller, 2004).

Building on those ideas, I assume that humans are rational, self-interested, sociable actors who pursue strategies to maximize their control over resources (social, material, and political), subject to constraints (Jackman, 1994, 2001). Those who are resource-advantaged (e.g., with more material resources, superior technology, or greater physical strength) cooperate with those who are similarly endowed to establish and maintain stable institutions that expropriate social, material, and political resources from the vulnerable resource-disadvantaged who fall within their grasp. The resulting institutional structure may take a variety of forms as it evolves strategically in response to the specific exigencies that dominants confront, but it is designed to provide a continuing flow of benefits by constraining subordinates' options. Ensnared subordinates, from their weaker position, are driven to follow strategies that are directed toward protecting their current holdings from further incursions, while working to ameliorate or improve their conditions of life when opportunity permits. Expropriative institutions also inevitably embroil the practice of violence, but it too is organized so as to co-opt rather than alienate subordinates.

Sustenance of the dominant group's privileged standing in an unequal social relationship depends critically on the continued presence of subordinates and their compliance with the institutionalized transfer of resources to dominants. Recalcitrant subordinates who must have resources dragged from them through clenched fingers are more costly to control and must be guarded more vigilantly. Subordinates, for their part, are cognizant of their weaker resource base and their subsequent vulnerability. In a world in which uncertainty hovers menacingly, these realities make compliance less risky than resistance, but at the same time subordinates bear the everyday costs of compliance in their foreshortened opportunities and quality of life. The task for dominants is to tip these delicately posed alternatives in the direction of ready compliance. In this context, incendiary hostility is counterproductive. Dominants prefer to befriend, love, or reason with the subordinates on whose cooperation they depend.

There are some intergroup relations that approximate the conditions created by the Sherifs at Robbers' Cave (e.g., some competing ethnicities in the former African colonies) and that thus contain incentives for the expression of hostility and conflict (Jackman, 1994). However, the racial inequality in the United States that has been the focal concern of prejudice scholars (as well as other long-term inequalities such as those based on class and gender) is structured by constraints that deter open expressions of hostility. Because dominant and subordinate groups are politically interdependent, both sides have no choice but to be attentive to the other as they pursue their mutually opposed, mutually contingent goals. As a dynamic ideological exchange is set in motion, the specific organizational structure of the relationship presents constraints and opportunities that favor some strategies and subvert the efficacy of others. While some individual variation in experiences and attitudes is to be expected, people do not operate freelance. Most people's attitudes are selected from a menu that has been forged by the organizational constraints of the intergroup relationship in which they live. Those constraints shape the historical and contemporaneous experiences of the groups to which people belong, and hence their behavior and attitudes (Jackman, 1994).

In long-term expropriative relations structured with frequent one-on-one contact across group lines (as in contemporary gender relations, and in race relations in America in the antebellum South and Jim Crow South), social distance mechanisms prevail and dominant group members exploit their close access to subordinates' daily lives to establish a *paternalistic* regime (Jackman, 1994). Dominants define the needs and interests of subordinates in relation to their position in the status hierarchy and division of labor, and then claim to supply those needs. Subordinates are praised and rewarded for manifesting the attributes that have been categorically assigned to them, and punished for lapsing into behaviors deemed inappropriate. The rewards and punishments are primarily social: compliant subordinates are rewarded with social inclusion, admiration, friendship, affection, or even love, while subordinates who flaunt the rules face social exclusion, ridicule, humiliation, or stigmatization. Human self-interest, sociability, and rationality ensure that most subordinates comply readily with expectations. The costs of noncompliance are bitter, while compliance offers individuals their best prospects for social success. Under these crushing constraints, the vast majority of subordinates take it upon themselves to meet or exceed the demands made by dominants, even competing with each other to excel in their designated duties and attributes.

The ideological mold of paternalism holds a shimmering allure for dominant groups because of its unparalleled effectiveness in using *positive* beliefs and feelings to coerce subordinates. However, when the system of expropriation dictates a shift to spatial segregation and a more aggregated pattern of interaction across group lines, the paternalistic system of conditional love loses its coercive potency because subordinates are afforded more opportunity to develop their own systems of social support, freed from the overbearing presence of dominants. Under these conditions, subordinates begin to dissociate emotionally from the dominant group and to formulate challenges to the expropriative arrangements that have cost them so dearly. Dominant group members are obliged to confront a changed political environment in which the comfortable old avenues are slipping away. The initial disbelief and sense of umbrage (as in the indignant diary entries of slave-owners in the 1860s when their apparently loyal slaves escaped behind Union lines during the Civil War; see Litwak, 1979) yield slowly to the regretful realization that a new way must be found to communicate with and control subordinates. Dominants are goaded to try to mitigate, divert, and diffuse the potentially disruptive challenge that subordinates have begun to introduce. With the failure of love, dominants gravitate to reason to blunt subordinate discontent. Variants of the *reasoned persuasion* ideological strategy (which emphasizes individual rights at the expense of group equality) developed in twentieth-century American class relations and in urbanized American race relations in the post-Jim Crow era, as group differentiation depended increasingly on spatial segregation.

Under paternalism, the group basis of social life is exalted by dominants as they exhort subordinates to abide by and honor its precepts. But when that comes under challenge from subordinates, dominants move to deny the group basis of social life and the legitimacy of group-based demands. Individualism is elevated to a lofty moral principle. This renders subordinates' new demand for equality of outcomes morally unacceptable because of its brazen disrespect for the rights of individuals (e.g., "reverse discrimination"), and political debate is rechanneled into less threatening questions about the degree to which equality of opportunity is available to all individuals (e.g., the conservative call for a "color-blind" society). The new defense of the status quo manipulates the idealistic goal of equal treatment espoused by Allport, Martin Luther King, Jr., and others in the 1950s. The idea of equality of opportunity only has meaning in a world in which *in*equality of *outcomes* is a given, and ironically, the latter renders the former unattainable because of the handicaps it dispenses unequally to the various competitors (Schaar, 1967). This catch-22 is obscured by the emphasis that is placed on procedures rather than outcomes, thus muddying the assessment of equality-of-opportunity policies (Dorn, 1979). Significantly, it undermines the moral credibility of demands made on behalf of groups and thus channels subordinates into focusing on individual opportunities and personal achievement. Individualism, with all its appearance of being reasonable, principled, and unbiased, becomes the new organizing principle for the defense of the status quo.

The specific configuration and character of the intergroup attitudes expressed by dominant groups is thus altered under different ideological regimes. The reshaping of stereotypes illustrates this point. Because paternalism builds on the reification of group differences, it calls for categorical stereotypes. Subordinates are stereotyped as having – and praised for exhibiting – positive, communal traits that are appropriate to their subservient position (such as being supportive, nurturing, loyal, compliant, deferential). The specificity of the embedded injunction is learned cruelly by individual subordinates who mistakenly manifest an abundance of agentic traits and are rewarded with dominants' wrath (Eagly & Diekman, ch. 2

this volume; Rudman, ch. 7 this volume; Van Deburg, 1979, pp. 73–5). When the ideological regime shifts to dissent and individualism, dominants' stereotypes about subordinates are gradually reshaped. The embedded message changes from "Vive la différence!" to "Too bad you aren't more like us – try harder." Negative attributions become more common, as restive subordinates must be reminded that they lack the agentic traits required to support their demands for equality, and, besides, complaining subordinates who fail to live up to the communal attributes demanded of them are no longer as likeable as they once were. What used to be a latent fear about loss of control (prompting watchful assertions about the emotional volatility or violence-propensity of subordinates) is sharpened and crystallized when subordinates have manifestly become less docile. At the same time, dominants simultaneously shed categorical attributions: rigid stereotypes are an embarrassment to a political defense that hinges on the assertion of individual rights. Dominants slip into a probabilistic style of attribution that is consistent with individualism.

A comparison of the stereotypes of women and Blacks in late twentieth-century America illustrates this dynamic. The former are still paternalistic (due to social, rather than spatial, segregation of the sexes), whereas the latter have shifted away from paternalism (as Blacks have become spatially segregated from Whites). As a result, women are more likely to have positive, communal traits categorically attributed to them (with little dissent from women), while Whites' stereotypes about Blacks are both more negative (focusing on their alleged deficits in agentic traits) and more probabilistic, with significant dissent from Blacks (Jackman, 1994).

The forms of violence that mark an intergroup relationship are also constrained by the overarching institutional structure. Far from being the uncontrolled eruption of extreme animosity, physical violence is a routine component of social inequality that finds form within the constraints and opportunities presented by key intergroup institutions. For example, in gender relations, the institution of the family provides a private niche in which individual males may indulge in moments of physical violence to reassert their dominance with little fear of outside sanction, despite strongly stated societal norms that forbid violence against women and a general lack of antipathy toward women (Jackman, 1999, 2001). Similarly, paternalistic sanctions and incentives in gender relations drive self-interested women to compete with one another in the self-infliction of bodily injuries in order to avoid stigmatization and earn the social rewards that come from meeting or exceeding the beauty standards of their day. In systems of inequality that rely more on spatial distance mechanisms, the dominant group cannot invade the psyches of subordinates as successfully, and there is a heavier reliance on formal institutions (such as the judicial system) to enforce control (Sidanius & Pratto, 1999). However, institutionalized chains of command still co-opt subordinates by offering them individual incentives to act as the frontline henchmen for the dominant group (e.g. as police officers, prison guards).

Has Allport Been Supported?

Allport argued that dominants' irrational hostility toward outgroups drove them to reject such groups, with the more extreme forms of rejection reflecting the most deep-seated, intense animosity. Evidence suggests instead that dominants who enjoy the benefits of unequal social relations prefer not to manifest hostility and are moved to act *inclusively* and amicably toward the groups over whom they dominate. Even as dominants must employ some mechanism to differentiate themselves from subordinates and maintain status boundaries, their dependence on those same subordinates for the continued flow of benefits leads them to strive for amicable relations. They are driven not by hostility but by the desire to control subordinates. In this endeavor, dominants adapt their ideological regime to respond to subordinates' political stance. The dynamic exchange between groups is set in motion by the constraints and opportunities that inhere in the structure of their expropriative relations. When Allport noted signs of ideological malleability among dominants (as in his hypothetical conversation between Mr. X and Mr. Y, 1954/1979, pp.13–14), he misread them as indicating that intergroup attitudes were intrinsically irrational and driven by deep-seated animosity. Instead, the malleability of intergroup ideology reflects its rational, strategic nature, as dominant and subordinate group members adapt to changing political exigencies.

Discrimination and violence also adapt to structural constraints. For example, the system of labor use in American antebellum slavery led to a reliance on social distance mechanisms (a variant of what is found in gender relations today), but when Blacks were disgorged into the urban working class in twentieth-century America, race relations were gradually pushed into a system of discrimination based on pervasive spatial distance rules. Similarly, the forms of violence that are practiced within an intergroup relationship do not reflect the underlying degree of hostility but the strategic possibilities carved out by the institutional structure of the relationship. For example, in the United States today, there is more interpersonal dominant-to-subordinate violence in gender relations than in race relations, and yet men display considerably less animosity toward women than do Whites toward Blacks. The key lies in the institutional structure of gender relations, which affords men the opportunity to indulge in interpersonal violence against the women they love in an intimate setting screened from the view of credible witnesses. Self-interested, rational subordinates are also routinely induced to act as the dominant group's henchmen in carrying out malevolent actions against other members of their own group, or even to inflict physical injuries on themselves or their children – with benevolence, not malice – in order to be successful players by the rules of the game in which they have been ensnared by their relations with dominants.

Future Directions for Research

The Allport tradition has neglected the part played by group-level political constraints in shaping the dynamic evolution of intergroup behaviors and attitudes. We need more empirical research addressing the influence of the social organization of intergroup relations.

First, there should be more attention to the exchange of attitudes between dominant and subordinate groups, instead of treating the former as unilateral actors. Second, the dynamic nature of intergroup attitudes calls for investigation. The historical evolution of the exchange of attitudes between groups in specific intergroup relations needs closer attention, although the paucity of representative population data in the historical record calls for both ingenuity and caution in locating and interpreting sources. Third, comparative analysis across differently structured intergroup relations should be extended.

The experimental paradigm offers an efficient, controlled way to simulate and manipulate key structural attributes and measure the human response. Experiments engineering power or status differentials in the lab (e.g., Molm, 1988; Ridgeway, 2001) have been productive and offer great promise. It would also be helpful to analyze other kinds of real-world intergroup relations (e.g., other ethnic divisions, sexual-orientation groups) as well as intergroup relations in other industrialized democracies, poorer nondemocratic nations, and nations marked by different configurations of group divisions (e.g., different relative group sizes or numbers of embroiled groups) based on ethnicity, religion, language, or gender. We need more information about group-level constraints emanating from (a) contextual factors in social and political institutions that frame an intergroup relationship and (b) the structure of the intergroup relationship itself (e.g., degree of resource parity or inequality between the groups, degree and type of economic and social independence/interdependence between groups, types of institutions regulating intergroup relations, and volume and type of intergroup contact).

Research on these issues should reveal a broader array of intergroup behaviors and attitudes than those encompassed by the current state of knowledge. I posit that the significance of intergroup hostility will recede when we identify the precise conditions under which it is displayed and the range of emotions, beliefs, discrimination, and violence that mark various intergroup relations. As wary, resourceful humans configure their behavioral and attitudinal strategies under the weight of their interests and political constraints, free-ranging hostility should be recognized as a probable liability. This is especially true in longstanding relations of inequality. The dearth of hostility in such relations in no way diminishes their human toll.

REFERENCES

Adorno, T. W., Frenkel-Brunswik, E., Levinson, D. J., & Sanford, R. N. (1950). *The authoritarian personality.* New York: Harper & Row.

Allport, G. (1954/1979). *The nature of prejudice.* Cambridge, MA: Perseus Books.

Arrow, K. (1951). *Social choice and individual values.* New York: Wiley.

Barstow, A. L. (1995). *Witchcraze.* San Francisco: Harper Collins.

Blumer, H. (1958). Race prejudice as a sense of group position. *Pacific Sociological Review,* 1, 3–7.

Bobo, L. D. (1999). Prejudice as group position. *Journal of Social Issues, 55(3),* 445–72.

Bobo, L. D. & Johnson, D. (2000). Racial attitudes in a prismatic metropolis. In L. D. Bobo, M. L. Oliver, J. H. Johnson, Jr., & A. Valenzuela, Jr. (eds.), *Prismatic metropolis* (pp. 81–163). New York: Russell Sage.

Centers, R. (1949). *The psychology of social classes.* Princeton: Princeton University Press.

Deutsch, M. & Collins, M. E. (1951). *Interracial housing.* Minneapolis: University of Minnesota Press.

Dorn, E. (1979). *Rules and racial equality.* New Haven, CT: Yale University Press.

Downs, A. (1957). *An economic theory of democracy.* New York: Harper & Row.

Duckitt, J. (2003). Prejudice and intergroup hostility. In D. O. Sears, L. Huddy, & R. Jervis (eds.), *The Oxford handbook of political psychology* (pp. 559–600). New York: Oxford University Press.

French, M. (1992). *The war against women.* New York: Ballantine Books.

Glick, P. & Fiske, S. T. (2001). Ambivalent sexism. *Advances in experimental social psychology* (vol. 33, pp. 115–88). San Diego, CA: Academic Press.

Goldhagen, D. J. (1996). *Hitler's willing executioners*. New York: Knopf.

Gramsci, A. (1971). *Selections from the prison notebooks of Antonio Gramsci*, ed.& tr. Q. Hoare and G. N. Smith. New York: International Publishers.

Grofman, B. (ed.) (1995). *Information, participation, & choice*. Ann Arbor, MI: University of Michigan Press.

Hamilton, D. L. (ed.) (1981). *Cognitive processes in stereotyping and intergroup behavior*. Hillsdale, NJ: Lawrence Erlbaum.

Jackman, M. R. (1978). General and applied tolerance. *American Journal of Political Science, 22*, 302–32.

Jackman, M. R. (1994). *The velvet glove*. Berkeley, CA: University of California Press.

Jackman, M. R. (1999). Gender, violence, and harassment. In J .S. Chafetz (ed.), *Handbook of the sociology of gender* (pp. 275–317). New York: Plenum.

Jackman, M. R. (2001). License to kill. In J. T. Jost & B. Major (eds.), *The psychology of legitimacy* (pp. 437–67). New York: Cambridge University Press.

Jackman, M. R. & Muha, M. J. (1984). Education and intergroup attitudes. *American Sociological Review, 49*, 751–69.

Jackman, R. W. & Miller, R. A. (2004). *Before norms*. Ann Arbor, MI: University of Michigan Press.

Kinder, D. R. & Sanders, L. M. (1996). *Divided by color*. Chicago, IL: University of Chicago Press.

Krysan, M. (2000). Prejudice, politics, and public opinion. *Annual Review of Sociology, 26*, 135–68.

Lipset, S. M. (1960). *Political man*. London: Heinemann.

Litwack, L. F. (1979). *Been in the storm so long*. New York: Knopf.

Marx, K. & Engels, F. (1888/1959). Manifesto of the communist party. In L. S. Feuer (ed.), *Marx and Engels: Basic writings on politics and philosophy* (pp. 1–41). New York: Anchor.

Massey, D. S. & Denton, N. A. (1993). *American apartheid*. Cambridge, MA: Harvard University Press.

Milgram, S. (1974). *Obedience to authority*. New York: Harper & Row.

Myrdal, G. (1944). *An American dilemma*. New York: Harper & Bros.

Molm, L. D. (1988). The structure and use of power. *Social Psychology Quarterly, 52*, 108–22.

Ridgeway, C. L. (2001). The emergence of status beliefs. In J. T. Jost & B. Major (eds.), *The psychology of legitimacy* (pp. 257–77). New York: Cambridge University Press.

Schaar, J. H. (1967). Equality of opportunity and beyond. In J. R. Pennock & J. W. Chapman (eds.), *Equality*, NOMOS IX (pp. 228–49). New York: Atherton Press.

Schuman, H., Steeh, C., & Bobo, L. (1985). *Racial attitudes in America*. Cambridge, MA: Harvard University Press.

Sherif, M. & Sherif, C. (1953). *Groups in harmony and tension*. New York: Harper.

Sidanius, J. & Pratto, F. (1999). *Social dominance*. New York: Cambridge University Press.

Sniderman, P. M. & Carmines, E. G. (1997).*Reaching beyond race*. Cambridge, MA: Harvard University Press.

Stephan, W. G. (1985). Intergroup relations. In G. Lindzey & E. Aronson (eds.), *Handbook of social psychology*, 3rd ed., vol. II (pp. 599–658). New York: Random House.

Tajfel, H. (1969). Cognitive aspects of prejudice. *Journal of Social Issues, 25*, 79–97.

Van Deburg, W. L. (1979). *The slave drivers.* Westport, CT: Greenwood Press.

van den Berghe, P. L. (1960). Distance mechanisms of stratification. *Sociology and Social Research, 44,* 155–64.

Weingast, B. R. (1997). Constructing trust. In V. Haufler, K. Soltan, & E. Uslaner (eds.), *Where is the new institutionalism now?* (pp. 163–200). Ann Arbor, MI: University of Michigan Press.

Williams, R. M., Jr. (1947). *The reduction of intergroup tensions.* New York: Social Science Research Council.

Wilner, D. M., Walkley, R. P., & Cook, S. W. 1955. *Human relations in interracial housing.* Minneapolis: University of Minnesota Press.

Zimbardo, P. G. (2004). A situationist perspective on the psychology of evil. In A. Miller (ed.), *The social psychology of good and evil* (pp. 21–50). New York: Guilford.

Chapter Seven

Rejection of Women? Beyond Prejudice as Antipathy

Laurie A. Rudman

Throughout this volume, there are impressive examples of how Allport, in *The Nature of Prejudice* (1954), not only effectively summarized the existing state of knowledge but also anticipated the major developments in the field, such as the important role of normal social-cognitive and social-identity processes in prejudice – perspectives that represented dominant frameworks 25 years later.

Nevertheless, in part because of the social conditions at the time he wrote his book (see Eagly & Diekman's chapter 2 in this volume), there are aspects of prejudice that Allport completely overlooked. In particular, although Allport considered biases toward many groups (e.g., based on race, religion, and occupation), he largely ignored gender bias. The present chapter considers the issue of prejudice against women, first in the context of Allport's framework and then in terms of recent developments.

Allport's Views on Prejudice Against Women

While Allport's chapter 4, "Rejection of Out-Groups," contains many alarming instances of discrimination, nowhere does he address the pervasiveness of sex discrimination. In his sole reference to gender, Allport noted that misogynists viewed women as their inferiors, but he characterized them as rare, stating that, for these men, "the cleavage between male and female was a cleavage between accepted in-group and rejected out-group. But for many people this 'war of the sexes' seems totally unreal. *They do not find in it a ground for prejudice*" (Allport, 1954/1979, p. 34, emphases added). Indeed, although Allport lists official forms of discrimination (as recognized by the United Nations), including inequality in "access to public office," "the enjoyment of free choice of employment," and "the regulation and treatment of ownership" (p. 52), he failed to acknowledge how they readily applied to half the population – women.

Moreover, this oversight led to a narrow view of prejudice – prejudice as antipathy – that failed to encompass more subtle, but equally pernicious, manifestations of prejudice. The current chapter builds upon Eagly and Diekman's and Jackman's chapters by providing a history of gender prejudice research, and then discussing recent approaches that challenge Allport's definition of prejudice as "an antipathy based upon a faulty or inflexible generalization" (p. 9).

How did Allport miss the ordinariness of gender prejudice? Historically and cross-culturally, women have traditionally been subordinate to men, creating a situation for Allport like that of the proverbial fish, blind to the water he swims in. Further, women themselves appeared to be content with the water, so Allport was not ignoring their complaints. But the fact that sexism is now highly recognized as a social problem despite women's long-lived compliance suggests two gaping holes in Allport's framework. First, his definition of prejudice as antipathy is overly restrictive, because it cannot fully account for gender prejudice (Eagly & Diekman, ch. 2 this volume). Second, he overlooked the teamwork engaged in by members of subordinate and dominant groups that promotes the status quo (Jackman, ch. 6 this volume).

Developments Since Allport: The Birth of Sexism Research

Gender prejudice research began serendipitously, with a cocktail party and a *New Yorker* cartoon (Helmreich, 1999). Janet Spence and Robert Helmreich met at a party, and both were struck by a cartoon in which a man said to a woman during a dinner date, "You are really stupid. I like that in a woman." Helmreich had recently found that competent men were liked more than incompetent men, and the two wondered whether the effect would generalize to women. The result was their seminal study, "Who Likes Competent Women?" (Spence & Helmreich, 1972a). To test their hypothesis that only gender egalitarians would like competent women, they designed the first individual difference measure of sexism, the (misnamed) Attitudes Toward Women Scale (Spence & Helmreich, 1972b), which assesses attitudes toward the rights and roles of women. Spence and Helmreich not only found support for their hypothesis, they effectively launched gender research within social psychology.

Gender Prejudice as Antipathy Toward Women

Spence and Helmreich's initial endeavors set the stage for gender prejudice researchers' concern with two broad themes for the next 30 years. The first is a focus on attitudes toward gender equality rather than attitudes toward women *per se*. The second theme concerns perceptions that men and women are different, resulting in a wealth of literature on sex stereotypes (i.e., beliefs about men and women; Ashmore, Del Boca, & Wohlers, 1986). These two themes are linked by the common assumption that sexism involves antifemale attitudes that stem from the belief that men are superior to women (e.g., more capable intellectually and physically). Thus, historically, gender prejudice researchers tailored their approach to Allport's view of prejudice as antipathy. This antipathy may be reflected in sexist attitudes, as assessed by a number of different scales, and gender beliefs and stereotypes.

Sexist attitudes

The Attitudes Toward Women Scale (Spence & Helmreich, 1972b) measures blatantly sexist attitudes regarding women's status in society (e.g., "Women should be concerned with their duties of childbearing and house tending, rather than with desires for professional and business careers"). Consistent with the argument that it reflects antipathy toward women, higher scores are associated with greater male aggression toward women (Scott & Tetreault, 1987) and more favorable perceptions of those who aggress toward women (e.g., rapists; Weidner & Griffitt, 1983; and domestic abusers; Hillier & Foddy, 1993). However, the measure is limited in the scope of its predictive utility (see Spence, 1999, for a review). For example, it does not predict gender identity, women's career choices, or gender stereotypes, perhaps because it measures attitudes toward women's rights, not attitudes toward women.

A further limitation is the measure's transparency, which affords contamination from social desirability bias. Not surprisingly, scores on the Attitudes Toward Women Scale have consistently decreased over time; indeed, the measure no longer shows appreciable variability in college student samples (Spence, 1999). To counter social desirability bias, researchers have developed more subtle instruments that tap antipathy toward women's progress and the policies that support it (e.g., affirmative action). Modeled after McConahay's (1986) approach to assessing racism, the Modern Sexism Scale (Swim, Aiken, Hall, & Hunter, 1995) and the

Neo-Sexism Scale (Tougas, Brown, Beaton, & Joly, 1995) assess opposition to feminist demands, including the belief that women are no longer discriminated against and therefore do not need affirmative action. Nonetheless, like the Attitudes Toward Women Scale, these instruments are more concerned with attitudes toward gender equality than attitudes toward women.

Gender stereotypes

By contrast, gender stereotype research has more directly targeted beliefs about women as a group. Compared with men, women have historically been perceived as less intelligent, competent, independent, and ambitious – in a word, *agentic* (Bakan, 1966). The putative absence of female agency underscored the (once prominent) misconception that women lacked intrinsic motivation to succeed (Horner, 1972). Later research has clarified that women do not "fear success" so much as they avoid the appearance of deviance (as do men; Cherry & Deaux, 1978). Women are also likely to strive to succeed in areas in which they are culturally supported (Eccles, 1987). Because men and women have traditionally been socialized to assume different roles in society, with men serving as breadwinners and women as homemakers, expectations for their behavior differ (Eagly, 1987). As a result, agency continues to be more associated with men than with women (Rudman & Kilianski, 2000; Spence & Buckner, 2000).

The socioeconomic implications of this discrepancy were immediately clear to gender researchers. Gutek (1985) argued that the tendency for gender-based expectations to influence work roles (termed "sex-role spillover") was costly for women. For example, female supervisors are expected to be more nurturant and sympathetic than men in the same positions, which may undermine their authority. Heilman's (1983) "lack of fit" hypothesis argued that women were not considered to be suitable managers because they were perceived as insufficiently agentic. As a consequence, for women to gain entry into male-dominated positions, it was necessary for them to disconfirm gender stereotypes – in short, to act more like men. In fact, unless a woman provides evidence that she is not a "typical" female, she may not be seriously considered as a candidate for jobs that require leadership skills (Glick, Zion, & Nelson, 1988; Rudman & Glick, 1999). Writing in the 1970s, Seyfried and Hendrick (1973) optimistically forecast the following solution to gender inequity:

> At present, the role of women in society is hotly debated by members and students of the various women's liberation movements. The central issue

hinges on a redefinition of the role of woman as a person – on what she should be. There are only two traditional models of the person readily available, that of the male and that of the female, and the traditional model of the female is under attack. The great difficulty in constructing a viable third model . . . suggests a simple answer to the debate. The modern female of the future will be very much like the male – in sex-role attitudes, general value orientation, and philosophy of life. (p. 20)

From this perspective, to undermine gender hegemony, women need only present themselves as independent, competitive, and forceful creatures (i.e., "act like men"). Although this solution sounds simple, it has turned out to be untenable for women because agency is not only more expected of men, it is more accepted in men. For example, women who self-promote, argue assertively, or defend themselves aggressively are viewed less favorably than identical male counterparts (see Rudman, 1998; Rudman & Fairchild, 2004, for reviews). Likewise, agentic women (but not men) are discriminated against when vying for leadership positions, even though agency is necessary for being viewed as competent and qualified (Rudman & Glick, 1999). When women do obtain leadership positions, they have a difficult time balancing the requisites of the work role with their gender role (Gutek, 1985). For example, female supervisors who lead in a task-oriented (versus a people-oriented) style are evaluated more negatively than male counterparts (Eagly, Makhijani, & Klonsky, 1992). These findings have led gender researchers to posit that sex stereotypes are not only descriptive (delineating what men and women are), but also prescriptive (delineating how men and women should be; Eagly, 1987). Thus, gendered beliefs overlap with attitudes, resulting in more prejudice directed toward women in masculine than feminine roles (Eagly & Diekman, ch. 2 this volume). As a consequence, the remedy for gender inequity in the workplace is not as straightforward as was once presumed.

A New Sexism Framework: Benevolent Gender Prejudice

Although the Allportian approach to sexism has been fruitful, the limitations of treating sexism purely as antipathy toward women are twofold. First, it does not take into account the fact that people often hold positive attitudes toward and beliefs about women. Second, it does not explain why women themselves are prone to maintaining the status quo. Recent advances in social-structural theories of prejudice address how seemingly benevolent forms of prejudice undermine women's socioeconomic progress. These approaches are supported by new methodologies, including response latency techniques, such as the Implicit Association Test (IAT; Greenwald, McGhee, & Schwartz, 1998) that assess reactions that may be unconscious and automatic, and thus are not susceptible to impression management strategies. Because this task measures the time it takes people to make decisions about pairs of stimuli (e.g., men and agentic traits) rather than directly asking people their opinions, the IAT (along with similar methods) has the advantage of overcoming people's inability (or unwillingness) to report their attitudes and beliefs (see also Fiske, ch. 3 this volume; Batson & Stocks, ch. 25 this volume). Thus, implicit measures provide unique insights into the psychology of prejudice beyond the direct, explicit measures that were the tools of social psychology when *The Nature of Prejudice* was written.

Pro-Female Attitudes and Benevolent Sexism

Conceptualizing sexism as antipathy did not prepare researchers for the (originally shocking) finding that men and women alike tend to report favorable beliefs about and attitudes toward "the fairer sex." In their initial demonstration of the *women are wonderful* effect, Eagly and Mladinic (1989) found that people viewed women as nicer, more supportive, and interpersonally sensitive, compared with men – in a word, more communal (see also Eagly & Diekman, ch. 2 this volume). As a result, people reported liking women more than they liked men. That is, female communality beliefs were associated with pro-female bias. This was shocking because it suggested the prevalence of *reverse* sexism – a phenomenon that has been supported even when researchers use implicit methods that do not rely on asking people for their preferences (Rudman & Goodwin, 2004).

Similarly, Glick and Fiske (1996) found that women were viewed as more moral, pure, and worthy of protection, compared with men. They termed this *benevolent* sexism (as opposed to hostile sexism). How can benevolence be bad? First, Glick and Fiske argue that it represents an assumption that women are child-like and weak and, therefore, reflects paternalist prejudice. Second, cross-cultural research revealed that benevolent sexism positively correlates with hostile sexism around the world (Glick et al., 2000). That is, people who have antifemale attitudes (e.g., who view women as trying to gain control over men) also view women benevolently. The authors interpret this pattern as suggesting ambivalence toward women, and they call their scale the Ambivalent Sexism Inventory.

But there is also evidence that female subtypes can explain the coincidence of hostile and benevolent sexism. Specifically, hostile sexism is directed toward career women and feminists, whereas benevolent sexism is directed toward traditional women (Glick, Diebold, Bailey-Werner, & Zhu, 1997). Thus, a way of synthesizing these lines of research is to dub it "the women are wonderful *when*" effect – when they are not in power. That is, women are wonderful provided they are communal and stick to traditional female roles (Eagly & Diekman, this volume).

Benevolent prejudice is insidious and stealthy, operating beneath the social radar to undermine the progress of women, particularly those with ability and ambition – the very women Seyfried and Hendrick (1977) predicted would succeed. For example, in one study, applicants for management positions (either male or female) described themselves as competitive and gave strong examples of their leadership ability (Rudman & Glick, 2001). As in the past (Rudman, 1998), results showed that women risk backlash effects if they "act like a man." Although women were rated as highly competent, men were viewed as more likable and, as a result, they were more likely to be hired. Moreover, people who scored higher on the implicit measure of gender stereotyping, the IAT, tended to dislike masterful women more; there were no effects for the explicit (self-reported) stereotyping measure. These findings are consistent with the hypothesis that agentic women are rejected because they violate prescriptive stereotypes (i.e., are viewed as insufficiently nice) and implicate the importance of *nonconscious* gender beliefs as barriers to gender parity.

Interestingly, Allport (1954/1979) also acknowledged possible resistance to efforts aimed at eliminating prejudicial social dynamics, which might "stiffen opposition in defense of existing attitudes"; he called it the *boomerang effect* (p. 508). However, his treatment of boomerang was optimistically naive. He wrote, "Such evidence as we have indicates that this effect is relatively slight . . . it seems probable, too, that 'boomerangs' occur chiefly in minds with paranoid trends" (p. 508). Clearly, Allport missed not only the systemic oppression of women, but also the possibility that women's efforts to overcome it (e.g., by adopting agency) would incur backlash from psychologically healthy men and women alike.

Paternalistic Prejudice Co-opts Women

Although women make up 46 percent of the workforce, they are underrepresented in positions of power and prestige (Eagly & Diekman, ch. 2 this volume). Gender prejudice helps to perpetuate this fact, as backlash research makes clear. However, women's own choices (i.e., self-selection bias) may also be an important factor. Compared with men, women tend to shy away from positions that carry the highest rewards, both social and economic (Pratto, Stallworth, Sidanius, & Siers, 1997). For as long as they do, gender hegemony will persist. Therefore, it is important to investigate why women might be less interested in positions of authority and leadership, compared with men.

The explanation that women receive positive reinforcement for communal behaviors and adopting traditional roles is consistent with social-structural theories of sexism (Eagly, 1987; Gutek, 1985). In particular, Jackman (1994) argues that benevolence toward subordinates in general (not only women) serves to reinforce the dominant group's position of superiority and control. Whites in the American Old South once stereotyped Blacks as cheerful and loyal, but also as ignorant, submissive, and in need of protection. Most perniciously, these beliefs were internalized by Blacks, and resulted in their helping to maintain a system of own-group oppression. Similarly, stereotyping women as nice (but weak) and treating them in a benevolent (but patronizing) manner serves to maintain gender hegemony, in at least two ways. First, it undermines perceptions of female competence and authority, relegating women to low-status, nurturing roles. Second, it may lead women themselves to uphold the status quo. Certainly oppression is more palatable for subordinates when it is "sugar-coated," compared with when it is overtly hostile (Jackman, ch. 6 this volume).

Moreover, women may not recognize that a prescription for female niceness underscores their subordinate status in society. Instead, they may view it as a means of favorably distinguishing themselves from men (Brewer, 1991), as well as a means of receiving positive reinforcement (Kilianski & Rudman, 1998). As a result, women may be just as susceptible to forming attitudes based on prescriptive stereotypes as are men. For example, in the foregoing research on prejudice toward masterful women, women were no less prejudiced than were men. Moreover, women and men are equally likely to favor male over female bosses (Gallup, 1996; Sherman & Spence, 1997), and to show an automatic preference for male over female authority figures (Rudman & Kilianski, 2000). Finally, cross-cultural research shows that women, compared with men, often report equal (or higher) levels of benevolent sexism (although their hostile sexism scores are routinely lower; Glick & Fiske, 1996; Glick et al., 2000). Each of these findings is consistent with the argument that sexism cannot be fully explained by viewing prejudice solely as antipathy toward women, in the Allportian tradition. Instead, a perhaps more insidious form of prejudice, involving benevolent and paternalistic beliefs about and attitudes toward women, is necessary to account for the pervasiveness of gender hegemony, including the role that women themselves play in maintaining the status quo (Jackman, ch. 6 this volume).

This paternalism may be transmitted and reinforced by fundamental cultural ideologies (see Jost & Hamilton, ch. 13 this volume). A cultural worldview that is largely overlooked concerns romance, a putatively positive ideology for women. Traditionally, romance has idealized femininity, placing women "on a pedestal." However, it may also teach them (e.g., through romantic fairytales) to depend on men for economic and social rewards. In particular, the romantic idealization of men as chivalric rescuers of women (e.g., Prince Charming) might encourage women to seek their fortune indirectly, through men. If so, romantic fantasies might be negatively linked to women's interest in personal power. Consistent with this hypothesis, Rudman and Heppen (2003) found that even women who were reluctant to explicitly associate male romantic partners with chivalry (e.g., Prince Charming, White Knight, protector, hero) demonstrated this association implicitly (on the IAT). Furthermore, women who possessed implicit romantic beliefs also showed less interest in personal power, across multiple measures. For example, women with high IAT scores expected to make less income in their careers, and had lower educational goals. They also showed less interest in prestigious occupations (e.g., CEOs, corporate lawyers, and politicians), and were less willing to volunteer for a leadership role in an upcoming experiment. Taken together, the results provide tentative support for a possible "glass-slipper" effect, such that women who implicitly idealize men may be more interested in pursuing power indirectly, through their romantic relationships, than by seeking their own fortunes. Because romantic ideologies are subjectively pro-female, they represent an important example of how women can be co-opted by benevolent sexism in ways that can be harmful for gender equity.

Has Allport Been Supported?

Following the Allportian tradition, seminal gender prejudice research centered on antipathy toward women's civil rights and negative female stereotypes. Although this approach has been productive, it has not been able to account for the positive attitudes and beliefs that people possess about women, or why women themselves might unwittingly perpetuate gender hegemony. To do so, researchers had to begin to consider the role that benevolent beliefs play in maintaining women's lower status (Jackman, ch. 6 this volume). Because Allport overlooked the power of benevolence to reinforce the status quo, it is fair to say that he was not "supported" because he did not think beyond hostile prejudice, or consider how subordinates might be wooed into supporting their own oppression. It is even possible that these oversights contributed to his blind spot with respect to sex discrimination, and thus, to his dismissal of gender conflict.

To complement the theoretical analyses of Eagly and Diekman and of Jackman, this chapter considered evidence for two benevolent barriers to gender equity. Each has implications for women's progress and, in each case, their presence was revealed when implicit (but not explicit) beliefs and attitudes were assessed. First, perceivers who possess automatic female benevolent stereotypes may devalue masterful women (the backlash effect). Second, women who implicitly rely on men for power and prestige may hinder their own aspirations, perhaps due to a belief that "someday their prince will come" (the glass-slipper effect). In concert, these barriers help to explain why women continue to be largely employed in low–status occupations at the turn of a new millennium.

Less obvious, but equally important, are the ways in which these effects may be intertwined. For example, women who have experienced backlash may curb agentic behaviors in the presence of both prospective and actual employers, resulting in misperceptions of incompetence. To the extent that women are not able to disconfirm negative stereotypes by adopting agency, they may remain under the glass ceiling. As a result, they may be forced to depend on men in order to gain status and prestige. If so, romanticizing men may be a more palatable option for women than bitterness about sexism. In addition, men's romantic and economic lives are more consistent with respect to agency than are women's. For example, men are encouraged to be assertive (e.g., to promote themselves) whether they are interviewing for a job, negotiating a contract, or approaching potential dating partners. By contrast, women are encouraged to be more modest and self-effacing in romantic situations. If women in performance settings are judged by criteria more suited to romantic roles, female agency may be viewed harshly by men and women alike. As a result, romance may be viewed as a means of achieving power more so for women than it is for men. Thus, although Allport's view of "prejudice as antipathy" still applies effectively to some types of contemporary prejudices, this view does not adequately encompass basic and prevalent forms of contemporary prejudice and discrimination, including sexism.

Future Directions

The analysis presented in this chapter suggests that benevolent attitudes toward women can block their advancement, even while, on the surface, appearing to be favorable. Yet, this is such a recent development in prejudice theory that it has not yet undergone systematic research attention. Hopefully, 50 years from now, the discrepancy between the amount of research on benevolent compared with hostile prejudice will have been greatly reduced. Because nearly all of the roads have been untaken, there are numerous directions in which to go.

For example, implicit beliefs that women are nicer (but weaker) than men no doubt influence a much broader array of outcomes than backlash toward masterly women. Their explanatory power might be extended to understanding why women are less likely than men to ask for what they want (including promotions and salary increases), and to be considered for positions that require physical labor or risk-taking (although these positions are often necessary for advancement, such as in the military or blue-collar trades; see Babcock & Laschever, 2003, for reviews). Female communality prescriptions may undercut women's ability to advance economically, in part, because women themselves are afraid of appearing to be "too demanding" or "too competitive."

However, and consistent with the idea that these prescriptions may be nonconscious, women may not be aware of the extent to which they restrict themselves to conform to gender norms. For example, a large web-based survey found that men were four times more likely than women to be actively engaged in negotiating better outcomes for themselves. When these findings were discussed with college-aged women, many predicted that this sex difference would apply only to "boomer" women, not to their generation. Yet, the actual findings showed that younger women were even less likely than their elders to be proactive on their own behalf, suggesting that "the tendency among women to accept what they're offered and not ask for more is far from just a 'boomer' problem" (Babcock & Laschever, 2003, p. 4). A direction for future research, then, is to uncover the multifarious ways in which implicit gender stereotypes influence behaviors on the part of perceivers and actors alike. Because these may affect decisions and actions without people's awareness or intentions, implicit assessment techniques, such as the IAT, will likely play a critical role.

Another domain ripe for research attention is the entanglement of close relationships and sexism. Researchers have scratched the surface by arguing that heterosexual interdependence leads to benevolent sexism. It is simply unfeasible for men to be overtly hostile toward women, on whom they depend for a variety of services, including sexual gratification, emotional intimacy, child-raising, and domestic labor (Glick & Fiske, 1996). Similarly, women depend on men for romantic love, economic stability, and social prestige. Thus, one could hardly invent a stronger context in which dominant and subordinate group members are equally invested in preserving the status quo (Jackman, ch. 6 this volume). Nonetheless, the door is wide open for empirically investigating the nexus of romance and sexism. For example, in light of the glass-slipper effect, it might be fruitful to explore the relationship between romantic ideology and gender competition. One possibility is that women are reluctant to change the gender dynamic from benevolence (men protecting women) to hostility (competing with men for economic resources) for fear that it will curb their love life, including their ability to marry. Because men are even more vested in gender hegemony, they might also be resistant to a change in this dynamic.

In conclusion, the presence of benevolent barriers to gender equity is significant because it broadens our definition of prejudice, and forces us to consider that prejudice is more heterogeneous than Allport acknowledged. From a practical standpoint, if prejudice is not monolithic, society is faced with a wider variety of potentially effective responses to it. In other words, thinking outside Allport's antipathy box expands potential causes of prejudice and intervention strategies alike. However, the benevolent barriers discussed in this chapter are likely to be difficult to counteract. This is due to both the valence of the beliefs and the process by which they appear to influence judgments and behaviors. Because viewing women as nicer than men casts women in a favorable light, and because romantic ideologies idealize women and men alike, they are likely to be overlooked as potential causes of gender inequity. Awareness is the first step to counteracting bias, so the fact that positive ideologies are likely to "sneak past" even vigilant egalitarians as a source of oppression is a significant one (see also Devine, ch. 20 this volume). In addition, the fact that each benevolent barrier was evident only when measured implicitly suggests that nonconscious beliefs about female niceness or male chivalry may be more powerful sources of influence, compared with beliefs that are more readily accessible (Greenwald & Banaji, 1995). Again, this represents a difficulty in overcoming benevolent barriers to gender equity by sheer virtue of their relative invisibility.

This is not meant to imply hopelessness. On the contrary, expanding theoretical frameworks to include patronizing (as well as antagonistic) forms of prejudice bodes well for the future. Furthermore, the growing interest in implicit assessment tools is an exciting development for prejudice researchers. Uncovering potentially hidden sources of gender prejudice, and calling attention to the ways in which treating women differently from men can harm them – even when this appears, on the surface, to be benevolent – can only further the aim of conquering gender inequity.

REFERENCES

Allport, G. W. (1954/1979). *The nature of prejudice.* Cambridge, MA: Perseus Books.

Ashmore, R. D., Del Boca, F. K., & Wohlers, A. J. (1986). Sex stereotypes. In R. D. Ashmore & F. K. Del Boca (eds.), *The social psychology of male–female relations* (pp. 69–120). Orlando, FL: Academic Press.

Babcock, L. & Laschever, S. (2003). *Women don't ask: Negotiation and the gender divide.* Princeton, NJ: Princeton University Press.

Bakan, D. (1966). *The duality of human existence: An essay on psychology and religion.* Chicago: Rand McNally.

Brewer, M. B. (1991). The social self: On being the same and different at the same time. *Personality & Social Psychology Bulletin, 17,* 475–82.

Cherry, F. & Deaux, K. (1978). Fear of success versus fear of gender-inappropriate behavior. *Sex Roles, 4,* 97–101.

Eagly, A. H. (1987). *Sex differences in social behavior: A social role interpretation.* Hillsdale, NJ: Lawrence Erlbaum.

Eagly, A. H., Makhijani, M. G., & Klonsky, B. G. (1992). Gender and the evaluation of leaders: A meta-analysis. *Psychological Bulletin, 111,* 3–22.

Eagly, A. H. & Mladinic, A. (1989). Gender stereotypes and attitudes toward women and men. *Personality and Social Psychology Bulletin, 15,* 543–58.

Eccles, J. S. (1987). Gender roles and women's achievement-related decisions. *Psychology of Women Quarterly, 11,* 135–72.

Gallup, G. H. (1996). *The Gallup poll.* Wilmington, DE: Scholarly Resources.

Glick, P., Diebold, J., Bailey-Werner, B., & Zhu, L. (1997). The two faces of Adam: Ambivalent sexism and polarized attitudes toward women. *Personality and Social Psychology Bulletin, 23,* 1323–34.

Glick, P. & Fiske, S. T. (1996). The Ambivalent Sexism Inventory: Differentiating hostile and benevolent sexism. *Journal of Personality and Social Psychology, 70,* 491–512.

Glick, P., et al. (2000). Beyond prejudice as simple antipathy: Hostile and benevolent sexism across cultures. *Journal of Personality and Social Psychology, 79,* 763–75.

Glick, P., Zion, C., & Nelson, C. (1988). What mediates sex discrimination in hiring decisions? *Journal of Personality and Social Psychology, 55,* 178–86.

Greenwald, A. G. & Banaji, M. R. (1995). Implicit social cognition: Attitudes, self-esteem, and stereotypes. *Psychological Review, 102,* 4–27.

Greenwald, A. G., McGhee, D., & Schwartz, J. L. K. (1998). Measuring individual differences in implicit cognition: The Implicit Association Test. *Journal of Personality and Social Psychology, 74,* 1464–80.

Gutek, B. A. (1985). *Sex and the workplace.* San Francisco: Jossey-Bass.

Heilman, M. E. (1983). Sex bias in work settings: The lack of fit model. *Research in Organizational Behavior, 5,* 269–98.

Helmreich, R. L. (1999). The many faces of Janet Taylor Spence. In W. B. Swann, J. H. Langlois, & L. A. Gilbert (eds.), *Sexism and stereotypes in modern society: The gender science of Janet Taylor Spence* (pp. 35–43). Washington, DC: American Psychological Association.

Hillier, L. & Foddy, M. (1993). The role observer attitudes in judgments of blame in cases of wife assault. *Sex Roles, 29,* 629–44.

Horner, M. S. (1972). Toward an understanding of achievement-related conflicts in women. *Journal of Social Issues, 28,* 157–75.

Jackman, M. R. (1994). *The velvet glove: Paternalism and conflict in gender, class, and race relations.* Berkeley, CA: University of California Press.

Kilianski, S. E. & Rudman, L. A. (1998). Wanting it both ways: Do women approve of benevolent sexism? *Sex Roles, 39,* 333–52.

McConahay, J. B. (1986). Modern racism, ambivalence, and the Modern Racism Scale. In J. F. Dovidio & S. L. Gaertner (eds.), *Prejudice, discrimination, and racism* (pp. 91–126). Orlando, FL: Academic Press, Inc.

Pratto, F., Stallworth, L. M., Sidanius, J., & Siers, B. (1997). The gender gap in occupational role attainment: A social dominance approach. *Journal of Personality and Social Psychology, 72,* 37–53.

Rudman, L. A. (1998). Self-promotion as a risk factor for women: The costs and benefits of counterstereotypical impression management. *Journal of Personality and Social Psychology, 74,* 629–45.

Rudman, L. A. & Fairchild, K. (2004). Reactions to counterstereotypic behavior: The role of backlash in cultural stereotype maintenance. *Journal of Personality and Social Psychology, 87(2),* 157–76.

Rudman, L. A. & Glick, P. (2001). Prescriptive gender stereotypes and backlash toward agentic women. *Journal of Social Issues, 57,* 743–62.

Rudman, L. A. & Glick, P. (1999). Feminized management and backlash toward agentic women: The hidden costs to women of a kinder, gentler image of middle-managers. *Journal of Personality and Social Psychology, 77,* 1004–10.

Rudman, L. A. & Goodwin, S. A. (2004). Gender differences in automatic ingroup bias: Why do women like women more than men like men? *Journal of Personality and Social Psychology, 87,* 494–509.

Rudman, L. A. & Heppen, J. (2003). Implicit romantic fantasies and women's interest in personal power: A glass slipper effect? *Personality and Social Psychology Bulletin, 29,* 1357–70.

Rudman, L. A. & Kilianski, S. E. (2000). Implicit and explicit attitudes toward female authority. *Personality and Social Psychology Bulletin, 26,* 1315–28.

Sherman, P. & Spence, J. T. (1997). A comparison of two cohorts of college students in responses to the Male–Female Relations Questionnaire. *Psychology of Women Quarterly, 21,* 265–78.

Scott, R. & Tetreault, L. A. (1987). Attitudes of rapists and other violent offenders toward women. *Journal of Social Psychology*, *127*, 375–80.

Seyfried, B. A. & Hendrick, C. (1973). When do opposites attract? When they are opposite in sex and sex-role attitudes. *Journal of Personality and Social Psychology*, *74*, 15–20.

Spence, J. T. (1999). Thirty years of gender research: A personal chronicle. In W. B. Swann, J. H. Langlois, & L. A. Gilbert (eds.), *Sexism and stereotypes in modern society: The gender science of Janet Taylor Spence* (pp. 255–90). Washington, DC: American Psychological Association.

Spence, J. T. & Buckner, C. E. (2000). Instrumental and expressive traits, trait stereotypes, and sexist attitudes. *Psychology of Women Quarterly*, *24*, 44–62.

Spence, J. T. & Helmreich, R. (1972a). Who likes competent women? Competence, sex-role congruence of interest, and subjects' attitudes toward women as determinants of interpersonal attraction. *Journal of Applied Social Psychology*, *2*, 197–213.

Spence, J. T. & Helmreich, R. (1972b). The Attitudes Toward Women Scale: An objective instrument to measure attitudes toward the rights and roles of women in contemporary society. *JSAS Catalog of Selected Documents in Psychology*, *2*, 66–7 (Ms. 153).

Swim, J. K., Aiken, K. J., Hall, W. S., & Hunter, B. A. (1995). Sexism and racism: Old-fashioned and modern prejudice. *Journal of Personality and Social Psychology*, *68*, 199–214.

Tougas, F., Brown, R., Beaton, A. M., & Joly, S. (1995) Neosexism: Plus ça change, plus c'est pareil. *Personality and Social Psychology Bulletin*, *21*, 842–9.

Weidner, G. & Griffitt, W. (1983). Rape: A sexual stigma? *Journal of Personality*, *51*, 152–66.

GROUP DIFFERENCES

Chapter Eight

Group Differences and Stereotype Accuracy

Charles M. Judd and Bernadette Park

A central concern in the study of prejudice is whether individuals perceive stereotypic differences between groups and, if so, whether those perceived differences are biased views or accurately reflect actual group differences that may exist. Allport considered this issue in chapters 6 ("The Scientific Study of Group Differences") and 7 ("Racial and Ethnic Differences") of his classic treatise, discussing whether the perception of group differences justifies prejudice and how the scientific study of group differences might proceed. We revisit these concerns, turning first to the writings of early theorists and their views on whether the perception of group differences is necessarily problematic. Next we review conceptual and methodological issues in the assessment of the accuracy with which perceivers judge group differences. Finally, we explore whether it is necessary to eliminate or minimize perceived group differences in order to reduce prejudice.

Allport's (and Other Early) Views on the Perception of Group Differences

One of the most notable aspects of Allport's book is his understanding of the role that categorization plays in maintaining the negative consequences of prejudice (see Fiske, ch. 3 this volume). He recognized the power of categories to structure intergroup relations and he anticipated decades of research showing that cognitive processes associated with categorization facilitate the harm done by prejudices. But importantly, he maintained that prejudice is the fundamental problem of intergroup relations, not categorization. Allport argued that categories and their attendant stereotypes operate in the service of prejudice, noting that the purpose of stereotypes "is to justify (rationalize) our conduct in relation to that category" (1954/ 1979, p. 191).

In thinking about where perceived groups differences come from, Allport argued that there exists a core of actual group differences which become magnified by prejudice so that the resulting stereotypic beliefs about outgroups are more extreme, negative, and overgeneralized than warranted by the data. He gave the example of mutual perceptions by the Russians and the Americans during the Cold War. Each group started with an observed difference rooted in reality, but these perceptions became negative caricatures of what the groups were actually like. The prejudiced person then comes to *invoke* group differences as a justification for his or her prejudiced attitude (see also Jost & Hamilton, ch. 13 this volume). According to Allport, "Difference alone does not make for hostility . . . and yet the prejudiced person almost always *claims* that some alleged difference is the cause of his attitude" (1954/1979, p. 87). Trying to alter the stereotype content is like treating the symptom rather than the root cause. Allport suggested that although beliefs can be challenged, typically "they have the slippery propensity of accommodating themselves somehow to the negative attitude which is much harder to change" (p. 13).

Consistent with Allport's views, Krech and Crutchfield (1948) argued that "The *grouping* of people in perception does not, in itself make for racial prejudice – it merely makes such beliefs and attitudes possible" (p. 506, emphasis in original). They noted that social grouping can just as easily lead to favorable attitudes toward a group and argued that it is the "nature of the cue that supports the grouping" that is critical to whether or not racial prejudice follows. It is not the cue "black skin" that leads to prejudice, but rather, Krech and Crutchfield argued, the supporting or correlated cues of poverty, lack of education, and low social status. What is important then is to eliminate these correlated cues:

> The significance of this formulation lies in the suggestion that in our attempt to control racial prejudice through changing the percepts involved, we are not necessarily forced to adopt a program that will eliminate all racial differences. Although it is true that if such an end were achieved, racial prejudice would also necessarily disappear, nevertheless racial prejudice can be eliminated through a process far short of such an "expunging solution" of the problem. Racial prejudice can be eliminated through the differential elimination or control of cues without erasing all the perceptible difference among races. (pp. 506–7)

In a wonderfully insightful article, Campbell (1967) echoed many of the same sentiments expressed by Allport. Campbell argued that actual differences between groups exist, an obvious point from an anthropological perspective. These actual group differences are reflected in stereotypes to some degree (a "kernel of truth"). For various motivational reasons, outgroups tend to be disliked. Accordingly, Campbell argued that this negative affect tends to color outgroup stereotypic beliefs. Because it is possible to represent almost any semantic content with either a positive or negative valence (e.g., *stingy* versus *thrifty*: Peabody, 1967), dislike of the outgroup ensures that a negative valence is attached to the perceived differences that are in part based in reality. In general, in addition to the kernel of truth, stereotypes are almost always also partially inaccurate (sometimes in large part). In an effort to denounce these inaccurate beliefs, "There has grown up in social and educational psychology a literature and teaching practice which says that all stereotypes of group differences are false, and, implicitly, that all groups are on average identical." (Campbell, 1967, p. 823; Allport, 1954/1979, p. 87, made essentially the same point.) Campbell noted that while social psychologists have been right in emphasizing the general errorfulness of stereotypes, the "problem is how to state the errors, without claiming that all groups are identical" (p. 824).

Campbell (1967) highlighted various factors that contribute to the "wrongfulness" of stereotypes. One of these, which he judged to be particularly important, is the tendency of the prejudiced individual to believe that it is the attributes of the group (i.e., stereotype content) that generate dislike, when in fact it is the dislike that generates the negative stereotypic beliefs about the group:

> The naive ingrouper perceives the different characteristics of the outgroup as causing his hostility (Ichheiser, 1949). He feels that were it not for these despicable traits, the outgroup would be loved . . . The social scientist sees the opposite causal direction: Causally, first is the hostility toward the outgrouper, generated perhaps by real threat, perhaps by ethnocentrism, perhaps by displacement. In the service of hostility, all possible differences are opportunistically interpreted as despicable. . . . So flexible is our emotional language that a difference in almost any direction can be anathematized. An outgroup can be hated as too lazy or as too industrious, as too dumb or as too shrewd, as too forward or too reclusive, as too emotional or as too cold, as too generous or as too thrifty (Merton, 1949). (p. 825)

In summary, Allport and other prominent theorists argued early on that the fundamental problem in intergroup relations was the intense feeling of antipathy and prejudice that can be associated with outgroups. They argued that beliefs about the existence of group differences were not in and of themselves problematic. Rather, those beliefs became problematic only in the service of prejudice, when they served to justify prejudicial attitudes.

Allport clearly recognized the power of social categories to reinforce and exacerbate group hostilities. But the core problem to rectify was intergroup animosity. Although the elimination of all social categories would logically be a way to do this, doing away with social categories was recognized not to be a feasible solution, because categorization is fundamental to perception. Finally, attempts to change negative outgroup stereotypes, without changing the underlying hostility, would do little good, because negative stereotypes are not the cause of prejudice. Rather they are a consequence of prejudice.

Developments Since Allport: The Study of Actual and Perceived Group Differences

As Campbell (1967) articulated, from an anthropological point of view, it is obvious that groups differ. They differ in their histories, customs, habits, preferences, values, traits, and goals. Of course, groups are themselves made up of diverse individuals, and certainly within groups there is considerable variability in those same characteristics along which groups differ from each other. Accordingly, while groups differ, undoubtedly distributions of group members show considerable overlap.

Someone who is an accurate social perceiver will appropriately recognize both the prototypic differences that exist between groups and the variability within groups. To recognize both group differences and within-group variability, and to gauge their magnitudes correctly, is to perceive the intergroup world in a veridical manner.

Following Allport, we can define stereotypes as beliefs about the attributes that differentiate groups from each other. An accurate intergroup perceiver is one who holds group stereotypes that reflect the actual group distributions and mean differences. Accordingly, the perception of group differences is not itself indicative of prejudice. However, in line with the views of Allport and Campbell, prejudice may very well lead to biased perceptions of group differences, i.e., stereotypes that are erroneous in part because they operate in the service of prejudice.

From this point of view, not only is the assessment of stereotype accuracy possible, but indeed it is critical in order to gauge the impact of prejudice on stereotypic beliefs. The simple possession of beliefs about group differences is not in and of itself a prejudiced view of the intergroup world. Rather, the prejudiced individual is one whose stereotypic beliefs about group differences (and within-group variability) are biased and inaccurate, relative to some reality, because they are in the service of prejudice.

In 1993 we published an article in the *Psychological Review* (Judd & Park, 1993) that defined the various ways in which beliefs about group differences may or may not be accurate. Additionally, we developed a research design called the full ingroup–outgroup accuracy design that permits an assessment of the accuracy of beliefs about group differences. In the following paragraphs, we review this approach, concentrating on the ways in which prejudice or outgroup hate may bias intergroup beliefs. We then review research that explores these issues with variants of our proposed approach.

Forms of Inaccuracies in Beliefs about Group Differences

Assume for the moment a single attribute continuum on which individuals, who are nested into two social groups, vary. For the time being we will not define this attribute continuum, we will simply assume that individuals' locations along the continuum represent fairly stable individual differences. Additionally, while there are differences among individuals within the two groups, there is also a stable mean difference along the continuum between the groups. Schematically the situation is portrayed in the overlapping group distributions (assumed to be roughly normal within each group) presented in figure 8.1.

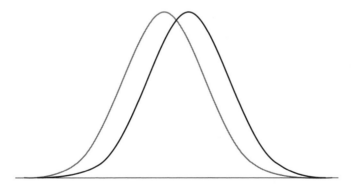

Figure 8.1 Hypothetical distributions of members of two groups on an attribute dimension

The question of the accuracy of social beliefs about group differences (i.e., stereotypes) concerns the ways in which the *perceived* distributions of group members along the attribute continuum differ from the actual distributions as portrayed in figure 8.1. For the moment, we will put aside the very thorny issue of how one might assess the actual distributions. Instead we will assume that the actual distributions, as displayed in figure 8.1, are known and we will focus on how perceived distributions may depart from these, i.e., how beliefs about stereotypic differences between groups may be inaccurate.

Initially one can define two ways in which perceived distributions may depart from the actual distributions. First, one may overestimate or underestimate the magnitude of the actual mean differences between the two distributions: one may see the groups as more different or less different on average than they actually are along the continuum. If the perceiver judges that there is a greater difference than there actually is between the two groups, this can be labeled as *stereotypic inaccuracy*: overestimating the degree to which groups differ along a stereotypic dimension on which there is in fact a mean difference between them. This sort of inaccuracy, of course, could also go in the opposite direction: failing to perceive a mean difference between the two groups when there is one.

The second sort of inaccuracy focuses on the perceiver's estimate of the within-group variability of individuals along the attribute continuum. One may underestimate or overestimate the degree to which individuals who are members of the groups are dispersed along the continuum, and this error may characterize perceptions of one of the groups more than perceptions of the other. This sort of error is known as *dispersion inaccuracy*.

A useful analogy in thinking about these two forms of inaccuracy derives from statistics, where the significance of a group difference depends on the size of the mean difference between the groups, relative to the within-group(s) variability. In the stereotyping literature, this ratio has come to be known as the *metacontrast ratio* (Oakes, Haslam, & Turner, 1994; Turner et al., 1987). The exaggeration of group differences in stereotypic beliefs can occur either when the stereotypic mean difference between the groups along the attribute continuum is overestimated or when the within-group dispersion of individuals along the continuum is underestimated. On the other hand, one might also underestimate group differences along the continuum, either by underestimating the magnitude of the mean difference between the groups or by overestimating the within-group dispersion of individuals along the continuum.

To this point, we have deliberately avoided discussing the content of the attribute dimension underlying the actual group differences in figure 8.1.

To define the third type of stereotype accuracy, however, we must focus on content, and in particular on the valence of the attribute in question. Although we agree with Allport (and Campbell) that many attribute dimensions can be defined in positively valenced or negatively valenced terms (e.g., stingy versus thrifty), it is nevertheless the case that there exists broad agreement about the valence of certain fundamental attributes. In particular, two fundamental and broad dimensions seem to underlie social perception, both at the individual (Rosenberg, Nelson, & Vivekananthan, 1968) and group (Fiske, Cuddy, Glick, & Xu, 2002) levels, and there is widespread agreement about the valence of these dimensions. People and groups seems to differ in the degree to which they are seen to possess positively valued agentic attributes (with the positive pole of the dimension including attributes such as motivated, intelligent, organized, capable; and the negative pole including attributes such as lazy, slow, disorganized) and communal attributes (with the positive pole including attributes such as warm, friendly, supportive; and the negative pole including attributes such as hostile, uncaring, and cold).

With social groups, it is likely that actual group differences along these valenced dimensions (as portrayed in figure 8.1) tend to cancel one another out across multiple attribute dimensions. That is, social groups on average are probably more or less evaluatively equivalent. Consider two social groups, A and B. On some valenced attribute dimensions A is likely to be higher than B, while on others the group difference would be reversed. Nevertheless, social perceivers may be biased in reporting these valenced group differences, such that they may tend to see systematically larger group differences on dimensions that favor one group over the other (say A over B) and smaller group differences on dimensions that favor the other group (say B over A). We use the term *valence inaccuracy* to refer to the systematic tendency to overestimate the evaluative difference between groups across multiple valenced attribute dimensions.

These three forms of stereotype *in*accuracy – stereotypic inaccuracy, dispersion inaccuracy, and valence inaccuracy – tend to take on certain expected directions in the intergroup literature, based on the notions that prejudice guides intergroup stereotypes. The most obvious effect of intergroup hostilities should be on valence inaccuracy, with actual group differences between the ingroup and the outgroup overestimated on dimensions that favor the ingroup and underestimated on dimensions that favor the outgroup. It may also be the case that more prejudiced social perceivers see larger group differences in general than actually exist, regardless of the valence of the attribute dimensions. In particular, prejudiced perceivers may tend to overestimate the relative degree to which outgroups possess stereotypic attributes and underestimate the extent to which they manifest within-group variability. Such a bias would be consistent with the well-documented tendency towards *outgroup homogeneity* (Park & Judd, 1990; Park & Rothbart, 1982): perceiving the outgroup to be more stereotypic and less dispersed than the ingroup.

Practical Difficulties in Assessing the Accuracy of Perceived Group Differences

While the various forms of stereotype inaccuracies can be defined relatively easily, their estimation is fraught with difficulties. Two primary difficulties occur. The first and more major of the two concerns the assessment of the actual distributions of groups (both the between-group differences and the within-group variability) on attribute dimensions. How do we figure out what groups are really like on the relevant dimensions of judgment? The second issue concerns the fact that various scaling and measurement issues may affect perceivers' judgments and these may make direct comparisons between actual distributions and judged distributions difficult.

To assess the actual distributions of groups on some attribute dimension, as portrayed in figure 8.1, we would need to draw representative samples from both groups and then accurately assess the location of each sampled individual on the attribute dimension. This is difficult from two points of view: sampling and measurement. Socially significant groups that figure in stereotyping and prejudice are often vaguely and imprecisely defined. If we are to sample individuals to assess their actual location along an attribute dimension, how do we define the population of all group members from which we should representatively sample? For instance, how do we define ethnic group membership in the United States? Drawing a random sample clearly depends on defining who is in the population and who is not.

And then there is the issue of how we are to accurately measure where the sampled individuals truly are located on the attribute dimension. How do we measure someone's true standing on trait dimensions such as "intelligent," "friendly," or "unmotivated." Do we use their own self-report? Do we interview their friends and neighbors? Do we ask experts to observe them and judge them? Do we give them tests or personality inventories? Although in different situations all of these might be reasonable choices, they also all undoubtedly have associated biases (see Allport, 1954/1979, pp. 89–94). The bottom line is that there is no perfect way to know where individuals (and groups) actually stand on relevant attribute dimensions.

And once we have assessed the criterion (i.e., where representative samples of group members actually are located on the relevant dimensions), what questions do we ask perceivers about the groups (and the individuals within them), and then how do we compare their responses to the criterion? One would ideally like to ask perceivers to locate groups (and their individual members) on the same attribute dimensions (using the same continua endpoints and metrics) as were used to assess the criterion (i.e., the actual group distributions). Then one could simply calculate the three forms of stereotype inaccuracies by computing difference scores. Collapsing across multiple attribute dimensions, balanced in their valence, are the groups seen to be more different than they actually are (stereotypic inaccuracy)? Do people perceive less within-group variability than there actually is (dispersion inaccuracy)? And is the perceived ingroup–outgroup difference on valenced attributes exaggerated on ones that favor the ingroup and understated on ones that favor the outgroup (valence inaccuracy)?

It is clear from previous research that has explored pitfalls in the assessment of judgmental accuracy (Cronbach, 1955) that these kinds of direct comparisons between judgments and a criterion can be problematic because of scale usage issues – people use scales differently because they idiosyncratically define the metrics of judgmental scales. We have proposed two tactics to address this problem. One is that the interpretations of direct comparisons (i.e., discrepancy scores) is less problematic in the context of a "full accuracy design," in which judgments are collected from both ingroup and outgroup members evaluating both target groups on positively and negatively valenced stereotypic and counterstereotypic attributes. This design avoids many typical scale usage problems because the comparisons are fundamentally *relative*, such that we ask, for example, whether members of both groups demonstrate valence inaccuracy, overestimating group differences on attributes that favor their respective ingroup, and underestimating them on dimensions that favor their respective outgroup. The relative nature of the comparisons means that differences due to scale usage are essentially cancelled out.

A second alternative to direct difference comparisons between judgments and the criterion is to use correlational methods. We have called such correlational assessments sensitivity correlations. Across multiple attribute dimensions, one can assess for each perceiver the degree to which judgments covary with the criterion. In terms of stereotypic accuracy, substantial correlations would indicate that perceivers are sensitive to the varying prevalence of particular attributes within a group: perceivers judge there to be a greater prevalence of attribute dimensions that are in fact more prevalent. While these sorts of sensitivity correlations have the potential to overcome judgmental scale usage problems, they of course make directional comparisons between the criteria and judgments impossible. For instance, if there are inaccuracies, one cannot determine whether judgments overestimate or underestimate the stereotypic differences between groups.

Recent Stereotype Accuracy Research

In our 1993 paper (Judd & Park, 1993), we reviewed a number of early studies that presented evidence relevant to the issue of the accuracy of stereotypic group judgments. We will not repeat that review here. Rather we will concentrate on studies that have generally adopted the perspective outlined above. In all of this work, the criterion measurement issue has been dealt with by asking group members to rate themselves and then aggregating these ratings. Thus stereotypic judgments of a group are compared to aggregated self-judgments. As discussed previously, there are certainly pitfalls in this approach.

An initial study (Judd, Ryan, & Park, 1991) involved participants from two majors on campus, business and engineering. These had been randomly sampled from all such majors, and they were asked to report both self-ratings on various stereotype-relevant attribute dimensions, as well as judgments of the prevalence and variability of these attributes in each group. The attributes were all positively valenced (e.g., analytical and extroverted). Accordingly, while stereotypic and dispersion inaccuracies were examined, there were no negatively valenced attributes to examine valence inaccuracy.

Participants reported that stereotypic attributes were more prevalent in the outgroup than they in fact were, suggesting stereotypic inaccuracies in perceptions of the outgroup. Sensitivity correlations also suggested greater inaccuracies in outgroup stereotypes, for both groups of participants, than in ingroup stereotypes. Additionally, outgroup homogeneity was found such that outgroup dispersion was underestimated in comparison to ingroup dispersion, resulting in greater dispersion inaccuracy for the outgroup than the ingroup. Also, there was a tendency for dispersion sensitivity correlations to be lower in the case of the outgroup than the ingroup. All these results suggest stereotyped exaggeration of the outgroup, which was perceived more stereotypically and as more homogeneous than it ought to be.

Stereotypical beliefs about campus majors probably do not involve strong intergroup antipathies; ethnic stereotypes are a different matter. Ryan

(1996) examined stereotype accuracy with samples of African American and white college students. Participants were representative samples of first-year students at the University of Colorado, half of them African American and half white. Once again aggregate self-ratings were used as the criterion. The target groups that participants rated were "first-year African American" or "first-year white" students at the University. Both self-ratings and perceived target group ratings were collected on attributes that varied in valence and stereotypicality for the two target groups.

Focusing on perceived stereotypic discrepancies, both target groups were seen more stereotypically by all participants than they self-described. Thus all participants viewed the groups as more different than in fact their self-ratings revealed them to be. This difference was especially true on the part of African American participants, who particularly overestimated the stereotypicality of both target groups. Interestingly, this overestimation did not depend on target group: both the ingroup and the outgroup were seen more stereotypically than the criterion suggested they ought to be. When attribute valence was taken into account, perceivers tended to over-estimate negatively valenced attributes and underestimate positively valenced ones (relative to self-reports). This tendency was particularly strong in the perceptions of the white target group and particularly when judged by African American participants.

In terms of within-group dispersion, participants generally under-estimated the actual variability in both target groups, again suggesting that they overestimated the relative difference between the two groups. And this underestimation was found for both positively and negatively valenced attributes. Interestingly, this underestimation of variability was particularly strong toward the African American target group compared to the white target group.

The analysis of sensitivity correlations suggested that African American perceivers were more accurate in judging between-attribute differences in stereotypicality. Thus, the larger discrepancy scores can be attributed to the tendency for African American participants to judge all targets, but particularly white targets, negatively. At the same time, however, African American perceivers were more sensitive to the variation from attribute to attribute in the degree to which the target groups self-reported that they possessed those attributes.

The combination of these results suggests a set of theoretically provocat-ive conclusions about perceived ethnic differences. Views of both target groups by all participants tended to exaggerate the stereotypic differences between the groups. Additionally, participants generally overestimated the prevalence of negative attributes, compared to positive ones, but this difference was particularly found for African American participants in judging whites. At the same time, however, African Americans manifested considerable sensitivity in judging the differences between attributes in the extent to which targets self-reported the presence of these attributes. This combination suggests both more negative intergroup views but also a heightened sensitivity to the actual stereotypic makeup of both target groups on the part of African American participants.

The final set of results that explores these issues did so longitudinally, examining the accuracy of ingroup and outgroup judgments with group members who were new initiates into sororities (the target and participant groups). These participants were followed over the course of a year so that it was possible to examine how their group views changed as they became more firmly ensconced as group members (Ryan & Bogart, 2001). Again, comparisons were made with actual self-reports of all group members in the sororities.

For all target groups, participants overestimated the degree to which there were stereotypic differences between them. Additionally, as in the dataset involving majors, the tendency to overestimate stereotypicality was more true for outgroup perceptions than ingroup ones. Interestingly, while the general tendency to overestimate stereotypicality decreased over time, for both the ingroup and the outgroup targets, the outgroup–ingroup difference in stereotype exaggeration did not diminish over time.

In terms of valence differences, views of the ingroup were biased in a positive direction, compared to views of the outgroup, but this valence difference decreased over time, with views of the ingroup becoming less positive as participants' membership status in the groups became more secure.

In terms of within-group variability, initially there was a tendency to underestimate within-group dispersion more for the ingroup than for the outgroup. Over time this difference declined, with participants more accurately judging within-group dispersion for the ingroup at later time points.

While the results from these three studies are provocative, they probably do not permit conclusions that could be generalized to other target and subject groups. Perhaps these data suggest a general tendency to exaggerate actual group differences. And there is a suggestion of ingroup–outgroup differences in perceptions of stereotypicality. In sum, these studies suggest that the analysis of perceived group differences, and comparisons of those differences with alternative estimates of actual group differences, can yield fruitful insights into the biases encountered in intergroup perception.

Group Differences and Prejudice Reduction

With this discussion of stereotype accuracy in mind, we now return to issues raised in the beginning of this chapter and specifically, to the nature of the relationship between perceived group differences and prejudice. Given the arguments of Allport and others, and our own analysis of the relevant issues, the following conclusions can be drawn. First, group differences obviously exist (Campbell, 1967). Second, although the prejudiced perceiver often begins with some true core difference, this is then exaggerated such that between-group differences are accentuated and within-group differences are minimized (Tajfel, 1969; Tajfel & Wilkes, 1963). Third, because the valence of attributed characteristics is somewhat malleable, the social perceiver can slant the evaluative quality of group differences by his or her choice of descriptors. Fourth, it is the prejudiced sentiments of the social perceiver that motivates these exaggerated group differences, not the other way around. In the end, then, as Allport suggested, understanding the accuracy of perceived group differences is important because it is informative about where there are problems in intergroup perceptions. Inaccuracies serve as a barometer of sorts, an indicator of the magnitude of manipulated social reality.

Perhaps as important as the degree of accuracy in social perception are the attributions made for group differences. Suppose one were to ask perceivers about racial disparities in high-school dropout rates. And these estimates were then compared with actual rates. It may well be the case that perceivers (particularly white majority participants) would overestimate the differences between racial groups. Yet this stereotypic exaggeration might be only part of the story. To aptly characterize the intergroup dynamics operating, it would be important to know not only how accurate perceptions are, but what attributions are made for perceived differences. Two perceivers may be inaccurate to exactly the same extent but one may believe the group differences are caused by poverty and an unsupportive social environment, whereas the other may believe the group differences reflect an underlying difference in intellectual ability.

If the ultimate goal is to bring about more harmonious relations between social groups, is the only way to achieve this goal to eliminate group stereotypes and suggest that all groups are equivalent? We think not, both because real group differences do exist, and because, as Allport (1954/ 1979) has noted, even if negative outgroup stereotypes could be eliminated, new ones would come along to justify the felt antipathy. While a laudable goal might be to increase the accuracy of intergroup beliefs, the real objective is to eliminate the intergroup antipathy.

To be clear, there are two critical aspects of intergroup perceptions with which the social scientist is concerned. The first is a general feeling of liking or disliking for an outgroup, that is, whether or not prejudiced sentiments are present. The second is the group stereotype or the semantic content of the attributes seen as characteristic of the group. Although these two are clearly linked (Fiske, 1998), they can operate somewhat independently of one another, as evidenced by the literature on the contact hypothesis (see ch. 16 by Pettigrew & Tropp and ch. 17 by Kenworthy, Hewstone, Turner, & Voci, this volume). In an extensive meta-analysis, Pettigrew and Tropp (2000) argued that contact seems to be effective in bringing about more positive evaluations of outgroups, but contact may not change the content of group stereotypes. In an empirical investigation of this issue, we found that moderately positive contact with a Latino confederate was sufficient to produce more positive attitudes towards Latinos as a group. Change in stereotype strength, however, occurred only when certain further conditions were met. Specifically, it was necessary for the Latino confederate to behave in a manner that disconfirmed the group stereotype, and at the same time, for the participant to continue to see the Latino as typical of his group (Wolsko, Park, Judd, & Bachelor, 2003).

Together with the arguments presented earlier in this chapter, this suggests that changing the negative affect often associated with outgroups is likely to be a more attainable and more proximal goal than directly attempting to change stereotype content (see also Smith & Mackie, ch. 22 this volume). In fact, it would be extremely interesting to examine the time course of change in group perceptions, and specifically, change in stereotype inaccuracies as a function of changes in group evaluations. It would seem likely that reducing animosity toward an outgroup can eventually result in less exaggerated group stereotypes, and thus, perhaps, more accurate intergroup perceptions.

This line of reasoning has profound consequences for models of prejudice reduction. Specifically, it suggests that eliminating perceived group differences, and the boundaries that separate social groups, may not in fact be necessary or even desirable. Rather, the focus of intervention efforts might best be placed on changing group sentiments, encouraging group members to develop a sense of acceptance and tolerance for one another even while acknowledging group differences on both positive and negative dimensions (Park & Judd, in press; Wolsko, Park, Judd, & Wittenbrink, 2000). We have some evidence from our lab that category boundaries can be made more salient even while leaving the evaluative differentiation between two groups intact (Deffenbacher, Park, Judd, & Correll, 2003). In the current political and social climate it seems critical to acknowledge that social groups differ in important and meaningful ways. At issue is whether we can find the means for producing acceptance of groups even while acknowledging group differences.

REFERENCES

Allport, G. W. (1954/1979). *The nature of prejudice.* Cambridge, MA: Perseus Books.

Campbell, D. T. (1967). Stereotypes and the perception of group differences. *American Psychologist, 22,* 817–29.

Cronbach, L. J. (1955). Processes affecting scores on "understanding of others" and "assumed similarity." *Psychological Bulletin, 52,* 177–93.

Deffenbacher, D. M., Park, B., Judd, C. M., & Correll, J. (2003). Does the accentuation of category boundaries necessarily increase intergroup bias? Unpublished MS, Boulder, CO.

Fiske, S. T. (1998). Stereotyping, prejudice, and discrimination. In D. T. Gilbert, S. T. Fiske, & G. Lindzey (eds.), *The handbook of social psychology* (4th ed., vol. 2, pp. 357–414). Boston, MA: McGraw-Hill

Fiske, S. T., Cuddy, A. J. C., Glick, P., & Xu, J. (2002). A model of (often mixed) stereotype content: Competence and warmth respectively follow from perceived status and competition. *Journal of Personality and Social Psychology, 82,* 878–902.

Ichheiser, G. (1949). Misunderstandings in human relations: A study of false social perception. *American Journal of Sociology, 55,* part 2, no. 2.

Judd, C. M. & Park, B. (1993). Definition and assessment of accuracy in

social stereotypes. *Psychological Review, 100,* 109–28.

Judd, C. M., Ryan, C. S., & Park, B. (1991). Accuracy in the judgments of in-group and out-group variability. *Journal of Personality and Social Psychology, 61,* 366–79.

Krech, D. & Crutchfield, R. S. (1948). *Theory and problems of social psychology.* New York: McGraw-Hill.

Merton, R. K. (1949). *Social theory and social structure* (2nd ed., 1957). Glencoe, IL: Free Press.

Oakes, P. J., Haslam, S. A., & Turner, J. C. (1994). *Stereotyping and social reality.* Malden, MA: Blackwell.

Park, B. & Judd, C. M. (1990). Measures and models of perceived group variability. *Journal of Personality and Social Psychology, 59,* 173–91.

Park, B. & Judd, C. M. (in press). Rethinking the link between categorization and prejudice within the social cognition perspective. *Personality and Social Psychology Review.*

Park, B. & Rothbart, M. (1982). Perception of out-group homogeneity and levels of social categorization: Memory for the subordinate attributes of in-group and out-group members. *Journal of Personality and Social Psychology, 42,* 1051–68.

Peabody, D. (1967). Trait inferences: Evaluative and descriptive aspects.

Journal of Personality and Social Psychology, 7, 1–18.

Pettigrew, T. F. & Tropp, L. R. (2000). Does intergroup contact reduce prejudice?: Recent meta-analytic findings. In S. Oskamp (ed.), *Reducing prejudice and discrimination* (pp. 93–114). Mahwah, NJ: Lawrence Erlbaum.

Rosenberg, S., Nelson, C., & Vivekananthan, P. S. (1968). A multidimensional approach to the structure of personality impressions. *Journal of Personality and Social Psychology, 9,* 283–94.

Ryan, C. S. (1996). Accuracy of Black and White college students' in-group and out-group stereotypes. *Personality and Social Psychology Bulletin, 22,* 1114–27.

Ryan, C. S. & Bogart, L. M. (2001). Longitudinal changes in the accuracy of new group members' in-group and out-group stereotypes. *Journal of Personality and Social Psychology, 37,* 118–33.

Tajfel, H. (1969). Cognitive aspects of prejudice. *Journal of Social Issues, 25,* 79–98.

Tajfel, H. & Wilkes, A. L. (1963). Classification and quantitative judgment. *British Journal of Psychology, 54,* 101–14.

Turner, J. C., Hogg, M. A., Oakes, P. J., Reicher, S. D., & Wetherell, M. S. (1987). *Rediscovering the social group: A self-categorization theory.* Oxford: Blackwell.

Wolsko, C., Park, B., Judd, C. M., & Bachelor, J. (2003). Intergroup contact: Effects on group evaluations and perceived variability. *Group Processes & Intergroup Relations, 6,* 93–110.

Wolsko, C., Park, B., Judd, C. M., & Wittenbrink, B. (2000). Framing interethnic ideology: Effects of multicultural and color-blind perspectives on judgments of groups and individuals. *Journal of Personality and Social Psychology, 78,* 635–54.

Chapter Nine

The Psychological Impact of Prejudice

Brenda Major and S. Brooke Vick

In *The Nature of Prejudice*, Allport devoted but a single chapter to the psychological impact of prejudice on those who are its targets: chapter 9, titled "Traits Due to Victimization." Despite its brevity, this seminal chapter anticipated many of the research questions that scholars interested in responses to prejudice pursue today. The present chapter outlines Allport's contribution to a growing body of literature that has begun to yield answers to the question he asked at the beginning of his chapter, "Ask yourself what would happen to your own personality if you heard it said over and over again that you were lazy, a simple child of nature, expected to steal, and had inferior blood?" (Allport, 1954/1979, p. 142).

Allport's Views on Prejudice from the Target's Perspective

Drawing on the self-fulfilling prophecy and other reflected appraisal theories that emphasize the importance of others' opinions on the development of the self-concept (see Crocker & Major, 1989, for a review), Allport (1954/ 1979) assumed that "no one can be indifferent to the abuse and expectations of others" (p. 142). Further, he believed that prejudice inevitably has an effect on the personality of its victims. "One's reputation, whether false or true," he observed, "cannot be hammered, hammered, hammered, into one's head without doing something to one's character" (p. 142).

Interestingly, Allport did not believe that the traits that targets of prejudice develop as a result of their persecution are necessarily unpleasant or lead to poor mental health. Rather, he argued that targets develop ego defenses in response to ridicule, disparagement, and discrimination, some of which (e.g., ingroup solidarity) help to protect their mental health. Allport asserted that the type of ego defenses that develop is largely an individual rather than group matter, dependent upon an individual's particular life circumstances, worldviews, and environment. In particular, he emphasized targets' personality as the driving force behind reactions to prejudice in his suggestion that extropunitive and intropunitive people would respond to prejudice differently. He hypothesized that people who tend to be "extropunitive" (i.e., who characteristically attribute the cause of personal events to things outside of themselves) will likely adopt outwardly focused defenses (e.g., aggression against the outgroup), whereas people who characteristically tend to be "intropunitive" (i.e., who attribute responsibility for events to themselves) will likely adopt inwardly focused defenses (e.g., denial of membership, self-hate, and ingroup aggression). However, he acknowledged that targets might display a blend of extra- and intropunitive strategies to protect themselves from being victimized by prejudice. As will be seen in the subsequent sections, researchers have found substantial support for Allport's seminal taxonomy of responses to prejudice (see also Jones's ch. 10 in this volume).

Developments Since Allport

In the decades following publication of *The Nature of Prejudice*, social-psychological research, with a few notable exceptions (Goffman, 1963; Rosenberg & Simmons, 1972) continued to emphasize the causes of prejudice rather than the consequences for its victims. This emphasis began to shift in the 1980s with the publication of several books and articles devoted to the psychology of stigmatization (e.g., Jones et al., 1984; Crocker & Major, 1989). Since then, a substantial and growing literature on the psychological implications of prejudice and negative stereotypes has emerged (see Crocker, Major, & Steele, 1998, for a review).

Many of Allport's ideas and assumptions are reflected in this new literature. For example, although contemporary scholars no longer use the psychodynamic term "ego defense" (see Newman & Caldwell's ch. 23 in this volume), many focus, as Allport did, on how victims respond to prejudice, and on the strategies that they adopt to defend themselves from the threat that it imposes. Like Allport, contemporary researchers also tend to conceptualize targets of prejudice not as passive victims, but as *motivated* (i.e., strategic) agents attempting to make sense of their world and to protect their identities from threat. Contemporary researchers address questions such as: to what extent do members of stigmatized groups protect their self-esteem by attributing negative outcomes to prejudice of others, comparing outcomes within their own stigmatized group, select-ively devaluing domains in which their ingroup fares poorly, and identify-ing more strongly with their devalued ingroup, among other strategies? (See Crocker, Major, & Steele, 1998, for a review.) Research derived from Social Identity Theory investigates strategies such as pursuing indi-vidual mobility, social competition with outgroups, and social creativity (redefining what traits are valued), all of which are used in the service of maintaining a positive social identity (Tajfel & Turner, 1986; see also chs. 4, 5, and 11 in this volume, by Brown & Zagefka, Gaertner & Dovidio, and Yzerbyt & Corneille, respectively).

Allport's assumption of *individual variability* in targets' responses to pre-judice also is reflected in contemporary approaches (see Major, Quinton, & McCoy, 2002). Consistent with Allport's idea that targets' responses to prejudice differ as a function of their personality characteristics, individual differences in dispositions such as optimism (Kaiser, Major, & McCoy, 2004), rejection sensitivity (Mendoza-Denton et al., 2002), social-dominance orientation (Overbeck, Jost, Mosso & Fizlik, 2004), social mobility beliefs (Major, Gramzow, et al., 2002), and group identification (McCoy & Major, 2003) moderate responses to prejudice. For example, members of low-status groups who endorse the belief in individual mobility, i.e., that anyone can get ahead in society (a belief that holds people personally responsible for their outcomes) express more ambivalence toward their ingroup and are less likely to see themselves or their ingroup as victims of prejudice, than are members of low-status groups who reject this belief (Major, Gramzow, et al., 2002).

Many contemporary perspectives also share Allport's assumption that targets of prejudice do not necessarily have poor mental health. Qualitative (Crocker & Major, 1989) and meta-analytic (Twenge & Crocker, 2000) reviews of the literature conclude that some devalued groups, such as African Americans, have *higher* self-esteem than nonstigmatized groups. Other groups that are targets of prejudice (e.g., White women, over-weight people), however, have lower self-esteem than the nonstigmatized (see Major, Quinton, & McCoy, 2002). An important question for future research is to identify why these group differences occur.

A New Framework

Despite the many assumptions that contemporary perspectives share with Allport, important differences can be found. Most notably, Allport believed that prejudice is internalized, at least to some extent, by its targets. In his view, prejudice inevitably, inescapably, and irrevocably alters the personality of its victims. This perspective predicts considerable cross-situational consistency in behavior. In contrast, most contemporary scholars adopt a more social-psychological, or situational, perspective. These scholars propose that stigma exposes its bearers to *situational threats*, i.e., situations where one's membership in a particular stigmatized group could influence how one is treated and judged (see Steele, Spencer, & Aronson, 2002). No internalization of stigmatizing stereotypes is assumed to be necessary for prejudice to influence the person's experience and behavior. Thus, quite different responses may be observed within the same individual as the context changes (Steele et al., 2002).

This situationist perspective is reflected in research and theory on "stereotype threat." Stereotype threat is a psychological predicament that occurs when people are aware of the negative stereotypes that others hold of their social group and are anxious that they may confirm them, either in their own or others' eyes. This anxiety, in turn, may interfere with their performance. It is not necessary that a person endorse the stereotype for stereotype threat to occur, or for it to impair performance. Importantly, stereotype threat is a situation-specific predicament, rather than a personality trait. It is experienced only in situations where a negative stereotype is relevant. Thus, a member of a minority group may perform badly on an intelligence test when stereotypes are salient, but not when stereotypes are not (see Steele et al., 2002, for a review).

Another development is the application of stress and coping frameworks to understand targets' psychological responses to prejudice (see Major, Quinton, & McCoy, 2002, for a review). According to these frameworks, being a target of prejudice is a stressful predicament. How individuals respond and adapt to this stressor differs depending on their cognitive appraisals (e.g., how threatening they perceive an event to be) and the coping strategies they employ in response to events appraised as stressful. Coping refers to volitional efforts to manage stress, and can be distinguished from nonvolitional responses to prejudice (e.g., stress responses). Within stress and coping frameworks it is theoretically possible for people to be exposed to prejudice but not perceive it, as well as to perceive themselves as targets of prejudice but not experience this as stressful. In sum, contemporary approaches view the psychological effects of prejudice as less permanent, less internalized, less inevitable, and less universal than did Allport.

Has Allport Been Supported?

Allport organized the bulk of his chapter around various responses that he believed targets of prejudice employ in response to their situation. To ascertain whether he has been supported, we will use a similar approach. Some of the responses that he identified have been the focus of substantial empirical inquiry over the last 50 years, whereas others have been ignored. Here we provide a selective overview, focusing on the responses identified by Allport that have received the most attention. First we review existing evidence on the development of *obsessive concern*, or hypersensitivity for cues to prejudice. We follow with a contemporary examination of group-relevant responses to prejudice, including *strengthening ingroup ties, denial of membership, identification with the dominant group, and aggression against own group*. We conclude with a discussion of research on *enhanced striving* and *disengagement* as responses to prejudice.

Obsessive Concern

Allport postulated that chronic targets of prejudice are haunted by feelings of anxiety over whether they will suffer insult and humiliation at the hands of the nonstigmatized, and as a consequence, experience deep feelings of insecurity. He wrote, "Alertness is the first step the ego takes for self-defense. It must be on guard. Sometimes the sensitiveness develops to an unreal pitch of suspicion; even the smallest cues may be loaded with feeling" (Allport, 1954/1979, pp. 144–5). In response to these feelings of insecurity, he proposed that the stigmatized become alert for and sensitive to signs of prejudice in others and preoccupied with the possibility that they are or will become a target of prejudice. Further, he proposed that in some cases this preoccupation becomes excessive, leading to vigilance, hypersensitiveness, and deep distrust of all members of the dominant group. He labeled this response *obsessive concern*.

Elements of these ideas can be found in contemporary approaches that assume that among members of chronically stigmatized groups, the possibility of being a target of negative stereotypes or a victim of prejudice is a highly accessible cognitive construct (see Stangor et al., 2003, for a review). Crocker, Major, and Steele (1998), for example, observed that objective experiences with prejudice and discrimination led members of stigmatized groups to develop "states of mind" that influence their emotions, cognitions, and actions. These states of mind include (a) awareness of the negative value that others place on their social identity, (b) "stereotype threat," and (c) "attributional ambiguity," i.e., uncertainty about whether their outcomes (both positive and negative) are due to their own merits or shortcomings, or to prejudice and discrimination based on their social identity. These predicaments have important implications for performance in stereotyped domains (Steele et al., 2002), and for self-esteem (e.g., Major, Quinton, & Schmader, 2003) among stigmatized groups.

Contemporary scholars question Allport's assumption that chronic targets of prejudice are "hypersensitive" to prejudice, and suggest instead that targets often minimize or deny the extent to which they are targets of prejudice (see Major, Quinton, & Schmader, 2002, for a review). Consistent with this latter view, many studies find that women and ethnic minorities see less discrimination directed against themselves personally than they do against members of their group (e.g., Crosby, 1984). This discrepancy is reliable across a variety of groups (see Taylor, Wright, & Porter, 1994, for a review). Women and ethnic minorities also often have difficulty recalling times when they were targets of prejudice (Stangor et al., 2003), avoid labeling negative treatment as discrimination, even when the treatment legally qualifies as such (Magley, Hulin, Fitzgerald, & DeNardo, 1999), and fail to recognize when they are interacting with a highly prejudiced (vs. low-prejudiced) partner, even though they feel greater discomfort when interacting with the former (Vorauer & Kumhyr, 2001). Furthermore, when placed in similar situations (e.g., rejection by an outgroup under ambiguous circumstances), members of stigmatized groups are no more likely than members of nonstigmatized groups to attribute their rejection to prejudice (Major, Quinton, & McCoy, 2002). Collectively, these findings are inconsistent with Allport's claim that targets of prejudice are hypersensitive to prejudice directed against themselves.

Other studies, however, lend some support for Allport's hypothesis. For example, one study found that compared to European Americans, African Americans were more sensitive to the differences between high- versus low-prejudiced European American interviewers who were interviewing an African American on a muted videotape (Rollman, 1978). Women and African Americans also were more likely to label ambiguous actions as prejudice than were men and European Americans, even when the targets were not members of their own group (Inman & Baron, 1996).

New research demonstrating that individuals differ in their chronic sensitivity to prejudice reconciles these contradictory findings. People who score highly on the Stigma Consciousness Questionnaire, for example, expect to be stigmatized and stereotyped on the basis of their stigma (Pinel, 1999). Among ethnic minorities, women, gays, and lesbians, high scores on the Stigma Consciousness Questionnaire correlate positively with perceptions of discrimination against the self and ingroup as well as with distrust of others (Pinel, 1999). A related measure, the Race Rejection Sensitivity Questionnaire, assesses a tendency to anxiously expect, readily perceive, and intensely react to rejection based on race (Mendoza-Denton et al., 2002). Scores on the Race Rejection Sensitivity Questionnaire among African American students prior to entering college prospectively predicted the extent to which they reported experiencing negative race-related events during their first three weeks of college, as well as the extent to which they felt negatively toward their peers and professors (Mendoza-Denton et al., 2002).

In summary, rudiments of Allport's idea that targets of prejudice are anxious about and alert for signs of prejudice in others can be found in contemporary theory and research on stereotype threat and attributional ambiguity. His belief that targets of prejudice become obsessively concerned with and hypersensitive to prejudice has received less support. Evidence of individual differences in chronic concerns about being a target of prejudice, however, suggests that some individuals may display the "obsessive concern" and vigilance that Allport described. Whether these individuals are "hypersensitive" to prejudice, or merely "accurate" perceivers of prejudice, however, is difficult to disentangle.

Coping with Prejudice Through Group Identification or Disidentification

Allport (1954/1979) noted that strengthening ingroup ties was a common response to prejudice in his observation, "Misery finds balm through the closer association of people who are miserable for the same reason. Threats drive them to seek protective unity within their common membership" (p. 148). As long as targets of prejudice cohere and affiliate with their ingroup, Allport speculated, they are not haunted by their problem, can put up with rebuffs from outside the group, and maintain positive mental health. Thus, he suggested that minority groups might develop a special solidarity as a form of coping with prejudice.

Contemporary research supports these ideas. For example, members of stigmatized or low status groups (e.g., African Americans, Latino Americans, women, blue-collar workers) typically report being more identified with their ingroup (i.e., say that their group is more important to them) than do members of nonstigmatized or high-status groups (e.g., Whites, men, white-collar workers) (e.g., Gurin, Miller, & Gurin, 1980). Members of low-status groups also often show more ingroup bias on self-report measures than do members of high-status groups (Mullen, Brown, & Smith, 1992).

Allport's idea that threats to the group increase group identification among devalued groups also has received support. For example, perceptions of discrimination are positively correlated with group identity in naturally occurring groups such as gender and ethnic groups, in minimal groups, and in chosen or self-selected groups (see Schmitt & Branscombe, 2002, for a review). Furthermore, group identification increases in response to perceived discrimination against the ingroup, at least among those who are already highly identified with their group (e.g., Jetten, Branscombe, Schmitt, & Spears, 2001). For example, among Latino Americans who read an article describing pervasive discrimination against Latinos, those initially high in group identification *increased* their identification with their ethnic group, whereas those low in initial group identification *decreased* their identification with their ethnic group compared to those who read about prejudice against a nonself-relevant group (McCoy & Major, 2003). This latter finding demonstrates that although some individuals strengthen their ties to the ingroup in response to prejudice, other individuals do the reverse.

One way in which targets of prejudice may distance themselves from a devalued ingroup is to *deny membership in the stigmatized group*. Allport (1954/1979) argued, "Perhaps the simplest response a victim can make is to deny his membership in a disparaged group" (p. 145). This response, however, is also perhaps the most psychologically costly a target of prejudice can make. People who deny or conceal a stigma from close others may experience more distress that those who do not deny or conceal it (Major & Gramzow, 2000). Targets of prejudice may also distance themselves from their group by altering their self-definitions. For example, when warned of the possibility of being negatively evaluated by a sexist evaluator, women subsequently described themselves as less stereotypically feminine compared to women who were not threatened with the possibility of being a target of prejudice (Kaiser & Miller, 2001). Similarly, African Americans whose race was made salient in the context of an intellectual test described themselves in less stereotypical ways than those whose race was not made salient (Steele, Spencer, & Aronson, 2002).

Allport also proposed two other responses to prejudice that involve distancing the self from the devalued group. One is to *identify with the dominant group*, i.e., to see one's own group through the eyes of the dominant group and to agree with their view. A second is to *aggress against own group*, i.e., to look down on and distinguish oneself from members of one's own group who are seen to "possess" the group qualities that are despised in society. Allport perceived the dominant western ideology of individual responsibility as contributing to these coping mechanisms. He noted, "They [victims of prejudice] have heard so frequently that they are lazy, ignorant, dirty, and superstitious that they may half believe the accusations, and since the traits are commonly despised in our western culture . . . some degree of in-group hate seems almost inevitable" (1954/ 1979, p. 152). By self-hate, Allport meant feelings of shame for possessing the despised qualities of one's group, or repugnance for other members of one's group because they possess those qualities.

Allport's idea that targets of prejudice display self-hate has not been supported by studies using explicit (self-report) measures of either personal or collective self-esteem (e.g., Crocker & Major, 1989). However, on implicit measures (i.e., measures not under volitional control), members of low-status groups sometimes evaluate higher-status outgroups more favorably than their own group (e.g., Rudman, Feinberg, & Fairchild, 2002). Moreover, even when outgroup favoritism is not observed, members of low-status groups routinely show considerably less automatic ingroup bias, compared with high-status group members, suggesting that societal evaluations can influence people's implicit cognitive systems (e.g., Ashburn-Nardo, Knowles, & Monteith, 2003; Jost, Pelham, & Carvallo, 2002). Targets of prejudice also sometimes display prejudice against their own groups by creating ingroup class distinctions that correspond to the views of the dominant group. One example is "colorism" in the African American and Latino communities (e.g., Hall, 2002). African Americans and Latinos often prefer light skin to dark skin within their own ethnicities (e.g., Uhlmann et al., 2002). This preference, in turn, is related to lower self-esteem and self-efficacy in darker-skinned minorities (Thompson & Keith, 2001). Low-status groups also self-stereotype on negative ingroup attributes (e.g., Dion & Earn, 1975). Preferring higher-status groups over one's own (lower-status) ingroup, and self-stereotyping on negative group attributes, are consistent with theories that posit that people justify the existing social structure, even when so doing goes against self-enhancement or group-enhancement concerns (see Jost & Hamilton, ch. 13 this volume).

Coping with Prejudice via Enhanced Striving vs. Domain Disengagement

Of the numerous ways in which targets of prejudice can cope, Allport believed that *striving* to overcome the negative implications of stigma is the response most highly approved in our culture. He wrote, "To redouble one's efforts is a healthy response to an obstacle" (1954/1979, p. 156). He proposed that in every minority group, some individuals perceive their devalued status as a handicap to be surmounted by extra effort rather than as an inevitable determinant of their fate. In response to the threat of prejudice, these individuals work harder than their competitors to run an equal race.

Research on compensation illustrates the use of this strategy. For example, one study found that when overweight women believed their stigma might have a negative impact on an interaction, they compensated for their obesity (and accompanying negative stereotypes) by bolstering their social skills (Miller, Rothblum, Felicio, & Brand, 1995). Further, self-affirmation research (Steele, 1988) illustrates that when threatened in one domain, people often defend their self-esteem by bolstering themselves in another domain. For example, members of low-status groups often acknowledge their group's inferiority on status-relevant dimensions like competence and intelligence, but compensate for it by expressing ingroup favoritism on other, status-irrelevant dimensions, such as warmth and friendliness (Ellemers & Van Rijswijk, 1997).

Directly consistent with Allport's views, many minority groups in the United States endorse hard work and determination as a means of overcoming their minority status (Kleugal & Smith, 1986). This value is reflected in the African American community in the legendary story of John Henry, a nineteenth-century steel driver, who beat a machine in a steel-driving competition only to drop dead of exhaustion. A dispositional preference to work harder to achieve success and advancement, despite sometimes overwhelming obstacles, has been called "john-henryism" (James, Hartnett, & Kalsbeek, 1983). Research linking john-henryism to hypertension among African Americans suggests that adopting this coping strategy may be physically harmful, even though it may indeed be the coping strategy most approved of in society (James, Hartnett, & Kalsbeek, 1983).

Although some targets of prejudice enhance their striving in response to prejudice, others withdraw their efforts from domains in which they are negatively stereotyped, devalued, or unfairly treated. Withdrawal of effort is likely to be one byproduct of psychologically disengaging self-esteem from a domain (Major et al., 1998). Psychological disengagement refers to detaching self-esteem from external feedback in a domain such that feelings of self-worth are not dependent on successes or failures in that domain (Major et al., 1998). One method of disengaging self-esteem from a domain is to *discount* the validity of feedback received in that domain; a second method is to *devalue* or reduce the importance in one's self-concept of a domain in which one is stigmatized. Either process may lead to unlinking self-esteem from feedback in domains where prejudice is possible. Consistent with this process, African Americans' self-esteem is affected less than that of European Americans by feedback on intelligence tests when race is salient, but not when it is not salient (Major et al., 1998).

Other Responses to Prejudice

Allport identified several other responses to prejudice in addition to those we discussed above. Although they are relatively ignored by researchers, we believe several are worthy of attention. Two of these are the "ego-defenses" of *prejudice toward outgroups* and *sympathy*. Allport (1954/1979) asserted, "*Victimization can scarcely leave an individual with a merely normal amount of prejudice*" (p. 155). Compared to members of dominant groups, Allport believed that victims of prejudice would either be *more* or *less* prejudiced against weaker others. Greater than average prejudice among minorities, he believed, would result from their greater need for a sense of power and status. Less than average prejudice, he believed, would result from their sympathy with other groups that suffer oppression. Allport also asserted that sharing hatred of a common outgroup with the dominant group may afford stigmatized group members a bond with the high-status group. Sympathizing with fellow minority groups, on the other hand, may increase the perception of an extended ingroup, which can be self-protective in the face of prejudice.

Although scarce, some research provides support for these speculations. For example, some studies found African Americans to be more preju-diced against women, and Asian Americans to be less comfortable interact-ing with members of other minority groups (compared to Latinos, African Americans, and Whites; e.g., Mack et al., 1997). Other studies, in contrast, found that compared to Whites and men, minorities and women are less prejudiced against other minorities, including homosexuals (e.g., Michalos & Zumbo, 2001). One reason for the neglect of this topic is researchers' perception that the more important problem of prejudice is one of high-status groups' mistreatment of low-status groups, rather than the reverse (Judd et al., 1995). We concur. Nonetheless, prejudice among members of lower-status groups, including aggression against dominant group members, is an issue worthy of attention.

In summary, contemporary research confirms many, but not all, of Allport's ideas about how targets respond to prejudice. As he speculated, targets of prejudice do appear to develop feelings of insecurity, facilitating such experiences as stereotype threat and attributional ambiguity. Contrary to Allport, however, there is little evidence that this develops into *obsessive concern* with prejudice, at least for most people. Also, while research supports Allport's idea that minority groups respond to group threats by increasing ingroup solidarity, it also supports his speculation that some people respond to the same threats by distancing themselves from their group. Finally, as Allport proposed, some targets of prejudice redouble their efforts in response to prejudice. Others, in contrast, appear to disengage their self-esteem from threatening domains and withdraw from those domains. Both individual and situational characteristics moderate these responses.

Future Directions

Allport's influential chapter examined a number of potential responses to prejudice that targets may adopt in the interest of protecting themselves from the consequences of having a devalued social identity. Despite 50 years of research since his original publication, a number of important questions about the nature of targets' responses to prejudice remain. We believe that the most promising directions for future research in this area involve attempts to better understand which individual and situational circumstances will predict a particular type of prejudice response, and how certain characteristics of the stigma (e.g., perceived controllability) affect group differences in responses to prejudice.

As noted above, research largely supports Allport's contention that responses to prejudice are largely an individual rather than a group matter. At the same time, his extropunitive/intropunitive typology has not been pursued. For example, people who are high on sensitivity to race rejection appear to be vigilant *vis-à-vis* prejudice, but whether this signals "extropunitiveness" as a personality trait or experience with prejudice (i.e., consciousness raising) is not known. Beyond personality differences, researchers have also begun to specify structural conditions that predict differences in responses among members of devalued groups. Social Identity Theory, for example, predicts that members of low-status groups are more likely to identify with their group and show ingroup favoritism to the extent that they see group boundaries as impermeable, and group status differences as unstable and illegitimate (e.g., Bettencourt, Charlton, Dorr, & Hume, 2001).

Group differences in responses to prejudice as a function of stigma type also merit further research attention. Characteristics of the stigmatizing attribute, such as its perceived controllability (either in onset or offset), visibility, entitativity, and perceived danger are likely to be important determinants of the types of coping strategies that targets of prejudice employ. For example, whereas African Americans who receive negative feedback from a White evaluator often attribute it to discrimination, overweight women who receive negative feedback from a male evaluator do not (see Major, Quinton, & McCoy, 2002). Compared to members of ethnic minority groups, overweight women also are less likely to identify with their ingroup (others who are overweight) and more likely to display prejudice against their ingroup on both explicit and implicit measures (Crandall, 1994; Rudman, Feinberg, & Fairchild, 2002). These group differences in responses to prejudice, we believe, are due in part to differences in the perceived controllability of and responsibility for weight.

In sum, contemporary research on targets of prejudice echoes many of the ideas Allport proposed in his classic chapter on "traits due to victimization." As he predicted, targets of prejudice respond in various ways, motivated by their desire to protect their self-esteem and make sense of their world. There is no uniform response to prejudice. An important agenda for future research is to identify the personal, situational, and structural antecedents of these different responses to prejudice and to identify coping strategies that are most adaptive.

NOTES

Preparation of this chapter was supported by a grant from the National Science Foundation (BCS-9983888) to Brenda Major, and a predoctoral fellowship from the Ford Foundation to S. Brooke Vick.

REFERENCES

Allport, G. W. (1954/1979). *The nature of prejudice.* Cambridge, MA: Perseus Books.

Ashburn-Nardo, L., Knowles, M. L., & Monteith, M. J. (2003). Black Americans' implicit racial associations and their implications for intergroup judgment. *Social Cognition, 21*, 61–87.

Bettencourt, B. A., Charlton, K., Dorr, N., & Hume, D. L. (2001). Status differences and in-group bias: A meta-analytic examination of the effects of status stability, status legitimacy, and group permeability. *Psychological Bulletin, 127*, 520–42.

Crandall, C. S. (1994). Prejudice against fat people: Ideology and self-interest. *Journal of Personality and Social Psychology, 66*, 882–94.

Crocker, J. & Major, B. (1989). Social stigma and self-esteem: The self-protective properties of stigma. *Psychological Review*, *96*, 608–30.

Crocker, J., Major, B., & Steele, C. (1998). Social stigma. In D. Gilbert, S. T. Fiske, & G. Lindzey (eds.), *Handbook of social psychology* (4th ed., pp. 504–53). Boston: McGraw-Hill.

Crosby, F. (1984). The denial of personal discrimination. *American Behavioral Scientist*, *27*, 371–86.

Dion, K. L. & Earn, B. M. (1975). The phenomenology of being a target of prejudice. *Journal of Personality and Social Psychology*, *32*, 944–50.

Ellemers, N. & Van Rijswijk, W. (1997). Identity needs versus social opportunities: The use of group-level and individual-level identity management strategies. *Social Psychology Quarterly*, *60*, 52–65.

Goffman, E. (1963). *Stigma: Notes on the management of spoiled identity.* Englewood Cliffs, NJ: Prentice-Hall.

Gurin, P., Miller, A. H., & Gurin, G. (1980). Stratum identification and consciousness. *Social Psychology Quarterly*, *43*, 30–47.

Hall, R. E. (2002). A descriptive methodology of color bias in Puerto Rico: Manifestations of discrimination in the new millennium. *Journal of Applied Social Psychology*, *32*, 1527–37.

Inman, M. L. & Baron, R. S. (1996). Influence of prototypes on perceptions of prejudice. *Journal of Personality and Social Psychology*, *70*, 727–39.

James, S. A., Hartnett, S. A., & Kalsbeek, W. D. (1983). John Henryism and blood pressure differences among Black men. *Journal of Behavioral Medicine*, *6*, 259–78.

Jetten, J., Branscombe, N. R., Schmitt, M. T., & Spears, R. (2001). Rebels with a cause: Group identification as a response to perceived discrimina-tion from the mainstream. *Personality and Social Psychology Bulletin*, *27(9)*, 1204–13.

Jones, E. E., Farina, A., Hastorf, A. H., Markus, H., Miller, D. T., & Scott, R. A. (1984). *Social stigma: The psychology of marked relationships.* New York: Freeman.

Jost, J. T., Pelham, B. W., & Carvallo, M. R. (2002). Non-conscious forms of system justification: Implicit and behavioral preferences for higher status groups. *Journal of Experimental Social Psychology*, *38*, 586–602.

Judd, C. M., Park, B., Ryan, C. S., Brauer, M., & Kraus, S. (1995). Stereo-types and ethnocentrism: Diverging interethnic perceptions of African American and White American youth. *Journal of Personality and Social Psychology*, *69*, 460–81.

Kaiser, C. R., Major, B., & McCoy, S. K. (2004). Expectations about the future and the emotional conse-quences of perceiving prejudice. *Personality and Social Psychology Bulletin*, *30*, 173–84.

Kaiser, C. R. & Miller, C. T. (2001). Reacting to impending discrimina-tion: Compensation for prejudice and attributions to discrimination. *Personality & Social Psychology Bulletin*, *27*, 1357–67.

Kleugel, J. R. & Smith, E. R. (1986). *Beliefs about inequality: Americans' view of what is and what ought to be.* Hawthorne, NJ: Aldine de Gruyer.

Mack, D. E., Tucker, T. W., Archuleta, R., DeGroot, G., Hernandez, A. A., & Oh Cha, S. (1997). Interethnic relations on campus: Can't we all get along? *Journal of Multicultural Counseling & Development*, *25*, 256–68.

Magley, V. J., Hulin, C. L., Fitzgerald, L. F., & DeNardo, M. (1999). Outcomes of self-labeling sexual harassment. *Journal of Applied Psychology, 84(3),* 390–402.

Major, B. & Gramzow, R. (1999). Abortion as stigma: Cognitive and emotional implications of concealment. *Journal of Personality and Social Psychology, 77,* 735–46.

Major, B., Gramzow, R., McCoy, S. K., Levin, S., Schmader, T., & Sidanius, J. (2002). Perceiving personal discrimination: The role of group status and status legitimizing ideology. *Journal of Personality and Social Psychology, 82,* 269–82.

Major, B., Quinton, W. J., & McCoy, S. K. (2002). Antecedents and consequences of attributions to discrimination: Theoretical and empirical advances. In M. P. Zanna (ed.), *Advances in Experimental Social Psychology* (vol. 34, pp. 251–330). San Diego, CA: Academic Press.

Major, B., Quinton, W. J., & Schmader, T. (2003). Attributions to discrimination and self-esteem: Impact of group identification and situational ambiguity. *Journal of Experimental Social Psychology, 39,* 220–31.

Major, B., Spencer, S., Schmader, T., Wolfe, C., & Crocker, J. (1998). Coping with negative stereotypes about intellectual performance: The role of psychological disengagement. *Personality & Social Psychology Bulletin, 24(1),* 34–50.

McCoy, S. K. & Major, B. (2003). Group identification moderates emotional responses to perceived prejudice. *Personality & Social Psychology Bulletin, 29,* 1005–17.

Mendoza-Denton, R., Downey, G., Purdie, V. J., Davis, A., & Pietrzak, J. (2002). Sensitivity to status-based rejection: Implications for African

American students' college experience. *Journal of Personality and Social Psychology, 83,* 896–918.

Michalos, A. C. & Zumbo, B. D. (2001). Ethnicity, modern prejudice and the quality of life. *Social Indicators Research, 53,* 189–222.

Miller, C. T., Rothblum, E. D., Felicio, D., & Brand, P. (1995). Compensating for stigma: Obese and nonobese women's reactions to being visible. *Personality and Social Psychology Bulletin, 21,* 1093–106.

Mullen, B., Brown, R., & Smith, C. (1992). Ingroup bias as a function of salience, relevance, and status: An integration. *European Journal of Social Psychology, 22,* 103–22.

Overbeck, J. R., Jost, J. T., Mosso, C. O., & Flizlik, A. (2004). Resistant versus acquiescent responses to ingroup inferiority as a function of social dominance orientation in the USA and Italy. *Group Processes and Intergroup Relations, 7,* 35–54.

Pinel, E. C. (1999). Stigma consciousness: The psychological legacy of social stereotypes. *Journal of Personality and Social Psychology, 76,* 114–28.

Rollman, S. A. (1978). The sensitivity of black and white Americans to nonverbal cues of prejudice. *The Journal of Social Psychology, 105,* 73–7.

Rosenberg, M. & Simmons, R. G. (1972). *Black and white self-esteem: The urban school child.* Washington, DC: American Sociological Association.

Rudman, L. A., Feinberg, J., & Fairchild, K. (2002). Minority members' implicit attitudes: Automatic ingroup bias as a function of group status. *Social Cognition, 20,* 294–320.

Schmitt, M. T. & Branscombe, N. R. (2002). The meaning and consequences of perceived discrimination in disadvantaged and privileged so-cial groups. In W. Stroebe & M. Hewstone (eds.), *European Review of Social Psychology* (vol. 12, pp. 167–200). Chichester, UK: Wiley.

Stangor, C., Swim, J. K., Sechrist, G. B., DeCoster, J., Van Allen, K. L., & Ottenbreit, A. (2003). Ask, answer, and announce: Three stages in perceiving and responding to dis-crimination. In W. Stroebe & M. Hewstone (eds.), *European Review of Social Psychology* (vol. 14, pp. 277–311). Chichester, UK: Wiley.

Steele, C. M. (1988). The psychology of self-affirmation: Sustaining the in-tegrity of the self. In L. Berkowitz (ed.), *Advances in experimental social psy-chology*, vol. 21: *Social psychological stud-ies of the self: Perspectives and programs* (pp. 261–302). San Diego, CA: Aca-demic Press.

Steele, C. M., Spencer, S., & Aronson, J. (2002). Contending with group image: The psychology of stereotype and social identity threat. In M. Zanna (ed.), *Advances in experimental social psychology* (vol. 34). New York: Aca-demic Press.

Tajfel, H. & Turner, J.C. (1986). The social identity theory of intergroup behavior. In S. Worchel & W. G. Austin (eds.), *The psychology of inter-group relations* (pp. 7–24). Chicago: Nelson-Hall.

Taylor, D. M., Wright, S. C., & Porter, L. E. (1994). Dimensions of perceived discrimination: The per-sonal/group discrimination discrep-ancy. In M. P. Zanna & J. M. Olson (eds.), *The psychology of prejudice: The Ontario symposium* (vol. 7., pp. 233–55). Hillsdale, NJ: Lawrence Erlbaum.

Thompson, N. S. & Keith, V. M. (2001). The blacker the berry: Gen-der, skin tone, self-esteem and self-efficacy. *Gender & Society*, 15, 336–57.

Twenge, J. & Crocker, J. (2002). Race, ethnicity, and self-esteem: Meta-analyses comparing Whites, Blacks, Hispanics, Asians, and Native Amer-icans, including a commentary on Gray-Little and Hafdahl (2000). *Psy-chological Bulletin*, *128*, 371–408.

Uhlmann, E., Dasgupta, N., Elgueta, A., Greenwald, A. G., & Swanson, J. (2002). Subgroup prejudice based on skin color among Hispanics in the United States and Latin America. *Social Cognition*, *20*, 198–225.

Vorauer, J. & Kumhyr, S. M. (2001). Is this about you or me? Self- versus other-directed judgments and feelings in response to intergroup interaction. *Personality and Social Psychology Bulletin*, *27*, 706–19.

Chapter Ten

Mechanisms for Coping with Victimization: Self-Protection *Plus* Self-Enhancement

James M. Jones

As with virtually every aspect of this classic treatise, Allport cast a broad and compelling net over the subject of how targets of discrimination and oppression may respond. In chapter 9 of *The Nature of Prejudice*, "Traits Due to Victimization," Allport outlined a number of possible ways that victims of prejudice might respond and mechanisms they might engage. He mentioned a number of alternative responses, including a focus on the self (e.g., obsessive concern), avoidant reactions (e.g., denial of membership, withdrawal), conforming or compliant responses (e.g., clowning, self-hate), enhanced ingroup solidarity (e.g., strengthening ingroup ties, militancy), negative orientations toward the majority group (e.g., prejudice against the outgroup), and social action (e.g., enhanced status striving). What these mechanisms have in common is a trait-based characterization of "ego-defenses."

In this chapter I will summarize Allport's analysis and suggest broadly that (a) he was on target by examining the wide variety of ego-defenses that might be recruited to sustain psychological well-being against the relentless nature of racism, but that (b) his personality-based analysis was not fully adequate to capture the dynamic, multidimensional connections between individuals and their groups. These connections among personal cognitions and collective actions, and the recurring role that cultural patterns play in shaping adaptive responses to racism, are critical in understanding the responses of victims of discrimination. Theories and research about African Americans will be used to illustrate the dynamics of the experience of and response to victimization.

Allport's Views on Victimization

Allport offered his prime assumption about coping with victimization as a hypothetical example:

> Suppose you heard it said over and over again that you were lazy, a simple child of nature, expected to steal, and had inferior blood. Suppose [further] this opinion were forced on you by the majority of your fellow citizens. And suppose nothing you could do would change this opinion – *because you happen to have Black skin.* (Allport, 1954/1979, p. 142)

Allport assumed that the constancy of denigration and discrimination took a psychological toll on Black children and Black people generally. This was a prevailing premise in the 1940s and 1950s among social scientists.

But whereas most theorists assumed that negative effects were universal, Allport instead argued for the basic human motivation to cope with, adapt to, and survive oppressive circumstances. Therefore his ideas about the effects of prejudice on its targets were a broad mixture of ego-defenses, strategic manipulations, and collective actions that preserved psychological and physical well-being.

Allport's enlightened approach contrasts with other perspectives that spawned the "self-hatred" hypothesis. For example, Kardiner and Ovesy (1951) claimed that the psychological toll was *inexorably* adverse, noting:

> The Negro, in contrast to the White, is an unhappy person; he has a harder environment to live in, and internal stress is greater. By "unhappy" we mean he enjoys less, he suffers more. There is not one personality trait of the Negro the source of which cannot be traced to his difficult living conditions. *There are no exceptions to this rule.* The final result is a wretched internal life. (p. 81, emphasis added)

Allport, in contrast, considered a variety of possible responses under the more general proposition that "ego-defenses" must be developed to cope with the daily assaults on well-being, dignity, and human value. He discussed some 16 different defense mechanisms that covered the gamut of possibilities from passive withdrawal to aggressive, action–oriented redress. Only one of these was labeled "self-hatred."

Allport summarized the operation of his defense mechanisms in a simple diagram (see figure 10.1). Broadly speaking, targets of racism are sensitized to and concerned with assaults on their basic humanity, as well as real and implied threats to their physical and psychological well-being. Discrimination

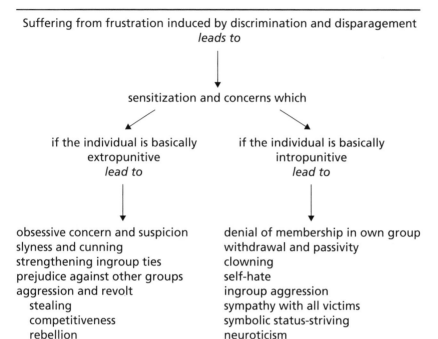

Suffering from frustration induced by discrimination and disparagement
leads to

sensitization and concerns which

if the individual is basically
extropunitive
lead to

if the individual is basically
intropunitive
lead to

obsessive concern and suspicion
slyness and cunning
strengthening ingroup ties
prejudice against other groups
aggression and revolt
   stealing
   competitiveness
   rebellion
enhanced striving

denial of membership in own group
withdrawal and passivity
clowning
self-hate
ingroup aggression
sympathy with all victims
symbolic status-striving
neuroticism

Figure 10.1 Allport's summary of ego-defense mechanisms of victims of discrimination (from Allport, 1954/1979, ch. 9; fig. 9, p. 160)

in all its aspects is conceived as a fundamental threat, and reactions to it fall under the broad label of "self-protection." Allport's inquiry then, focused on the mechanisms by which targets of discrimination and dehumanization protect themselves psychologically.

Allport proposed two basic modes of psychic self-protection. In the first, which he labeled *extropunitive*, the targets place blame for their degraded and threatened existence on external sources (e.g., Whites in general, bigots, systemic discrimination). In the second, which he labeled *intropunitive*, targets take responsibility for their plight, either by feeling that somehow they deserve it (i.e., false consciousness; Jost & Banaji, 1994) or that, whether deserved or not, they must take responsibility for self-protection.

As figure 10.1 suggests, *extropunitive* mechanisms are more aggressive, planful, and strategic, and, one might think in our individualistic culture, more likely to promote positive self-esteem. *Intropunitive* responses, by contrast, seem more destructive, passive, and less able to draw strength from common plight and cause. A substantial literature has grown up that seems at its core to explore one or the other of these modes of adaptation. The _extropunitive_ path has developed into research and theory that proposes and finds relatively positive psychological well-being among Black Americans (see Twenge & Crocker, 2002). This research has further shown that the sociocognitive mechanisms that identify external sources of individual and collective disadvantage may have self-protective psychological effects (Crocker & Major, 1989). Research that has explored the _intropunitive_ path more often finds that experiencing or perceiving prejudice has adverse psychological effects (see Branscombe, Schmitt, & Harvey, 1999).

Although this simple dichotomy is a convenient way to summarize much of the research on target perspective that has followed Allport's analysis, even he saw its shortcomings. He noted that a person might show combinations of mechanisms that cross over the intropunitive/extropunitive modalities. Allport (1954/1979) suggested that some targets of prejudice:

> Do not regard their marginality as fatal in their pursuit of a wholesome and enjoyable life. Their basic values are human and universal . . . [when] they encounter discrimination and prejudice, they react with dignity and broad understanding . . . There develops an intelligent pursuit of one's goals, including efforts to reduce discrimination in society and increase democracy. There develops a broad compassion for oppressed people whoever they are. In short, sympathy, courage, persistence, and dignity mark such a personality . . . a fully developed personality is one that can handle its suffering without inflicting suffering in return. (p. 161)

What Allport roughly sketched is a two-factor model of targets' responses to prejudice. One recurring response is _self-protective_, as it protects a person from the most negative effects of discrimination, oppression, and disadvantage. The second, which social scientists have spent far less time thinking about, can be considered _self-enhancement_, the mechanisms by which one maintains a positive outlook and a wholesome pursuit of well-being and human dignity. I have labeled the disparaging and threatening circumstances of prejudice the "universal context of racism." The universal context of racism implies the continuous "availability" of patterns of discrimination and disadvantage that become chronically accessible as explanatory constructs for personal experience. Consistent with Allport, this model proposes that both self-protective and self-enhancement motives arise in response to the universal context of racism (see Jones, 2003). Below, I will briefly review some of the core issues relating to theoretical and empirical developments on self-protective processes and mechanisms employed by targets of prejudice.

Developments Since Allport

Contrary to the prevailing views of Allport's contemporaries, in this section, I will first describe evidence that the mental health of victims is on par with that of nonvictimized groups, including their self-esteem and psychological well-being. I will next consider the mechanisms that sustain or challenge self-esteem, including intropunitive mechanisms (e.g., self-hate and system justification mechanisms), which are generally associated with negative self-esteem, and extropunitive mechanisms (e.g., perceived discrimination and system-blame), which are generally associated with positive self-esteem and psychological well-being. In general, how victims understand and perceive the influence that systemic institutional practices have on their well-being adds a level of analysis that Allport did not directly address.

Maintaining Self-Esteem in the Face of Stigma and Discrimination

It is significant that Allport's *The Nature of Prejudice* was published the same year that *Brown v. Board of Education* declared that racial segregation in public education was *inherently unequal*. The basis for that conclusion rested partly on the research reported in the Social Science Statement (*Brown v. Board of Education*, 1954, fn. 11), which cited (among other research) the famous doll studies by Clark and Clark (1947). In that work, Black children who chose a White, blond haired, blue-eyed doll in response to the directive to "show me the doll that is pretty, nice and you want to play with" were determined to have *damaged self-esteem*. This damage, it was argued, reflected the inevitable consequence of legally enforced racial segregation.

Many similar investigations followed the doll studies conducted in the 1940s. The collective findings suggest that choosing dolls of different colors may be an imprecise measure of racial identity or awareness. In general, they show a tendency toward within-race preferences that is importantly influenced by the race of the experimenter, whether a child is in a multicultural or desegregated learning environment, or has been involved in race-pride programs. Thus, the intropunitive defenses outlined by Allport and implied in the *Brown* decision have not withstood the test of time.

More generally, theorizing about the damaging psychological effects of being a target of prejudice, discrimination, and stigma was widespread following Allport's book, but empirical research since 1954 has had difficulty confirming the damaged self-esteem hypothesis. Indeed, based on several studies that support the *positive* self-esteem of Blacks, Twenge and Crocker (2002) provided a comprehensive meta-analysis that compellingly makes the opposite case. They found that Blacks, on average, have higher self-esteem than Whites, who in turn have higher self-esteem than Asians, American Indians, and Hispanics. Moreover, the Black–White self-esteem gap has actually *increased* since 1980.

Recent studies of mental health reveal a similar overall pattern. Major epidemiological surveys of incidences of depression among Black and White Americans (Kendler, Gallagher, Abelson, & Kessler, 1996) show that national lifetime prevalence rate of major depression is actually lower for Blacks (about 12 percent) than for Whites (about 16 percent). With this strong evidence for psychological protection among Blacks, the question turns to understanding the mechanisms that sustain self-esteem.

Mechanisms for Maintaining Self-Esteem

It appears that internalizing stigma either does not occur or does not have the negative effects previously theorized. A fairly robust debate has arisen about whether stigma can itself be self-protective (see Crocker & Major, 1989; Gray-Little & Hafdahl, 2000; see also Major & Vick, ch. 9 this volume). That is, if people perceive, as Allport proposed, that others generally devalue their social group, and by extension themselves, it could lead them either to internalize that devaluation (thus diminishing self-esteem) or to reject the prejudiced other as a standard of evaluation or comparison. In the latter case, negative feedback from people believed to be prejudiced is discounted; victims of discrimination can dismiss the other's views as irrational and unfounded because they can be attributed to bias (Crocker & Major, 1989). By this analysis, being sensitive to and vigilant about biased perceptions, beliefs, and behaviors is adaptive and preserves self-esteem against a backdrop of prevalent discrimination (see Major & Vick, ch. 9 this volume).

Nonetheless, several studies demonstrate that perceptions of racial discrimination are associated with a variety of adverse outcomes (e.g., Sellers & Shelton, 2003; Taylor & Turner, 2002). The critical issue seems to be the level of analysis. Perceiving discrimination in a specific setting or situation may enable people to discount the judge's assessment as unfairly biased. However, if the perceived discrimination is systemic and long-term, they may internalize these assessments, making it difficult to maintain integrity and optimism. Branscombe and her colleagues (1999) have proposed Rejection-Identification Theory to account for the dual role that perceiving discrimination can have on psychological well-being. Consistent with Crocker and Major's (1989) theorizing, they find that positive effects of attributing outcomes to prejudice are found if the outcome is discrete or situationally specific, whereas adverse psychological responses are likely when discrimination is enduring and pervasive (see also Taylor & Turner, 2002). Nevertheless, even the adverse effects of pervasive discrimination are not inevitable. The potential negative psychological impact of pervasive discrimination can be mitigated by diverse coping strategies, such as by strengthening ingroup identification (Leonardelli & Tormala, 2003) or, alternatively, by disidentifying with one's group (McCoy & Major, 2003).

As opposed to Allport's intrapersonal level of analysis, research over the past several decades has implicated macrolevel perceptions of structural and enduring elements of discriminatory practice. What is now known as "institutional racism" more broadly implicates the effects of systemic bias that are not necessarily linked to a given person or even racial group (Jones, 1997). In particular, system blaming and justification are two types of systems perception that have been investigated. System blame, the tendency to perceive structural inequalities as a source of individual and group disadvantage, has been associated with positive self-esteem in Blacks (Crocker, Luhtanen, Brodnax & Blaine, 1999). Targets of discrimination are more likely to believe that outcomes (positive or negative) are due more to structural determinants than personal character (Kleugel & Smith, 1986). Whether this perception is an ego-defensive projection or ideological perception, it is not one of the defenses proposed by Allport.

A recently identified problem for prejudice victims stems from *false consciousness* – the idea that one may hold a complex set of beliefs that are both false and contrary to one's social interest. In general, these beliefs justify a system of inequality in which victims find themselves (see Jackman and Jost & Hamilton, chs. 6 and 13 this volume). The net result is that actions based on such beliefs further one's disadvantaged position in society. System justification is characterized by psychological tendencies that include failure to perceive injustice and disadvantage, justification of social roles, false attribution of blame, identification with the oppressor, and resistance to change. System justification helps to explain negative self-stereotyping by disadvantaged group members and implicates an unwitting complicity of victims in their victimization. The influence of social-structural dynamics (such as racial segregation or socio-economic status) is known to have an effect on cognitive processes, but with greater subtlety and nuance than was envisioned by Allport.

What is clear from current research is that the pervasiveness of racial discrimination (i.e., the universal context of racism) has a generally adverse impact on psychological well-being. Although distancing oneself from the outgroup (i.e., strengthening ties to the ingroup) can have positive psychological benefits for targets of discrimination, as Allport suggested, this can lead to outgroup prejudice, which may exacerbate the negativity of interracial relations. For example, Blacks might take solace in segregating themselves from Whites (and may feel completely justified in doing so), but self-protective behaviors can undermine opportunities for Blacks to disconfirm negative stereotypes possessed by Whites (and vice versa).

New Frameworks: Racial Identity as a Multidimensional Strategy

In this section, I will briefly discuss three racial and cultural identity models specifically geared toward understanding the complexities of Blacks' responses to racism, each of which rests on conceptual advances since Allport that emphasize processes for maintaining positive self-esteem for members of devalued groups (e.g., social-identity theory; see Brown & Zagefka, ch. 4 this volume).

Nigresence Model

Cross (1991; Vandiver, Cross, Worrell, & Fhagen-Smith, 2002) proposed a developmental *Nigresence Model* in which identity evolves over time, and the relation of stages of racial identity to self-esteem varies. The first stage is labeled Pre-Encounter and consists of Assimilation (associated with racelessness) or Anti-Black identities (related to "mideducation," often based on system justification; see Jost & Hamilton, ch. 13 this volume). Early stages represent a repressed racial status or racelessness. This corresponds to Allport's intropunitive defenses of "denial of membership in own group" and "self-hate," which would be expected to be less successful in protecting self-esteem. Research tends to support this idea: Self-hatred is linked directly to lowered self-esteem (Vandiver et al., 2002). In addition, Arroyo and Zigler (1995) found that whereas a measure of racelessness was positively related to academic achievement, it was also related to poorer psychological well-being and weakened ingroup ties.

The middle stage of the Nigresence Model, Immersion-Emersion, depicts two dynamics – intense Black involvement and anti-White sentiment. This stage maps directly onto Allport's strengthening ingroup ties and outgroup prejudice. However, these are not intropunitive, and they are not related to self-esteem. The last stage, Internalization, consists of two subidentities, Black Nationalist – an activist orientation with high race salience – and Multiculturalist, in which positive race salience combines with activism in concert with other groups. This last set of identities seems to address the strategies of empowerment more than the psychological feelings of inferiority or well-being. These subidentities reflect extropunitive mechanisms outlined by Allport, but have not been directly tied to specific psychological outcomes.

Multidimensional Model of Black Identity

Sellers and colleagues (Sellers et al., 1997; see also Rowley, Sellers, Chavous, & Smith, 1998) proposed a Multidimensional Model of Black Identity that is composed of three major aspects: (a) race centrality (My destiny is tied to the destiny of other Black people); (b) racial regard (I feel good about Black people); and (c) race ideology, how Blacks *ought* to act, which is comprised of four subdimensions: *Assimilation* (Blacks should view themselves as being Americans first and foremost); *Humanist* (Blacks and Whites have more commonalities than differences); *Oppressed Minority* (Black people should treat other oppressed people as allies); *Nationalist* (Black people must organize). Race centrality is assumed to be situationally influenced, whereas regard and ideology are considered to be beliefs that are relatively stable across situations.

The Multidimensional Model of Black Identity argues for bidirectional effects of race on psychological well-being. Situations can influence race centrality, which in turn can moderate other psychological outcomes, such as self-esteem. But it is likely that one's stable ideological beliefs may influence the likelihood of perceiving race-relevant cues, and more, how one responds when they are salient. Finally, the ideological dimensions of identity represent a "worldview"; that is, a system of thought that dictates the desirability of individual and collective behaviors as a preferred pathway to well-being. One can find similar thoughts in Allport's writings, but his conjectures about how intro- and extro-punitive mechanisms combine were quite conceptually primitive. Moreover, because Allport's model focused on the intrapsychic dynamics of ego-defenses, he did not capture the interplay of multiple levels of analysis and synthesis.

Universal Context of Racism Model

Targets of racism live daily with the possibility of threat, bias, denigration, and diminished opportunity. Individual and collective histories of targets are psychologically available at any given moment, and thus are part of the situation that influences behavior and forms the basis of the Universal Context of Racism Model (UCR; Jones, 2003).

This model posits that *racism is an accessible, explanatory construct with motivational consequences*. Belonging to a group that is socially salient and historically stigmatized renders the possibility of race-bias highly accessible, with the potential to influence interpretations of one's experiences, expectations of outcomes, goal-setting, and attainment. Although every negative experience is not attributed to or interpreted by racism, it is often a plausible explanation whether applied to the self or to others in one's racial group.

Two motivational consequences of the universal context of racism are proposed: (a) *self-protective* motivations, by which one is oriented to detecting the occurrence of, protecting oneself from, avoiding, and conquering racism; and (b) *self-enhancing* motivations by which one is oriented toward expressing and enhancing one's self-worth and humanity. Self-protective mechanisms are triggered by the perception of a race-based threat in a given situation, or a chronic state of unfairness or discrimination based on race. Deployment of these defense mechanisms will depend on the cues in the situation as interpreted by one's race-based schema (racial centrality), as well as by more enduring belief systems (system blame, system justification, and race ideology processes). Individual and situational influences and their interactions are projected in self-protective mechanisms.

Self-enhancing mechanisms are conceptualized as the active process of maintaining positive self-regard. This mechanism may include social comparison processes by which self-enhancers perceive themselves more positively than they perceive others; or they believe that others perceive them more positively than they in fact do (Kwan et al., 2004). This approach emphasizes the discrepancy between self-judgments and other judgments (i.e., self-enhancement bias), which can lead to "positive illusions" (Taylor, 1989). The evidence that self-enhancement is generally associated with mental and physical health and longevity is substantial (Taylor et al., 2003)

The Universal Context of Racism Model is driven by two real or imagined threats: (a) a threat to personal control and freedom, and (b) a threat to personal and/or collective worth. As with Allport's claim that both intro- and extro-punitive mechanisms may operate singly or in combination, I propose that self-protective and self-enhancement mechanisms may work in similar fashion. Self-protective and self-enhancing motives converge when self-enhancement operates in a threatening context. This can happen in two ways. First, it can occur by altering the negative elements of a threatening environment so that one's personal sense of security is enhanced. For example, creating microcontexts in which one feels comfortable is one way to enable self-enhancing motives to be served (see Tatum, 2002). By creating a nonthreatening environment within a threatening one, a greater degree of comfort follows when self-defining values are a standard for self-judgment and freedom of self-expression adheres to core individual or collective principles. Second, one may align with others in the group to alter the values attached to certain behaviors so that self-worth is not based on matching an "other-group standard" but depends upon embracing an "ingroup criterion" (Jones, 1999).

Attempts to explain African Americans' adaptation to racism have traditionally been ahistorical and culturally neutral. In contrast, the patterns of adaptations to the universal context of racism, I argue, are culturally derived from African origins and applied in a functional way to the challenges presented by this pervasive context. Over time, the adaptations to the human challenges of slavery, Jim Crow, and contemporary forms of dominative and aversive racism have molded and shaped those originating cultural patterns of behavior (Jones, 1986).

I propose a quintet of characteristics that are considered originating cultural patterns of behavior (Jones, 2003): Time, Rhythm, Improvisation, Orality, and Spirituality (TRIOS). These culturally derived qualities combine to create adaptation potential in circumstances characterized by lack of control and denigrated human worth. By staying focused in the present, employing creative and flexible problem-solving strategies in unpredictable and threatening situations, utilizing oral communication to transmit cultural values and political self-protective courses of action, and sustaining the human spirit through connection to a higher being and the natural rhythms of nature and the soul, are the qualities that I argue are utilized in the adaptation and coping of African Americans.

The Universal Context of Racism Model assumes a cultural pattern of adaptation that takes into account the challenges of discrimination and the need to establish internalized standards of human worth. TRIOS is proposed as a worldview that directs both self-protective and self-enhancing mechanisms. In this model, self-enhancement is a complex intersection of self–other, as well as own-race and other-race comparisons. That is, a Black person may self-enhance relative to Whites or relative to Blacks. For example, a Black person may self-enhance by perceiving that one is regarded more favorably by Whites than other Blacks are, or more favorably by other Blacks than Whites are.

The Universal Context of Racism Model proposes that one's TRIOS level moderates the intersections of self-protective and self-enhancement mechanisms. The UCR model also argues that self-enhancement is not exclusively a social comparison process, but can also express a fundamental internalized feeling of worth that is based on connection to a higher authority, ingroup affirmation, or meeting one's own standards of being.

A self-report rating scale was developed to assess the degree to which one endorses the dimensions of TRIOS (Jones, 2003). Early evidence shows that Blacks endorse the dimensions more than other race/ethnic groups, with Hispanics slightly less, and Whites and Asians similar to each other and lower still. TRIOS level has been related to prosocial values, ego-resiliency, and lower levels of self-reported stress. TRIOS level is associated with more active and spiritual coping styles in *positive* events (behavior designed to prolong the positive outcomes of good events), which is consistent with the current meaning of self-enhancement. Further, TRIOS level is shown to moderate the relationship between stress and well-being so that when stress level is high, the decline in well-being is less for those high than those low in TRIOS. In some cases (e.g., with Improvisation), well-being remains positive even at high levels of self-reported stress. This moderation effect is shown to be the greatest in a sample of college students in Africa (Jones, Campbell, & Turner, 2004).

In sum, the models described above build from the most microlevel of analysis (Nigrescence) to the most macro (Universal Context of Racism). Together, they postulate a variety of mechanisms that link self and other judgments within and across race; incorporate cognitive representations of systemic forces in personal outcomes; and base well-being on a calculus of these multilevel representations. Although these approaches are not contrary to Allport, they take us well beyond his analysis of ego-defensive tactics.

Has Allport Been Supported?

Allport argued that the frustration suffered by victims of discrimination caused them to be sensitized and concerned with the sources of disparagement as well as means of coping with it. He further proposed that this sensitivity was determined by the degree to which one possessed traits that were intropunitive or extropunitive. The former often lead to self-destructive, lowered self-esteem and group identification. The latter are associated with more favorable outcomes that promoted ingroup ties while disparaging biased outgroups. Allport has been supported in part and contradicted in part. His ideas generally transcended in the scope and complexity of victim-based theories.

Allport is supported principally in his analysis of extropunitive responses. As described above, ample evidence supports the idea that ingroup ties are central to racial identity theories and have been shown to organize and moderate reactions to discrimination. It is also true that group identity may moderate the adaptive responses to perceived discrimination, and that outgroup prejudice may result from dynamic racial identity processes. Allport also proposed that rebellion and revolt were adaptations as well, and evidence for the link between system blame and positive self-esteem suggests that acting against the system of discrimination is an effective response (system-justification, though, is an important consideration that suggests systemic processes may also have adverse, group-defeating effects [see Jost & Hamilton, ch. 13 this volume]).

But a principal claim by Allport is that self-hate and other forms of intropunitive self-destructive ego-defenses were common. If we accept damaged self-esteem as a reflection of this idea, the evidence is clearly contradictory. As already noted, researchers have found that Blacks have higher (not lower) self-esteem, relative to Whites, and that the Black–White disparity has grown in recent years.

Nonetheless, Allport suggested that intropunitive and extropunitive mechanisms may combine to create a dynamic personality constellation. To some degree, this is a basic tenet of modern racial identity theories. For example, multidimensional models of racial identity incorporate intropunitive mechanisms such as race salience, racelessness, and self-hatred with extropunitive mechanisms such as racial ideologies, ingroup bias, and outgroup rejection. Perhaps it is the combination of mechanisms that confers self-esteem protection.

Finally, Allport did not directly address the complex representations of systemic unfairness in his analysis, nor did he address the role that shared meaning, action, and belief systems may play in generating a family of strategies for coping with discrimination. He also did not directly speak to the concept of social identity generally, and racial identity more specifically. The incorporation of social identity principles into racial identity theories represents a major advance since Allport.

Future Directions

One dramatic change in the nature of prejudice and discrimination is the substantial evidence of subtle or aversive racism (see Gaertner & Dovidio, ch. 5 this volume). Allport wrote in the context of blatant, public, and legally sanctioned patterns of discrimination. For the most part, this old-fashioned racism has been transformed into less obvious threats to opportunity and well-being. What are the adaptive strategies that targets employ to create or maintain psychological safety and self-worth in this more nebulous but palpable world of psychological threat?

I have proposed that TRIOS represents a patterned worldview that plays an adaptive role in such circumstances. Subtle racism may require flexibility of response styles, and self-determined standards of self-worth. Blatant forms of racism compelled Allport's theorizing to focus on patterns of self-protection, but the more subtle forms may require more self-enhancing mechanisms. Self-enhancement is commonly considered to be a social comparison process, but I believe future research should explore noncomparative forms of self-enhancement. For example, spirituality may confer positive self-regard in ways that are internally motivated and do not depend on relative worth. It is possible that social comparative mechanisms are rejected by stigmatized groups to avoid unfavorable outcomes in a system of reward allocation biased against them. Crocker and colleagues have already suggested as much and shown that Blacks are more inclined to base self-worth on _non_contingent criteria than Whites are (Crocker & Wolfe, 2001).

A related question concerns how ingroup comparisons can become standards for conferring self-worth. This may be related to Reference Group Orientation (Vandiver et al., 2002). Cross and colleagues argue that reference group orientation is independent of personal identity, but others argue they are intertwined. I propose that preferred modes of personal expression, values, and the like, can become standards of conduct (cultural patterns or designs for living) and may thus provide standards for psychological well-being that do not rely on cross-racial comparative processes. I propose that affirming the values and cultural ethos of the collective, including individualistic forms of self-expression, may also serve self-enhancing functions (Jones, 1999). An important general research direction is to explore the conditions under which intergroup versus interpersonal comparisons are made by members of stigmatized social groups. That is, when does one compare with mainstream standards or ingroup standards as a measure of self-worth? It is probable that the hypothesized low self-esteem of minority group members stemmed from assuming they made intergroup social comparisons as standards of personal worth.

Another research question concerns how members of stigmatized groups can create contexts of comfort. In the Universal Context of Racism model, self-protective mechanisms are elicited by the accessibility of racist explanations for personal and collective outcomes. If one can create a context where either (a) racism is not likely to occur or (b) if racism does emerge, its impact is significantly reduced, then one may be freer to use self-enhancement as a means of preserving psychological well-being. Research might be fruitful that explores the mechanisms by which one creates safe physical and psychological contexts and how they facilitate self-enhancing behaviors that have positive effects on well-being.

Finally, this approach need not be limited to African Americans but has general application to any identifiable human group that is a target of systemic group-based loss of control or freedom and physical and psychological denigration of their collective human worth. When a group faces such circumstances, it will necessarily draw upon its known and practiced cultural patterns as a means of coping with these challenges. It could be that the TRIOS qualities are uniquely suited to adapting to dehumanizing circumstances. It also could be that different groups will find ways to employ their cultural tendencies to successfully cope with similarly challenging circumstances. Indeed, the framework I propose is that understanding the responses of victims of systematic discrimination must take into account the group's historical-cultural patterns and mechanisms in order to have an adequate and accurate understanding of their psychological life.

REFERENCES

Allport, G. W. (1954/1979). *The nature of prejudice*. Cambridge, MA: Perseus Books.

Arroyo, C. & Zigler, E. (1995). Racial identity, academic achievement, and the psychological well-being of economically disadvantaged adolescents. *Journal of Personality and Social Psychology, 69*, 903–14.

Branscombe, N. R., Schmitt, M. T., & Harvey, R. D. (1999). Perceiving pervasive discrimination among African Americans: Implications for group

identification and well-being. *Journal of Personality and Social Psychology, 77(3)*, 135–49.

Clark, K. B. & Clark, M. P. (1947). Racial identification and preference in negro children. In T. M. Newcomb & E. L. Hartley (eds.), *Readings in social psychology* (pp. 602–11). New York: Holt.

Crocker, J., Luhtanen, R., Brodnax, S., & Blaine, B. E. (1999). Belief in U.S. government conspiracies against Blacks among Black and White college students: powerlessness or system-blame? _Personality and Social Psychology Bulletin, 25(8)_, 941–53.

Crocker, J. & Major, B. (1989). Social stigma and self-esteem: The self-protective properties of stigma. _Psychological Review, 96_, 608–30.

Crocker, J. & Wolfe, C. T. (2001). Contingencies of self-worth. _Psychological Review, 108(3)_, 593–623.

Cross, W. E. (1991). _Shades of Black: Diversity in African American identity._ Philadelphia, PA: Temple University Press.

Gray-Little, B. & Hafdahl, A. R. (2000). Factors influencing racial comparisons of self-esteem: A quantitative review. _Psychological Bulletin, 126_, 26–54.

Jones, J. M. (1986). Racism: The problem and an approach to the solution. In J. Dovidio & S. L. Gaertner (eds.), _Prejudice, discrimination and racism_ (pp. 279–314). New York: Academic Press.

Jones, J. M. (1997). _Prejudice and racism_ (2nd ed.). New York: McGraw-Hill.

Jones, J. M. (1999). Cultural racism: The intersection of race and culture in intergroup conflict. In D. Prentice and D. Miller (eds.), _Culture divides: Understanding and overcoming group conflict_ (pp. 465–90). New York: Russell Sage.

Jones, J. M. (2003). TRIOS: A psychological theory of African legacy in American culture. _Journal of Social Issues, 59_, 217–41.

Jones, J. M., Campbell, S. D., & Turner, C. E. (2004). TRIOS moderates the relationship between stress and well being. Unpublished MS, University of Delaware.

Jost, J. T. & Banaji, M. (1994). The role of stereotyping in system-justification and the production of false consciousness. _British Journal of Social Psychology, 33(1)_, 1–27.

Kardiner, A. & Ovesey, L. (1951). _The mark of oppression._ New York: Norton.

Kendler, K. S., Gallagher, T. J., Abelson, J. M., & Kessler, R. C. (1996). Lifetime prevalence, demographic risk factors, and diagnostic validity of non-affective psychosis as assessed in a US community sample: The National Comorbidity Survey. _Archives of General Psychiatry, 53_, 1022–31.

Kleugel, J. R. & Smith, E. R. (1986). _Beliefs about inequality: Americans' view of what is and what ought to be._ New York: Aldine de Gruyter.

Kwan, V. S. Y., John, O. P., Kenny, D. A., Bond, M. H., & Robins, R. W. (2004). Reconceptualizing individual differences in self-enhancement bias: An interpersonal approach. _Psychological Review, 111(1)_, 94–110.

Leonardelli, G. J. & Tormala, Z. L. (2003). The negative impact of perceiving discrimination on collective well-being: The mediating role of perceived group status. _European Journal of Social Psychology, 33(4)_, 507–14.

Rowley, S., Sellers, R. M., Chavous, T. M., & Smith, M. A. (1998). The relationship between racial identity and self-esteem in African American college and high school students. _Journal of Personality and Social Psychology, 74(3)_, 715–24.

Schmitt, M. T., Spears, R., & Branscombe, N. R. (2003). Constructing a minority group identity out of shared rejection: The case of international students. _European Journal of Social Psychology, 33(1)_, 1–12.

Sellers, R. M., Rowley, S. A., Chavous, T. M., Shelton, J. N., & Smith, M. A.

(1997). Multidimensional inventory of Black identity: A preliminary investigation of reliability and construct validity. *Journal of Personality and Social Psychology, 73(4)*, 805–15.

Sellers, R. M. & Shelton, J. N. (2003). The role of racial identity in perceived racial discrimination. *Journal of Personality and Social Psychology, 84(5)*, 1079–92.

Taylor, J. & Turner, R. J. (2002). Perceived discrimination, social stress and depression in the transition to adulthood: Racial contrasts. *Social Psychology Quarterly, 65(3)*, 213–25.

Taylor, S. E. (1989). *Positive illusions: Creative self-deception and the healthy mind.* New York: Basic Books.

Taylor, S. E., Lerner, J. S., Sherman D. K., Sage, R. M., & McDowell, N. K. (2003). Are self-enhancing cognitions associated with healthy or unhealthy biological profiles? *Journal of Personality and Social Psychology, 85(4)*, 605–15.

Twenge, J. M. & Crocker, J. (2002). Race and self-esteem: Meta-analyses comparing Whites, Blacks, Hispanics, Asians and American Indians and comment on Gray-Little and Hafdal (2000). *Psychological Bulletin, 128(3)*, 371–408.

Vandiver, B. J., Cross, W. J., Worrell, F. C., and Fhagen-Smith, P. E. (2002) Validating the crossracial identity scale. *Journal of Counseling Psychology, 49(1)*, 71–85.

PERCEIVING AND THINKING ABOUT GROUP DIFFERENCES

Chapter Eleven

Cognitive Process: Reality Constraints and Integrity Concerns in Social Perception

Vincent Yzerbyt and Olivier Corneille

Recent reviews and textbooks celebrate the ubiquitous implications of cognitive processes in the formation, use, and modification of stereotypes. Gordon Allport was in many ways the source of this "monomania" since he first drew scholars' attention to the role of cognition in stereotypes, prejudice, and discrimination. Interestingly, Allport suggested that not only twisted and sick minds rely on unwarranted generalizations. Rather, he emphasized the normality of people's faulty perceptions of social groups. In so doing, he claimed the study of prejudice and stereotyping as part of mainstream social psychology. Importantly, although Allport is known to have anticipated much of the later work on cognitive processes, he also emphasized the influence of motivational concerns in social perception. Over the years, it has become increasingly clear that motivational concerns must be fully integrated with cognitively-tuned approaches to stereotyping and prejudice. The field is only now achieving this kind of integration.

In the present chapter, we first provide a brief overview of the main ideas developed in Allport's chapter 10, "The Cognitive Process." As will become clear, cognitive limitations and partisanship are the recurrent themes of this founding text. In a second section, we discuss the most significant subsequent advances in understanding the process of categorization and stereotyping. In the third section, we emphasize the role of motivation in stereotyping and illustrate how current research provides evidence for the interplay of cognitive and motivational factors in the use of stereotypes. We conclude by suggesting promising avenues for future research.

Allport's Views on the Cognitive Process . . . and Motivated Cognition

In the opening section of his chapter "The Cognitive Process," Allport emphasized the idea, also developed by the New Look movement (Bruner, 1957), that perceivers are active witnesses of their environment. Perception is as much affected by the perceiver, "the light within" as Allport called it, as by the object of perception, "the light without" (1954/1979, p. 165). Allport stressed the role of meaning construction in social perceptions as well, noting that both cognitive and motivational factors determine people's interpretation of the social environment. After Allport, cognitively oriented social psychologists long concentrated on the former aspects and compared people's cognitive performance to so-called objective accounts of the surrounding world (Hamilton & Trolier, 1986). More recently, the role of motivation in social judgment has very much been rediscovered. Nowadays, most students of stereotyping and prejudice would agree that *reality constraints* (i.e., the light without) and *integrity concerns* (i.e., the light within) both shape social judgment (Leyens, Yzerbyt, & Schadron, 1992, 1994).

As a matter of fact, several propositions in Allport's chapter are quite cognitive in tone and can be seen as prefiguring later social-cognition work (see Fiske, ch. 3 this volume). First, he proposed that categories and categorization are tools that not only help people to deal with the complexity of the environment but also guide their thoughts and actions. Second, Allport discussed the structural aspects of categories, such as the appropriate features thought to define a category (similarity and association) and the hierarchical relations among categories (subordinate and superordinate). A central idea regarding the internal characteristics of categories is that people sometimes hold "monopolistic" categories in which all category members are thought to be interchangeable. It is in this sense that people's reliance on categories is supposedly based on the "principle of least effort": in order to reduce at low cost the uncertainty of their social environment, perceivers treat all members of a social group as being alike. A final section linked cognitive processes to dispositional factors, a theme that still is at the heart of many contemporary efforts in the field (see Duckitt, ch. 24 this volume).

In addition to the emphasis on cognition, several portions of Allport's chapter alluded to the influence of vested interests on social impressions and judgments. One section dealt with the consequences of people's attachment to preexisting knowledge. It is in this context that Allport discussed the role of "selection, accentuation, and interpretation" as providing a way to keep mental categories largely intact. Specifically, people rely on categorical thinking not only to overcome the limitation of their attentional capacities, but also to avoid repeated modifications of their views about others. Perhaps most illustrative of the intrusion of motivational concerns in people's thinking is what Allport called "autistic" thinking. In contrast to rational, so-called "directed" thinking, perceivers often reason in self-serving terms. "There is nothing passive about thinking," Allport noted (1954/1979, p. 167). The rationalization process that accompanies autistic thinking crystallizes around some form of simple human agency (e.g., blaming a scapegoat for one's problems), and neglects complex situational factors that may enter the picture (see Glick, ch. 15 this volume).

Again, whereas researchers' curiosity initially concerned the cognitive processes responsible for perceivers' *partial* appraisal of their social environment, the latest research efforts also aimed at better understanding the motivational factors that contribute to people's *partisan* view of the social world. To the extent that Allport considered the interplay of cognition and motivation to be the hallmark of social perception, the more balanced view advocated in contemporary work comes across as a tribute to the perspective he already championed half a century ago.

Developments Since Allport:
What Have We Learned?

One of Allport's most provocative and inspiring ideas was that stereotyping is grounded in a basic, unavoidable, categorization process. People are not capable of thought in the absence of concepts. New experiences remain meaningless unless they are incorporated into preexisting categories. Open-mindedness, Allport noted, "is considered to be a virtue. But strictly speaking, it cannot occur. A new experience must be redacted into old categories" (1954/1979, p. 20).

Categorical Thinking: The Cognitive Side of the Coin

Categorization is a prerequisite for human thinking for it gives meaning to new experiences. It also facilitates learning and guides people's adjustments to the social world. By abstracting sensory inputs, categorization allows individuals to quickly interpret, and react to, their environment. The act of categorization, however, deprives people of the ability to perceive some aspects of the world: stimuli can be assimilated to the category only if their peculiarities are overlooked. Here resides the dual nature of categorization: "Categorical thinking is a natural and inevitable tendency of the human mind" and "has property of guiding daily adjustments" (Allport, 1954/ 1979, pp.170–1), but it also impoverishes experiences and leads to a host of perceptual, judgmental, and memory biases.

One famous piece of evidence for the biasing impact of categorization on perception comes from a study by Tajfel and Wilkes (1963). Like Allport, Tajfel and Wilkes conceived categorization (and stereotyping) to result in the overestimation of intergroup differences and intragroup resemblances. Participants estimated the length of a series of lines that varied from each other by regular increments. When shorter lines (As) were systematically given a different label than longer lines (Bs), participants overestimated the differences between the categories. This basic categorization effect applies to estimates about attitudes, traits, or even physical values (e.g., Krueger & Clement, 1994) and points to the biasing influence of categorization. However, it seems most pronounced when the judgment is uncertain, such as when participants communicate their estimates in an unfamiliar measurement unit (Corneille, Klein, Lambert, & Judd, 2002). This is consistent with Allport's view that the "whole purpose [of categories] seems to be to facilitate perception and conduct – in other words, to make our adjustment to life speedy, smooth, and consistent" (1954/1979, p. 21).

Whereas Tajfel and Wilkes provided evidence that categorization leads perceivers to overestimate the difference between groups, later work confirmed that categorization also reduces the perceived variability within categories. For instance, stimuli belonging to the same category are more perceptually confusable than are cross-category stimuli (Harnad, 1987). This effect is consistent with Allport's claim that "categories assimilate as much old and new experience as possible to themselves" (1954/1979, p. 170). Beyond the implications of categorization for perception and judgment, Allport also noted that the categorization process implies a comparison between an old and an incoming representation. Categorization therefore involves a memory component. A straightforward illustration of the biasing impact of categorization on memory can be found in the "who-said-what" paradigm: people are more likely to misremember face–statement associations within than between groups (e.g., Taylor, Fiske, Etcoff, & Ruderman, 1978). For instance, individuals are more likely to misattribute a statement by a female speaker to another female than to another male speaker. More recently, categorization has also been shown to bias people's visual memory. Faces that are moderately typical of an Asian person will be misremembered as being more Asian-like than they are (Corneille, Huart, Bécquart, & Brédart, 2004). Research in social cognition has demonstrated a growing interest in how categorical thinking moderates basic memory processes.

Categorization is aimed at reducing uncertainties, but uncertainty reduction comes at the cost of increased inaccuracy in perceptions, judgments, and memories. As Allport acknowledged, inaccuracy is difficult to estimate in the context of social judgments: "nature does not tell us which [categorical] attributes are defining, which merely probable, and which totally fallacious" (1954/1979, p. 172; see Judd & Park, ch. 8 this volume, for a discussion of stereotype accuracy). Allport further suggested that as pragmatic perceivers, people choose when to make this trade-off. He noted,

> While most of us have learned to be critical and open-minded in *certain* regions of experience we obey the law of least effort in others. A doctor will not be swiped by folk generalizations concerning arthritis, snake bite, or the efficacy of aspirin. But he may be content with overgeneralizations concerning politics, social insurances, or Mexicans . . . Life is just too short to have differentiated concepts about everything. A *few* pathways are enough for us to walk in. (p. 173)

Because, by definition, people are experts in different and limited domains, a logical consequence of Allport's view is that most social concepts are underdifferentiated. Accordingly, Allport noted that: "One consequence of least effort in group categorizing is that a *belief in essence* develops." (1954/1979, p. 173–4). This subjective essentialism argument, i.e., the view that people tend to overestimate the homogeneity, consistency, and durability of social categories, has become a lively topic of research in recent intergroup relations work (for a collection, see Yzerbyt, Judd, & Corneille, 2004).

The idea of differentiated thinking and expertise is also at the heart of the numerous efforts on the contact hypothesis (Pettigrew & Tropp, 1998, and ch. 16 this volume; Kenworthy, Hewstone, Turner, & Voci, ch. 17 this volume) and of abundant research on stereotype change (Hewstone, 1994). According to Allport, perceivers avoid simplifications when given a chance to acquire rich sets of information. That is, "the more they know about a group the *less* likely they are to form monopolistic categories" (Allport, 1954/1979, p. 172, emphasis original). The belief that people stay away from inflexible categories if they become acquainted with members of a stigmatized group is of course very optimistic. As anticipated by

Allport, research has shown that a series of stringent conditions need to be met in order to change people's views about social groups. Clearly, one has to do more than provide information about members of a stigmatized group when attempting to change people's representations about this group (Gaertner & Dovidio, 2000), if only because perceivers are biased in their incorporation of group-attribute covariations (Hamilton & Gifford, 1976; but see McGarty, 2002).

In the early 1980s, researchers examined in more detail the cognitive factors that may be responsible for the inertia of stereotypes. The first paradigm to be used asked whether perceivers would disregard their faulty generalizations more or less as a function of the magnitude and distribution of counterstereotypical information about group members (Hewstone, 1994). As many studies revealed, people's reactions are best described in terms of the so-called "subtyping strategy" according to which people resist changing their stereotypes if they can group inconsistencies together in a few individuals. This strategy elaborates on Allport's notion that exceptional individuals are "fenced off" as not being like the rest of the group. This "structural" paradigm inspired a closer examination of the way perceivers approach information about groups. Do they favor a consideration of various subgroups within a larger group, a strategy commonly encountered when people's own group is at stake, or do they subtype the "deviants" so as to oppose a majority of stereotypic group members (all students) to a limited number of exceptions to the rule (Park, Wolsko, & Judd, 2001). For instance, there are various subgroups among university students, like "nerds," "party-animals," or "artists," to name but a few, allowing to accommodate for a great range of behaviors among students. In contrast to a subtyping strategy, approaching a group in terms of its diversity is a good way to ensure a moderate view, one that keeps all group members under the same umbrella and offers limited room for oversimplified conceptions regarding group members.

Because Allport considered stereotypes to be mainly a matter of (non)expertise, he appeared somewhat less sensitive to the circumstances under which categorical thinking is more or less prevalent within a given individual. Modern social cognition has been extremely prolific on this front. The thrust of the message is that the initial selection of a particular category (stereotype activation) and its further use (stereotype application) depend on a number of factors that relate to the perceiver, to the structure of the information, and to the circumstances in which information processing takes place (for integrative models, see Bodenhausen & Macrae, 1998; Brewer, 1988; Fiske & Neuberg, 1990; Kunda & Spencer, 2003).

Stereotype activation

As far as stereotype activation is concerned, the intrinsic salience of certain characteristics (such as race, age, or gender; Brewer & Lui, 1989) or their temporary salience in a situation due to their rarity or surprising nature (Taylor & Fiske, 1978) influence people's selection of one specific category over another. Chronic or transient goals are also important factors that orient the way perceivers approach other people in a given situation. Finally, stereotypic knowledge can become accessible even when perceivers remain unaware that it has been evoked in the first place.

Although category activation was long thought to require basically no intellectual resources, this assumption has now been challenged (Gilbert & Hixon, 1991). Interestingly, it has been proposed that the activation of a particular category may inhibit the activation of competing categories. In an illustrative experiment, Macrae and Bodenhausen had participants look at an Asian woman putting on make-up (to make gender salient) or eating rice (to make ethnicity salient). This encounter made stereotypically related words more accessible than control words. In contrast, the words associated with the opposing stereotype became less accessible (Bodenhausen & Macrae, 1998).

Stereotype application

Although category activation may well be pervasive in social life, people do not invariably use their stereotypic knowledge once a category label has been activated. Not surprisingly, assimilation to the activated constructs will depend on a host of situational constraints (Dijksterhuis & van Knippenberg, 2000; Macrae & Johnston, 1998) and personal characteristics (Smeesters et al., 2003).

In general, enhanced motivation and sufficient capacity to process fine-grained information increase perceivers' likelihood of attending to individuating information (rather than applying stereotypes). A striking example comes from a demonstration that "morning people" (vs. "night people") are more likely to be influenced by their stereotypes when confronted with a judgment task late (vs. early) in the day (Bodenhausen, 1990). In other words, more stereotyping is obtained when perceivers lack the energy to fulfill the judgment task than when they can count on their full intellectual vigor.

As Allport anticipated, applying stereotypes saves intellectual resources. Not only do stereotypes intrude more on judgments when there is a dearth of cognitive energy (Gilbert & Hixon, 1991; Macrae, Milne, & Bodenhausen, 1994) but access to categorical labels may free intellectual resources that can be redirected toward other tasks. Although circumstances in which resources are scarce encourage the use of stereotypic knowledge (see also Dijksterhuis & Bargh, 2001), people may switch to more sophisticated (and costly) forms of thinking if able and motivated to do so (Sinclair & Kunda, 1999). Social-cognition work conducted over the last two decades provides ample evidence that strategic, individual, and situational factors moderate people's inclination toward "differentiated thinking." As we show in the next section, research on the role of integrity concerns lends even more credence to this assertion.

A New Framework: Autistic Thinking, the Motivational Side of the Coin

A noteworthy aspect of Allport's cognitive approach of intergroup perceptions is the view that categorical thinking is often directed at serving self-interests. This form of reasoning, which Allport called "autistic thinking," is at the heart of various recent lines of work (Leyens, Yzerbyt, & Schadron, 1992, 1994) and is nicely illustrated in the research conducted by Kunda and her colleagues on "motivated reasoning with stereotypes" (Kunda & Spencer, 2003). When confronted with a member of a stigmatized category (e.g., an Asian doctor), people may choose to appraise this target using one among several categorical bases (e.g., doctor or Asian). The selection of a particular category depends upon the way the interaction unfolds. If the target somehow frustrates the well-being of the perceiver or counters self-enhancement goals, the more derogatory category will impose itself whereas the more flattering category will be inhibited. Of importance too is the fact that, although stereotypes may well be activated at early stages of an interaction, activation is not always found to last very long (Kunda, Davies, Adams, & Spencer, 2002). Chances are then that stereotypes will not be applied to a target at a later stage of the interaction unless some event (e.g., the emergence of a disagreement) triggers a need for people to fall back on their *a priori* views. That perceivers switch back and forth to stereotypes as a function of their relevance for the task at hand is consistent with the view that stereotypes are used when they prove useful in guiding perceivers' behavior.

In the above work, the reactions *vis-à-vis* the target person result from the nature of the interaction. Sometimes personal threats or frustrations influence judgments even when they are only incidentally related to the interaction. Research confirms that people change the way they perceive an outgroup member when their self-worth has been challenged in an otherwise unrelated episode. Indeed, Fein and Spencer (1997) found that compared to people who initially receive positive feedback about their intelligence, those who learn that they have failed a test express more derogatory judgments when the feedback provider is Jewish (a stigmatized category) than when she is not. Moreover, the more the threatened individuals derogate the Jewish candidate, the better they feel afterwards. Whereas the above work establishes the impact of self-threats on stereotype application, similar conclusions have been reported at the activation level.

Allport hypothesized that "the process of perception-cognition is distinguished for three operations that it performs on the 'light without.' It selects, accentuates, and interprets the sensory data" (1954/1979, p. 166). This claim is supported by work on hypothesis confirmation (Snyder, 1981). People working under the guidance of a particular hypothesis, and a stereotyped category would certainly qualify here, tend to rely on strategies that uncover evidence that supports rather than questions the validity of this hypothesis.

Numerous studies confirm that people are indeed highly selective in the information they collect to test their hypotheses about others, and that accentuation, biased interpretation, and selective memory often favor confirmatory evidence. In a study by Darley and Gross (1983), participants watched an ambiguous video showing a girl performing a number of scholastic tests. Participants who had initially been told that the girl was from a poor socioeconomic background saw a much poorer performance than those who believed she was from a wealthy family (see also Yzerbyt, Schadron, Rocher, & Leyens, 1994). A disturbing message emanating from hypothesis-confirmation work is that perceiver's initial hypotheses are likely to create a reality that eventually confirms their initial stereotypical expectations.

In sharp contrast with a simple-minded "energy-saving device" view sometimes advocated by social-cognition researchers, a view by which cognitive resources would be associated with a decreased impact of stereotypes, the work on hypothesis confirmation suggests that, when confronted with contradictory evidence, people may devote considerable resources in order to *save* the structure and content of their categories. Indeed, people have been found to exert a substantial amount of cognitive work in order to avoid revising their current views (Ditto & Lopez, 1992; Yzerbyt & Leyens, 1991).

Consistent with Allport's view on stereotype preservation, various studies on stereotype change have emphasized the active role that perceivers play in keeping their preconceptions intact. Kunda and Oleson (1995) found that the presence of an irrelevant piece of information facilitated perceivers' work in fencing off the deviant. Initially neutral, the irrelevant information was now deemed to "explain" the deviance, allowing perceivers to keep their general expectations intact. Only when no irrelevant information was provided were perceivers forced to integrate the information about the deviant in their representation of the group as a whole. There are thus limits to people's ability to bend reality.

The issue is not only whether additional information gives room for the reinterpretation of the evidence, but also whether perceivers enjoy the necessary cognitive resources to actively salvage their cherished beliefs. As a matter of fact, research reveals that perceivers confronted with a deviant group member manage to dismiss this inconsistency (thereby retaining the original stereotype unaltered) unless they face another cognitively demanding task (in which case their general stereotype is weakened) (Yzerbyt, Coull, & Rocher, 1999). "Fencing off" a deviant is a job that comes with its attentional cost, one that people are nevertheless willing to pay if this can help them to maintain their preconceptions.

That people are ready to invest resources to keep with their initial views and feel compelled to work hard when unexpected evidence pops up is not only detailed in work on person memory, hypothesis confirmation, and stereotype change. This pattern has been reported in many other areas, such as attribution and persuasion. All in all, social-cognition work is thus strongly compatible with the idea that perceivers have a vested interest in the inertia of their beliefs. In line with lessons from attitude change research, our prediction is that stereotypes are likely to be even more resistant if they survive a stage of thorough examination during which perceivers actively reaffirm them. It would thus seem that stereotypes can emerge in two rather different contexts. Besides being handy interpretations of the evidence, highly susceptible to being abandoned or modified whenever more attention is devoted to the stimulus information, they may also result from a thorough rationalization process and should then be seen as deeply rooted beliefs likely to resist most contradictory facts.

Does this mean that people are never motivated to stay away from stereotypes? Not necessarily. Whereas contemporary work acknowledges the role of integrity concerns and enhancement goals on stereotype maintenance, other studies suggest that perceivers can be eager to avoid stereotyping. This can occur because people are motivated to live up to personal standards or social prescriptions of fairness, resulting in attempts at stereotype suppression (for a review, see Monteith, Sherman, & Devine, 1998; Devine, ch. 20 this volume). Research on mental control suggests that this commendable line of action may not always be the ideal strategy it seems to be at first sight. Indeed, because suppression apparently activates the very stereotype people wish to combat, stereotypic materials can become even more accessible during later encounters with members of the target group, causing a "rebound" effect of stereotypes on judgment and behavior when suppression is no longer enforced (Macrae, Bodenhausen, Milne, & Jetten, 1994). The paradoxical consequences of suppression are also demonstrated in studies showing that perceivers initially asked to suppress a stereotype later preferentially recalled (Macrae et al., 1996) and recognized (Sherman et al., 1997) stereotype-consistent over stereotype-inconsistent materials presented during the suppression episode.

Is it then best to forgo suppression altogether? This would be a premature conclusion as some people seem able to suppress activated stereotypes without incurring the cost of rebound effects (for a review, see Monteith, Sherman, & Devine, 1998). For instance, Monteith, Spicer, and Tooman (1998) found that low-prejudice participants are less susceptible to rebound effects than high-prejudice participants. Presumably, low-prejudice people are more motivated to control the application of cultural stereotypes and have more practice with such control than their high-prejudice counterparts. To be sure, the impact of egalitarian goals or norms may also be situated at the activation stage in that low-prejudice people may simply never evoke the derogatory stereotype in the first place (Lepore & Brown, 1997; Moskowitz, Gollwitzer, Wasel, & Schaal, 1999). Also, it seems that not all target categories lend themselves to rebound effects, as stereotype control is likely to be maintained on a spontaneous basis for categories that are highly sensitive (e.g., race).

Has Allport Been Supported?

Over the five decades that followed the publication of *The Nature of Prejudice*, researchers have embraced Allport's ideas regarding the role of cognitive processes and accumulated an impressive series of findings establishing the central role of categorization and stereotypes in the formation, use, and change of beliefs about groups. As key tools in people's dealings with the social environment, stereotypes are likely to prevail not only when perceivers lack the ability and motivation to deal in a scrupulous and impartial way with the stimuli they encounter, but also when they are attached to a particular interpretation of the world or are otherwise frustrated in their pursuit of a positive view of themselves and their reference groups.

The gap in conceptualization and indeed often-mentioned tension between seeing stereotypes as a energy-saving cognitive shortcuts or cherished explanations of the surrounding world has probably fueled some misunderstanding between the two most productive lines of work on stereotypes and intergroup relations, namely social cognition and social identity (for a similar point, see Abrams & Hogg, 1998; Leyens, Yzerbyt, & Schadron, 1994). For the latter strand of research, stereotypes are used for the purpose of giving meaning, asserting perceived hierarchies between groups, and emphasizing group identities. For the former, stereotypes are simplifying devices that allow individual perceivers to deal with incoming stimuli in a manner that alleviates the burden of complexity. The growing role afforded to self-promoting goals or even social concerns within social-cognition work and a closer consideration for the cognitive dimensions of stereotyping within social-identity work offers great promise for future convergence of these two approaches.

Future Directions

In our opinion, four research topics have started to attract and will increasingly draw the attention of researchers in the next few years. The first concerns the impact of people's social position on their processing of social information. Factors as diverse as the power people have (e.g., Corneille & Yzerbyt, 2002; Fiske, 1993; Guinote, Judd, & Brauer, 2002), the immediate audience they have to face (Stangor, Sechrist, & Jost, 2001; Yzerbyt & Carnaghi, 2003), or the moral credentials they enjoy (Monin & Miller, 2001) have all been shown to shape people's reactions to groups and group members (see also Jackman's and Rudman's chapters 6 and 7 in this volume). In our view, research on these and related topics will likely receive enhanced attention in the forthcoming years.

Second, we see a growing interest in how people's communication about the reality of groups and group members is affected by and indeed shapes social representations. The way stereotypes are formed, established, and changed through communication is a fascinating – yet quite neglected – issue that researchers have just started to examine (Kashima, 2000; Ruscher, 2001). A better recognition of the fact that categories about groups are a social product as much as they are an outcome of individual cognitive processes is a central endeavor for future research (McGarty, Yzerbyt, & Spears, 2002).

Third, emotions have received an increasing amount of attention in the domain of intergroup relations (see also Smith & Mackie, ch. 22 this volume). This research has concerned the impact of people's mood on their processing of category and individual information (e.g., Bodenhausen, 1993), the beliefs people hold about the nature of emotions experienced by members of different groups (Leyens et al., 2000), or the emotions people experience as a function of their self-categorization into, and identification with, groups (e.g., Mackie, Devos, & Smith, 2000; Yzerbyt, Dumont, Gordijn, & Wigboldus, 2001).

Finally, the possibilities offered by the tools of mental imagery, and the current attention devoted to neuroscience issues, suggest a growing interest in the psychophysiological and neurophysiological correlates of stereotyping and prejudice. This emerging area has been the subject of recent symposia (e.g., see the special issue of the *Journal of Personality and Social Psychology: Attitudes and Social Cognition*, October 2003, on this topic).

Half a century ago, the path opened by Allport in his groundbreaking work made clear that the boundaries of people's cognitive apparatus and the restrictions imposed by self-interest likely join together to shape social judgment. For the many travelers that embraced social cognition, the journey has been every bit as fascinating as Allport advertised it to be. Our intuition of what future research holds similarly stresses the interplay of reality constraints and integrity concerns in the perception of groups and group members. The promise is thus for even more integration of cognition and motivation, a perspective Allport would surely have liked.

REFERENCES

Abrams, D. & Hogg, M. A. (1998). *Social identity and social cognition.* Oxford: Blackwell.

Allport, G. W. (1954/1979). *The nature of prejudice.* Cambridge, MA: Perseus Books.

Bodenhausen, G. V. (1990). Stereotypes as judgmental heuristics: Evidence of circadian variations in discrimination. *Psychological Science, 1,* 319–22.

Bodenhausen, G. V. (1993). Emotions, arousal, and stereotypic judgments: A heuristic model of affect and stereotyping. In D. M. Mackie & D. L. Hamilton (eds.), *Affect, cognition, and stereotyping: Interactive processes in group perception* (pp. 13–37). San Diego, CA: Academic Press.

Bodenhausen, G. V. & Macrae, C. N. (1998). Stereotype activation and inhibition. In R. S. Wyer (ed.), *Stereotype activation and inhibition: Advances in social cognition* (Vol. 11, pp. 1–52). Mahwah, NJ: Erlbaum.

Brewer, M. B. (1988). A dual process model of impression formation. In R. S. Wyer, Jr. & T. K. Srull (eds.), *Advances in social cognition* (vol. 1, pp. 1–36). Hillsdale, NJ: Erlbaum.

Brewer, M. B. & Lui, L. N. (1989). The primacy of age and sex in the structure of person categories. *Social Cognition, 7,* 262–74.

Bruner, J. S. (1957). On perceptual readiness. *Psychological Review, 64,* 123–52.

Corneille, O., Huart, J., Becquart, E., & Brédart, S. (2004). When memory shifts towards more typical category exemplars: Accentuation effects in the recollection of ethnically ambiguous faces. *Journal of Personality and Social Psychology, 86,* 236–50.

Corneille, O., Klein, O., Lambert, S., & Judd, C. M. (2002). On the role of familiarity with units of measurement in categorical accentuation: Tajfel and Wilkes (1963) revisited and replicated. *Psychological Science, 4,* 380–4.

Corneille, O. & Yzerbyt, V. (2002). Dependence and the formation of stereotyped beliefs about groups: From interpersonal to intergroup perception. In C. McGarty, V. Yzerbyt, & R. Spears (eds.), *Stereotypes as explanations: The formation of meaningful beliefs about social groups* (pp. 111–26). Cambridge, UK: Cambridge University Press.

Darley, J. M. & Gross, P. H. (1983). A hypothesis-confirming bias in labeling effects. *Journal of Personality and Social Psychology, 44,* 20–33.

Devine, P. G. (1989). Stereotypes and prejudice: Their automatic and controlled components. *Journal of Personality and Social Psychology, 56,* 5–18.

Dijksterhuis, A. & Bargh, J. A. (2001). The perception–behavior expressway: Automatic effects of social perception on social behavior. In M. Zanna (ed.), *Advances in experimental social psychology* (vol. 33, pp. 1–40). Hillsdale, NJ: Lawrence Erlbaum Associates.

Dijksterhuis, A. & van Knippenberg, A. (2000). Behavioral indecision: Effects of self-focus on automatic behavior, *Social Cognition, 18,* 55–74.

Ditto, P. H. & Lopez, D. F. (1992). Motivated skepticism: Use of differential decision criteria for preferred and nonpreferred conclusions. *Journal of Personality and Social Psychology, 63,* 568–84.

Fein, S. & Spencer, S. J. (1997). Prejudice as self-image maintenance: Affirming the self through derogating others. *Journal of Personality and Social Psychology, 73,* 31–44.

Fiske, S. T. (1993). Controlling other people: The impact of power on stereotyping. *American Psychologist, 48,* 621–8.

Fiske, S. T. & Neuberg, S. L. (1990). A continuum model of impression formation from category-based to individuating processes: Influences of information and motivation on attention and interpretation. In M. P. Zanna (ed.), *Advances in experimental social psychology* (vol. 3, pp. 1–74). San Diego, CA: Academic Press.

Gaertner, S. L. & Dovidio, J. F. (2000). *Reducing intergroup bias: The common Ingroup Identity Model.* Philadelphia, PA: Psychology Press.

Gilbert, D. T. & Hixon, J. G. (1991). The trouble of thinking: Activation and application of stereotypic beliefs. *Journal of Personality and Social Psychology, 60,* 509–17.

Guinote, A., Judd, C. M., & Brauer, M. (2002). Effects of power on perceived and objective group variability: Evidence that more powerful groups are more variable. *Journal of Personality and Social Psychology, 82,* 708–21.

Hamilton, D. L. & Gifford, R. K. (1976). Illusory correlation in interpersonal perception: A cognitive basis of stereotype judgments. *Journal of Experimental Social Psychology, 12,* 392–407.

Hamilton, D. L. & Trolier, T. K. (1986). Stereotypes and stereotyping: An overview of the cognitive approach. In J. F. Dovidio & S. L. Gaertner (eds.), *Prejudice, discrimination, and racism* (pp. 127–63). New York: Academic Press.

Harnad, S. (1987). Introduction: Psychophysical and cognitive aspects of categorical perception: A critical overview. In S. Harnad (ed.), *Categorical perception: The groundwork of cognition.* New York: Cambridge University Press.

Hewstone, M. (1994). Revision and change of stereotypic beliefs: In search of the elusive subtyping model. In W. Stroebe & M. Hewstone (eds.), *European review of social psychology* (vol. 5, pp. 69–109). Chichester, UK: Wiley.

Kashima, Y. (2000). Maintaining cultural stereotypes in the serial reproduction of narratives. *Personality and Social Psychology Bulletin, 26,* 594–604.

Krueger, J. & Clement, R. W. (1994). Memory-based judgments about multiple categories: A revision and extension of Tajfel's accentuation theory. *Journal of Personality and Social Psychology, 67,* 35–47.

Kunda, Z., Davies, P. G., Adams, B. D., & Spencer, S. J. (2002). The dynamic time course of stereotype activation: Activation, dissipation, and resurrection. *Journal of Personality and Social Psychology, 82,* 283–99.

Kunda, Z. & Oleson, K. C. (1995). Maintaining stereotypes in the face of disconfirmation: Constructing grounds for subtyping deviants. *Journal of Personality and Social Psychology, 68,* 565–79.

Kunda, Z. & Spencer, S. J. (2003). When do stereotypes come to mind and when do they color judgment? A goal-based theoretical framework for stereotype activation and application. *Psychological Bulletin, 129,* 522–44.

Lepore, L. & Brown, R. (1997). Category and stereotype activation: Is prejudice inevitable? *Journal of Personality and Social Psychology, 72,* 275–87.

Leyens, J.-P., Paladino, M.-P., Rodriguez, R. T., Vaes, J., Demoulin, S., Rodriguez, A. P., & Gaunt, R. (2000). The emotional side of prejudice: The attribution of secondary emotions to ingroups and outgroups. *Personality and Social Psychology Review, 4,* 186–97.

Leyens, J.-P., Yzerbyt, V. Y., & Schadron, G. (1992). The social judgeability approach to stereotypes. In W. Stroebe & M. Hewstone (eds.), *European review of social psychology* (vol. 3, pp. 91–120). Chichester, UK: Wiley.

Leyens, J.-P., Yzerbyt, V. Y., & Schadron, G. (1994). *Stereotypes and social cognition.* London: Sage.

Mackie, D. M., Devos, T., & Smith, E. R. (2000). Intergroup emotions: Explaining offensive action tendencies in an intergroup context. *Journal of*

Personality and Social Psychology, 79, 602–16.

Macrae, C. N., Bodenhausen, G. V., Milne, A. B., & Jetten, J. (1994). Out of mind but back in sight: Stereotypes on the rebound. *Journal of Personality and Social Psychology*, 67, 808–17.

Macrae, C. N., Bodenhausen, G. V., Milne, A. B., & Wheeler, V. (1996). On resisting the temptation for simplification: Counterintentional effects of stereotype suppression on social memory. *Social Cognition*, 14, 1–20.

Macrae, C. N. & Johnston, L. (1998). Help, I need somebody: Automatic action and inaction. *Social Cognition*, 16, 400–17.

Macrae, C. N., Milne, A. B., & Bodenhausen, G. V. (1994). Stereotypes as energy-saving devices: A peek inside the tool-box. *Journal of Personality and Social Psychology*, 66, 37–47.

McGarty, C. (2002). Stereotype formation as category formation. In C. McGarty, V. Y. Yzerbyt, & R. Spears (eds.), *Stereotypes as explanations: The formation of meaningful beliefs about social groups* (pp. 16–37). Cambridge: Cambridge University Press.

McGarty, C., Yzerbyt, V. Y., & Spears, R. (2002). *Stereotypes as explanations: The formation of meaningful beliefs about social groups*. Cambridge: Cambridge University Press.

Monin, B. & Miller, D. T. (2001). Moral credentials and the expression of prejudice. *Journal of Personality and Social Psychology*, 81, 33–43.

Monteith, M. J., Sherman, J. W., & Devine, P. G. (1998). Suppression as a stereotype control strategy. *Personality and Social Psychology Review*, 2, 63–82.

Monteith, M. J., Spicer, C. V., & Tooman, G. (1998). Consequences of stereotype suppression: Stereotypes on AND not on the rebound. *Journal of Experimental Social Psychology*, 34, 355–77.

Moskowitz, G. B., Gollwitzer, P. M., Wasel, W., & Schaal, B. (1999). Preconscious control of stereotype activation through chronic egalitarian goals. *Journal of Personality and Social Psychology*, 77, 167–84.

Park, B., Wolsko, C., & Judd, C. M. (2001). Measurement of subtyping in stereotype change. *Journal of Experimental Social Psychology*, 37, 325–32.

Pettigrew, T. F. (1998). Intergroup contact theory. *Annual Review of Psychology*, 49, 65–85.

Ruscher, J. B. (2001). *Prejudiced communication: A social psychological perspective*. New York: Guilford Press.

Sherman, J. W., Stroessner, S. J., Loftus, S. T., & Deguzman, G. (1997). Stereotype suppression and recognition memory for stereotypical and nonstereotypical information. *Social Cognition*, 15, 205–15.

Sinclair, L. & Kunda, Z. (1999). Reactions to a Black professional: Motivated inhibition and activation of conflicting stereotypes. *Journal of Personality and Social Psychology*, 77, 885–904.

Smeesters, D., Warlop, L., Van Avermaet, E., Corneille, O., & Yzerbyt, V. Y. (2003). Do not prime hawks with doves: The interplay of construct activation and consistency of social value orientation on cooperative behavior. *Journal of Personality and Social Psychology*, 84, 972–87.

Snyder, M. (1981). Seek and ye shall find: Testing hypotheses about other people. In E. T. Higgins, C. P. Herman, & M. P. Zanna (eds.), *Social cognition: The Ontario Symposium on Personality and Social Psychology* (vol. 1, pp. 277–303). Hillsdale, NJ: Erlbaum.

Stangor, C., Sechrist, G. B., & Jost, J. T. (2001). Changing racial beliefs by providing consensus information. *Personality and Social Psychology Bulletin*, *27*, 486–96.

Tajfel, H. & Wilkes, A. L. (1963). Classification and quantitative judgment. *British Journal of Psychology*, *54*, 101–14.

Taylor, S. E. & Fiske, S. T. (1978). Salience, attention, and attribution: Top of the head phenomena. In L. Berkowitz (ed.), *Advances in experimental social psychology* (vol. 11, pp. 250–89). New York: Academic Press.

Taylor, S. E., Fiske, S. T., Etcoff, N. L., & Ruderman, A . J. (1978). Categorical bases of person memory and stereotyping. *Journal of Personality and Social Psychology*, *36*, 778–93.

Yzerbyt, V. Y. & Carnaghi, A. (2003). Social consensus and the maintenance of stereotypic beliefs: Knowing whom you'll talk to affects what you do with the information. MS submitted for publication. Catholic University of Louvain at Louvain-la-Neuve.

Yzerbyt, V. Y., Coull, A., & Rocher, S. J. (1999). Fencing off the deviant: The role of cognitive resources in the maintenance of stereotypes. *Journal of Personality and Social Psychology*, *77*, 449–62.

Yzerbyt, V. Y., Dumont, M., Gordijn, E., & Wigboldus, D. (2002). Intergroup emotions: The impact of self-categorization on reactions to victims. In D. M. Mackie & E. R. Smith (eds.), *From prejudice to intergroup emotions: Differentiated reactions to social groups* (pp 67–88). Philadelphia, PA: Psychology Press.

Yzerbyt, V., Judd, C. M., & Corneille, O. (eds.) (2004). *The psychology of group perception: Homogeneity, entitativity, and essentialism.* London: Psychology Press.

Yzerbyt, V. Y. & Leyens, J.-P. (1991). Requesting information to form an impression: The influence of valence and confirmatory status. *Journal of Experimental Social Psychology*, *27*, 337–56.

Yzerbyt, V. Y., Schadron, G., Leyens, J.-P., & Rocher, S. (1994). Social judgeability: The impact of meta-informational cues on the use of stereotypes. *Journal of Personality and Social Psychology*, *66*, 48–55.

Chapter Twelve

Linguistic Factors: Antilocutions, Ethnonyms, Ethnophaulisms, and Other Varieties of Hate Speech

Brian Mullen and Tirza Leader

"Prejudice squints when it looks, and lies when it talks."
—Laure Junot, Duchess d'Abrantes

Ethnophaulisms (Roback, 1944; from the Greek roots meaning "a national group" and "to disparage") are the words used as ethnic slurs to refer to outgroups in hate speech. These are distinct from *ethnonyms* (Levin & Potapov, 1964; from the Greek roots meaning "a national group" and "name"), which are the names an ingroup gives itself to distinguish itself from outgroups. *Antilocutions* (Allport, 1954/1979; from the Greek root meaning "against" and the Latin root meaning "to speak") are prejudiced speech, which include ethnophaulisms as well as other linguistic factors in hostile prejudice, such as derogatory outgroup jokes. Even in a "politically correct" cultural climate, the popular media continue to report the use of hate speech in interethnic conflicts (e.g., Associated Press, 2003; Fuquay, 2003). Palmore (1962, p. 442) went so far as to state that "it is probably safe to say that there is no known group which does not use ethnophaulisms." Indeed, popular fiction often employs antilocutions in the form of fictional ethnophaulisms as a telegraphic shorthand for hostile prejudice (e.g., "changeling" in the television show *Star Trek: Deep Space Nine*; "coppertop" in the film *The Matrix*; "mudblood" in the *Harry Potter* books and films).

These linguistic factors of intergroup hostility were unequivocally of central importance in Allport's (1954/1979) conceptualization of hostile prejudice. On the one hand, it should be acknowledged that only one (chapter 11, "Linguistic Factors") of 31 chapters, and only 10 of 480 pages, were devoted to a discussion of the role of language in prejudice. On the other hand, the frequency with which Allport used antilocutions to illustrate his thinking on intergroup hostility is remarkable. For example, Allport (1954/1979) noted: "In the ethnic sphere even plain labels such as

Negro, Italian, Jew, Catholic, Irish-American, French-Canadian may have emotional tone . . . But they all have their higher key equivalents: nigger, wop, kike, papist, harp, cannuck. When these labels are employed we can be almost certain that the speaker *intends* not only to characterize the person's membership but also to disparage and reject him" (p. 181, italics in original). Ethnophaulisms are employed for illustrative purposes in 14, or about half, of his 31 chapters. On average, Allport (1954/1979) covers no more than 11 pages between uses of ethnophaulisms to illustrate some element of prejudice. In the present chapter, we will reflect upon the past 50 years of theory and research regarding linguistic factors in prejudice.

Allport's Views on Linguistic Factors in Prejudice

Allport's consideration of the linguistic factors in prejudice was complex and variegated. He hypothesized that linguistic factors served a range of functions and had a number of different consequences. Antilocutions were hypothesized to reflect social categorization; to express hostile prejudice; to promote exclusion; to precipitate violence; and to directly harm the targets.

One of the most straightforward aspects of Allport's perspective is his notion that the use of antilocutions is a reflection of social categorization. This notion is illustrated in Allport's (1954/1979) signature phrase, "nouns that cut slices" (p. 174), referring to the group labels that cluster the social world into meaningful groups for the perceiver. This is also illustrated in direct statements, such as "until we label an outgroup it does not clearly exist in our minds" (p. 49).

However, beyond reflecting social differentiation, antilocutions can also directly reflect prejudice. As Allport (1954/1979) observed, these are "emotionally toned labels" (p. 181), and, as a consequence, the use of antilocutions represents an expression of prejudice. According to Allport, "intense hostility is reflected in the antilocution of name-calling" (p. 49). Moreover, Allport proposed that the use of antilocutions towards a target outgroup precipitates subsequent exclusion of that target outgroup. Allport stated, "It seems a safe generalization to say that an ethnic label arouses a stereotype which in turn leads to rejective behavior" (p. 316). The use of antilocutions towards a target outgroup can also subsequently facilitate violence towards that group. For instance, Allport wrote, "Although most barking [antilocution] does not lead to biting, yet there is never a bite without previous barking" (p. 57).

Allport also recognized the deleterious impact of antilocutions on targets. He wrote, "The basic feeling of members of minority groups who are the object of prejudice is one of insecurity . . . 'I wait in fear for an anti-Jewish remark'" (1954/1979, p. 140). A more complex facet of Allport's perspective is his notion of verbal realism, or the tendency for responses to words to be as strong as the responses to the things represented by the words. This proposition is illustrated by Allport's description of ethnophaulisms as "fighting words" that evoke as much response in their targets as actual physical attacks.

Allport also considered two other aspects of antilocutions – their potential effects on the perpetrator and how others could intervene. Regarding the former issue, the propositions that antilocutions precipitate subsequent hostile prejudice, exclusion, and violence towards the target outgroup suggest that they facilitate further expressions of antipathy. However, Allport also considered the possible cathartic role of the use of antilocutions. He explained that the explosion of feeling that occurs during an act of antilocution "has a quasi-curative effect. It temporarily relieves the tension and may prepare the individual for a change of attitude" (1954/1979, p. 460). Thus, Allport seemed to recognize a paradox in the use of antilocutions: On the one hand, the use of antilocutions may promote subsequent hostile prejudice. On the other hand, the use of antilocutions may serve as a "safety valve" which prevents subsequent hostile prejudice.

In terms of interventions, Allport considered rebuttals which bystanders might use in response to overhearing someone else employ antilocutions. Citing the work of Citron, Chein, and Harding (1950), Allport concluded that the most effective way to respond to someone else's use of ethnophaulisms was to point out that such prejudiced remarks are not in the American tradition (1954/1979, p. 314).

Developments Since Allport

Although the number of pages Allport explicitly devoted to linguistic factors in *The Nature of Prejudice* was limited, his ideas have stimulated a considerable amount of theoretical analysis and empirical work. In this section, we consider recent developments in each of the areas Allport discussed: social categorization, the promotion of exclusion, the precipitation of violence, effects on targets, effects on perpetrators, and interventions.

With respect to social categorization, in traditional cultures, the ethnonyms an ingroup gives itself often derive from native words for "real humans" or "the people," whereas the ethnophaulisms given to outgroups often derive from native words for "beast" or "animal" (Fried, 1975). This parallels the recent finding that ingroup members are attributed complex "uniquely human" emotions, whereas outgroups are assumed to exhibit more simple and primary animal-like emotions (Leyens et al., 2001). The interplay between ethnonyms and ethnophaulisms across social categories is poignantly captured by the pairings of "Christian" vs. "heathen," "Muslim" vs. "infidel," and "Jew" vs. "goyim" (Cardona, 1989).

Other research confirms the basic premise that the use of ethnophaulisms is a reflection of social categorization across a range social groups beyond ethnic groups. Ethnophaulisms have been documented in the context of artificial laboratory groups (e.g., Mullen & Johnson, 1995), as well as in terms of derision by physicians towards undesirable patients (e.g., Coombs et al., 1993), by normal weight individuals towards overweight individuals (e.g., Cossrow, Jeffery, & McGuire, 2001), and by men and women towards one another (e.g., Grossman & Tucker, 1997). In each case, these non-ethnic ingroups and outgroups are defined by clear social categorizations.

Also supportive of Allport's analysis, the current evidence indicates that antilocutions can promote exclusion. In the first effort to explicitly examine the relationship between exclusion and ethnic labels, Mullen and Rice (2003) showed that the use of ethnophaulisms towards ethnic immigrant outgroups in the US did indeed predict the exclusion of those outgroups from the host American society. Ethnic immigrant groups that were referred to with less complex (and, to a lesser degree, more negative) ethnophaulisms were less likely to marry native-born Americans, more likely to be segregated into ethnic neighborhoods, and more likely to be deemed suitable for hazardous work. More recently, Mullen (2004) showed that the use of ethnophaulisms towards ethnic immigrant groups in the US also predicted a more subtle form of exclusion, the portrayal of ethnic immigrants to children. For example, members of ethnic immigrant outgroups that were cognitively represented with less complex (and, to a lesser degree, more negative) ethnophaulisms were less frequently present in children's literature, described more in terms of physical appearance than in terms of personal traits, and portrayed with smaller heads and with lower verbal complexity. These results confirm Allport's position that the use of ethnophaulisms towards a target group can facilitate subsequent exclusion of that target group.

The possible link between antilocutions and violence is highlighted in some recent papers that explicitly assume a causal link between the two phenomena, as in Owen's (1998) "The speech that kills," and Scott's (1999) "From hate rhetoric to hate crime: A link acknowledged too late."

The tragic shooting rampage in April 1999, which resulted in the deaths of 12 students and the wounding of 23 others at Columbine High School in Littleton, Colorado, is often cited to illustrate the link between hate speech and violence: The shooters, Eric Harris and Dylan Klebold, referred to one of the victims, Isaiah Shoels, with ethnophaulisms as they killed him (Associated Press, 1999). Even though the titles of these papers and these anecdotes seem to be persuasive, the fact remains that they clearly fall short of establishing a compelling *empirical* link between antilocutions and violence. It should be noted that, in more general terms, the relationship between the way people think and talk about outgroups and the way they behave towards those outgroups is far from straightforward (see Mackie & Smith, 1998). To date, there has been no systematic study of the association between antilocutions and violence.

The impact of prejudice on targets of discrimination is, as illustrated by the chapters by Major & Vick and by Jones in this volume (chs. 9 and 10 respectively), often profound. Antilocutions represent a critical mechanism by which prejudice can injure targets. As compellingly illustrated in Matsuda, Lawrence, Delgado, and Crenshaw's (1993) *Words That Wound*, self-reports of the victims of hate speech are universal in conveying the breadth and depth of these deleterious effects. It is not at all surprising that evidence has confirmed that being the target of hate speech results in harmful effects, ranging from negative emotional responses (Nielsen, 2002), to physiological reactivity (Clark, Anderson, Clark, & Williams, 1999), to lowered collective self-esteem (Boeckmann & Liew, 2002; see also Leets & Giles, 1997).

This evidence of the impact of ethnophaulisms on the people towards whom they are directed also provides indirect support for Allport's notion of verbal realism, the tendency to respond as strongly to words as to the actions they represent. In a historical example of culinary verbal realism, the First World War inspired many in the US to rename sauerkraut as "victory cabbage," hamburgers as "victory steaks," and frankfurters as "hot dogs." More recently, the refusal on the part of France to support the US war on Iraq led Representative Bob Ney (a Republican from Ohio) to propose that US government restaurants rename french fries as "freedom fries" and french toast as "freedom toast." Despite these salient examples, there have been no empirical investigations of the prevalence, the antecedents, or the consequences of this tendency for verbal realism.

Similarly, Allport's ideas about how antilocutions can produce either an escalation or an attenuation of negative feelings and behavior have not been directly tested empirically in the intervening 50 years since the publication of *The Nature of Prejudice*. In a peripherally relevant study, Loew

(1967) showed that participants trained to speak aggressive verbs during a learning task delivered more extreme electric shocks to a peer. While these results seem to disconfirm the notion of catharsis in the expression of hostility, the target of hostility in Loew's study was explicitly not an ethnic outgroup member, and the aggressive verbs were explicitly not ethnophaulisms. Nevertheless, these results suggest that intergroup hostility is exacerbated, and not cathartically ameliorated, by the use of antilocutions. More generally, "releasing" aggression has been shown to increase, not to decrease, subsequent aggression (Bushman, 2002).

Evidence relating to Allport's notions about interventions, such as rebuttals to the use antilocutions, has also been more anecdotal than empirical (see also Guerin's, [2003] discussion of possible rebuttals, and Stephan & Stephan's chapter 26 in this volume). This approach was vividly illustrated when, in response to the hate-motivated drive-by murders by White supremacist Benjamin Smith in July of 1999, President Clinton commented that the shooting spree was "a rebuke of American ideals" (Cable Network News, 1999). However, there has been relatively little research examining the way that people (targets or bystanders) rebut the use of antilocutions. Notable exceptions are studies indicating that an important element in the parenting of ethnic-minority children is preparing, and assisting, children to deal with being the targets of ethnophaulisms (e.g., Pankiw & Bienvenue, 1990; Phinney & Chavira, 1995; see also Aboud's ch. 19 in this volume). Also of note is Leets's (2002) recent study that showed that adults who were the targets of ethnophaulisms most often employed passive response strategies.

In summary, many of Allport's propositions have been confirmed by the weight of subsequent evidence. Others of these positions have not even been subjected to empirical scrutiny. Other recent work has challenged Allport's ideas. Nevertheless, regardless of whether the work supports or challenges these ideas, it is a testament to the enduring relevance of Allport's influence that the majority of these empirical papers cited *The Nature of Prejudice*.

New Frameworks

As far-ranging as Allport's speculations about the role of linguistic factors in prejudice were, several recent frameworks have developed that have expanded the scope of work on this topic both theoretically and empirically. Theoretically, work in this area has examined the basic dimensions of ethnophaulisms used for different groups, and it has revealed new insights about how the use of language both reflects and perpetuates bias (see also Ruscher, 2001).

Dimensions of Ethnophaulisms

In terms of the general structure of ethnic labels, paralleling research on stereotypes (see Judd & Park's ch. 8 in this volume), ethnophaulisms reflect two basic dimensions: On the one hand, the array of ethnophaulisms used for an ethnic group can vary in complexity, which indicates the type of cognitive representation being used for the ethnic groups (Mullen & Johnson, 1993, 1995; Mullen, Rozell, & Johnson, 2000, 2001). The ethnophaulisms for some ethnic groups are distributed across different semantic categories, indicating a relatively higher level of complexity in cognitive representation. For example, two of the four ethnophaulisms applied to Spanish immigrants in the US refer to some aspect of a group name ("spanisher" and "spinach") while the other two ethnophaulisms refer to personal names ("diego" and "josé"). Alternatively, the ethnophaulisms for other ethnic groups are clustered into relatively few semantic categories, indicating a relatively lower level of complexity in cognitive representation. For example, all of the four ethnophaulisms applied to Belgian immigrants in the US refer to some aspect of a group name ("belgeek," "belgie," "blemish," and "flamingo"). As suggested by Graumann and Wintermantel (1989), the use of ethnophaulisms provides a gauge of prototype representation of ethnic groups: "Typing [a member of a social category] by nouns fixates the other person as a *typical* instance of a social category" (p. 192, emphasis added). This simplified cognitive representation of an ethnic outgroup seems to be exaggerated when the ethnophaulisms for that outgroup are clustered into relatively few semantic categories.

On the other hand, the array of ethnophaulisms used for an ethnic group can vary in valence, which indicates the negativity of the cognitive representation being used for the ethnic groups (Mullen, Rozell, & Johnson, 2000, 2001). The ethnophaulisms for some ethnic groups are relatively moderate in valence, indicating a relatively benign cognitive representation. For example, ethnophaulisms applied to Welsh immigrants in the US have tended to be relatively neutral in valence (such as "cousin jack" and "taffy"). Alternatively, the ethnophaulisms for other ethnic groups are extremely negative in valence, indicating a relatively derogatory cognitive representation. For example, ethnophaulisms applied to Greek immigrants in the US have tended to be extremely negative in valence (such as "greaseball" and "asshole-bandit"). As suggested by Greenberg, Kirkland, and Pyszczynski (1988), ethnophaulisms "probably constitute the most direct and effective expression of prejudice in everyday discourse" (p. 75). This derogatory cognitive representation of an ethnic outgroup seems to be exaggerated when the ethnophaulisms for that outgroup are extremely negative in valence.

The complexity and valence of ethnophaulisms, while conceptually distinct, are often interrelated. That is, ethnic immigrant outgroups characterized by more negative ethnophaulisms tend to be characterized by ethnophaulisms that cluster together with less complexity (Mullen, 2001, 2004; Mullen & Johnson, 1993, 1995; Mullen & Rice, 2003; Mullen, Rozell, & Johnson, 2000, 2001). In addition, valence and complexity are affected by many of the same factors. Groups that are more salient because they are smaller, less familiar, and more foreign tend to be cognitively represented with less complexity, and more negativity, in ethnophaulisms (Mullen & Johnson, 1993, 1995; Mullen et al., 2000, 2001). This combination of low complexity and negative valence in ethnophaulisms clearly resonates with Allport's (1954/1979, p. 3403) depiction of the hated outgroup as something despicable and less than fully human. The tendency to use ethnophaulisms of low complexity and negative valence for salient ethnic outgroups may reflect the same basic process by which people ascribe human essence to their ingroup while "infrahumanizing" outgroups (see also Leyens et al., 2001).

As noted earlier, the use of ethnophaulisms predicts the exclusion of immigrant outgroups (Mullen, 2004; Mullen & Rice, 2003). In addition, simply overhearing ethnophaulisms can influence people to devalue the targets of these antilocutions (Greenberg & Pyszczynski, 1985; Simon & Greenberg, 1996). This pernicious influence of overheard hate speech on bystanders led Greenberg and Pyszczynski (1985, p. 70) to conclude that ethnophaulisms "are not merely symptoms of prejudice but carriers of the disease as well." Relatedly, research has begun to examine differential responses to derogatory jokes about target outgroups as varied as immigrants (Fuehr, 1998), Poles (Bier, 1988), and African Americans (Jaret, 1999).

The evidence to date indicates that ethnophaulism complexity tends to be a stronger predictor of the negative consequences of ethnophaulisms than ethnophaulism valence. In both Mullen and Rice (2003) and Mullen (2004), across 150 years of archival data, ethnophaulism complexity was a better predictor of the exclusion of ethnic immigrant outgroups than ethnophaulism valence. This pattern of results was recently replicated in the controlled experimental examination of the use of ethnophaulisms. Mullen, Leader, and Rice (2004) had participants use ethnophaulisms for an ethnic immigrant outgroup. Increasing the negativity of the ethnophaulisms had no apparent effect, but decreasing the complexity of the ethnophaulisms led to greater subsequent exclusion of the group.

Linguistic Intergroup Bias

A second new direction in research on linguistic factors in prejudice, one not anticipated by Allport in *The Nature of Prejudice*, involves the way that people make different types of attributions for the behaviors of ingroup and outgroup members. This approach is represented by research on the *linguistic intergroup bias* (Maass, Salvi, Arcuri, & Semin, 1989), which involves the tendencies to describe ingroup and outgroup behaviors at different levels of abstractness. Specifically, desirable ingroup and undesirable outgroup behaviors tend to be communicated more abstractly (e.g., "we are helpful," "they are aggressive"), while undesirable ingroup and desirable outgroup behaviors tend to be communicated more concretely (e.g., "we pulled their hair," "they opened the door").

The more abstract statements may imply greater stability over time and greater generalizability across settings. Thus, on the one hand, "we are helpful" conveys a consistent, predictable, positive attribute of the ingroup, and ingroup members could be expected to show related helpful behaviors like sharing resources or providing useful information. On the other hand, "they are aggressive" conveys a consistent, predictable negative attribute of the outgroup, and outgroup members could be expected to show related aggressive behaviors like kicking or hitting. Such dispositional inferences about positive attributes for the ingroup or negative attributes for the outgroup provide a subtle means of enhancing the ingroup and derogating the outgroup (von Hippel, Sekaquaptewa, & Vargas, 1997). The linguistic intergroup bias effect reflects an intriguing approach to the linguistic transmission and maintenance of intergroup hostilities. This effect is reinforced by general tendencies regarding the attribution for positive or negative behavior by an ingroup member or outgroup member: Ingroup members' positive outcomes tend to be attributed to internal, stable causes and their negative outcomes to unstable, external causes, whereas outgroup members' negative outcomes tend to be attributed to internal causes, and their positive outcomes to external causes (Hewstone, 1990).

Has Allport Been Supported?

As we have illustrated in previous sections, Allport's general perspective that antilocutions play important and multiple roles in prejudice has received considerable support. However, many of his ideas have yet to be comprehensively tested. Moreover, recent research has refined many of his ideas, such as identifying how the underlying dimensions of complexity and valence contribute to the effects of ethnophaulisms, and has identified new linguistic factors in prejudice, such that the linguistic intergroup bias. The indirect influence of Allport's work can be seen in the subsequent development of research on additional linguistic factors related to prejudice which derive from, but were not directly anticipated by, Allport's work.

Differences in language, accent, or dialect typically elicit responses associated with prejudice and intergroup hostility. Despite the occasional passing reference (e.g., "Unfamiliar dialects strike us as ludicrous," p. 177), the effects of language differences did not seem to loom large in Allport's thinking. A considerable number of studies have employed the "matched-guise" paradigm (Lambert, Hodgson, Gardner, & Fillenbaum, 1960), in which participants listen to and evaluate verbal material spoken in different languages or accents by a single speaker. The rationale for this paradigm is that it can elicit responses to different languages or accents while holding constant the vocal attributes of the single speaker. The basic tendency to exhibit an ingroup bias of preference for one's ingroup language or accent has been demonstrated repeatedly (e.g., Larimer, 1970; Lambert et al., 1960; Larimer, Beatty, & Broadus, 1988). This linguistic facet of intergroup hostility is obviously of particular importance in bi- or multi-lingual environments (e.g., Canada: Bourhis, 1991; France: Gardner-Chloros, 1985).

Speech accommodation, or language switching, refers to the sometimes subtle and unspoken negotiation by which a language is selected for communication between bilinguals from two ethnolinguistic groups. Often, the selection of the language of one's ingroup, and the corresponding rejection of the language of the outgroup, represents a unique linguistic form of ingroup bias (e.g., Giles, Taylor, & Bourhis, 1973). For example, in the Gaeltacht (Gaelic-speaking) west coast of Ireland where speaking in Gaelic was a criminal offense for generations, a sign common in many inns and taverns reads, "Irish spoken. English understood." Hogg, D'Agata, and Abrams (1989) documented that Italian immigrants to Australia responded negatively to fellow Italian immigrants who engaged in an "ethnolinguistic betrayal" by speaking the dominant (English) language of the host receiving nation. Once again, this linguistic facet of intergroup hostility is obviously of particular importance in bi- or multi-lingual environments.

Directions for Future Research

Several of the propositions derived from Allport's consideration of linguistic factors in prejudice have received empirical confirmation. However, it should be emphasized that most of the research examining the proposition that the use of antilocutions is a reflection of social categorization (e.g., Mullen, 2001; Mullen & Johnson, 1993, 1995; Mullen et al., 2000, 2001) has focused exclusively on the use of ethnophaulisms towards those salient outgroups. It remains for future research to determine whether other forms of antilocution are similarly influenced by outgroup salience. For example, future studies should determine the extent to which the linguistic intergroup bias effect of describing negative outgroup behaviors in more abstract terms (e.g., Maass et al., 1989), or the use of derogatory outgroup jokes (e.g., Fuehr, 1998), are also exacerbated towards target outgroups that are more rare, unfamiliar, or more foreign. Similarly, most of the research examining the effects of antilocutions on targets has focused exclusively on the effects of the use of ethnophaulisms towards those outgroup targets. Future studies might determine whether the linguistic intergroup bias, or the use of derogatory outgroup jokes, also create negative emotional responses or harm the collective self-esteem of targets, and whether they exacerbate hostile prejudice towards and exclusion of outgroup targets.

Psychologists still understand relatively little about the effective rebuttal of antilocutions, on the part of either outgroup targets or ingroup by-standers to those antilocutions. In addition, while the effects of the use of ethnophaulisms on hostile prejudice and on exclusion have received empirical confirmation, the plausible and very serious link between antilocutions and violence is woefully in need of research. Finally, Allport maintained that these various forms of intergroup enmity were arrayed on an escalating scale, where attaining one level predisposed the prejudiced person to move on to the next level of hatred. However, the interrelations between hostile prejudice towards, exclusion of, and violence towards outgroups (especially as such effects occur in the context of antilocution towards outgroups) remain poorly understood.

The effects of ingroup speaker antilocution on hostile prejudice on the part of the ingroup bystander (Greenberg & Pyszczynski, 1985) represent a singular development in the study of linguistic factors in prejudice. How-ever, once again, it should be emphasized that the research examining these effects has focused exclusively on the effects of the use of ethno-phaulisms. It remains for future research to determine whether other forms of antilocution (e.g., derogatory outgroup jokes) exert similar effects on hostile prejudice on the part of ingroup bystanders. Moreover, no research to date has examined the effects of overhearing the use of antilocutions on bystander exclusion of, or violence towards, outgroup targets.

It remains an empirical question as to how much of the aversive effect of antilocution is due to a direct effect (representing Allport's notion of verbal realism) versus how much of the aversive effect of antilocution is due to more indirect effects. In other words, is the primary harm inflicted by hate speech due to the direct hurtful nature of the words, or is the primary harm inflicted by hate speech due to the more indirect effects of hate speech leading to other hurtful social behaviors like exclusion and/or violence?

Future research still needs to determine whether the patterns discovered in the use of ethnophaulisms in hate speech for ethnic immigrants in the US are replicated for other nonimmigrant groups in the US, or for other ethnic minorities in other parts of the world. We need to examine the correspondences between what we know about the use of ethnophaulisms and what we know about the linguistic intergroup bias, the use of derogatory outgroup jokes, or "ethnolinguistic betrayal" in language switching. The relative importance of complexity and valence in ethnophaulisms is an intriguing development in this arena and may be paralleled by analogous asymmetries in the complexity and valence of derogatory outgroup jokes. The general absence of research on verbal realism represents an important direction for future efforts. Finally, we should highlight the importance of the essentially unexplored comparisons between ethnophaulisms as derogatory outgroup names and ethnonyms as complimentary ingroup names.

Additional research might also focus on how the vehicle by which hate is expressed can influence its impact. A development that obviously occurred after Allport's (1954/1979) time is the recent scrutiny of hate speech on the internet (e.g., Glaser & Dixit, 2002; Leets, 2001), or what has come to be called "cyberhate" (Levin, 2002). White racist internet chat rooms and websites (e.g., www.Stormfront.org) include music, graphics, and videogames, which may enhance the extent to which hate groups can appear to be mainstream and thereby recruit young members. Benjamin Smith, who committed the hate-motivated drive-by murders in July of 1999, told documentary filmmaker Beverly Peterson months before his spree, "It wasn't really 'til I got on the Internet, read some literature of these groups that . . . it really all came together" (www.adl.org/internet/ extremism_rw/inspiring.asp). It is too soon to determine whether hate speech on the internet represents a genuinely different, or merely a technologically more advanced, version of traditional linguistic factors of prejudice. It is encouraging to note that groups promoting tolerance (e.g., www.PartnersAgainstHate.org, www.Tolerance.org) are employing the same online technologies employed by hate groups.

In conclusion, the prevalence, and the potential consequences, of the use of antilocutions, ethnonyms, and ethnophaulisms make the empirical study of hate speech one of the most timely and vital topics of social-psychological research. It should be emphasized that a considerable amount of the evidence summarized in this chapter was derived from the use of both archival and experimental research methodologies. On the one hand, the relative contributions of complexity and valence ethnophaulisms, and the impact of ethnophaulisms on exclusion, could only have been discovered by scrutinizing the existing historical record of hate speech. On the other hand, these patterns, once observed, were confirmed and further explored in controlled laboratory experiments. In the present context it is important to note that while Allport was willing to incorporate experimental social-psychological evidence, he was not shy about going outside the laboratory in his effort to understand the nature of prejudice. A reflection on his efforts encourages social psychologists to entertain the value and the legitimacy of occasionally returning to their theoretical and methodological roots. The ideas formulated by Allport have generated a considerable legacy of subsequent empirical research, and these ideas continue to provide a foundation for future efforts in the study of linguistic factors in prejudice.

NOTES

The authors would like to thank Jack Dovidio, Peter Glick, Laurie Rudman, and especially Howie Giles, for helpful comments on earlier drafts of this chapter.

REFERENCES

Allen, I. L. (1983). *The language of ethnic conflict: Social organization and lexical culture.* New York: Columbia University Press.

Allport, G. W. (1954/1979). *The nature of prejudice.* Cambridge, MA: Perseus Books.

Associated Press (1999). Boy tells how friend was killed. Associated Press, April 22.

Associated Press (2003). Vanbiesbrouck quits after using racial slur. Associated Press, March 10.

Bier, J. (1988). The problem of the polish joke in derogatory American

humor. *Humor: International Journal of Humor Research, 1,* 135–41.

Boeckmann, R. J. & Liew, J. (2002). Hate speech: Asian American students' justice judgements and psychological responses. *Journal of Social Issues, 58,* 363–81.

Bourhis, R. Y. (1991). Organizational communication and accommodation: Toward some conceptual and empirical links. In H. Giles & J. Coupland (eds.), *Contexts of accommodation: Developments in applied sociolinguistics* (pp. 270–303). New York: Cambridge University Press.

Bushman, B. J. (2002). Does venting anger feed or extinguish the flame? Catharsis, rumination, distraction, anger, and aggressive responding. *Personality and Social Psychology Bulletin, 28*, 724–31.

Cable Network News (CNN) (1999). Clinton calls shooting spree "a rebuke" of American ideals. Cable Network News (CNN), July 6.

Cardona, G. R. (1989). Noms de peuples et noms de langues. In G. Calame-Griaule (ed.), *Graines de paroles: Puisance du verbe et traditions orales*. Paris: Editions du CNRS.

Citron, A. F., Chein, I., & Harding, J. (1950). Anti-minority remarks: A problem for action research. *Journal of Abnormal and Social Psychology, 45*, 99–126.

Clark, R., Anderson, N. B., Clark, V., & Williams, R. R. (1999). Racism as a stressor for African Americans: A biopsychosocial model. *American Psychologist, 54*, 805–16.

Coombs, R. H., Chopra, S., Schenk, D. R., & Yutan, E. (1993). Medical slang and its functions. *Social Science and Medicine, 36*, 987–98.

Cossrow, N. H. F., Jeffery, R. W., & McGuire, M. T. (2001). Understanding weight stigmatization: A focus group study. *Journal of Nutritional Education, 33*, 208–14.

Fried, M. (1975). *The notion of tribe*. Menlo Park, CA: Cummings.

Fuehr, M. (2001). Some aspects of form and function of humor in adolescence. *Humor: International Journal of Humor Research, 14*, 25–36.

Fuquay, J. (2003). LP&L chief faces profanity complaint weeks after ethnic slur. *Avalanche Journal*, Lubbock, TX, May 16.

Gardner-Chloros, P. (1985). Language selection and switching among Strasbourg shoppers. *International Journal of the Sociology of Language, 54*, 117–35.

Giles, H., Taylor, D. M., & Bourhis, R. (1973). Towards a theory of interpersonal accommodation through language: Some Canadian data. *Language in Society, 2*, 177–92.

Glaser, J. & Dixit, J. (2002). Studying hate crime with the internet: What makes racists advocate racial violence? *Journal of Social Issues, 5*, 177–93.

Graumann, C. F. & Wintermantel, M. (1989). Discriminatory speech acts: A functional approach. In D. Bar-Tal et al. (eds.), *Stereotyping and prejudice: Changing conceptions*. New York: Springer.

Greenberg, J., Kirkland, S. L., & Pyszczynski, T. (1988). Some theoretical notions and preliminary research concerning derogatory ethnic labels. In G. Smitherman-Donaldson & T. A. van Dijk (eds.), *Discourse and discrimination*. Detroit, MI: Wayne State University Press.

Greenberg, J. & Pyszczynski, T. (1985). The effects of an overheard ethnic slur on evaluations of the target: How to spread a social disease. *Journal of Experimental Social Psychology, 21*, 61–72.

Grossman, A. L. & Tucker, J. S. (1997). Gender differences and sexism in the knowledge and use of slang. *Sex Roles, 37*, 101–10.

Guerin, B. (2003). Combating prejudice and racism: New interventions from a functional analysis of racist language. *Journal of Community and Applied Social Psychology, 13*, 29–45.

Hewstone, M. (1990). The "ultimate attribution error"? A review of the literature on intergroup attributions. *European Journal of Social Psychology*, 20, 311–25.

Hogg, M. A., D'Agata, P., & Abrams, D. (1989). Ethnolinguistic betrayal and speaker evaluations among Italian Australians. *Genetic, Social, & General Psychology Monographs*, 115, 153–81.

Jaret, C. (1999). Attitudes of Whites and Blacks towards ethnic humor: A comparison. *Humor: International Journal of Humor Research*, 12, 385–409.

Lambert, W. E., Hodgson, R. C., Gardner, R. C., & Fillenbaum, S. (1960). Evaluational reactions to spoken languages. *Journal of Abnormal and Social Psychology*, 60, 44–51.

Larimer, G. S. (1970). Indirect assessment of intercultural prejudices. *International Journal of Psychology*, 5, 189–95.

Larimer, G. S., Beatty, E. D., & Broadus, A. C. (1988). Indirect assessment of interracial prejudices. *Journal of Black Psychology*, 14, 47–56.

Leets, L. (2001). Response to internet hate sites: Is speech too free in cyberspace? *Communication Law and Policy*, 6, 287–317.

Leets, L. (2002). Experiencing hate speech: Perceptions and responses to anti-Semitism and antigay speech. *Journal of Social Issues*, 58, 341–61.

Leets, L. & Giles, H. (1997). Words as weapons: When do they wound? Investigations of harmful speech. *Human Communication Research*, 24, 260–301.

Levin, B. (2002). Cyberhate: A legal and historical analysis of extremists' use of computer networks in America. *American Behavioral Scientist*, 45, 958–88.

Levin, M. G. & Potapov, L. P. (1964). *The peoples of Siberia*. Chicago: University of Chicago Press.

Leyens, J. P., Rodriguez-Perez, A., Rodriguez-Torres, R., Gaunt, R., Paladino, M. P., Vaes, J., & Demoulin, S. (2001). Psychological essentialism and the differential attribution of uniquely human emotions to in groups and outgroups. *European Journal of Social Psychology*, 31, 395–411.

Loew, C. A. (1967). Acquisition of a hostile attitude and its relation to aggressive behavior. *Journal of Personality and Social Psychology*, 5, 335–41.

Maass, A., Salvi, D., Arcuri, L., & Semin, G. (1989). Language use in intergroup contexts: The linguistic intergroup bias. *Journal of Personality and Social Psychology*, 57, 981–93.

Mackie, D. M., & Smith, E. R. (1998). Intergroup relations: Insights from a theoretically integrative approach. *Psychological Review*, 105, 499–529.

Matsuda, M. J., Lawrence, C. R., Delgado, R., & Crenshaw, K. W. (1993). *Words that wound: Critical race theory, assaultive speech, and the first amendment*. Boulder, CO: Westview.

Mullen, B. (2001). Ethnophaulisms for ethnic immigrant groups. *Journal of Social Issues*, 57, 457–75.

Mullen, B. (2004). Sticks and stones can break my bones, but ethnophaulisms can alter the portrayal of immigrants to children. *Personality and Social Psychology Bulletin*, 30, 250–60.

Mullen, B. & Johnson, C. (1993). Cognitive representation in ethnophaulisms as a function of group size: The phenomenology of being in a group. *Personality and Social Psychology Bulletin*, 19, 296–304.

Mullen, B. & Johnson, C. (1995). Cognitive representation in ethnophaulisms and illusory correlation in stereotyping. *Personality and Social Psychology Bulletin, 21*, 420–33.

Mullen, B., Johnson, C., & Anthony, T. (1994). Relative group size and cognitive representations of ingroup and outgroup: The phenomenology of being in a group. *Small Group Research, 25*, 250–66.

Mullen, B., Leader, T., & Rice, R. R. (2004). An experimental examination of the effects of ethnophaulism complexity on exclusion. Paper to be presented at the annual meeting of the Society of Personality and Social Psychology, Austin, TX.

Mullen, B. & Rice, D. R. (2003). Ethnophaulisms and exclusion: The behavioral consequences of cognitive representation of ethnic immigrant groups. *Personality and Social Psychology Bulletin, 29*, 1056–67.

Mullen, B., Rozell, D., & Johnson, C. (2000). Ethnophaulisms for ethnic immigrant groups: Cognitive representation of "the minority" and "the foreigner." *Group Processes and Intergroup Relations, 3*, 5–24.

Mullen, B., Rozell, D., & Johnson, C. (2001). Ethnophaulisms for ethnic immigrant groups: The contributions of group size and familiarity. *European Journal of Social Psychology, 31*, 231–46.

Nielsen, L. B. (2002). Subtle, pervasive, harmful: Racist and sexist remarks in public as hate speech. *Journal of Social Issues, 58*, 265–80.

Owen, U. (1998). The speech that kills. *Index on Censorship, 27*, 32–9.

Palmore, E. B. (1962). Ethnophaulisms. *American Journal of Sociology, 67*, 442–5.

Pankiw, B. & Bienvenue, R. M. (1990). Parental responses to ethnic name-calling: A sociological inquiry. *Canadian Ethnic Studies, 22*, 78–98.

Phinney, J. S. & Chavira, V. (1995). Parental ethnic socialization and adolescent coping with problems related to ethnicity. *Journal of Research on Adolescence, 5*, 31–53.

Roback, A. A. (1944). *A dictionary of international slurs*. Cambridge: Sci-Art Publishers.

Ruscher, J. B. (2001). *Prejudiced communication: A social psychological perspective*. New York: Guilford.

Scott, J. (1999). From hate rhetoric to hate crime: A link acknowledged too late. *The Humanist, 59*, 8–14.

Simon, L. & Greenberg, J. (1996). Further progress in understanding the effects of derogatory ethnic labels: The role of preexisting attitudes toward the targeted group. *Personality and Social Psychology Bulletin, 22*, 1195–1204.

Von Hippel, W., Sekaquaptewa, D., & Vargas, P. (1997). The linguistic intergroup bias as an implicit indicator of prejudice. *Journal of Experimental Social Psychology, 33*, 490–509.

Chapter Thirteen

Stereotypes in Our Culture
John T. Jost and David L. Hamilton

Allport's *The Nature of Prejudice* is not merely a "classic" well worth re-
membering for its historical significance; the magnitude of its contribution
has increased steadily over time, especially with regard to the structure and
functions of stereotypes. It was in chapter 12, entitled "Stereotypes in Our
Culture," that Allport famously proposed that the "rationalizing and justifying function of a stereotype exceeds its function as a reflector of group
attributes" (1954/1979, p. 196). There were two major themes that Allport
sought to develop and, to some degree, integrate in this chapter: (a) that
categorization is a fundamental process that gives rise to stereotyping and
prejudice; and (b) that the contents of stereotypes are, above all, culturally
shared forms of justification that often turn out to be false. Putting these
two points together, we see that categorization is a necessary but not
sufficient cause of prejudicial attitudes. The cultural context is crucial, for
stereotypes operate in relation to societal and ideological systems. The
overwhelming effect of both categorization and justification processes is
that existing forms of inequality tend to be reinforced and perpetuated
(e.g., Eagly & Steffen, 1984; Hamilton & Trolier, 1986; Jost & Banaji,
1994; Snyder, Tanke, & Berscheid, 1977; Yzerbyt, Rocher, & Schadron,
1997). In this chapter, we critically examine the validity of Allport's claims
concerning societal and cultural factors that shape social categorization and
the contents of stereotypes.

Allport's Views on Categorization Processes in Stereotyping and Prejudice

Among the most unique and compelling features of Allport's analysis is his
emphasis on the fundamental role of categorization as a basic process

underlying intergroup perception. In this respect he was clearly attuned to developments in other areas of psychology that addressed the ways in which concepts are learned, stored in memory, retrieved, and applied (see Fiske, ch. 3 this volume). In "Stereotypes in Our Culture," Allport advanced his ideas concerning the nature of relations between categorization and stereotyping in pivotal fashion; the significance of these ideas is confirmed in several areas of contemporary research, as we illustrate below.

Although he stressed categorization processes, Allport insisted that "a stereotype is not identical with a category; it is rather a fixed idea that accompanies the category" (1954/1979, p. 191). A stereotype is a belief system in which psychological characteristics are ascribed more or less indiscriminately to the members of a group. According to Allport, it "acts both as a justificatory device for categorical acceptance or rejection of a group, and as a screening or selective device to maintain simplicity in perception and in thinking" (p. 192). In this way, the categorization (or simplification) and justification functions are compatible and mutually reinforcing. "The fault," as Allport pointed out, lies "not in any malicious intent" but in "culture-bound traditions" (p. 202). This is because people use stereotypes both to maximize cognitive efficiency and to explain and justify cultural and institutional forms of prejudice in which members of some groups are accepted while others are rejected (Jost & Banaji, 1994).

In the next section, we review developments in the study of categorization and stereotyping since Allport. This work builds on the notion that people form social categories on the basis of similarity and related cues but also go further to develop intuitive theories and explanations about how and why members of a social category belong together. These explanations often take tautological, essentialistic forms. Anti-Semitism, for example, invariably "finds its rationalization in some presumed aspect of 'Jewish essence'" (Allport, 1954/1979, p. 195). The same perceiver may criticize Jews (or Asians, or whomever) at one convenient moment for being inherently "clannish" and at other times for intrusively forcing themselves upon others. The categorization function explains why stereotypes are undifferentiated and overgeneralized; the justification function explains why they are so often illogical and contrary to fact.

Developments Since Allport's Work

Much of the work on cognitive processes underlying the development of stereotypes and prejudice since the publication of *The Nature of Prejudice* has focused on the perceptions of people as members of social categories. The central idea is that stereotypes are belief structures that influence the processing of information about stereotyped groups and their members. What this means is that expectations formed on the basis of early experience tend to guide subsequent perceptions. As Allport pointed out, "A stereotype is sustained by selective perception and selective forgetting" (1954/ 1979, p. 196). These mechanisms explain how even false stereotypes can be perpetuated over time.

The impact of stereotypes on social cognition is probably even more profound than Allport knew. The last two decades of research have demonstrated that stereotypes: (a) direct attention to certain aspects of the available information, (b) color the interpretation of that information, (c) influence the way in which the information is retained in memory, (d) shape judgments and subsequent actions, (e) serve as hypotheses that are tested and disproportionately favored in the interpretation of new information, and (f) play an important role in eliciting from target persons the very same behavior that confirms the perceiver's biased expectations (for reviews, see Fiske, 1998; Hamilton & Sherman, 1994; Macrae & Bodenhausen, 2000). The overwhelming effect of stereotypes, therefore, is to perpetuate prior beliefs and prejudices; the *status quo* is bolstered through information processors' reliance upon stereotypes as a convenient way of organizing information about the social world.

Whereas other chapters in this book focus on the consequences of stereotypes, we explore the origins and contents of stereotypes in the remainder of this chapter. In particular, we demonstrate that stereotyping has its origins in social categorization, but the specific contents of stereotypes and their prejudicial flavor are best accounted for in terms of social and cultural functions that these attitudes serve. In this section and the next, we first consider social categorization processes and then examine societal forces – including demands for system justification – that partially determine stereotype contents.

The Perception of Group Entitativity

Recent developments in understanding social categorization processes have focused on how individuals become recognized as a group or entity in the first place, how the process of categorization (as an entity or as a group) affects perceptions, how people infer the essential characteristics of group membership, and how they use these characteristics as intuitive explanations.

A few years after *The Nature of Prejudice* was published, Donald Campbell (1958) grappled with the issue of how people perceive groups as coherent entities. He suggested that perceptions of entitativity could be based on cues such as proximity and similarity as well as conceptual cues such as cohesiveness and interdependence. The fundamental issue of how the "groupness" of a group is perceived – after lying dormant for an extended period – has become the focus of a great deal of research in the last decade (for reviews, see Hamilton, Sherman, & Castelli, 2002; Yzerbyt, Corneille, & Estrada, 2001).

This recent work has established evidence for several important points: (a) groups vary considerably in the extent to which they are perceived as possessing entitativity (Lickel et al., 2000); (b) a variety of cues – for example, extent of interaction among group members, member similarity, importance of the group to members, shared goals – can and do serve as the basis for perceiving the "groupness" of groups (Castano, Yzerbyt, & Bourguignon, 2003; Lickel et al., 2000); (c) perceivers spontaneously recognize qualitatively different types of groups (e.g., groups based on friendship, task groups, social categories), and these group types differ in the extent to which they possess entitativity (Sherman, Castelli, & Hamilton, 2002); (d) the extent to which a group is perceived as being entitative has important implications for the generalization of qualities across individual group members and the perceived interchangeability of group members (Crawford, Sherman, & Hamilton, 2002); and (e) perceived group entitativity plays a central and mediating role in the stereotyping of groups (Hamilton, Sherman, & Rodgers, 2004).

From Perception to Explanation

Following Lippmann's (1922) influential analysis, Allport observed that the members of a group, once categorized, are assumed to be similar to one another. The accentuation of within-category similarity ("They're all alike") and between-category differences ("They're different from other folks") is now a well-documented effect (e.g., Judd & Park, ch. 8 this volume).

Theories of categorization differ in how "grouping" is cognitively achieved. Some accounts posit that categories, both social and nonsocial, are mentally represented by a single prototype, that is, a generalized mental representation of the ideal member of a category. Each individual is then compared to the prototype, and if the "family resemblance" is adequate, the individual is categorized as a member of that group (Rosch, 1978). Other perspectives downplay the necessity of forming an abstract, generalized prototype and instead emphasize the role of exemplars in categorization. On this view, perceptions of individual cases are compared to other instances retrieved from memory, and the individual is categorized into a group on the basis of whether it fits the retrieved exemplars (e.g., Smith & Zárate, 1992). In both types of theories, similarity is the driving principle on which social categorizations are based.

Although similarity is without question an important feature on which the categorization process relies, more recent work has shown that similarity alone is not sufficient for fully understanding the categorization process. In other words, a category consists of more than a simple listing of the features that are shared by category members. The category must also provide some intuitive theory, some rationale, some *explanation* as to why these category members belong to the same category, that is, some causal means for understanding how and why these features are related to each other (Murphy & Medin, 1985).

For example, social stereotypes often ascribe a wide array of attributes to the members of some target group, even when these specific attributes would not normally be classified together on the basis of semantic meaning, frequency of co-occurrence, or even shared valence. Historically, African Americans were said to be lazy, religious, unintelligent, and musical (e.g., Katz & Braly, 1933). These attributes do not normally "go together," either in people's actual behavioral patterns or in their implicit personality theories. As a cluster of beliefs, they would have no meaning for the stereotype holder if it were not for an intuitive theory that ties them together (e.g., Kunda, Miller, & Claire, 1990).

How people respond to the members of a particular group is determined in part by the intuitive theory that the person holds. For instance, people who subscribe to the intuitive theory that Blacks lack the ability and/or motivation to achieve (a view often associated with political conservatism) and those who believe that discrimination limits Blacks' economic progress (a view associated with liberalism) process and interpret information about Blacks in fundamentally different ways (Wittenbrink, Gist, & Hilton, 1997). Thus, some stereotypes go beyond the mere description of groups in terms of commonly associated traits to explain the origins of those traits in such a way that the group's social position is seen as justified or unjustified.

From Explanation to Essentialism

Another development in categorization theory has been to identify different types of categories and to distinguish among various consequences of these different types. Researchers have, for example, differentiated natural kinds from artifactual categories. Natural kinds are categories of objects whose existence is somehow defined by nature; the members all share some category-defining feature(s). Robins are robins because of their natural make-up, their genetic structure, their physical being. In contrast, artifactual categories consist of objects created by humans, typically to perform some function or meet some need. Cars, for example, were invented to enable people to move about, to meet their transportation needs. As a result, people do not tend to have the same kinds of theories about automobiles that they do about biological and racial groups.

If people believe that a category is a natural kind, then two important principles follow. First, a natural category affords inductive potential; that is, one can infer a lot about members of the category because such things are true of all members. When people see a robin sitting on a branch, they can assume certain things about it (e.g., it can fly, eats worms, chirps, etc.). Such inductive potential is greater for natural kinds than for artifactual categories. Second, membership in a natural kind is unalterable. A robin is a robin, and no amount of blue spray-paint will transform it into a blue-bird. In contrast, the fundamental "nature" of an artifactual category object can be changed, for the simple reason that it has no underlying essence (apart from its function).

Although most social groups (including racial groups) are, in reality, artifactual categories rather than natural kinds, people often perceive groups as natural kinds and therefore endow their members with some kind of essence (Rothbart & Taylor, 1992). Thus, historically, people have talked about the "Jewishness" of Jews and have applied the "single drop of blood" criterion for race; in these cases, ethnic group differences "are regarded as innate, indelible, and unchangeable" (Frederickson, 2002, p. 5). Once a group is perceived as a natural kind – as having some unalterable inner essence – then it affords greater confidence in drawing inferences (inductive potential) about its members. As a result, perceivers make sweeping gener-alizations (of the kind Allport stressed) about all group members, who are seen as being very similar to one another, especially on attributes related to the "essential" basis for category membership (see also Haslam, Rothschild, & Ernst, 2002; Yzerbyt, Rocher, & Schadron, 1997). Perceptions of social groups as natural categories significantly shape the operation and content of stereotypes through the development of "intuitive theories."

Our review of the categorization process has highlighted the ways in which stereotypes function as categories that provide intuitive theories that, while aiding in understanding and navigating the complexities of intergroup life, bias the interpretation and use of information. In some cases, the stereotyped group is ascribed an inner essence that conveys something about group members' basic nature. The group's essence is seen as relatively immutable and as providing an explanation for why groups differ in terms of resources and opportunities. This observation moves us closer to more fully appreciating Allport's remark that, "the rationalizing and justifying function of a stereotype exceeds its function as a reflector of group attributes" (1954/1979, p. 196). This is because, as Yzerbyt et al. (1997) note, "rationalization is best served by an essentialistic approach to social categories" (p. 39). More specifically, essentialism has a strong capacity to contribute to "system-justification" processes, which in turn mold the specific contents of stereotypes (Jost & Banaji, 1994).

A New Framework: System Justification Processes and Stereotype Content

To understand where the specific *contents* of stereotypes come from, a social, cultural analysis is needed to supplement our cognitive analysis of categorization. Hamilton and Gifford (1976) confirmed Allport's claim that "It is possible for a stereotype to grow in defiance of all evidence" (1954/1979, p. 189). They demonstrated that people could develop false stereotypes through a process of "illusory correlation" (by mistakenly forming a mental association between two or more relatively infrequent events) without there being even a "kernel" of truth. These cognitive biases are shaped and exacerbated by actual inequalities of opportunity in society (which prevent group memberships and achieved outcomes from varying freely) as well as by selective reporting in the mass media (e.g., Iyengar & Kinder, 1987). Members of US society, for example, are disproportionately exposed to associations between "Black" and "criminal" and between "White man" and "politician" or "celebrity" (Banaji & Bhaskar, 2000). As Allport observed, stereotypes are "socially supported, continually revived and hammered in, by our media of mass communication" (p. 200). In addition, there is a tendency for people, both media representatives and their audiences, to spontaneously explain and justify social and economic inequality in such a way that the legitimacy of the existing social system is seldom – if ever – called into question (e.g., Jost, Banaji, & Nosek, 2004).

Three Types of Justification

Theoretical and empirical advances in social psychology sustain Allport's contention that a stereotype acts as a "justificatory device" (1954/1979,

p. 192), probably in many more ways than Allport himself could have anticipated. He focused almost exclusively on perceivers' use of stereotypes to justify liking or disliking of outgroup members, that is, the justification of "love-prejudice" or "hate-prejudice" (p. 189). In seeking to understand the origins of these intense evaluative responses, Allport's analysis drew heavily on the psychoanalytic assumptions of the day, including Bettelheim and Janowitz's (1950, p. 42) speculation that "ethnic hostility is a projection of unacceptable inner strivings onto a minority group" (quoted with evident approval by Allport, p. 199).

Jost and Banaji (1994) proposed that there are three major ways in which stereotypes serve as "justificatory devices," namely as forms of ego-justification, group-justification, and system-justification. Only the first of these functions (ego-justification) had received any real attention from psychologists of Allport's generation, and insights concerning the second function (group-justification) coalesced later (e.g., Tajfel, 1981). Skeletal versions of the third function (system-justification) are discernible in Allport's (1954/1979) discussions of the "exploitation theory of prejudice" on pp. 209–11 and of "structural views" on pp. 504–6, but it seems that he could not quite integrate a sociological perspective on the American class system with his psychological analysis of rationalization.

Work on the ego-justification function suggests that people engage in stereotyping and prejudice at least in part because it allows them to feel better about themselves by derogating others. This view originated in psychoanalytic theories of the kind Allport favored, including the notion that stereotypes "serve as projection screens for our personal conflict" (1954/1979, p. 200). The more general idea that stereotypes rationalize the individual's own interests, actions, and psychological needs is also consistent with more recent theories of self-esteem maintenance. Experimental studies demonstrate, for example, that threats to one's self-esteem stimulate enhanced levels of stereotyping and discrimination (Fein & Spencer, 1997; Oakes & Turner, 1980).

Tajfel (1981) elaborated a group-based version of Allport's (1954/1979) argument that a stereotype's "function is to justify (rationalize) our conduct in relation to that category" (p. 191). Specifically, Tajfel proposed that stereotypes justify "actions, committed or planned, against outgroups" (p. 156). Stereotypes, on this view, serve group-justifying ends. They are used to rationalize discrimination against outgroup members, enhance positive group distinctiveness, and allow people to feel good about themselves and their fellow group members through intergroup social comparison processes.

In addition to serving ego-justifying and group-justifying functions, Jost and Banaji (1994) noted that stereotypes fulfill the *system-justifying* function of rationalizing the status quo. According to this view, stereotypes arise not merely in order to justify "love-prejudice" or "hate-prejudice" but also to provide legitimacy for institutional forms such as slavery, segregation, apartheid, the caste system, capitalism, patriarchy, heterosexual marriage, etc. The system-justification view is consistent with historical evidence indicating that full-fledged prejudicial ideologies tend to come *after*, not before, institutionalized forms of tyranny and exploitation. For example, anti-Semitism as a racial ideology first arose in the eleventh century to justify the Medieval Crusades, and virulent forms of anti-Black prejudice were not developed until the fifteenth century to justify the European enslavement of Africans (Frederickson, 2002). System-justifying forms of stereotyping and prejudice render cultural practices and institutions legitimate, rational, and sometimes even necessary and noble.

Several consequences follow from taking system-justification seriously as a social-psychological phenomenon. First, to the extent that members of disadvantaged as well as advantaged groups possess at least some needs for system justification, they should internalize a sense of inferiority and experience considerable ambivalence concerning their own group membership. Second, specific stereotype contents should emerge to rationalize particular divisions of labor and unequal distributions of social roles. Third, complementary stereotypes – stereotypes of both disadvantaged and advantaged groups that have both favorable and unfavorable content – should be fairly common, insofar as these lend legitimacy to the system as a whole. Fourth, essentialist forms of stereotyping should be especially effective at satisfying system-justification needs, insofar as they render intergroup differences not only substantial and real but also natural and necessary.

Internalization of Inequality and Attitudinal Ambivalence

The most provocative aspect of Jost and Banaji's (1994) theory was that members of disadvantaged groups would themselves engage in system justification (at least under some circumstances), even at the expense of personal or collective interests and esteem. Members of disadvantaged groups should therefore internalize attitudes about themselves and each other that are more similar than dissimilar to the attitudes held by members of advantaged groups. As Allport put it, "so heavy is the prevailing cultural pressure that members of minority groups sometimes look at themselves through the same lens as other groups" (1954/1979, p. 198). Indeed, this does seem to be the case; stereotypical attitudes evince a remarkable degree of consensus across perceiver groups. It is extremely common for members of disadvantaged groups to hold favorable attitudes toward more advantaged outgroup members and unfavorable attitudes toward ingroup members, especially (but not solely) on dimensions that explain and justify the success of the former and the relative failure of the latter.

Allport's insight concerning the role of societal and cultural pressures helps to explain the prevalence of "self-hatred" and outgroup favoritism among members of low-status groups (e.g., Jost & Banaji, 1994; Jost, Banaji, & Nosek, 2004; Lewin, 1948; Sidanius & Pratto, 1999). Experimental and field studies have demonstrated that members of disadvantaged groups often hold ambivalent, conflicted attitudes about their own group memberships and surprisingly favorable attitudes toward members of more advantaged groups (e.g., Jost & Burgess, 2000; Jost, Pelham, & Carvallo, 2002). For instance, Sniderman and Piazza (1993) found in a large, nationally representative sample that African American respondents generally accepted unfavorable stereotypes of their own group as lazy, irresponsible, and violent. In fact, they endorsed these stereotypes even more strongly than European American respondents did. Jost et al. (2004) found that 37.5 percent of gay and lesbian respondents held implicit attitudes that were more favorable toward heterosexuals than homosexuals, and 39.3 percent of African Americans held implicit attitudes that were more favorable toward the European American outgroup than the African American ingroup.

Allport observed that Blacks (and other groups) "have heard so frequently that they are lazy, ignorant, dirty, and superstitious that they may half believe the accusations, and since the traits are commonly despised in our western culture – which, of course, Negroes share – some degree of in-group hate seems almost inevitable" (1954/1979, p. 148). To the extent that members of disadvantaged groups face a conflict between opposing needs for group and system justification, Jost and Burgess (2000) hypothesized that members of disadvantaged groups would exhibit stronger ingroup ambivalence than would members of advantaged groups. They also predicted that for members of disadvantaged groups ambivalence toward the ingroup would increase as system-justification tendencies increased (measured in terms of perceived legitimacy of the *status quo* and scores on the Belief in a Just World and Social Dominance Orientation scales; see aslo Duckitt, ch. 24 this volume). For members of advantaged groups, it was expected that ingroup ambivalence would decrease as system-justification tendencies increased. These hypotheses were supported in two studies. Work on the internalization of inequality and attitudinal ambivalence supports Allport's observation that in at least some cases, "the victim instead of pretending to agree with his 'betters' actually *does* agree with them, and sees his own group through their eyes" (p. 150).

Stereotyping and the Rationalization of Social Roles

That consensual stereotypes not only describe but also justify and rationalize existing hierarchical structures in society has been established experimentally over the past two decades. Eagly and Steffen (1984), for example,
demonstrated that observers inferred "communal" characteristics from feminine roles (e.g., homemaker) and "agentic" characteristics from masculine
roles (e.g., employee; see also Eagly & Diekman, ch. 2 this volume).
Hoffman and Hurst (1990) used an experimental paradigm in which participants made trait ratings of fictional groups described as "child raisers"
and "city workers." They found that perceivers spontaneously stereotyped
the group of child raisers as more patient, kind, and understanding than
the city workers, and they stereotyped the group of city workers as more
self-confident and forceful than the child raisers – especially when perceivers
were first asked to explain _why_ the groups occupied different roles.

Conway, Pizzamiglio, and Mount (1996) demonstrated in a variety of
occupational and non-occupational settings that members of low-status
groups in general were consistently stereotyped in more communal, socioemotional terms, whereas members of high-status groups were stereotyped
in agentic, achievement-oriented terms. Jost and Kay (2005) found that
exposure to communal stereotypes of women and agentic stereotypes of
men leads people to show increased levels of support for the current state
of gender relations as well as for the American political and economic
system in general. These studies are among the first to demonstrate that
a cause-and-effect relationship exists between exposure to specific stereotypical beliefs and support for the societal status quo (see also Kay & Jost,
2003). This work also suggests that the link between stereotypes and the
status quo can be largely implicit, nonconscious, and unexamined (see also
Jost et al., 2004).

Complementary Stereotypes

Gender stereotypes are not unique in ascribing different but complementary characteristics to members of high-status and low-status groups (e.g.,
agentic and communal traits, respectively). This leads us to yet another
important observation made by Allport, who wrote that: "Stereotypes are
by no means always negative. They may exist together with a favorable
attitude" (1954/1979, p. 191). We know from recent work that attitudes
toward members of lower-status groups (like women) can be highly

favorable and at the same time contribute to ideological support for the system (see Glick & Fiske, 2001; also chapters by Eagly & Diekman, Jackman, and Rudman, chs. 2, 6, and 7 this volume). The system justification function may explain other seemingly anomalous stereotypes identified by Allport, including the belief that African Americans are "more cheerful and more humorous" than members of other groups (1954/1979, p. 198). Kay and Jost (2003) suggested that "poor but happy" and "poor but honest" stereotypes would serve to increase support for the status quo, insofar as such stereotypes maintain the belief that every group in society has some rewards, and no group has a monopoly on valued characteristics. The authors demonstrated in four experiments that exposure to "poor but happy," "poor but honest," "rich but miserable," and "rich but dishonest" stereotype exemplars led people to score higher on a general, diffuse measure of system justification, compared to control conditions.

The System-Justifying Function of Essentialism

Allport (1954/1979) pointed out that stereotypes concerning the "essence" of racial, ethnic, and religious groups are particularly nefarious and that it is difficult to disabuse people of them (pp. 169, 191; see also Frederickson, 2002). Drawing on the research of cognitive and social psychologists, we have noted that essentialism often follows from acts of categorization and explanation (e.g., Murphy & Medin, 1985; Rothbart & Taylor, 1992) and that it contributes to system justification processes (e.g., Yzerbyt et al., 1997). Once an explanation exists for why certain groups occupy various social positions, the explanation becomes a justification for keeping people "in their place." If members of certain groups are *inherently* agentic, communal, etc., then their current position is not only well-explained but also natural and unlikely ever to change. The *status quo* begins to acquire a strong sense of legitimacy and even inevitability.

Mahalingam (2003) examined essentialism in the context of the caste system in India and found that Brahmins endorsed a selective form of essentialism that justified their group's position of privilege in the system. Research by Haslam, Rothschild, and Ernst (2002) indicated that American participants endorsed (to varying degrees) two general classes of essentialist beliefs, namely *natural kind* beliefs (naturalness, discreteness, immutability, historical stability, and necessary features) and *entitativity* beliefs (uniformity, informativeness, and inherence), and that at least some of these beliefs were correlated with anti-Black and antigay prejudice. Keller (2004) obtained stronger and more consistent support in Germany for the hypotheses that endorsement of essentialist beliefs (operationalized in terms of belief in genetic determinism) would be associated with (a) increased stereotyping and prejudice, especially with regard to gender and race, and (b) increased endorsement of system-justifying ideologies, such as the Protestant Work Ethic, Social Dominance Orientation, patriotism, and nationalism. Taken as a whole, these recent findings suggest that while essentialism varies according to specific cultural contexts in the US, Germany, and India, it does seem to contribute to system justification processes in general.

Have Allport's Views Been Supported?

A careful rereading of Allport's chapter on "Stereotypes in Our Culture" leads one to admire not only his intellectual prescience in anticipating the trajectories of empirical research programs for several decades but also his uncanny ability to meaningfully link societal and cultural levels of analysis to a psychological investigation of the thoughts, feelings, and behaviors of individuals and groups. This is perhaps the most important achievement of *The Nature of Prejudice*, although it is underappreciated. At the same time, Allport did not integrate his ideas concerning rationalization, the internalization of inferiority, prejudice as an ideology, and the deleterious consequences of inequality in society into a comprehensive theoretical framework. In short, he did not recognize that system justification (in addition to ego justification and group justification) is an important motive for individuals. In retrospect, we can say that Allport's analysis of the justification function of stereotyping was incomplete at best and naive – from a political, institutional perspective – at worst (see also Jackman, ch. 6 this volume). Stereotypes are used – implicitly and explicitly – to justify much more than "love-prejudice" and "hate-prejudice." They imbue existing forms of social arrangements with meaning and legitimacy; they preserve and bolster the status quo. It took several decades of experimental and field research to elucidate the connection between social structure and stereotype contents, and there is still more to be done.

Future Directions

Because today's researchers possess a fuller appreciation of the ways in which stereotyping and prejudice emanate from individual and collective needs to rationalize social and cultural institutions, the opportunities to cross levels of analysis are greater than ever before. From basic cognitive and perceptual processes that underlie social categorization to broad-based ideologies that grip entire nations of people, we need to better understand the interplay of evolutionary, cultural, and historical mechanisms and constraints. Social psychology is well-poised to play a broker role in integrating and reconciling different disciplinary perspectives on the causes and consequences of group-based discrimination. To do so effectively, it will have to go well beyond the two major dimensions of intergroup attitudes (agency vs. communion or, what is nearly the same, competence vs. warmth) that have been investigated almost exclusively in systematic research on the contents of stereotype. The insight that prejudice and other ideological forms operate nonconsciously will be a hallmark of a new approach that recognizes the centrality of system justification in social and political life (e.g., Jost et al., 2004).

It follows from a cultural, systemic approach to the study of stereotyping that substantive change in the contents of intergroup attitudes – if it is to come at all – requires qualitative social change. Prejudice may be, among other things, a problem of the individual, but it is also a problem that is "stitched into the fabric of social living" (Allport, 1954/1979, p. 506). Any effective attempt to ameliorate prejudice must take into account its unmistakably societal origins and lead ultimately to an unraveling of the familiar justifications, both petty and grand, that provide cover for any cultural system that relies, either directly or indirectly, on inequality and exploitation.

REFERENCES

Allport, G. W. (1954/1979). *The nature of prejudice*. Cambridge, MA: Perseus Books.

Banaji, M. R. & Bhaskar, R. (2000). Implicit stereotypes and memory: The bounded rationality of social beliefs. In D. L. Schacter & E. Scarry (eds.), *Memory, brain, and belief* (pp. 139–175). Cambridge, MA: Harvard University Press.

Bettelheim, B. & Janowitz, M. (1950). *Dynamics of prejudice: A sociological study of veterans*. New York: Harper and Brothers.

Campbell, D. T. (1958). Common fate, similarity, and other indices of the status of aggregates of persons as social entities. *Behavioral Science, 3*, 14–25.

Castano, E., Yzerbyt, V., & Bourguignon, D. (2003). We are one and I like it: The impact of ingroup entitativity on ingroup identification. *European Journal of Social Psychology, 33*, 735–54.

Conway, M., Pizzamiglio, M. T., & Mount, L. (1996). Status, communality, and agency: Implications for stereotypes of gender and other groups. *Journal of Personality and Social Psychology, 71,* 25–38.

Crawford, M. T., Sherman, S. J., & Hamilton, D. L. (2002). Perceived entitativity, stereotype formation, and the interchangeability of group members. *Journal of Personality and Social Psychology, 83,* 1076–94.

Eagly, A. & Steffen, V. J. (1984). Gender stereotypes stem from the distribution of women and men into social roles. *Journal of Personality and Social Psychology, 46,* 735–54.

Fein, S. & Spencer, J. (1997). Prejudice as self-image maintenance: Affirming the self through derogating others. *Journal of Personality and Social Psychology, 73,* 31–44.

Fiske, S. T. (1998). Stereotyping, prejudice, and discrimination. In S. T. Fiske, D. T. Gilbert, & G. Lindsey (eds.), *The handbook of social psychology* (vol. 2, pp. 357–411). New York: McGraw-Hill.

Frederickson, G. M. (2002). *Racism: A short history.* Princeton, NJ: Princeton University Press.

Glick, P. & Fiske, S. T. (2001). An ambivalent alliance: Hostile and benevolent sexism as complementary justifications for gender inequality. *American Psychologist, 56,* 109–18.

Hamilton, D. L. & Gifford, R. K. (1976). Illusory correlation in interpersonal perception: A cognitive basis of stereotypic judgments. *Journal of Experimental Social Psychology, 12,* 392–407.

Hamilton, D. L. & Sherman, J. W. (1994). Stereotypes. In R. S. Wyer, Jr., & T. K. Srull (eds.), *Handbook of social cognition* (2nd ed., vol. 2, pp. 1–68). Hillsdale, NJ: Lawrence Erlbaum.

Hamilton, D. L., Sherman, S. J., & Castelli, L. (2002). A group by any other name – The role of entitativity in group perception. *European Review of Social Psychology, 12,* 139–66.

Hamilton, D. L., Sherman, S. J., & Rodgers, J. (2004). Perceiving the groupness of groups: Entitativity, homogeneity, essentialism, and stereotypes. In V. Yzerbyt, C. M. Judd, & O. Corneille (eds.), *The psychology of group perception: Contributions to the study of homogeneity, entitativity and essentialism* (pp. 39–60). Philadelphia, PA: Psychology Press.

Hamilton, D. L. & Trolier, T. K. (1986). Stereotypes and stereotyping: An overview of the cognitive approach. In J. F. Dovidio & S. L. Gaertner (eds.), *Prejudice, discrimination, and racism.* New York: Academic Press.

Haslam, N., Rothschild, L., & Ernst, D. (2002). Are essentialist beliefs associated with prejudice? *British Journal of Social Psychology, 41,* 87–100.

Hoffman, C. & Hurst, N. (1990). Gender stereotypes: Perception or rationalization? *Journal of Personality and Social Psychology, 58,* 197–208.

Iyengar, S. & Kinder, D. (1987). *News that matters: Television and American opinion.* Chicago: University of Chicago Press.

Jackman, M. R. (1994). *The velvet glove: Paternalism and conflict in gender, class, and race relations.* Berkeley, CA: University of California Press.

Jost, J. T. & Banaji, M. R. (1994). The role of stereotyping in system-justification and the production of false consciousness. *British Journal of Social Psychology, 33,* 1–27.

Jost, J. T., Banaji, M. R., & Nosek, B. A. (2004). A decade of system justification theory: Accumulated evidence of conscious and unconscious bolstering of the status quo. *Political Psychology, 25,* 881–919.

Jost, J. T. & Burgess, D. (2000). Attitudinal ambivalence and the conflict between group and system justification motives in low status groups. *Personality and Social Psychology Bulletin, 26,* 293–305.

Jost, J. T. & Kay, A. C. (2005). Exposure to benevolent sexism and complementary gender stereotypes: Consequences for specific and diffuse forms of system justification. *Journal of Personality and Social Psychology,* in press.

Jost, J. T., Pelham, B. W., & Carvallo, M. (2002). Non-conscious forms of system justification: Cognitive, affective, and behavioral preferences for higher status groups. *Journal of Experimental Social Psychology, 38,* 586–602.

Katz, D. & Braly, K. (1933). Racial stereotypes of one hundred college students. *Journal of Abnormal and Social Psychology, 28,* 280–90.

Kay, A. C. & Jost, J. T. (2003). Complementary justice: Effects of "poor but happy" and "poor but honest" stereotype exemplars on system justification and implicit activation of the justice motive. *Journal of Personality and Social Psychology, 85,* 823–37.

Keller, J. (2004). In genes we trust: The biological component of psychological essentialism and its relationship to processes of system justification. MS under review, University of Mannheim.

Kunda, Z., Miller, D. T., & Claire, T. (1990). Combining social concepts: The role of social reasoning. *Cognitive Science, 14,* 551–77.

Lewin, K. (1948). Self-hatred among Jews. In *Resolving social conflicts* (pp.

186–200). New York: Harper & Brothers. (First published 1941.)

Lickel, B., Hamilton, D. L., Wieczorkowska, G., Lewis, A., Sherman, S. J., & Uhles, A. N. (2000). Varieties of groups and the perception of group entitativity. *Journal of Personality and Social Psychology, 78,* 223–46.

Lippmann, W. (1922). *Public opinion.* New York: Harcourt, Brace, Jovanovitch.

Macrae, C. N. & Bodenhausen, G. V. (2000). Social cognition: Thinking categorically about others. *Annual Review of Psychology, 51,* 93–120.

Mahalingam, R. (2003). Essentialism, culture, and power: Representations of social class. *Journal of Social Issues, 59,* 733–49.

Murphy, G. L. & Medin, D. L. (1985). The role of theories in conceptual coherence. *Psychological Review, 92,* 289–316.

Oakes, P. J. & Turner, J. C. (1980). Social categorization and intergroup behavior: Does minimal intergroup discrimination make social identity more positive? *European Journal of Social Psychology, 10,* 295–301.

Rosch, E. (1978). Principles of categorization. In E. Rosch & B. B. Lloyd (eds.), *Cognition and categorization.* Hillsdale, NJ: Lawrence Erlbaum.

Rothbart, M. & Taylor, M. (1992). Category labels and social reality: Do we view social categories as natural kinds? In G. R. Semin & K. Fiedler (eds.), *Language, interaction and social cognition.* Thousand Oaks, CA: Sage.

Sherman, S. J., Castelli, L., & Hamilton, D. L. (2002). The spontaneous use of a group typology as an organizing principle in memory. *Journal of Personality and Social Psychology, 82,* 328–42.

Sidanius, J. & Pratto, F. (1999). *Social dominance: An intergroup theory of social hierarchy and oppression.* New York: Cambridge University Press.

Smith, E. R. & Zárate, M. A. (1992). Exemplar-based model of social judgment. *Psychological Review, 99,* 3–21.

Sniderman, P. M. & Piazza, T. (1993). *The scar of race.* Cambridge, MA: Belknap Press.

Snyder, M., Tanke, E. D., & Berscheid, E. (1977). Social perception and interpersonal behavior: On the self-fulfilling nature of social stereotypes. *Journal of Personality and Social Psychology, 35,* 656–66.

Tajfel, H. (1981). *Human groups and social categories.* Cambridge: Cambridge University Press.

Wittenbrink, B., Gist, P. L., & Hilton, J. L. (1997). Structural properties of stereotypic knowledge and their influences on the construal of social situations. *Journal of Personality and Social Psychology, 72,* 526–43.

Yzerbyt, V., Corneille, O., & Estrada, C. (2001). The interplay of subjective essentialism and entitativity in the formation of stereotypes. *Personality and Social Psychology Review, 5,* 141–55.

Yzerbyt, V., Rocher, S., & Schadron, G. (1997). Stereotypes as explanations: A subjective essentialistic view of group perception. In R. Spears & P. J. Oakes (eds.), *The social psychology of stereotyping and group life* (pp. 20–50). Oxford, UK: Blackwell.

SOCIOCULTURAL FACTORS

Chapter Fourteen

Instrumental Relations Among Groups: Group Competition, Conflict, and Prejudice

Victoria M. Esses, Lynne M. Jackson, John F. Dovidio, and Gordon Hodson

The nature of relations between groups has a profound effect on intergroup attitudes and behavior. As Allport (1954/1979) observed, competitive relations lead to prejudice and discrimination, whereas cooperative relations promote integration and reduced prejudice (see also Pettigrew & Tropp, and Kenworthy, Turner, Hewstone, & Voci, chs. 16 and 17 this volume). In chapter 14 of *The Nature of Prejudice*, "Social Structure and Cultural Pattern," Allport focused on when and how conflicts of interest between groups create, sustain, and magnify prejudice. Following from this work, in this chapter, we provide an overview of the theorizing and research on group conflict and competition from the time that *The Nature of Prejudice* was first published, propose a unified model that places these perspectives within one framework, and consider promising directions for future research.

Allport's Perspective on Instrumental Intergroup Relations

In a world of limited resources, conflicts of interest between groups, as well as between individuals, may be inevitable. Allport suggested that in heterogeneous societies in which group distinctions are noticeable, there is a tendency for people to link their individual material and identity needs to the interests of their group. Consequently, when collective social mobility is possible, people are especially attuned to actual or potential changes in the status of their own and other groups. These concerns for group status produce competition between groups for material resources and for value dominance. According to Allport, this competition exacerbates prejudice between groups.

Allport observed that it is often difficult to disentangle genuine conflicts of interest between groups from prejudice, in part because they often operate in concert. Once initiated, Allport suggested, genuine conflicts of interest tend to take on "excess baggage" in the form of prejudice, so that the conflict is magnified. Nevertheless, Allport (1954/1979) further argued that it is important, both conceptually and practically, to distinguish between the "inherently competitive elements in the situation" (p. 231) and prejudice.

Allport noted that group relations may be realistically competitive in two respects. First, demands for resources often exceed their supply. For example, the number of people seeking employment may be greater than the number of jobs available. Although in such a case the competition actually exists between individual rivals for jobs, these individuals may nonetheless *perceive* the competition to be at an intergroup level. Thus, Allport described realistic group conflict as reflecting the common perception that competition for resources involves group identities and has collective consequences. Second, Allport also considered competitive relations between groups to be realistic when the competition involves less tangible qualities, such as religious or political belief systems. Belief systems may be seen as in direct conflict by those who endorse the relevant beliefs. For example, the fundamentalist belief that there is only one true religion (Altemeyer & Hunsberger, 1992) may generate realistic competition between religious groups for "soul winning." Similarly, individuals on the political left and right realistically compete through voting and other mechanisms for representation of their views.

Much of Allport's analysis of instrumental relations between groups involved explication of the social conditions that prompt competition and subsequent prejudice. He reasoned that diverse societies are particularly vulnerable to intergroup clashes because salient group differences (e.g., in appearance or clothes that identify group memberships) help define group boundaries and mark others as potential competitors (see Mullen & Leader, ch. 12 this volume). Allport (1954/1979) observed, "In the United States – probably the most heterogeneous and complex society on earth – conditions are ripe for abundant group conflict and prejudice. Differences are numerous and visible. The resulting clash of customs, tastes, ideologies cannot help but engender friction" (p. 222). We note that such a diverse, complex society involving visible differences and potential clashes of customs is not unique to the United States, but exists in many parts of the world. Allport further proposed that when minority groups are densely populated or separated from the dominant culture in ethnic communities, the ingroup/

outgroup boundary is reinforced (see Brown & Zagefka, and Gaertner & Dovidio, chs. 4 and 5 this volume). He also indicated that increases in visible minority populations (e.g., through immigration) exacerbate perceptions of competition given both the increased salience of the group, and the fact that resources are often construed as finite in availability.

Prevailing ideologies and social structures can aggravate competition, Allport argued. In particular, he suggested that in social contexts in which equality of opportunity is prized and social mobility is encouraged, perceived competition is likely. Allport (1954/1979) wrote, "But, when men [*sic*] are viewed as potentially equal, and by national creed are guaranteed equal rights and equal opportunity . . . members of even the lowest group are encouraged to put forth effort, to rise, and to demand their rights" (p. 222). Allowance, or encouragement, of upward social mobility makes evident the possibility of downward mobility, which, in the presence of a visually salient outgroup, generates competition and animosity. Although Allport acknowledged that there are contexts in which oppression is stable and institutionalized (see Jackman, ch. 6 this volume), and that in these contexts subtle forms of prejudice arise as justifications of inequality (see Jost & Hamilton, ch. 13 this volume), his emphasis was clearly on the active, overt animosity that follows mobilization and change in an open society that prizes freedom.

Following this line of reasoning, the outcome of competition is stereotyped and/or overtly hostile attitudes toward competitor groups. Although Allport did not articulate the instrumental nature of such prejudice in detail, he did acknowledge that prejudice can serve many functions for dominant groups, such as maintaining economic and political dominance, social status, and sexual access. Moreover, Allport gave some credit to the Marxist notion that because systems involving social stratification tend to be exploitative, members of dominant groups may be motivated, consciously or unconsciously, to maintain their advantage by promoting myths about disadvantaged groups that imply that the exploitation is in fact fair, deserved, and necessary. He concluded that "there lies at the heart of any diversified and stratified social system the tempting possibility that economic, sexual, political, and status gains may result from a deliberative (and even from unconscious) exploitation of minorities. To achieve those gains, prejudice is propagated by those who stand to win the most advantage" (Allport, 1954/1979, p. 234).

In summary, Allport proposed that in diverse societies in which social mobility is possible, intergroup competition invariably arises because of finite resources and varied value systems. Conflict between groups generates hostility, which further reinforces perceptions of competition. Although

Allport distinguished between real intergroup competition and the resulting prejudice, he acknowledged the often clouded nature of perceptions
of conflict. He suggested that intergroup competition is "like a note on an
organ . . . it sets all prejudices that are attuned to it into simultaneous
vibration" (1954/1979, p. 233). Allport's analysis clearly acknowledged
the complexities of social reality. Correspondingly, theory and research
during the past half century have illuminated how many of these complexities operate.

Allport's Foundation for Subsequent Developments in the Field

The importance of functional relations between groups was already well
established by the work of Sherif (e.g., Sherif et al., 1961) and others at the
time that *The Nature of Prejudice* was produced. In a series of studies
beginning in 1949, including the classic Robber's Cave experiment, Sherif
and his colleagues demonstrated that functional relations between groups
are critical in determining intergroup attitudes. In particular, competition
between groups produces prejudice and discrimination, whereas intergroup
interdependence and successful cooperative interaction reduce intergroup
bias. Allport's insights, however, laid the foundation for two fundamental
new developments on this topic: (a) a focus on *perceptions* of group conflict
and competition, rather than *inherent* conflict and competition, and (b) an
emphasis on the role of collective identity in intergroup conflict.

Perceptions of Intergroup Conflict

Work on the critical role of perceptions of conflict in the development
of prejudice and discrimination has been conducted at both distal and
proximal levels. Distal perspectives emphasize functional explanations for
perceptions of intergroup conflict in general and in specific contexts.
Proximal approaches concentrate on the way in which these perceptions
of conflict relate to prejudice and discrimination in more specific situations.
    Distal-level theories such as Social Dominance Theory (Pratto, 1999;
Sidanius & Pratto, 1999), System Justification Theory (e.g., Jost & Banaji,
1994; see Jost & Hamilton, ch. 13 this volume), and Terror Management
Theory (Greenberg, Solomon, & Pyszczynski, 1997) have sought to explain
how ideologies that promote group conflict and competition are maintained,

and the functions they may serve. Social Dominance Theory suggests that in most societies, socially constructed groups are hierarchically organized so that certain groups receive a disproportionate percentage of positive outcomes (e.g., money, power). To maintain these hierarchies, it is argued, ideologies are developed that sustain the stability of the system. For dominant group members, these ideologies include beliefs about the legitimacy of their position in society and beliefs about inherent zero-sum competition among groups (i.e., that for dominants to prosper, others must suffer and, conversely, that if other groups prosper, it is necessarily at the expense of the dominant group). A belief in group conflict and competition thus serves to maintain the group dominance and inequality in society.

Relatedly, System Justification Theory (Jost & Banaji, 1994) discusses the processes that ensure that members of both privileged and disadvantaged groups believe that the hierarchically structured society in which they live is legitimate and fair. In particular, the theory proposes that stereotypes justify the positive outcomes of dominant groups, the negative outcomes of subordinate groups, and the exploitation of subordinate groups by dominant groups. For example, dominant group members may be stereotyped as intelligent and hard-working, whereas subordinate group members may be stereotyped as unintelligent and lazy (see also Jost & Hamilton, ch. 13 this volume). Threats to the *status quo* may lead to heightened endorsement of these stereotypes in an attempt to defend and strengthen the system (see also Bobo, 1999).

Terror Management Theory takes a different perspective, focusing on less tangible resources and outcomes (Greenberg et al., 1997). The theory proposes that awareness of death causes people to experience the terror of their own meaninglessness. To counteract this terror, it is argued, people create cultural worldviews that give meaning and significance to their lives. These worldviews provide the possibility of symbolic or actual immortality to those who meet the group's standards of value. Because of their often absolute nature, however, they are not impervious to threat and competition from other group's worldviews. Group conflict and competition arise, then, because those with different worldviews are seen as suggesting that our worldview is incorrect, threatening the very basic premises on which the meaning and significance of our lives are based.

At a more proximal level, psychologists have also examined how situations that promote perceived competition and threat can lead to prejudice and discrimination, and vice versa. The Instrumental Model of Group Conflict (Esses, Jackson, & Armstrong, 1998) proposes that resource stress – the perception that there are not enough resources to go around – and the presence of a potentially competitive outgroup, lead to perceived competition. A variety of resources may be seen to be at stake, including more tangible resources, such as jobs and power, and more symbolic resources, such as values. In either case, perceptions of group competition are proposed to lead to prejudice and discrimination that are instrumental in their attempt to eliminate group competition (e.g., restrictive immigration policies to prevent job competition from immigrants).

The Integrated Threat Theory of Prejudice (Stephan & Stephan, 2000) stresses intergroup threats and fears as major causes of prejudice and discrimination, focusing on realistic threats, symbolic threats, intergroup anxiety, and negative stereotypes of outgroups as sources of threat and fear. Relatedly, the Stereotype Content Model (Fiske, Cuddy, Glick, & Xu, 2002) suggests that the stereotypes of groups are captured by two dimensions, competence and warmth, with groups perceived as competing with one's ingroup seen as low in warmth. This perception then has implications for emotional reactions to outgroups, with low-warmth outgroups eliciting envy or contempt, depending on their perceived competence.

In line with the focus on *perceptions* of group competition and threat, contemporary research has also highlighted the importance of individual differences in perceptions of group competition and threat that may lead to prejudice (see Duckitt, ch. 24 this volume). For example, research has shown that individuals who are high in Social Dominance Orientation (i.e., those who believe in group inequality and support group hierarchies in society) tend to see the world in terms of inherent competition among groups for dominance and power, and are thus especially likely to display prejudice and discrimination (e.g., Esses et al., 1998; Sidanius & Pratto, 1999). Research has also shown that individuals who are high in Right-Wing Authoritarianism are especially sensitive to threats to their traditional values, and display negative attitudes and behavior toward those seen to hold values different from their own (e.g., Altemeyer, 1996; Esses, Haddock, & Zanna, 1993).

Collective Identity

Allport proposed that identification with groups makes salient the link between individuals' own needs and interests and those of the groups to which they belong. As a result, contemporary researchers have also focused on group identification, and the link between self-interest, group interest, and prejudice.

The central role of identification with groups was highlighted and developed in Tajfel and Turner's (1979) Social Identity Theory. The basic premise of Social Identity Theory (see also Self-Categorization Theory: Turner et al., 1987) is that people have important collective as well as personal identities. Moreover, with respect to collective identity, people obtain a sense of self-worth from the groups to which they belong, so that self and group identity are linked. Individuals therefore seek to belong to groups that are evaluated more positively than other groups, and will denigrate other groups and limit their opportunities in order to obtain this outcome.

Contemporary work on group identification and its implications has also explored the idea that outgroup derogation and ingroup favoritism are conceptually and empirically distinguishable (see Brown & Zagefka, ch. 4 this volume). For example, Brewer (1999, 2001) has proposed that ingroup love does not necessarily entail outgroup hatred, and that intergroup discrimination can indicate preferential treatment of the ingroup, rather than direct hostility toward outgroups. In line with this suggestion, research on discrimination in the minimal group paradigm (in which group memberships are created in the laboratory using criteria as minimal as an alleged shared preference for different styles of art or random assignment) used to test the premises of Social Identity Theory has found that people are generally more willing to discriminate by providing more rewards or positive outcomes to the ingroup than to outgroups, versus providing more costs or negative outcomes to outgroups than to the ingroup (Buhl, 1999; Mummendey & Otten, 1998). Notably, individuals who are highly identified with the ingroup are especially likely to discriminate for positive outcomes, but ingroup identification does not necessarily relate to discrimination for negative outcomes (Hodson, Dovidio, & Esses, 2003). Thus, in examining intergroup relations and resource allocation, it is important to consider both collective identity and the nature of the resources at stake.

A New Framework: Unified Instrumental Model of Group Conflict

The various perspectives discussed and researched since Allport's time are not necessarily alternative contenders for explaining group conflict and competition, but instead may each contribute to a more unified model of group conflict, as depicted in figure 14.1. We suggest that ideologies and situational factors may be mutually reinforcing in initiating the process of perceiving group competition and conflict. In order for perceptions of group competition to arise, however, a relevant outgroup must be available.

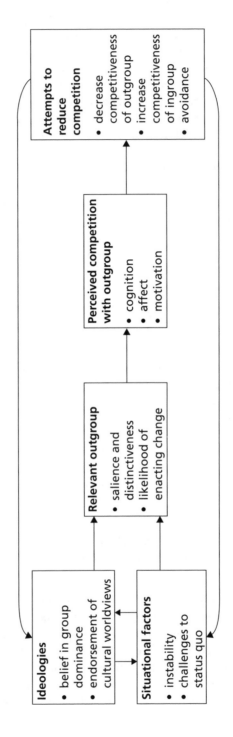

Figure 14.1 Unified instrumental model of group conflict

Once this outgroup is identified, perceived competition with that group will be experienced. As a result, various attempts will be made to eliminate this competition, including the expression of prejudice and discrimination. The resulting attitudes and behaviors may then feed back on the ideologies and situational factors, reducing or exacerbating the factors that initiated the process. This model can be applied to understand a broad range of intergroup relations, including relations between immigrants and members of host countries (Esses, Dovidio, Jackson, & Armstrong, 2001), as well as the social prejudices (e.g., racism, anti-Semitism) that Allport emphasized. We discuss each of these steps in more detail below.

As illustrated in figure 14.1, the process is initiated by ideologies and situational factors that predispose people to perceive competition. With respect to ideologies, belief systems that promote group dominance and cultural worldviews may both facilitate the development of chronic perceptions of group competition, though the resources seen to be primarily at stake may differ. Belief systems that promote group dominance may primarily lead to perceived competition over relatively tangible resources, such as money and power. In order for some groups in society to dominate others, they must have disproportionate access to valued resources. It is not sufficient for them to have a great deal in an absolute sense; they must have more than others in a relative sense. As a result, in societies in which group dominance is evident, there is likely to be a perception that there are not enough valued resources to go around, fueling the belief that groups are chronically competing for valued and scarce resources.

Dominant group members are especially likely to be high in Social Dominance Orientation and to hold a belief in zero-sum competition between groups because it is in their interests to maintain the hierarchy (Sidanius & Pratto, 1999; Duckitt, ch. 24 this volume). These zero-sum beliefs mediate the relation between Social Dominance Orientation and negative attitudes toward outgroups, particularly outgroups seen to be succeeding in society (Esses et al., 1998, 2001; Esses, Hodson, & Dovidio, 2003). Although belief systems that promote group dominance often lead to perceived competition over tangible resources, in the context of relations with immigrants, high social dominance oriented individuals not only perceive zero-sum competition for resources such as jobs and power, they also perceive zero-sum competition for value dominance (Esses et al., 2003). Thus, it seems that group dominance is not only a matter of having wealth and power, but of having moral hegemony.

Cultural worldviews may be at the heart of perceived competition over more symbolic factors such as values. Worldviews often have an absolute nature so that they not only prescribe appropriate modes of thinking and behaving, but proscribe others (Greenberg et al., 1997; see also Batson & Stocks, ch. 25 this volume). As a result, cultures (and subcultures) may be seen as competing for obtaining "truth." The correctness of a cultural worldview may be promoted, then, by proving the incorrectness of opposing views. Of importance, there are individual differences in the extent to which people endorse and seek to defend their cultural perspectives, as assessed by such measures as Right-Wing Authoritarianism and religious fundamentalism (Altemeyer, 1996; Altemeyer & Hunsberger, 1992). Right-wing authoritarians and religious fundamentalists not only strongly endorse particular values, but also perceive outgroups as a threat to their values (e.g., Esses et al., 1993; Jackson & Esses, 1997). As a result, they are likely to express prejudice and discrimination toward these groups (Altemeyer & Hunsberger, 1992; Esses et al., 1993; Jackson & Esses, 1997).

Ideologies related to group dominance and cultural worldviews may lead to a chronic belief in group competition. However, situational factors (see figure 14.1) also play an important role by making salient and heightening perceived competition among groups. We propose that social instability and perceived challenges to the status quo are likely to have such effects. For example, major events such as economic upheaval or threat of war may lead not only to increased protection of tangible resources held by one's group (whose finite nature may become especially salient under such conditions), but also protection of more symbolic factors such as values and positive group distinctiveness (Rothgerber, 1997; Worchel & Coutant, 1997; see also Glick, ch. 15 this volume). Less dramatic situational influences, such as media reports of unemployment rates in different segments of the population or debate over men's and women's roles in society, may have similar effects (e.g., Esses et al., 1998). In both cases, the increased motivation to protect group interests is likely to increase perceived competition with other groups.

In addition, as illustrated by the reciprocal arrows between these elements in figure 14.1, ideologies and situational factors that promote perceived group competition may be mutually reinforcing so that the ideologies heighten sensitivity to situational factors, and the situational factors reinforce and strengthen the ideologies. For example, right-wing authoritarians are particularly sensitive to perceived threats to their values (Esses et al., 1993), and conversely, national threat and uncertainty have been shown to lead to increased expressions of authoritarianism (Altemeyer, 1996; Doty, Peterson, & Winter, 1991).

The influence of ideologies and situational factors is further shaped by the nature of the relevant outgroup (see figure 14.1). Although ideologies and situational factors may promote the likelihood of perceiving zero-sum competition among groups, some groups are more likely to be perceived as competitors than are others. Groups that are salient and distinct from the ingroup are especially likely to stand out as potential competitors. For example, groups that are large or are increasing in size, and are distinctive in appearance or behavior, are especially likely to be perceived as potential competitors. In addition, however, outgroups must be seen as relevant to enacting changes in the status quo in terms of likelihood of success in order to be viewed as competitors. Thus, for example, as Blacks have made gains in the United States, they are more likely to be seen as a competitive threat to Whites (Bobo, 1999; Sidanius & Pratto, 1999). Similarly, as the likelihood of legalized same-sex marriage in Canada increases, discussion of values in terms of zero-sum outcomes seems to be on the rise (e.g., Take Back Canada, 2004).

In our model, the propensity to perceive group competition due to ideological and situational factors, and the availability of a relevant outgroup, together lead to perceived competition with that outgroup. This perceived competition has cognitive, affective, and motivational components. The cognitive component may involve beliefs about the nature of the competition (e.g., zero-sum beliefs about the resources at stake; Esses et al., 2003) and stereotypes associated with perceived competitor groups, including lack of warmth (Fiske et al., 2002; Glick, ch. 15 this volume). The affective component may involve anxiety and fear (Stephan & Stephan, 2000), as well as more specific emotions directed toward the group, such as envy or contempt (Fiske et al., 2002; see also Smith & Mackie, ch. 22 this volume). Finally, perceived competition is likely to elicit a motivation to eliminate the sense of group competition and emotions that may accompany it.

Perceptions of group competition motivate actions to reduce competition. As shown in figure 14.1, attempts to eliminate group competition may take a variety of forms, reflecting various manifestations of prejudice and discrimination toward outgroups. We discuss three general strategies here, though others may certainly exist. The first two strategies correspond to the distinction between outgroup derogation and discrimination versus ingroup enhancement and preferential treatment (Brewer, 1999, 2001). First, a group may attempt to reduce the outgroup's perceived competitiveness by expressing negative attitudes and attributions about the other group in order to establish the competitor's lack of worth. This may include heightened endorsement of stereotypes about the outgroup used to justify the system as it currently exists (Jost & Banaji, 1994). Attempts to eliminate the outgroup's competitiveness may also entail overt discrimination and opposition to programs and policies that might change the status quo

(Bobo, 1999; Jackson & Esses, 2000; Pratto & Lemieux, 2001). Second, a group may attempt to increase the ingroup's competitiveness through the expression of ingroup-enhancing attitudes aimed at justifying the ingroup's entitlement to the resources at stake, whether tangible resources or more symbolic moral certainty and social value (Jost & Banaji, 1994). Attempts to increase the ingroup's competitiveness may also entail preferential treatment in the allocation of positive outcomes (Mullen, Brown, & Smith, 1992; Sidanius & Pratto, 1999). The third strategy that may be used to eliminate group competition is avoidance. The competitor outgroup may be denied access to the ingroup's territory or kept at a distance (e.g., Esses et al., 1998). In addition, the outgroup may be denied voice so that its challenges to the status quo are silenced (McFarland & Warren, 1992). As a result, competition (or its salience) may be reduced.

Finally, as illustrated by the outer arrows in figure 14.1, our model is cyclical and iterative. Attempts to eliminate group competition may feed back to the ideologies and situational factors that initially elicited the competition. For example, outgroup derogation, ingroup enhancement, and avoidance may reinforce ideologies of group dominance and strengthen the perceived "correctness" of one's worldview, increasing the likelihood of further perceptions of competition. In terms of situational factors, however, successful attempts to eliminate competition may increase the stability of the system and reduce challenges to the status quo, so that situational factors promoting group competition no longer operate. Thus, as a result of mutual effects of group ideologies and situational factors, further group competition may be promoted or attenuated.

Has Allport Been Supported?

Considerable progress has been made in understanding group conflict and competition since Allport wrote *The Nature of Prejudice*. Yet the foundation established by Allport remains as important and influential as ever. First, Allport's discussion of ideologies and social structures that are likely to exacerbate group conflict foreshadowed theories of group dominance (e.g., Bobo, 1999; Jost & Banaji, 1994; Sidanius & Pratto, 1999). Second, Allport maintained a broadly inclusive conception of group conflict and competition, recognizing that they can occur over economic resources, social power, religious values, group status, and social identity. Recent theorizing has tended to subsume these conflicts within two categories: conflict over relatively tangible resources, such as economic resources and power, and conflict over more symbolic factors, such as values and positive group distinctiveness (e.g., Esses et al., 2003; Stephan & Stephan, 2000; Scheepers, Spears, Doosje, & Manstead, 2003; Tajfel & Turner, 1979). Whereas Allport primarily identified these different sources of conflict, considerable recent research has attempted to pit symbolic or social-identity explanations for prejudice against explanations based on tangible conflicts of interest between groups (e.g., Gagnon & Bourhis, 1996; Rabbie, Schot, & Visser, 1989). Most recently, however, attempts have been made to reconcile and integrate these perspectives (e.g., Esses et al., 2003; Scheepers et al., 2003; Stephan & Stephan, 2000; Zárate, Garcia, Garza, & Hitlan, 2004). Thus whereas Allport identified key factors that contribute to competition, current work has gone beyond his initial insights to understand the dynamic relations between different sources of conflict and the more proximate mechanisms that translate conflict into prejudice and discrimination.

Future Research Directions

Our analysis of Allport's thinking about instrumental relations between groups and of the 50 years of research since Allport's time raises five general issues that may help to guide future research. First, one important direction will be a move away from the tendency to consider different explanations of intergroup conflict as mutually exclusive. For example, rather than pitting symbolic and tangible conflict explanations against each other, it is more fruitful to explore how perceived symbolic and resource conflicts work in concert to maintain group boundaries. One possibility is that symbolic threat may give rise to material threat, and vice versa. In the context of social change in which the dominance of one's value system may be threatened, identity may be protected by targeting outgroups as competitors for more tangible resources. Gaining resources (e.g., social power) may allow groups to ensure that their values have representation and status. Moreover, competition for resources may generate exaggerated perceptions of value differences to justify conflict. The emerging legality of same-sex marriage in Canada provides an example of these dynamics. Canadians who value the preservation of tradition and those who value social progress have responded differently to same-sex marriage, and may consequently view one another as rivals for political representation. Although the majority heterosexual population stands neither to gain nor lose materially as a function of same-sex marriage, the perceived threat to value dominance among critics of same-sex marriage may translate into real competition for a resource (e.g., votes for politicians with a relevant stance), thereby generating animosity among critics and supporters of change. Moreover, in the context of competition for the real resource of political representation, opponents may exaggerate value differences.

Second, sustaining the recent trend toward differentiating many forms of problematic intergroup attitudes and responses will likely continue to prove instructive in reconciling seemingly contradictory ideas. For example, Allport proposed that upward social mobility is associated with greater tolerance, whereas downward social mobility generates prejudice. The former situation, he reasoned, provides a safe platform from which to extend benevolence, whereas the latter, more vulnerable position generates a focus on group interest and competition. Yet, a provocative line of recent research suggests that upward mobility may also be associated with prejudice. Guimond and colleagues (e.g., Guimond & Dambrun, 2002) found that relative gratification – a comparison that results in a favorable outcome – is associated with increases in expressed prejudice. They reason that people whose groups are overbenefited may generate justifications, including prejudiced beliefs that protect their advantage. Future research may thus address the ways in which specific forms of prejudice correspond to different types of social change. For example, change from which dominant groups benefit may be especially likely to create subtle, ideological forms of prejudice, whereas change involving losses in power or status may generate more open hostility.

Third, it will be useful for future work to incorporate within one framework instrumental relations at different levels of analysis, including international relations, relations among groups within a nation (e.g., ethnic, religious groups), and relations among members within a group. Competition at one level may have different implications for group relations at other levels of analysis. For example, following Allport, we anticipate that whereas internal instability is likely to generate antagonism between groups within a nation, international instability may foster recategorization at the national level that leads to more inclusive ingroup representations (Gaertner & Dovidio, 2000) and to more harmonious internal relations. Our models may need to incorporate multiple outgroups and outcomes to allow for these cross-level of analysis effects.

Fourth, it is our hope that evolving models of the instrumental nature of intergroup relations will be applied with flexibility. For example, the preceding analysis makes clear that many of the relations among variables in competition models are reciprocal, such as the relation between perceived competition and ideologies that support competition. Thus, models ought not to be interpreted in a mechanistic, linear fashion. In addition, our models will more accurately reflect the complexity of social reality to the extent that they allow for varying realizations of similar psychological constructs to emerge in different ways. For example, belief in hierarchical, zero-sum relations between groups in general (typical, for example, among people high in Social Dominance Orientation) may give rise, under specified social conditions, to a heightened concern regarding negatively inter-dependent relations between specific groups.

Fifth, and finally, we hope that the next 50 years of research will generate as much attention to the cures for prejudice as the last 50 years have addressed to its causes. In this regard, increased examination of national strategies geared toward fostering social inclusion and respect, such as assimilation and multiculturalism, are needed. To the extent that such strategies function as ideologies, models of intergroup relations ought to specify the ways by which they may both reinforce and constrain perceived intergroup competition. It is our hope that an analysis of such possibilities may point the way toward the development of effective com-munity, national, and international strategies for minimizing group friction and maximizing cooperation and respect.

REFERENCES

Allport, G. W. (1954/1979). *The nature of prejudice*. Cambridge, MA: Perseus Books.

Altemeyer, B. (1996). *The authoritarian specter*. Cambridge, MA: Harvard University Press.

Altemeyer, B. & Hunsberger, B. (1992). Authoritarianism, religious funda-mentalism, quest, and prejudice. *The International Journal for the Psychology of Religion, 2*, 113–33.

Bobo, L. (1999). Prejudice as group position: Micro-foundations of a so-ciological approach to racism and race relations. *Journal of Social Issues, 55*, 445–72.

Brewer, M. B. (1999). The psychology of prejudice: Ingroup love or out-group hate? *Journal of Social Issues, 55*, 429–44.

Brewer, M. B. (2001). Ingroup identi-fication and intergroup conflict: When does ingroup love become outgroup hate? In R. E. Ashmore & L. Jussim (eds.), *Social identity, intergroup conflict, and conflict reduction. Rutgers series on self and social identity* (vol. 3, pp. 17–41). London: Oxford University Press.

Buhl T. (1999). Positive–negative asym-metry in social discrimination: Meta-analytic evidence. *Group Processes and Intergroup Relations, 2*, 51–8.

Doty, R. E., Peterson, B. E., & Winter, D. G. (1991). Threat and authoritarianism in the United States, 1978–1987. *Journal of Personality and Social Psychology, 61*, 629–40.

Esses, V. M., Dovidio, J. F., Jackson, L. M., & Armstrong, T. L. (2001). The immigration dilemma: The role of perceived group competition, ethnic prejudice, and national identity. _Journal of Social Issues_, 57, 389–412.

Esses, V. M., Haddock, G., & Zanna, M. P. (1993). Values, stereotypes, and emotions as determinants of intergroup attitudes. In D. M. Mackie & D. L. Hamilton (eds.), _Affect, cognition and stereotyping: Interactive processes in group perception_ (pp. 137–66). San Diego, CA: Academic Press.

Esses, V. M., Hodson, G., & Dovidio, J. F. (2003). Public attitudes toward immigrants and immigration: Determinants and policy implications. In C. M Beach, A. G. Green, & J. G. Reitz (eds.), _Canadian immigration policy for the 21st century_ (pp. 507–35). Montreal: McGill Queen's Press.

Esses, V. M., Jackson, L. M., & Armstrong, T. L. (1998). Intergroup competition and attitudes toward immigrants and immigration: An instrumental model of group conflict. _Journal of Social Issues_, 54, 699–724.

Fiske, S. T., Cuddy, A. J. C., Glick, P., & Xu, J. (2002). A model of (often mixed) stereotype content: Competence and warmth respectively follow from perceived status and competition. _Journal of Personality and Social Psychology_, 82, 878–902.

Gagnon A. & Bourhis, R. Y. (1996). Discrimination in the minimal group paradigm: Social identity or self-interest? _Personality and Social Psychology Bulletin_, 22, 1289–1301.

Greenberg, J., Solomon, S., & Pyszczynski, T. (1997). Terror management theory of self-esteem and cultural worldviews: Empirical assessments and cultural refinements. In M. P. Zanna (ed.), _Advances in experimental social psychology_ (vol. 29, pp. 61–139). Orlando, FL: Academic Press.

Guimond, S. & Dambrun, M. (2002). When prosperity breeds intergroup hostility: The effects of relative deprivation and relative gratification on prejudice. _Personality and Social Psychology Bulletin_, 28, 900–12.

Hodson, G., Dovidio, J. F., & Esses, V. M. (2003). Ingroup identification as a moderator of positive-negative asymmetry in social discrimination. _European Journal of Social Psychology_, 33, 215–33.

Jackson, L. M. & Esses, V. M. (1997). Of scripture and ascription: The relation between religious fundamentalism and intergroup helping. _Personality and Social Psychology Bulletin_, 23, 893–906.

Jackson, L. M. & Esses, V. M. (2000). The effect of economic competition on people's willingness to help empower immigrants. _Group Processes and Intergroup Relations_, 3, 419–35.

Jost, J. T. & Banaji, M. R. (1994). The role of stereotyping in system-justification and the production of false consciousness. _British Journal of Social Psychology_, 33, 1–27.

McFarland, S. G. & Warren, J. C. (1992). Religious orientations and selective exposure among fundamentalist Christians. _Journal for the Scientific Study of Religion_, 31, 163–74.

Mullen, B., Brown, R., & Smith, C. (1992). Ingroup bias as a function of salience, relevance and status: An integration. _European Journal of Social Psychology_, 22, 103–22.

Mummendey A. & Otten S. (1998). Positive-negative asymmetry in social discrimination. In W. Stroebe & M. Hewstone (eds.), _European review of social psychology_ (vol. 9, pp. 107–43). Chichester, UK: Wiley.

Pratto, F. (1999). The puzzle of continuing group inequality: Piecing together psychological, social, and cultural forces in social dominance theory. In M. P. Zanna (ed.), *Advances in experimental social psychology* (vol. 31, pp. 191–263). San Diego, CA: Academic Press.

Pratto, F. & Lemieux, A. F. (2001). The psychological ambiguity of immigration and its implications for promoting immigration policy. *Journal of Social Issues, 57,* 413–30.

Rabbie, J. M., Schot, J. C., & Visser, L. (1989). Social identity theory: A conceptual and empirical critique from the perspective of a behavioural interaction model. *European Journal of Social Psychology, 19,* 171–202.

Rothgerber, H. (1997). External intergroup threat as an antecedent to perceptions in in-group and out-group homogeneity. *Journal of Personality and Social Psychology, 73,* 1206–12.

Scheepers, D., Spears, R., Doosje, B., & Manstead, A. S. R. (2003). Two functions of verbal intergroup discrimination: Identity and instrumental motives as a result of group identification and threat. *Personality & Social Psychology Bulletin, 29,* 568–77.

Sherif, M., Harvey, O. J., White, B. J., Hood, W. R., & Sherif, C. W. (1961). *Intergroup conflict and cooperation: The Robbers Cave experiment.* Norman, OK: University of Oklahoma Book Exchange.

Sidanius, J. & Pratto, F. (1999). *Social dominance: An intergroup theory of social hierarchy and oppression.* New York: Cambridge University Press.

Stephan, W. G. & Stephan, C. W. (2000). An integrated threat theory of prejudice. In S. Oskamp (ed.), *Claremont symposium on applied social psychology* (pp. 23–46). Hillsdale, NJ: Lawrence Erlbaum.

Tajfel H. & Turner J. C. (1979). An integrative theory of intergroup conflict. In W. G. Austin & S. Worchel (eds.), *The social psychology of intergroup relations* (pp. 33–47). Monterey, CA: Brooks/Cole.

Take Back Canada. (2004). Family values. www.takebackcanada.com (retrieved Dec. 26, 2004).

Turner, J. C., Hogg, M. A., Oakes, P. J., Reicher, S. D., & Wetherell, M. S. (1987). *Rediscovering the social group: A self-categorization theory.* Oxford: Blackwell.

Worchel, S. & Coutant, D. (1997). The tangled web of loyalty: Nationalism, patriotism, and ethnocentrism. In D. Bar-Tal & E. Staub (eds.), *Patriotism in the lives of individuals and nations* (pp. 190–210). Chicago: Nelson Hall.

Zárate, M. A., Garcia, B., Garza, A. A., & Hitlan, R. T. (2004). Cultural threat and perceived realistic group conflict as dual predictors of prejudice. *Journal of Experimental Social Psychology, 40,* 99–105.

Chapter Fifteen

Choice of Scapegoats

Peter Glick

A decade before Allport wrote *The Nature of Prejudice*, the Nazis had attempted to exterminate Europe's Jews, whom they blamed for Germany's woes. A decade before this chapter was written, hundreds of thousands of Tutsi were murdered by Hutu neighbors, who blamed the Tutsi for Rwanda's economic and social problems. Both are examples of scapegoating, here defined as *an extreme form of prejudice in which an outgroup is unfairly blamed for having intentionally caused an ingroup's misfortunes.* Allport considered scapegoating to be one of the most important theories of prejudice, devoting considerable space to it (chapter 15, "Choice of Scapegoats," plus large portions of Part IV, "The Dynamics of Prejudice"), focusing (not surprisingly, given how recent the Holocaust was) on the Jews' long history of having been scapegoated.

Although he invoked "normal" cognitive (e.g., categorization) and social (e.g., conformity) processes to explain why people differentiate between groups (see Fiske, ch. 3 this volume), Allport believed that only scapegoating, which he attributed to irrational and maladaptive ego-defense mechanisms, could account for the most extreme forms of prejudice, such as genocide. Although subsequent prejudice researchers took up the cognitive-social strand of Allport's thought with zeal, research on scapegoating languished as psychodynamic views fell out of favor. This chapter first reviews Allport's synthetic view and incisive critique of scapegoat theory and then presents an alternative model of scapegoating that (a) is more in keeping with the dominant cognitive-social approach, (b) focuses on social conditions and group-level processes, rather than individual psychopathology, as root causes of scapegoating (and its most extreme manifestation, genocide), and (c) solves the problems Allport identified as major stumbling blocks for scapegoat theory.

Allport's View of Scapegoating

Allport noted the biblical origins of the term "scapegoat" – a sacrificial goat to which the ancient Israelites had symbolically transferred their sins. This anecdote illustrates the psychodynamic view of scapegoating: negative traits that people do not wish to acknowledge in themselves are psychologically projected onto others, thereby relieving feelings of guilt and frustration (see Newman & Caldwell, ch. 23 this volume). Allport embraced both the psychodynamic theory of scapegoating and a less complicated model in which external frustrations (not necessarily due to one's own sins) are displaced onto an innocent target, regarding these two versions as complementary.

Freudian Psychodynamics versus Frustration–Aggression

The two approaches to scapegoating Allport described, though overlapping, stem from different psychological approaches, one rooted in Freudian theory (the psychodynamic view) and the other in later drive-reduction models (the frustration–aggression view). Freud believed that frustration and guilt are the inevitable consequences of society's (necessary) restrictions of individuals' instinctual drives, most prominently for sex and aggression, which are collectively labeled as the *id*. To avoid social chaos, people must be socialized (predominantly by their parents) to restrict their natural impulses and to redirect them in socially approved ways. These parental and societal strictures become internalized, creating the *superego*, the individual's conscience, which strives to enforce good behavior. Thus an overly punitive upbringing guarantees continuing conflicts between a highly restrictive superego and the instinctual drives of the id. The superego (with limited success) attempts to repress even simple awareness of the id's unacceptable impulses, resulting in frustration, guilt, and aggressive feelings that need to be vented, setting the stage for scapegoating.

Later drive-reduction models agreed with Freud that various drives sought discharge in behavior. In contrast to the psychodynamic view, however, frustration–aggression theory characterized aggression as a response to circumstances that block goal-directed behavior, not as an innate drive (Dollard et al., 1939). External frustrations (rather than internal psychodynamic conflict) evoke aggression, typically against the source of frustration. Like Freud, however, Dollard et al. believed that aggression would be displaced onto an innocent target if the true source of frustration was powerful and therefore likely to retaliate.

Both the psychodynamic and frustration–aggression views of scapegoating invoke the notions of *displaced aggression* (directing aggressive impulses toward an innocent target) and *projection* (attributing negative characteristics and blame to targets to justify aggressing against them). The Freudian approach, however, emphasized what Allport termed "direct projection," in which the individual's own unacceptable impulses are projected onto others, allowing people to deny their own faults. Direct projection requires a complicated set of ego-defense mechanisms, including repression (eliminating conscious awareness that the faults are one's own) as well as displacement. The frustration–aggression approach concentrated instead on what Allport termed "complementary projection" in which perceivers explain feelings (of which they are consciously aware) by projecting complementary, causal traits onto others (e.g., I am fearful, therefore you must be hostile). Because the source of frustration is external (circumstances that block attainment of goals, rather than "character-conditioned" internal psychodynamic conflict) there is no need for repression. In both views, however, derogatory beliefs about scapegoats reveal more about the perceiver (either their faults or their fears) than they do about the actual traits of the scapegoated group, which merely serves as a projective screen.

An example of the psychodynamic view is the idea that antihomosexual prejudice results from the perceiver's own "latent homosexuality." Individuals who have internalized the notion that homosexuality is immoral yet themselves experience homosexual impulses would try to deny these desires in themselves and displace their self-loathing onto others. Adams, Wright, and Lohr (1996) found that avowedly heterosexual male participants' antihomosexual attitudes were correlated with greater penile tumescence when viewing videos of homosexual sex. This study is consistent with the idea that men who had repressed their own homosexual impulses had (at least in part) transformed self-loathing into hostility toward others.

In contrast, Bettleheim and Janowitz's (1950) findings (cited by Allport) that men experiencing downward social mobility (an external source of frustration) expressed both more anti-Semitism and racism, is a prime example of the frustration–aggression approach. Presuming that Jews and Blacks were not the direct cause of their downward mobility, these men's greater anti-Semitism and racism was an example of displaced aggression. The targets of their aggression were assumed to be chosen because they were weak, vulnerable, and already deprecated minority groups.

In sum, the major difference between the psychodynamic and frustration–aggression theories of scapegoating is whether frustration is due to internal psychodynamic conflict or to external sources that block goal-directed behavior. Otherwise, both views suggest that: (a) aggression against the true source of frustration is inhibited, (b) aggression is displaced toward others who are weak and therefore unable to retaliate, and (c) negative stereotypes of scapegoated groups are mere projections or rationalizations that obscure the real reasons for hostility toward them. Overall, both accounts view scapegoating as irrational – an infantile, maladaptive, and emotionally driven response to (either internal or external) frustration.

Despite his frequent use of scapegoat explanations and willingness to synthesize psychodynamic and frustration–aggression approaches, Allport provided an extensive critique of scapegoat theory (based partly on concerns expressed by Zawadzki, 1948), summarized below:

> (1) Frustration does not always lead to aggression . . . (2) Aggression is not always displaced [but rather is more likely to be directed at the true source of frustration] . . . (3) Displacement does not . . . actually relieve the feeling of frustration [because it does not address frustration's underlying causes] . . . (4) The theory says nothing concerning the choice of scapegoats . . . (5) It is not true that a defenseless minority is always chosen for displacement purposes [powerful groups are sometimes blamed] . . . (6) Available evidence does not indicate that the displacement tendency is any more common among people high in prejudice than among those low in prejudice . . . (7) Finally, the theory itself overlooks the possibility of realistic social conflict. (1954/1979, pp. 350–1)

In the decades following Allport's book, progress addressing the problems listed above was slow in coming, but recent theoretical advances are beginning to suggest resolutions.

Developments Since Allport

Theoretical developments since the 1950s suggest that scapegoating ought to be viewed as a collective rather than individual process (though for more on the latter, see Newman & Caldwell, ch. 23 this volume). Subsequent work has accepted the fundamental role of frustration in scapegoating, but with a focus on the roles of shared (collective) frustrations (e.g., economic collapse, social disorder) that produce social movements with scapegoating ideologies that lead to organized persecution. Frustration's role thus becomes indirect, with ideology being the proximal cause of aggression. This section reviews post-Allport developments related to collective scapegoating and explains how they begin to address some of Allport's criticisms.

Staub's (1989) refinement of the frustration–aggression perspective suggests one answer to Allport's first criticism that (contrary to frustration–aggression theory) frustration does not always turn into aggression against scapegoats. Staub theorized that genocides and mass killings require widespread, extremely "difficult life conditions" (due to social, political, and/or economic upheavals) that frustrate a host of basic needs, for physical well-being, safety, a sense of belonging, self- and group esteem, and hope for the future. Mundane frustrations are insufficient to spawn scapegoating movements, which gain adherents by promising to fulfill the heightened needs of a mass of people (e.g., safety and prosperity will be achieved by attacking the "enemy"). Terror management theory (Pyszczynski, Greenberg, & Solomon, 1999), which proposes that asserting their ingroup's superiority is one means by which people defend against awareness of their own mortality, can be incorporated into Staub's view. The difficult life conditions that precede scapegoating movements often include widespread disease or wars, making mortality highly salient. Deeply frustrated basic motives can attract masses of people to movements that blame an outgroup for current difficulties, affirm the ingroup's superiority, and offer the promise of a better future.

Consistent with Staub's (1989) viewpoint, social-identity theorists (Billig, 1976; Tajfel, 1981) have posited that only collective frustrations (those shared by many) lead to organized scapegoating. Based upon social-identity theorists' general critique of Allport's (and others') individualistic approach to prejudice (as rooted in personality), Tajfel and Billig argued that scapegoating is a group-based process. These theorists highlighted a problem Allport had not articulated – why does the scapegoating of a particular outgroup become socially shared or consensual within a society? Although Freudian psychodynamics or the frustration–aggression hypothesis might explain why a particular individual lashes out against a convenient target, how can this account for mass movements in which a significant portion of a society's members join together in attacking a specific group? As Billig observed about the Holocaust, "It is too fanciful to imagine that the Germans were kept in an increasing state of emotional arousal for fifteen years, and at the end of this time simultaneously millions happened to rid themselves of these tensions in an identical manner" (1976, p. 150). The most horrendous examples of scapegoating (from medieval witch-hunts to the attempted genocides of the twentieth century) involve coordinated mass movements.

Allport imagined that all levels of frustration could promote scapegoating, including intensely personal causes. For instance, he noted that a "short stature" could be "a life-long cause for irritation" (1954/1979, p. 344). In contrast, Tajfel (1981) hypothesized that individual frustrations lead people to blame other individuals for their problems, whereas shared (group-level) frustrations predispose people to blame other groups. For example, a woman might blame her boss for firing her if other members of her ethnic group remain gainfully employed, but might blame an outgroup if she loses her job during an economic downturn that affects many members of her (but not of another) ethnic group. Events that people interpret as applying to their group as a whole (rather than to themselves as individuals) arouse group-based emotions (see Smith & Mackie, ch. 22 this volume).

Tajfel termed the process by which frustration becomes group blame "social attribution," situating it firmly within the social-cognitive approach favored by social psychologists. Attribution theory (e.g., Kelley, 1967) posits that people seek to understand the causes of events, especially negative ones. This makes adaptive sense: when bad events happen, people try to diagnose why they occurred, which may indicate how to correct the problem. When goals are blocked, frustration energizes the individual to diagnose and overcome obstacles. Like physical pain, frustration is an aversive state that indicates something is amiss and motivates the individual to attend to the problem.

Although Tajfel did not get the chance to further refine or empirically test the concept of social attribution, he pointed out how "normal" social-identity and cognitive-social processes, rather than infantile rage or the random venting of frustrations, could precipitate scapegoating. For example, when people are classified as members of a salient outgroup, they are perceived in a less individualized fashion so that their similarities to one another are exaggerated (see Gaertner & Dovidio, ch. 5 this volume), and are often ascribed less "human" qualities than are ingroup members (Leyens et al., 2000). These consequences of social categorization facilitate negative stereotyping and dehumanization and often provide system-justifying ideologies (see Jost & Hamilton, ch. 13 this volume) that act as catalysts for scapegoating. Staub (1996) identified the systematic devaluation and dehumanization of members of another group as key elements in the "psychology of evil" leading to open, and often mass, violence against the group (see also Sternberg's, 2003, duplex model of intergroup hate).

Further, social-identity theory links these cognitive processes to powerful motivations (e.g., the need for a positive group identity) of the sort Staub (1989) also hypothesized shared frustrations to arouse. The link between attributions and emotions can also be understood using appraisal theories of emotion, which Smith and Mackie (ch. 22 this volume; see also Cottrell & Neuberg, 2004) have incorporated in their intergroup emotions theory. For example, if another group's actions are appraised as a deliberate attempt to harm the ingroup, ingroup members will experience fear (if the other group is powerful) or anger (if the other group is weak). Social attribution is an initial link in a chain that produces intergroup emotions.

The theories outlined above suggest that *group-level frustrations* create *shared attributions and appraisals* that, in turn, lead to scapegoating. They effectively address Allport's first criticism (that not all frustrations lead to scapegoating), but not the other questions Allport asked: Why are innocent groups targeted? Why is aggression ever displaced? How are scapegoats chosen? Are scapegoats always defenseless and vulnerable?

Heider's (1958) foundational insights into the attribution process and recent work on the stereotype content model of prejudice (Fiske, Cuddy, Glick, & Xu, 2002; see Fiske, ch. 3 this volume) help to address many of Allport's concerns. Heider reasoned that to explain the cause of an event, people look for a causal agent (e.g., another person) who possesses the power (or ability) and intent to bring about that event. Thus, for example, an infant is unlikely to be blamed for knocking a plate off of a 6-foot-high, secure shelf because of her inability to reach it, even if she is known generally to have the intent to knock things over. Extending Heider's analysis to social (or intergroup) attribution suggests that only groups perceived as having the power and intent to cause widespread frustrations will be scapegoated.

The stereotype content model (see Fiske, ch. 3 this volume) suggests which groups are likely to be scapegoated. This model states that the structural relations between groups – their relative status and type of interdependence (competitive or cooperative) – determine the content of group stereotypes. High status or powerful (e.g., socioeconomically successful) minorities that are viewed as competing with the dominant group are subjected to *envious* prejudice: they are admired for their success, but also resented for it; stereotyped as highly competent, but as having hostile motives. Because envied minorities are viewed as having the power and intent to harm, they are at risk of being blamed for causing group-level frustrations. Additionally, a sense of relative deprivation (Runciman, 1966) can play into the scapegoating of successful minorities, who may be perceived as being less affected by or even as benefiting from the suffering endured by the ingroup, inflaming resentment and lending plausibility to the belief that the scapegoated group intentionally brought about the ingroup's misfortunes. In contrast, low-status groups – whether paternalized (see Jackman, ch. 6 this volume; Rudman, ch. 7 this volume) or treated with contempt – are stereotyped as incompetent, suggesting less ability and power to cause widespread misfortunes, making them less likely to be chosen as scapegoats.

Allport identified the Jews as history's most frequently scapegoated group. In retrospect, his historical analysis of European anti-Semitism (from the Jews' special theological position as the Bible's "chosen people" to their professional success in pre-Nazi Germany) is consistent with the notion of envious prejudice. The nineteenth-century anti-Semitic forgery, *The Protocols of the Learned Elders of Zion* (which purports to describe a meeting of a Jewish group bent on world domination), perfectly illustrates the character of envious prejudice. Far from being disparaged as inept, the Jews' power and abilities are exaggerated to a hysterical degree. Currently, difficult life circumstances in the Muslim world combined with Israel's military might, close alliance with the United States, and occupation of the West Bank and Gaza have reinvigorated these anti-Semitic canards. For example, at a summit of 57 Islamic nations the Malaysian Prime Minister contended that the Jews control the world (Rhode, 2003). Conspiracy theories and related rumors that blame disliked events on the machinations of a group are the hallmark of envious prejudice and scapegoating. Intergroup emotion theory (Smith & Mackie, ch. 22 this volume) suggests that an outgroup that is perceived as intentionally having brought about calamities for the ingroup will elicit strong (group-based) anger. If a scapegoated group is viewed as both powerful and malevolent, even the most extreme actions against them (e.g., murder) can be rationalized as self-defense.

A New Framework for Scapegoating Theory

The theoretical developments described above can be synthesized into a new model of scapegoating that addresses the problems Allport identified with older versions of the theory, an *ideological model of scapegoating* (Glick, 2002). This model views scapegoating, even in its most extreme and unwarranted versions, as stemming from ordinarily adaptive cognitive tendencies and motives, rather than inherently irrational, maladaptive processes. It downplays Freudian defense mechanisms, emphasizing instead the role of culturally shared beliefs, stereotypes, and ideologies. Finally, it focuses on scapegoating as a collective process by which commitment to hateful ideologies becomes widely shared within a community, creating a consensus that spawns political movements (e.g., Nazism) and coordinated hostile actions (e.g., discriminatory laws, organized mass killings, etc.).

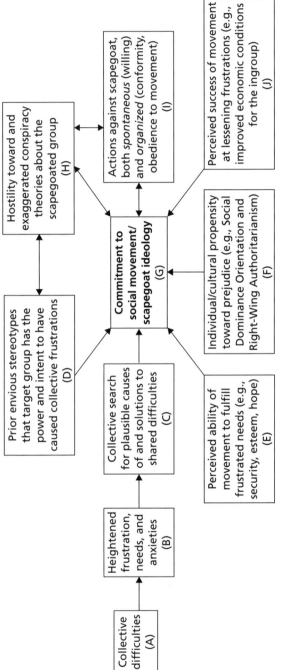

Figure 15.1 An ideological model of scapegoating (adapted from Glick, 2002)

Causes of Commitment to Scapegoating Ideology

Figure 15.1 illustrates the proposed ideological model of scapegoating (the letter labels in the figure correspond to the text below). The model begins with (A) widespread, shared frustrations, the kind of group-level events that Staub (1989) and Tajfel (1981) viewed as a prerequisite for scapegoating. These difficult life conditions (B) frustrate basic needs and arouse shared anxieties (Staub, 1989) that (C) lead to a collective search for explanations and solutions (Tajfel, 1981). How and why the third step leads to the heart of the model, (G) *commitment to scapegoat ideologies*, is the unique contribution of this framework.

Allport suggested that "the commonest reaction to frustration is . . . a simple and direct attempt to surmount the obstacle in our path" (1954/1979, p. 348), but this first requires identifying the obstacle. In cases of widespread misfortune, the nature of the "obstacle" and how to overcome it is often obscure. In their collective search for plausible explanations and courses of action, people may come to inaccurate, even (to those with better or different information) objectively ridiculous, conclusions that scapegoat an innocent group. Incorrect attributions may occur because information and people's cognitive abilities to process it are limited, especially when coping with large-scale problems in complex, modern societies. For example, even professional economists may be unable adequately to explain an economic crisis. Complex explanations involving largely uncontrollable, impersonal forces are difficult to fathom and may fail to suggest a clear solution, rendering them unattractive (because they do not fulfill heightened psychological needs for control and optimism). Scapegoat movements attract followers by offering simpler, culturally plausible explanations and solutions for shared negative events.

The ideological model suggests that the choice of scapegoat is primarily determined by (D) prior envious stereotyping (Fiske et al., 2002) of groups that are viewed as having the power and intent to cause widespread harm. Thus the perceived plausibility of a scapegoat ideology is influenced by cultural context. When Medieval Europe was decimated by plague, people blamed witches because witches were already believed to have the capability (via supernatural powers) and desire to cause such harm. Within the cultural context, blaming witches made "sense." Even though blame was wholly (and horribly) misplaced, rational faculties were not abandoned. For example, the well-documented witchcraft claims made in Salem, Massachusetts, in the seventeenth century were subjected to rigorous and, if basic premises about witches are granted, arguably rational tests, as well as trials that adhered to the legal standards of the day (Karlsen, 1987).

Similarly, a history of envious stereotyping is evident in most of the large-scale genocide attempts of the twentieth century. The Armenians in Turkey and the Jews in Germany filled strikingly similar social niches; both were economically successful minorities, often in "middleman" roles as merchants and traders. Perceived as a powerful minority, the Armenians were blamed for weakening the Ottoman Empire during the years of its decline (Adanir, 2001) much as Nazis blamed the loss of the First World War on a Jewish conspiracy (the "stab in the back" theory). In Rwanda (see Prunier, 2001), the Tutsi are a high-status minority, who (having been favored during Belgian colonization) are typically better educated, wealthier, and more likely to hold high-status jobs in comparison to the Hutu majority. The *genocidaires* among Rwanda's Hutus characterized the Tutsi as a powerful minority profiting off of the majority's misery. Cambodia's *Khmer Rouge*, who had their roots in the peasantry, resented and specifically targeted those with wealth and social influence, such as intellectuals (Kiernan, 2001).

Thus, Allport's critique that it "is not true that a defenseless minority is always chosen" (p. 351) is turned into a much stronger claim in the model presented here – it is precisely the perceived power of a group (not its perceived weakness) that makes it likely to be scapegoated. Earlier views dismissed perceptions of the scapegoat's power and malevolence as mere projections (of perpetrators' own megalomania and murderous intentions), but for the genocides listed above, envious stereotypes can be traced to prior historical circumstances (e.g., a middleman role) that conditioned the structural relations between groups. Envious stereotypes are here viewed more as a cause (increasing the likelihood that a group will be blamed for misfortunes) than a consequence of scapegoating. When a history of envious prejudice collides with a precipitous decline in a society's life conditions, successful minorities are at grave risk.

In the ideological model, the tendency to seek a scapegoat is also conditioned by (E) a scapegoat movement's ability to address a host of psychological and social needs. Although past theorists focused on the destructiveness of scapegoating, a utopianism that promises the fulfillment of people's basic needs is an equally important feature of scapegoating movements (see Staub, 1989). For example, Friedländer (1997) argued that Nazi anti-Semitism was "redemptive" – the Nazis promised Germans a "Thousand Year Reich" in which the problems of the present would be solved by eliminating their source, the Jews. Similarly, Fritzsche (1999) contends that most Germans were more directly attracted by the Nazis' promise to satisfy their current needs and provide a better tomorrow than by their hostility toward the Jews *per se* (though the former was inextricably intertwined with the latter in Nazi ideology).

As Staub (1989) has noted, difficult times heighten needs for security and physical well-being, for self- and group esteem, to believe that life is controllable and predictable, and to have hope for the future. Pyszczynski et al. (1999) add psychological defense against mortality salience to this list. Scapegoat movements address frustrated needs for esteem, belonging, and transcendence by reasserting the ingroup's superiority and offering membership in a wider social movement that promises symbolic immortality. Security, physical well-being, and hope are addressed by identifying and combating the "enemy" that has putatively caused the ingroup's misfortunes. The Nazis, for example, were masterful at creating a sense of belonging (everyone, children included, could belong to a subgroup, e.g., the Hitler Youth), group esteem and transcendence (through pageantry and an ideology of racial superiority), and optimism (through economic progress spurred by re-armament).

Thus parts A–E of the current model answer many of Allport's critiques of earlier scapegoat theory (corresponding to Allport's numbered critiques): (1) Why does frustration not always lead to intergroup aggression? Because only widely shared (not individual) frustrations are likely to lead to scapegoating. (2) Why is aggression ever "displaced"? Aggression may be better characterized as *misplaced* as a result of prior cultural stereotypes that characterize an outgroup as having the ability and intent to cause harm to the ingroup. (3) Why would human nature include an inherently maladaptive displacement tendency? It does not; a generally adaptive attribution process, due to limited cognitive capacity, imperfect knowledge, and motivational and cultural biases, results in misplaced blame. (4) Which groups are likely to be scapegoated? Successful but resented minorities. (5) Are groups always chosen for their perceived vulnerability? No, precisely the opposite – groups are scapegoated because they are (often falsely) perceived to be powerful and malevolent.

Allport's criticism (6), that "[a]vailable evidence does not indicate that the displacement tendency is any more common among people high in prejudice than among those low in prejudice" (p. 351), is also solvable if ideological commitment, not projection and displacement, is the central mediator of scapegoating. For Allport, the prejudiced personality was high in authoritarianism, a personality syndrome then thought to be dominated by low frustration tolerance, repression of one's own desires, and psychodynamic conflict. Authoritarians were assumed to be especially prone to displace and to project their own failings onto others. As Allport noted, however, there has been little support for this view.

In contrast, the current model (F) is consistent with contemporary theories of the prejudiced personality (see Duckitt, ch. 24 this volume). Altemeyer (1981) has reconceptualized the authoritarian personality as being rooted in ideology, rather than psychodynamics. Right-Wing Authoritarianism (Altemeyer, 1981) assesses a tendency toward group conformity and the acceptance of conservative political ideologies that demean cultural outgroups. People high in Right-Wing Authoritarianism are hypervigilant toward perceived threats to the ingroup, and therefore (especially during difficult life conditions that threaten the ingroup) are likely to scapegoat outgroups. The other most prominent individual difference measure of prejudice, Social Dominance Orientation (Sidanius & Pratto, 1999), assesses a preference for group-based hierarchy. People high in Social Dominance Orientation seek to preserve established dominance hierarchies (which are threatened during times of social upheaval) and may scapegoat to restore ingroup dominance.

Authoritarianism and Social Dominance Orientation are strongly related to the mediator of scapegoating proposed here, endorsement of nationalistic and xenophobic political ideologies (Duckitt, ch. 24 this volume). Further, rather than indicating individual psychopathology, current research reveals these individual differences to be socialized belief systems (Duckitt, this volume), suggesting that cultures (as well as individuals) differ on these dimensions and therefore in their proneness to scapegoating (Staub, 1989). As Duckitt (this volume) notes, people's endorsement of authoritarianism and social dominance may increase when the ingroup is threatened (authoritarianism) or the status of the ingroup is diminished (social dominance), increasing attraction to and social consensus in scapegoating. Thus, people who endorse these belief systems are likely to be prominent among the willing adherents of scapegoat movements (Staub, 1989).

Allport's last criticism, (7), was that scapegoat theory ignores the possibility of realistic social conflict. In the model proposed here, realistic conflict is part of a continuum that can result in scapegoating. For instance, during war the enemy is reasonably defined as a source of problems. At the same time, exaggerated stereotypes and inaccurate conspiracy theories are also likely to arise. Realistic conflict increases the perceived plausibility that an outgroup caused the ingroup's woes and exacerbates envious stereotyping. Just when realistic conflict becomes unreasonable scapegoating is a difficult judgment to make, but similar psychological processes are at work and the former can easily develop into the latter.

Consequences (and Reinforcers) of Commitment to Scapegoat Ideologies

Commitment to a scapegoat ideology (G) mediates the negative consequences of scapegoating. Although already resented due to prior envious stereotypes, hostility toward scapegoated groups (H) increases in direct proportion to prejudiced perceivers' endorsement of an ideology that blames them for current shared misfortunes. Such ideologies (and increased hostility) cohere around political movements that act against the scapegoated group (I). Genocides, for example, are not spontaneous events, but top-down affairs, organized and ordered by a state. The perpetrators may be a mixture of ideologically-motivated true-believers (Goldhagen, 1997) and those who merely follow orders (Milgram, 1974). These motivations, however, may typically act in concert to produce a *willing obedience* to authority in which perpetrators' acceptance of a scapegoat ideology and commitment to a political movement motivates zealous compliance with orders (and, for some, spontaneous sadistic acts that exceed those orders).

The persecution of scapegoats launches perpetrators along a "continuum of destruction" in which initial, less severe actions spiral into increasingly violent behavior (Staub, 1989). Harming another creates psychological pressures to rationalize one's behavior, resulting in further derogation of victims (Lerner & Miller, 1978) and increased commitment to scapegoat ideologies that portray targets as powerful, implacable enemies who deserve what they get (hence the double-tipped arrows in figure 15.1). A vicious loop between ideological commitment, hostility, and violence, can devolve into mass murder, which is justified by the movement as moral and necessary, a matter of self-defense against an inherently malevolent "enemy."

Finally, if ideological commitment is the proximal cause of scapegoating, an important implication follows. Older scapegoat theories assumed that the lessening of frustrations would decrease subsequent scapegoating. The current model suggests, however, that if the scapegoating movement itself is viewed as having improved general life conditions (J), thereby "proving" its effectiveness, ideological commitment is likely to increase. For example, the Nazis' economic successes in the 1930s increased Germans' faith in Hitler's policies, encouraging the Nazis to take increasingly harsh and, finally, murderous actions against the Jews.

Has Allport Been Supported?

The model proposed here is quite different from the scapegoating theory Allport described. Importantly, it yields several implications that directly contradict earlier versions. First, only collective, not individual-level frustrations are likely to foster scapegoating. Second, groups that are perceived to be powerful (not weak and vulnerable) are likely to be victimized. Third, because frustration is an underlying, but not the proximal, cause of aggression, the lessening of frustrations may actually increase (not decrease) scapegoating (if improved conditions are attributed to the scapegoat movement).

Although the model proposed here differs significantly from Allport's view, frustration is still conceived to be a critical precondition for scapegoating. Further, the current model is strongly indebted to Allport's incisive critique of the original theory, which pointed the way forward. Although this model eschews projection as a central mechanism in scapegoating, it is important to note that researchers have recently constructed careful empirical tests of projection, yielding evidence that it may play a role in prejudice (see Newman & Caldwell, ch. 23 this volume). This revival of psychodynamic views is exciting, but although projection may account for individual differences in prejudice, it may not be a central mediator of consensual, organized scapegoating.

Future Directions

Although this chapter has focused on scapegoating as a collective process, individual-level scapegoating ought not to be abandoned as a topic of study. At the individual level, momentary frustrations, such as threats to self-esteem, can exacerbate derogation of outgroups (Fein & Spencer, 1997) and daily frustrations can lead individuals to respond disproportionately to minor provocations, especially by outgroup members (Miller, Pederson, Earleywine, & Pollock, 2003). However, such individual-level processes must be distinguished from collective processes; whereas the former explain when individuals are likely spontaneously to act on their prejudices, the latter explain when frustrations lead to organized persecution of outgroups.

Studying collective scapegoating presents significant methodological challenges, especially to laboratory-based experimental approaches. Specific components of the theory, such as the attribution of blame, may be amenable to experiments, but laboratory simulations of the entire model may be difficult or impossible to construct. To study the most extreme manifestations of scapegoating, such as genocide, requires a social-historical analysis of stereotypes and mass political movements. Allport himself suggested that "[i]t is chiefly the historical method that helps us to understand [scapegoating]" (1954/1979, p. 246). A rigorous social-scientific approach could, however, be applied to archival data. For example, content analysis of the propaganda directed at scapegoated groups, either historically (e.g., *Mein Kampf* and *Der Stürmer*) or currently (e.g., conspiracy theories on the internet) could test whether scapegoats are stereotyped in the manner the model predicts. Comparisons of scapegoat movements from different cultures and time periods might reveal (or disconfirm) the underlying social-psychological similarities the ideological model proposes.

The twentieth century was marred by increasingly frequent genocide attempts inspired by nationalism and fascism. In the current century, terrorism rooted in religious fundamentalism poses an equally grave threat. The ideologies differ, but their underlying dynamics have something in common – the scapegoating of groups who are viewed as powerful and malevolent, and who therefore must be annihilated. The persistence and destructiveness of such movements makes it tempting to conclude that people are inherently irrational, aggressive, and malicious. Despite his appeal to psychodynamics to explain scapegoating, however, Allport concluded that "human nature seems, on the whole, to prefer the sight of kindliness and friendliness to the sight of cruelty" (1954/1979, pp. xv–xvi). The perspective presented here – which explains fanatical ideological commitment to destructive ideologies as a result of "normal" social psychological processes in response to extreme circumstances – is consistent with Allport's cautious optimism that intergroup hostility is not an inevitable outcome of the human condition.

REFERENCES

Adams, H. E., Wright, L. W., & Lohr, B. A. (1996). Is homophobia associated with homosexual arousal? *Journal of Abnormal Psychology*, *105*, 440–5.

Adanir, F. (2001). Armenian deportations and massacres in 1915. In D. Chirot & M. E. P. Seligman (eds.), *Ethnopolitical warfare: Causes, consequences, and possible solutions* (pp. 71–81). Washington, DC: American Psychological Association.

Allport, G. W. (1954/1979). *The nature of prejudice*. Cambridge, MA: Perseus Books.

Altemeyer, B. (1981). *Right-wing author-itarianism*. Winnipeg: University of Manitoba Press.

Bettelheim, B. & Janowitz, M. (1950). *Dynamics of prejudice: A sociological study of veterans*. New York: Harper and Brothers.

Billig, M. (1976). *Social psychology and intergroup relations*. London: Academic Press.

Cottrell, C. A. & Neuberg, S. L. (2004). Different emotional reactions to different groups: A sociofunctional threat-based approach to "prejudice." Unpublished MS, Arizona State University.

Dollard, J., Doob, L. W., Miller, N. E., Mowrer, O. H., & Sears, R. R. (1939). *Frustration and aggression*. New Haven, CT: Yale University Press.

Fein, S. & Spencer, S. (1997). Prejudice as self-image maintenance: Affirming the self through derogating others. *Journal of Personality & Social Psychology*, 73, 31–44

Fiske, S. T., Cuddy, A. J. C., Glick, P., & Xu, J. (2002). A model of (often mixed) stereotype content: Competence and warmth respectively follow from perceived status and competition. *Journal of Personality and Social Psychology*, 82, 878–902.

Friedländer, S. (1997). *Nazi Germany and the Jews: The years of persecution, 1933–39* (vol. 1). New York: Harper Collins.

Fritzsche, P. (1999). *Germans into Nazis*. Boston: Harvard University Press.

Glick, P. (2002). Sacrificial lambs dressed in wolves' clothing: Envious prejudice, ideology, and the scapegoating of Jews. In L. S. Newman & R. Erber (eds.), *Understanding genocide: The social psychology of the Holocaust* (pp. 113–

42). New York: Oxford University Press.

Goldhagen, D. J. (1997). *Hitler's willing executioners: Ordinary Germans and the Holocaust*. New York: Random House.

Heider, F. (1958). *The psychology of interpersonal relations*. New York: John Wiley and Sons.

Karlsen, C. F. (1987). *The devil in the shape of a woman: Witchcraft in colonial New England*. New York: W. W. Norton & Co.

Kelley, H. H. (1967). Attribution theory in social psychology. In D. Levine (ed.), *Nebraska symposium on motivation* (vol 15., pp. 192–238). Lincoln: University of Nebraska Press.

Kiernan, B. (2001). The ethnic element in the Cambodian genocide. In D. Chirot & M. E. P. Seligman (eds.), *Ethnopolitical warfare: Causes, consequences, and possible solutions* (pp. 83–91). Washington, DC: American Psychological Association.

Lerner, M. J. & Miller, D. T. (1978). Just world research and the attribution process: Looking back and ahead. *Psychological Bulletin*, 85, 1030–51.

Leyens, J. P., Paladino, P. M., Rodriguez, R. T., Vaes, J., Demoulin, S., Rodriguez, A. P., & Gaunt, R. (2000). *Personality and Social Psychology Review*, 4, 186–97.

Milgram, S. (1974). *Obedience to authority*. New York: Harper and Row.

Miller, N., Pedersen, W. C., Earleywine, M., & Pollock, V. E. (2003). A theoretical model of triggered displaced aggression. *Personality and Social Psychology Review*, 7, 75–97.

Prunier, G. (2001). Genocide in Rwanda. In D. Chirot & M. E. P. Seligman (eds.), *Ethnopolitical warfare:*

Causes, consequences, and possible solutions (pp. 109–16). Washington, DC: American Psychological Association.

Pyszczynski, T., Greenberg, J., & Solomon, S. (1999). A dual process model of defense against conscious and unconscious death-related thoughts: An extension of terror management theory. *Psychological Review, 106*, 835–45.

Rhode, D. (2003). Radical Islam gains a seductive new voice. *The New York Times*, Oct. 26, D4–5.

Runciman, W. G. (1966). *Relative deprivation and social justice: A study of attitudes and social inequality in twentieth century England*. Berkeley: University of California Press.

Sidanius, J. & Pratto, F. (1999). *Social dominance: An intergroup theory of social hierarchy and oppression*. Cambridge: Cambridge University Press.

Staub, E. (1989). *The roots of evil: The psychological and cultural origins of genocide*. Cambridge: Cambridge University Press.

Staub, E. (1996). Cultural-societal roots of violence: The examples of genocidal violence and of contemporary youth violence in the United States. *American Psychologist, 51*, 117–32.

Sternberg, R. J. (2003). A duplex theory of hate: Development and application to terrorism, massacres, and genocides. *Review of General Psychology, 7*, 299–328.

Tajfel, H. (1981). *Human groups and social categories: Studies in social psychology*. Cambridge: Cambridge University Press.

Zawadzki, B. (1948). Limitations of the scapegoat theory of prejudice. *Journal of Abnormal and Social Psychology, 43*, 127–41.

Chapter Sixteen

Allport's Intergroup Contact Hypothesis: Its History and Influence

Thomas F. Pettigrew and Linda R. Tropp

What happens when groups interact? In a single chapter in *The Nature of Prejudice* (chapter 16, "The Effect of Contact"), Allport set the stage for researchers' efforts to answer this question by presenting his "intergroup contact hypothesis." This seminal chapter inspired a vast research literature that has spread far beyond race relations. In the present chapter, we will trace the origins of Allport's formulation by considering the 1950's intellectual climate in which he was working. We will also present a meta-analysis of intergroup contact studies that reveals strong support for his intergroup contact theory, while suggesting modifications to guide future research (see also Kenworthy, Turner, Hewstone, & Voci's ch. 17 in this volume).

Allport's Views: The Seeds of Intergroup Contact Theory

Theorists and practitioners began to speculate about the effects of intergroup contact long before there was a research base to guide them. Nineteenth-century thinking, dominated by Social Darwinism, was quite pessimistic. William Graham Sumner (1906) held that intergroup contact almost inevitably led to conflict. This followed from his famous contention that hostility toward outgroups is a reciprocal function of an ingroup's sense of superiority. Because Sumner also believed that most groups felt themselves to be superior, his theory viewed intergroup hostility and conflict to be natural and inevitable outcomes of contact. More recent perspectives make similar predictions (see Jackson, 1983; Levine & Campbell, 1972).

Twentieth-century writers continued to speculate about intergroup contact without empirical evidence. Some persisted in believing that contact between the races, even under conditions of equality, would only breed "suspicion, fear, resentment, disturbance, and at times open conflict" (Baker, 1934, p. 120). Others, especially following the Second World War, were more optimistic. Lett (1945) held that shared interracial experiences with a common objective led to "mutual understanding and regard" (p. 35). Instead, when groups "are isolated from one another," Brameld (1946) wrote, "prejudice and conflict grow like a disease" (p. 245).

The newly emerging discipline of social psychology soon began to study intergroup contact. This interest followed logically from the field's emphases on intergroup relations and interactions between people. University of Alabama researchers were among the first to conduct a study focused specifically on the effects of contact (Sims & Patrick, 1936). Their initial results were not encouraging. With each year students from the north attended the southern university, their anti-Black attitudes increased. Because the university's faculty and student body were then all White, northern students were likely to have met only lower-status Blacks and to respond according to Alabama's racist norms of that period.

Later studies investigated Black–White contact under more favorable conditions. After the desegregation of the Merchant Marine in 1948, close bonds developed between Black and White seamen on the ships and in the maritime union (Brophy, 1946). Consequently, the more voyages the White seamen took with Blacks, the more positive their racial attitudes became. Similarly, White police in Philadelphia who had worked with Black colleagues differed sharply from other White police (Kephart, 1957). They showed fewer objections to teaming with a Black partner, having Blacks join their previously all-White police districts, and taking orders from qualified Black officers.

The Social Science Research Council then asked the Cornell University sociologist, Robin Williams Jr., to review the research on intergroup relations. Williams's (1947) monograph, *The Reduction of Intergroup Tensions*, offers 102 testable "propositions" on intergroup relations that included the initial formulation of intergroup contact theory. Based on the scant research available, Williams (1947) stressed that intergroup contact would maximally reduce prejudice when: (a) the two groups share similar status, interests, and tasks; (b) the situation fosters personal, intimate intergroup contact; (c) the participants do not fit the stereotyped conceptions of their groups; and (d) the activities cut across group lines. These general principles will be familiar to anyone versed in Gordon Allport's framework.

In 1949, Stouffer et al.'s extensive study of "the American Soldier" provided the first massive field test of intergroup contact's effects. Using an ingenious quasi-experimental design, Stouffer showed that the experience of fighting side-by-side with African American soldiers in the desperate Battle of the Bulge during the winter of 1944–5 sharply changed the attitudes of White American soldiers. Though limited to the fighting situation, these altered attitudes were found among southerners as well as northerners, and among officers as well as enlisted men. Later field studies of racially desegregated public housing projects provided additional evidence for contact's ability to diminish racial prejudice among both Blacks and Whites (Deutsch & Collins, 1951; Wilner, Walkley, & Cook, 1955; Works, 1961).

This intellectual climate of the 1950s provided the foundation and context for Allport's thinking. Armed with this early work, he introduced in 1954 the most influential statement of contact theory in *The Nature of Prejudice*. The 24 notes of the book's chapter 16 on the effects of contact reveal what directly shaped Allport's formulation. He was well aware of Williams's initial statement; and he cited the Brophy, Stouffer et al., and housing studies.[1] But he also relied on the work of his doctoral students – Bernard Kramer (1950) and Barbara MacKenzie (1948). And, true to his belief in the richness of personal documents and idiographic methods, he also cited papers on personal intergroup contact experiences written for him by students in his annual graduate seminars on morale and prejudice.

From the student papers especially, Allport noted the contrasting effects of intergroup contact – often reducing but sometimes exacerbating prejudice. To account for these inconsistencies, Allport adopted a "positive factors" approach. Reduced prejudice will result, he held, when four positive features of the contact situation are present: (a) equal status between the groups, (b) common goals, (c) intergroup cooperation, and (d) the support of authorities, law, or custom.

Developments Since Allport

Allport's Contact Conditions

Studies conducted since Allport's original formulation generally support the importance of his four key conditions for intergroup contact to reduce prejudice. We shall consider each condition in detail.

Equal group status in the situation

Equal status" is often difficult to define and researchers use the term in different ways (Riordan, 1978). What is critical is that both groups perceive equal status in the situation (Cohen, 1982; Riordan & Ruggiero, 1980;

Robinson & Preston, 1976). Some writers emphasize that the groups should be of equal status *coming into* the contact situation (Brewer & Kramer, 1985; Foster & Finchilescu, 1986). But research demonstrates that equal status in the situation is effective in promoting positive intergroup attitudes even when the groups initially differ in status (Patchen, 1982; Schofield & Eurich-Fulcer, 2001).

Common goals

Effective contact usually involves an active effort toward a goal the groups share. Athletic teams furnish a prime example (Chu & Griffey, 1985; Patchen, 1982). In striving to win, teams comprising members of different groups must work together and rely on each other to achieve their shared goals. This consideration leads to the third characteristic of effective intergroup contact.

Intergroup cooperation

Attainment of common goals should be an interdependent effort based on cooperation rather than competition. Sherif et al. (1961) demonstrated this principle in their famous Robbers' Cave field study. These researchers cleverly devised barriers to such common goals as a planned picnic that could only be surmounted with the cooperation of both groups. The intergroup cooperation that then took place encouraged the development of positive relations between the groups.

Intergroup cooperation in schools provides more evidence (Brewer & Miller, 1984; Johnson, Johnson, & Maruyama, 1984; Schofield, 1989; Slavin, 1983). Guided by Allport's contentions, Elliot Aronson's "jigsaw" approach structures classrooms so that diverse groups of students strive cooperatively for common goals (Aronson & Patnoe, 1997; Stephan & Stephan, ch. 26 this volume). This direct application of contact theory has led to positive results for children around the globe, including those in Australia (Walker & Crogan, 1998), Germany (Eppler & Huber, 1990), Japan (Araragi, 1983), and the United States (Aronson & Gonzalez, 1988).

Support of authorities, law, or custom

Intergroup contact will also have more positive effects when it is backed by explicit support from authorities and social institutions. Authority sanction establishes norms of acceptance and guidelines for how members of different groups should interact with each other. Field research has demonstrated the importance of authority sanction in military (Landis, Hope, & Day, 1984), business (Morrison & Herlihy, 1992), and religious settings (Parker, 1968).

More broadly, the passage of civil-rights legislation has been instrumental in establishing antiprejudicial norms in contemporary American society – just as Allport predicted in his chapter 29 ("Ought There to be a Law?").

Incorporating these principles, Allport's formulation has guided research on intergroup contact for the past half-century. And interest in the potential for intergroup contact to reduce prejudice has continued to grow over these years. Researchers have pursued studies of intergroup contact using a wide range of research approaches, including field studies (e.g., Deutsch & Collins, 1951), laboratory experiments (e.g., Cook, 1969), surveys (e.g., Pettigrew, 1997), and archival research (e.g., Fine, 1979). Indeed, the research literature on intergroup contact has expanded substantially over the past half-century, both in the number of contact studies conducted and the range of groups examined.

A Meta-Analysis of Intergroup Contact Effects

We recently completed a meta-analysis of intergroup contact effects to review and evaluate this vast research literature (Pettigrew & Tropp, 2004a).[2] Meta-analysis is a statistical technique for determining the size and consistency of effects across tests of hypotheses. To perform a meta-analysis, researchers first attempt to find every study conducted on a particular topic. Then, they statistically pool the results to examine the overall patterns of effects and to uncover additional variables that moderate those effects (Rosenthal, 1991; Johnson & Eagly, 2000). We applied this technique first to evaluate the overall effects of intergroup contact on prejudice, and then we used this approach to assess support for the specific factors identified by Allport as important for successful contact.

For our meta-analysis, we conducted a 5-year search from which we uncovered 515 studies (including 714 independent samples and 1,365 nonindependent tests) that examined relationships between intergroup contact and prejudice. These cases were gathered from the 1940s through the year 2000, and, together, they represent responses from 250,493 individuals in 38 nations.

Close examination of these cases reveals that contact studies have increased steadily in number over the last several decades. Of the 515 studies, only 35 (7%) were conducted before 1960, 55 (11%) during the 1960s, 106 (21%) during the 1970s, 126 (26%) during the 1980s, and 178 of the studies (35%) were conducted between 1990 and 2000. Given the enormous expansion in published social science research of all types over the past half-century, this growth in contact studies probably reflects a fairly consistent proportion of published research devoted to the subject.

In our analysis, we used two indicators of effect size (Cohen's *d* and Pearson's *r*), with larger effect sizes signifying stronger relationships between intergroup contact and prejudice. Cohen's *d* represents the difference between the means of the contact and noncontact groups given in standard score units (or *z*-scores). For typical effects found in psychological research, a *d* of 0.25 is a small effect, 0.50 a medium effect, and 0.75 a large effect (Cohen, 1988). Results reported here derive from a fixed-effects model.

We also examined the effects at three distinct levels of analysis. Analyses conducted at the level of *studies* represent the overall effects for all data reported in each paper. Analyses at the level of *samples* represent the overall effects for *each independent sample* reported in each paper; since studies often include multiple samples, analyzing data at the level of samples offers larger numbers of cases for conducting more detailed comparisons of effects. Analyses conducted at the level of *tests* represent effects for *each individual test* of the relationship between intergroup contact and prejudice. Analyzing data at the test level offers even more cases for detailed comparisons. But because multiple tests from the same sample violate statistical assumptions of independence, we use tests as our unit of analysis when variables can only be measured at that level.

Overall, results from the meta-analysis reveal that greater levels of intergroup contact are typically associated with lower levels of prejudice across the three levels of analysis: studies (mean $d = -0.43$, mean $r = -0.21$), samples (mean $d = -0.43$, mean $r = -0.21$), and tests (mean $d = -0.42$, mean $r = -0.20$). Additional analyses indicate that these results are unlikely to be due to participant selection or publication biases; also, the more rigorous research studies reveal stronger contact–prejudice relationships. Moreover, these effects typically generalized, such that contact with individual outgroup members contributed to less prejudice toward the entire outgroup – an issue that has been debated extensively in the research literature (Pettigrew & Tropp, 2004a).

Contact studies have also extended far beyond their original focus on racial and ethnic groups to test the effects of contact with groups that differ in terms of age, sexual orientation, disability, and mental illness. The relationships between contact and prejudice vary significantly depending on the specific groups involved. Figure 16.1 provides mean effect sizes for studies and samples across the many types of target groups studied in the contact literature. The largest effects emerge for contact between heterosexuals and gays and lesbians (mean $d = -0.51$, mean $r = -0.25$). Indeed, these effects are significantly larger than those for studies involving racial and ethnic groups (mean $d = -0.45$, mean $r = -0.22$) and young people

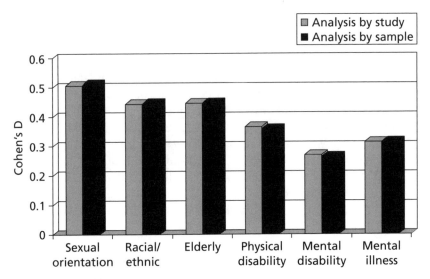

Figure 16.1 Negative mean effect sizes across different target groups by studies and samples

and the elderly (mean $d = -0.45$, mean $r = -0.22$), which show the next largest mean effects.

By contrast, research involving other groups produces much smaller average effects. In particular, studies involving contact between those with and without physical disabilities (mean $d = -0.36$, mean $r = -0.18$), mental disabilities (mean $d = -0.27$, mean $r = -0.13$) and mental illness (mean $d = -0.32$, mean $r = -0.16$) reveal significantly lower mean effect sizes than those of other target groups. Nonetheless, these contact–prejudice relationships for disabled targets remain statistically significant. It may be especially difficult to achieve truly equal status between groups in these intergroup contexts due to an exaggerated focus on the stigma, and the perceptions of unpredictability and dangerousness often associated with these stigmatizing conditions (Hebl & Kleck, 2000; Corrigan et al., 2003).

Has Allport Been Supported?

The primary thrust of our meta-analysis centered on the effectiveness of Allport's conditions for achieving positive intergroup outcomes. We began by attempting to rate each of Allport's four conditions individually for each study, but this approach proved impossible due to limitations in the information provided in most studies. Consequently, we employed two global indicators of Allport's proposed conditions – intergroup friendship and structured programs for optimal contact. These ratings actually offer more direct tests of the theory than our original approach, since Allport held that his four conditions should be integrated and implemented together, rather than listing them as variables to be considered individually. In addition, these two indices offer a stringent test of Allport's contentions, because they are *negatively* related to each other ($p < 0.001$). Indeed, only 4 of the 134 samples that experienced optimal structured contact used friends as the measure of contact.

The two authors conducted all ratings and achieved high estimates of inter-rater reliability for these two variables (kappas = 0.96 and 0.88, for intergroup friendship and structured programs for optimal contact, respectively). All discrepancies between the raters were then resolved through further discussion.

Intergroup friendship

As our first indicator of Allport's conditions, we compared effects for tests that either did or did not use cross-group friendships as the measure of intergroup contact. Here we assume that friendship requires the operation of conditions that approach Allport's specifications for optimal contact. Intergroup friendship is likely to involve cooperation and common goals, and it is likely to indicate repeated, equal-status interactions in a variety of settings over an extended period of time (Pettigrew, 1997).

The left bars in figure 16.2 present the results. We find that the 149 tests in which friendship was used as the contact measure revealed markedly stronger effects (mean $d = -0.55$, mean $r = -0.27$) than the remaining tests using other indicators of contact (mean $d = -0.37$, mean $r = -0.18$), a statistically significant difference.

Structured programs for optimal contact

Next we rated for all samples whether the contact situations included structured programs designed to approximate all or most of Allport's four optimal conditions. Here, we did not require that the contact situation specifically address each of Allport's conditions. Rather, we rated samples as to whether explicit efforts were made to create a contact situation that generally reflected the conditions outlined by Allport, such that it would maximize the potential for optimal intergroup contact.

The right bars in figure 16.2 present the mean effect sizes for samples that correspond to our ratings of structured contact programs. The 134 samples with contact situations structured to meet Allport's conditions

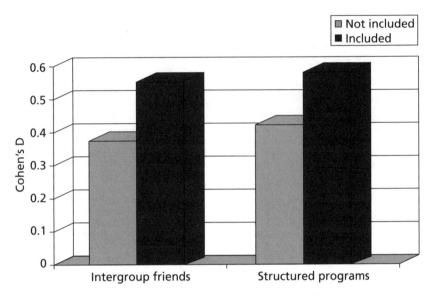

Figure 16.2 Negative mean effect sizes for intergroup friendship (tests) and structured contact programs (samples)

yielded significantly stronger contact–prejudice effects (mean $d = -0.58$, mean $r = -0.28$) than the remaining samples (mean $d = -0.42$, mean $r = -0.21$), a statistically significant difference.[3] Moreover, the samples involving structured contact programs provided relatively consistent effects. Their effect sizes become homogeneous once only 11 outliers (8 percent) are trimmed. And the average effect size for this homogenous subset (mean $d = -0.49$, mean $r = -0.24$) remains significantly larger than that for samples involving contact without structured programs.

In addition, it is important to observe in figure 16.2 that the inverse relationship between contact and prejudice persisted – thought not as strongly – when friendship was *not* the contact measure and when the contact situation was *not* structured to match Allport's key conditions. These findings suggest modifications of Allport's original conceptualization of intergroup contact theory.

Future Directions in Intergroup Contact Theory

Considered together, the meta-analytic results suggest a somewhat different perspective on intergroup contact than the view Allport held when he was constructing the initial theory. Although he taught sociology as a young man in Turkey (Nicholson, 2003), Allport emphasized proximal, immediate causes and generally disregarded distal, societal causes. So he looked to features of the immediate situation as determinants of intergroup contact's effects on prejudice. Additionally, both he and Williams (1947) before him doubted whether contact would generally reduce prejudice. Thus, they sought to specify the positive conditions that were necessary for intergroup contact to diminish prejudice.

However, a problem with this "positive factors" approach is that it puts forward an open-ended theory – that is, it invites the addition of further situational conditions thought to be crucial. This weakness has allowed subsequent researchers to propose a host of additional conditions needed to achieve positive contact outcomes (e.g., Foster & Finchilescu, 1986; Wagner & Machleit, 1986). But, with an ever-expanding list of necessary conditions, it becomes increasingly unlikely that any contact situations could meet these highly restrictive conditions (Pettigrew, 1986, 1998; Stephan, 1987).

Moreover, Allport's formulation specified neither the processes involved in intergroup contact's effects nor how these effects generalize to other situations, the entire outgroup, and other outgroups not involved in the contact (Pettigrew, 1998). Indeed, these omissions explain why he called it a "hypothesis" and not a "theory."

Instead, our meta-analytic findings suggest a reorientation for future contact research. Several key points illustrate our view of a reformulated approach to intergroup contact theory that builds on Allport's formulation while it exploits the research findings of the last five decades.

First, we noted in figure 16.2 that intergroup contact typically leads to positive outcomes even when no intergroup friendships were reported and in the absence of Allport's proposed conditions. Indeed, 95 percent of the 714 samples included in our meta-analysis reported that greater intergroup contact corresponds with lower intergroup prejudice; but only 10 percent of the contact measures involved intergroup friendship and only 19 percent of the samples reported contact under Allport's conditions. In his formulation, Allport held his optimal factors to be essential conditions for intergroup contact to diminish prejudice. But our results indicate that, while these factors are important, they are not necessary for achieving positive effects from intergroup contact. Instead, Allport's conditions are better thought of as *facilitating*, rather than essential, conditions for positive contact outcomes to occur.

This shift in perspective challenges the original "positive factors" approach taken by Allport in *The Nature of Prejudice*. But this revised view is consistent with the contentions of other theorists who propose that greater contact and familiarity typically contribute to increased liking (e.g., Homans, 1950; Zajonc, 1968). And presently, with only a minute number of contact studies showing contact leading to *greater* prejudice, the "negative factors" that curb reductions in prejudice now appear to be the most problematic theoretically, yet the least understood. Thus, future contact research must grant more attention to the negative factors operating in contact situations to enhance understanding of the conditions that may inhibit the development of positive contact outcomes.

In many ways, this stance reverses Allport's approach. It starts with the prediction that intergroup contact will generally diminish prejudice, but the magnitude of this effect will depend on the presence or absence of a large array of facilitating factors – not just the four emphasized by Allport. In particular, this approach focuses special attention on those negative factors that can subvert contact's typical reduction of prejudice.

Thus, this approach leads to an emphasis on the need for further research on the moderators and mediators of intergroup contact's effects. This emerging emphasis in intergroup contact research addresses directly those questions left unanswered by Allport concerning the generalization of contact's effects and the processes underlying these effects (Pettigrew, 1998; Dovidio, Gaertner, & Kawakami, 2003; see also Gaertner & Dovidio's ch. 5 and Kenworthy, Turner, Hewstone, & Voci's ch. 17 in this volume). For instance, increased salience of group representations during intergroup contact typically leads to greater reductions in prejudice toward the outgroup as a whole (Brown, Vivian, & Hewstone, 1999). And participants who do not think intergroup contact is important show far less prejudice reduction than those who regard it as important (Van Dick et al., 2004).

Emotions such as anxiety and threat are especially important negative factors in the link between contact and prejudice (Blair, Park, & Bachelor, 2003; Stephan et al., 2002; Stephan & Stephan, 1992; Voci & Hewstone, 2003; see also Stephan & Stephan's ch. 26 in this volume). Moreover, reducing anxiety during contact acts as an important mediator for contact's effects on prejudice. Examining studies from our meta-analysis that tested for anxiety, we estimate that the mediation by lowered anxiety explains roughly one-fifth to one-fourth of contact's effects in reducing prejudice (Pettigrew & Tropp, 2004b). Kenworthy, Turner, Hewstone, and Voci (ch. 17 this volume) consider these important advances in contact theory in more detail.

Finally, to broaden our understanding of contact's effects, our meta-analytic results indicate the need for greater attention to the specific groups under study. We noted in figure 16.1 that the outcomes of contact vary substantially across different intergroup contexts. In line with this view, emerging intergroup research has begun to examine the ways in which people show different emotional reactions to outgroups, depending on their perceptions of those groups and histories of relations with them (see Mackie & Smith, 2002 and Smith & Mackie, ch. 22 this volume, for recent reviews). These perspectives suggest a need to extend Allport's approach beyond a general conceptualization of contact's effects, to examine distinct points of concern and responses to intergroup contact across different intergroup relationships. As such, future contact research should consider the ways in which contact situations might best be tailored to accommodate the diverse concerns that are likely to be relevant when different groups come into contact.

NOTES

1   As his graduate assistant "go-for" (not for coffee but for books from the library), the first author remembers well that the Deutsch and Collins (1951) volume on interracial contact in public housing made an especially important impact on Allport's thinking about intergroup contact. It also should be noted that Allport himself valued this chapter on contact. When he had to condense by 40 percent *The Nature of Prejudice* for its 1958 abridged paperback edition (Allport, 1958), he reduced chapter 16 on contact only slightly and retained all but three of the original references.

2   A preliminary report of this work, using fewer than half of the studies, appeared in Pettigrew and Tropp (2000).

3   It may seem surprising that only 134 (19 percent) of our samples followed Allport's model. But this result reflects the fact that 70 percent of the samples in our file rely on participants reporting on their contact without information concerning the conditions of the contact.

REFERENCES

Allport, G. W. (1954/1979). *The nature of prejudice*. Cambridge, MA: Perseus Books.

Allport, G. W. (1958). *The nature of prejudice*. Garden City, NY: Doubleday Anchor Books.

Araragi, C. (1983). The effect of the jigsaw learning method on children's academic performance and learning attitude. *Japanese Journal of Educational Psychology*, *31*, 102–12.

Aronson, E. & Gonzalez, A. (1988). Desegregation, jigsaw, and the Mexican-American experience. In P. A. Katz & D. A. Taylor (eds.), *Eliminating racism: Profiles in controversy* (pp. 301–14). New York: Plenum Press.

Aronson, E. & Patnoe, S. (1997). *The jigsaw classroom: Building cooperation in the classroom* (2nd ed.). New York: Addison Wesley Longman.

Baker, P. E. (1934). *Negro–White adjustment*. New York, NY: Association Press.

Blair, I. V., Park, B., & Bachelor, J. (2003). Are some people more anxious than others? *Group Processes and Intergroup Relations, 6,* 151–69.

Brameld, T. (1946). *Minority problems in the public schools*. New York: Harper.

Brewer, M. B. & Kramer, R. M. (1985). The psychology of intergroup attitudes and behavior. *Annual Review of Psychology, 36,* 219–43.

Brewer, M. B. & Miller, N. (1984). Beyond the contact hypothesis: Theoretical perspectives on desegregation. In N. Miller & M. B. Brewer (eds.), *Groups in contact: The psychology of desegregation* (pp. 281–302). Orlando: Academic Press.

Brophy, I. N. (1946). The luxury of anti-Negro prejudice. *Public Opinion Quarterly, 9,* 456–66.

Brown, R. J., Vivian, J., & Hewstone, M. (1999). Changing attitudes through intergroup contact: The effects of group membership salience. *European Journal of Social Psychology, 17,* 131–42.

Chu, D. & Griffey, D. (1985). The contact theory of racial integration: The case of sport. *Sociology of Sport Journal, 2,* 323–33.

Cohen, E. G. (1982). Expectation states and interracial interaction in school settings. *Annual Review of Sociology, 8,* 209–35.

Cohen, J. (1988). *Statistical power analysis for the behavioral sciences*. Hillsdale, NJ: Erlbaum.

Cook, S. W. (1969). Motives in a conceptual analysis of attitude-related behavior. In J. Brigham & T. Weissbach (eds.), *Racial attitudes in America: Analyses and findings of social psychology* (pp. 250–60). New York: Harper & Row.

Corrigan, P., Markowitz, F. E., Watson, A., Rowan, D., & Kubiak, M. A. (2003). An attributional model of public discrimination toward persons with mental illness. *Journal of Health and Social Behavior, 44,* 162–79.

Deutsch, M. & Collins, M. (1951). *Interracial housing: A psychological evaluation of a social experiment*. Minneapolis: University of Minnesota Press.

Dovidio, J. F., Gaertner, S. L., & Kawakami, K. (2003). Intergroup contact: The past, present, and the future. *Group Processes and Intergroup Relations, 6(1),* 5–21.

Eppler, R. & Huber, G. L. (1990). Wissenserwerb im Team: Empirische Untersuchung von Effekten des Gruppen-Puzzles. [Knowledge acquisition in a team: Empirical investigation of the effects of group puzzles.] *Psychologie in Erziehung und Unterricht, 37,* 172–8.

Fine, G. A. (1979). The Pinkston settlement: An historical and social psychological investigation of the contact hypothesis. *Phylon, 40,* 229–42.

Foster, D. & Finchilescu, G. (1986). Contact in a "non-contact" society: The case of South Africa. In M. Hewstone & R. Brown (eds.), *Contact and conflict in intergroup encounters* (pp. 119–36). Oxford: Blackwell.

Hebl, M. R. & Kleck, R. E. (2000). The social consequences of physical disability. In T. F. Heatherton, R. E.

Kleck, M. R. Hebl, & J. G. Hull (eds.), *The social psychology of stigma* (pp. 419–39). New York: Guilford.

Homans, G. C. (1950). *The human group.* New York: Harcourt, Brace & World.

Jackson, J. W. (1983). Contact theory of intergroup hostility: A review and evaluation of the theoretical and empirical literature. *International Journal of Group Tensions, 23*, 43–65.

Johnson, B. T. & Eagly, A. H. (2000). Quantitative synthesis of social psychological research. In H. T. Reis & C. M. Judd (eds.), *Handbook of research methods in social psychology* (pp. 496–528). Cambridge: Cambridge University Press.

Johnson, D. W., Johnson, R. T., & Maruyama, G. (1984). Goal interdependence and interpersonal-personal attraction in heterogeneous classrooms: A meta-analysis. In N. Miller & M. B. Brewer (eds.), *Groups in contact: The psychology of desegregation* (pp. 187–212). Orlando: Academic Press.

Kephart, W. M. (1957). *Racial factors and urban law enforcement.* Philadelphia: University of Pennsylvania Press.

Kramer, B. M. (1950). Residential contact as a determinant of attitudes toward Negroes. Unpublished doctoral dissertation, Harvard University.

Landis, D., Hope, R. O., & Day, H. R. (1984). Training for desegregation in the military. In N. Miller & M. B. Brewer (eds.), *Groups in contact: The psychology of desegregation* (pp. 258–78). Orlando: Academic Press.

Lett, H. A. (1945). Techniques for achieving interracial cooperation. In *Proceedings of the Institute on Race Relations and Community Organization.* Chicago, IL: University of Chicago

and the American Council on Race Relations.

Levine, R. A. & Campbell, D. T. (1972). *Ethnocentrism: Theories of conflict, ethnic attitudes, and group behavior.* New York: John Wiley.

MacKenzie, B. K. (1948). The importance of contact in determining attitudes toward Negroes. *Journal of Abnormal and Social Psychology, 43*, 417–41.

Mackie, D. M. & Smith, E. R. (eds.) (2002). *From prejudice to intergroup emotions: Differentiated reactions to social groups.* New York: Psychology Press.

Morrison, E. W. & Herlihy, J. M. (1992). Becoming the best place to work: Managing diversity at American Express travel related services. In S. E. Jackson and associates (eds.), *Diversity in the workplace: Human resources initiatives* (pp. 203–26). New York: Guilford.

Nicholson, I. A. M. (2003). *Inventing personality: Gordon Allport and the science of selfhood.* Washington, DC: American Psychological Association.

Parker, J. H. (1968). The interaction of Negroes and Whites in an integrated church setting. *Social Forces, 46*, 359–66.

Patchen, M. (1982). *Black–white contact in schools.* West Lafayette, IN: Purdue University Press.

Pettigrew, T. F. (1971). *Racially separate or together?* New York: McGraw-Hill.

Pettigrew, T. F. (1986). The contact hypothesis revisited. In H. Hewstone & R. Brown (eds.), *Contact and conflict in intergroup encounters* (pp. 169–95). Oxford: Blackwell.

Pettigrew, T. F. (1997). Generalized intergroup contact effects on prejudice. *Personality and Social Psychology Bulletin, 23*, 173–85.

Pettigrew, T. F. (1998). Intergroup contact theory. *Annual Review of Psychology, 49*, 65–85.

Pettigrew, T. F. & Tropp, L. R. (2000). Does intergroup contact reduce prejudice? Recent meta-analytic findings. In S. Oskamp (ed.), *Reducing prejudice and discrimination: Social psychological perspectives* (pp. 93–114). Mahwah, NJ: Erlbaum.

Pettigrew, T. F. & Tropp, L. R. (2004a). A meta-analytic test of intergroup contact theory. Unpublished manuscript under review, University of California, Santa Cruz, CA.

Pettigrew, T. F. & Tropp, L. R. (2004b). Intergroup anxiety as a mediator for contact–prejudice relationships. Manuscript in preparation.

Riordan, C. (1978). Equal-status interracial contact: A review and revision of the concept. *International Journal of Intercultural Relations, 2*, 161–85.

Riordan, C. & Ruggiero, J. (1980). Producing equal-status interracial interaction: A replication. *Social Psychology Quarterly, 43*, 131–6.

Robinson, J. W. & Preston, J. D. (1976). Equal status contact and modification of racial prejudice: A reexamination of the contact hypothesis. *Social Forces, 54*, 911–24.

Rosenthal, R. (1991). *Meta-analytic procedures for social research* (rev. ed.). Newbury Park, CA: Sage.

Schofield, J. W. (1989). *Black and White in school: Trust, tension, or tolerance?* New York: Teachers College Press.

Schofield, J. W. & Eurich-Fulcer, R. (2001). When and how school desegregation improves intergroup relations. In R. Brown & S. L. Gaertner (eds.), *Blackwell handbook of social psychology: Intergroup processes* (pp. 475–94). Malden, MA: Blackwell.

Sherif, M., Harvey, O. J., White, B. J., Hood, W. R., & Sherif, C. W. (1961). *Intergroup conflict and cooperation: The Robbers Cave experiment.* Norman, OK: University of Oklahoma Book Exchange.

Sims, V. M. & Patrick, J. R. (1936). Attitude toward the Negro of northern and southern college students. *Journal of Social Psychology, 7*, 192–204.

Slavin, R. E. (1983). *Cooperative learning.* New York: Longman.

Stephan, C. W. & Stephan, W. G. (1992). Reducing intercultural anxiety through intercultural contact. *International Journal of Intercultural Relations, 16*, 89–106.

Stephan, W. G. (1987). The contact hypothesis in intergroup relations. In C. Hendrick (ed.), *Review of personality and social psychology: Group processes and intergroup relations* (vol. 9, pp. 13–40). Newbury Park, CA: Sage.

Stephan, W. G., Boniecki, K. A., Ybarra, O., Bettencourt, A., Ervin, K. S., Jackson, L. A., McNatt, P. S., & Renfro, C. L. (2002). The role of threats in the racial attitudes of Blacks and Whites. *Personality and Social Psychology Bulletin, 28*, 1242–54.

Stouffer, S. A., Schuman, E. A., DeVinney, L. C., Star, S. A., & Williams, R. M., Jr. (1949). *The American soldier: Adjustment during army life* (vol. 1). Princeton: Princeton University Press.

Sumner, W. G. (1906). *Folkways.* New York: Ginn.

Van Dick, R., Wagner, U., Pettigrew, T. F., Christ, O., Wolff, C., Petzel, T., Castro, V., & Jackson, J. S. (in press). The role of perceived importance in intergroup contact. *Journal of Personality and Social Psychology, 87*, 211–27.

Voci, A. & Hewstone, M. (2003). Intergroup contact and prejudice toward immigrants in Italy: The mediational role of anxiety and the moderational role of group salience. *Group Processes and Intergroup Relations, 6*, 37–52.

Wagner, U. & Machleit, U. (1986). "Gastarbeiter" in the Federal Republic of Germany: Contact between Germans and migrant populations. In M. Hewstone & R. Brown (eds.), *Contact and conflict in intergroup encounters* (pp. 59–78). Oxford: Blackwell.

Walker, I. & Crogan, M. (1998). Academic performance, prejudice, and the jigsaw classroom: New pieces to the puzzle. *Journal of Community and Applied Social Psychology, 8*, 381–93.

Williams, R. M., Jr. (1947). *The reduction of intergroup tensions.* New York: Social Science Research Council.

Wilner, D. M, Walkley, R. P., & Cook, S. W. (1955). *Human relations in interracial housing: A study of the contact hypothesis.* Minneapolis, MN: University of Minnesota Press.

Works, E. (1961). The prejudice-interaction hypothesis from the point of view of the Negro minority group. *American Journal of Sociology, 67*, 47–52.

Zajonc, R. B. (1968). Attitudinal effects of mere exposure. *Journal of Personality and Social Psychology, 9*, Monograph supplement, no. 2, part 2: 1–27.

Chapter Seventeen

Intergroup Contact: When Does it Work, and Why?

Jared B. Kenworthy, Rhiannon N. Turner, Miles Hewstone, and Alberto Voci

In his 1954 volume *The Nature of Prejudice*, Allport proposed that, under certain conditions, bringing together individuals from opposing groups could reduce intergroup prejudice. Prior to Allport's formulation of contact theory, researchers had already considered the impact of contact through field research when, following the Second World War, attentions turned to the domestic social problem of race relations in the United States (e.g., Williams, 1947; see also Pettigrew & Tropp, ch. 16 this volume). By specifying some critical situational conditions necessary for intergroup contact to reduce prejudice, however, it was Allport's theory that emerged as the most influential. Despite his optimism about the potential benefits of contact, Allport warned that superficial contact between members of different groups would, in fact, reinforce stereotypes, by failing to provide new information about each group, or via a self-fulfilling prophecy whereby cautious avoidance of intimacy is mutually interpreted as distrust or dislike, confirming initial suspicion. Thus he wrote, "the casual contact has left matters worse than before" (Allport, 1954/1979, p. 264).

Given that the ideas initially proposed by Allport were based on the quite limited literature available in the early 1950s, the fact that its predictions have held up over the past half-century is rather impressive. By contrast, contemporary researchers and theorists have the advantage of 50 years of extensive contact research (see Pettigrew & Tropp, 2000, for a detailed meta-analysis of these data; see also Pettigrew & Tropp, ch. 16 this volume) on which to base extensions and reformulations of the hypothesis (see Pettigrew, 1998).

Our chapter builds upon the ideas developed in Allport's chapter 16, "The Effect of Contact," and complements the meta-analytic review of the existing empirical literature that appears in the chapter by Pettigrew and Tropp. We begin with a brief presentation of Allport's ideas regarding how contact might reduce intergroup bias, then we discuss both theoretical developments and empirical findings relevant to his contact hypothesis. Finally, we suggest some avenues of research that will further illuminate the processes by which contact reduces intergroup prejudice.

Allport's Views on Contact

Allport was cautiously optimistic about the role of contact in reducing prejudice. He began his discussion of contact by citing work by sociologists, whose "peaceful progression" model (Allport, 1954/1979, p. 261) described a series of steps through which groups in contact progress until the intergroup relationship is a peaceful one: "At first, there is *sheer contact*, leading soon to *competition*, which in turn gives way to *accommodation*, and finally to *assimilation*" (p. 261, emphases in original). But, he warned, "whether or not the law of peaceful progression will hold seems to depend on the *nature of the contact*" (p. 262).

Allport's chapter on contact dealt primarily with considerations of contact across several kinds of social situations, but he summarized his thinking in a general hypothesis about when contact will yield the most positive results:

> Prejudice . . . may be reduced by equal status contact between majority and minority groups in the pursuit of common goals. The effect is greatly enhanced if this contact is sanctioned by institutional supports (i.e., by law, custom or local atmosphere), and provided it is of a sort that leads to the perception of common interests and common humanity between members of the two groups. (1954/1979, p. 281)

Thus, the basic formulaic version of the contact hypothesis had four elements: (a) equal status, (b) common goals, (c) institutional support, and (d) a perception of similarity between the two groups.

Research since then has extended Allport's ideas about *when* contact will be most effective. For example, three distinct lines of research examined the nature of perceivers' cognitive representations of groups, each proposing different ideas about how the categorization of "us" and "them" will be optimally effective in reducing prejudice (see also Gaertner & Dovidio, ch. 5 this volume). The *decategorization* model (Brewer & Miller, 1984) proposed minimizing the use of category labels altogether, and instead interacting on an individual basis. The *recategorization* model (e.g., Gaertner, Mann, Murrell, & Dovidio, 1989) suggested that intergroup contact could be maximally effective if perceivers rejected the use of "us" and "them" in favor of a more inclusive, superordinate "we" category. These two models can be seen as extensions to Allport's notions of perceived similarity between groups and, to a lesser degree, equality of status. Another model (Hewstone & Brown, 1986), called *categorization* (or sometimes mutual intergroup differentiation) pointed out practical problems with personalized, as opposed to group-based, interactions, and instead promoted keeping group boundaries intact and salient during intergroup encounters. Nevertheless, despite their conceptual differences, all of the various models that followed Allport paid a tribute to his ideas in some fundamental way.

In addition to studying *when* contact works, researchers have recently taken a keen interest in understanding *how* contact works. In other words, social psychologists began to ask, "What are the psychological processes and mechanisms that underlie the effectiveness of contact as a means of reducing intergroup prejudice?" Our focus in this chapter will be on both when and how contact reduces prejudice.

Developments Since Allport

In this section, we discuss some empirical findings related to when and how contact produces beneficial effects for intergroup relations. As mentioned above, Allport (1954/1979) noted that simple contact *per se* with a member of the outgroup would not necessarily be sufficient to change attitudes towards that group. He even asserted that "the bare fact of equal-status contact" (1954/1979, p. 276) would not necessarily improve intergroup relations. He seemed to believe deeply that "contact must reach below the surface in order to be effective in altering prejudice" (p. 276). Some contemporary theoretical approaches, discussed below, have attempted to optimize contact by getting "below the surface" in various ways.

The proponents of an interpersonal approach (e.g., Brewer & Miller, 1984), which is often called *decategorization*, predicted optimal contact under conditions of minimized salience of group membership and group boundaries. This would allow those involved in the intergroup interaction to focus on personal information that individuates outgroup members and makes them unique and distinct from their group as a whole. Hewstone and Brown (1986) argued, in contrast, that by focusing solely on individuating information, the outgroup member would not be seen as an outgroup member at all, and thus any positive outcomes that result from the interaction would fail to generalize to other members of the category. In other words, they are likely to be subtyped, or cognitively processed as separate from the group as a whole, or treated as an individual with no connection to the overall group. Indeed, a real concern is that individuals may discount positive experiences with outgroup members as an exception to the rule. Consequently, Hewstone and Brown (1986) argued that, under decategorized contact, attitudes towards the outgroup as a whole would remain unchanged, due to the very conditions intended to produce the attitude change. Nevertheless, practically, for categories that are visually salient (e.g., race, gender), complete decategorization is unlikely to occur, thus providing some basis for the benefits of positive personalized interaction to generalize to attitudes to the group as a whole (Miller, 2002).

Hewstone and Brown's (1986) alternative general theoretical solution – *categorization* – proposed that for the positive effects of contact to generalize to the entire outgroup, it is vital that category salience remains relatively high during the interaction. Although it is not necessary that category salience be maintained at all times (see van Oudenhoven, Grounewoud, & Hewstone, 1996), ideally it should occur before the outgroup individual is perceived as atypical of their group.

Methodologically and practically, category salience is easier to induce than is decategorization because ignoring group membership is often perceptually difficult to achieve, and may be resisted by those who strongly identify with their group. Emphasizing categorization during contact, however, is not without its own dangers. Making categories salient risks exacerbating and reinforcing perceptions of group differences, which may result in anxiety, discomfort, and fear (Hewstone & Brown, 1986). This would effectively serve to undermine Allport's notion of the importance of a perceived common humanity between groups during contact.

These reactions themselves have a number of subsequent negative consequences, including cognitive and motivational information-processing biases, emotional reactions, defensive behaviors, and even avoidance of future intergroup contact (see Stephan & Stephan, 1985). A theoretical paradox had thus arisen: whereas interpersonal encounters were likely to be pleasant, they might fail to generalize without some salience of group membership; conversely, salient intergroup encounters could generalize to the whole outgroup, but might be undermined by the concomitant generation of *intergroup anxiety* (viz., "anxiety stemming from contact with outgroup members"; see Stephan & Stephan, 1985, p. 158; see also Smith & Mackie, ch. 22 this volume).

Several studies sought to demonstrate how the effects of positive contact would better generalize to the outgroup when those involved were aware of the intergroup nature of the interaction (see Pettigrew, 1998, for a review). These studies manipulated or measured factors which produce "intergroup" rather than "interpersonal" contact. For example, research has investigated the effect of increasing the salience of one's group membership (e.g. van Oudenhoven et al., 1996), perceiving the outgroup target of intergroup contact as typical of the entire group (e.g., Ensari & Miller, 2002), or perceiving the outgroup individual's category as highly homogenous, reducing the likelihood of cognitive subtyping (i.e., "exceptional" contact; Allport, 1954/1979, p. 263). Cross-sectional survey data also reveal the importance of category salience in moderating the effects of intergroup contact (Brown, Vivian, & Hewstone, 1999). In Brown et al. (1999), Europeans were generally more likely to express an interest in living in another country when they had greater contact with people from that country and the quality of that contact (measured as intimacy) was high, particularly among respondents who reported high outgroup salience during contact (see Brown & Zagefka, ch. 4 this volume).

Recent empirical work has considered the *combined* impact of the intergroup and interpersonal approaches. Specifically, Ensari and Miller (2002, study 1, involving traditional Islamic versus secularist students in Turkey) had a traditional Islamic confederate, whose attire and description of herself were either typical or atypical of her group, disclose either personal and unique information or impersonal and general information to a participant, prior to undertaking a cooperative task (see Miller, 2002). The combined perceptions of disclosure (interpersonal) and typicality (intergroup) reduced subsequent bias toward new outgroup members, who themselves had no connection to the confederate other than shared group membership. Recent research shows cross-group friendship (i.e., intimate contact with a member of the outgroup) to be a particularly effective form of intergroup contact (Pettigrew, 1997). Moreover, even indirect contact (i.e., the mere *knowledge* that other ingroup members have friends in the outgroup; Wright, Aron, McLaughlin-Volpe, & Ropp, 1997), can lead to more positive intergroup attitudes. These findings indicate the importance of the intimacy of contact and its potential to personalize the outgroup member, but they also suggest that despite the importance of a personalized interaction, some level of category salience must also be maintained if positive attitudes are to generalize to other members of the outgroup category.

The research presented here thus suggests that ignoring or overlooking group membership during contact may not necessarily result in better intergroup attitudes and relations. Even if eliminating category salience can seem theoretically advantageous, group memberships are frequently both subjectively and collectively meaningful and emotionally significant, and in such cases group members are reluctant to surrender their identity and distinctiveness (Brewer, 1991). Allport himself foresaw this dilemma between eliminating categories via assimilation and retaining important group memberships, and proposed that "for those who wish to assimilate, there should be no artificial barriers placed in their way; for those who wish to maintain ethnic integrity, their efforts should be met with tolerance and appreciation" (1954/1979, p. 517). Moreover, even if avoiding group salience seems theoretically desirable, it may be perceptually impossible for certain groups, such as race, age, and gender, for which even a minimal cue to group membership is asymptotically and unambiguously high. The elimination of group membership is not only impractical and threatening (Brewer, 1991), but it also limits the impact of intergroup contact on generalization. Therefore, retaining group salience in a positive, intimate, cross-group interaction appears to be the best way to optimize intergroup contact. The findings presented here indicate that interpersonal (Brewer & Miller, 1984; Miller, 2002) and intergroup (Hewstone & Brown, 1986) approaches are not incompatible, and should be employed conjunctively to produce the most effective intergroup contact that truly reaches "below the surface" (Allport, 1954/1979, p. 276; see Brown & Hewstone, in press, for a detailed review).

A New Framework:
How Does Intergroup Contact Work?

Based on meta-analytic findings (Pettigrew & Tropp, 2000), as well as on recent primary-level investigation (Voci & Hewstone, 2003), it is clear that contact *per se* typically has a reliable and independent effect (e.g., bottom path of figure 17.1) on the reduction of prejudice. Nevertheless, recent modifications of the contact hypothesis have included an emphasis on moderation (i.e., when it works; see previous section) and mediation (i.e., how it works). Although affective factors are now considered to be particularly important (see Pettigrew, 1998), individuation and self-disclosure – factors that have both cognitive and affective elements – have also been found to mediate the relationship between intergroup contact and improved outgroup attitudes (e.g., Turner, Hewstone, & Voci, 2005).

Pettigrew (1998) suggested a three-stage model in which an optimal contact experience is developed gradually. Decategorization and individuation (Brewer & Miller, 1984) should occur first. Although the interaction initially may be characterized by anxiety, the effects of decategorization

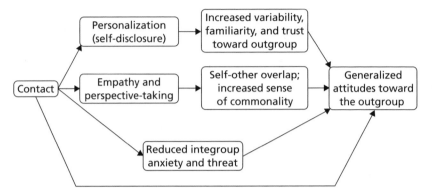

Figure 17.1 Model of mediating processes linking contact and improved intergroup attitudes. Previous work (Voci & Hewstone, 2003) has indicated that the direct paths from contact to anxiety and to outgroup attitudes are moderated by group salience: they are stronger when group salience is high, as compared to when it is low. Such moderational tests remain to be conducted for other mediators shown.

should reduce this negative affect. If successful, this initial contact should then develop into a stage during which group salience will result in generalized positive attitudes towards the outgroup via categorization (Hewstone & Brown, 1986). Finally, recategorization (Gaertner & Dovidio, 2000) should occur during which a perception of a common ingroup is achieved. Pettigrew's model suggests that mediators and moderators might work together to produce the optimal contact situation (see Brown & Hewstone, in press).

Dovidio, Gaertner, and Kawakami (2003) argue for a unified frame-work which explains how the contact conditions proposed by Allport might achieve their effect. In this proposal, the several explanatory variables (i.e., mediators) fall into five key categories: functional relations (such as cooperation), behavioral factors (such as cognitive dissonance), affective factors (such as empathy and anxiety), and two cognitive factors: (a) learning new information and social representations via decategorization or personalization and (b) recategorization. Dovidio et al.'s (2003) reformulation suggests that the four prerequisite conditions (discussed earlier in this chapter), friendship, and personal interaction, lead to the five mediating processes, which result in more positive outgroup attitudes and reduced stereotyping. In the final stage, these attitudes are generalized from the individual to the outgroup as a whole. Both cognitive and affective factors are important aspects of the process by which this generalization occurs.

Cognitive Factors

"Learning about the outgroup" was originally considered to be a key process involved in reducing prejudice, because general knowledge about the outgroup as a whole was thought to counteract ignorance, and thus undermine stereotypes. Although meta-analytic findings (see Pettigrew & Tropp, ch. 16 this volume) reveal that increasing knowledge about the outgroup has some effect, it is not a primary mechanism by which contact changes intergroup attitudes. Nevertheless, other types of information, such as the acquisition of knowledge about unique attributes of specific individuals that distinguishes them from other group members, has been found to effectively reduce ingroup bias (e.g., Miller, Kenworthy, Stenstrom, & Canales, in press) by helping to disconfirm stereotypes about the outgroup.

Relatedly, exchanges between members of different groups in which the members reveal meaningful aspects of themselves through self-disclosure (see figure 17.1) have been demonstrated to be important in the development of interpersonal relationships that lead to successful intergroup contact. Self-disclosure may reduce prejudice by increasing the complexity and differentiated perception of the outgroup target, thus overriding the use of stereotypes to categorize and evaluate an individual. Consistent with this explanation, a cross-sectional survey study of the orientation of White elementary and high school students to South Asians revealed that cross-group friendship was associated with greater self-disclosure, which subsequently resulted in more positive intergroup attitudes towards South Asian people (Turner et al., 2005). Self-disclosure also increased the perceived differences among South Asian people, rendering homogenous perceptions of the outgroup, such as those based on stereotypes, less tenable.

Although there is evidence that changes in cognitions are an important mechanism by which contact improves attitudes toward other groups, other processes, such as those related to affect and emotion, may also operate. For instance, self-disclosure might decrease prejudice by increasing familiarity, thereby reducing the threat often associated with intergroup contact. Self-disclosure may also improve intergroup relations because the disclosed information is rarer, and therefore has higher subjective value than less intimate, and more common, information (Petty & Mirels, 1981), making the exchange more rewarding for the individuals involved in the contact because it implies a trust that is shared usually only with friends. Similarly, when members of different groups accommodate each other (the adaptation of oneself to meet the needs of a communicative partner) during intergroup contact, the interaction is likely to be enjoyable and productive for both partners, producing positive affect that undermines negative intergroup attitudes. In the next section, we consider such affective processes.

Affective Factors

Pettigrew and Tropp's (2000; ch. 16 this volume) meta-analysis has revealed that, although cognitive processes did appear to contribute somewhat to the effects of intergroup contact, affective factors appeared to be much more influential. Specifically, Pettigrew and Tropp (2000) concluded that *anxiety* appears to be a more important link between contact and reduced prejudice than is increased knowledge of the outgroup. They estimated that 20–25% of the effect of contact in reducing prejudice is explained by a reduction in intergroup anxiety. In addition, cross-group friendship is thought to be one of the best predictors of better intergroup attitudes because of its impact in terms of reducing anxiety and threat (see figure 17.1).

Intergroup anxiety is thought to stem from the anticipation of negative consequences during contact, such as embarrassment, rejection, discrimination, or misunderstanding, and may therefore be exacerbated by minimal prior contact with the outgroup and large status or numerical differences between the ingroup and the outgroup (Stephan & Stephan, 1985). Anxiety may also result from intergroup threat, either symbolic or realistic, a distinction that is prominent in Stephan and Stephan's (2000) Integrated Threat Model. *Symbolic threat* is conceptualized as a threat to the value system, belief system, or worldview of the ingroup, whereas *realistic threat* is a threat to the political and economic power, or physical well-being, of the ingroup.

In general, intergroup anxiety is associated with a number of negative outcomes that may harm the impact of contact, including information-processing biases such as a narrowed focus of attention and simplified, expectancy-confirming cognitive processing, which may lead to avoidance of contact and polarized group judgments (Stephan & Stephan, 1985). In contrast, positive intergroup contact, in terms of both greater quantity and better quality, is associated with lower levels of intergroup anxiety, which has positive implications for intergroup relations (see Islam & Hewstone, 1993).

Although cognitive and affective processes are conceptually distinct, they frequently operate in concert. For example, in a cross-sectional survey study of Protestant and Catholic students in Northern Ireland, direct and indirect friendship were both found to predict less prejudice toward, as well as greater cognitive representations of variability of, the other religious community; these relationships were both largely accounted for by reduced intergroup anxiety (Paolini, Hewstone, Cairns, & Voci, 2004). These findings support the argument put forward by Wright et al. (1997), namely, that when one observes a fellow ingroup member interacting with an outgroup member, not only is there less immediate anxiety because the observer is not directly involved in the contact situation, but anxiety about future possible intergroup interactions will also be lessened by reducing the fear (affect) and negative expectations (cognition) that tend to cause anxiety prior to actual contact.

Similarly, the beneficial effects of taking the perspective of a member of another group during intergroup contact can occur through both affective and cognitive mechanisms. Empathy is generally defined as a vicarious emotional state triggered by witnessing the emotional state of another. Empathy is thought to be the result of perspective-taking, which is imagining how another person perceives their situation and how they might feel as a result. Allport (1954/1979) informally defined empathy as an "ability to put [oneself] in other people's shoes" (1954/1979, p. 436) or a "capacity to know the other person's state of mind, and adapt to it" (p. 436); he cited a positive relationship between empathic ability and tolerance for social differences.

Perspective-taking and empathy (see figure 17.1) have a number of positive consequences for intergroup relations (see Galinsky & Moskowitz, 2000, for a review). By inducing a merging of, or a perception of increased overlap between, the self and the other (see Aron et al., in press), perspective-taking makes thoughts about the target individual become more self-like (Galinsky & Moskowitz, 2000). Consequently, this increased self–target overlap means that a greater percentage of traits used to describe the self will be attributed to the target individual. Because one of the main causes of ingroup bias is thought to be the association of the ingroup with the self (Cadinu & Rothbart, 1996), attributing traits associated with the self to the outgroup target is likely to lead to a more positive evaluation of her or him, which may then generalize to the outgroup as a whole. The increased cognitive accessibility of the self-concept after perspective-taking might also result in the preferential use of the self-concept rather than a stereotype schema to guide the categorization and evaluation of an outgroup member.

Perspective taking and empathy can operate through other routes as well. They can increase the perception that a common humanity and destiny is shared with the other group; experimental findings (e.g., Gaertner, Mann, Dovidio, Murrell, & Pomare, 1990) show that creating a sense of common identity can reduce prejudice and discrimination. Empathy is also likely to evoke altruistic motivation to relieve any difficulties experienced by the person for whom empathy is felt (Batson, Early, & Salvarani, 1997) or motivations to restore justice in response to discrimination (Dovidio et al., in press).

Has Allport Been Supported?

As is the case in any scientific endeavor, good ideas promote initial validational research, and the findings themselves spawn new ideas as well as methodological and technical innovations. Furthermore, as time passes, the society and culture in which the research is carried out change, creating new and unforeseen needs and scientific challenges; this is especially so in social science research. These processes lead to a research program that often does not resemble the original project, except in superficial ways. This change and openness is in fact a hallmark of good science, but the degree to which progressing and continuing research programs retain ideas from original theories is also an indication of the intellectual merit of those upon whose shoulders we, as scientists, stand. In the case of Gordon Allport, his ideas about intergroup contact have been formulated into testable, and indeed potentially falsifiable (Popper, 1974), hypotheses. Notably, although researchers have taken many new and fruitful directions since his ideas were published, many of his original ideas have stood up over time and are, in fact, retained in contemporary thinking about intergroup contact.

The final words of Allport's chapter on contact are the suggestion that contact will reduce prejudice "provided it is of a sort that leads to the perception of common interests and common humanity between members of the two groups" (1954/1979, p. 281). This contention is borne out most directly in the research examining decategorized, personalized interaction (Brewer & Miller, 1984; Miller, 2002), and in that which advocates recategorization of group structures (Gaertner et al., 1989). Allport (1954/ 1979) also foresaw research which promotes intergroup encounters that retain relatively high levels of group salience (Hewstone & Brown, 1986) when he included in his comprehensive list of key "Kinds of Contact" that it was important to ask, "Is the contact perceived in terms of intergroup relations or not perceived as such?" (p. 263). As discussed, although the issue is not simple, all of these models contribute to the understanding of the types of intergroup contact that maximize commonalities and reduce both perceived differences as well as negative feelings associated with outgroups.

Whereas Allport focused primarily on the descriptive issue of *whether* contact can reduce intergroup bias, more recent work has examined the explanatory matters of *when* and *how* contact reduces bias. This work has identified the conditions under which contact can most effectively improve attitudes not only to the outgroup members present during the contact situation but also to the outgroup as a whole. Much of the most recent research has investigated how contact reaches "below the surface" (Allport, 1954/1979; p. 276) to alter prejudice, considering both the factors that moderate and mediate its effects (i.e., category salience, self-disclosure, anxiety, etc.). See also Pettigrew and Tropp's chapter 16 in this volume for a discussion of meta-analytic data with respect to these and other ideas (viz., the original conditions) in the research since Allport.

Future Directions

The consistent pattern of the data described herein provides strong support for continuing and expanding research into intergroup contact processes, even where there is intergroup conflict and a high degree of segregation between the different communities (see Tausch, Kenworthy, & Hewstone, in press). As discussed, there is evidence that, primarily through affective processes, contact can reduce prejudice and hostility between groups.

A recent analytical trend concerns the simultaneous consideration of moderation (i.e., when contact works best) and mediation (i.e., how contact works) using advanced statistical techniques. Voci and Hewstone (2003) examined group salience and intergroup anxiety, a moderator variable and a mediator variable respectively, while looking at the effect of contact on Italians' attitudes towards immigrants in their country. Using Structural Equation Modeling procedures, they found that intergroup anxiety mediated the impact of combined quality and quantity of contact in reducing subtle prejudice and improving outgroup attitudes. They then tested the effect of group membership salience as a moderator for each path in the model. They found that between contact and anxiety, positive frequent contact reduced anxiety more when group membership was salient than when it was not. The direct path from contact to attitudes was also stronger when group salience was high compared to when it was low. Thus, a combination of positive contact and group salience during that contact resulted in the most positive evaluations of the outgroup. This methodological innovation can make a unique contribution to the future understanding of the contact hypothesis.

Although Allport suggested that stereotypes about outgroups would change via positive intergroup contact, relatively few studies have examined stereotypes as dependent measures. Although contact with outgroup members is generally associated with less negative stereotypes of the outgroup as a whole, we think that as stereotypes and group variability estimates are assessed in the future, our understanding of the processes underlying them will continue to expand. We expect, and support, efforts towards more theoretical development and precision regarding the impact of contact on cognitive variables, as well as the interplay between cognitive and affective variables.

One potentially fruitful trajectory of research concerns the nature of anxiety in intergroup contexts. Specifically, we think that researchers should examine intergroup anxiety versus general anxiety. Intergroup anxiety (aroused as a direct result of the intergroup context) may elicit group-protecting behaviors and group-serving attributions, whereas general anxiety (if it is correctly attributed to non-intergroup sources) may not have such consequences. Do these potentially differentiated types of anxiety have different predictive qualities with respect to contact and prejudice reduction (see Plant & Devine, 1998)?

We are hopeful that (hitherto) antagonistic theoretical positions will continue to be integrated in a coherent and convergent understanding of intergroup contact (e.g., Miller, 2002; Brown & Hewstone, in press). As part of that program, we suggest that intervention programs should promote contact under conditions that promote positive affect (e.g., lower anxiety, greater perspective-taking and empathy), and that encourage the presentation of uniqueness and differentiation among outgroup members (e.g., via individuation and self-disclosure), while at the same time ensuring that participants remain aware of their own and others' group memberships. To consider the true implications of the contact hypothesis, the impact of interventions which systematically include these elements must also be investigated.

REFERENCES

Allport, G. W. (1954/1979). *The nature of prejudice.* Cambridge, MA: Perseus Books.

Aron, A., McLaughlin-Volpe, T., Mashek, D., Lewandowski, G., Wright, S. C., & Aron, E. N. (in press). Including others in the self. In W. Stroebe & M. Hewstone (eds.), *European Review of Social Psychology* (vol. 14). Hove, UK: Psychology Press.

Batson, C. D., Early, S., & Salvarani, G. (1997). Perspective taking: Imagining how another feels versus imagining how you would feel. *Personality and Social Psychology Bulletin, 23*, 751–8.

Brewer, M. B. (1991). The social self: On being the same and different at the same time. *Personality and Social Psychology Bulletin, 17*, 475–82.

Brewer, M. B. & Miller, N. (1984). Beyond the contact hypothesis: Theoretical perspectives on segregation. In N. Miller & M. B. Brewer (eds.), *Groups in contact: The psychology of desegregation.* Orlando, FL: Academic Press.

Brown, R. & Hewstone, M. (in press). An integrative theory of intergroup contact. In M. Zanna (ed.), *Advances in experimental social psychology.* San Diego: Academic Press.

Brown, R., Vivian, J., & Hewstone, M. (1999). Changing attitudes through intergroup contact: The effects of group membership salience. *European Journal of Social Psychology, 29*, 741–64.

Cadinu, M. R. & Rothbart, M. (1996). Self-anchoring and differentiation processes in the minimal group setting. *Journal of Personality and Social Psychology, 70*, 661–77.

Dovidio, J. F., Gaertner, S. L., & Kawakami, K. (2003). Intergroup contact: the past, present and future. *Group processes and intergroup relations, 6*, 5–21.

Dovidio, J. F., ten Vergert, M., Stewart, T. L., Gaertner, S. L., Johnson, J. D., Esses, V. M., Riek, B. M., & Pearson, A. R. (in press). Perspective and prejudice: Antecedents and mediating mechanisms. *Personality and Social Psychology Bulletin.*

Eisenberg, N. & Strayer, J. (1987). Critical issues in the study of empathy.

In N. Eisenberg & J. Strayer (eds.), *Empathy and its development. Cambridge studies in social and emotional development* (pp. 3–13). New York: Cambridge University Press.

Ensari, N. & Miller, N. (2002). The outgroup must not be so bad after all: The effect of disclosure, typicality and salience on intergroup bias. *Journal of Personality and Social Psychology, 83*, 313–29.

Gaertner, S. L. & Dovidio, J. F. (2000). *Reducing intergroup bias: The Common Ingroup Identity Model.* Philadelphia, PA: The Psychology Press.

Gaertner, S. L., Mann, J. A., Dovidio, J. F., Murrell, A. J., & Pomare, M. (1990). How does cooperation reduce intergroup bias? *Journal of Personality and Social Psychology, 59*, 692–704.

Gaertner, S. L., Mann, J., Murrell, A., & Dovidio, J. F. (1989). Reducing intergroup bias: The benefits of recategorization. *Journal of Personality and Social Psychology, 57*, 239–49.

Galinsky, A. D. & Moskowitz, G. B. (2000). Perspective-taking: Decreasing stereotype expression, stereotype accessibility and ingroup favouritism. *Journal of Personality and Social Psychology, 78*, 708–24.

Hewstone, M. & Brown, R. (1986). Contact is not enough: An intergroup perspective on the "contact hypothesis." In M. Hewstone and R. Brown (eds.), *Contact and conflict in intergroup encounters.* Oxford: Blackwell.

Islam, M. R. & Hewstone, M. (1993). Dimensions of contact as predictors of intergroup anxiety, perceived outgroup variability and outgroup attitudes: An integrative model. *Personality and Social Psychology Bulletin, 19*, 700–10.

Miller, N. (2002). Personalization and the promise of contact theory. *Journal of Social Issues, 58*, 387–410.

Miller, N., Kenworthy, J. B., Stenstrom, D. M., & Canales, C. J. (in press). Explaining the effects of crossed categorization on ethnocentric bias. In R. J. Crisp, & M. Hewstone (eds.), *Multiple social categorization: Processes, models and applications*. Hove, UK: Psychology Press (Taylor & Francis).

Paolini, S., Hewstone, M., Cairns, E., & Voci, A. (2004). Effects of direct and indirect cross-group friendships on judgements of Catholics and Protestants in Northern Ireland: The mediating role of an anxiety-reduction mechanism. *Personality and Social Psychology Bulletin, 30*, 770–86.

Pettigrew, T. F. (1997). Generalized intergroup contact effects on prejudice. *Personality and Social Psychology Bulletin, 23*, 173–85.

Pettigrew, T. F. (1998). Intergroup contact: Theory, research and new perspectives. *Annual Review of Psychology, 49*, 65–85.

Pettigrew, T. F. & Tropp, L. R. (2000). Does intergroup contact reduce prejudice? Recent meta-analytic findings. In S. Oskamp (ed.), *Reducing prejudice and discrimination* (pp. 93–114). Hillsdale, NJ: Lawrence Erlbaum.

Petty, R. E. & Mirels, H. L. (1981). Intimacy and scarcity of self-disclosure: Effects on interpersonal attraction for males and females. *Personality and Social Psychology Bulletin, 7*, 493–503.

Plant, E. A. & Devine, P. G. (2003). The antecedents and implications of interracial anxiety. *Personality and Social Psychology Bulletin, 29*, 790–801.

Popper, K. R. (1974). *Conjectures and refutations: The growth of scientific knowledge*. London: Routledge.

Stephan, W. G. & Stephan, C. W. (1985). Intergroup anxiety. *Journal of Social Issues, 41*, 157–76.

Stephan, W. G. & Stephan, C. W. (2000). An integrated threat theory of prejudice. In S. Oskamp (ed.), *Reducing prejudice and discrimination* (pp. 23–46). Hillside, NJ: Erblaum.

Tausch, N., Kenworthy, J. B., & Hewstone, M. (in press). Conflict resolution and prevention: The role of intergroup contact. In M. Fitzduff and C. E. Stout (eds.), *Psychological approaches to conflict and war*. New York: Praeger.

Turner, R. N., Hewstone, M., & Voci, A. (2004). The impact of cross-group friendship on explicit and implicit prejudice in children. MS under review.

Van Oudenhoven, J. P., Groenewoud, J. T., & Hewstone, M. (1996). Co-operation, ethnic salience and generalization of interethnic attitudes. *European Journal of Social Psychology, 26*, 649–61.

Voci, A. & Hewstone, M. (2003). Intergroup contact and prejudice towards immigrants in Italy: The mediational role of anxiety and the moderational role of group salience. *Group Processes and Intergroup Relations, 6*, 37–54.

Williams, R. M., Jr. (1947). *The reduction of intergroup tensions*. New York: Social Science Research Council.

Wright, S. C., Aron, A., McLaughlin-Volpe, T., & Ropp, S. A. (1997). The extended contact effect: Knowledge of cross-group friendships and prejudice. *Journal of Personality and Social Psychology, 73*, 73–90.

ACQUIRING PREJUDICE

Chapter Eighteen

Conformity and Prejudice

Christian S. Crandall and Charles Stangor

In chapter 17, titled "Conforming," Allport (1954/1979) targeted conformity as a primary cause of prejudiced behaviors and belief, stating, *"about half of all prejudiced attitudes are based only on the need to conform"* (p. 286). By the 1950s, psychologists had long known that people adapt their behavior to the social norms of the situation; Allport applied this principle to prejudice. Relying both on anecdote and empirical research, Allport cogently argued that conformity was one of the most important causes of prejudice. In this chapter, we will review theorizing and research on the role of conformity in intergroup attitudes from Allport to the present day.

Allport's Views on Conformity

Allport was not alone in his views; most early social psychologists agreed that prejudice was the result of societal norms (Chein, 1946; Lewin, 1952; Marrow & French, 1945). For example, Minard (1952) studied coal miners in West Virginia. While below the ground, Black and White miners worked together in complete integration without substantial racial conflict, but above ground practiced almost complete segregation. It may seem the miners were inconsistent: they were racist above ground and antiracist below. However, the miners were *consistent* with prevailing social norms in different contexts. Underground work rules had developed that tolerated and promoted integration, but societal rules above ground promoted segregation. The workers moved between the two worlds without conflict because they adhered to the norms in both places.

Allport's own analysis extended beyond observing a connection between conformity and prejudice. He was interested in *why* people conform and in how conformity helps people meet their psychological needs and social goals. He speculated that prejudice has Darwinian "survival value." He pondered whether conformity was "skin deep or marrow deep" (1954/ 1979, p. 285). Allport also wondered what types of people are most likely to conform and what types to maintain their individuality even in the face of strong pressures to give in. In general, he viewed conformity as a sign of a weak, authoritarian personality, prone to unreflective obedience.

Allport and others focused on conformity as a root cause of prejudice for a number of reasons. First, the group-relevant information that people are exposed to every day must shape their views of other groups. The child, Allport noted, is profoundly influenced by the opinions of their parents and close others, "If their design for living is tolerant, so too is his; if they are hostile toward certain groups, so too is he" (1954/1959, p. 293; see also Aboud, ch. 19 this volume). In present society, the media bombard us with information promoting stereotypes and prejudice, and this information is echoed in everyday conversation. With prejudice literally "in the air," it is not surprising that people often adopt prejudiced views.

Second, and as many of Allport's anecdotes in chapter 17 illustrate, people from the same social culture tend to hold the same prejudices. Many Americans, for instance, harbor prejudices against Iraqis, gay men and lesbians, and drunk drivers (Crandall, Eshleman, & O'Brien, 2002) that influence their judgments and behavior. People also tend to choose relationship partners from their own racial group, live in racially segregated neighborhoods, and have friends of similar social class and education level (Feagin & Vera, 1995). Race and other social categories are important and defining features for people, and the beliefs that individuals hold about different social groups are remarkably similar to other members of their own social groups. These beliefs and attitudes are substantially shaped by interaction with others.

Finally, Allport recognized that conformity provides a promising avenue for changing prejudice. Just as conformity to prejudicial norms produces prejudice, when social norms become more tolerant, prejudice is reduced. Allport thought that people learned prejudice primarily from family ties (see Aboud, ch. 19 this volume), but was cautiously hopeful that people might "unlearn" prejudice by exposure to other influences. He wrote, "The primacy of the family does not mean that school, church, and state should cease practicing or teaching the principles of democratic living. Together, their influence may establish at least a secondary model for the child to follow" (1954/1979, p. 296).

Developments Since Allport

This section reviews developments since Allport that have created a new understanding of conformity and how it affects the development of prejudice. Because conformity applies to the social norms of a *particular* group, we also consider what happens when a person is part of more than one group, whose norms are in conflict with each other. These developments suggest three basic arguments: (1) conformity is a normal and common process, (2) people's attitudes and prejudices change when the groups that they are members of change, and (3) behavior that appears to be due to prejudiced personality traits or internal conflict may actually reflect peoples' attempts to conform to different groups' norms.

What is Conformity?

Perhaps the most radical development since Allport concerns his moral evaluation of conformity. Although Allport considered conformity to be a sign of deviance, that stance is no longer held by social psychologists. In fact, conformity is now seen as perhaps the most important *normal* social process. In 1954, Allport needed to explain why a person might not actively seek individual expression as a weakness of the soul or spirit. Shortly after Allport's book appeared, however, one of his students, Thomas Pettigrew, embarked on a decades-long program of research on normative theory and prejudice. Pettigrew looked at white racial attitudes in the American South and apartheid-era Republic of South Africa (Pettigrew, 1958, 1959). He showed that differences in authoritarian personality could not account for the large regional differences in racial attitudes between North and South in the USA, nor the large national differences in attitudes between the USA, Europe, and South Africa. Instead, Pettigrew has focused on how historical, political, and social factors shape social norms, which in turn play a large role in determining racial attitudes, social policy, and interpersonal conduct (Pettigrew, 1991).

By the 1970s, the tremendous power of the social situation, and its ability to elicit conformity, were well accepted. Stanley Milgram had shown in 1963 that most people will obey an authority, even to the point of delivering potentially lethal shocks to a hapless victim; Asch (1952) had shown that people will apparently believe their peers instead of their own eyes; and Zimbardo and his colleagues (Haney, Banks & Zimbardo, 1973) demonstrated in the Stanford Prison Experiment how easily people can fall into destructive social roles.

Conformity is prevalent because it has both individual and societal benefits. At the individual level, there are dire consequences for those who fail to conform. Those who do not follow social norms may be overtly punished or ostracized, may fail to gain respect, and be unable to advance in their careers (see Rudman, ch. 7 this volume). Conformity is also useful at the cultural level because it helps create a smoothly functioning society. Conformity transmits cultural values and mores, the important "group beliefs" of the society (Bar-Tal, 1990). It guides speech and actions, making social interactions predictable. Taken this way, conformity simply means that a person adheres to the prevailing social norms in a given situation, as would be expected of any upstanding society member. Conformity does not necessarily imply weakness, dependency, or a lack of creativity; it occurs as a normal part of everyday existence.

Following the norms of prejudice is just as pervasive and effortless as following any other social norm. In many ways, conformity to prevailing ethnic, racial, religious, and other beliefs is no different than driving on the right side of the road, paying for items in stores, or acting pleasantly to one's boss. To the extent that people want to belong to social groups they must adhere to the rules, and new group members will want to – and work to – conform; although they might initially merely "act the part," they will eventually come to internalize the group's attitudes and make them their own (Crandall, Eshleman, & O'Brien, 2002; Sherif & Sherif, 1953).

Conformity and Prejudice

The view that prejudice is "normal" creates a seeming contradiction – according to popular belief, a "prejudice" is something that breaks social norms; prejudice is *deviant*. In fact, Allport seemed to concur with this assessment by defining prejudice as an irrational, negative reaction to others based on their group membership. But according to our perspective, prejudice *is* a social norm. Sometimes this disconnect between viewing prejudice as normative versus deviant occurs as a result of changes in norms over time, creating different segments of society that disagree about what is acceptable. Although most Americans today would see slavery as a violation of decency and tolerance norms, slave owners in the antebellum American South did not think that their attitude toward enslaved Black was prejudiced; it was the common, accepted, prevalent attitude (Jordan, 1977).

To the extent that conformity is normal, prejudice is too. Crandall et al. (2002) had college students indicate the prevailing social norms of the acceptability of prejudice toward 105 different social groups. Students agreed that some prejudices were acceptable (e.g., rapists, child molesters, drug dealers, thieves) and others (e.g., African Americans, blind people, Jews, Canadians) were not. A second group of college students' ratings of how they, personally, felt about the same groups showed a near perfect relationship between the social norm ratings and people's personal prejudices toward the 105 groups, $r = 0.96$. Thus, people's reports of their own prejudices were an almost perfect reflection of norms designating which prejudices are appropriate or inappropriate.

Because what is acceptable and normal in one context may be unacceptable in another, it is important to untangle the psychological process of negative feelings toward a person or group (prejudice) from whether or not these feelings are generally sanctioned (social norms). Many researchers define prejudice as _unjustified_ negative attitudes toward social groups or their members. Similarly, Allport (1954/1979) defined prejudice as "thinking ill of others without sufficient warrant," and ethnic prejudice as "an antipathy based upon a faulty and inflexible generalization" (p. 9; see also Eagly & Diekman, ch. 2 this volume). The problem is that what is commonly perceived to be "justified" or "warranted" depends primarily on the cultural rules about the acceptability of prejudice (see Crandall & Martinez, 1996). In practice, "justifiable" is a very flexible, norm-sensitive standard (Crandall & Eshleman, 2003). What appears justified to some people does not to others.

Of course, conformity does not always imply prejudice – many group norms, and indeed the American credo itself (e.g., Tocqueville, 1839/ 1969), are based on tolerance, egalitarianism, and recognizing the humanity of all people, regardless of race, religion, ethnicity, or class. As a result, in America (as in other societies), in addition to norms that suggest that there are real, valid, group differences (prejudice norms), there are other norms that promote egalitarianism and equality (see Devine, ch. 20 this volume). Thus, cultural norms provide no easy answers to questions such as how White and Black Americans should treat each other, or whether race and cultural differences ought to be respected or derided. Allport (1954/1979) wrote, "Anti-attitudes alternate with pro-attitudes. Often the see-saw and zig-zag are almost painful to follow . . . such inconsistency is bewildering . . . it must be awkward to live with" (pp. 326–7). Because people are forced to follow a contradictory set of internalized rules about how to think, feel, and behave, it can be difficult for people to know what to do. Conformity to social norms about treatment of ethnic groups leads to prejudice in some cases but antiprejudice in others. Because most Americans conform in various situations to both norms, they feel the conflict (Devine, ch. 20 this volume; Gaertner & Dovidio, ch. 5 this volume).

Conformity and Conflict

The research we have reviewed to this point is consistent with the idea that norms can either create or reduce prejudice. But internalized norms frequently conflict with external norms, especially when the social dynamic is in flux. As a result, people do not always act on their inner beliefs. This conflict cuts both ways – sometimes people express more prejudice than they believe is proper (for instance, when they agree with or fail to confront others who are acting in prejudicial ways), and other times they may express less prejudice than they believe proper (for instance, when they invoke principles of political correctness or endorse affirmative-action policies even when they do not agree with them). Not surprisingly, which way the pendulum swings depends entirely on perceptions of prevailing social norms. The careful attention Allport paid to inner conflict (e.g., in his chapter 20) is essential, because the inner conflict often refers to competing conformity pressures – a conflict of internalized social norms and values with the norms and values of the immediate situation. This approach to understanding prejudice has been fruitfully mined by several authors in this volume, and will be considered below (see Devine, ch. 20, and Gaertner & Dovidio, ch. 5, this volume).

A New Framework: Consensus, Groups, Individuals, and Conformity

One of the most important advances in thinking about conformity comes from research on *perceived consensus*. Most people do not have complete access to, nor even a random sample of, their peers' beliefs and attitudes. This next section reviews research on how prejudice and stereotyping is affected by obtaining information about whether or not the perceived consensus of peers matches one's own attitudes. This research shows how easily consensus can be manipulated to create strong conformity effects. Another important advance has been the study of the motives people report for moderating their prejudices. Together, these two lines of research illuminate how people psychologically experience the process of conformity.

The Ease of Expressing Shared Prejudices

When people are not sure how to behave, the conflict between inner and outer norms can be particularly vexing. However, it might not take much social prompting to assure people that their prejudices are justified, or even to create prejudicial norms to begin with. For example, dynamic social-impact theory specifies how social norms can spread rapidly through a culture (Latané, 1996; Nowak, Szamrej, & Latané, 1990). According to this model, people develop their opinions in large part through their interactions with others. Furthermore, beliefs are determined through the "force" or "impact" of others, where the force is itself a function of the *strength* (for instance, how persuasive an individual is), the *immediacy* (that is, how far away in space someone is), as well as the *number* of the others in the environment who hold the belief.

Dynamic social-impact theory applies this idea of social impact to understanding the development and sharing of beliefs within a large group of individuals, such as a culture. Latané and his colleagues assume that relevant beliefs are spread throughout the culture because individuals communicate with other individuals (usually those who are in close physical contact with them). And, in line with the power of social influence, it is expected that over time the size of the majority endorsing a belief will increase and the size of the minority will decrease. However, in comparison to what would be expected in smaller groups, dynamic social-impact theory does not predict that a society will become completely homogeneous in their beliefs. Rather, because individuals share ideas with others who are nearby (their "neighbors"), it specifically predicts that clusters (or subcultures) of individuals who hold similar beliefs will develop within the larger culture, and thus that there will be cultural diversity. Furthermore, as a result of the frequent communication among their neighbors, the subclusters will develop sets of beliefs that they share with each other, even if the culture as a whole holds different beliefs.

One implication of dynamic social-impact theory for conformity and prejudice is that different groups in a society will have different patterns of prejudices. It would be a mistake to suggest that, for example, US culture has a strong norm against having prejudices based on race and religion. Some groups in the US have powerful norms suppressing these kinds of prejudices, and others do not (Ezekiel, 1996). Different social groups, living in different places, will have a stable set of prejudices and beliefs (that may conflict with the dominant social view in society), and people in contact with a subgroup will conform to the norms close around them, rather than the general norms that describe American values. Thus, for example, extremist groups, such as the Ku Klux Klan or other white-pride groups, Black separatist groups, and secessionist movements persist in the US, despite their deviation from the culture-at-large. Different subgroups have their own prejudices, and people who are part of the local culture will share the local culture's values. By limiting their contact with the rest of the culture, the prejudices of extremist groups can persist and even flourish (Myers & Bishop, 1970).

Perceiving (at least local) social consensus validates people's beliefs and encourages them to translate their attitudes into action. Sechrist and Stangor (2001) manipulated perceived consensus to explore the extent to which it can create consistency between people's attitudes and behaviors. They found that highly prejudiced college students who were provided with information that their anti-Black beliefs were shared by other students at their university subsequently sat farther away from an African American target than participants who were informed that their beliefs were not shared. That the correspondence between scores on a prejudice questionnaire and seating distance was greater when people believed that most other students shared their beliefs, suggests that knowing that others share one's prejudices gives social permission for those prejudices to be acted upon.

The Role of Conformity in Changing Prejudice

Although Allport thought that the *combined* influence of extrafamilial pressure (e.g., peer groups, social institutions, and mass media) might sway prejudiced people's opinions, he underestimated the power of social consensus as a force for change. Recent research suggests that changing the perception of social norms (to create consensus) can result in immediate and long-lasting changes in prejudice. Stangor, Sechrist, and Jost (2001a, 2001b) had White/European American students first indicate their beliefs about positive and negative stereotypes of African Americans, and then estimate the beliefs of fellow students at their university. One week later, they provided participants with (false) information indicating that, according to research, they had either under- or over-estimated the prejudice of their peers. Because of a (bogus) "computer error," the students were told their initial data had been lost and were asked to report their racial beliefs again. As expected, participants attitudes moved substantially in the direction of the bogus social consensus information – becoming either more positive or more negative toward African Americans depending on what the local consensus was said to be. These changes were strong and persisted for up to two weeks (Stangor et al., 2001b). Follow-up work showed that people do not follow the social norms of just any group. Instead, it has to be a group that is meaningful to them; that is, of which they are (or aspire to be) a member, suggesting that these effects are based on conformity, rather than motivated simply by a desire to be accurate (Stangor et al., 2001b).

Finally, perceived consensus can enhance (or reduce) prejudice, but it can also make prejudices more resistant to change (Stangor et al., 2001a, experiment 3). One week after reporting their prejudice levels toward African Americans, students were given information that their beliefs were either shared or were *not* shared by other students at their university. Then, in an attempt to change their beliefs, they were given allegedly "objective" (research-based) information about the actual traits possessed by African Americans. People who were told that others at their university agreed with them showed less opinion change as a result of the "objective" information than people who were told that others did not share their beliefs. The type of information (e.g., concerning positive or negative stereotypes) did not influence the findings.

In sum, conformity creates prejudice; social norms and prevailing cultural values play a strong role in determining people's internal values, beliefs, and prejudices. The same pathway can be used to undermine, reduce, and eliminate prejudices. Moreover, people who believe that others support their prejudices tend to persist steadfastly in their views, whereas people who do not feel that support are more easily swayed.

Can a Single Communication Influence Prejudice?

If the communication of social norms is important in creating and potentially reducing prejudice, then even a single statement might be expected to have an influence on attitudes. Research suggests that this is indeed the case. Greenberg and Pyszczynski (1985) examined the influence of overhearing an ethnic slur or derogatory ethnic label on individuals' perceptions of a member of the targeted group. White participants read about a vignette in which a Black or a White person was said to have either won or lost a debate. Participants then overheard either an ethnic slur ("nigger") describing the debater, a neutral remark, or did not overhear any comment. Following this manipulation, participants rated the debaters' skills. Results showed that when the Black debater had lost, participants rated him more negatively when they overheard the ethnic slur than when the ethnic slur was absent. The ethnic slur had no effect when the Black debater won, or on ratings of the White debater. Thus, simply overhearing a derogatory ethnic label can affect attitudes towards members of that ethnic group, at least when the target's behavior is consistent with the group stereotype, because it sets up a norm in which expressing racist attitudes is acceptable (Kirkland, Greenberg, & Pyszczynski, 1987; see also Mullen & Leader, ch. 12 this volume).

If a single expression of prejudice can reinforce prejudice, can confronting individuals who make prejudicial statements or who behave in prejudicial ways diminish it? There are naturally costs to such confronting, because doing so breaks the established social norm of generally accepting the behavior of others. But even a single dissenter can be effective at promoting changes in prejudiced norms. Blanchard, Crandall, Brigham, and Vaughn (1994) arranged for White students to hear another student either condone or condemn racism before answering five questions about how their college should respond to acts of racism. Hearing another student condemn racism increased participants' expressed antiracist opinions, and hearing someone condone racism reduced antiracist expressions, compared to a control condition in which no information about others' opinions was provided. In addition, these changes occurred not only in participants' oral responses in the presence of the person making the comment, but also on their privately expressed attitudes. This suggests that the attitude change was not simply based on public conformity, but reflected a real change in private attitudes.

Individual Differences: Not Everyone is Equally Conforming

As noted earlier, Allport pondered individual differences in people's tendencies to be influenced by prejudiced social norms. The dispositional factor most commonly researched today is one that Allport considered, whether people "suppress" prejudice due to external pressures or to internal motives to be egalitarian (see Devine, ch. 20 this volume). But what makes people feel external pressure to suppress their prejudice? And where do the internal motives to conform come from? Crandall et al. (2002) looked at University of Kansas students' attempts to suppress their prejudices. Many of the students come to this relatively progressive university town from rural communities with more tolerance for racial, religious, and ethnic prejudices than their peers possess. Students are often surprised by the lack of tolerance for the racism, sexism, and other prejudices that they have grown up with quite comfortably. At first, their expressions of counternormative prejudice (e.g., too much prejudice toward women and Blacks, but also too little prejudice toward, say, date rapists) are met with argument, even derision and social rejection. Soon newcomers publicly conform, keeping these beliefs to themselves. This is externally motivated conformity. In time, however, to the extent that students want to belong at the university, they must conform to norms about proper conduct. Crandall et al. (2002) found that as students became less identified with their hometowns and old high school, and more identified with the university, their internal motives to suppress prejudice increased. In this case, the "internal motives to suppress prejudice" function less like a personality variable and more as an indicator that people are trying to fit themselves into local group norms.

Another study by Crandall et al. (2002) confirms that the "internal suppression of prejudice" is less a personality trait than a good marker for conformity. Students' internal suppression scores were assessed at the beginning of the semester. Much later, they participated in an "unrelated" experiment, in which they filled out a petition asking whether or not racist acts on campus should be punished as hate speech, or tolerated as free speech. The petition ostensibly already had the responses of four previous "participants," which either strongly condemned or condoned the racist acts. One might think that the more students were motivated to suppress prejudice, the more they would condemn the racist acts and vigorously recommend punishing the miscreants. This is not what happened; instead, those highly motivated to suppress prejudice showed high rates of conformity. Thus, whether previous participants recommended punishing or tolerating racist acts, the suppressors followed suit. This suggests that people who are suppressing prejudice are those who are carefully trying to adapt to group norms of prejudice. Thus, when the group is prejudiced, people will sometimes increase their own displays of prejudice to adapt to their group. As a result, the presumed dispositional nature of motives to be egalitarian might be better described as a reflection of where people are in a process of readjusting to local norms (cf. Devine, ch. 20 this volume).

Has Allport Been Supported?

There can be no doubt that Allport's contention that conformity is important in prejudice has been supported. However, conformity may be even more important than Allport originally suggested. Conformity in matters of prejudice is not occasional, and is probably not to blame for merely half of all prejudices, but instead seems to form the very core of the majority of people's prejudices. As a cause of prejudice, it is normal, widespread, and powerful. Knowing that one is deviant (e.g., by holding exceptionally tolerant views) can motivate substantial behavioral and attitudinal change; by contrast, the knowledge that others agree with one's beliefs and attitudes can make an individual resistant to change.

Where modern social psychologists part company with Allport concerns his pathological view of conformity. Allport wrote about the conformist as weak, psychologically needy, deviant, or incomplete. Today, psychologists do not consider conformity unusual or deviant; instead, conformity is viewed as normal, acceptable, and essential to smooth functioning in society.

On the facts, Allport clearly had it right. But in conceptual terms, Allport may have underestimated the importance of normal conformity and the pervasiveness of everyday imitation. Around the same time, the work of Chein (1946), Sherif and Sherif (1953), and others had pointed in this direction. By contrast, Allport presented a careful balance of personality and social factors underlying prejudice, although it must be said that when Allport assigned half of all prejudices to conformity, he deemed it the single most important factor in the acquisition of prejudice. Even given this very high standard, social psychologists might now point to a wide range of research (reported here and elsewhere throughout this volume) that emphasizes social processes even more strongly than he did.

Future Directions in Conformity and Prejudice Research

There is still much to learn about prejudice, especially prejudice acquisition. What might this research program look like for the next 50 years? One area of research that is just now taking shape concerns the experiences that people have as they begin to conform to new social norms about prejudice. To paraphrase an old social-psychological question, What makes which people conform when? There are still several basic questions about conformity to prejudice norms: which reference groups do people conform to, how do people negotiate competing references groups, and how do people manage switches from one group to another? Furthermore, we know very little about how people psychologically experience the process of conformity, especially with respect to prejudice. There is much opportunity to follow how people's emotions and self-images track advancing stages of conformity to prejudice norms.

The suppression of prejudice is closely related to conformity. How is it motivated, is the audience the self or others? There is a blurring between self and others when it comes to internally motivated prejudice suppression, and this process of prejudice socialization and how it relates to identity formation needs to be better researched. How people come to adapt to new prejudice norms is still poorly understood; that they do adapt is well-demonstrated. But people's reports of this experience are quite at variance with the empirical fact of conformity.

What are the emotions people experience when they conform: do they feel reactance or a sense of choice? Because the mere fact of conformity is so powerful, despite the lack of people's reports of their conformity, are there biases and processes that people use to feel comfortable about conforming? What are the internal costs of deviating from social norms? Do people change their view of themselves as they conform and deviate? We know from research on value violations that people experience guilt when they violate their own prejudice standards (see Devine, ch. 20 this volume), but we know little about the exact social consequences of violating social norms about prejudice. Does violating prejudice norms create social rejection? Are value-laden norms more likely to create ostracism? Are social norms that are fraught with ambivalence (as racial norms are in the USA) more or less powerful, more or less punished?

Finally, the most important research to be derived from theory on conformity and prejudice involves developing techniques and programs that will serve to reduce prejudice. Recently, researchers have had success convincing college students that the social norms for alcohol should be for moderate drinking; when norms are established as moderate, binge drinking on campus appears to shrink (Marlatt, 1998). What is needed is a program of solid application of social norms and conformity theory to similarly attack prejudices, reduce their effect, and in short, to convince people to curb their prejudices because they are deviant (see Bassili, 2003).

There are three important themes that emerge in this chapter. First, that conformity is normal, not an abnormal personality weakness. Like any other belief, attitude, and behavior, we learn how to feel about others and social groups from our family, our peers, and our culture. Having attitudes and beliefs that are very different from our friends is uncomfortable, and we are likely to change them to fit our friends, or change our friends to fit our beliefs. To desire to fit in is normal, natural, and leads to highly adaptive social behavior. Second, norms operate on a societal level; norms change over time and different "subcultures" create different local norms that can make competing demands on individuals when they cross those subcultures. When people make major life transitions, whether at school or at work, when they become married, parents, or empty-nesters, when they move to a new neighborhood, area, or country, the norms about what attitudes are proper are likely to change, and adapting to these new norms is a significant challenge of everyday life. Third, what may seem like inconsistency and "inner conflict" may actually reflect attempts to be consistent with local norms. When people make these changes, when they adapt to new groups and changing norms, the motives they report and the experiences that they have in conforming to new norms may sometimes appear to be enduring personality traits, motive profiles or value configurations. Instead, they may often be simply attempts to conform to a new set of norms.

Allport argued that conformity is the primary source of prejudice. We agree. However, he may have underestimated the power of social consensus as a basis for prejudice; most of people's prejudices are acquired from the local social norms and the culture in which people live. In addition, the manipulation of social consensus and social norms has been shown to be a powerful means by which to reduce prejudice. There is still much to learn about how to wield this normative power for reducing prejudice.

REFERENCES

Aboud, F. (1988). *Children and prejudice.* Oxford: Blackwell.

Allport, G. W. (1954/1979). *The nature of prejudice.* Cambridge, MA: Perseus Books.

Asch, S. (1952). *Social psychology.* Englewood Cliffs, NJ: Prentice-Hall.

Bar-Tal, D. (1990). *Group beliefs: A conception for analyzing group structure, processes, and behavior.* New York: Springer-Verlag.

Bassili, J. N. (2003). The minority slowness effect: Subtle inhibitions in the expression of views not shared by others. *Journal of Personality and Social Psychology, 84,* 261–76

Blanchard, F. A., Crandall, C. S., Brigham, J. C., & Vaughn, L. A. (1994). Condemning and condoning racism: A social context approach to interracial settings. *Journal of Applied Psychology, 79,* 993–7.

Brewer, M. B. (1979). Ingroup bias and the minimal group situation: A cognitive-motivational analysis. *Psychological Bulletin, 86,* 307–24.

Brown, R. (1995). *Prejudice: Its social psychology.* Oxford: Blackwell.

Chein, I. (1946). Some considerations in combating intergroup prejudice. *Journal of Educational Sociology,* 412–19.

Crandall, C. S. & Eshleman, A. (2003). A justification-suppression model of the expression and experience of prejudice. *Psychological Bulletin, 129,* 414–46.

Crandall, C. S., Eshleman, A., & O'Brien, L. T. (2002). Social norms and the expression and suppression of prejudice: The struggle for internalization. *Journal of Personality and Social Psychology, 82,* 359–78.

Crandall, C. S. & Martinez, R. (1996). Culture, ideology, and anti-fat attitudes. *Personality and Social Psychology Bulletin, 22,* 1165–76.

Ezekiel, R. (1996). *The racist mind.* New York: Penguin.

Feagin, J. R. & Vera, H. (1995). *White racism*. New York: Routledge.

Greenberg, J. & Pyszczynski, T. (1985). The effect of an overheard ethnic slur on evaluations of the target: How to spread a social disease. *Journal of Experimental Social Psychology, 1*, 61–72.

Haney, C., Banks, C., & Zimbardo, P. (1973). Interpersonal dynamics in a simulated prison. *International Journal of Criminology and Penology, 1*, 69–97.

Jordan, W. D. (1977). *White over Black: American attitudes toward the Negro, 1550–1812*. New York: Norton.

Kirkland, S. L., Greenberg, J., & Pyszczynski, T. (1987). Further evidence of the deleterious effects of overheard derogatory ethnic labels: Derogation beyond the target. *Personality & Social Psychology Bulletin, 2*, 216–27.

Latané, B. (1996). Dynamic social impact: The creation of culture by communication. *Journal of Communication, 46*, 13–25.

Lewin, K. (1952). Group decision and social change. In G. Swanson, T. Newcomb, & E. Hartley (eds.), *Readings in social psychology* (pp. 197–211). New York: Henry Holt.

Marlatt, G. A. (1998). *Harm reduction: Pragmatic strategies for managing high-risk behaviors*. New York: Guilford Press.

Marrow, A. J. & French, J. R. P. (1945). Changing a stereotype in industry. *Journal of Social Issues, 1*, 33–7.

Milgram, S. (1963). Behavioral study of obedience. *Journal of Abnormal and Social Psychology, 67*, 371–8.

Minard, R. D. (1952). Race relations in the Pocahontas Coal Field. *Journal of Social Issues, 8*, 29–44.

Myers, D. G. & Bishop, G. D. (1970). Discussion effects on racial attitudes. *Science, 3947*, 778–9.

Nowak, A., Szamrej, J., & Latané, B. (1990). From private attitude to public opinion: A dynamic theory of social impact. *Psychological Review, 97(3)*, 362–76.

Pettigrew, T. F. (1958). Personality and sociocultural factors in intergroup attitudes: A cross-national comparison. *Journal of Conflict Resolution, 2*, 29–42.

Pettigrew, T. F. (1959). Regional differences in anti-Negro prejudice. *Journal of Abnormal and Social Psychology, 59*, 28–36.

Pettigrew, T. F. (1991). Normative theory in intergroup relations: Explaining both harmony and conflict. *Psychology and Developing Societies, 3*, 3–16.

Sechrist, G. & Stangor, C. (2001). Perceived consensus influences intergroup behavior and stereotype accessibility. *Journal of Personality and Social Psychology, 80*, 645–54.

Sherif, M. & Sherif, C. (1953). *Groups in harmony and tension*. New York: Harper.

Stangor, C., Sechrist, G., & Jost, J. (2001a). Changing racial beliefs by providing consensus information. *Personality and Social Psychology Bulletin, 27*, 484–94.

Stangor, C., Sechrist, G. B., & Jost, J. T. (2001b). Social influence and intergroup beliefs: The role of perceived social consensus. In J. P. Forgas & K. D. Williams (eds.), *Social Influence* (pp. 235–52). Philadelphia, PA: Psychology Press.

Tocqueville, A. (1839/1969). *Democracy in America*, ed. J. P. Mayer, tr. G. Lawrence. Garden City, NY: Doubleday.

Chapter Nineteen

The Development of Prejudice in Childhood and Adolescence

Frances E. Aboud

Allport began his chapter on "The Young Child" (chapter 18) by asking: How is prejudice learned? Allport's readers might have expected to hear about the common mechanisms of learning: paired association, reinforcement, observational imitation. Indeed, Allport emphasized what he called the direct "transfer" of parental words, emotions, and ideas to children through learning and conformity. He also described how a child–rearing environment that promotes insecurity and hatred provides fertile ground for prejudicial emotions. Because Allport wrote during a time when it was the norm for White Americans to express prejudice openly, most of his proposed routes led to prejudice toward, rather than respect for, minorities. However, he also wrote that prejudice was "not merely a matter of specific parental teaching . . . blind imitation, or mirroring the culture" (1954/1979, p. 318). Allport was referring to influences internal to the child, specifically emotional/cognitive stages of development and internal motivational influences such as the need for status and identity. These two processes were less well formulated but foreshadowed current research and theory. Thus, Allport described many routes to prejudice, learning being only one.

Allport most convincingly argued for three social mechanisms of acquisition: learning, conformity, and contact. He proposed that parents were most influential as children learned and conformed to societal rules, yet peers were most likely to provide contact in biracial schools. Although Allport touched on the more psychological processes of identity and developmental sequencing, the cognitive revolution that gave full force to such constructs was a decade away.

Allport's Views on the Development of Prejudice

In *The Nature of Prejudice*, Allport considered a broad range of influences that shape the nature and extent of a child's prejudices. These factors included (a) learning, (b) conformity, (c) intergroup experiences, (d) identity and status, and (e) developmental stages.

Learning

Allport emphasized learning principles, as one would expect from a psychologist in the 1950s. He assumed that most parents freely express their views, and so children learn to associate a racial label with an emotion, both of which become associated with a referent person. In later years, the emotion and person descriptors are generalized to an entire social category. Further, paired associate learning might be reinforced or punished by parents. Allport recognized that some children were more predisposed to learn prejudice because their early family life emphasized relationships based on power and authority rather than individuality and trust (see Adorno, Frenkel-Brunswik, Levinson, & Sanford, 1950) . Allport thereby distinguished between those who simply learned prejudiced responses *per se* and those who developed a prejudice-prone personality.

Conformity

Allport viewed conformity as second only to learning as the mechanism by which attitudes are acquired. Children become aware of family and then peer and societal norms (i.e., implicit rules for how people in the group think and act) and, as a result of identification with these groups and the desire for approval, children conform. They also learn social stereotypes (e.g., for class and race). This was Allport's only attempt to introduce the society-wide racial caste system which provides easy solutions to those who need to categorize, project, and raise their self-esteem at others' expense. Allport felt that conformity was the likely mechanism when parents passed on prejudices without consciously intending to, because children imitate parents in order to be like them. Together, conforming to and learning from the home environment were "undoubtedly the most important . . . source of prejudice" (1954/1979, p. 294).

Intergroup Experiences

Allport rightly dismissed as a *post-hoc* rationalization people's justification that their prejudice arose from early traumatic experiences. In his contact theory (see Pettigrew & Tropp, ch. 16 this volume), he elaborated on the other side of the coin, namely the benefits of positive intergroup experiences. However, Allport's anecdotes about early biracial schooling suggest that though White children freely play with minority children (1954/ 1979, p. 309) and are "interested, curious, and appreciative of differences" (p. 304), they are also becoming aware of societal and parental views that contradict their actions and will eventually override their openness.

Identity and Status

Allport saw identification with one's parents and social group as the psychological mechanism that promotes learning attitudes from and conformity to a kinship group. Identification refers to the emotional merging of child with parent; at times Allport describes the child as "mirroring" and "mimicking" parental attitudes for lack of any of his or her own (1954/ 1979, pp. 293–4). The need for status on which to base high self-esteem leads children (and adults) to compare themselves with people who are lower in social standing, making children more willing to adopt the racial hierarchy and social groupings of their peers. Once their values and self-identity become stable, adolescents adopt a level of prejudice that is compatible with their personalities – children who are affectionate, trusting, and democratic may learn about others' stereotypes and prejudices but personally reject them during adolescence as being incompatible with their self-identity.

Developmental Stages

Allport is not well known for his stage-like descriptions of how children learn and apply prejudice, but he describes them clearly. They include the pregeneralized learning of emotions attached to labels (around 4–6 years), overgeneralization of these emotions to all people with that label (6–12 years), differentiation within the category (post-12), and then the tailoring of attitudes to fit the individual's self-image, status seeking, and values. These stages fit what developmental psychologists know about the ages associated with category development, yet Allport meant them to be learning rather than cognitive stages (see pp. 307–9). Very little was made of these stages in subsequent research until Katz (1976) demonstrated their utility in her theory and research on the overgeneralization and differentiation of prejudice.

Developments Since Allport: New Directions in Thinking and Research

Since 1954, theories of child and adolescent prejudice have benefited from extensive research, though only after 1975 was a standardized measure of prejudice used with young children. Allport's theorizing was largely inductive. And he was forced to rely on fewer than 10 child studies, supplemented by anecdotes, to bolster his arguments. Since 1954, theoretical frameworks incorporating Allport's main routes to prejudice have been sharpened and elaborated based on empirical findings. The cognitive revolution put a new twist on almost all of Allport's mechanisms for acquiring prejudice. Since the 1960s, greater emphasis has been placed on how children and adolescents are influenced by social input from parents and peers through the filters of cognitive maturation and identity. Theories have been tested, but the relative merits of theories in comparison with one another have not been. These new directions are briefly outlined in this section. It should be kept in mind that ways of thinking about prejudice in youngsters do not remain static for long.

How is Child Prejudice Different from Adolescent and Adult Prejudice?

With better understanding of the development of prejudice, theorists now recognize the less sophisticated and more tentative prejudice experienced by children compared to adults (see Eagly & Diekman, ch. 2 this volume). Prejudice can take many forms, as Brown (1995, p. 8) defines it: "the holding of derogatory social attitudes or cognitive beliefs, the expression of negative affect, or the display of hostile or discriminatory behavior towards members of a group on account of their membership of that group." Among children and adolescents, the most overt level includes racial conflicts and name-calling. Less overt but equally damaging is avoidance of outgroup peers. Because children lack the emotional and verbal sophistication of adolescents and adults, their prejudice does not usually take the form of anger, hostility, and verbal taunts. Rather, it is experienced as suspicion, fear, sadness, and disapproval, and expressed as avoidance, social exclusion, and negative evaluation. Consequently, qualitative methods that use participant observation and open-ended interviews reveal little obvious prejudice among young children (e.g. Holmes, 1995), though these were the sources of Allport's anecdotes.

Since Allport's book, there has been a decline in the use of qualitative methods and the simple doll technique that asks children which of two racially different dolls is "nice," "bad," and so forth. Currently used multi-item tests include appropriate positive and negative evaluative terms and do not force a single selection. Prejudice in children may be revealed through the expression of outright negative evaluations or the withholding of positive evaluations normally made of ingroup peers (Aboud, 2003; see also Brown and Zagefka, ch. 4 this volume). Discriminatory behavior has been measured in the context of peer relations, including rejection, companionship, and friendship quality (Aboud, Mendelson, & Purdy, 2003). Also the distinction between implicit and explicit prejudice, so important in the mental make-up of egalitarian-minded adults (see Rudman, ch. 7 this volume), is currently being examined in light of new implicit measures for children (Skowronski & Lawrence, 2001). Finally, children often do not show consistency between attitudes and behavior. Theoretically this reflects children's weaker cognitive systems, but this explanation has not yet been explored. For example, children's behavior may be driven more by concrete situational cues than by attitudes, as is the case with children's sense of identity and morality. Moreover, children may have several cross-race friends with whom they play on a daily basis, but they may not integrate and generalize this information.

The Use of Differing Research Designs to Examine Acquisition and Reduction of Prejudice

Allport referred mostly to observational studies recording children's words and behavior. However, the conclusions one can draw from this design are limited. Attitudes are not generally expressed unless triggered by the situation, so the number of spontaneous expressions does not reveal the prevalence or intensity of prejudice in children. Subsequent research used structured measures of prejudice along with cross-sectional and longitudinal designs to pin down the prevalence and development of prejudice. At the other extreme, laboratory studies of learning show that children *can* learn to associate an evaluative term with a category label – one mechanism thought to underlie the acquisition of prejudice in children – but not that children *do* learn this way or that such associations are maintained after the experimental situation. Given that evaluative forms of prejudice seem to be prevalent and strong at 5 years, we might ask: Why do children learn a label–evaluation pairing at 5 years and not at 4 or 3 years? Why do they not equally well learn the positive associations? Cognitive processes may be partly able to account for age and association differences. Children of 5 years are less self- and more group-centered than 4- or 3-year-olds and more motivated to use good–bad dichotomies. Likewise, negative evaluations are taken to be more informative and therefore given more weight, perhaps because negative behaviors are unexpected and less frequent. It is important that experiments mimic as closely as possible the actual conditions of children's lives in order to show convincingly which mechanisms explain prejudice (Bigler, Brown, & Markell, 2001).

Research that tests Allport's hypotheses about prejudice prevention and reduction, rather than acquisition, is becoming more important. He assumed that if children learn to become prejudiced through observation and reinforcement, they can learn to become unprejudiced through similar mechanisms, i.e. by building up "contrary associations" (Allport, 1954/1979, p. 304). Studies have evaluated the impact of children's exposure to positive outgroup models and respectful attitudes, but the outcomes were not always encouraging (Cole et al., 2003; Persson & Musher-Eizenman, 2003). Psychologists now realize that to change an already-existing attitude requires overcoming a stubborn obstacle, namely the tendency to dismiss contradictory attitudes and attend only to evidence confirming the existing attitude. While greater success has been achieved in reducing prejudice through cooperative intergroup contact (see Pettigrew & Tropp, ch. 16 this volume; Kenworthy, Turner, Hewstone, & Voci, ch. 17 this volume), where this is not feasible, the combined elements of several theories may be needed to bring about change.

Examining the Processes Underlying Minority Children's Identity and Bias

Allport had very little of value to say about minority children, except that they were sophisticated and social in biracial preschools. Allport observed, "Negro children are, by and large, 'racially aware' earlier than are white children. They tend to be confused, disturbed, and sometimes excited by the problem" (1954/1979, p. 302). Recent studies primarily on African

American children, but also Hispanic, Native, and Asian Americans, have focused on their complex identity development (Phinney, 1990; Quintana, 1999), as well as reactions to their unfair treatment in schools and the media (e.g. Graves, 1996). Parents of young minority children were found to play a very overt role in preparing their youngsters for the discrimination they will inevitably face. Similarly peers exert strong conformity pressures on adolescents. Nonetheless, minority children neither mirror nor mimic fully their environment; most studies indicate that minority identity and attitudes show considerable individual variation (see chapters by Major & Vick and by Jones, chs. 9 and 10 this volume). Reactions to discrimination have also been widely studied. Research on stereotype threat points to the deleterious effects of differential treatment, verbal insults, and the potential for fulfilling a negative stereotype on performance (Steele, 1997; Stephan & Stephan, 2000). Increasingly, studies are examining the conditions under which "leveling the playing field" enhances minority outcomes.

Sharpening of Theories on the Acquisition and Development of Prejudice

Exciting theoretical advances have occurred since Allport's book. Although most people accepted the learning-theory explanation for a gradual increase in prejudice with age, as summarized by Brand, Ruiz, and Padilla (1974), this was challenged by findings that the increase was not so gradual (e.g. Asher & Allan, 1966; Clark, 1955) and that there was little correlation between the attitudes of parents and children (see Aboud & Amato, 2001). Clearly the validity and scope of Allport's learning and conformity explanations needed to be reexamined. An expanded understanding of cognitive processes allowed psychologists to elaborate on concepts such as norms, social motives, identity, and personality. This led to the sharpening, elaboration, and testing of alternative theories, which had been described in only a cursory fashion by Allport in chapters 18 ("The Young Child") and 19 ("Later Learning").

Several milestones of theory development have recently occurred. One approach concerns the impact of norms that could have an immediate conformity effect in any particular situation. Costanzo and Shaw (1966) demonstrated that even children of 6 years conformed to group pressure by adopting an incorrect judgment about the length of a line, and that conformity to subjective opinions increased between 6 and 13 years but declined thereafter. Norm theory has recently become of greater value as psychologists discover the powerful impact of ingroup in contrast to outgroup sources of messages, the role of ingroup peers who demand conformity in exchange for group belonging, and developmental changes in children's understanding of social regularities and moral rules (Killen, Pisacane, Lee-Kim, & Ardila-Rey, 2001). Whereas Allport used conformity and learning almost interchangeably, current researchers would say that the children's awareness of the need to follow social rules may motivate them quickly to learn such rules, but that the two are distinct: learning is the acquisition of a novel response, whereas conformity is following the assumed rules.

Intergroup experiences have been studied extensively since the 1950s, particularly once Sherif (1966) demonstrated so vividly the conditions that led both to hostility and acceptance in a boys' camp. Laboratory studies by Cook (1985) highlighted the importance of equal status and cooperation for reducing prejudice, which were also found to be critical conditions in school settings (e.g., Schofield & Eurich-Fulcer, 2001). Friendship, as the optimal form of contact, has been examined more closely by Pettigrew (1998; Pettigrew & Tropp, ch. 16 this volume), as have other forms of contact, to determine what psychological processes mediate the effect of contact on prejudice reduction. Thus, a new, more elaborated, theory of contact is being developed and tested (Hewstone, 2002; see Kenworthy, Turner, Hewstone, & Voci, ch. 17 this volume).

Identity and status are the centerpiece of Tajfel's (1978) social-identity theory of discrimination. He demonstrated that young boys' identification with even a meaningless social category could lead to discrimination (Tajfel, 1970). His explanation for the connection between identification and prejudice centered not on conflict but on the process of social comparison/competition whereby children attempt to attain a positive social identity by enhancing their ingroup status relative to the outgroup. In the "minimal" laboratory context, which intentionally eliminates all social groups, identities, and reactions, other than the ones being studied, identity and discrimination are strongly connected (see Bourhis & Gagnon, 2001). After this research, developmentalists could no longer assume, as Allport did, that group identity is salient, strong, and automatic, and that children understand their group's social status

Developmental stages of prejudice now refer to stages in cognitive development rather than learning stages. Katz (1976) was the first to pick up on Allport's sequence, demonstrating its utility in her research on overgeneralization and differentiation. The current view, however, arose from applying Piaget's theory to prejudice (Piaget & Weil, 1951) and to social development more generally. Social-cognitive and social-emotional development determine what children are able to learn from others and to retain once the model and the reinforcement disappear. Research has highlighted psychological processes of learning and motivation, such as the need to make sense of the social world and one's place in it. Peer influences are given more weight than previously, recognizing the importance of peer play and conflict in the learning process. Also, social developmentalists noticed the positive outcomes, such as fairness and perspective-taking, that come with cognitive development. This view of the child and adolescent required major changes in how psychologists understood learning and conformity. Furthermore, because Piaget's stages are based not only on category development, but on changing self–other perspectives, they are relevant to identity concerns and intergroup contact. So, Allport's stages of learning were transformed to age-related stages of category development, and finally to stages of self, social identity, and perspective taking. All three formulations require some social input, but they differ in the extent of readiness of the child to seek and make use of that input.

A New Framework for Integrating Current Research and Theory

Rebecca Bigler, Sheri Levy, and I have developed an integrated framework to organize variables that are important to the acquisition and reduction of prejudice that prominently features all five theories raised previously (see figure 19.1). This framework points out how these theories can be tested in combination and in comparison to one another.

The framework outlined in figure 19.1 assumes that people and events are located within a social time and place, which alters the likelihood that socializers will be ingroup or outgroup members and that events and messages about the outgroup will be positive or negative. These elements have changed since Allport's time, though the relations of the constructs may not have.

It is generally accepted that learning, conformity, and contact are common mechanisms of acquisition, and so identifying one specific mechanism may not be informative. More valuable is knowing how prejudiced messages and behaviors are transmitted by different socializers and why they are differentially adopted by youth who vary in age and identity. The importance of the child or adolescent is highlighted by the fact that at each age developmental tasks influence the meaning of messages. Five-year-olds are intent on figuring out social rules and regularities, whereas young adolescents search for meaningful identities in their social space. Learning

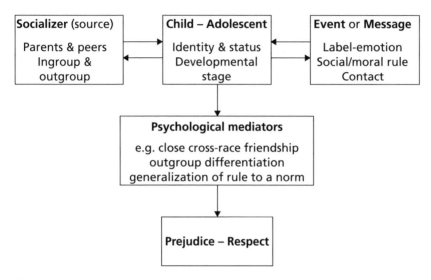

Figure 19.1 Framework for organizing theoretical variables in child and adolescent prejudice

from parental emotions and observation of their surroundings may be more important for 5-year-olds, whereas conformity to ingroup peer norms and contact with outgroup peers may be more influential with adolescents. Consequently, the framework emphasizes the need to combine variables from two or three boxes in order to compare mechanisms and theories.

As illustrated in figure 19.1, the framework places the child and adolescent at the center of various social forces. Cognitive-developmental research continues to demonstrate age-related changes in basic social-cognitive processes and the way youth understand themselves, other individuals, and social groups. These perceptions and understandings, in turn, may influence children's motivations for adopting alternative attitudes and behaviors. Thus, antibias programs may have the desired effect only if the message is geared to the child's developmental level, or a higher developmental level is primed with practice (Aboud, 2002). The real value of a cognitive or emotional stage theory is in combination with other theories, in that it helps to specify age-related constraints and readiness to attend to a certain socializer and to receive a specific message.

Identity and status determine which socializers and messages are readily received. Identity refers to the cognitive and emotional representation of oneself in terms of an organized network of (relatively stable) interrelated descriptors and evaluations. However, under certain conditions one or more social identities become salient (see Gaertner & Dovidio, ch. 5 this volume). The strength of one's group identity and the potential for multiple identities change with age and racial status, but little is known about how children develop an understanding of status based on criteria such as occupation, power, and numbers. In addition to identity, child psychologists have begun to search for character structures that might predispose a child or adolescent to prejudice. Social dominance, for example, is evident during play in children as young as 4 years, but is rarely studied in relation to prejudice and gender segregation. Ways of cognitively interpreting the basic nature and behavior of others, such as in static or dynamic terms, are also relevant to the tendency to stereotype or not (Levy & Dweck, 1999; Levy et al., 2001).

An important question is how children learn bias in the first place, even under circumstances in which their parents do not express overt prejudice. It is not enough to show that paired associate learning can occur in 10-year-olds, because prejudice may first be learned differently (e.g., emotionally, making it harder to eliminate) than the way it can be learned later. Other forms of observational learning may be more common if, for example, children notice that people of the same racial/ethnic group congregate in families and friendship groups. Thus, illusory correlations (Johnston & Jacobs, 2003) and actual regularities will be quickly observed by preschoolers, who are noted for their eagerness to acquire language and social rules. Children may assume that because their family has fewer associations with outgroup members, the latter are to be avoided and disliked. Such a minimal learning environment may be a sufficient explanation for young children who give meaning to social regularities, yet it may not explain later learning. Learning processes may be moderated by developmental and identity characteristics of the child learner. Because children have a different understanding and evaluation of self and social information at 5 years compared to 9 years, they will pick out different messages to adopt.

Conformity research poses questions about the persuasiveness of ingroup over outgroup messages, yet again this varies with age and identity. Children and adolescents are motivated to understand the rules governing social behavior, and peers rather than parents are often the source of these rules. Research on the norms underlying gender segregation and gender clothing preferences, for example, demonstrates the power of rules imposed by young peers, particularly those who are socially dominant and articulate. Several areas of norm research converge to demonstrate how ingroup peers impose social rules in the light of identity and developmental concerns. Mackie and Wright's (2001) research suggests that children, like adults, are motivated to attend to and are persuaded by the message of an ingroup member, regardless of supporting arguments. So, children may very quickly, rather than gradually, adopt prejudiced attitudes from peer groups. This may be strengthened by social forces whose impact on prejudice acquisition is not yet clear. For example, pluralistic ignorance, the faulty perception of a high level of agreement among ingroup members (e.g., family and friends), may increase conformity (Prentice & Miller, 1993). Further, research by Abrams, Rutland, Cameron, and Marques (2003) exposed group processes whereby ingroup members uphold extreme ingroup—outgroup attitudes by derogating those with balanced attitudes. This derogation is particularly strong among children in middle childhood, when conformity increases, and among group members who do not yet have a positive consensual identity. It will be important to test how developmental and identity moderators affect these processes.

Countering norms of prejudice is important for reducing racial bullying in the schoolyard (Aboud & Fenwick, 1999). Figure 19.1 suggests that when identity concerns are high, an ingroup peer socializer will be more effective at countering the bully than an outgroup peer, who for reasons of empathy might be more likely to side with the bullied victim. Research with adults highlights the need for behavior that explicitly disagrees with the insults or exclusions and demonstrates a new norm. But motivations for conformity differ by age. The age at which young children identify themselves with their peer group and conform willingly or unwillingly follows an inverted-U curve (Costanzo & Shaw, 1966; Gavin & Furman, 1989). One motivation is to maintain positive peer relations and social evaluation. Older children know that moral reasons against exclusion and bullying are preferable to social convention and conformity (Killen, Lee-Kim, McGlothlin, & Stangor, 2002), so the former might successfully be used to counter norms of prejudice. However, conformity to another's attitude also occurs among younger children, possibly with a different motivation (Aboud, 1981). Because of developmental constraints on the ability to take more than one perspective, young children are often not aware that an alternative is possible or better. They may also not see the difference between a rule that derives from social convention as opposed to moral considerations.

Intergroup contact in a school setting has become the most informative and challenging context for studying prejudice and its reduction that cries out for psychological analysis and theoretical explanation. Hewstone's (2002; Kenworthy, Turner, Hewstone, & Voci, ch. 17 this volume) theory includes variables proposed as mediators in figure 19.1 that are known to reduce prejudice, though their mediatonal role is not always clear. However, age and identity must always be considered. For example, Bigler and colleagues (Bigler, Brown, & Markell, 2001; Brown & Bigler, 2002) arranged for children to wear either blue or yellow t-shirts at school for several weeks, thus manipulating social categories and identity. Only when teachers used t-shirt color to organize class activities did children use these categories for a more positive, but not less negative, ingroup evaluation. Social status was manipulated in a naturalistic way with posters distinguishing high- and low-status personnel according to t-shirt color; high- but not low-status children made differential group evaluations. In contrast, when numerical status was manipulated, those who were significantly outnumbered by their classmates used the categories regardless of the teacher's use of them. This research comes closest to testing variables from three boxes in our integrated framework, namely the child (ages/stages and identity/status) and peer intergroup contact.

Has Allport Been Supported?

Most of Allport's ideas have been modified and extended. That is precisely why his writings are so seminal – he provided tidbits of tantalizing evidence for all sorts of mechanisms without nailing any one down convincingly. His claim that prejudice is learned is well supported, along with the proposal that prejudice often reflects conformity to a perceived consensus among one's ingroup. Beyond this, psychologists have come a long way in identifying major constructs and sharpening distinctions between them. Researchers have also recognized the important role of the center box in figure 19.1, namely the cognitive and socioemotional abilities and needs of children as they develop into adolescents and adults. Contemporary scholars have also given more weight to the influence of peers, particularly ingroup peers. Finally, research on the development of racial-minority children, along with their growing identity needs, has progressed almost independently of Allport's work, which showed little insight into minority prejudice and responses to prejudice.

Future Directions: Promising Avenues for Research

In the next 20 years developmentalists must continue to elaborate and test theories that include variables from more than one box of the integrated framework proposed here, eventually comparing the validity and scope of different theories. Some theories may be more valuable in race-salient societies and others in societies where race is less of a social issue. Certain theories may be more applicable to the formation of prejudice (e.g. learning plus developmental theory) and others more relevant to the reduction of prejudice (e.g. intergroup contact plus identity and norms). Although there is enough evidence now to support the basic mechanisms of each theory, the predictive power of different theories needs to be compared in the same experiment.

In addition to comparing different theories, psychologists need to examine how the variables from several boxes of figure 19.1 interact with one another. For example, how explicit must an antibias message be when delivered to a 5- versus a 9-year-old by an ingroup compared to an outgroup peer/adult? The answer to this question requires systematically varying message clarity, child age, and socializer group, and measuring the effects on attitude change. If there are age and socializer differences, researchers should then try to evaluate potential underlying mechanisms (i.e., possible mediators). Young children may not attend to or recall messages from outgroup members; they may dismiss antibias messages from ingroup members as non-normative and socially disapproved; or they may be unable to reconcile differences of opinion and so not process anyone's opinion that differs from their own. Identifying underlying processes will strengthen theoretical explanations.

Field experiments also should be conducted once laboratory experiments have demonstrated the efficacy of a manipulation under controlled conditions. It is inefficient to implement a school intervention, with its multiple uncontrolled inputs, before showing that the intervention changes attitudes or behavior under well-scrutinized laboratory conditions. Success in the laboratory does not guarantee effectiveness in the field, but it would seem to be a necessary precondition (see Stephan & Stephan, ch. 26 this volume).

Prejudice is a multifaceted construct that includes not only cognitive but emotional and behavioral processes that are becoming more prominent in research (see Smith & Mackie, ch. 22 this volume). The role of affect has been acknowledged, but rarely studied. Presumably many different emotions come into play when experiencing prejudice, yet we have no widely accepted measures for these. Emotions are more salient and may predict behavior better than cognitions. Measures of behavior also need to become more diversified. Currently, psychologists use self-reports or observations of cross-race friendship, exclusion, conflict, and helping. If prejudice and discrimination arise partly from ingroup pressures, then discrimination could be measured through support for or conflict with ingroup peers who express prejudice through racist jokes and epithets (see Mullen & Leader, this volume). Researchers also need to assess the circumstances under which evaluations influence behavior and vice versa. Under many circumstances behavior directed toward outgroup members is unrelated to evaluations. Some would say that this is due to poor measurement. But it is theoretically more interesting to hypothesize that with age, behavior comes under more cognitive control, whereas with younger children it is under emotional control. Perhaps differences in implicit and explicit attitudes arise in children when cognitions become strong and salient enough to diverge from emotions.

My hope is that we will not be studying ethnic prejudice 50 years from now, that psychologists will have solved the problem and overcome current divides as societies become increasingly blended. Of course, the cognitive processes of categorization and identity will remain, though they need not trigger generalized and discriminatory evaluation.

REFERENCES

Aboud, F. E. (1981). Egocentrism, conformity, and agreeing to disagree. *Developmental Psychology, 17,* 791–799.

Aboud, F. E. (1988). *Children and prejudice.* New York: Blackwell.

Aboud, F. E. (2002). Changing racial attitudes of young children with anti-bias messages. Paper presented at the annual meeting of the Society for the Psychological Study of Social Issues, Toronto, June.

Aboud, F. E. (2003). The formation of in-group preference and out-group prejudice in young children: Are they distinct attitudes? *Developmental Psychology, 39,* 48–60.

Aboud, F. E. & Amato, M. (2001). Developmental and socialization influences on intergroup bias. In R. Brown & S. L. Gaertner (eds.), *The Blackwell handbook of social psychology: Intergroup processes* (pp. 65–85). Malden, MA: Blackwell.

Aboud F. E. & Fenwick, V. (1999). Exploring and evaluating school-based interventions to reduce prejudice in preadolescents. *Journal of Social Issues, 55,* 767–85.

Aboud, F. E., Mendelson, M. J., & Purdy, K. T. (2003). Cross-race peer relations and friendship quality. *International Journal of Behavioral Development, 27,* 165–73.

Abrams, D., Rutland, A., Cameron, L., & Marques, J. M. (2003). The development of subjective group dynamics: When in-group bias gets specific. *British Journal of Developmental Psychology, 21,* 155–76.

Adorno, T. W., Frenkel-Brunswik, E., Levinson, D. J., & Sanford, R. N. (1950). *The authoritarian personality.* New York: Harper.

Allport, G. W. (1954/1979). *The nature of prejudice.* Cambridge, MA: Perseus Books.

Asher, S. R. & Allen, V. L. (1966). Racial preference and social comparison processes. *Journal of Social Issues, 25,* 157–67.

Bigler, R. S., Brown, C. S., & Markell, M. (2001). When groups are not created equal: Effects of group status on the formation of intergroup attitudes in children. *Child Development, 72,* 1151–62.

Bourhis, R. & Gagnon, A. (2001). Social orientations in the minimal group paradigm. In R. Brown & S. L. Gaertner (eds.), *The Blackwell handbook of social psychology: Intergroup processes* (pp. 89–111). Malden, MA: Blackwell.

Brand, E. S., Ruiz, R. A., & Padilla, A. M. (1974). Ethnic identification and preference: A review. *Psychological Bulletin, 81,* 860–90.

Brown, C. S. & Bigler, R. S. (2002). Effects of minority status in the classroom on children's intergroup attitudes. *Journal of Experimental Child Psychology, 83,* 77–110.

Brown R. (1995). *Prejudice: Its social psychology.* Cambridge, MA: Blackwell.

Clark, K. B. (1955). *Prejudice and your child.* Boston, MA: Beacon Press.

Cole, C., Arafat, C., Tidhar, C., Tafesh, W., Fox, N., Killen, M., Ardila-Rey, A., Leavitt, L., Lesser, G., Richman, B., & Yung, F. (2003). The educational impact of *Rechov Sumsmn/ Shara's Simsim*: A Sesame Street television series to promote respect and understanding among children living in Israel, the West Bank, and Gaza. *International Journal of Behavioral Development, 27,* 409–29.

Cook, S. W. (1985). Experimenting on social issues. *American Psychologist, 40,* 452–60.

Costanzo, P. R. & Shaw, M. E. (1966). Conformity as a function of age level. *Child Development, 37,* 967–75.

Doyle, A. B. & Aboud, F. E. (1995). A longitudinal study of White children's racial prejudice as a social-cognitive development. *Merrill-Palmer Quarterly, 41,* 209–28.

Gavin, L. A. & Furman, W. (1989). Age differences in adolescent's perceptions of their peer groups. *Developmental Psychology, 25,* 827–34.

Graves, S. B. (1996). Diversity on television. In T. MacBeth (ed.), *Tuning in to young viewers* (pp. 61–86). Thousand Oaks, CA: Sage.

Hewstone, M. (2002). Intergroup contact to improve intergroup relations: How and when it works. Presentation at the annual meeting of the Society for the Psychological Study of Social Issues, Toronto, June.

Holmes, R. M. (1995). *How young children perceive race.* Thousand Oaks, CA: Sage.

Johnston, K. E. & Jacobs, J. E. (2003). Children's illusory correlations: The role of attentional bias in group impression formation. *Journal of Cognition & Development, 4,* 129–60.

Katz, P. A. (1976). The acquisition of racial attitudes in children. In P. A. Katz (ed.), *Toward the elimination of racism* (pp. 125–54). New York: Pergamon Press.

Killen, M., Lee-Kim, J., McGlothlin, H., & Stangor, C. (2002). How children and adolescents evaluate gender and racial exclusion. *Monographs for the Society for Research in Child Development* (serial no. 271, vol. 67, no. 4). Malden, MA: Blackwell Publishers.

Killen, M., Pisacane, K., Lee-Kim, J., & Ardila-Rey, A. (2001). Fairness or stereotypes?: Young children's priorities when evaluating group exclusion and inclusion. *Developmental Psychology, 37*, 587–96.

Levy, S. R. & Dweck, C. (1999). The impact of children's static versus dynamic conceptions of people on stereotype formation. *Child Development, 70*, 1163–80.

Levy, S. R., Plaks, J. E., Hong, Y., Chiu, C., & Dweck, C. S. (2001). Static versus dynamic theories and the perception of groups: Different routes to different destinations. *Personality & Social Psychology Review, 5*, 156–68.

Mackie, D. M. & Wright, C. L. (2001). Social influence in an intergroup context. In R. Brown & S. L. Gaertner (eds.), *The Blackwell handbook of social psychology: Intergroup processes* (pp. 281–300). Malden, MA: Blackwell.

Persson, A. & Musher-Eizenman, D. R. (2003). The impact of a prejudice prevention television program on young children's racial attitudes and knowledge. *Early Childhood Research Quarterly, 18*, 530–46.

Pettigrew, T. F. (1998). Intergroup contact theory. *Annual Review of Psychology, 49*, 65–85.

Phinney, J. S. (1990). Ethnic identity in adolescents and adults: Review of research. *Psychological Bulletin, 108*, 499–514.

Piaget, J. & Weil, A. M. (1951). The development in children of the idea of the homeland and of relations to other countries. *International Social Science Journal, 3*, 561–78.

Prentice, D. A. & Miller, D. T. (1993). Pluralistic ignorance and alcohol use on campus: Some consequences of misperceiving the social norm. *Journal of Personality and Social Psychology, 64*, 243–56.

Quintana, S. M. (1999). Role of perspective-taking abilities and ethnic socialization in development of adolescent ethnic identity. *Journal of Research on Adolescence, 19*, 161–84.

Schofield, J. W. & Eurich-Fulcer, R. (2001). When and how school desegregation improves intergroup relations. In R. Brown & S. L. Gaertner (eds.), *The Blackwell handbook of social psychology: Intergroup processes* (pp. 475–94). Malden, MA: Blackwell.

Sherif, M. (1966). *Group conflict and cooperation*. London: Routledge & Kegan Paul.

Skowronski, J. J. & Lawrence, M. A. (2001). A comparative study of the implicit and explicit gender attitudes of children and college students. *Psychology of Women Quarterly, 25*, 155–65.

Steele, C. M. (1997). A threat in the air: How stereotypes shape intellectual identity and performance. *American Psychologist, 52*, 613–29.

Stephan, W. G. & Stephan, C. W. (2000). An integrated threat theory of prejudice. In S. Oskamp (ed.), *Reducing prejudice and discrimination* (pp. 23–45). Mahwah, NJ: Erlbaum.

Tajfel, H. (1970). Experiments in intergroup discrimination. *Scientific American, 223*, 96–102.

Tajfel, H. (1978). Social categorization, social identity, and social comparison. In H. Tajfel (ed.), *Differentiation between social groups* (pp. 61–98). New York: Academic Press.

Chapter Twenty

Breaking the Prejudice Habit:
Allport's "Inner Conflict" Revisited

Patricia G. Devine

Many chapters in Allport's *The Nature of Prejudice* leave readers with the impression that prejudice is rather commonplace and essentially guaranteed by virtue of both how the mind works and how society is structured. For example, early chapters revealed prejudgment and categorical thinking to be ordinary, if not necessary, cognitive processes. In still other chapters, prejudice was observed to be woven into the fabric of society and individual learning histories, if not the fundamental structure of personality. Ordinary and normal, however, do not imply acceptable – and this fact is the starting point for Allport's analysis of what he referred to as *inner conflict*. To the extent that one views prejudice as deplorable, these ordinary processes can lead to troubling intrapsychic outcomes.

Allport's Views on Inner Conflict

In recognition of the very real possibility that prejudice may be viewed as unacceptable, Allport opened the "Inner Conflict" chapter, chapter 20, with the following observation: "The course of prejudice in a life seldom runs smoothly. For prejudiced attitudes are almost certain to collide with deep-seated values that are often equally or more central to the personality" (1954/1979, p. 326). The types of deep-seated values that create problems for prejudice are those of fairness, justice, and the humane treatment of others as prescribed by the American Creed and Judeo-Christian values – values that Allport claimed are integral in our socialization as Americans. To the extent that people subscribe to these values, possessing group-based prejudices would by definition collide with them and would reveal those with such prejudices to be hypocrites. Being exposed as a hypocrite is, according to Allport, discomforting to people. More than simply discomforting, Allport anticipated that this type of inner conflict would lead to the experience of prejudice with *compunction* (i.e., accompanied by shame, guilt, and regret). Such self-inflicted punishment Allport believed would serve as a powerful motivating force to reduce the conflict. He cautioned, however, that the process of resolving the conflict would be both difficult and fraught with internal tension.

Historical Context: Questioning the Morality and Legality of Prejudice

It is important to place Allport's observations in the historical, social, and political context in which experiences of prejudice with compunction arose. The world was still reeling from the events of the Second World War in which unspeakable atrocities were perpetrated against Jews *because* they were Jews. The Holocaust, largely viewed as a crime against humanity, led many Americans to seriously question the morality of group-based prejudice. How could the nation fight against such crimes against humanity while, on its own soil, entire groups of people were denied rights and opportunities because of their skin color? Quite simply, the American Creed, although revered in the abstract, was being violated in practice.

Legislators and lay-people alike had long being struggling with these issues. In 1896, for example, the Supreme Court, in the case of *Plessy vs. Ferguson*, handed down a ruling that undermined racial discrimination while affording segregation by establishing "separate but equal" facilities (e.g., schools, water fountains, restaurants) for White and Black Americans. Over time, however, it became evident that "separate but equal" was a fiction that was fundamentally at odds with the constitutional proclamation that "all men [*sic*] are created equal." Indeed, in the same year that Allport published his book, the Supreme Court ruled in the case of *Brown vs. The Board of Education* that separate is inherently *unequal* and, in 1955, they decreed that schools should be desegregated with "all deliberate speed." These decisions legitimized remediation for race-based educational discrimination and, in tandem with the Civil Rights Legislation of the 1960s, they contributed to a social and political context in which group-based prejudice was questioned on both legal and moral grounds.

Allport's Inner Conflict: Prejudice with Compunction

Against the backdrop of the American Creed and an emerging social context that discouraged overt expressions of prejudice, Allport noted that although prejudice without compunction may exist among true bigots, more common was the experience of prejudice with compunction. To illustrate the power of this conflict, Allport reviewed anecdotal evidence abstracted from essays written by college students and suburban women concerning their experiences with and attitudes toward minority groups in America. Indeed, Allport was struck by what he referred to as the almost bewildering inconsistencies observed in these essays. With each example cited, the reader easily gets caught up in the conflict as people explain how they actually often express biases and then quickly explain that they know they shouldn't express or wished that they didn't express them. Consider just one example: "Every rational voice within me says the Negro is as good, decent, sincere, and manly as the white, but I cannot help but notice a split between my reason and my prejudice" (Allport, 1954/1979, p. 327). Indeed, as the essayists confess to the injustice (and often irrationality) of their biases, their tension is palpable. Abstracting from these anecdotal examples, Allport concluded that "defeated intellectually, prejudice lingers emotionally" (p. 328). Allport was impressed by the essayists' self-insight, but was careful to note that self-insight is a necessary but insufficient step toward overcoming prejudice; instead, it serves as a prelude to a period of conflict during which self-dissatisfaction with one's biases will motivate efforts to reduce the conflict and bring one's responses in line with one's values.

Developments Since Allport

A great many years passed following the publication of Allport's book before social psychologists took up the issues explored in the "Inner Conflict" chapter. Eventually, however, these issues came to occupy the center of contemporary discussions concerning both the nature of prejudice and efforts to overcome prejudice.

The impetus to revisit Allport's discussion of "inner conflict" was an effort to address a perplexing set of research findings concerning expressions of prejudice in the wake of the legislative and normative changes that made overt expressions of prejudice both illegal and socially taboo. Social scientists were struggling to explain the disparity between people's reports of their racial attitudes (i.e., what they say) and their behavior (i.e., what they do; see Crosby, Bromley, & Saxe, 1980). That is, although White Americans often reported relatively positive attitudes toward Black Americans on surveys, their behaviors often belied these statements and revealed substantial evidence of prejudice – perhaps direct evidence of the "split between reason and prejudice." These findings served as the cornerstone for modern theories of prejudice (see also Sears, ch. 21 this volume). Each theory offers a different analysis of the reasons why people may withhold overt expressions of race bias in response to social norms that proscribe prejudice. Allport's discussion of strategies for handling inner conflict anticipated, at least indirectly, some of these modern conceptions of prejudice.

Repression of Inner Conflict and Aversive Racism

Allport noted that one way to obviate the need for conscious attention to or distress over inner conflict was to *repress* evidence of it. This strategy reflects a denial of prejudice within the self. For example Allport noted that "no one wants to be at odds with his own conscience" (Allport 1954/ 1979, p. 334). An important component of repression as a strategy for handling conflict is that in deploying it, people fail to recognize their prejudices. According to Allport, repression is a protective rather than truly effective resolution of the conflict and leaves people vulnerable to responding with prejudice and, hence, inner conflict.

This line of reasoning has conceptual parallels in Gaertner and Dovidio's (1986) analysis of aversive racism, which proposes that many White Americans simultaneously hold anti-Black feelings and a sincere belief that people should be treated equally (see also Dovidio & Gaertner, 2004). Although these negative feelings are largely disavowed and consequently unacknowledged by many White people, they are nevertheless activated during interactions with Black people. This juxtaposition of prejudice and egalitarianism leads to *aversive racism*, such that the conflict between simultaneously-activated prejudiced and egalitarian views causes aversive feelings, such as discomfort, unease, and sometimes fear. Aversive feelings can motivate people to avoid future interactions with Black people in order to avoid evoking negative emotions.

Defensive Rationalization

Whereas the repression strategy represents a wholesale disavowal of prejudice, Allport identified other strategies that drew on people's flexible cognitive processes to construe evidence to fit with preferred preconceptions. These strategies, Allport suggested, involve *defensive rationalizations*. Defensive rationalizations do not truly resolve the conflict, but rather allow people to make sense of inconsistencies by marshalling evidence to justify negative views of outgroup members. People can, for example, selectively cite examples to support negative views of outgroup members while simultaneously ignoring or distorting contrary evidence. Such selective consideration and interpretation of "evidence" enables people to maintain the illusion that they are objective and fair-minded. For example, evidence of a highly accomplished Black person who contradicts the stereotype of Blacks as lazy is easily handled by viewing that individual as the "exception that proves the rule." Contemporary authors refer to this process as subtyping (Rothbart & John, 1985). Once subtyped, the person no longer threatens the validity of stereotypic thinking. Allport recognized that this strategy enables people to recognize their negative beliefs but to view them as valid rather than prejudiced. The contemporary literature is replete with examples of the deployment of such strategies to maintain stereotypes and prejudice (see Fiske, ch. 3 this volume).

Alternation and Ambivalent Racism

Explaining away inconsistent evidence can be challenging and requires a vigilance that may be taxing to social perceivers. An alternative strategy is to accept negative beliefs about outgroup members as valid while simultaneously viewing oneself as egalitarian and fair-minded. Because these views are likely to collide, Allport suggested that people who use this type of strategy would need to *alternate between their conflicting views of outgroup members*. Indeed, Allport suggested that this was likely the most common strategy used to address the threat of inner conflict because it allowed people to maintain a fair and just self-concept yet still respond in prejudiced ways. Using this strategy, people vacillate between their egalitarian values and their prejudiced beliefs based on situational factors that make one or the other salient.

Katz and Hass (1988; Katz, Wackenhut, & Hass, 1986) developed this theme and provided evidence for what they referred to as *ambivalent racism*, defined as the simultaneous possession of positive and negative attitudes toward Black people. Katz and Hass argued that people's pro- and anti-Black attitudes were derived from their commitment to alternative values cherished by Americans, humanitarianism and Protestant Work Ethic values, respectively. Katz and Hass (1988) developed two separate measures to assess respondents' positive and negative attitudes. They found that *anti*-Black attitudes were correlated with beliefs in the Protestant Work Ethic (the idea that personal success is gained through hard work and self-reliance), whereas *pro*-Black attitudes correlated with humanitarianism and egalitarianism. The authors hypothesized – and found – that highly ambivalent people were prone to extreme pro- or anti-Black responses, depending on the situation. For example, in situations emphasizing egalitarianism, ambivalent racists were particularly positive toward Black people, whereas in situations emphasizing the merits of self-reliance, they were especially harsh toward Black people (Katz et al., 1986).

According to Allport, none of the above strategies provides a true or effective resolution of inner conflict. Instead, each of these strategies and their contemporary theoretical counterparts explain how the conflict between thought and action remains intact and nonthreatening. Hence, they are explanations for how prejudice persists rather than how prejudice is reduced. Each of the modern theories, for example, presumes that in the context of normative pressure, people's prejudices are forced "underground," such that they are expressed in subtle, indirect, or covert ways. Thus, prejudice does not truly decline; rather, the form in which prejudice is expressed is changed.

In this regard, none of these approaches offer insights into strategies for prejudice reduction. Allport recognized, however, that for some people, overcoming rather than circumventing prejudice was the overarching goal. For example, Allport (1954/1979) noted that some people are likely to find their defenses wanting such that "they can neither repress, rationalize, nor compromise with any comfort" (p. 338). These people are aware of, and do not hide from, the conflict between their values and their actions. Indeed, awareness of the conflict is a prerequisite to overcoming prejudice. According to Allport, successful resolution of inner conflict – true prejudice reduction – requires taking stock of one's biases and doing the hard work to achieve an integrated personality in which there is consistency between values and actions. The true resolution or prejudice reduction theme was taken up in another of the modern approaches to understanding the disparity between verbal reports of people's attitudes and covert indicators of prejudice (Devine, 1989). And in our unfolding program of research, a modern analysis of inner conflict and efforts to achieve its true resolution are found.

A New Framework: Automatic and Controlled Processes in Prejudice

In developing an analysis of how nonprejudiced beliefs and prejudiced thoughts may coexist within the same individual, Devine's (1989) dissociation model of prejudice drew on the distinction between automatic and controlled cognitive processes. My goal was to provide a theoretical analysis of how those who sincerely renounce prejudice may remain vulnerable to unintentional activation of stereotyped thoughts and prejudiced feelings. To do so, I recast Allport's "internal conflict" as reflecting a struggle between automatic and controlled processes. According to the model, whether people are consciously prejudiced or not, they are vulnerable to the automatic activation of the cultural stereotype of African Americans. This type of automatic stereotype activation is a legacy of our common socialization experiences and occurs without people's consent or bidding. The model assumes that adoption of nonprejudiced beliefs or values does not immediately eliminate automatic prejudiced responses. Importantly, the model does not presume that people who adopt egalitarian values hide from or deny automatic biases; instead, the biases are recognized, viewed as unacceptable, and motivate corrective efforts. Provided low-prejudice people have sufficient time and cognitive resources available, they will use controlled processes to censor automatic processes and respond on the basis of their nonprejudiced beliefs.

In developing this analysis, I argued that eliminating prejudice "as a first response" requires overcoming a lifetime of socialization experiences, which, unfortunately, promote automatic prejudice (Devine, 1989). I likened the process of overcoming prejudice to the breaking of a bad habit in that people must make a decision to eliminate the habit and then learn to inhibit the habitual response. Thus, the change from being prejudiced to nonprejudiced is not an all-or-none event, but unfolds as a process during which those who have renounced prejudice remain vulnerable to the conflict engendered between automatic negative responses and consciously endorsed nonprejudiced beliefs – a conflict that has been well-established in recent years (see Blair, 2001, for a review). In the following section, the consequences of this conflict for prejudice reduction are considered.

Prejudice with Compunction Revisited

Although Allport assumed that the essayists who reported inconsistencies between their "reason and their prejudice" experienced compunction, this assumption was first tested directly by Devine, Monteith, Zuwerink, and Elliot (1991). Their empirical strategy was to assess how people who vary in self-reported level of prejudice believe they *should* respond in interpersonal situations involving minority group members, and how they actually *would* respond in these same situations. On average, low-prejudice people believe that they should not feel uncomfortable sitting next to an African American on a bus, but that they likely would. High-prejudice people disagree, indicating that is it acceptable to feel uncomfortable in this situation. Devine et al. also measured people's affective reactions to the match or mismatch between their *should* and *would* responses. The critical items focused on the extent to which people felt guilty, self-critical, and regretful – in short, the compunction Allport believed to be associated with inner conflict.

When actual responses were discrepant from people's personal standards, Devine et al. (1991) found that low-prejudice people experienced compunction but high-prejudice people did not. Moreover, the greater the violation of nonprejudiced standards, the more guilt low-prejudice people reported. For low-prejudice people, then, the conflict between their *should* and *would* reactions threatens their nonprejudiced self-concepts and they hold themselves personally accountable for these failures. In tandem with considerable similar evidence (for a review, see Devine & Monteith, 1993), it appears that many people are embroiled in the arduous process of prejudice reduction. Further, in line with Allport's prescient observations, the adoption and internalization of nonprejudiced standards is clearly only the first step in breaking the prejudice habit. As outlined below, subsequent work has directly addressed the processes involved in breaking the prejudice habit, with a specific focus on control and regulation of automatic processes that give rise to prejudiced responses.

Breaking the Prejudice Habit: "Putting the Brakes on Prejudice"

During the period of conflict in which people struggle with the inconsistencies between their values and their prejudice, Allport presumed that guilt would engender efforts to bring responses and values in line. People would, in effect, "put brakes upon their prejudices" (Allport, 1954/1979, p. 332). Allport was not terribly specific about how this would occur, merely suggesting that people "do not act [their prejudices] out – or act them out only to a certain point. Something stops the logical progression somewhere" (p. 332). Putting the brakes on prejudice requires exerting some type of control. In recent years, two specific lines of research have directly addressed what it means to "put the brakes" on prejudice (Devine & Monteith, 1999). Although these approaches similarly aim to understand specific prejudice reduction mechanisms, the resulting models differ in their attention to the postconscious and preconscious processes involved in establishing control over automatic prejudiced responses.

Postconscious cues for control

Monteith and her colleagues (Monteith, 1993; Monteith, Ashburn-Nardo, Voils, & Czopp, 2002) argued that low-prejudice people learn to overcome their automatic prejudiced tendencies through self-regulatory outcomes that follow from an awareness of the failure to control stereotyping or prejudice. Specifically, this program of research has revealed that awareness of a prejudiced response elicits not only guilt but other outcomes that enable low-prejudice people to exert control over future, potentially prejudiced responses. These other outcomes include heightened self-focus, a momentary disruption of ongoing behavior coupled with *retrospective* reflection on why the failure occurred, and careful attention to the stimuli or cues present when the failure occurred. Learning to associate a prejudice-related failure with guilt and self-regulatory mechanisms establishes *cues for control* (Monteith et al., 2002). When these cues are present in future situations, they lead to an immediate interruption in ongoing behavior and *prospective* reflection, which leads to response slowing and a careful consideration of how to respond with the goal of preventing a prejudiced response. This work is important because it provides a theoretical account of how controlled processes may be recruited to disrupt automatic processes in the presence of cues for control such that prejudiced responses are prevented and replaced with egalitarian responses. Across a number of experiments, Monteith and colleagues have provided compelling evidence that low-prejudice people can effectively learn to "put the brakes on their prejudices" (see also Kawakami et al., 2000).

Preconscious conflict detection

To the extent that cues for control become well learned, low-prejudice people should become highly efficient at eliminating prejudice and should, in effect, break the prejudice habit. However, evidence suggests that there is considerable variability in the effectiveness with which low-prejudice people regulate behavioral expressions of prejudice (e.g., Devine & Monteith, 1999; see also Dovidio, Kawakami & Gartner, 2002). Whereas some low-prejudice people are good at regulating prejudice (i.e., effective at inhibiting prejudice), others are less effective (see, for example, Amodio, Harmon-Jones, & Devine, 2003; Devine et al., 2002). Drawing on insights from the cognitive neuroscience literature, Amodio, Devine, and Harmon-Jones (2004; Amodio, Harmon-Jones, et al., 2004) explored the possibility that examining differences in underlying brain activity can help to clarify the types of processes used to exert control and reveal differences among effective and less effective prejudice regulators in the use of such processes.

Cognitive neuroscience evidence suggests that the process of control involves two mechanisms, each associated with activity in separate neural structures (e.g., Botvinick et al., 1999). The first is a conflict detection system, which monitors ongoing responses and is sensitive to competition between automatic and consciously intended responses. The conflict detection system, which has been associated with activity in the anterior cingulate cortex (ACC), is constantly active, requires few resources, and may operate below the level of awareness. When the ACC detects conflict, it alerts a second, resource-dependent system designed to inhibit unintended responses and replace them with intended responses. This regulatory system has been shown to involve prefrontal cortical activity. Amodio et al. (2004) found that good regulators were more effective at responding without race bias than poor regulators, and that this difference was mediated by the sensitivity of the conflict detection system's response to race-biased tendencies (i.e., responses indicative of differences in ACC activity). That is, good regulators were more sensitive to the fact that their automatically activated stereotypes were at odds with their intended nonstereotypic responses and they were more efficient in recruiting controlled processes online as the response unfolded. Because the ACC operates automatically, these findings suggest that mechanisms of control are set in motion very early in the response stream and do not necessarily require conscious appraisals for the engagement of control. In this case, "putting the brakes on prejudice" involves preconscious mechanisms which both detect the potential for failure and recruit the needed controlled processes to avert biased responses and replace them with intended responses.

To the extent that these pre- and postconscious strategies are effective, over time they may enable people personally motivated to overcome prejudice to fully break the prejudice habit and achieve the type of *true resolution* (integration) of inner conflict envisioned by Allport. As anticipated by Allport, this process is likely to be a long one and certainly requires a major commitment among those for whom responding with prejudice is abhorrent.

Has Allport Been Supported?

In responding to this question, it is worth noting that Allport offered his analysis of inner conflict and speculations concerning strategies for resolving it largely without the benefit of empirical data. This fact makes reexamination of his analysis and speculations an interesting exercise. To facilitate this exercise, note that Allport's chapter addressed the following four general themes, each of which has since been addressed in the contemporary literature: (a) the source of inner conflict, (b) the nature of inner conflict, (c) strategies for conflict reduction, and (d) issues concerning prejudice control. With regard to each of these themes, it is fair to say that Allport was right in large measure. Indeed, one could argue that his ideas and suppositions were nothing short of prescient. In reading Allport's "Inner Conflict" chapter, one can't help but be impressed with Allport's presaging of many of the major themes explored by subsequent generations of scholars.

Allport's insights about both the origins and the nature of inner conflict were right on target. He identified the necessary ingredients for the experience of prejudice with compunction. People who sincerely embrace egalitarian values prescribed by the American Creed hold themselves personally accountable for prejudice within themselves. As described above, Devine and colleagues' work provided direct empirical support for Allport's speculations. Allport also anticipated that the discomforting nature of inner conflict would lead some people to develop strategies to circumvent rather than to fully acknowledge the violation of values. Yet for others, he anticipated that working around the conflict would be an inadequate way to address inner conflict. These individuals, he argued, would need to "put the brakes on their prejudices" and work toward true resolution of the conflict.

It should be noted that the impetus to the study of these issues did not always follow directly from Allport's writings. That is, although Allport's analysis appears to have anticipated many of these themes, without the normative changes that followed in the wake of the 1954 Supreme Court Ruling on school desegregation and Civil Rights legislation of the early 1960s, these themes may not have emerged as central to the study of prejudice and its control. In other words, the issues that directly led to many of the more recent developments grew out of questions concerning the extent to which changes in personal attitudes kept pace with legal and normative changes. Allport could not have fully anticipated these changes and, indeed, this may be what makes his foreshadowing of contemporary themes all the more extraordinary.

Nonetheless, the contemporary literature has a number of strengths not evident in Allport's chapter. For example, the contemporary literature has provided much more detailed theoretical analyses of the disparity between one's reason and one's prejudice and the modern conceptualizations of this conflict have been subjected to empirical tests. Indeed, some of the most exciting developments have come from fleshing out the process issues involved in "breaking the prejudice habit." Because Allport did not speak to automaticity, he did not anticipate these advances.

Future Directions

Though the contemporary literature has borne out many of Allport's insights, the most exciting developments are yet to come. For example, the research programs described above have drawn attention to postconscious and preconscious processes involved in controlling automatic processes that give rise to prejudiced responses even among those who consciously renounce prejudice. Future work will be needed to integrate postconscious control mechanisms (in which people effectively learn from their mistakes to avoid future discrepant responses) and the rapid onset of preconscious mechanisms that function to prevent a prejudice response as it unfolds. Is it the case, for example, that good regulators have established strong cues for control through the postconscious processes outlined by Monteith and colleagues and that, over time, these cues engage the conflict detection processes explored by Amodio and colleagues? A complete model of control will likely require integrating these programs of research, and doing so may ultimately provide insights concerning how to help poor regulators, who have similar nonprejudiced values, to develop sensitive conflict detection and control mechanisms to prevent prejudiced responses.

Another matter ripe for future research concerns an issue Allport largely overlooked. That is, although the bulk of Allport's chapter focused on the personal or internal reasons for renouncing prejudice and deploying mechanisms to address the attendant inner conflict, in a number of instances, Allport also alluded to the effect others' views may have in discouraging expressions of prejudice. Though Allport clearly recognized the power of both *inner* (personal) and *outer* (normative) forces discouraging the expression of prejudice as alternative types of cues for "putting the brakes on prejudice," he did not consider outer forces in any depth. Time, however, has revealed that the presence of others who discourage prejudice may be among the strongest cues for engaging controlled processes to prevent expressions of prejudice (see Crandall & Stangor, ch. 18 this volume).

Recent work has shown the importance of distinguishing between intra- and interpersonal processes when examining prejudice regulation. Plant and Devine (1998), for example, showed that people vary in the extent to which they are motivated to respond without prejudice for internal compared with external reasons. Further, internal motives to respond without prejudice are strongly and negatively correlated with self-report measures of prejudice, whereas external motives are much less correlated with self-reported prejudice (and neither measure correlates strongly with general measures of self-presentation or social evaluation). Interestingly, the internal and external motive measures are largely independent; that is, people can be motivated to respond without prejudice for primarily internal reasons, primarily external reasons, both reasons, or simply be unmotivated.

Plant, Devine, and their colleagues' evolving program of research examines the utility of this individual difference approach for understanding the challenges involved in controlling prejudice (Devine et al., 2002; Devine, Brodish, & Vance, 2005; Plant & Devine, 1998, 2001, 2004). For example, low-prejudice people who are internally motivated experience compunction when they respond with prejudice, whereas people who are externally motivated experience threat – a qualitatively distinct form of affective distress. This distinction suggests the possibility that threat might serve as an effective cue for control for externally motivated people, whereas guilt might serve this function primarily for internally motivated people. Plant and Devine's (1998) work, then, may lead to new insights concerning the cues and the processes involved in controlling prejudice among those who lack the personal motivation to overcome prejudice.

Plant and Devine's (1998) measures have also proved useful in identifying who is most likely to respond with prejudice and, hence, needs to engage controlled processes to overcome its pernicious, if often unintended, effects. In Amodio et al.'s (2004) research on preconscious control processes, Plant and Devine's measures were used to identify who among the low-prejudice were good regulators of prejudice. Specifically, people high in internal but low on external motivation to respond without prejudice are generally effective in responding without prejudice, whereas people high on both motives are much more prone to responding with prejudice (Devine et al., 2002). Key questions remain, however, concerning how or why the presence of external motivation interferes with effective control of prejudice (or why its absence leads to effective control). Related questions concern the developmental antecedents of possessing internal and external motivation to respond without prejudice. Allport assumed that most people embraced the tenets of the American Creed and, hence, were vulnerable to inner conflict. Yet, the contemporary work suggests that there is some variability in the extent to which people internalize these ideals, and little is currently known about the characteristics of those who strongly internalize nonprejudiced standards and those who do so less strongly.

Finally, Allport took for granted that social norms would be influential in cuing the need to "put the brakes on prejudice." And, while these cues can be effective, they are not completely without costs. For example, Plant and Devine (2001) showed that people who are not privately motivated to respond without prejudice but who are sensitive to external mandates proscribing prejudice (i.e., low internal/high external), comply with pressure from others to respond without prejudice but do not do so happily. That is, their compliance is accompanied by feelings of anger and resentment, and sadly, this anger fuels their prejudice and their tendency to show a backlash against the pressure. As the study of prejudice and efforts to reduce it move forward, it is important to recognize that this type of external pressure can produce some counterintentional and counterproductive consequences. Such knowledge may prove useful in addressing perhaps the most enduring and difficult challenge faced by social scientists in the study of prejudice – namely, how to create internal motivation to be nonprejudiced. Without internal motivation, many of the processes explored in the "Inner Conflict" chapter are moot. It seems clear that merely applying pressure from outside encourages resistance to change. Future efforts to combat prejudice will need to strike a delicate balance between outer and inner forces for "putting the brakes on prejudice."

In conclusion, there are several noteworthy features of Allport's "Inner Conflict" chapter. First, in this chapter Allport confronted directly the paradox of racism in a nation founded on the fundamental principle of equality. He explored how ordinary people grapple with the paradox when they discover it within themselves (Myrdal, 1944). After all, to the extent that "all men [sic] are created equal," considering some (e.g., Black Americans) less equal (i.e., three-fifths of a man) shouldn't add up and *should* provide a challenge to one's sense of self as reasoned, fair, and just. Second, Allport's analysis is impressive in that, although he focused primarily on the experience of inner conflict and the compunction that it engenders, he also recognized the importance of social, cultural, religious, and political forces that questioned the morality (and ultimately, legality) of prejudice, which helped to set the stage for experiencing prejudice with compunction. In so doing, Allport recognized that prejudice is at once a personal and social phenomenon and that the two are inextricably intertwined. Finally, the "Inner Conflict" chapter provides a kind of optimism not fully evident in other chapters – an optimism about the potential to reduce prejudice among those who struggle with the moral uneasiness created by conflict between their values and their prejudice. One comes away with the impression the intrapersonal battle to conquer prejudice, though arduous, can be won.

REFERENCES

Allport, G. W. (1954/1979). *The nature of prejudice*. Cambridge, MA: Perseus Books.

Amodio, D., Devine, P. G., & Harmon-Jones, E. (2004). Individual differences in the regulation of race bias among low-prejudice people: The role of conflict detection and neural signals for control. Paper under review.

Amodio, D. M., Harmon-Jones, E., & Devine, P. G. (2003). Individual differences in the activation and control of affective race bias as assessed by startle eyeblink responses and self-report. *Journal of Personality and Social Psychology, 84,* 738–53.

Amodio, D. M., Harmon-Jones, E., Devine, P. G., Curtin, J. J., Hartley, S., & Covert, A. (2004). Neural signals for the control of unintentional race bias. *Psychological Science, 15,* 88–93.

Blair, I. (2001). Implicit stereotypes and prejudice. In G. Moskowitz (ed.), *Cognitive social psychology: On the tenure and future of social cognition* (pp. 359–74). Mahwah, NJ: Erlbaum.

Botvinick, M. M., Nystrom, L. E., Fissel, K., Carter, C. S., & Cohen, J. D. (1999). Conflict monitoring versus selection-for-action in anterior cingulate cortex. *Nature, 402,* 179–81.

Crosby, F., Bromely S., & Saxe, L. (1980). Recent unobtrusive studies of Black and White discrimination and prejudice: A literature review. *Psychological Bulletin, 87,* 546–563.

Devine, P. G. (1989). Prejudice and stereotypes: Their automatic and controlled components. *Journal of Personality and Social Psychology, 56,* 5–18.

Devine, P. G., Brodish, A. B., & Vance, S. L. (2005). Self-regulatory processes in interracial interactions. In J. Forgas, K. Williams, and S. Laham (eds.), *Social motivation: Conscious and unconscious processes* (Sixth Sydney Symposium on Social Psychology) (pp. 249–73). New York: Psychology Press.

Devine P. G. & Monteith, M. J. (1993). The role of discrepancy associated affect in prejudice reduction. In D. M. Mackie & D. L. Hamilton (eds.), *Affect, cognition, and stereotyping: Interactive processes in intergroup perception* (pp. 317–44). New York: Academic Press.

Devine, P. G. & Monteith, M. M. (1999). Automaticity and control in stereotyping. In S. Chaiken & Y. Trope (eds.), *Dual process theories in social psychology* (pp. 339–60). New York: Guilford Press.

Devine, P. G., Monteith, M., Zuwerink, J. R., & Elliot, A. J. (1991). Prejudice with and without compunction. *Journal of Personality and Social Psychology, 60,* 817–30.

Devine, P. G., Plant, E. A., Amodio, D. M., Harmon-Jones, E., & Vance, S. L. (2002). The Regulation of Explicit and Implicit Race Bias: The Role of Motivations to Respond without Prejudice. *Journal of Personality and Social Psychology, 82,* 835–48.

Dovidio, J. F. & Gaertner, S. L. (2004). Aversive racism. In M. Zanna (ed.), *Advances in experimental social psychology*. San Diego, CA: Academic Press.

Dovidio, J. F., Kawakami, K., & Gaertner, S. L. (2002). Implicit and explicit prejudice and interracial interaction. *Journal of Personality and Social Psychology, 82,* 62–68.

Gaertner, S. L. & Dovidio, J. F. (1986). The aversive form of racism. In J. F. Dovidio & S. L. Gaertner (eds.), *Prejudice, discrimination, and racism* (pp. 61–89). San Diego: Academic Press.

Katz, I. & Hass, R. G. (1988). Racial ambivalence and American value conflict: Correlational and priming studies of dual cognitive structures. *Journal of Personality and Social Psychology, 55,* 893–905.

Katz, I., Wakenhut, J., & Hass, R. G. (1986). Racial ambivalence, value duality, and behavior. In J. F. Dovidio & S. L. Gaertner (eds.), *Prejudice, discrimination, and racism* (pp. 35–60). San Diego: Academic Press.

Kawakami, K., Dovidio, J. F., Moll, J., Hermsen, S., & Russin, A. (2000). Just say no (to stereotyping: Effects of training on the negation of stereotypic associations on stereotype activation. *Journal of Personality and Social Psychology, 78,* 871–88.

Monteith, M. J. (1993). Self-regulation of stereotypical responses: Implications for progress in prejudice reduction. *Journal of Personality and Social Psychology, 65,* 469–85.

Monteith, M. J., Ashburn-Nardo L., Voils, C. I., & Czopp, A. M. (2002). Putting the brakes on prejudice:

On the development and operation of cues for control. *Journal of Personality and Social Psychology, 83,* 1029–50.

Monteith, M. J. & Voils, C. I. (1998). Proneness to prejudice responses: Toward understanding the authenticity of self-reported discrepancies. *Journal of Personality and Social Psychology, 75,* 901–16.

Myrdal, G. (1944). *An American dilemma.* New York: Harper & Row.

Plant, E. A. & Devine, P. G. (1998). Internal and external motivation to respond without prejudice. *Journal of Personality and Social Psychology, 75,* 811–32.

Plant, E. A. & Devine, P. G. (2001). Responses to other-imposed pro-Black pressure: Acceptance or backlash? *Journal of Experimental Social Psychology, 37,* 486–501.

Plant, E. A. & Devine, P. G. (2004). Regulatory concerns for interracial interactions: Approaching egalitarianism versus avoiding overt bias. Unpublished MS, University of Wisconsin-Madison.

Rokeach, M. (1973). *The nature of human values.* New York: Free Press.

Rothbart, M. & John, O. P. (1985). Social categorization and behavioral episodes: A cognitive analysis of effects of intergroup contact. *Journal of Social Issues, 41,* 81–104.

Chapter Twenty-One

Inner Conflict in the Political Psychology of Racism

David O. Sears

In this chapter, I will reflect on Allport's chapter 20, "Inner Conflict," focusing, as he did, on racism in the United States. I will present a complementary view to that of Devine's chapter (ch. 20 this volume). The main differences between our chapters are that her emphasis is on experimental social psychology, whereas mine stems from survey research on the general population, and that my primary focus is on the role of racial prejudice in political life. Although our reflections dovetail in many respects, our conclusions about the current state of intrapsychic conflict for White Americans diverge substantially. This discrepancy, of course, only underscores the fact that the nature of prejudice remains complex and intriguing. In this chapter I review important new developments in the nature of racism that have occurred since the publication of *The Nature of Prejudice*, and promising new directions for theory and research.

Allport's View of the Role of "Inner Conflict" in White Americans' Prejudice

Allport's analysis of intrapsychic conflict in *The Nature of Prejudice* owed a great deal to Gunnar Myrdal's (1944) monumental work, *An American Dilemma*. Myrdal's central theme was that most White Americans experience inner conflict over race because their prejudice conflicts with their equally deep-seated democratic and Christian values. The American Creed, in principle, spoke to the equality of all people, and especially to equal opportunity rather than to ascribed status hierarchies. The result, as Allport noted, is that "the United States holds a unique position among the nations of the world in its *official* morality. No other country has such ringing expressions of the creed of equality in its historic papers of State. The laws, the executive orders, and the Supreme Court decisions have not often departed from this creed . . . in the United States, discrimination is *unofficial*, illegal, and, in a profound sense, regarded as un-American" (1954/ 1979, p. 330–1; emphases in original).

Allport recognized that high-minded national and Christian egalitarian precepts often conflict with the realities of life on the ground; that is, with the self-interests, jealousies, and conformity to conventional prejudices that drive discrimination in practice. As a result, the influence of the school may conflict with parental influence, and religious teachings may contradict established social hierarchies. Sometimes bias predominates, but, in Allport's view, prejudice with compunction, in which positive attitudes alternate with negative attitudes, is far more common. This inconsistency is awkward to live with, because, as Allport (1954/1979) noted, even if it is "defeated intellectually, prejudice lingers emotionally" (p. 328). Allport further observed, "The average [White] American, therefore, experiences moral uneasiness and 'a feeling of individual and collective guilt.' He lives in a state of conflict" (p. 330).

We do not always practice what we preach. However, this inner conflict restrains people's behavior, checking their tendencies toward ingroup favoritism and overt discrimination against outgroups when they threaten to go too far and violate social norms or personal standards. Such "situational brakes" are most likely to be applied when face-to-face contact with individual Blacks is involved, and less likely when minority groups are impersonal and abstract. Moreover Allport argued that often the best retort to bigotry is an appeal to the American Creed. To be sure, Allport felt that Myrdal may have overstated the extent of this inner conflict, and its beneficial effects. Most Whites feel little guilt for a system they did not create. Still, he felt that many Americans were in a state of conflict.

How do Americans resolve this conflict? Allport's answer stressed that it can be handled through various defense or conflict-resolution mechanisms (see Esses, Jackson, Dovidio, & Hodson, ch. 14 this volume). These include repression and denial ("I have no prejudice; we have no problem"); defensive rationalization, in which selective perception biases evidence in favor of prejudice while "bifurcation" allows for exceptions; and compromises that allow for the coexistence of charity and prejudice, and for gradualism as a political strategy. Optimally, inner conflict would be resolved through true consistency and integration in personality, wherein genuine enemies are recognized, while racial bogeymen, traditional scapegoats, and designated villains are dispensed with.

Developments Since Allport

Over time, prejudice has adapted to changes in legislation and societal norms that no longer authorize discriminating against people on the basis of their race. This section reviews legal and political developments since the publication of *The Nature of Prejudice*, considers the nature of contemporary types of prejudice, examines the ways in which Allport's inner conflict is currently conceptualized, and addresses the difficulties of measuring prejudice directly.

Society Has Changed

In the first quote given above from Allport's chapter 20, published in the year of the watershed *Brown v. Board* Supreme Court decision, Allport seems oddly naive about America's racial situation, describing discrimination as "unofficial" and even "illegal." The continuing support, both passive and aggressive, for legalized discrimination and segregation by governments at all levels was a harsh reality of his day. To be sure, elsewhere in the book he acknowledges the complicity of legal and political authorities in maintaining the racial caste system, such as in the mob lynchings of Blacks, and in the Supreme Court's extraordinarily narrow interpretations of the fourteenth and fifteenth amendments and in its precedent-setting *Plessy v. Ferguson* decision. However devoted White Americans of his day were to the preamble to the Declaration of Independence, they largely acquiesced to a government-supported racial caste system.

Much changed in the next decade and a half. Developments in post-Allport social psychology must be understood in that context. The civil rights movement increasingly acted directly against that racial caste system. Pivotal court decisions, such as *Brown v. Board of Education*, and sweeping federal legislation, such as the Civil Rights Act of 1964, the Voting Rights Act of 1965, and the Fair Housing Act of 1967, as well as many other lower-profile executive and judicial actions at the federal level and legislative actions at the state and local levels, ultimately eliminated official support for the two-caste system. As profound as these changes were, they did not eliminate all discrimination or *de facto* segregation. But losing the active support of the political and legal systems ultimately forced changes in the nature of prejudice.

New Forms of Sociocultural Prejudice

The intrapsychic conflict described by Allport and Myrdal was represented at the time principally by "old-fashioned racism," or "Jim Crow racism," the racial ideology held by a majority of Whites in the US before the Second World War. It had three main tenets: (a) belief in the biological inferiority of African Americans; (b) support for formal discrimination against Blacks in many domains of life such as schools, public accommodations, and housing; and (c) racial segregation of Blacks in those domains, as well as in private domains such as marriage. After the Second World War, support for that ideology began to wane in the North, and later, after the mid-1960s, gradually in the White South as well. Most of it was gone by the 1990s (Schuman, Steeh, Bobo, & Krysan, 1997).

Although the evidence of the gradual disappearance of old-fashioned racism is rarely disputed, a debate ensued about whether or not racial prejudice was disappearing with it. Many social psychologists concluded that it had not disappeared but had changed its form. Various new forms were proposed, having much in common although variously labeled as "symbolic racism," "racial resentment," "modern racism," "laissez-faire racism," or "subtle prejudice." Their conceptualizations shared three common elements: (a) general replacement of old-fashioned racism with acceptance of formal racial equality, and (b) continuing negative affect toward Blacks (whether animosity, uneasiness, or distancing), mixed in some way with (c) nonracial values, such as traditional morality, individualism, and the Protestant Ethic. The manifest contents of these forms of contemporary racism do not differ a great deal, and they are all assessed with very similar self-report questions. Considerable research showed these "new racisms" predicted opposition to racial policies and to Black political candidates. As a result, they were interpreted as having taken over the political role once played by old-fashioned racism (for reviews, see Hutchings & Valentino, 2004; Krysan, 2000; Sears & Henry, in press).

Traces of Intrapsychic Conflict

Several other research developments in social psychology since 1954 rest more centrally on the conflict between egalitarian values and racial prejudice that Allport described. First, other concepts of a "new racism," though sharing many of the same assumptions, were built more directly on Allport's idea of a conflicted racism. "Aversive racism" (Dovidio & Gaertner, 2004) assumes that most Whites today sincerely hold an egalitarian value system, but that negative racial affect remains common, perhaps more often taking the form of discomfort or uneasiness than of hostility. Whites have trouble acknowledging anti-Black feelings, so aversive racism is often expressed in subtle ways that protect nonprejudiced self-images. For example, people racially discriminate by avoiding minority-group members in distress when failure to help can be explained on the basis of some factor other than race (e.g., the belief that someone else might intervene). In contrast, "ambivalent racism" describes many Whites as having both humanitarian and individualistic beliefs, and priming either can cause people to express either pro-Black or anti-Black opinions in a seemingly inconsistent way (Katz, 1981).

Recent research on implicit social cognition also suggests that Whites may be truly unaware of their biased racial feelings, which may be inconsistent with their sincere, conscious, and publicly expressed beliefs. The distinction in cognitive psychology between largely conscious, voluntary, deliberate "controlled processing" and largely nonconscious, involuntary, "automatic processing" has been extended to *explicit prejudice*, measured with traditional direct questions, and *implicit prejudice*, measured indirectly (e.g., using response latency measures; see chapters by Fiske and by Rudman, chs. 3 and 7 this volume).

This contrast has brought considerable attention to the issue of the measurement of prejudice. Allport, as far as I can tell, was relatively unconcerned about the validity of standard measures of prejudice, although he admitted that prejudice is an "embarrassing" topic for people, and that estimating the prevalence of prejudice requires careful consideration of specific question wording (ch. 5, pp. 74–7). How the universality of the norm of equality produces *social desirability biases* in expressed prejudice has been a prominent concern of social psychology since Allport wrote his classic book. To avoid social censure, racially prejudiced Whites may express falsely tolerant attitudes. Some claim that even the lower levels of prejudice expressed by highly educated Whites merely reflect sophisticated dissembling, not greater tolerance (Jackman & Muha, 1984).

Social desirability biases have been shown to influence survey responses. White respondents generally express more positive racial attitudes to Black interviewers than to White interviewers, as if trying not to offend (Kinder & Sanders, 1996; Schuman et al., 1997). Also, prejudiced Whites may hide behind "no opinion" responses (Berinsky, 2004). Unobtrusive measures typically reveal more evidence of bias than do explicit self-reports (Crosby, Bromley, & Saxe, 1980). Like models of repressed, suppressed, or unconscious prejudice, the social desirability perspective highlights an inconsistency between publicly expressed attitudes and personal prejudices.

When attitudes involve inconsistent components, the external environment has the power to alter the expression of prejudice by heightening the salience of one aspect over the other (Katz, 1981). For example, experiments have shown how racial prejudice can be primed by different kinds of television news or political advertising (e.g., Valentino, Hutchings, & White, 2002). But overtly racist appeals may not be necessary to prime racial prejudice if ostensibly nonracial issues have been racialized, as "welfare" and crime have been (Gilens, 1999; Mendelberg, 2001).

To this point, the inner conflict with principles of equality has been described only as stemming from animosity toward racial outgroups. But Myrdal believed that self-interest also provided a strong foundation for prejudice and the racial caste system in general. Much research has tested the proposition that political support for the racial status quo is motivated by threats posed by Blacks to White privilege, such as feeling threatened by nearby crime-ridden ghettos or fearing that family members may lose opportunities because of affirmative action for Blacks. However, such indices of Whites' self-interests in racial issues generally have only weak political effects, as reflected in weak associations with racially-relevant political preferences or with votes against Black candidates in mixed-race campaigns (Sears & Funk, 1991).

New Framework

Where does this leave us today? In this section, first I will describe how the two elements of Allport's intrapsychic conflict, egalitarianism and prejudice, inform the symbolic racism perspective on contemporary prejudice. Second, I will explore the meaning of the concept of egalitarianism at the individual and intergroup levels, and how it serves as a powerful force against formal racial hierarchy. Third, I ask whether the widespread co-existence of symbolic racism and egalitarianism reflects a new form of inner conflict. And finally I examine the possibility that White identity promotes another new form of inner conflict. References to empirical findings not otherwise attributed are to analyses done specifically for this chapter using the 2000 National Election Studies (NES) survey.

Symbolic Racism

In the years since the concept of symbolic racism was developed, much research has been done refining and testing its claims, as well as responding to critiques (see Sears & Henry, in press, for a detailed review). Symbolic racism was originally inductively derived to describe public opinion, and so not rigorously conceptualized. For this reason, and partly as a result of the popularity of the Reagan era's market-based political conservatism, the idea of symbolic racism came under vigorous attack (e.g., Sniderman & Tetlock, 1986). Overall, however, those critiques of the symbolic racism concept have not been strongly supported once tested empirically (for reviews, see Hutchings & Valentino, 2004; Krysan, 2000; Sears & Henry, in press).

The concept of symbolic racism has evolved over time with accumulated evidence. In recent years, it has been conceptualized and measured in terms of four themes: (a) the denial of discrimination, (b) criticism of Blacks' work ethic, (c) resentment of Blacks' demands, and (d) resentment of unfair advantages given to Blacks by the broader society (Henry & Sears, 2002). Typical items include "If blacks would only try harder, they could be as well off as whites," and "Blacks are getting too demanding for equal rights." These are usually interpreted as sincere beliefs rather than as efforts to cloak underlying prejudice. Empirical evidence confirms that these four themes together form a logically, psychologically, and statistically coherent belief system (Tarman & Sears, in press). Symbolic racism is quite different from old-fashioned racism, which now receives far less support than in the past and whose political effects are now dwarfed by those of symbolic racism (Sears, van Laar, Carrillo, & Kosterman, 1997).

Symbolic racism is rooted in racial affect and individualistic values, which contribute to it both additively and through perceptions of Blacks that merge the two (Sears & Henry, 2003). Although once criticized as merely reflecting political conservatism, symbolic racism empirically relates about equally to it and to traditional prejudice (Sears & Henry, 2003). The effects of symbolic racism on racially relevant dependent variables are not materially reduced by controlling for political conservatism (Sears et al., 1997).

Egalitarianism

Most writers today describe a post-civil-rights era consensus among Whites on support for general principles of racial equality. But things are not quite that simple. It depends on which version of equality is in question. The principle of *equal treatment for individuals* is often measured with items from the NES surveys, such as "Our society should do whatever is necessary to make sure that everyone has an equal opportunity to succeed" or "If people were treated more equally in this country we would have many fewer problems." A strong majority of Whites, but far from all of them, support equality in these terms. On a scale created from such items in the 2000 NES, 67 percent of Whites agreed, on average, and 22 percent disagreed (Sears, Henry, & Kosterman, 2000).

Social dominance theory focuses on attitudes toward equality for groups rather than individuals (Sidanius & Pratto, 1999). Its central construct, "social dominance orientation," is partly constituted by opposition to *equal treatment for groups*, and measured with items (which, if disagreed with, indicate a social dominance orientation) such as "It would be good if groups could be equal" and "We should do what we can to equalize conditions for different groups." In general, support for equal treatment for groups receives far more support than does the notion of equal treatment of individuals, and indeed is almost unanimous, supported by an average of 89 percent of Whites in one survey (Sears et al., 2000). The greater support for group than individual equality is even clearer concerning differences that may affect people's life chances. Most White Americans comfortably accept such differences among individuals. For example, in one national survey, 93 percent agreed that "Some people are better at running things and should be allowed to do so," and 85 percent that "Some people are just better cut out than others for important positions in society" (Sears et al., 2000, p. 93). Unequal life chances are simply accepted as the way of the world. But almost all Whites feel that imposing inequalities among *groups* is unacceptable. When these same questions were reworded to refer to racial groups rather than to individuals, only 14 percent agreed that "some Whites are better at running things than Blacks are and should be allowed to do so" and 8 percent that "some Whites are just better cut out than Blacks for important positions in society." That is, a broad consensus of Whites repudiates privileged access for advantaged groups. That repudiation is not limited to the case of race; similar items yielded almost as much opposition to privileged access for men over women.

Finally, the most distinctive construct in social dominance theory is the belief that subordinate groups should be kept in their proper place, by force if necessary. This *dominance* construct is measured with such items as, "Inferior groups should stay in their place" and "Sometimes other groups must be kept in their place." Dominance and opposition to group equality are not highly correlated, so they should be considered as conceptually separate components of social dominance orientation. The notion of "dominance" is overwhelmingly rejected by White Americans; in one survey, only 15 percent of Whites accepted it (Sears et al., 2000). "Dominance" is peripheral to contemporary partisan and racial politics. It does not correlate strongly with political-party identification, political ideology, or racial policy preferences. It does, however, correlate significantly with old-fashioned racism, which also has little remaining acceptance or political influence in today's society (Sears et al., 2000; Sears & Henry, in press).

In sum, three main points seem clear about the contemporary status of the egalitarian side of Allport's inner conflict. First, a majority of Whites do support general principles of equality for all individuals, but support for formal *group* equality is far broader, and indeed overwhelming. Second, almost all Whites recognize that individual differences in abilities naturally affect life chances, but almost none are willing to endorse privileged access for Whites or for men as groups. Third, dominance of subordinate groups, in terms of "keeping them in their place," is now almost entirely repudiated by White Americans, and plays little role in either conventional partisan or racial politics. Thus, and in contrast to Allport's day, the politics of intergroup relations today begin with the near-universal support for equal treatment of all groups, not explicit support for a racial caste system.

Inner Conflict *Redux*

Myrdal and Allport were primarily concerned about the conflict between the general principle that "all men [*sic*] are created equal" and old-fashioned racism. Today the latter is nearly non-existent, so that source of conflict is rare. Do the "new racisms" produce a more contemporary form of inner conflict with the consensual support for group equality? That was the view taken nearly two decades ago by McConahay (1986), although not tested empirically. On the other hand, it is possible that the new racisms are not widely perceived as conflicting with equal treatment. That is, there may be little conflict between believing in equal opportunity for all groups and believing that Blacks, because of their own lack of effort, are simply not performing at a level that would allow them to take advantage of it. Therefore, there may be little moral uneasiness in symbolic racism.

To be sure, the survey evidence shows that the correlations of egalitarianism with symbolic racism are always negative and substantial, suggesting that they are in conflict. And many Whites today seem to hold beliefs analogous to the "Myrdal ambivalents" of Allport's day. In the 2000 NES, 38 percent of all Whites fell simultaneously above the absolute midpoints of both the symbolic racism and the "equal treatment" scales. But among Whites as a whole, symbolic racism dominates egalitarianism as a determinant of attitudes toward racial policies such as affirmative action and busing (Sears & Henry, in press). Still, people whose egalitarian beliefs conflict with their racial animosity might have different political preferences than those who have consistent attitudes, because of the psychological tension produced by their conflict. But among today's versions of the "Myrdal ambivalents," symbolic racism has a much stronger effect on policy attitudes than do beliefs in equal treatment. In other words, symbolic racism does not seem to be widely perceived as inconsistent with support for equal treatment in the abstract. And it dominates Whites' responses to concrete public policies.

Also contrary to Myrdal's view, intense Christian faith now seems to promote racial prejudice rather than conflict with it. Evangelical Christians are higher in symbolic racism than any other White Americans, and White Southern Christian fundamentalists are the highest in the nation. Southern fundamentalists also show stronger opposition to policies intended to increase racial equality than do either other White Southerners or Northern fundamentalists. This exceptionally high opposition is due to their high levels of symbolic racism (Sears & Valentino, 2002).

A final possible source of inner conflict is not the new racisms, but vestiges of the old racism that remain psychological hot buttons for White Americans because they conflict with the American Creed. Many Whites might accept subtle racist messages because they do not perceive them as inconsistent with the norm of racial equality. But, as Allport suggested, the best retort to bigotry may be an appeal to the Creed. If the underlying racism in subtly racist messages was revealed, they might be repudiated for violating it. The 1988 Republican presidential campaign exploited a horrific crime of sexual violence against a white woman by Willie Horton, a black convict, to attack the Democrats for being "soft on crime." Though ostensibly a message about crime, the message had a strongly racial subtext. When Jesse Jackson pointed this out, some Whites turned against the Republican campaign (Mendelberg, 2001). Egalitarians also successfully appealed to Whites' consensual opposition to old-fashioned racism after David Duke's membership in the KKK was publicized during his statewide campaigns in Louisiana in the 1990s, and in 2000, after Senate Majority Leader Trent Lott's public nostalgia for Strom Thurmond's 1948 segregationist campaign was revealed. Interestingly enough, Duke's and Lott's fellow Republicans seemed the most nervous, as if being associated with old-fashioned racism is the political kiss of death today. However, such appeals to the Creed also have sometimes failed, as with a recent Alabama miscegenation referendum and the Confederate flag controversies in South Carolina, Georgia, and Mississippi.

Whiteness and Ingroup Identity

Today many theories of intergroup relations imply a central role for self-conscious ingroup identity, such as "whiteness," in group members' political preferences (Bobo, 1999; LeVine & Campbell, 1972; Sidanius & Pratto, 1999). For instance, recent work has focused on *White guilt* about Blacks' disadvantages as a subset of the broader category of collective guilt (Branscombe & Doosje, 2005). In contrast, a symbolic-politics theory views ingroup identity as being historically contingent rather than psychologically hard-wired (Sears, 1993). Sometimes group norms emphasize it; in the old South, Whites' racial identity was perhaps their primary social identity. But sometimes not, as in the waning attachment to national origins among today's descendants of nineteenth-century European immigrants. Does White identity resonate politically among ordinary White Americans?

In fact, "whiteness" appears not to be politically significant in America today. In recent research it has been indexed in terms of self-categorization as a White, a sense of White identity (using such items as "How often do you think of yourself as White?" or "How strongly do you identify with other Whites?"), or pro-White affect (using a feeling thermometer). In several NES and Los Angeles surveys, these variables have had small and usually nonsignificant correlations, averaging below $r = 0.05$, with either symbolic racism or racial policy preferences. In contrast, outgroup antagonism, as indexed by symbolic racism, almost invariably correlates with racial policy preferences at 0.40 or higher (Sears & Henry, in press).

In short, Whites' racial politics today are all about antagonism toward Blacks. Neither a self-conscious sense of "whiteness" nor a positive evaluation of Whites has much to do with either symbolic racism or opposition to liberal racial policies. It is unlikely that psychological tensions between the principle of group equality and a self-conscious protection of a privileged White ingroup produce high levels of inner conflict today.

Has Allport Been Supported?

Allport made four essential points in his chapter on inner conflict. The first was that White Americans have a high sense of principled morality about equality. That claim seems even more true now than in his day. Most White Americans now believe that formal group inequality is illegitimate, as is formalized dominance by any high-status group such as Whites or men.

Second, Allport claimed widespread intrapsychic conflict in Americans' attitudes about race. Has this continued to be the case? Not very often, if defined in the old form of subscribing both to equality in general and to a racial caste system. True, over a third of White Americans are modern versions of the "Myrdal ambivalents," endorsing both the principle of equal treatment and symbolic racism. However, this conflict seems not to be troubling to such people, since symbolic racism dominates egalitarianism in determining their preferences about such racial policies as busing and affirmative action. Allport, writing at the height of the Cold War, also felt that moral uneasiness about "an American dilemma" was exacerbated by international pressures from socialist ideologies that privileged equality. Contemporary scholarship sustains that view for his era (e.g., Klinkner & Smith, 1999). But with the demise of the Soviet Union, and the triumph of free-market values over socialism throughout the world, that is no longer so true. Even the Europeans are backing away from the welfare state, and have their own issues of internal ethnic strife and ethnocentrism. Many parts of the Third World exhibit far deadlier ethnocentrism than does America, as in the genocide in Rwanda. There is no longer much international moral pressure on the United States to become more racially egalitarian.

Third, Allport observed that Americans' high official morality was inconsistent with their poor practice. That seems to me to have changed substantially. Compared to the immediate postwar period, White Americans' behavior tends to be formally egalitarian (though discriminatory at the margins; Sidanius & Pratto, 1999). But Allport's insight about people drawing the line and controlling their behavior, using "situational checks," seems still to be on target (see Devine, ch. 20 this volume). So is his view that prejudice expresses itself more powerfully about Blacks as a category than in direct interpersonal contact. Symbolic racism reflects people's attitudes toward abstract and impersonal social objects, rather than behavior toward a specific individual. And an appeal to the American Creed still seems to be the best retort to bigotry, as Mendelberg's (2001) analysis suggests. Ironically, however, such appeals are sometimes used today as a justification for racially conservative political positions. The California campaign against affirmative action in 1996 appealed to Martin Luther King, Jr., and "color-blind" public policies.

Finally, Allport discussed psychological mechanisms of conflict resolution at some length. Although such ideas were common at the time in psychoanalytic theory, he anticipated later developments in cognitive consistency theory (see Devine, ch. 20 this volume). But Allport's emphasis on modes of resolution of intrapsychic conflict is no longer so prominent in social psychology. He did hold out hope for "true integration" of genuine egalitarianism with an absence of prejudice, at least at the intrapsychic level. But what constitutes "true egalitarianism" depends on the eye of the beholder. Many people today believe they are truly nonprejudiced, although social psychologists are often skeptical about their claims.

Future Research

One valuable area for future research concerns the measurement of prejudice. Social desirability biases in measures of racial attitudes have been reasonably well documented. But do they normally occur in sufficient magnitude to threaten the main findings of survey research? Race-of-interviewer comparisons show that Whites express more liberal attitudes to Black than to White interviewers. But relatively few Whites are interviewed by Blacks. For example, in the 1986 NES survey that is often analyzed in studies of racial attitudes, only 4 percent of the White respondents had non-White interviewers. Social desirability pressures could lead some Whites to express no opinion at all rather than expressing their true prejudices (Berinsky, 2004). But in practice relatively few Whites fail to answer questions on prejudice or racism (e.g., in the 1986 NES, an average of only 3 percent of White respondents gave a "no opinion" response to the symbolic racism and old-fashioned racism items). At this point, the existing evidence does not indicate that such biases are powerful enough to render survey measures invalid, though clearly more research is needed.

What about specific measures of prejudice? Measures of traditional prejudice continue to be used in academic surveys, including "feeling thermometers" measuring liking of Blacks and Whites, and trait stereotyping indexes. At first blush they yield the expected results: in the 2000 NES, ingroup favoritism on the feeling thermometers (evaluating Whites more favorably than Blacks) was more common (37 percent) than is the reverse (10 percent), and the same was true on a composite stereotype index (59 percent vs. 8 percent). However, the number who failed to differentiate Whites and Blacks at all was almost as large as the number showing ingroup favoritism. On the thermometer scales, 53 percent of the Whites gave exactly the same response to both groups, as did an average of 50 percent on the stereotype scales. The usefulness of thermometer and stereotype measures is therefore uncertain, both because they are so blatant and because about half of the White respondents fail to differentiate Blacks and Whites on them for unknown (possibly social desirability) reasons.

At present, we know little about self-perceptions of inner conflict, ambivalence, and one's own racism. Most survey researchers infer such dimensions from responses to closed-ended items, and have little faith in people's own professions about such matters. But the researchers' closed-ended items often give little insight into the respondent's own phenomenology.

In the prejudice domain, as in most other aspects of psychology, little is known about the role of religion. In particular the linkage of religious values to egalitarianism, or to prejudice and discrimination, has not received adequate attention, despite the claims made by Myrdal and Allport (cf. Batson & Stocks, ch. 25 this volume). The growing political role of religion across the globe, intermixed as it often is with ethnocentrism and xenophobia, merits greater attention.

Finally, although I have mainly focused on White Americans' prejudice toward African Americans, Allport plainly believed his book was a general psychological account of "the nature of prejudice." It would be useful to know how well the "new racism" concepts travel to such domestic intergroup venues as relations between and among other American minority groups, and to other cultures across the world.

REFERENCES

Allport, G. W. (1954/1979). *The nature of prejudice*. Cambridge, MA: Perseus Books.

Berinsky, A. J. (2004). *Silent voices: Public opinion and political participation in America*. Princeton: Princeton University Press.

Bobo, L. (1999). Prejudice as group position: Micro-foundations of a sociological approach to racism and race relations. *Journal of Social Issues*, *55*, 445–72.

Branscombe, N. R. & Doosje, B. (eds.) (2005). *Collective guilt: International perspectives*. New York: Cambridge University Press.

Crosby, F., Bromley, S., & Saxe, L. (1980). Recent unobtrusive studies of black and white discrimination and prejudice: A literature review. *Psychological Bulletin*, *87*, 546–63.

Dovidio, J. F. & Gaertner, S. L. (2004). Aversive racism. In M. P. Zanna (ed.), *Advances in experimental social psychology*. San Diego, CA: Academic Press.

Gilens, M. (1999). *Why Americans hate welfare*. Chicago, IL: University of Chicago Press.

Henry, P. J. & Sears, D. O. (2002). The symbolic racism 2000 scale. *Political Psychology*, *23*, 253–83.

Hutchings, V. L. & Valentino, N. A. (2004). The centrality of race in American politics. *Annual Review of Political Science*, 7, 383–408.

Jackman, M. R. & Muha, M. J. (1984). Education and intergroup attitudes: Moral enlightenment, superficial democratic commitment, or ideological refinement? *American Sociological Review*, 49, 751–69.

Katz, I. (1981). *Stigma: A social psychological analysis*. Hillsdale, NJ: Lawrence Erlbaum.

Kinder, D. R. & Sanders, L. M. (1996). *Divided by color: Racial politics and democratic ideals*. Chicago: University of Chicago Press.

Klinkner, P. A. & Smith, R. M. (1999). *The unsteady march: The rise and decline of racial equality in America*. Chicago: University of Chicago Press.

Krysan, M. (2000). Prejudice, politics, and public opinion: Understanding the sources of racial policy attitudes. *Annual Review of Sociology*, 26, 135–68.

LeVine, R. A. & Campbell, D. T. (1972). *Ethnocentrism*. New York: Wiley.

McConahay, J. B. (1986). Modern racism, ambivalence, and the modern racism scale. In J. F. Dovidio & S. L. Gaertner (eds.), *Prejudice, discrimination, and racism* (pp. 91–126). New York: Academic Press.

Mendelberg, T. (2001). *The race card: Campaign strategy, implicit messages, and the norm of equality*. Princeton: Princeton University Press.

Myrdal, G. (1944). *An American dilemma*. New York: Harper and Row.

Schuman, H., Steeh, C., Bobo, L., & Krysan, M. (1997). *Racial attitudes in America: Trends and interpretations* (rev. ed.). Cambridge, MA: Harvard University Press.

Sears, D. O. (1993). Symbolic politics: A socio-psychological theory. In S. Iyengar & W. J. McGuire (eds.), *Explorations in political psychology* (pp. 113–49). Durham, NC: Duke University Press.

Sears, D. O. & Funk, C. L. (1991). The role of self-interest in social and political attitudes. In M. Zanna (ed.), *Advances in experimental social psychology* (vol. 24, pp. 1–91). Orlando, FL: Academic Press.

Sears, D. O. & Henry, P. J. (2003). The origins of symbolic racism. *Journal of Personality and Social Psychology*, 85, 259–75.

Sears, D. O. & Henry, P. J. (in press). Over thirty years later: A contemporary look at symbolic racism. In M. P. Zanna (ed.), *Advances in experimental social psychology* (vol. 35).

Sears, D. O., Henry, P. J., & Kosterman, R. (2000). Egalitarian values and contemporary racial politics. In D. O. Sears, J. Sidanius, & L. Bobo (eds.), *Racialized politics: The debate about racism in America*. Chicago: University of Chicago Press.

Sears, D. O. & Valentino, N. A. (2002). Is the proof in the pulpit? Race, religion, and party realignment in the South. Presented at the annual meeting of the American Political Science Association, Boston, MA, Aug. 31.

Sears, D. O., van Laar, C., Carrillo, M., & Kosterman, R. (1997). Is it really racism? The origins of white Americans' opposition to race-targeted policies. *Public Opinion Quarterly*, 61, 16–53.

Sidanius, J. & Pratto, F. (1999). *Social dominance: An intergroup theory of social hierarchy and oppression.* New York: Cambridge University Press.

Sniderman, P. M. & Tetlock, P. E. (1986). Symbolic racism: Problems of motive attribution in political debate. *Journal of Social Issues, 42,* 129–50.

Tarman, C. & Sears, D. O. (in press). The conceptualization and measurement of symbolic racism. *Journal of Politics.*

Valentino, N. A., Hutchings, V. L., & White, I. K. (2002). Cues that matter: How political ads prime racial attitudes during campaigns. *American Political Science Review, 96,* 75–9.

THE DYNAMICS OF PREJUDICE

Chapter Twenty-Two

Aggression, Hatred, and Other Emotions

Eliot R. Smith and Diane M. Mackie

Allport's Views About Emotion

Although Gordon Allport's *The Nature of Prejudice* is probably best known for its prescient emphasis on cognitive factors such as stereotypes, chapter 22, entitled "Aggression and Hatred," presents Allport's analysis of some of the "hotter" factors in prejudice. First, Allport believed that aggression stems from general frustration. He rejected a simplistic quasi-Freudian metaphor of a "steam boiler" in which pressure (frustration) builds up until some outlet (aggression) is necessary. However, Allport was very clear that aggression is often displaced – that is, directed against some target other than the source of the original frustration. "When we meet an individual who is full of complaints, resentment, and has many out-group prejudices, we can safely assume he has much unresolved reactive aggression, undoubtedly built up through a long series of chronic frustrations" (1954/1979, p. 357). Allport discussed in particular middle-class Americans, hypothesizing that they face many frustrations due to cultural pressures, for example, to achieve status and wealth. These frustrations are ready for displacement as aggression against convenient outgroups (see Glick, ch. 15 this volume).

Second, in addition to frustration, Allport identified socialization, particularly for boys, as an additional source of aggression. Despite the initial closeness of a young boy's ties to his mother, he must learn to be a man, which often involves expressing toughness and aggression. These are certainly part of the cultural definition of maleness, and may be specifically taught by the father, worried about the possibility of his son being regarded as a "sissy."

Both general frustration and socialization for aggressiveness thus set the stage for people to experience hostile feelings toward outgroups. What form do those feelings take? Allport distinguished two, anger and hatred. Anger is a transitory emotion that is ordinarily directed toward individuals; thus, a person might be angry at a driver who irresponsibly cuts her off on the highway. Hatred, in contrast, is more longstanding than anger, involving bitter feelings as well as accusatory thoughts that serve to rationalize these feelings. It is held without compunction or guilt because it is viewed as justified. Finally, hatred is more often directed at groups than individuals. Allport, citing Aristotle for this point, argued that people more readily empathize with individuals (even those who are members of a hated group) than with groups (see Sternberg, 2003).

Citing Fromm, Allport further distinguished rational hatred (for those who pose severe, realistic threats to one's life or values) from "character conditioned" hatred arising from a lifetime of disappointments and frustration (see Duckitt, ch. 24 this volume). In the latter case, hatred is not meaningfully connected to the source of the frustration; rather, the individual "thinks up some convenient victim and some good reason. The Jews are conspiring against him, or the politicians are set on making things worse" (1954/1979, p. 364). In other words, hatred of this type is a function of personality abnormalities rather than being rationally targeted at groups that pose realistic threats.

Closing the chapter, Allport asks a deeply philosophical question: since people need and want to love and be loved, why do they so often end up hating? He gives three answers to this riddle. First, because of the many frustrations of life, Allport noted that people seek "an island of security" (1954/1979, p. 365) by psychologically excluding most others, defining them as outgroups. Second, children brought up in rejecting homes, or learning prejudices directly from their parents, will naturally develop negative outlooks on other people or groups.* Finally, Allport held that there is "a kind of economy in adopting an exclusionist approach" (1954/1979, p. 365) to other people. For example, if one thinks of all members of a particular group as inferior and unworthy, there is no need to bother to distinguish among them, or to decide how to act toward any individual group member.

Developments Since Allport

Allport's emphasis on the emotional component of prejudice was shared by several lines of theory and research during the 1950s. In particular, the highly influential Authoritarian Personality approach (Adorno, Frenkel-

Brunswik, Levinson, & Sanford, 1950), based in psychodynamic thinking, also emphasized inner psychic conflicts as the fuel for negative emotional reactions to outgroups, similar to Allport's description of "character conditioned" hatred. With the decline in this perspective's popularity due to conceptual and methodological critiques in the late 1950s (see Duckitt, ch. 24 this volume), other viewpoints came to the fore.

It is a story that is told many times in the chapters in this volume: the cognitive revolution of the 1960s and 1970s in North American psychology (especially social psychology) changed everything. In the area of prejudice and intergroup relations, the most prominent change was an intense focus on the nature of perceivers' beliefs about outgroups (i.e., their stereotypes) and on the consequences of those beliefs for prejudice and discrimination. Research in this tradition has led to great advances in psychology's understanding of how stereotypes and prejudice are acquired, activated, applied, and (sometimes) altered. In many ways, the focus on such processes in this approach reflected Allport's allusion to the resource "economy" of categorization and generalization. Attitude theory proved a natural source of conceptual tools and research methods to investigate these issues, and so "prejudice" came to be defined as an attitude – the perceiver's evaluation, positive or (more often) negative – of a group as a whole or of its members. Although attitude theory is flexible enough to accommodate emotions as determinants of attitudes, research on stereotyping and prejudice clearly shifted away from emotion.

Around the same time (the late 1960s and early 1970s) another approach emerged, originally in Europe. Inspired by Henri Tajfel (Tajfel, Billig, Bundy, & Flament, 1971), Social Identity Theory has spawned its own descendants and variants, including self-categorization theory (Turner et al., 1987). But in all versions, the emphasis is on the effects of social context – specifically, important and salient group memberships – on the ways people think, feel, and act toward themselves and others. Both laboratory studies using temporary groups and real-world investigations of live, interacting social groups generated broad support for Social Identity Theory's predictions (see Brown & Zagefka, ch. 4 this volume). This tradition has produced tremendous insights into the ways that group membership shapes perceptions and actions toward other people. In fact, its key tenets are reminiscent of Allport's ideas about the psychological benefits of seeking "an island of security" distinct from outgroups. However, although Tajfel's original definition of social identity included a reference to the "emotional significance" of group membership, emotions received relatively little emphasis in the research generated by Social Identity Theory.

The change in theoretical focus from the 1950s to these newer perspectives stemmed in part from an implicit shift in the focal phenomenon under study. Both Allport (in his chapter on aggression and hatred) and the Authoritarian Personality researchers focused on the overt bigot – the Nazi, the Ku Klux Klan member – one who hates without compunction while feeling his hatred to be justified. Emotions, culturally viewed since the days of the ancient Greeks as irrational, naturally seemed an important part of explanations for these people's disturbed thinking and despicable behavior. However, through the 1960s the research focus shifted gradually toward less extreme types of prejudice and more seemingly "normal" psychological processes. Learning stereotypes of outgroups from the surrounding culture and desiring esteem for one's ingroups are processes that affect virtually all people, not only a handful of extreme bigots. In fact, one of the chief points of emphasis of both the stereotype-based and social-identity approaches was the normality of the psychological processes underlying prejudice, and the corollary fact that most people (even those who are fundamentally well-intentioned and liberal-minded) are at risk of succumbing to them. Emotions may have fallen out of favor in theories of prejudice in part because of this shift in focus from the extreme bigot to the more "normally" prejudiced person.

Beginning in the late 1980s, though, and continuing with ever greater momentum into the early and middle 1990s, researchers rediscovered the importance of emotions in intergroup relations. One early example is research by Dijker (1987) on the specific emotions (such as irritation and resentment) that people feel in encounters with individual outgroup members. Around the same time, Gaertner and Dovidio (1986) developed "aversive racism" theory, which posits that many Whites avoid interaction with Blacks or other minorities not because they hate them, but simply because interacting with outgroup members arouses negative emotions of unease, anxiety, and uncertainty (see also the concept of intergroup anxiety, Stephan & Stephan, 1985, and ch. 26 this volume). Also in the 1980s, Sears (ch. 21 this volume) developed "symbolic racism" theory, which holds that early-socialized negative affect toward outgroups is an important component of current forms of prejudice. Within a few years, Mackie and Hamilton (1993) edited a volume collecting numerous chapters on the theme of affective-cognitive interactions in stereotyping and prejudice. A new area for investigation had clearly opened up, and new theoretical ideas began to emerge, which considered a broader range of emotions – such as irritation, anxiety, guilt, and even positive emotions– and not only the anger and hatred that Allport had discussed.

A New Framework: Integrating Current Research and Theory on Emotions

The rediscovery of emotions in the field of prejudice and intergroup relations has involved contributions from numerous researchers and groups, operating from several theoretical perspectives. At least three general approaches can be conceptually distinguished. First, some researchers focused on the effects of "incidental" affect – affect arising from outside of the intergroup encounter itself – on stereotyping, prejudice, or related processes (e.g., Bodenhausen, 1993; Mackie, Queller, Stroessner, & Hamilton, 1996). Studies of incidental affect are important in demonstrating how general emotional processes influence thoughts, judgments, and behavior, including those in intergroup situations. However, these studies leave open the question of whether emotion in an intergroup context operates in the same way when it is caused specifically by that context (Bodenhausen, 1993).

A second approach stays at the individual level but investigates the causes and consequences of individuals' emotional reactions, for example, in face-to-face encounters with members of outgroups. A number of approaches have emphasized different emotions that can arise in intergroup encounters. These emotions are assumed to be largely negative, but can include several distinct emotions (beyond just anger and hate). Dijker (1987), for example, found that irritation often resulted from personal encounters with outgroup members (especially those who are culturally different). For example, in one study, Dutch respondents reported feeling irritation especially in encounters with Turks and Moroccans, the minority groups most culturally different from the Dutch themselves. The aversive racism (Gaertner & Dovidio, 1986) and the intergroup anxiety (Stephan & Stephan, 1985) approaches both focus on feelings of unease and anxiety in intergroup interaction. These emotions arise from more or less "innocent" (at least nonracist) causes, such as a lack of knowledge about the outgroup, fear of unintentionally giving offense, and general lack of necessary interactional skills for intergroup interaction. In a related vein, Devine and Monteith (1993) and others have studied the ways in which individual emotions (such as guilt) aroused by one's own stereotypic thoughts might motivate people to work to change their stereotypes. All these approaches have added immeasurably to our understanding of emotions that might be caused by intergroup concerns and actions, and have also contributed to the more general issue of how emotions affect thoughts, judgments, and behavior.

Table 22.1 Summary of current models of emotion in intergroup relations

Theory and key citations	Emotions experienced by	Specific emotions assumed	Key points of emphasis
Emotions in intergroup interaction (Dijker, 1987, others)	An individual (individual-level emotions)	Irritation, resentment	Emotions experienced in personal encounters with outgroup members
Aversive racism (Gaertner & Dovidio, 1986); intergroup anxiety (Stephan & Stephan, 1985)	An individual (individual-level emotions)	Anxiety, unease, discomfort	Emotions experienced because of lack of knowledge or skills in intergroup interaction, not because outgroup is hated
Intergroup Emotions Theory (Smith, 1993; Mackie, Devos, & Smith, 2000)	An individual who identifies with a social group (group-based emotions)	Any and all emotions can be experienced at group as well as individual level	Draws on appraisal theories of emotion to understand conditions under which group-based emotions will be experienced and their consequences for action
Stereotype Content Model (Fiske, Cuddy, Glick, & Xu, 2002)	An individual taking the perspective of the societal mainstream (group-based emotions)	Pride, pity, envy, contempt	Relates emotions to 2 dimensions (warmth, competence) of stereotypes of groups
Biocultural model (Neuberg & Cottrell, 2002)	An individual who identifies with a social group (group-based emotions)	Fear, anger, contempt, disgust, guilt	Evolutionary analysis of why people identify with groups and respond emotionally to group threats
Integrated threat theory (Stephan & Stephan, 2000)	An individual responding either as an individual or as a group member	Fear, anger	Integrates individual and group-level threats; analysis of preconditions for threat perceptions

While dealing with emotions generated as a direct result of intergroup relations, these theories nevertheless continue to treat such emotions as individual-level phenomena. A third approach, and the one on which we focus predominantly in this chapter, borrows the general assumptions of Social Identity Theory and assumes that emotions can be experienced by people on behalf of their ingroups – that is, that the "collective self" defined by a group identification can trigger emotional reactions (Smith, 1993). From this perspective, emotions can be group-level as well as individual-level phenomena. The distinction between the group-based and individual emotion approaches is analogous to the distinction drawn by Runciman (1966) and others between "fraternal" (group-based) and individual or "egoistic" relative deprivation – the sense that one's group in society or oneself as an individual has relatively poorer outcomes compared to other groups or individuals. From this group-based, perspective, emotion can arise because of group belonging, and thus emotions can be group-level as well as individual-level phenomena. All of these approaches are summarized in table 22.1.

Among group-based approaches, Intergroup Emotions Theory (Mackie, Devos, & Smith, 2000; Smith, 1993, 1999) follows the Social Identity Theory approach in taking the notion of a socially extended self as its starting point. When a group membership is salient, people think of themselves as interchangeable members of the ingroup, rather than in terms of their unique personal identities. This "depersonalization" process in turn makes group membership function in all the ways that the psychological self does, as several studies have demonstrated. For example, people tend to think of themselves in terms of attributes that characterize the entire ingroup (Smith & Henry, 1996). That is, the person responds to the world in terms of a collective rather than an individual self. Importantly, this makes the group play a role in the regulation of emotional responses.

To the fundamental postulate of the socially extended self, Intergroup Emotions Theory adds the assumptions of appraisal theories of emotions. Intergroup Emotions Theory posits that when a group membership is salient, people appraise the effects that events, objects, and groups have on the *ingroup* (not just the individual self). Appraisals, which may be conscious or nonconscious, have two significant characteristics. First, they are subjective interpretations of objects or events. Thus, two different people (or one person at different times) may appraise the identical event differently – say, as a dangerous threat versus an energizing challenge – leading to different emotional reactions. Second, appraisals are not perceptions of an object's inherent characteristics, but rather of the object's implications for the perceiver (or the perceiver's group), so that a generally positive object or event may still give rise to negative emotions if it is appraised as impinging negatively on the perceiver. Intergroup Emotions Theory holds that group-based emotions are generated by this appraisal process, in exactly the same way as individual emotions are generated by appraisals of objects or events that impinge on the individual self (Frijda, 1986; Roseman, 1984). For example, if someone who thinks of himself or herself as a group member perceives that the ingroup is threatened by an outgroup's goals or actions and believes that the ingroup is strong, he or she may experience group-based anger (Mackie et al., 2000). Consequently the individual may desire to attack or confront the outgroup. Group-based emotions may be directed at the ingroup as well. For example, people may feel collective pride if they see their group as responsible for an important accomplishment, or collective guilt if they appraise their group as having violated important moral principles (Doosje, Branscombe, Spears, & Manstead, 1998).

In summary, Intergroup Emotions Theory postulates that when people identify with a group, they will appraise social objects or events in terms of their implications for the group. These appraisals generate group-based emotions and, in turn, collective action tendencies. Emotions are predicted to mediate the effects of the appraisals on the action tendencies, demonstrating that the emotions play a functional role in the overall process. We sketch some of the existing evidence supporting Intergroup Emotions Theory here; fuller summaries are available elsewhere (Devos, Silver, Mackie, & Smith, 2002; Mackie, Silver, & Smith, 2004).

Yzerbyt and his colleagues (Yzerbyt, Dumont, Gordijn, & Wigboldus, 2002) showed that when a particular self-categorization is salient, people experience emotional reactions to events that affect other ingroup members – even if the events have no direct effect on the perceiver personally. Participants read about an event that harmed another person with whom they shared one group membership (a fellow psychology student) but differed on another (a student at a rival university). Only when a subtle manipulation made their common group membership with the victim salient did participants experience anger and unhappiness, reactions based on the collective self (group membership) shared with the victim.

Evidence also suggests that identification with, rather than mere cognitive categorization in, the group produces intergroup emotions. Shortly after the September, 2001, attacks on the US, Mackie, Silver, Maitner, and Smith (2002) measured students' identification as "Americans" and asked about their emotions in reaction to a hypothetical future terrorist attack on their country. Group identification with "Americans" strongly predicted both fear and anger responses. As suggested by Intergroup Emotions Theory, increased identification with the group led to more intense emotions experienced on behalf of the group.

Additional studies (Mackie et al., 2000) investigated the nature and impact of intergroup appraisals, as well as the distinctiveness of specific intergroup emotions and their action tendency consequences. Specifically, we examined the appraisal of the ingroup's relative strength or weakness, which is hypothesized to determine whether perceived threats create anger or fear. Participants identified themselves as members of one of two opposing groups. Perception of ingroup or outgroup strength was manipulated by having participants read alleged newspaper headlines, which appeared to reflect popular and political support either for their own group or for the out-group. We then assessed emotions toward the out-group. Analyses of emotion responses revealed three distinct factors representing fear (fearful, anxious, worried, frightened), anger (annoyed, irritated, angry, mad), and contempt (disgusted, contemptuous, repulsed). Perceived ingroup strength increased anger toward the other group, whereas ingroup weakness led to less anger. Moreover, these emotions were associated with distinct action tendencies. Participants who reported feelings of anger were more likely to want to take action against the out-group (e.g., confront or argue with them), while anger had no impact on behavioral tendencies to avoid the out-group. Importantly, the relation between appraisals and action tendency was significantly mediated by experienced emotion.

In summary, several types of evidence currently support the central claims of Intergroup Emotions Theory that intergroup appraisals (appraisals of other groups or intergroup situations as they affect the perceiver's ingroup) can trigger group-based emotions and, in turn, group-based action tendencies. Intergroup Emotions Theory, as well as other current approaches, postulates that a wide range of emotions, and not just anger and hatred, can be experienced with respect to people's group identities and can have consequences for intergroup relations.

Other approaches also consider that emotions can be based in perceivers' group memberships, and directed at other distinct groups in society. Fiske, Cuddy, Glick, and Xu (2002) developed the Stereotype Content Model, which links two dimensions of group stereotypes (warmth and competence) to emotional reactions to groups (see also Fiske, ch. 3 this volume). A group's perceived competence is closely connected to its societal status, and warmth to the degree of competitive relationship between the perceiver's own group and the target group. Warm and competent groups (e.g., middle-class Americans) elicit pride, while groups attributed competence plus a lack of warmth (e.g., Asian Americans, Jews) are targets of envy. Incompetent (low-status, helpless) groups may elicit warm feelings of pity (e.g., the elderly), whereas incompetent groups that are perceived as competing for resources and therefore as cold (e.g., welfare recipients) elicit contempt. Importantly, the Stereotype Content Model posits that some subjectively positive feelings toward disadvantaged groups (e.g., pity and sympathy) may nevertheless reinforce inequality by casting these groups as incompetent (worthy only of pity rather than respect). Jackman (1994; ch. 6 this volume) provides a general analysis of paternalistic aspects of racist, classist, and sexist prejudices and their effects on undermining disadvantaged groups' resistance to social inequality. Glick and Fiske's (1996) ambivalent sexism theory presents an in-depth analysis of one such paternalistic prejudice, benevolent sexism (the notion that women are "wonderful but weak"). Benevolent sexism involves positive feelings toward women, but is nevertheless associated across nations with gender inequality that disadvantages women (Glick et al., 2000).

Although both the Stereotype Content Model and Intergroup Emotions Theory postulate emotional reactions to other groups, there are at least two major distinctions between these perspectives. One is that the Stereotype Content Model conceptualizes emotional reactions to specific groups from the viewpoint of "society as a whole." Indeed, studies testing this approach have typically asked respondents to describe how society in general reacts to various groups such as welfare recipients, rather than how those respondents *themselves* react emotionally (either as individuals or as members of their own particular ingroups, which is the focus of Intergroup Emotions Theory). Second, the Stereotype Content Model focuses specifically on the two dimensions of warmth and competence, and on four specific resulting emotions, while Intergroup Emotions Theory assumes that any and all emotions that can occur to individuals can also occur in intergroup contexts, based on a wide range of possible appraisal dimensions.

Neuberg and Cottrell (2002) developed a biocultural model of intergroup threat and the resulting discrete emotions. They emphasize the group context in which humans evolved, and hypothesize that people are tuned by evolution to respond emotionally to group-level as well as individual-level threats. This model distinguishes different types of threats; for example, directed at the ingroup's resources versus the group's integrity, which may elicit systematically different emotions. Neuberg and Cottrell (2002, see p. 272) hypothesize a wide range of emotions that could be experienced in group contexts, including anger, fear, disgust, sadness, and pity. Their approach is generally consistent with Intergroup Emotions Theory, while also offering a further evolutionary analyses of functionality that explains why people tend to psychologically identify with ingroups as well as to respond emotionally to group-level threats.

Similar ideas are part of Stephan and Stephan's (2000) Integrated Threat Theory. This hypothesizes a number of antecedent factors such as prior intergroup relations, individual differences, and cultural and situational contexts, which result in either symbolic or realistic group threats. These threats in turn predict the psychological (e.g., prejudice) and behavioral (e.g., discrimination) responses of groups and group members. Integrated Threat Theory is both a group-level and an individual-level theory of emotions in that group members can perceive that they as individuals, their group, or both are being threatened. Similarly, responses can be at either the individual or the group level.

Other investigators have looked at specific emotions in group contexts. For example, Doosje et al. (1998) investigated collective guilt, an emotion that people experience when they regard their ingroup as having morally transgressed in an important way. Notably, the research shows that the most highly identified group members may be the least likely to experience this emotion, because they are motivated to find ways to reinterpret events and evaluate the ingroup's actions as morally acceptable. This finding indicates that experiencing emotions as a member of a group is not inevitable for an individual; people may seek to reinterpret or reappraise the situation, or even to disidentify with a group, if the resulting group-based emotion is unwelcome.

Has Allport Been Supported?

We have summarized and briefly reviewed current research on the role of emotion in prejudice and intergroup relations. The work of the past half-century shows that Allport was right on several key points. Hot emotions are part of the picture of intergroup reactions – this is perhaps the key idea of his chapter and, surprisingly, it was neglected until the last decade or so. Notably, recent research (e.g., on aversive racism and on Intergroup Emotions Theory and the Stereotype Content Model) establishes that emotions are important components of even the more "normal," everyday types of stereotyping and prejudice that afflict so many of us, not only for understanding the Nazis or other extreme bigots who were the focus of research attention in the 1950s.

Allport was also right about some of the causes of aggression. Angry feelings and aggression, we now know, can be induced or intensified by negative affect stemming from frustration or discomfort (from pain, high temperature, etc.) that have no connection to the target of the aggression

(Berkowitz, 1998). Whatever their causes, aggression and anger are often rationalized by beliefs adopted after the fact (Alexander, Brewer, & Hermann, 1999). As Allport also held, emotional reactions can have different time courses; recall his distinction of episodic anger from more enduring feelings of hatred. We discuss the time-dependent nature of intergroup emotions in detail elsewhere (Smith & Mackie, in press). Finally, Allport was correct that researchers need to distinguish feelings about individuals from feelings about whole groups. Allport's idea that it is easier to hate groups than individuals anticipated later research by Sears (1983) on the "person positivity bias."

Allport missed some things, however. Perhaps the most important new insight is that many emotions, not only hatred, are involved in intergroup relations. Moreover, these differentiated emotions have distinct causes and effects. Allport's model focused on hatred and considered negative emotions to be largely interchangeable, driven by a single inner "pool" of frustration that seeks an expression, even against a displaced target. However, current thinking on emotion distinguishes anger from fear, disgust, contempt, guilt, and other possibilities, as distinct emotions with different determinants (people's appraisals of intergroup situations) and different effects (action tendencies). The current focus on the antecedents and consequences of differentiated emotional reactions provides predictive power beyond Allport's more narrow focus on hatred. Recent work even demonstrates that prejudice can involve subjectively positive emotions; as noted earlier, research on the Stereotype Content Model shows that women, the elderly, and the handicapped often elicit sympathetic reactions that coexist with stereotypes of these groups' incompetence (Fiske et al., 2002).

Allport also neglected the role of identification with an ingroup, and instead considered emotions as experienced by an isolated individual toward other individuals or groups. In current thinking, people have "selves" at several levels (individual, collective, possibly relational) and any or all of these selves can be activated in specific contexts, arousing emotions. In a comment that may anticipate this idea, Allport noted that hatred never arises without love, meaning love for the values or other objects that are threatened by the hated other (see Brown & Zagefka, ch. 4 this volume). This love may be equivalent to ingroup identification, which attaches value and emotional salience to the ingroup, and is therefore a necessary although not sufficient cause for hate and other negative reactions to the outgroup (Brewer, 2001). In general, however, Allport's analysis was profoundly individualistic.

Future Directions

Considering prejudice and intergroup relations as involving emotion opens up several new research directions. First, emotions are time-dependent states. Self-evidently, they ebb and flow across time, over scales ranging from seconds to perhaps hours or days. This contrasts with stereotypes and prejudice (conceptualized as an attitude), which are notoriously stable and therefore difficult to change even when change is desired. Emphasizing the role of emotion suggests measuring reactions to groups across time, perhaps using daily diary measures or experience-sampling methods (Smith & Mackie, in press). People may be particularly likely to perform emotion-driven behaviors or to show biases in judgment processes precisely when they are experiencing intense group-based emotions.

Second, the line between emotions experienced with regard to the individual and collective selves can be difficult to draw. (Even an interaction between two individuals can be intergroup rather than interpersonal, if the individuals construe themselves and each other as representing their groups.) For this reason, lines of research that focus primarily on individual-level determinants of emotional reactions very likely have implications for group-based emotions as well. As one example, we suggest that feelings of guilt and compunction due to unwanted stereotypic thoughts could be experienced not only as an individual (Devine & Monteith, 1993), but also as a member of a dominant group (e.g., a White American might feel a sense of collective guilt for that group's general tendency to stereotype ethnic minority groups). The latter would be a group-based emotion (Doosje et al., 1998).

Third, much research will be required to work out the relations of intergroup emotions to more traditional concepts such as stereotypes and attitudes. Certainly these can all affect each other on many different time scales. For example, a stereotype that portrays an outgroup as both capable and threatening may well contribute to emotional reactions of fear and hostility toward that group (Fiske et al., 2002). However, as Allport claimed, stereotypes can also emerge as rationalizations, constructed after the fact to justify the emotions that one experiences toward a group. Another possibility is that prejudices are of different types. Reactions to some groups may be more stereotype-driven and others more emotion-driven, depending on the particular circumstances and the nature of the target group.

Fourth, considering the role of emotion in prejudice and intergroup relations opens up a new set of approaches to the goal of prejudice reduction. Traditional approaches emphasized the need to change negative stereotypes to reduce prejudice. However, we now know stereotypes are resistant to change as a result of psychological mechanisms such as subtyping (Johnston & Hewstone, 1992; Rothbart & John, 1985). Changing emotions present a different set of challenges. Drawing from the clinical literature and research on emotional self-regulation, researchers might apply such strategies as reappraisal, misattribution, or desensitization to the emotions involved in intergroup relations. Misattribution (being led to interpret one's emotions and feelings as due to extrinsic causes, such as medication or the music that is playing) has been shown to reduce the effects of those feelings on judgments and behaviors. Desensitization, or systematic and repeated exposure to an object that arouses strong emotions, can diminish those emotions and their effects.

Obviously these strategies may or may not succeed if applied to emotions experienced with respect to social groups and their members, but at least they offer a novel set of approaches to the difficult yet supremely important goal of reducing prejudice. We can obtain some encouragement in this regard from Pettigrew and Tropp's meta-analysis of intergroup contact and prejudice (ch. 16 this volume), which revealed that contact is most effective in prejudice reduction when it has positive affective consequences (e.g., by building friendships). This pattern may indicate that prejudice is more effectively undermined by changing emotions than by changing stereotypes. These and other research directions indicate the potential fruitfulness of the idea that emotions are a key part of prejudice and other intergroup phenomena.

REFERENCES

Adorno, T. W., Frenkel-Brunswik, E., Levinson, D. J., & Sanford, R. N. (1950). *The authoritarian personality*. New York: Harper.

Alexander, M. G., Brewer, M. B., & Hermann, R. K. (1999). Images and affect: A functional analysis of outgroup stereotypes. *Journal of Personality & Social Psychology, 77*, 78–93.

Allport, G. W. (1954/1979). *The nature of prejudice*. Cambridge, MA: Perseus Books.

Berkowitz, L. (1998). Affective aggression: The role of stress, pain, and negative affect. In R. G. Geen &

E. Donnerstein (eds.), *Human aggression: Theories, research, and implications for social policy* (pp. 49–72). San Diego, CA: Academic Press, Inc.

Bodenhausen, G. V. (1993). Emotions, arousal and stereotyping judgments: A heuristic model of affect and stereotyping. In D. M. Mackie & D. L. Hamilton (eds.), *Affect, cognition, and stereotyping: Interactive processes in group perception* (pp. 13–37). San Diego, CA: Academic Press.

Brewer, M. B. (2001). Ingroup identification and intergroup conflict: When does ingroup love become outgroup hate? In R. D. Ashmore & L. Jussim (eds.), *Social identity, intergroup conflict, and conflict reduction* (pp. 17–41). Rutgers Series on Self and Social Identity, vol. 3. New York: Oxford University Press.

Devine, P. G. & Monteith, M. J. (1993). The role of discrepancy-associated affect in prejudice reduction. In D. M. Mackie & D. L. Hamilton (eds.), *Affect, cognition, and stereotyping* (pp. 317–44). San Diego, CA: Academic Press.

Devos, T., Silver, L. A., Mackie, D. M., & Smith, E. R. (2002). Experiencing intergroup emotions. In D. M. Mackie & E. R. Smith (eds.), *From prejudice to intergroup emotions* (pp. 111–34). New York: Psychology Press.

Dijker, A. J. (1987). Emotional reactions to ethnic minorities. *European Journal of Social Psychology, 17,* 305–25.

Doosje, B., Branscombe, N. R., Spears, R., & Manstead, A. S. R. (1998). Guilty by association: When one's group has a negative history. *Journal of Personality and Social Psychology, 75,* 872–86.

Fiske, S. T., Cuddy, A. J. C., Glick, P., & Xu, J. (2002). A model of (often mixed) stereotype content: Competence and warmth respectively follow from perceived status and competition. *Journal of Personality and Social Psychology, 82,* 878–902.

Frijda, N. H. (1986). *The emotions.* Cambridge: Cambridge University Press.

Gaertner, S. L. & Dovidio, J. F. (1986). The aversive form of racism. In J. F. Dovidio & S. L. Gaertner (eds.), *Prejudice, discrimination, and racism* (pp. 61–90). Orlando, FL: Academic Press.

Glick, P. & Fiske, S. T. (1996). The Ambivalent Sexism Inventory: Dif-
ferentiating hostile and benevolent sexism. *Journal of Personality & Social Psychology, 70,* 491–512.

Glick, P., Fiske, S. T., Mladinic, A., Saiz, J. A. D., Masser, B., Adetoun, B., et al. (2000). Beyond prejudice as simple antipathy: Hostile and benevolent sexism across cultures. *Journal of Personality and Social Psychology, 79,* 763–75.

Jackman, M. R. (1994). *The velvet glove: Paternalism and conflict in gender, class, and race relations.* Berkeley, CA: University of California Press.

Johnston, L. & Hewstone, M. (1992). Cognitive models of stereotype change: III. Subtyping and the perceived typicality of disconfirming group members. *Journal of Experimental Social Psychology, 28,* 360–86.

Mackie, D. M., Devos, T., & Smith, E. R. (2000). Intergroup emotions: Explaining offensive action tendencies in an intergroup context. *Journal of Personality and Social Psychology, 79,* 602–16.

Mackie, D. M. & Hamilton, D. L. (1993). *Affect, cognition, and stereotyping: Interactive processes in group perception.* San Diego, CA: Academic Press.

Mackie, D. M., Queller, S., Stroessner, S. J., & Hamilton, D. L. (1996). Making stereotypes better or worse: Multiple roles of positive affect in group impressions. In R. M. Sorrentino & E. T. Higgins (eds.), *Handbook of motivation and cognition* (vol. 3, pp. 371–96). New York: Guilford Press.

Mackie, D. M., Silver, L. A., Maitner, A. T., & Smith, E. R. (2002). *Intergroup emotions in response to and as a predictor of intergroup aggression.* Unpublished MS, Santa Barbara, CA.

Mackie, D. M., Silver, L. A., & Smith, E. R. (2004). Intergroup emotions: Emotion as an intergroup phenomenon. In L. Z. Tiedens & C. W. Leach (eds.), *The social life of emotions*. Cambridge: Cambridge University Press.

Neuberg, S. L. & Cottrell, C. A. (2002). Intergroup emotions: A biocultural approach. In D. M. Mackie & E. R. Smith (eds.), *From prejudice to intergroup emotions* (pp. 265–84). New York: Psychology Press.

Roseman, I. J. (1984). Cognitive determinants of emotion: A structural theory. *Review of Personality and Social Psychology, 5*, 11–36.

Rothbart, M. & John, O. P. (1985). Social categorization and behavioral episodes: A cognitive analysis of the effects of intergroup contact. *Journal of Social Issues, 41*, 81–104.

Runciman, W. G. (1966). *Relative deprivation and social justice*. Berkeley, CA: University of California Press.

Sears, D. O. (1983). The person-positivity bias. *Journal of Personality and Social Psychology, 44*, 233–40.

Smith, E. R. (1993). Social identity and social emotions: Toward new conceptualizations of prejudice. In D. M. Mackie & D. L. Hamilton (eds.), *Affect, cognition, and stereotyping: Interactive processes in group perception* (pp. 297–315). San Diego, CA: Academic Press.

Smith, E. R. (1999). Affective and cognitive implications of group membership becoming part of the self: New models of prejudice and of the self-concept. In D. Abrams & M. Hogg (eds.), *Social identity and social cognition* (pp. 183–96). Oxford: Blackwell.

Smith, E. R. & Henry, S. (1996). An in-group becomes part of the self: Response time evidence. *Personality and Social Psychology Bulletin, 22*, 635–42.

Smith, E. R. & Mackie, D. M. (in press). Intergroup emotions theory: Intergroup emotions as time-dependent phenomena. In D. Capozza & R. Brown (eds.), *Social identities: Motivational, emotional, cultural influences*.

Stephan, W. G. & Stephan, C. W. (1985). Intergroup anxiety. *Journal of Social Issues, 41*, 157–75.

Stephan, W. G. & Stephan, C. W. (2000). An integrated threat theory of prejudice. In S. Oskamp (ed.), *Reducing prejudice and discrimination* (pp. 23–45). Mahwah, NJ: Lawrence Erlbaum.

Sternberg, R. J. (2003). A duplex theory of hate: Development and application to terrorism, massacres, and genocide. *Review of General Psychology, 7*, 299–328.

Tajfel, H., Billig, M. G., Bundy, R. P., & Flament, C. (1971). Social categorization and intergroup behavior. *European Journal of Social Psychology, 1*, 149–78.

Turner, J. C., Hogg, M. A., Oakes, P. J., Reicher, S. D., & Wetherell, M. S. (1987). *Rediscovering the social group: a self-categorization theory*. Oxford: Blackwell.

Yzerbyt, V. Y., Dumont, M., Gordijn, E., & Wigboldus, D. (2002). Intergroup emotions and self-categorization: The impact of perspective-taking on reactions to victims of harmful behavior. In D. M. Mackie & E. R. Smith (eds.), *From Prejudice to Intergroup Emotions* (pp. 67–88). New York: Psychology Press.

Chapter Twenty-Three

Allport's "Living Inkblots": The Role of Defensive Projection in Stereotyping and Prejudice

Leonard S. Newman and Tracy L. Caldwell

Not long after Nazi Germany's ill-fated assault on the Soviet Union in 1941, the climactic exterminatory phase of Hitler's campaign against the Jews was launched. Over the next few years, Poland, the locus of the bulk of the killings, became a graveyard for Jews (who made up approximately 10 percent of the country's pre-war population). A significant portion of the violence towards Poland's Jewish inhabitants, however, did not come at the hands of Germans or even from people doing the Nazis' bidding; instead, it was spontaneously generated by Poles themselves. (Although it should also be noted that almost half of the "righteous gentiles" recognized by Israel for helping Jews during the Holocaust were also Poles.)

One explanation offered for the murderous hostility some Poles felt toward the country's Jewish population is that it was in revenge for the Jews' alleged collaboration with the earlier and extremely brutal Soviet occupation of 1939–41. Historian Jan Gross (2001), however, found no evidence to support the claim that a disproportionate number of Jews cooperated with the Soviets. Instead, he found ample evidence for a different wartime collaboration. He concluded that in eastern Poland, "it is manifest that the local non-Jewish population enthusiastically greeted entering Wehrmacht units in 1941 and broadly engaged in collaboration with the Germans." Gross goes on to say that "it appears that the local non-Jewish population projected its own attitude toward the Germans in 1941 . . . onto an entrenched narrative about how the Jews allegedly behaved vis-à-vis the Soviets in 1939." This, he suggests, is "a fascinating subject for a social psychologist" (Gross, 2001, p. 104).

This story would certainly have been of interest to Gordon Allport. Although in recent years social psychologists have typically framed their discussions and analyses of intergroup hostility in terms of anti-Black prejudice, Allport's classic book *The Nature of Prejudice* was written in the shadow of the Second World War. As a result, his discussion of stereotyping, prejudice, and discrimination was more likely to take anti-Semitism as its point of departure. In addition, he wrote at a time when psychoanalytic ideas had a very different status in mainstream social psychology than they do today. Allport took psychodynamic theorizing and its implications for understanding prejudice very seriously, and was especially intrigued with projection.

Jan Gross was right: projection should be a "fascinating subject" for social psychologists. Allport would undoubtedly have agreed. Unfortunately, projection and other defensive processes have not played particularly prominent roles in the last half-century of research on stereotyping and prejudice (Hamilton, Stroessner, & Driscoll, 1994; Monteith, Zuwerink, & Devine, 1994). Indeed, for many years, psychodynamic concepts were taboo for experimental psychologists, and some still see them as being incompatible with contemporary cognitive approaches to understanding social behavior. In this chapter, we review Allport's treatment of projection, and critically analyze some of his distinctions between different forms of projection. Then we will briefly discuss how and why projection went out of fashion among social psychologists. Recent years have seen a modest revival of interest in the topic; we will discuss some of the recent research on defensive projection and the development of negative stereotypes and suggest an important direction for future research. Finally, we will suggest that Allport anticipated the rekindling of interest in defensive and unconscious processes that has taken place over the last decade or so.

Allport's Views on the Psychodynamic Approach

The Nature of Prejudice does not offer – nor does it pretend to offer – a grand theory of prejudice. Allport repeatedly made the point that prejudice is a multidetermined phenomenon that can be analyzed at many different levels (e.g., historical, cultural, situational, and individual). Furthermore, he made clear, at any one of those levels, no one variable or process can totally account for the existence or intensity of prejudice.

Thus, the psychodynamic approach was just one of many complementary ways of thinking about the topic. As defined by Allport (1954/1979), psychodynamic theories of prejudice emphasized internal motivational variables, especially those involving "unconscious mental operation in the individual" (p. 352). Psychodynamic theories, he said, could explain how a person might not be "aware of the psychological function that prejudice serves in his life," so that when he explained his reasons for feeling hostility towards outgroups, those explanations would be "merely rationalizations" (p. 352). In short, psychodynamic theories emphasize that prejudice can be a byproduct of people's attempts to feel good about themselves, and more generally, to avoid threatening thoughts. A core assumption is that sometimes what one hates about other groups of people is related to the things that one hates about oneself.

Given the status of psychodynamic ideas (and psychoanalytic theory in general) in contemporary social psychology, one might assume that Allport included the approach in his review merely to be comprehensive, or for "balance." Nothing could be further from the truth. Although he expressed reservations about the "exuberance of the theorizing," Allport also urged social psychologists not to forget their "indebtedness to Freud and to psychoanalysis" (1954/1979, pp. 352, 353). Indeed, in an earlier study of people's reactions to catastrophic social change (specifically, the Nazis' consolidation of power in Germany), Allport, Bruner, and Jandorf (1941) liberally invoked defense mechanisms such as suppression, rationalization, isolation, and displacement to account for their research subjects' thoughts, feelings, and behaviors.

The prominent place of psychodynamic ideas in *The Nature of Prejudice* should not be surprising, though, given the context in which it was written. Psychoanalytic accounts of behavior were quite popular among social psychologists at the time, even though they are almost invisible today. A comparison of the 1954 and 1998 editions of the *Handbook of Social Psychology* vividly illustrates this point. The earlier edition (Lindzey, 1954) – published during the same year as Allport's book – includes the chapter "Psychoanalytical Theory and its Applications in the Social Sciences" (Hall & Lindzey, 1954). Even excluding that chapter, references to Sigmund Freud appear on 70 of the other 1,137 pages (excluding the index), or every 16 pages or so. The more recent handbook (Gilbert, Fiske, & Lindzey, 1998) does not include a chapter on psychoanalytic theory, and overall, references to Freud appear on only 17 of the book's 1,853 pages, or every 109 pages.

Psychodynamic thinking played an important role in Allport's treatment of a number of topics, including the selection of scapegoats (Glick, ch. 15 this volume) and individual differences in prejudice (Duckitt, ch. 24 this volume). The most extensively discussed psychodynamic process, however – and one that has been central to most psychodynamic analyses of stereotyping and prejudice – was *projection*.

Allport on Projection

Sometimes the nasty characteristics people attribute to outgroups are more revealing about the nature of the prejudiced perceivers than they are about the targets of their prejudice. As Allport (1954/1979) stated, "One may imagine qualities in a group and hate the group for them because one is in conflict over the same qualities in oneself" (p. 200). And in the case of both anti-Semitism and anti-Black prejudice, "accusations and feelings of revulsion against both groups symbolize our dissatisfaction with the evil in our own nature" (p. 199). Allport provided some vivid illustrations of these ideas. In one, a gentile businessman uses shady tactics to force a Jewish competitor out of business, but feels justified – because after all, who is more unethical then the Jews? Another example, in the tradition of classic psychodynamic theorizing, focused on sexual motivation. A White man violates what to him is a taboo: he has had sex with a Black woman. Whatever agitation might be caused by that indiscretion, however, is overshadowed by his rage at "the lecherous Negro male" who "would deflower white womanhood" (p. 376).

Why, then, did projection not prove to be a "fascinating subject" for social psychologists in the years following publication *The Nature of Prejudice*? As we discuss below, the marginalization of the topic had much to do with the status of psychodynamic theorizing in the field more generally. However, it also is necessary to point out some problematic aspects of Allport's treatment of projection. Some of his distinctions and definitions have either not withstood the test of time or were too fuzzy to begin with. For example, Allport insisted on differentiating between "direct projection" and "mote-beam projection." Direct projection was said to occur when the trait attributed to another person or group is actually "not at all" (1954/1979, p. 387) characteristic of the target. Mote-beam projection, on the other hand, was said to involve an exaggeration of traits that the target of projection does in fact possess to some extent. Although Allport argued that "it is worthwhile to observe the distinction" (p. 390), it is not clear why. First of all, personality psychologists would be hard-pressed to come up with criteria that could be used to determine whether a trait existed "not at all" versus "just a little bit" in some person or group. In addition, it strikes us as more feasible to view the two "types" as simply falling on a continuum defined by the applicability of the trait to the target in question. While the distinction might be meaningful for the predicament of the target (undoubtedly, it would seem like more of an injustice – and more bewildering – to be labeled with a trait that has next to nothing to do with what motivates one's behavior), the underlying projective process is likely to be the same.

Allport's discussion of another form of projection, "complementary projection," also muddied the waters. He defined complementary projection as incorrectly attributing the cause of one's internal state to another person's behavior. Allport illustrated this idea with a study in which children described their impressions of photographs of unfamiliar men. They did so both before and after they played a scary game in a darkened house. When the photos were rated after the activity, the men were seen as being more sinister. But as Allport himself pointed out (1954/1979, p. 350), complementary projection differs in an important way from what he called direct projection. Only the latter process is directly fueled by self-concept threats. In the case of direct or "classical" projection, one's thoughts, feelings, and behaviors suggest that one might have certain undesirable characteristics (lustfulness, cruelty, stupidity, etc.), and one seeks to avoid awareness of that possibility. Complementary projection, on the other hand, emerges from the desire to understand the cause of an internal state, a state that has typically been activated by some external stressor. It seems more similar to what social psychologists later came to refer to as misattribution of arousal (Dutton & Aron, 1974).

Developments Since Allport: Problems With Projection

Allport was not alone in the difficulty he had defining projection and distinguishing it from other related phenomena. Sigmund Freud himself was famously fuzzy on the topic. Anna Freud (1936) elaborated on projection in *The Ego and the Mechanisms of Defence*, but that definitive work also failed to provide a detailed or thorough explanation of projection. For the 50th anniversary of that volume, an extensive series of discussions on defense mechanisms involving Anna Freud and other psychoanalysts was published. When the conversation turned to projection, however, the participants concluded that there was no consensus on how to explain or even define the phenomenon (see Sandler & Freud, 1985, pp. 136–46).

Following the publication of Allport's book, the most extensive discussions of projection in the psychology literature (outside of psychoanalytical journals) could be found in a series of papers by Holmes (1968, 1978, 1981). Among other things, Holmes preserved Allport's distinction between complementary projection and direct projection (called "similarity projection" by him), and he also attempted to clearly define the latter. Unfortunately, the result was that direct projection was essentially defined out of existence. Holmes's first criterion was trait possession; in other words, direct projection could only be labeled as such if the projector actually possessed the trait being attributed to someone else. It was not enough for a person to simply *fear* possessing the trait. Unfortunately, the usefulness of this criterion is dependent on there being a definitive method for deciding that a person "has" a trait, and as has already been noted, that is not the case. Holmes's other criterion was that direct projection had to take place without awareness. Projection, though, may result from a number of interrelated psychological processes, and a person's level of awareness of each one might not be identical (Newman, 2001b). Holmes concluded that there was no empirical evidence for defensive projection, but given the definition he promoted, it is easy to see why no studies met his criteria. For example, it was not even clear what the "awareness" criterion referred to: Awareness of having the trait? Awareness of attributing it to someone else? Awareness of the connection between one's own self-concept and the impressions one forms of others?

In sum, although Allport made a strong case for projection as a process that should be of interest to students of prejudice, his more specific definitions and distinctions did not necessarily provide a solid foundation for later research. Others had no more luck taming the concept. In the end, all such attempts suffered from the same limitation: a lack of a clear description of the cognitive and motivational processes underlying projection. Without a more process-oriented approach, and without specification of the mental mechanisms involved, efforts to clarify the nature of projection were doomed to failure.

A New Framework:
A Contemporary Approach to Projection

Although there were sporadic attempts to empirically investigate projection in the 1950s and 1960s, Holmes's critiques more or less closed the book on this kind of research. Even though the study of the cognitive and motivational processes underlying the impressions people form of other individuals and groups came to occupy center stage in social psychology (see Gilbert, 1998; Newman, 2001a), projection was still seen as a questionable psychoanalytic idea for which there was not – and perhaps never could be – empirical evidence.

More recently, though, projection has been reconceptualized in social-cognitive terms, and perhaps not coincidentally, is enjoying a revival of interest. Newman, Duff, and Baumeister (1997) formulated and tested a model of defensive projection in which the tendency to overperceive one's own undesired traits in others is a byproduct of another defense: thought suppression. When individuals confront evidence indicating they may not be the type of people they want to be, they might attempt to suppress thoughts of that evidence. But research by Wegner and colleagues (e.g., Wegner, 1992) indicates that actively trying to keep a thought out of awareness can backfire; suppression of a thought can ironically increase the accessibility of that thought. The frequency with which unwanted thoughts are activated causes them to become chronically accessible (Higgins, 1989) and to therefore dominate people's perceptions of others, resulting in projection. Individuals with repressive coping styles, by virtue of their tendency to avoid thinking about threats to their self-esteem by suppressing such thoughts, are even more prone to projection. It should be noted that an undesired trait does not even have to be "possessed" in any way by the person projecting it; it is enough to simply fear the trait and/or be motivated not to be characterized by it.

The Newman et al. (1997) model's validity was demonstrated in a series of six studies. Repressors, who (Study 1) spend as little time as possible thinking about their own threatening traits and (Study 2 and Study 6) insist that they do not possess those traits (in spite of contrary evidence), are more likely than nonrepressors to interpret ambiguous behaviors of others in terms of those very traits (i.e., were more likely to project; Studies 3 and 4). This occurred despite the fact that repressors were actually somewhat charitable in their attributions concerning traits that were *not* threatening. Importantly, thought suppression seemed to underlie this effect; instructing participants to suppress thoughts of unfavorable traits that they were said to have (suggested to them by means of false feedback) had the effect of essentially turning all of them into repressors, causing them to project more (Study 5). Participants seemed to be unaware of the extent to which they were projecting; indeed, when their attention was called to their own unwanted traits, they seemed to bend over backwards not to let those traits color their perceptions of others (Study 4). In sum, the Newman et al. model can explain why responding to the fear that one might be (for example) selfish or dull-witted by suppressing those disturbing thoughts can result in concluding that *other* people have those nasty characteristics.

Converging evidence for the model has been reported. Mikulincer and Horesh (1999) found that individuals with avoidant attachment styles (who tend to deny or repress their need for close relationships) also project unwanted traits more than other people, probably because of their tendency to suppress unwanted thoughts. Smart and Wegner (1999) demonstrated that participants who attempted to conceal stigmas were more likely to project their stigmas onto other people than those who did not attempt to conceal them. Women with eating disorders were interviewed, and some of them were asked to play the role of a person without an eating disorder. Participants in this condition were subsequently more likely than others to suspect that the *interviewer* had an eating disorder. In other words, having to hide or suppress aspects of themselves caused eating disordered participants to project those traits. Finally, to investigate whether projection can actually serve to distance individuals from threatening traits, Schimel, Greenberg, and Martens (2003) examined the consequences of projection for the accessibility of the projected traits. They found that individuals who had been told they had "repressed hostility" (an undesirable trait) showed decreased accessibility of this trait if given the opportunity to project it onto others. Specifically, when completing a series of word fragments, they were less likely to think of anger-related words. In addition, they rated themselves as less hostile than participants who had not been given an opportunity to project.

The Role of Projection in Stereotyping and Prejudice: A First Study

Caldwell, Newman, Griffin, and Chamberlin (2001) recently attempted to extend this research to shed light on the development of stereotypes. Groups of three or four individuals were told (based on questionnaire responses) that they had the same personality type, "Epsilon." They were then provided with five trait ratings said to be the typical Epsilon personality profile. Of the five trait ratings, two fillers were always mildly positive (conscientiousness and extroversion). But within each group, feedback on the remaining three traits – agreeableness, emotional stability, and intellectance (intelligence and sophistication) – varied: one rating was always clearly positive, whereas two were always clearly negative. Participants were later asked to think about and discuss how well they felt those five trait ratings characterized their group. However, they were instructed to suppress comments and even thoughts about one of the two negative trait ratings. Following this discussion, they were asked to rate an outgroup ("Gammas") on the same five traits after being exposed to an ambiguous set of behaviors said to be performed by members of that group. As expected, participants rated the outgroup most harshly on the trait they were instructed to suppress, even more harshly than on the trait related to the unfavorable rating that they were allowed to discuss. Importantly, this finding was strongest for those groups who most scrupulously complied with the instructions not to dwell on the trait (assessed by coding the contents of their conversations), providing strong support for a motivational account of stereotype development. In other words, trying to suppress negative thoughts about their group indirectly caused these individuals to overperceive that very trait in other groups.

Projection as a Group-Level Phenomenon

Stereotypes about outgroups are not simply formed in the minds of individual people; the construction of a specific stereotype involves interpersonal, not just intrapsychic, processes (Schaller & Conway, 1999). Allport (1954/1979) himself stated that "Prejudice is a social fact, and seems to require a social context" (p. 344). Most thinking on the topic of defensive projection, however (including the Newman et al. model), has focused exclusively on the individual. For example, according to classic psychodynamic approaches, prejudice in a given society arises when many different people individually have experiences (e.g., punitive parenting; Adorno, Frenkel-Brunswik, Levinson, & Sanford, 1950) that motivate derogation of other groups. Not surprisingly, these theories could more easily account for generalized prejudices than the specific consensual stereotypes associated with those prejudices (Ashmore & Del Boca, 1981). To be more concrete: It is one thing to imagine that a number of individuals who were subjected to harsh parenting might respond by repressing hostile thoughts and feelings that are difficult to bottle up, but it is another to explain how this will result in collective agreement that Jews are dishonest and stingy, Blacks are hostile and lazy, and gay people are weak and immoral. Allport noted that "When all the anxious Georges in a community put their fears together and agree on an imagined cause (the Negro, the Jew, the communist), a great deal of fear-produced hostility may result" (pp. 369–70). But how do all of those Georges reach those agreements?

Any analysis of projection's role in stereotyping and prejudice must eventually account for group consensus in stereotyping. Prejudice, after all, is to a great extent a function of stereotypes that are constructed, maintained, and enhanced in a group context. Caldwell et al. (2001) began to empirically investigate how projection might produce social consensus (see also Glick, ch. 15 this volume). We offer a brief sketch of the processes that may be involved.

As already discussed in detail, the tendency to project unwanted traits onto others is triggered by efforts to suppress thoughts about those traits. To a great extent, the precise traits involved are idiosyncratic, but certain undesired traits appear with great frequency in any group of people (Newman, Caldwell, & Griffin, 2000). More generally, it is reasonable to assume that through a complex interaction of historical, ecological, and psychological variables (Cohen, 2001), members of a particular culture will both value and despise certain social and psychological characteristics more than others. Thus, particular traits will be especially likely to be candidates for projection. A related observation was made by Allport (1954/1979), who noted that people always "paint the villain in the same way – as opposite to the cultural ideal" (p. 387).

And onto whom will these undesired traits be projected? As discussed at length by Fiske, Glick, and their colleagues (Fiske, Cuddy, Glick, & Xu, 2002; Glick, ch. 15 this volume), not all groups are equally susceptible to being slandered with a given unfavorable trait. The key variables determining stereotypes of particular groups are the relative statuses of the groups and the extent to which their relationships are cooperative or competitive. For example, some minority groups are economically, politically, and/or academically successful, but are perceived by the majority or dominant group as competitors for resources (e.g., Asians and Jews). Such groups – seen as competent yet hostile – are said to be the targets of *envious prejudice*. They will be feared and mistrusted, and viewed as dishonest, sinister, and selfish. Other minority groups might not be perceived as threatening, but also not be seen as competent. Those groups, the targets of *paternalistic prejudice*, are more likely to be stereotyped as being warm and childlike (e.g., traditional women). Finally, *contemptuous prejudice* is reserved for minority groups perceived to be lower in status than the majority but also a drain on resources. They will be both hated *and* disrespected, and possibly stereotyped as savages (e.g., African Americans). Overall, the main point is that as a result of the relationships between groups in a given society, certain groups will be magnets for the projection of specific stereotypical traits and not others.

Thus, it would actually not be surprising to find that at any given time or place, many members of a particular society had, as a result of defensive processes, independently formed the same initial hypotheses about the general characteristics of other specific groups. It would also be reasonable to assume that people will communicate with each other about their prejudiced beliefs. For example, according to shared reality theory, people are motivated to achieve "interpersonally achieved perceptions of common experience" (Hardin & Conley, 2001, p. 9). Establishing shared realities –

i.e., consensual attitudes and beliefs – serves at least two important purposes. The first is the fulfillment of epistemic needs; quite simply, beliefs are perceived to be more valid when endorsed by other people. In addition, a shared reality satisfies relational needs (sharing beliefs makes people feel connected to each other).

Hence, people will be motivated to exchange information with other ingroup members about outgroups. And in such interactions, what observations and beliefs are likely to emerge? Group discussions tend to be dominated by shared information – i.e., knowledge available to many members of a group – rather than by unshared information, or the idiosyncratic bits of knowledge possessed by individual people (Larson, Foster-Fishman, & Keys, 1994). Thus, if many individuals have projected specific traits onto an outgroup, those common perceptions are likely to be exchanged and discussed. As a result, stereotypes initially constructed at the level of the individual could be further developed and elaborated at the group level. Furthermore, research by Lambert et al. (2003) shows that when people think about groups in the presence (or even imagined presence) of others, the likelihood that stereotypes associated with those groups will come to mind and be expressed significantly increases.

Finally, specific unfavorable impressions of an outgroup might not only be a common topic of discussion with other ingroup members; they could become even *more* extreme after the discussion. As succinctly summarized by Isenberg (1986), "on decisions in which group members have, on the average, a moderate proclivity in a given direction, group discussion results in a more extreme average proclivity in the same direction" (p. 1141), a process known as *group polarization*. Indeed, Myers and Bishop (1970) found that White participants' attitudes towards Blacks polarized after discussion when they had talked about their attitudes with likeminded people (i.e., with people who were either low or high in prejudice).

Other processes might also be involved, and if projection is to be taken seriously as a source of intergroup tension and conflict, the role of those processes in transforming the biased perceptions of individuals into widely shared prejudices must be explored as well.

Has Allport Been Supported? Past, Current, and Future Directions in Research

Allport took projection quite seriously, but saw it as just one of many processes underlying intergroup bias. He would probably have been open to critiques of his treatment of the topic. However, he would have been less patient with doubts about the more general role of defensive and unconscious processes (of which projection was just one) in stereotyping and prejudice.

As already noted, in the years after the publication of *The Nature of Prejudice*, the popularity of the psychodynamic approach to stereotyping and prejudice declined. Previously, it had enjoyed at least some prominence among social psychologists. One example is research on the authoritarian personality (Adorno et al., 1950), in which prejudice was theorized to be characteristic of a particular kind of person (authoritarians) whose weak egos were in constant need of protection. Unfortunately, this research was criticized for methodological and psychometric flaws, including susceptibility to response sets and experimenter expectancies, and a reliance on a small unrepresentative sample for norming (see Duckitt, ch. 24 this volume).

After 1954, the sociocultural and cognitive approaches to stereotyping and prejudice became more prominent. Researchers in the sociocultural tradition conceptualized stereotypes as attitudes and values that are culturally transmitted and maintained. The focus was on how individuals acquire stereotypic beliefs from the same sources that influence the development of other attitudes and values: parents, teachers, peers, and other community and cultural institutions. (Indeed, the modern approach to authoritarianism as a personality-driven explanation for prejudice is couched firmly within social learning theory, not Freudian principles; see Altemeyer, 1988.) Researchers in the cognitive tradition (see Fiske, ch. 3 this volume) concentrated instead on the cognitive processes that underlie stereotype formation. They conceptualized stereotypes, both negative and positive, as social categories individuals develop as a byproduct of their need to simplify the vast amount of social information they encounter daily. Within this tradition, the mind was seen as a computer-like information processor; interest was directed toward how events in the outside world were consciously represented and processed by it. The unconscious, a concept integral to the psychodynamic approach, was no longer seen as relevant to understanding human cognition. Likewise, affect and motivation were generally ignored in favor of studying the cognitive processes that account for stereotyping and prejudice.

More recently, though, social psychologists are again embracing the ideas that (1) stereotypes can be shaped be people's desires to feel good about themselves and their groups (Yzerbyt & Cornielle, ch. 11 this volume), and (2) people are not always aware of the sources and manifestations of their prejudice (Fiske, ch. 3 this volume; Rudman, ch. 7 this volume). An example of the former is research on the motivated application of stereotypes, which tests whether defending the self affects perceptions of others. For instance, Fein and Spencer (1997) found that people who did not have the opportunity to affirm some positive aspect of their self-concepts following self-image threat were more likely than others to derogate and dislike members of stigmatized groups, which, in turn, boosted their self-esteem (see also Kunda & Sinclair, 1999). Other research indicative of a revival of interest in "hotter" aspects of stereotyping is that on the effects of mood and emotion on stereotyping and prejudice (Bodenhausen, Mussweiler, Gabriel, & Moreno, 2001; Smith & Mackie, ch. 22 this volume) and the motivation to suppress stereotype use (Devine, ch. 20 this volume).

Research on the unconscious aspects of attitudes and beliefs about different groups of people has become even more prominent (Devine, 2001; Greenwald et al., 2002; Solomon, Greenberg, & Pyszczynski, 2000), and promises to be a major area of investigation for years to come. It is now widely accepted that prejudice and stereotypes can be implicit rather than explicit, operating without perceivers' intent or awareness. Allport would not have been surprised by this conclusion, but undoubtedly would have been intrigued with the new methodological tools that have allowed researchers to reliably assess unconscious cognitive processes (e.g., Greenwald, McGhee, & Schwartz, 1998).

Conclusion

Allport (after Ackerman & Jahoda, 1950) proposed that groups of people can become "living inkblots" (1954/1979, p. 385) onto whom others can project their own fears, frustrations, and perceived inadequacies. A compelling idea, it nonetheless did not play a major role in the subsequent history of research on stereotyping, prejudice, and discrimination. In recent years, interest in the psychodynamic approach, broadly defined, has made a comeback, as has interest in defensive projection in particular. Full appreciation of the role of projection in stereotyping, however, will require multilevel, multivariate, and multimethod research strategies. In other words, it will require an approach to studying prejudice modeled for us by Gordon Allport.

REFERENCES

Ackerman, N. W. & Jahoda, M. (1950). *Anti-Semitism and emotional disorder.* New York: Harper.

Adorno, T. W., Frenkel-Brunswik, E., Levinson, D. J., & Sanford, R. (1950). *The authoritarian personality.* New York: Harper.

Allport, G. W. (1954/1979). *The nature of prejudice.* Cambridge, MA: Perseus Books.

Allport, G. W., Bruner, J. S., & Jandorf, E. M. (1941). Personality under social catastrophe: ninety life-histories of the Nazi revolution. *Character and Personality, 10,* 1–22.

Altemeyer, B. (1988). *Enemies of freedom: Understanding right-wing authoritarianism.* San Francisco: Jossey-Bass.

Ashmore, R. D. & Del Boca, F. K. (1981). Conceptual approaches to stereotypes and stereotyping. In D. L. Hamilton (ed.), *Cognitive processes in stereotyping and intergroup behavior* (pp. 1–35). Hillsdale, NJ: Lawrence Erlbaum.

Bodenhausen, G. V., Mussweiler, T., Gabriel, S., & Moreno, K. N. (2001). Affective influences on stereotyping and intergroup relations. In J. P. Forgas (ed.), *Handbook of affect and social cognition* (pp. 319–43). Mahwah, NJ: Lawrence Erlbaum.

Caldwell, T., Newman, L. S., Griffin, T. D., & Chamberlin, B. W. (2001). Thought suppression, projection, and the development of stereotypes. Paper presented at the annual meeting of the American Psychological Society, Toronto, Canada, June.

Cohen, D. (2001). Cultural variation: Considerations and implications. *Psychological Bulletin, 127,* 451–71.

Devine, P. G. (2001). Implicit prejudice and stereotyping: How automatic are they? Introduction to the special section *Journal of Personality and Social Psychology, 81,* 757–9.

Dutton, D. G. & Aron, A. P. (1974). Some evidence for heightened sexual attraction under conditions of high anxiety. *Journal of Personality and Social Psychology, 30,* 510–17.

Fein, S. & Spencer, S. J. (1997). Prejudice as self-image maintenance: Affirming the self through derogating others. *Journal of Personality and Social Psychology, 73,* 31–44.

Fiske, S. T., Cuddy, A. J. C., Glick, P., & Xu, J. (2002). A model of (often mixed) stereotype content: Competence and warmth respectively follow from perceived status and competition. *Journal of Personality and Social Psychology, 82,* 878–902.

Freud, A. (1936). *The ego and the mechanisms of defence.* London: Hogarth Press.

Gilbert, D. T. (1998). Ordinary personology. In D. T. Gilbert, S. T. Fiske, & G. Lindzey (eds.), *The Handbook of Social Psychology* (4th ed., vol. 2, pp. 89–150). New York: McGraw Hill.

Gilbert, D. T., Fiske, S. T., & Lindzey, G. (eds.) (1998). *The handbook of social psychology.* New York: McGraw Hill.

Greenwald, A. G., Banaji, M. R., Rudman, L. A., Farnham, S. D., Nosek, B. A., & Mellott, D. S. (2002). A unified theory of implicit attitudes, stereotypes, self-esteem, and self-concept. *Psychological Review, 109,* 3–25.

Greenwald, A. G., McGhee, D. E., & Schwartz, J. L. K. (1998). Measuring individual differences in implicit cognition. *Journal of Personality and Social Psychology, 74*, 1464–80.

Gross, J. T. (2001). *Neighbors: The destruction of the Jewish community in Jedwabne, Poland.* New York: Penguin Books.

Hall, C. S. & Lindzey, G. (1954). Psychoanalytical theory and its applications in the social sciences. In G. Lindzey (ed.), *The handbook of social psychology* (vol. 1, pp. 143–80). Cambridge, MA: Addison-Wesley.

Hamilton, D. L., Stroessner, S. J., & Driscoll, D. M. (1994). Social cognition and the study of stereotyping. In P. G. Devine, D. L. Hamilton, & T. M. Ostrom (eds.), *Social cognition: Impact on social psychology* (pp. 291–321). San Diego, CA: Academic Press.

Hardin, C. D. & Conley, T. D. (2001). A relational approach to cognition: Shared experience and relationship affirmation in social cognition. In G. B. Moskowitz (ed.), *Cognitive social psychology: The Princeton symposium on the legacy and future of social cognition* (pp. 3–17). Mahwah, NJ: Lawrence Erlbaum.

Higgins, E. T. (1989). Knowledge accessibility and activation: Subjectivity and suffering from unconscious sources. In J. S. Uleman and J. A. Bargh (eds.), *Unintended thought* (pp. 75–123). New York: Guilford.

Holmes, D. S. (1968). Dimensions of projection. *Psychological Bulletin, 69*, 248–68.

Holmes, D. S. (1978). Projection as a defense mechanism. *Psychological Bulletin, 85*, 677–88.

Holmes, D. S. (1981). Existence of classical projection and the stress-reducing function of attributive projection: A reply to Sherwood. *Psychological Bulletin, 90*, 460–6.

Isenberg, D. J. (1986). Group polarization: A critical review and meta-analysis. *Journal of Personality and Social Psychology, 50*, 1141–51.

Kunda, Z. & Sinclair, L. (1999). Motivated reasoning with stereotypes: Activation, application, and inhibition. *Psychological Inquiry, 10*, 12–22.

Lambert, A. J., Payne, B. K., Jacoby, L. L., Shaffer, L. M., Chasteen, A. L., & Kahn, S. R. (2003). Stereotypes as dominant responses: On the "social facilitation" of prejudice in anticipated public contexts. *Journal of Personality and Social Psychology, 84*, 277–95.

Larson, J. R. Jr., Foster-Fishman, P. G., & Keys, C. B. (1994). Discussion of shared and unshared information in decision-making groups. *Journal of Personality and Social Psychology, 67*, 446–61.

Lindzey, G. (ed.) (1954). *The handbook of social psychology.* Cambridge, MA: Addison-Wesley.

Mikulincer, M. & Horesh, N. (1999). Adult attachment style and the perception of others: The role of projective mechanisms. *Journal of Personality and Social Psychology, 76*, 1022–34.

Monteith, M. J., Zuwerink, J. R., & Devine, P. G. (1994). Prejudice and prejudice reduction: Classic challenges, contemporary approaches. In P. G. Devine, D. L. Hamilton, & T. M. Ostrom (eds.), *Social cognition: Impact on social psychology* (pp. 323–46). San Diego, CA: Academic Press.

Myers, D. G. & Bishop, G. D. (1970). Discussion effects on racial attitudes. *Science, 169*, 778–89.

Newman, L. S. (2001a). A cornerstone for the science of interpersonal behavior? Person perception and person memory, past, present, and future. In G. B. Moskowitz (ed.), *Cognitive social psychology: The Princeton symposium on the legacy and future of social cognition* (pp. 191–207). Mahwah, NJ: Lawrence Erlbaum.

Newman, L. S. (2001b). Coping and defense: No clear distinction. *American Psychologist, 56,* 760–1.

Newman, L. S., Caldwell, T. L., & Griffin, T. D. (2000). The psychological significance of the undesired self: Repressive coping as an illustrative example. Paper presented at the annual meeting of the American Psychological Society, Miami, FL, June.

Newman, L. S., Duff, K. J., & Baumeister, R. F. (1997). A new look at defensive projection: Thought suppression, accessibility, and biased person perception. *Journal of Personality and Social Psychology, 72,* 980–1001.

Sandler, J. & Freud, A. (1985). *The analysis of defense: The ego and the mechanisms of defense revisited.* New York: International Universities Press.

Schaller, M. & Conway, L. G. III (1999). Influence of impression-management goals on the emerging contents of group stereotypes: Support for a social-evolutionary process. *Personality and Social Psychology Bulletin, 25,* 819–33.

Schimel, J., Greenberg, J., & Martens, A. (2003). Evidence that projection of a feared trait can serve a defensive function. *Personality and Social Psychology Bulletin, 29,* 969–79.

Smart, L. & Wegner, D. M. (1999). Covering up what can't be seen: Concealable stigma and mental control. *Journal of Personality and Social Psychology, 77,* 474–86.

Solomon, S., Greenberg, J., & Pyszczynski, T. (2000). Pride and prejudice: Fear of death and social behavior. *Current Directions in Psychological Science, 9,* 200–4.

Wegner, D. M. (1992). You can't always think what you want: Problems in the suppression of unwanted thoughts. In M. Zanna (ed.), *Advances in experimental social psychology* (vol. 25, pp. 193–225). San Diego, CA: Academic Press.

PART VII

CHARACTER STRUCTURE

Chapter Twenty-Four

Personality and Prejudice
John Duckitt

Allport regarded the character structure or personality of individuals as a fundamental determinant of prejudice, devoting three chapters of his book to this topic: "The Prejudiced Personality," "Demagogy" (concerning the ideology and rhetoric to which this personality was particularly responsive), and "The Tolerant Personality." The empirical basis for his belief that personality powerfully influenced prejudice was, however, discussed in an earlier chapter dealing with the patterning and extent of prejudice. Here Allport described research reported in the great classic by Adorno, Frenkel-Brunswick, Levinson, and Sanford (1950), *The Authoritarian Personality*, published shortly before Allport's book, which showed that individuals' attitudes to completely different outgroups and minorities were strongly correlated.

Allport therefore concluded: "One of the facts of which we are most certain is that people who reject one out-group will tend to reject other out-groups. If a person is anti-Jewish, he is likely to be anti–Catholic, anti–Negro, anti any out-group" (1954/1979, p. 68). He also went on to assert that this "generality of prejudice" constituted a strong argument for saying that "prejudice is basically a *trait of personality*" (1954/1979, p. 73; italics in the original).

Allport's Views: The Prejudiced and the Tolerant Personality

Allport proposed two polar opposites: a personality chronically disposed to generalized prejudice versus one disposed to generalized tolerance. The prejudiced personality, which like Adorno et al. (1950) he also referred to as the "authoritarian personality," was someone for whom prejudice was psychologically functional and a direct response to deep-rooted underlying needs in the personality. At the core of this prejudiced personality were a set of traits Allport summed up as "ego weakness" – insecurity, fearfulness, anxiety and an inability to cope effectively with one's own inner tensions, conflicts, and anxieties, or with uncertainty, threat, change, and ambiguity in the external world.

Allport suggested that these intrapersonal dynamics of insecurity, anxiety, and threat would produce seven surface traits characteristic of the authoritarian personality: (1) *Emotional ambivalence*, particularly toward one's parents, with uncritical positivity on the surface contrasting with repressed underlying resentment; (2) *Moralism and rigid conventionality*, with punitiveness toward anything deviant or unconventional; (3) *Dichotomization*, a tendency to categorize the world into rigid, simplistic dichotomies of good–bad, right–wrong, us–them; (4) *Needs for definiteness, structure, order,* and an intolerance of ambiguity; (5) *Externalization*, a preference to explain behavior in terms of concrete external forces rather than subjective, inner, psychological processes; (6) *Institutionalization*, a tendency to seek order and security in organized and institutionalized groups with clear roles, norms, and rules, such as the "nation"; (7) *Authoritarianism*, a need for strong authority and leaders that would impose order, discipline, and cohesion in society and the nation.

While the core of the authoritarian personality was threat, insecurity, and ego weakness, the core of the tolerant personality was the exact opposite: a sense of inner security, freedom from threat, ego maturity, and therefore the inner confidence and strength to cope adequately with threat. In contrast to the typically harsh, punitive early life experience of the authoritarian, the tolerant person was the product of a permissive home characterized by security and unconditional acceptance from parents, leading to an empathic and accepting orientation toward others, a liberal ideological outlook, tolerance of ambiguity, psychological sophistication, and the capacity to think in shades of gray rather than simplistic, rigid categories.

Thus, it was ego strength versus weakness, or a sense of inner security as opposed to insecurity and threat, that comprised the dispositional basis for acceptance of others and tolerance of uncertainty and diversity. This also formed the basis for profoundly different philosophies of life or social worldviews. Allport proposed that the prejudiced or authoritarian person typically saw the social world as a threatening place in which people were evil and dangerous. On the other hand, the tolerant personality had a trusting and affiliative view of the world, with a generally positive and optimistic view of others.

But would the ego weakness, insecurity, fearfulness, and inadequacy of the authoritarian personality automatically translate into prejudice? Here Allport suggested that certain activating conditions might be important, and the one that he singled out in particular was exposure to racist, ethnocentric, and fascist demagogy.

The Role of Demagogy

Allport suggested that demagogues, and their racist, ethnocentric, nationalist, and fascist rhetoric, would arouse and direct the insecurity and fears of authoritarian personalities towards particular targets, and into particular channels. Demagogues would arise and be particularly successful in social conditions characterized by insecurity, change, innovation, diversity, unconventionality, and instability. "Authoritarian personalities," Allport argued, "cannot face all this indefiniteness, unconventionality, and loss of familiar anchorage" (1954/1979, p. 413). In these conditions the rhetoric of the demagogue would activate the authoritarians' yearnings for stability, security, cohesion, and order, and direct it towards the "familiar anchorage" of ethnocentric nationalism and traditionalism. Their dissatisfaction, frustration, and fearfulness would be channeled into blame and hate directed at minorities, immigrants, outgroups, liberals, intellectuals, and radicals. Thus, "demagogy invites the externalization of hatred and anxiety: it is an institutionalized aid to projection . . . By declaring that every social issue is the result of out-group misconduct, the demagogue consistently avoids focusing his followers' attention on their own painful inner conflicts" (1954/ 1979, p. 419).

In discussing the personality of the demagogue, Allport hinted at a second kind of prejudiced personality. While he viewed demagogues as typically also having authoritarian personalities, he attributed certain other characteristics to them that set them apart from their more conventional "authoritarian" followers. They were motivated by power, wealth, and success, and were cynical, manipulative, and charismatic enough to use others to try to achieve these goals

Allport and Adorno's Authoritarian Personalities Compared

Allport's concept of the authoritarian personality was very similar to that of Adorno et al. (1950). While Adorno et al.'s book was published first, both *The Authoritarian Personality* and Allport's *The Nature of Prejudice* were monumental works likely to have been many years in preparation. It seems probable therefore that Allport's ideas were not just derived from those of Adorno et al., but evolved simultaneously. Both accounts were also heavily based on ideas already expressed by earlier theorists, such as Fromm, Reich, and Maslow, that shared the same kind of personality-based explanation of why individuals might have a generalized disposition to prejudice, and described an authoritarian personality characterized by basic insecurity and ego weakness.

However, Allport and Adorno et al.'s accounts differed in several important respects. Adorno et al. placed greater emphasis on punitive early socialization, inner conflict, and defense. For Adorno et al. it was the young child's repression of anger towards punitive parental authority, identification with this authority, and consequent displacement of this hostility outward that accounted for the authoritarian's generalized prejudice. Adorno et al. also listed a set of surface traits of their authoritarian personality, many of them similar to Allport's, even if labeled differently. The main difference was that Allport's authoritarian traits included two that described restricted, limited cognitive styles – dichotomization (tendency to categorize the world into rigid, simplistic dichotomies) and a need for definiteness, structure, and intolerance of ambiguity – that did not have direct parallels in Adorno et al.'s list.

There are four interesting differences in Allport and Adorno et al.'s views of the authoritarian personality, all of which are relevant to subsequent research and theoretical developments on personality and prejudice. (1) For Allport, the fearfulness, inadequacy, and anxiety of the authoritarian was at the core of his or her prejudice, while for Adorno et al. it was displaced hostility and aggression. (2) Allport suggested that social environmental factors, such as demagogy and the social context, interacting with personality, created prejudice and aggression by activating and directing the fearfulness, anxiety, and inadequacy of the authoritarian, whereas social factors were largely ignored by Adorno et al. (3) Allport hypothesized that a particular worldview, specifically that people are basically bad and that the social world is a dangerous and threatening place, is an important component of the authoritarian syndrome, while Adorno et al. did not. (4) Allport's authoritarian surface traits emphasized a rigid, simplistic, and restricted cognitive style, which was a direct expression of the authoritarian's fearfulness, anxiety and inadequacy, while Adorno et al. did not (perhaps because they saw repressed hostility and aggression rather than fearfulness and anxiety as the core of the syndrome).

Developments Since Allport

Criticisms of the Authoritarian Personality and the F Scale

Adorno et al.'s great contribution was their famous F scale to measure the authoritarian personality and their extensive research showing that it correlated powerfully with anti-Semitism, generalized prejudice against minorities, chauvinistic nationalism, politico-economic conservatism, and right-wing extremism. Despite enormous initial interest, however, interest in this perspective and the F scale largely collapsed by the late 1960s. First, the psychodynamic processes (repressed and displaced aggression) on which the theory was built received little empirical support. Second, and perhaps most critically, the F scale was shown to be a psychometrically weak measure. When acquiescence due to the uniformly positive formulation of its items was controlled the F scale was neither adequately reliable nor unidimensional (Altemeyer, 1981).

Another weakness of the F scale attracted much less attention at the time. Its items did not pertain to behavior as personality measures typically do, but to social attitudes and ideological beliefs. Adorno et al. (1950) seem to have assumed that these reflected an underlying personality dimension, but this was never empirically demonstrated.

Rokeach's Dogmatism and Cognitive Style

Soon after its publication, Shills (1954) and others pointed out that Adorno et al.'s theory accounted only for authoritarianism of the right. This criticism had particular cogency at the time, because with fascism defeated, authoritarianism of the left (e.g., communism) seemed to pose the greater threat to democracy. Yet communists scored low on the F scale, indicating that it failed to capture authoritarianism of the left.

In response to this criticism, Rokeach (1954) conceptualized dogmatism as a cognitive style characterized by "a relatively closed cognitive organization of beliefs and disbeliefs about reality" that "provides a framework for patterns of intolerance towards others" (p. 195), and developed the D scale to measure it. Persons high on dogmatism would be highly susceptible to authoritarian ideologies of either right or left, and likely to reject persons who held beliefs different from their own. Like Allport, but not Adorno et al., Rokeach viewed cognitive style as a core trait of the "prejudiced personality." However, for Rokeach this cognitive style was the fundamental characteristic of this personality, and the direct cause of generalized prejudice, whereas for Allport cognitive style was merely a surface trait, and the authoritarian's prejudice was rooted more deeply in the personality.

However, like the F scale, the D scale was seriously criticized for its failure to control for acquiescence, poor internal consistency reliability, unstable and unclear multidimensional factor structure, and poor correlations with validity criteria (Altemeyer, 1981). In addition, the D scale was so highly correlated with the F scale as to suggest that it measured the same construct. As a result of these criticisms, research on the D scale largely collapsed during the 1960s, and the concept of dogmatism seemed relegated to obscurity.

Rokeach's research, however, stimulated the development of new measures of cognitive style, such as integrative complexity, intolerance of ambiguity, cognitive flexibility, need for structure, uncertainty tolerance, and need for cognitive closure, and new research on their relationships with prejudice, authoritarianism, and conservatism. This research found that restricted, limited, rigid cognitive styles were consistently associated with conservatism and authoritarianism (Jost, Glaser, Kruglanski, & Sulloway, 2003), but only relatively weakly associated with prejudice (Altemyer, 1998; Duckitt, 1992, pp. 188–90; McFarland, 1998). Moreover, with cognitive style controlled, authoritarianism still predicted prejudice significantly, while controlling authoritarianism eliminated the effects of cognitive style on prejudice (Altemeyer, 1998; McFarland & Adelson, 1996; McFarland, 1998). These findings suggest that rigid, limited cognitive styles are integral aspects of authoritarianism, but are not themselves responsible for the relationship of authoritarianism to prejudice. Interestingly, this is entirely consistent with Allport's original conceptualization that fearfulness and insecurity was responsible for authoritarians' prejudice as well as their rigid, limited cognitive styles.

Altemeyer's Revival of the Authoritarian Personality

After two decades of obscurity, Altemeyer (1981) revived the theory of the authoritarian. His research suggested that only three of the original nine facets of authoritarianism (conventionalism, authoritarian aggression, and authoritarian submission) described by Adorno et al. (1950) covaried strongly to form a unitary dimension, and he developed the Right-Wing Authoritarianism (RWA) scale to measure this dimension. Subsequent research by Altemeyer (1981, 1998) and others (cf. Duckitt, 1992) showed that the RWA scale is a unidimensional and reliable psychometric measure of authoritarianism that powerfully predicts a wide range of political, social, ideological, and intergroup phenomena, including generalized prejudice toward outgroups and minorities and chauvinistic ethnocentrism.

Altemeyer (1981, 1998) found that his own and others' research disconfirmed Adorno et al.'s psychoanalytic theory of the childhood origins of authoritarianism. He found no associations between authoritarianism and harsh, punitive parental socialization; rather, he suggested that authoritarianism results from social learning (i.e., from having been socialized to see the social world as a dangerous and threatening place). This finding has been well replicated (Duckitt, 2001; McFarland, 1998; McFarland & Adelson, 1996) and is consistent with earlier research that found significant associations between authoritarianism and perceived social threat (e.g., Feldman & Stenner, 1997; Sales, 1973).

These findings support Allport's original view that fearfulness, insecurity, and a threat orientation are core characteristics of authoritarianism, rather than Adorno's psychoanalytically based hypotheses about repressed and displaced aggression. However, Altemeyer's social-learning perspective also suggests that the insecurity, fear, and anxiety of the authoritarian might not reflect personal maladjustment and inadequacy, as Allport had hypothesized, but rather a learned set of beliefs about others and society.

Authoritarianism and Psychological Adjustment

Are authoritarians dispositionally anxious and maladjusted as Allport suggested? While some studies have reported significant but weak correlations between authoritarianism and maladjustment, most studies, especially those that tapped large general population samples, did not find significant associations (Duckitt, 1992, pp. 200–3). More recently, Jost et al. (2003) reviewed studies investigating the association between measures of conservatism, such as authoritarianism, and a variety of indices relating to needs to manage uncertainty and threat. Their meta-analysis did not separate dispositional indices of anxiety and maladjustment from indices of perceived social threat and dangers, or authoritarianism from conceptually different indices of conservatism such as social dominance. However, computing the associations separately shows that indicators of social threat, such as belief in a dangerous world, correlated powerfully with authoritarianism (e.g., averaged correlation with belief in a dangerous world was 0.48), while indicators of dispositional maladjustment, such low self-esteem or neuroticism, had weak and often nonsignificant correlations with authoritarianism (averaged correlations were 0.04). In addition, studies using large student and adult samples by McFarland (1998; McFarland & Adelson, 1996), which were not included in the Jost et al. (2003) review, also found no significant correlation between the RWA scale and low self-esteem or neuroticism (the weighted mean correlation for 1,311 participants was −0.03).

Overall, subsequent research supports Allport's view that threat, fear, and insecurity seem to be at the core of authoritarianism, but contradicts his view that this fearfulness and threat orientation stem from a "weak ego" or dispositional maladjustment and insecurity. Instead, the findings seem consistent with Altemeyer's proposal that the insecurity, fear, and threat orientation of authoritarian persons are socially learned and specific to their perceptions of others and the social world.

Social Dominance Orientation: A Second Prejudiced Personality?

During the 1990s an important new individual-difference construct, social dominance orientation (SDO), and measure, the SDO scale, were proposed to explain generalized prejudice (Pratto, Sidanius, Stallworth, & Malle, 1994). The SDO scale taps a "general attitudinal orientation toward intergroup relations, reflecting whether one generally prefers such relations to be equal, versus hierarchical" and the "extent to which one desires that one's ingroup dominate and be superior to outgroups" (Pratto et al., 1994, p. 742).

The SDO scale powerfully predicts a range of sociopolitical and intergroup phenomena similar to those predicted by the RWA scale. Nevertheless, the two scales are relatively independent (nonsignificantly or only weakly correlated) and predict prejudice independently of each other (Altemeyer, 1998; McFarland, 1998; Pratto et al., 1994). Moreover, studies using a large number of individual-difference variables (i.e., personality, cognitive style, or social values and attitudes) to simultaneously predict prejudice found that both RWA and SDO were powerful predictors of prejudice when all other variables were controlled, and no other psychological variables were able to explain materially significant variance in generalized prejudice once RWA and SDO were controlled (Altemeyer, 1998; McFarland, 1998; McFarland & Adelson, 1996). Thus, RWA and SDO appear to be the strongest individual-difference predictors of prejudice.

Altemeyer (1998) has noted that the RWA and SDO scales seem to relate to different sets of the original nine "trait" clusters listed by Adorno et al. (1950). He therefore concluded that these scales measure two different kinds of authoritarian personality dimensions (the "submissive" and the "dominant"), and that both directly cause generalized prejudice and ethnocentrism.

Are RWA and SDO Personality Traits or Social Attitudes?

The view that the RWA and SDO scales measure personality traits is consistent with Allport and Adorno et al.'s approaches; however, both RWA and SDO may be more accurately viewed as measuring social attitudes or ideological beliefs (Duckitt, 2001). The content of the RWA or F scales (e.g., "Obedience and respect for authority are the most important virtues children should learn") and the SDO scale ("It's OK if some groups have more of a chance in life than others") do not pertain to personality traits and behavior, but to social attitudes and beliefs of a broadly ideological nature (cf. also Feldman & Stenner, 1997; Saucier, 2000). Indeed, Pratto et al. (1994) have usually described the SDO scale as a measure of enduring beliefs.

Second, the social conservatism dimension of social attitudes, when reliably measured, has correlated powerfully with the RWA scale and scaled with it as a single general factor or dimension (Raden, 1999; Saucier, 2000). And third, the RWA scale and its predecessor, the F scale, are highly reactive to situational threat manipulations (Altemeyer, 1988; Duckitt & Fisher, 2003; Sales, 1973), while SDO scores react to the salience of membership in high-power and high-status groups (Schmitt, Branscombe, & Kappen, in press; Guimond, Dambrun, Michinov, & Duarte, 2003). Finally, Guimond et al. (2003) found that SDO did not predict prejudice regardless of the social situation, but mediated the impact of the social situation on prejudice. This situational variability is more consistent with measures of attitude than measures of personality traits.

Research on the Psychological Bases of RWA and SDO

During the past few decades research has cast light on the likely psychological bases of RWA and SDO, linking RWA and SDO to two distinctive social worldviews, motivational goals and social values, and underlying personality traits. Research by Altemeyer (1998) and others (Duckitt, 2001; Duckitt et al., 2002; Jost et al., 2003) shows strong associations between RWA and belief that the social world is dangerous and threatening. SDO has linked with a different (though related) belief about the social world, termed a competitive-jungle worldview (Duckitt, 2001). Research has found SDO to be strongly correlated with Machiavellianism (Saucier, 2000), power values (Duriez & Van Hiel, 2002; McFarland, 1998), and Altemeyer's (1998) "Personal Power, Meanness, and Dominance" and "Exploitive Manipulative, Amoral, Dishonesty" scales, all of which reflect a competitive, manipulative, cynical, social Darwinist, and power-oriented view of others and the social world. Thus, distinct worldviews – of the social world as a dangerous and threatening place (RWA) versus a competitive jungle (SDO) – may be underlying causes of RWA and SDO (Duckitt, 2001).

Research has also linked RWA and SDO to particular social motives and values. Jost et al.'s (2003) review found authoritarianism and conservatism to be strongly associated with measures of perceived social threat and fear, intolerance of uncertainty and ambiguity, low integrative complexity, low openness to experience, and needs for order, structure, and closure. They concluded that conservatism and authoritarianism are motivated by needs to control and manage uncertainty and threat. Research using Schwartz's (1992) well-validated values inventory (developed to measure universal values that express basic human motivational goals) supports this conclusion. His conservation values of security, conformity, and tradition correlate strongly with RWA but not with SDO, while his power and self-enhancement values correlate with SDO but not with RWA (Altemeyer, 1998; Duriez & Van Hiel, 2002; McFarland & Adelson, 1996; McFarland, 1998). In sum, people high in RWA value security, order, and control whereas people high in SDO value power, dominance, and group enhancement.

Personality Traits Linked to RWA and SDO

Heaven and Bucci (2001) found that RWA correlated with personality trait measures of dutifulness, orderliness, and moralism. This is consistent with Altemeyer's (1998) earlier findings that high RWAs are self-righteous, conscientious, agreeable, and low on openness, as well as Jost et al's (2003) review, which indicated that authoritarianism was associated with intolerance of ambiguity and uncertainty, needs for order, structure, and closure, and low scores on integrative complexity and openness to experience. These findings suggest a coherent trait pattern, which Duckitt (2001; Duckitt et al., 2002) captured in a single construct and trait (refined from one of Saucier's [1994] Big 5 personality dimensions): "Social

Conformity." The Social Conformity scale (including items such as "obedient," "respectful," "moralistic," versus "nonconforming," "rebellious," "unpredictable") is highly reliable, unidimensional, and highly correlated with the RWA scale, but nonsignificantly correlated with the SDO scale.

In contrast, studies have found SDO to be associated with low scores on personality measures of empathy, and high scores on Eysenck's psychoticism scale (Altemeyer, 1998; McFarland, 1998; McFarland & Adelson, 1996), which is indicative of being tough-minded, unempathic, cold, and hostile (Eysenck & Eysenck, 1975). Heaven and Bucci (2001) similarly found that SDO was correlated with low scores on personality measures of sympathy, cooperation, agreeableness, and morality. Duckitt (2001) developed a Tough versus Tender-mindedness trait rating scale to captured this trait pattern, consisting of items such as tough-minded, hard-hearted, uncaring, versus sympathetic, compassionate, forgiving. The Tough-mindedness scale is highly reliable, unidimensional, and correlates strongly with SDO but not with RWA.

Overall, research during the past decade suggests different psychological bases for RWA and SDO, with each associated with different sets of motivational goals and values, personality traits, and social belief systems or worldviews (referred to as "philosophies of life" by Allport). These findings have recently been integrated in a model of how motivational goals or values, personality traits, and social worldviews cause RWA and SDO, and how these in turn determine generalized outgroup prejudice.

New Framework: An Integrative Model of Personality, Ideology, and Prejudice

This dual-process cognitive motivational model proposes that RWA and SDO are two basic dimensions of social or ideological attitudes with each expressing motivational goals or values made chronically salient for individuals by their social worldviews and their personalities (Duckitt, 2001). High RWA expresses the motivational goal of establishing or maintaining social cohesion, stability, and security, which is made salient by seeing the social world as dangerous and threatening. The predisposing personality dimension is social conformity, which leads individuals to identify with the existing social order, be more sensitive to threats to it, and so to see the social world as dangerous and threatening. High social conformity also has a direct impact on authoritarian attitudes by making the motivational goal of social control, security, and stability salient to the individual. In

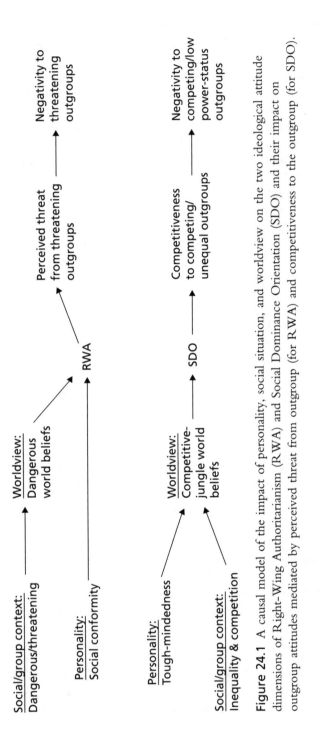

Figure 24.1 A causal model of the impact of personality, social situation, and worldview on the two ideological attitude dimensions of Right-Wing Authoritarianism (RWA) and Social Dominance Orientation (SDO) and their impact on outgroup attitudes mediated by perceived threat from outgroup (for RWA) and competitiveness to the outgroup (for SDO).

contrast, the model proposes that SDO stems from the underlying personality dimension of tough versus tender-mindedness. Tough-minded personalities view the world as a ruthlessly competitive jungle in which the strong win and the weak lose, which activates the motivational goals of group power, dominance, and superiority over others.

These two worldviews should generally be relatively stable, reflecting the influence of individuals' personality and socialization, but they should also be influenced by social situations. When the social world becomes markedly more dangerous and threatening, authoritarianism should be more prevalent, while situations characterized by inequality and competition over power and status should increase social dominance (see Glick, ch. 15 this volume). In both cases the effect ought to be mediated through change in individuals' corresponding worldviews. This causal model of personality, social situation, worldview, ideological attitudes, and prejudice is summarized in figure 24.1. In it, the influence of personality, the social situation, and individuals' worldviews on prejudice are indirect and mediated through their impact on the two ideological attitude dimensions of RWA and SDO.

Four recent studies using structural equation modeling with latent variables showed excellent overall fit for the causal relationships proposed among the two personality, two worldview, two ideological attitude dimensions, with each other and with intergroup attitudes for large samples in New Zealand, South Africa, and the USA (Duckitt, 2001; Duckitt et al., 2002). An experiment showed that manipulating social threat (using scenarios) increased RWA, but not SDO, with the effect being entirely mediated through a change in social worldview towards an increased perception of the social world as dangerous and threatening (Duckitt & Fisher, 2003).

According to this model, RWA reflects social cohesion and security motivation. Thus, RWA would drive prejudice towards outgroups seen as threatening or disrupting the stability, survival, and cohesion of the ingroup or society, and should be mediated through perceived threat from outgroups. SDO reflects competitive motivation to maintain or establish group dominance and superiority, and would therefore cause prejudice against competing or subordinate outgroups, who are viewed as inferior to the ingroup in power and status, and should therefore be mediated through competition for power, status, or resources with outgroups. Thus while RWA and SDO might often predict negative attitudes to the same groups (but for different reasons), they could also predict prejudice against quite different groups.

Recent findings support these predictions. For example, the effect of RWA on antigay prejudice is mediated by perceived threat (Esses, Haddock,

& Zanna, 1993), while the effect of SDO on anti-immigrant attitudes is mediated by economic competitiveness (Esses, Dovidio, Jackson, & Armstrong, 2001). More recently, RWA was found to predict negative attitudes to social categories rated as socially threatening but not socially subordinate (e.g., "rock stars," "drug dealers") while SDO did not, with the effect of RWA mediated by perceived threat from these groups, and not by competitiveness with them (Duckitt, 2003). In contrast, SDO predicted negative attitudes toward social categories rated as socially subordinate but not threatening (e.g., "housewives," "physically disabled persons," "unemployment beneficiaries") while RWA did not, with the effect of SDO mediated by competitiveness with these groups, and not by perceived threat. When social groups or categories were rated as threatening *and* socially subordinate (e.g., "feminists") both RWA and SDO predicted negative attitudes toward them with the effect of RWA mediated by perceived threat and of SDO by competitiveness.

In sum, the social attitude dimensions of authoritarianism and social dominance interact with outgroup characteristics to determine responses to those groups. Interestingly, this interactive hypothesis is consistent with Allport's original proposal that social environment (e.g., threat and uncertainty) activate and direct the fearfulness and anxieties of authoritarians. However, in contrast to Allport and other's early approaches to personality and prejudice, this model (and current research) suggests a more complex picture involving two empirically distinct individual-difference syndromes consisting of interrelated personality dispositions, social belief systems or worldviews, motivational goals or values, and social or ideological attitudes that interact with particular environmental and outgroup characteristics to cause prejudice.

Has Allport Been Supported?

In the middle of the twentieth century Allport and Adorno et al. produced personality theories of prejudice that were broadly similar but differed in important respects. At that time and for many years afterwards it was Adorno et al.'s theory that dominated the attention of social scientists. Yet, in retrospect, Allport's ideas have better stood the test of time. Of course, the view by both that one authoritarian personality dimension causes generalized prejudice was too simplistic. First, subsequent research has indicated that not just one, but two individual-difference syndromes, authoritarianism and social dominance, underlie generalized prejudice, with each involving quite different dynamics. Second, both Allport and Adorno et al. reduced what have turned out to be complex syndromes involving personality traits, social worldviews, motivational goals and values, and social-ideological attitudes into a single, oversimplified "personality" construct.

Still, Allport's ideas (compared to Adorno et al.'s) better captured the complexity revealed by later research. Most centrally, Allport's view that fearfulness and a threat orientation are the motivational core of the authoritarian syndrome has been substantially confirmed, whereas Adorno et al.'s hypothesis of repressed aggression has not. Allport's emphasis on fearfulness and insecurity also led him correctly to view a restricted, limited cognitive style as an essential aspect of this syndrome, whereas Adorno et al. did not. Allport also identified the "philosophy of life" of the social world as dangerous and threatening as an important component of the authoritarian syndrome, while Adorno et al. did not. And finally, Allport emphasized that social environmental uncertainties and threats interact with authoritarianism to elicit hostility toward particular groups and to activate support for authoritarian policies, while Adorno et al. largely ignored social environmental influences.

The major issue on which Allport appears to have been wrong is attributing the fearfulness, insecurity, and threat orientation characterizing the authoritarian syndrome to an underlying "ego weakness," or personal maladjustment, anxiety, and inadequacy. Subsequent research has shown authoritarians to be no lower on self-esteem and general adjustment than nonauthoritarians. Instead, as Altemeyer has shown, the fearfulness and threat orientation associated with the authoritarian syndrome seem to be learned beliefs about others and the social world.

However, Allport has certainly not been alone in assuming a single "prejudiced personality." Those who have studied individual differences in negative outgroup attitudes seem to have found it difficult to resist the attractively simple attribution to a disturbed or inadequate personality, broadly similar to that captured in the lay stereotype of the "bigot." It is ironic that similar negative essentialistic attributions seem to underlie the way in which prejudiced individuals think about the targets of their prejudice.

Future Directions

Since Allport's volume, two broad approaches to the study of prejudice have dominated social-psychological inquiry. One consists of the approach discussed here, which has seen prejudice as an attitude held by individuals that is determined by personality or other individual-difference factors. The other has seen prejudice as a group or intergroup phenomenon determined by intergroup dynamics and processes. Allport himself believed that different approaches and levels of analysis would need to be integrated into broader models for prejudice to be adequately understood. However, since the publication of his book there has been little connection or cross-fertilization between these two major approaches, with each characterized by different theories, research interests, and strategies.

Nevertheless, contemporary findings do seem to suggest important possibilities for future *rapprochement*. For example, the dual-process cognitive motivational model of personality, ideological attitudes, and prejudice described earlier sees RWA as influencing prejudice through sensitivity to perceived threat from outgroups, while SDO influences prejudice against outgroups through competitiveness, dominance, and superiority. It is interesting that the two dominant intergroup theories of prejudice, Realistic Conflict Theory and Social Identity Theory, suggest similar processes operating at the level of intergroup dynamics; the former sees prejudiced attitudes towards outgroups as being elicited by intergroup threat, whereas the latter sees intergroup attitudes as determined primarily by intergroup competitiveness over relative status and superiority. Both intergroup and individual-difference approaches may thus operate through the same motivational mechanisms, with one approach delineating the intergroup processes that activate these motives, and the other individual differences in proneness to their activation. The most important priority for future research and theory may therefore be the development and testing of such integrative models to provide a broader and more comprehensive understanding of the causes and dynamics of prejudice.

REFERENCES

Adorno, T., Frenkel-Brunswick, E., Levinson, D., & Sanford, N. (1950). *The authoritarian personality*. New York: Harper.

Allport, G. (1954/1979). *The nature of prejudice*. Cambridge, MA: Perseus Books.

Altemeyer, B. (1981). *Right-wing authoritarianism*. Winnipeg: University of Manitoba Press.

Altemeyer, B. (1998). The other "authoritarian personality." In M. P. Zanna (ed.), *Advances in experimental social psychology* (vol. 30, pp. 47–92). San Diego, CA: Academic Press.

Duckitt, J. (1992). *The social psychology of prejudice*. New York: Praeger.

Duckitt, J. (2001). A dual process cognitive-motivational theory of ideology and prejudice. In M. Zanna (ed.), *Advances in experimental social psychology* (vol. 33, pp. 41–113). San Diego, CA: Academic Press.

Duckitt, J. (2003). Authoritarianism, social dominance, and prejudice against social groups varying in threat and social subordination. MS submitted for publication.

Duckitt, J. & Fisher, K. (2003). The impact of social threat on worldview and ideological attitudes. *Political Psychology, 24,* 199–222.

Duckitt, J., Wagner, C., du Plessis, I.,& Birum, I. (2002). The psychological bases of ideology and prejudice: Testing a dual process model. *Journal of Personality and Social Psychology, 83,* 75–93.

Duriez, B. & Van Hiel, A. (2002). The march of modern fascism. A comparison of social dominance orientation and authoritarianism. *Personality and Individual Differences, 32,* 1199–1213.

Esses, V., Dovidio, J., Jackson, L., & Armstrong, T. (2001). The immigration dilemma: the role of perceived group competition, ethnic prejudice, and national identity. *Journal of Social Issues, 5,* 389–413.

Esses, V., Haddock, G., & Zanna, M. (1993). Values, stereotypes, and emotions as determinants of intergroup attitudes. In D. Mackie & D. Hamilton (eds.), *Affect, cognition, and stereotyping* (vol. 17, pp. 137–66). San Diego, CA: Academic.

Eysenck, H. & Eysenck, M. (1975). *Manual of the Eysenck Personality Questionnaire.* London: Hodder & Stoughton.

Feldman, S. & Stenner, K. (1997). Perceived threat and authoritarianism. *Political Psychology, 18,* 741–70.

Guimond, S., Dambrun, M., Michinov, N., & Duarte, S. (2003). Does social dominance generate prejudice? Integrating individual and contextual determinants of intergroup cognitions. *Journal of Personality and Social Psychology, 84,* 697–721.

Heaven, P. & Bucci, S. (2001). Rightwing authoritarianism, social dominance orientation and personality: An analysis using the IPIP measure. *European Journal of Personality, 15,* 49–56.

Jost, J., Glaser, J., Kruglanski, A., & Sulloway, F. (2003). Political conservatism as motivated social cognition. *Psychological Bulletin, 129,* 339–75.

McFarland, S. (1998). Toward a typology of prejudiced persons. Paper presented at the annual meeting of the International Society of Political Psychology, Montreal, Canada.

McFarland, S. & Adelson, S. (1996). *An omnibus study of personality, values, and prejudice.* Paper presented at the annual meeting of the International Society of Political Psychology, Vancouver, Canada.

Pratto, F., Sidanius, J., Stallworth, L., & Malle, B. (1994). Social dominance orientation: A personality variable predicting social and political attitudes. *Journal of Personality and Social Psychology, 67,* 741–63.

Raden, D. (1999). Is anti-Semitism currently part of an authoritarian attitude syndrome. *Political Psychology, 20,* 323–44.

Rokeach, M. (1954). The nature and meaning of dogmatism. *Psychological Review, 61,* 194–204.

Sales, S. (1973). Threat as a factor in authoritarianism. *Journal of Personality and Social Psychology, 28,* 44–57.

Saucier, G. (1994). Separating description and evaluation in the structure of personality attributes. *Journal of Personality and Social Psychology, 66,* 141–54.

Saucier, G. (2000). Isms and the structure of social attitudes. *Journal of Personality and Social Psychology, 78,* 366–85.

Schmitt, M., Branscombe, N., & Kappen, D. (in press). Attitudes toward group-based inequality: Social dominance or social identity? *British Journal of Social Psychology.*

Schwartz, S. (1992). Universals in the content and structure of values: Theoretical advances and empirical tests in 20 countries. In M. P. Zanna (ed.), *Advances in experimental social psychology* (vol. 25, pp. 1–65). San Diego, CA: Academic Press.

Shills, E. A. (1954). Authoritarianism: Right and left. In R. Christie & M. Jahoda (eds.), *Studies in the scope and method of "The Authoritarian Personality"* (pp. 24–49). Glencoe, IL: Free Press.

Chapter Twenty-Five

Religion and Prejudice
C. Daniel Batson and E. L. Stocks

We cannot speak sensibly of the relation between religion and prejudice without specifying the sort of religion we mean and the role it plays in the personal
life.

–Allport, 1954/1979, p. 456

Gordon Allport was a deeply religious man (see Allport, 1978). He was
also well aware of life's ironies. In chapter 28 of *The Nature of Prejudice*, he
addressed the paradoxical role of religion: "It makes prejudice and it
unmakes prejudice" (Allport, 1954/1979, p. 444). All major religions teach
universal tolerance and compassion. In practice, however, these same religions often promote intolerance and hatred.

Allport's own research on US college students in the mid-1940s revealed far higher prejudice among those who reported that religion was a
marked or moderate influence in their upbringing than among those who
reported that the influence of religion was slight or nonexistent (Allport &
Kramer, 1946). Many subsequent studies also found that individuals with
no religious affiliation showed less prejudice than did church members (for
a review, see Batson, Schoenrade, & Ventis, 1993, pp. 297–302.) These
findings suggest that religion makes prejudice.

Allport also found that some students in his research reported a more
positive religious influence. In the words of one: "The Church teaches
that we are all equal and there should be no persecution, for any reason, of
minority groups." And another: "It [religion] has helped me to understand
the way these groups feel and how they are human beings also" (Allport
& Kramer, 1946, p. 26). Such statements suggest that religion unmakes
prejudice.

Allport's Explanation of the Relation
Between Religion and Prejudice

To explain this paradox, Allport made a distinction between different ways of being religious – not between different religious beliefs but between different ways that religion can fit into the character or personality of the individual.

> Religion is a highly personal matter; it has quite different meanings in different lives. Its functional significance may range from its crutch-like ability to bolster infantile and magical forms of thinking to its support for a guiding and comprehensive view of life that turns the individual from his self-centeredness towards genuine love for his neighbor. (Allport, 1954/1979, p. 451–2)

Specifically, in *The Nature of Prejudice* Allport focused on two ways of being religious. One he called "institutionalized religion." An individual religious in this way is primarily concerned with the political and social aspects of religious activities. This way of being religious, Allport claimed, is associated with increased prejudice. The other he called "interiorized religion." An individual religious in this way has internalized his or her religious beliefs, is personally committed, and is devout. This way of being religious, he claimed, is associated with decreased prejudice. In his earlier book, *The Individual and His Religion* (1950), where Allport sought to explain the role of religion in character and personality development, he had called these two ways of being religious "immature" and "mature," respectively. "Some people seize upon the tribal investments of traditional religion for comfort and security; others take its universalistic teaching as an authentic guide to conduct" (1954/1979, p. 455). These two ways of being religious, and their respective relations to a personal disposition toward rigid, conventional adherence to authority and institutional structure, as well as toward ethnocentrism and prejudice, closely paralleled the distinction in the classic authoritarian personality research between "neutralized" religion and "internalized" or "real" religion (Adorno, Frenkel-Brunswik, Levinson, & Sanford, 1950; see also Duckitt's ch. 24 this volume).

Data, Doubts, and Developments Since 1954

In the decade and a half from the writing of *The Nature of Prejudice* to the end of his life in 1967, Allport continued to study the relation to prejudice of different ways of being religious. He extended his work both conceptually and empirically. Conceptually, he recast his distinction between different ways of being religious in more motivational, goal-oriented terms. By 1959, he had shifted from speaking of immature and mature religion to speaking of "extrinsic" and "intrinsic" religion (Allport, 1959).

> We borrow from axiology the concept of *extrinsic* value and *intrinsic* value. The distinction helps us to separate churchgoers whose communal type of membership supports and serves other, nonreligious ends, from those for whom religion is an end in itself – a final, not instrumental, good. (Allport, 1966, p. 454, italics in original)

Extrinsic religion involves using one's religion as an instrumental means to the self-serving ends of gaining social status and personal security. Intrinsic religion involves pursuing one's religion as an end in itself, a master motive in life. Allport (1966) claimed that, "both prejudice and religion are subjective formulations within the personal life. One of these formulations (the extrinsic) is entirely compatible with prejudice; the other (the intrinsic) rules out enmity, contempt, and bigotry" (p. 456).

Empirically, Allport and his students developed self-report questionnaire measures of both the extrinsic and intrinsic orientations to religion. The 11 items on the Extrinsic scale included, for example: "Although I believe in my religion, I feel there are many more important things in my life." "The church is most important as a place to formulate good social relationships." "What religion offers me most is comfort when sorrows and misfortune strike." The 9 items on the Intrinsic scale included, for example: "I try hard to carry my religion over into all my other dealings in life." "If I were to join a church group I would prefer to join a Bible study group rather than a social fellowship." "My religious beliefs are what really lie behind my whole approach to life." (For a full list of the items on each scale, see Batson et al., 1993, p. 162.)

A second method of measuring the extrinsic–intrinsic distinction was also developed. Gorsuch and McFarland (1972) suggested that a measure of this distinction could be obtained by simply asking people about the frequency of their involvement in religious activities. The extrinsically religious should limit their involvement to a moderate level because for them religion is subsumed under more important values and goals. The intrinsically religious should be highly involved because for them religion is the master motive in life. Employing this logic, a number of researchers used three levels of involvement in religious activities to assess the association with prejudice: no or low involvement (e.g., less than four times a

year), moderate involvement (e.g., less than weekly), and high involvement (e.g., at least weekly). The three levels were assumed to identify the
nonreligious, extrinsically religious, and intrinsically religious, respectively.
Consistent with this assumption, among religious individuals involvement
in religious activities has been found to be highly positively correlated
with scores on the Intrinsic scale but not the Extrinsic scale (Donahue,
1985; Gorsuch & McFarland, 1972).

Data

Empirical research using one or both of these two ways of operationalizing
the extrinsic versus intrinsic distinction has strongly supported Allport's
claim that extrinsic religion is associated with increased prejudice, whereas
intrinsic religion is associated with reduced prejudice. Batson et al. (1993)
reviewed 41 findings obtained across 32 different studies between 1949
and 1990 of individuals from Christian backgrounds (mostly US samples).
About one-third of these studies used some form of questionnaire or interview data to make the distinction between extrinsic and intrinsic religion.
In each, those who were classified as intrinsic scored lower on prejudice
than those classified as extrinsic. Two-thirds of the studies used level of
religious activity to make the distinction. Again, in the overwhelming
majority those who were highly involved in religious activities scored
lower on prejudice than those who were only moderately involved. Across
these 32 studies, prejudice of several types was assessed: racial and ethnic
prejudice, anti-Semitism, social distance, and ethnocentrism. Extrinsic religion (or moderate religious activity) was associated with higher prejudice
on all forms, whereas intrinsic religion (or high religious activity) was
associated with relatively low prejudice. It is hard to imagine stronger
support for Allport's claims.

Doubts

However, doubt has been cast on the meaning of these findings because of
the reactive nature of the self-report questionnaire measures of prejudice
used in these studies. (For critiques of self-report measures of prejudice see
Crosby, Bromley, & Saxe, 1980; Gaertner & Dovidio, 1986; Karlins,
Coffman, & Walters, 1969; Sigall & Page, 1971; Silverman, 1974.) In
subsequent research using less reactive measures (e.g., unobtrusive behavioral
responses rather than self-reports), the association between intrinsic

religion and relatively low prejudice has disappeared. This subsequent research has suggested that the association found with self-report measures of prejudice may have been produced by a desire on the part of the intrinsically religious to appear unprejudiced either to themselves or to other people – or both.

Doubts has also been cast on Allport's bipolar extrinsic–intrinsic model of ways of being religious. This model ran into problems early on, when Allport and Ross (1967) found that the extrinsic and intrinsic scales were not measuring opposite ends of the same continuum, as had been assumed, but defined two independent dimensions of personal religion. Associations with prejudice could be due to either or both of the underlying independent dimensions.

Developments

A three-dimensional model of ways of being religious proposed by Batson (1976) included two independent dimensions that corresponded conceptually to Allport's (1966) extrinsic and intrinsic orientations (and were measured principally by the Extrinsic and Intrinsic scales). These dimensions were called *religion as means* and *religion as end*, respectively.

Batson's model also included a third dimension, independent of the other two, called *religion as quest*. This third dimension of personal religion concerns the degree to which an individual seeks to face religious issues – such as issues of personal mortality and meaning in life – in all their complexity, resisting pat answers. An individual who approaches religion in this way recognizes that he or she does not know, and probably never will know, the final truth about such matters. Still, the questions are deemed important and, however tentative and subject to change, answers are sought. A number of writers, both theologians (e.g., Bonhoeffer, 1953; Niebuhr, 1963) and psychologists (e.g., Barron, 1968; Fromm, 1950), have suggested the importance of a quest dimension of religion. Indeed, this dimension was an important component of Allport's (1950) concept of mature religion, which he described as being "the outgrowth of many successive discriminations and continuous reorganization" (p. 59). This dimension was not, however, clearly represented in Allport's (1966) later concept of intrinsic religion, especially as that concept was operationalized using the Intrinsic scale.

Batson and colleagues developed a reliable and valid 12-item measure of the quest dimension, called the Quest scale (Batson & Schoenrade, 1991a; Batson & Schoenrade, 1991b; Batson et al., 1993). This scale included items such as: "It might be said that I value my religious doubts and uncertainties." "God wasn't very important to me until I began to ask questions about the meaning of my own life." "Questions are far more central to my religious experience than are answers." (For a full list of items on this scale, see Batson et al., 1993, p. 170.)

New Framework: A Revised View of the Religion–Prejudice Relationship

Research that employed this three-dimensional model of different ways of being religious, and at the same time assessed prejudice in less reactive ways, led to a revised view of the religion–prejudice relationship. Some of this research assessed the relations between the three dimensions of religion and one or another form of nonproscribed prejudice. Proscribed prejudices are those that are *explicitly opposed* by an individual's religious group. Nonproscribed prejudices are those that are either *endorsed* or *implicitly encouraged*. Nonproscribed prejudices include, for example, negative attitudes toward homosexuals on the part of church members in most Christian denominations in the United States (Herek, 1987) and negative attitudes toward non-Whites on the part of Afrikaner church members in South Africa during apartheid (Snook & Gorsuch, 1985).

In this research, the patterns of association with nonproscribed prejudices for the extrinsic/means and the intrinsic/end dimensions exactly reverse the patterns for extrinsic versus intrinsic religion found in the earlier studies that relied on self-report questionnaire measures of proscribed prejudices (e.g., racial prejudice in the US in the last half of the twentieth century). For nonproscribed prejudices, the extrinsic, means dimension showed no clear relation to prejudice; the intrinsic, end dimension showed a positive relation. Apparently, those scoring high on measures of intrinsic religion are less likely to report prejudicial attitudes when their religion tells them that they should not, but they are more likely to report prejudicial attitudes when these attitudes are permitted or encouraged by their religion. Only the quest dimension showed evidence of a negative relation to prejudices that were not proscribed by one's religious community (see Batson et al., 1993, pp. 317–23, for a review).

Other research assessed the relations between the three dimensions of religion and measures of both overt prejudice (e.g., self-report or obviously prejudicial behavior) and covert prejudice (e.g., subtly prejudicial behavior;

see also Rudman's ch. 7 this volume). Measures of covert prejudice include, for example, (a) assessing preference to avoid contact with a Black when this preference can be justified as due to some factor other than race or (b) being less willing to help someone who is homosexual even when the help in no way promotes homosexuality.

In this research, the relation between the extrinsic, means dimension and overt prejudice is inconsistent, but the relation between this dimension and covert prejudice is clearer. It tends to be positive. The relation between the intrinsic, end dimension and overt prejudice tends to be negative, but the relation between this dimension and covert prejudice tends to be positive. Only the quest dimension has shown a pattern suggesting a negative relation with covert prejudice (see Batson et al., 1993, pp. 324–9, for a review of 43 findings from 11 studies – also see Batson, Eidelman, Higley, & Russell, 2001; Batson, Floyd, Meyer, & Winner, 1999; and Goldfried & Miner, 2002).

In sum, studies to date that have attempted to look at the relation between religion and prejudice while avoiding the reactivity of self-report measures of proscribed prejudice – either by assessing forms of prejudice that are not proscribed by respondents' religious communities or by using covert measures of proscribed prejudice – suggest a more complex explanation of the religion–prejudice relationship than the one proposed by Allport. First, much research, starting with that of Allport and Ross (1967), suggests that an extrinsic, means orientation to religion and an intrinsic, end orientation are not the polar opposites or distinct types that Allport had assumed. Instead, they are independent dimensions of personal religion. Second, in addition to these two there is at least a third dimension to being religious, as an open-ended quest. There may, of course, be more than three dimensions.

Third, the relation to prejudice of these three dimensions of personal religion differs depending on whether prejudice is proscribed or not proscribed, and if proscribed, is measured overtly or covertly. The extrinsic, means dimension tends to be related to increased prejudice on both overt and covert measures, but only if the prejudice in question is proscribed, as is racial prejudice by mainstream religion in the US today. This dimension is not clearly associated with forms of prejudice not proscribed by one's religious community. The quest dimension tends to be related to decreased prejudice on both overt and covert measures of prejudice, both when the prejudice is proscribed and not proscribed. The intrinsic, end dimension tends to be related to decreased prejudice when that prejudice is proscribed by one's religious community and is measured overtly.

However, this dimension tends to be related to increased prejudice when that prejudice is not proscribed by one's religious community. It also tends to be related to increased prejudice when a proscribed prejudice is measured covertly.

What Would Allport Say?

Were Allport still with us, what might he say about this revised view of the relation between religion and prejudice? He would probably not be overly surprised at the finding that extrinsic and intrinsic religion are not polar opposites but are instead two independent dimensions of individual religion. His own research (Allport & Ross, 1967) indicated that there was not a strong negative correlation between scores on the Extrinsic and Intrinsic scales. This finding led Allport and Ross (1967) to attempt to patch up the extrinsic–intrinsic typology by creating a third type. Participants who scored high on both the Extrinsic and Intrinsic scales were typed as "indiscriminately pro-religious" (and described as "muddled-headed" – Allport, 1966, p. 456 – and "provokingly inconsistent" – Allport & Ross, 1967, p. 437). However, this typological patch does not seem appropriate because the relatively high self-report prejudice scores for participants typed as indiscriminately pro-religious can be predicted simply by their relatively high scores on the Extrinsic scale.

Allport might be a bit more surprised to find that a quest orientation to religion reflects a third independent dimension of individual religion. He would probably have expected responses on the Quest scale to correlate highly positively with responses on the Intrinsic scale. After all, the Intrinsic scale was intended to reflect his earlier concept of mature religion, and the Quest scale was developed to reflect an aspect of mature religion. It now seems clear, however, that these two scales tap two distinct dimensions of personal religion, each of which is a component of what Allport (1950) referred to as mature religion. Although it may be tempting to propose a typology in which individuals scoring high on both the Intrinsic and Quest scales would be typed as displaying mature religion, a typology once again seems inappropriate. Associations with prejudice seem best predicted by scores on one or the other of these scales, Intrinsic or Quest, not by a combination of the two.

Allport would not, we think, be surprised or troubled by the move toward using less reactive measures to assess prejudice when looking at the relation between religion and prejudice. Given that he was trying to find such measures shortly before he died (Allport & Ross, 1967), we think he would be quite pleased with this development. Indeed, he might encourage us to add the currently popular Implicit Association Test (IAT – Greenwald, McGhee, & Schwartz, 1998; see also Rudman's ch. 7 this volume) to our techniques for assessing the religion-prejudice relationship.

We suspect that Allport might be more surprised and troubled by what the use of less reactive measures has revealed about the relation between his Intrinsic scale and prejudice. It now seems that the relationship between higher scores on the Intrinsic scale and lower scores on measures of prejudice and ethnocentrism that he stated with such confidence during the 1960s applies only to reactive, overt measures of prejudices proscribed by one's religious community. When assessing prejudices not clearly proscribed or when using more covert measures, scores on the Intrinsic scale are more likely to be positively correlated with prejudice. Rather than the personal transformation toward tolerance that Allport assumed was associated with intrinsic religion, higher scores on the Intrinsic scale appear to be associated with an increased desire to look unprejudiced – or to look prejudiced only toward the right people and groups.

The consistent negative association between scores on the Quest scale and measures of prejudice, including nonproscribed and covertly measured prejudice, would likely please Allport. Indeed, we can almost imagine him saying, "Oh yes, that's what I meant when I was talking about a way of being religious that 'rules out enmity, contempt, and bigotry'" (Allport, 1966, p. 465). We can almost hear him saying that, but not quite. Allport thought that it was devotion and adherence to the universalistic teachings of religion as "an authentic guide to conduct" that unmade prejudice, not pursuit of an open-ended religious quest.

Moreover, it is not clear that a religious quest is actually the cause of the relatively low prejudice associated with higher scores on the Quest scale. Higher Quest scores and lower prejudice may each reflect a general disposition toward an open, tolerant approach to both people and ideas – a disposition that might characterize what Allport (1954/1979) called a "maturely democratic person" (p. 515).

There have, then, been developments in our understanding of the religion–prejudice relationship. But Allport's most basic insight about this relationship has stood the test of time: In order to understand the relation between religion and prejudice, we need to specify the sort of religion we mean and the role it plays in the personal life. This insight is as fundamental and important today as it was 50 years ago.

Future Directions: Where Would Allport Point Us?

Were he able, where might Allport point us for future research? First, we suspect he might point social psychologists interested in prejudice toward prejudice.

1. Toward Prejudice

The extensive, often clever theory and research on stereotyping produced over the past 25 years would doubtless impress and please Allport. However, we suspect he would encourage us to look beyond the relatively automatic processes of categorization and stereotyping to the more controlled and motivated processes of resistance to new information, defensiveness, rationalization, and biased decisions that he believed lay at the core of prejudice (Allport, 1954/1979, pp. 505–6). For him, prejudice was not simply a conditioned prejudgment about an individual or group, it was a felt or expressed "antipathy based upon a faulty and inflexible generalization" (1954/1979, p. 9; see also Eagly & Diekman's ch. 2 this volume). It was not simply a misperception or an expectation; it was a dislike or hatred. The basis for this aversion was factually wrong and impervious to correction because the aversion served important psychological functions for the prejudiced individual. Thus, Allport's analysis went well beyond attention to a predisposition to prejudice; he also considered the role that prejudice plays in the life of the individual. He considered the fears, anxieties, and inadequacies to which prejudice speaks that make it resistant to correction and a source of viscous, inhumane acts. He would probably suggest that contemporary analyses need to move beyond perceptual and cognitive factors to give more attention to motivational and personality factors involved in prejudice.

Allport might remind us that motivational and personality factors play important roles in both racism and sexism, by far the most commonly studied forms of prejudice. Even more obviously today, they play important roles in homophobia, xenophobia, ethnocentrism, and religious prejudice. In this post 9–11 era, mixed strains of xenophobia (reflected in nationalism and patriotism), ethnocentrism, and religious prejudice – whether of Protestants against Catholics or the reverse, Christians against Jews or the reverse, Christians and Jews against Muslims or the reverse, Muslims against Hindus or the reverse – are especially virulent. Few in our society are immune, including prejudice researchers. Yet this conspicuous form of prejudice has been the focus of only limited research. Have we avoided this form because it is too hot and too controversial – and too close to home? Allport had the courage to address forms of prejudice that in 1954 were hot, controversial, and close to home. He would probably encourage us to do the same.

2. Toward Integration of Personality and Social-Identity Perspectives

Second, Allport might point us toward an integration of personality and social-identity perspectives on the relation between religion and prejudice. His own thinking about religion focused on the role of religion in the life of the individual, a personality perspective, and it is not likely that he would want to relinquish that perspective. At the same time, he would likely embrace the current interest in the effects of social identity and group membership on the prejudice-religion relationship (e.g., Burris & Jackson, 2000; Jackson & Hunsberger, 1999). Rather than focusing on one of these perspectives and ignoring the other, Allport recognized the importance of each: "Are discrimination and prejudice facts of the social structure or of the personality structure? The answer we have given is *Both*" (Allport, 1954/1979, p. 514, italics in original). Specifically, he noted ways that interiorized religion may overcome in-group bias and ethnocentrism of membership-based institutionalized religion (pp. 446–9).

Allport thought that devotion to the essential teachings of one's religion, teachings of universal tolerance and compassion, could provide a personality-integrating master motive that would dissolve categories and barriers. In social-identity (Tajfel, 1981) and self-categorization (Turner, 1987) terms, one might say that such devotion both (a) meets esteem needs and (b) prompts recategorization of self away from the level of the group to the level of all humanity, leading one to see outgroup members as brothers and sisters.

An association of devout, intrinsic religion – the form of religion that Allport thought unmade prejudice – with higher self-esteem has been frequently reported (see Batson et al. 1993, pp. 257–90; Pargament, 2002). Its association with universal tolerance and compassion is less clear. The limited research that exists suggests the opposite (e.g., Batson et al., 1993, 1999, 2001; Burris & Jackson, 2000; Deconchy, 1980; Jackson & Hunsberger, 1999). Rather than a precondition for universal tolerance and compassion, the esteem boost associated with devout, intrinsic religion may be a product of a sense of privileged status in the eyes of God. Such a sense may heighten, not diminish, religion-based ethnocentric animosity.

3. Toward Consideration of the Religious Teachings Internalized

Perhaps in future research we need to consider the specific religious teachings internalized by the devout, intrinsic believer. All major world religious teach universal tolerance and compassion; such teachings are a defining feature of a world religion (Burtt, 1957). All major western religions also teach that the faithful follower has special status as one of "God's chosen people," the elect, or the saved. As Allport was well aware, religion can serve esteem-enhancing (see Brown & Zagefka's ch. 4 this volume) and system-justifying (see Jost & Hamilton's ch. 13 this volume; see also Sidanius & Pratto, 1999) functions. Internalization of a doctrine of universal compassion as a master motive may unmake prejudice; internalization of a doctrine of election may make it. Although a bit too neat, the relative emphasis placed on these two doctrines characterizes what are described as liberal and conservative branches of a given religion, respectively. Such a distinction may need to be taken into account in future research. (We focus here on core religious doctrines rather than on teachings that reflect a particular point in history or social order such as teachings about dietary, dress, and sexual practices, treatment of slaves, and gender roles.)

In his analysis of the religion–prejudice relationship, Allport was concerned with how a person believes, not with what. His research focused on Protestant Christians, but he thought that immature and mature religion, extrinsic and intrinsic religion, could be found in any religious tradition. Research over the past 50 years indicates that the means (extrinsic), end (intrinsic), and quest dimensions apply to Catholic respondents as well as Protestants, and may apply much more widely (e.g., Kaneko, 1990). However, research has also suggested that how one believes and what one believes (or does not believe) may not be as clearly separable as Allport thought.

Scores on his Intrinsic scale have been found to be highly correlated (typically 0.50 or higher) with scores on Orthodoxy and Fundamentalism scales (Altemeyer & Hunsberger, 1992; Batson et al., 1993). This finding has led some researchers to adopt a strategy of using partial correlations to assess the relationship between the Intrinsic scale and prejudice, adjusting for the relation with Orthodoxy or Fundamentalism. It is not clear that this strategy is wise, however, for two reasons. First, the correlations of the Intrinsic scale with Orthodoxy and Fundamentalism are so high that the adjusted Intrinsic scores may no longer measure the same construct. Second, to the extent that, as suggested above, how and what people believe are not independent, then adjusting for what people believe may undercut the attempt to measure how they believe. In future research, rather than throwing away that part of a given dimension of personal religion (means, end, quest) associated with given types of religious beliefs, it may be wise to focus attention on these associations. How and what one believes may be inextricably entwined.

4. Toward Application of What We Know

Fourth, Allport might point toward increased application of what we know about the relation to prejudice of different ways of being religious. He was committed to combating prejudice not simply to understanding it. If he was right in his belief that internalizing religious teachings of universal acceptance and compassion can unmake prejudice, then more attention needs to be given to religious institutions not as causes of intergroup antipathy and ethnocentrism but as possible contributors to solutions – at least in those areas of the world where religion remains an important part of people's lives. Allport would likely encourage us to develop programs in religious settings to reduce prejudice.

Of course, to do so we must solve some serious problems. First, as suggested above, we need to know which religious teachings encourage rather than discourage tolerance and compassion. Second, we need to get religious institutions to focus on these teachings. Third, we need to get people to take their religion seriously as a challenge and guide rather than to use it as a crutch and buffer. This last problem, arguably the most difficult, is the one Allport identified in 1954, the problem of what role religion plays in the personal life.

Nor are religious teaching and preaching likely to be sufficient, even if we can solve these substantial problems. It is important to keep in mind one of Allport's key observations, frequently voiced by others since. This observation is that direct, purposeful, positive interaction with and action on behalf of the targets of prejudice are more effective in reducing prejudice than is learning about prejudice (Allport, 1954/1979, p. 485) or hearing sermons about tolerance (p. 495). Even if one's religion talks the talk of universal acceptance and compassion, this talk needs to be combined with opportunities to walk the walk. As usual, Allport (1954/1979) said it very well: "When he *does* something, he *becomes* something" (p. 509, italics in original). Only through such a combination of action and personal transformation is religion likely to unmake prejudice.

REFERENCES

Adorno, T. W., Frenkel-Brunswik, E., Levinson, D. J., & Sanford, R. N. (1950). *The authoritarian personality.* New York: Norton.

Allport, G. W. (1950). *The individual and his religion.* New York: Macmillan.

Allport, G. W. (1954/1979). *The nature of prejudice.* Cambridge, MA: Perseus Books.

Allport, G. W. (1959). Religion and prejudice. *Crane Review, 2,* 1–10.

Allport, G. W. (1966). Religious context of prejudice. *Journal for the Scientific Study of Religion, 5,* 447–57.

Allport, G. W. (1978). *Waiting for the Lord: 33 meditations on God and man.* ed. P. A. Bertocci. New York: Macmillan.

Allport, G. W. & Kramer, B. (1946). Some roots of prejudice. *Journal of Psychology, 22,* 9–30.

Allport, G. W. & Ross, J. M. (1967). Personal religious orientation and prejudice. *Journal of Personality and Social Psychology, 5,* 432–43.

Altemeyer, B. & Hunsberger, B. (1992). Authoritarianism, religious fundamentalism, quest, and prejudice. *International Journal for the Psychology of Religion, 2,* 113–33.

Barron, F. (1968). *Creativity and personal freedom.* Princeton: Van Nostrand.

Batson, C. D. (1976). Religion as prosocial: Agent or double agent? *Journal for the Scientific Study of Religion, 15,* 29–45.

Batson, C. D., Eidelman, S. H., Higley, S. L., & Russell, S. A. (2001). "And who is my neighbor?" II: Quest religion as a source of universal compassion. *Journal for the Scientific Study of Religion, 40,* 39–50.

Batson, C. D., Floyd, R. B., Meyer, J. M., & Winner, A. L. (1999). "And who is my neighbor?": Intrinsic religion as a source of universal compassion. *Journal for the Scientific Study of Religion, 38,* 445–57.

Batson, C. D. & Schoenrade, P. A. (1991a). Measuring religion as quest: 1. Validity concerns. *Journal for the Scientific Study of Religion, 30,* 416–29.

Batson, C. D. & Schoenrade, P. A. (1991b). Measuring religion as quest: 2. Reliability concerns. *Journal for the Scientific Study of Religion, 30,* 430–47.

Batson, C. D., Schoenrade, P. A., & Ventis, W. L. (1993). *Religion and the individual: A social-psychological perspective.* New York: Oxford University Press.

Bonhoeffer, D. (1953). *Letters and papers from prison.* New York: Macmillan.

Burris, C. T. & Jackson, L. M. (2000). Social identity and the true believer: Responses to threatened self-stereotypes among the intrinsically religious. *British Journal of Social Psychology, 39,* 257–78.

Burtt, E. A. (1957). *Man seeks the divine: A study in the history and comparison of religions.* New York: Harper.

Crosby, F., Bromley, S., & Saxe, L. (1980). Recent unobtrusive studies of black and white discrimination and prejudice: A literature review. *Psychological Bulletin, 87,* 546–63.

Deconchy, J.-P. (1980). *Orthodoxie religieuse et sciences humaines* [*Religious orthodoxy, rationality, and scientific knowledge*]. The Hague: Mouton.

Donahue, M. J. (1985). Intrinsic and extrinsic religiousness: Review and meta-analysis. *Journal of Personality and Social Psychology, 48,* 400–19.

Fromm, E. (1950). *Psychoanalysis and religion.* New Haven: Yale University Press.

Gaertner, S. L. & Dovidio, J. F. (1986). The aversive form of racism. In J. F. Dovidio & S. L. Gaertner (eds.), *Prejudice, discrimination, and racism* (pp. 61–89). New York: Academic Press.

Goldfried, J. & Miner, M. (2002). Quest religion and the problem of limited compassion. *Journal for the Scientific Study of Religion, 41,* 685–95.

Gorsuch, R. L. & McFarland, S. (1972). Single- vs. multiple-item scales for measuring religious values. *Journal for the Scientific Study of Religion, 11,* 53–65.

Greenwald, A. G., McGhee, D. E., & Schwartz, J. L. K. (1998). Measuring individual differences in implicit cognition: The implicit association task. *Journal of Personality and Social Psychology, 74,* 1464–80.

Herek, G. M. (1987). Religious orientation and prejudice: A comparison of racial and sexual attitudes. *Personality and Social Psychology Bulletin, 13,* 34–44.

Jackson, L. T. & Hunsberger, B. (1999). An intergroup perspective on religion and prejudice. *Journal for the Scientific Study of Religion, 38,* 509–23.

Kaneko, S. (1990). Dimensions of religiosity among believers in Japanese folk religion. *Journal for the Scientific Study of Religion, 29,* 1–18.

Karlins, M., Coffman, T. L., & Walters, G. (1969). On the fading of social stereotypes: Studies in three generations of college students. *Journal of Personality and Social Psychology, 13,* 1–16.

Niebuhr, H. R. (1963). *The responsible self.* New York: Harper.

Pargament, K. I. (2002). The bitter and the sweet: An evaluation of the costs and benefits of religiousness. *Psychological Inquiry, 13,* 168–81.

Sidanius, J. & Pratto, F. (1999). *Social dominance: An intergroup theory of social hierarchy and oppression.* New York: Cambridge University Press.

Sigall, H. & Page, R. (1971). Current stereotypes: A little fading, a little faking. *Journal of Personality and Social Psychology, 18,* 247–55.

Silverman, B. I. (1974). Consequences, racial discrimination, and the principle of belief congruence. *Journal of Personality and Social Psychology, 29,* 497–508.

Snook, S. C. & Gorsuch, R. L. (1985). Religion and racial prejudice in South Africa. Paper presented at the 92nd Annual Convention of the American Psychological Association, Los Angeles, Aug.

Tajfel, H. (1981). *Human groups and social categories: Studies in social psychology.* Cambridge: Cambridge University Press.

Turner, J. C. (1987). *Rediscovering the social group: A self-categorization theory.* Oxford: Blackwell.

PART VIII

REDUCING GROUP TENSIONS

Chapter Twenty-Six

Intergroup Relations Program Evaluation

Walter G. Stephan and Cookie White Stephan

In this chapter, we discuss Gordon W. Allport's seminal contributions to the evaluation of programs designed to improve intergroup relations. We first introduce Allport's (1954/1979) chapter on this topic, and note the current conditions throughout the world that make these programs as necessary today as they were in Allport's time. Then we discuss four types of program that have been developed to improve intergroup relations – multicultural education, diversity training, intergroup dialogues, and co-operative learning groups – and detail some of the many ways Allport's work has influenced these programs. We also discuss Allport's views on evaluation, examine and evaluate the current research on each of these types of programs, and present a meta-analysis of the effectiveness of inter-group relations programs. We close by noting recent program develop-ments and drawing conclusions about the directions these programs and their evaluations should take in the future.

Allport's Views on Intergroup Program Evaluation

Allport's contributions to current intergroup relations programs and their evaluation are remarkable. If one were to take his landmark book, *The Nature of Prejudice*, and use it as a guide for designing intergroup relations programs, a set of programs that looks very much like those of today would result. Unfortunately, however, most of today's intergroup relations program evaluations fall short of the evaluation standards set forth by Allport.

Allport's chapter 30, "Evaluation of Programs," was written when intergroup relations programs and their evaluation were in their infancy. Allport started by discussing the problems associated with intergroup relations program evaluation, but he strongly advocated conducting evaluations, despite those problems. Allport detailed the perfect evaluation design: pretest/post-test measures, experimental and control groups, the use of carefully selected dependent variables, the careful collection of data, and the collection of longitudinal data. This design is still the evaluation gold standard.

Allport then discussed the fact that the existing programs were individual-level interventions, explaining that structural approaches to prejudice and discrimination are of great concern but not amenable to simple program interventions. This point will be taken up when we discuss new developments. Allport noted that intergroup relations programs could be either direct or indirect in their approach to improving intergroup relations. He outlined six types of program in existence at the time he was writing: formal educational methods, contact and acquaintance programs, group retraining methods, mass media, exhortation, and individual therapy. In assessing each type of program, Allport described the underlying theoretical foundation and any data that existed on the effectiveness of these programs. He ended the chapter by suggesting that catharsis could have positive effects on intergroup relations.

Developments Since Allport: Fifty Years of Intergroup Relations Programs

The history of intergroup relations shows that peaceful, productive relations between groups involving mutual respect do not come naturally. The recognition of this fact has led to the creation of a wide range of programs to improve intergroup relations among racial, ethnic, religious, cultural, and other types of groups. Intergroup relations programs began to appear in the mid-twentieth century, but it was not until the 1970s and 1980s that they started to appear in large numbers. Unfortunately, the social problems that these programs address – prejudice, stereotyping, and discrimination – are still widespread in all societies. Centuries-old tensions remain. New tensions are arising, fueled in part by increasing migration worldwide and the globalization of the world economy. In 2000, at least 160 million people were living outside their country of birth or citizenship (Martin & Widgren, 2002). The increasing internal diversity of the world's societies, and the continuation of longstanding prejudice, stereotyping, and discrimination, make the creation of effective intergroup relations programs an issue of paramount importance for the future welfare of our world.

In the following sections, we discuss four types of intergroup relations programs, labeling them by their current names as well as by the labels that Allport used (noted in parentheses). As in 1954, some of these programs confront prejudice, stereotyping, and discrimination directly, but others are more indirect in their approach and do not specifically address intergroup relations issues. Most of these programs attempt to implement the conditions Allport described by which face-to-face contact results in positive intergroup relations. Following Allport, we divide the programs into direct and indirect approaches. First, we discuss three programs taking a direct approach: multicultural education, diversity training, and intergroup dialogues. Both the programs and the basic techniques employed are described.

Multicultural Education (Formal Educational Methods)

"No person knows his own culture who only knows his own culture."
—Allport, 1954/1979, p. 486

Allport emphasized the importance of cultural ignorance as a barrier to true intercultural communication. He ended his landmark book on prejudice with a section entitled "Imperatives of Intercultural Education." In it, he argued for teaching about a number of issues regarding race, culture, prejudice, discrimination, and multiple loyalties. These were to be taught throughout the educational experience:

> If taught in a simple fashion all the [intercultural] points can be made intelligible to younger children and, in a more fully developed way, they can be presented to older students in high school or college. In fact, at different levels of advancement, through "graded lessons," the same content can, and should, be offered year after year. (Allport, 1954/1979, p. 511)

Today's multicultural education programs have similar goals. They are based on the premise that students of all groups should learn about the history and culture of other racial, ethnic, cultural, and religious groups (Banks, 1973; Katz, 1975). These programs often attempt to present history from the perspective of minority groups, to counter the more traditional approach to history that emphasizes the perspective of the dominant group. One of the primary goals of these programs is to improve intergroup relations by helping students to acquire the knowledge, attitudes, and skills needed to participate in the social, civic, and cultural life of a diverse society (Banks, 1997). In addition to providing knowledge about different racial, ethnic, religious, and cultural groups, these programs usually aim to educate students about systems of inequality. Consistent with Allport's belief that ingroup loyalty does not necessarily imply outgroup hostility, another goal of many of these programs is to increase students' identification with their own racial, ethnic, religious, and cultural groups.

Multicultural education relies heavily on didactic techniques, although more interactive techniques, such as group discussions, role-playing, and simulation games, are frequently employed. Typically, the students read about different ethnic groups and are taught about basic intergroup relations concepts such as prejudice, stereotypes, and racism. An attempt is often made to modify the structure and procedures of the school to reflect the egalitarian emphasis of the multicultural curriculum.

Studies of multicultural education have focused on four populations: Students in primary and secondary schools, graduate students in counseling, preservice teachers, and undergraduate students. The results of these studies show that multicultural education programs have predominantly, but not uniformly, positive outcomes. Of the 33 studies we have reviewed, 11 (33 percent) found positive effects, 14 (42 percent) found a mixture of positive effects and nonsignificant effects, 5 (15 percent) found only nonsignificant effects, one (3 percent) found mixed negative and nonsignificant effects, and 2 (6 percent) found negative effects on measures related to intergroup relations (Stephan & Stephan, 2004). Two of the three studies that had negative or partially negative effects were the only two published studies of preschool children.

Diversity Training (Group Retraining Methods)

"It is clear that group retraining cannot be used with people who resist both the method and its objectives."

—Allport, 1954/1979, p. 492

Allport believed that desegregation of the job market by federal law would only increase prejudice unless minorities of equal or higher status were hired. In addition, he was concerned that contact with minority-group members in the workplace would not generalize to the group as a whole. He advocated group retraining methods in which the content would be group dynamics. His discussion of group retraining makes clear that he felt these programs must be voluntary. Unfortunately, diversity training as we know it today is typically mandatory, usually does not focus on group dynamics, and still suffers from problems of generalization, thus potentially failing to fulfill the criteria Allport outlined.

Diversity training programs were first created for use in the US military (Landis et al., 1976; Tansik & Driskell, 1977), but later diversity training and diversity initiatives became popular in business organizations. Diversity training typically attempts to increase the participants' awareness of dissimilarities among racial, ethnic, and cultural groups, and encourages them to value these differences. These programs use both didactic (e.g., lectures and readings) and interactive techniques (e.g., role-playing, simulation games). The focus of diversity training programs is often on changing the attitudes and behaviors of members of the majority group. In some organizations, diversity training is accompanied by changes in the organizational structure and climate that reflect an emphasis on greater diversity. Diversity programs tend to be rather brief in duration, often only two or three days. Although many assessments of diversity programs have been conducted, only a small number of studies have been published on the effects of diversity training on intergroup relations. Although three of these programs reported considerable success in changing attitudes, three others obtained a mixture of positive and negative effects and one was unsuccessful in improving intergroup relations (for details, see Stephan & Stephan, 2001, 2004).

Based on these studies, it appears that diversity training programs are less successful with members of the dominant group than with members of targeted minority groups (see Major & Vick, ch. 9, and Jones, ch. 10, this volume). In addition, short programs appear to be less successful than longer programs. Because these studies suggest that the results grow stronger over time, evaluations with only immediate outcome measures may not capture the full effects of the program. Surprisingly, a survey of human resource managers in organizations that examined the perceived success of programs and the factors related to perceived success found that programs requiring mandatory attendance by managers were thought to be more successful than voluntary programs (Rynes & Rosen, 1995).

Intergroup Dialogues (Contact and Acquaintance Programs)

"Information seldom sticks unless mixed with attitudinal glue."
                                                        –Allport, 1954/1979, p. 485

Intergroup dialogues provide one example of programs that Allport labeled "contact and acquaintance programs." He argued that these programs needed to occur under optimal contact conditions, and he believed that informational components would not succeed without the inclusion of experiential, interactive components. All intergroup dialogue programs emphasize these interactive components. Most intergroup dialogue programs involve a series of face-to-face discussions and experiential exercises among members of two groups, facilitated by trainers. Typically, they take place in educational settings, although some are conducted in community settings. They are generally employed with adults. The goals of these dialogues range from solving a specific conflict to improving ongoing relations among members of groups with a history of negative relations. The contact in dialogue groups embodies some of the principles of Allport's contact hypothesis – equal status, collaboration on common goals, and support by authority figures (see also Pettigrew & Tropp, ch. 16, and Kenworthy, Hewstone, Turner, & Voci, ch. 17, this volume). The emphasis on social justice and social action in these programs is stronger than in most other programs. Unlike most other programs, conflict is often brought out into the open and discussed. Participants are encouraged to express their emotions and discuss their reactions to prejudice, stereotyping, and discrimination. Allport may have approved of this emphasis on conflict and emotions; his evaluation chapter includes a section on the benefits of emotional catharsis.

There have been empirical studies of dialogue groups conducted at the University of Michigan and dialogues involving Israeli Jews and Arabs. In the University of Michigan program, first-year students from groups with a history of conflict (e.g., Whites and African Americans) meet for a semester. Evaluation data indicate that this program has a number of positive effects on intergroup relations (e.g., changing intergroup attitudes and creating a better understanding of discrimination and its causes) (Gurin, Nagda, & Lopez, 2004; Gurin, Peng, Lopez, & Nagda, 1999; Lopez, Gurin, & Nagda, 1998; Nagda & Zuniga, 2003). One of these studies found predominantly positive effects three years after the completion of a one semester program, suggesting that such programs can have lasting effects (Gurin et al., 1999).

In the Neve Shalom/Wahat al Salam program in Israel, Jewish and Arab trainers conduct three-day conflict management dialogues for Jewish and Arab youths aged 16–17. Studies of this program suggest that it was generally more successful with each succeeding year, but there were clearly years when the program was not successful in changing attitudes (Bargal & Bar, 1992). A study of a related program in Israel obtained similarly mixed results (Hertz-Lazarowitz, Kupermintz, & Lang, 1998). This program involved mutual school visits by Jewish and Arab students in Israel. These meetings focused on understanding culture and customs, reducing stereotypes, and issues of identity. Although the meetings were designed to create mutual liking and increase empathy and understanding, pretest/post-test comparisons indicated that very few positive effects and some negative effects occurred among participants in the program when compared to nonparticipants. The mixed outcomes of the Israeli programs are a reminder of just how difficult it is to improve relations between groups that have a history of protracted conflict.

Next, we discuss cooperative learning groups, a type of program that takes an indirect approach to improving intergroup. Indirect programs do not explicitly address prejudice, stereotyping or discrimination and they do not cover differences or similarities among racial and ethnic groups. The direct programs often employ didactic techniques, in which teachers dominate the interaction. By contrast, the indirect techniques were devised specifically to enact the contact principles set out by Allport: equal-status contact in the pursuit of common goals, positively sanctioned by the institution and leading to "the perception of common interests and common humanity between members of the two groups" (Allport, 1954/1979, p. 281).

Cooperative Learning Groups
(Contact and Acquaintance Programs)

"The nub of the matter seems to be that contact must reach below the surface in order to be effective in altering prejudice."

–Allport, 1954/1979, p. 276

One of the most popular types of indirect program relies on cooperative learning techniques. Investigators in the US in Colorado, Minnesota, Maryland, and Texas independently developed these programs for use in schools (Aronson et al., 1978; Blaney et al., 1977; DeVries, Edwards, & Slavin, 1978; Johnson & Johnson, 1992; Weigel, Wiser, & Cook, 1975). Cooperative learning usually consists of placing students in small learning groups in which the task and reward structure require face-to-face interaction in a situation in which students are interdependent. That is, the students can only reach their individual goals through the success of the group. Typically, students from two or more ethnic groups, both sexes, and of varying academic abilities are brought together in groups of 4 to 6. The content of these programs does not concern intergroup relations *per se*, but is, instead, organized around traditional curricula taught in a new format. Cooperation guides the within-group interactions. In some cooperative learning techniques the small cooperative groups compete with each other, whereas in other cooperative learning techniques they do not. Cooperative techniques typically include pretraining of students – practice in cooperative techniques and team-building – as well training of teachers in their new roles as group facilitators.

Studies of the effects of cooperative learning groups are so numerous that they have been subjected to meta-analyses. In one analysis of 53 studies comparing cooperative and competitive conditions, intergroup liking was stronger and intergroup friendships were more frequent under cooperative learning than in traditional competitive classrooms (Johnson & Johnson, 1989). In later reviews, Johnson and Johnson (1992, 2000) found that cooperation produced more cross-racial friendships than competition or individualistic learning. In addition, they found that competition may actually reduce cross-racial friendships. Another review of studies of cooperative learning also found that cooperative learning generally had more positive effects on intergroup relations (e.g., increased intergroup friendships) than traditional competitive or individual learning (Slavin, 1995). Thus, there is compelling evidence that cooperative learning groups improve intergroup relations (see also Esses, Jackson, Dovidio, & Hodson, ch. 14 this volume).

Meta-Analysis of Intergroup Relations Programs

With the exception of the cooperative learning programs, studies of intergroup relations programs have not been subjected to meta-analysis. To remedy this deficit, we performed a meta-analysis of all other types of intergroup relations programs (see Stephan, Renfro, & Stephan, 2004, for details). We located 58 articles containing quantitative data. Of these, we excluded studies reporting interventions lasting less than three hours under the assumption that such short programs were unlikely to have lasting effects on intergroup attitudes or behaviors. We also excluded those in which the dependent variables did not measure intergroup relations attitudes or behaviors, studies in which the reported data were too incomplete to be included in the analyses, and those with design or analysis problems. We were able to include 35 studies in the meta-analysis.

These 35 remaining studies are quite diverse. The participants' ages ranged from kindergarten through adulthood. The treatment programs took place all across the US, as well as in several other countries, and ranged from 4 to 80 hours in length. The participants and the target groups included Whites and many types of ethnic minorities. The programs contained one or more of the following treatments: lectures, readings, library research, films/videos, discussions involving all the participants, small group discussions, experiential exercises (e.g., simulations, role-playing), and one-on-one dialogues. Most programs took place in educational institutions, but some were conducted in work and recreational (e.g., summer camp) settings.

The four dependent measures consisted of attitude change, behavior change, delayed attitude change (postmeasures assessed from 8 to 64 weeks after the intervention), and delayed behavior change. The goals of the programs differed greatly, and consequently the dependent measures were quite diverse. Examples of the measures include stereotypes, racial awareness, social distance, racial preference, perceived group differences, liking for members of an outgroup, the importance of diversity, knowledge of stereotype effects, outgroup attributes, discouraging racist comments, encouraging open discussion of cultural differences, and demonstrations of multicultural skills.

The meta-analysis indicated that these programs were generally effective, although the effect size was relatively modest. The average effect size was 0.25 for attitudinal measures and 0.38 for behavioral measures. The effect sizes for the small number of studies that included delayed measures (0.80 for attitudes, and 0.86 for behaviors) indicate that these programs can produce effects that endure over time. The programs that employed experiential techniques were somewhat more effective than programs that did not, but this difference was only of marginal statistical significance.

Although the studies were coded for a host of other factors that are thought to affect the impact of these programs (e.g., holding group discussions, providing information on cultural differences, viewing films/videos), none of these factors proved to be positively related to the effect sizes in these studies, perhaps because all of these studies employed multiple techniques, making it difficult to disentangle the effectiveness of any particular technique. In addition, the age of the participants and the duration of the programs were unrelated to effect sizes. These programs appeared to be equally effective with majority and minority group members. At the present state of our knowledge, it appears that the manner in which the programs are conducted may be more important than the specific techniques that are employed.

Although the results of this meta-analysis are encouraging, they must be regarded as tentative. All of the programs were quite different from one another, making it difficult to compare across programs. The programs employed an amazing array of different measures of intergroup relations. A number of these measures are not well-established and their reliability and validity remain in question. Nearly all of these studies used self-report measures of attitudes which are subject to social desirability biases. Although many of these studies employed pretest/post-test designs with experimental and control groups, few of them employed random assignment and a number of studies employed weaker designs (pre/post designs or post-test/control group designs). Thus, nearly all of them are subject to alternative explanations of one type or another. In addition, the sample sizes were sometimes rather small. Moreover, many of these programs were conducted by inexperienced personnel or were evaluated during their inaugural application. It seems likely that these programs would have had a greater impact if they had been conducted by experienced personnel or if they had been evaluated after they had been in use for a considerable period of time. Finally, it is probable that studies finding no effects or negative effects were less likely to have been published than studies finding positive effects, which may lead to overestimating the favorable effects of these programs.

New Frameworks: Advances in Programs and Evaluations

Allport's argument that intergroup relations programs were not able to address social-structural issues such as institutional prejudice and discrimination has proven not to be correct. Some techniques focus on group-level rather than individual-level relations, acknowledge that individuals are defined and limited by their group identification, and demonstrate that groups are embedded in systematic power politics. In these programs, emphasis is placed on creating a more equitable environment in the institutions in which the programs are conducted. They also engage the participants in social change efforts that extend beyond these institutions. We review two such programs: conflict resolution programs and moral education programs. Both are indirect in their approach to improving intergroup relations.

Conflict Resolution Techniques

Current conflict resolution techniques include programs designed to resolve intergroup disputes in community and school settings (Fisher, 1990; Johnson

& Johnson, 1996). Mediation, negotiation, and third-party consultation provide examples of these techniques. The goals of these techniques are to lessen conflict or to resolve conflicts in a positive manner. These goals are achieved through teaching conflict resolution skills to contending parties or by placing contending parties in situations in which a third party helps to resolve the problem to the mutual benefit of the contending parties. The approach is intensely interactive. Traditionally, this approach has not been explicitly oriented toward imparting intergroup relations skills or changing intergroup attitudes, although some programs directly address intergroup conflicts.

The existing literature mostly consists of evaluations of general school-based conflict resolution and peer mediation programs. Reviews of that literature show that these programs are typically effective in teaching students negotiation and mediation skills and that trained students tend to use these skills to reach constructive solutions to conflict (Carruthers, Sweeney, Kmitta, & Harris, 1996; Johnson & Johnson, 1996). The studies assessing school-based dispute resolution or mediation programs that focus on intergroup mediation usually report that participants are satisfied with these programs and find them useful (Lam, 1989). One large-scale program found that students in an alternative inner-city school who completed a mediation program were able to better manage their conflicts than those who had not completed the program (Coleman & Deutsch, 1998; Deutsch, 1992).

Moral Education

Most moral education programs are an outgrowth of Kohlberg's work on moral development (Kohlberg, 1969). For instance, the first "just community" schools were based on this theory (Kohlberg, 1981). These schools not only taught moral reasoning but were also designed to create egalitarian, caring learning communities. Other moral education programs emphasize moral discourse, attempt to inculcate respect and interpersonal sensitivity, promote tolerance and understanding of others, or place moral education in the historical context of the Holocaust (Battistich et al., 1989; Fine, 1995; Oser, 1985). The primary goal of these programs is to increase students' levels of moral reasoning, typically through discussions of moral dilemmas. These programs can improve intergroup relations indirectly through their emphasis on justice and egalitarianism.

A number of studies indicate that moral education programs do increase levels of moral reasoning (e.g., Bardige, 1981; Lieberman, 1981; Power,

Higgins, & Kohlberg, 1989). Several studies show that high levels of moral development are linked with low levels of prejudice (Davidson & Davidson, 1994) and acceptance of outgroups (Battistich et al., 1995), suggesting that increasing moral development may reduce prejudice. The only study we are aware of that assessed the effects of a moral education program on prejudice found that eighth-grade students who participated in the "Facing History and Ourselves" program (a program that examines moral issues in light of the Holocaust) had significantly lower scores on the modern racism scale than did a control group (Schultz, Barr, & Selman, 2001).

Has Allport Been Supported?

Allport's focus on the evaluation of intergroup relations programs and his attention to evaluation design seem completely modern. He stressed the necessity of conducting evaluations of all intergroup relations programs, despite the problems inherent in evaluations, and he was a strong advocate of the use of sophisticated methodologies in conducting this research. For example, Allport noted the importance of control groups, something that was missing from most evaluation research of the 1950s. Increasingly, programs are being evaluated in a manner which Allport would approve. We also think that Allport would be excited to see how the types of programs he identified in 1954 have flourished and become integrated into institutions such as schools and business organizations. In addition, Allport could not possibly have imagined the variety of intergroup relations programs that have been devised. In general, Allport's approach has stood the test of time, with the one exception noted in the preceding section – he did not anticipate how programs can address structural aspects of discrimination.

Future Directions: Recommendations for Programs and Evaluations

Following Allport, we argue that a concern for intergroup relations should be a recurring theme from childhood to adulthood and should extend into the workplace, recreational settings, and the community. These programs should be tailored to suit the emotional, social, and intellectual maturity of the participants and should take into consideration local conditions affecting intergroup relations.

Clearly, more and better research is needed on the effectiveness of intergroup relations programs in order to refine and improve them. The ideal quantitative study would follow Allport's specifications (pre- and post-test, the use of control groups, and longitudinal measurements). In addition, systematic qualitative and quantitative data on the specific processes that are believed to bring about favorable changes in attitudes and behavior are needed. Research has barely begun on the processes that mediate change in intergroup relations programs. The psychological literature is replete with candidates for these processes including: creating value–behavior discrepancies, reducing threat (see Smith & Mackie's ch. 22 this volume), increasing perceptions of ingroup–outgroup similarities, creating superordinate groups (see Gaertner & Dovidio's ch. 5 this volume), emphasizing multiple identities, reinforcing and modeling positive intergroup behaviors (see Crandall & Stangor's ch. 18 this volume), modifying deleterious associations between cognition and affect, creating dissonance to induce attitude change, creating empathy, correcting misattributions about outgroup members, counteracting negative expectancies, increasing the use of self-regulation (see Devine's ch. 20 this volume), and differentiating among outgroup members (for reviews see Dovidio, Gaertner, Esses, & Hodson, 2004; Stephan & Stephan, 2001).

In addition, comparative studies are needed. Currently, it is not known which programs are most effective with participants from specific racial and ethnic groups, with males or females, and with younger or older participants. Likewise, it is not known know which types of programs are most effective in educational, work, or community settings. Although some intergroup relations programs (e.g., cooperative learning) are used in many countries, we know of no studies comparing a particular program's outcomes across cultures.

The evaluations of these programs should cast a broader net. Most evaluations currently concentrate on short-term changes in perceptions and a limited range of self-reported behaviors (e.g., intergroup friendships). Considerably less in known about whether or not these programs improve intergroup relations skills, increase intergroup communication competence, and decrease intergroup conflicts. The effects of these programs on the institutions in which they are conducted should also be examined. Do institutions become more egalitarian, just, and caring as a consequence of these programs? In addition, a broader range of long-term effects of these programs should be studied, such as social activism, job choices, neighborhood choices, voting, philanthropic donations, adult friendships, and other indices of intergroup interaction at work and in recreational settings.

All of these programs would be more effective if they not only attempted to change the attitudes and behaviors of individuals, but sought to modify the institutions within which they are conducted and the society in which the participants live. Many of these programs would benefit from a greater emphasis on teaching about structural inequalities in society and their causes and cures. All of these programs should recognize that individual change is not sufficient; it must be accompanied by structural changes in society as well, especially changes that affect inequalities in income, education, political power, and healthcare (Phillips, 2002).

Intergroup relations programs show great promise of helping to achieve the goal of a society in which different groups coexist with mutual respect and understanding. These programs and their theoretical underpinnings owe an enormous debt to Gordon Allport's work. However, these programs are young yet, and much work remains to be done to refine, implement, evaluate, and disseminate them. Practitioners and researchers alike would do well to reread *The Nature of Prejudice* as they develop and evaluate intergroup relations programs.

REFERENCES

Allport, G. W. (1954/1979). *The nature of prejudice.* Cambridge, MA: Addison-Wesley.

Aronson, E., Blaney, N., Stephan, C., Sikes, J., & Snapp, M. (1978). *The jigsaw classroom.* Beverly Hills, CA: Sage.

Banks, J. A. (1973). *Teaching ethnic studies: Concepts and strategies.* Washington, DC: National Council for the Social Studies.

Banks, J. A. (1997). *Educating citizens in a multicultural society.* New York: Teachers College Press.

Bardige, B. (1981). Facing History and Ourselves: Tracing development through analysis of student journals. *Moral Education Forum, 6,* 42–8.

Bargal, D. & Bar, H. (1992). A Lewinian approach to intergroup workshops for Arab-Palestinian and Jewish youth. *Journal of Social Issues, 48,* 139–54.

Battistich, V., Solomon, D., Kim, D., Watson, M., & Schaps, E. (1995). Schools as communities, poverty levels of student populations, and students' attitudes, motives, and performance: A multilevel analysis. *American Educational Research Journal, 32,* 627–58.

Battistich, V., Solomon, D., Watson, M., Solomon, J., & Schaps, E. (1989). Effects of an elementary school program to enhance prosocial behavior on children's cognitive-social problem-solving skills and strategies. *Journal of Applied Developmental Psychology, 10,* 147–69.

Blaney, N., Stephan, C., Rosenfield, D., Aronson, E., & Sikes, J. (1977). Interdependence in the classroom: A field study. *Journal of Educational Psychology, 69,* 121–8.

Carruthers, W. L., Sweeney, B., Kmitta, D., & Harris, G. (1996). Conflict resolution: An examination of the research literature and a model for program evaluation. *School Counselor*, *44*, 5–18.

Coleman, P. T. & Deutsch, M. (1998). The mediation of interethnic conflict in schools. In E. Weiner (Ed.), *Handbook of Interethnic Coexistence* (pp. 447–63). New York: Continuum.

Davidson, F. H. & Davidson, M. M. (1994). *Changing childhood prejudice: the caring work of school*. Westport, CT: Bergin and Garvey.

Deutsch, M. (1992). *The effects of training in conflict resolution and cooperative learning in an alternative high school*. New York: Teachers College, Columbia University, International Center for Cooperation and Conflict Resolution.

DeVries, D. L., Edwards, K. J., & Slavin, R. E. (1978). Biracial learning teams and race relations in the classroom: Four field experiments on Teams-Games-Tournaments. *Journal of Educational Psychology*, *70*, 356–62.

Dovidio, J. F., Gaertner, S. L., Esses, V. M., & Hodson, G. (2004). From intervention to outcome: Processes in the reduction of bias. In W. G. Stephan & W. P. Vogt (eds.), *Learning together: Intergroup relations programs*. New York: Teachers College Press.

Fine, M. (1995). *Habits of the mind: Struggling over values in America's classrooms*. San Francisco: Jossey-Bass.

Fisher, R. J. (1990). *The social psychology of intergroup and international conflict resolution*. New York: Springer Verlag.

Gurin, P., Nagda, R., & Lopez, G. (2004). The benefits of diversity in education for democratic citizenship. *Journal of Social Issues*, *60*, 17–34.

Gurin, P., Peng, T., Lopez, G., & Nagda, B. R. (1999). Context, identity, and intergroup relations. In D. Prentice & D. Miller (eds.), *Cultural divides: The social psychology of intergroup contact* (pp. 133–70). New York: Russell Sage Foundation.

Hertz-Lazarowitz, R., Kupermintz, H., & Lang, J. (1998). Arab–Jewish coexistence: Beit Hagafen coexistence programs. In E. Weiner (ed.), *The handbook of interethnic coexistence* (pp. 565–84). New York: Continuum.

Johnson, D. W. & Johnson, R. T. (1989). *Cooperation and competition: Theory and research*. Edina, MN: Interaction Books.

Johnson, D. W. & Johnson, R. T. (1992). Positive interdependence: Key to effective cooperation. In R. Hertz-Lazarowitz and N. Miller (eds.) *Interaction in cooperative groups* (pp. 174–99). New York: Cambridge University Press.

Johnson, D. W. & Johnson, R. T. (1996). Conflict resolution and peer mediation programs in elementary and secondary schools: A review of the research. *Review of Educational Research*, *66*, 459–506.

Johnson, D. W. & Johnson, R. T. (2000). The three C's of reducing prejudice and discrimination. In S. Oskamp (ed.), *Reducing prejudice and discrimination* (pp. 239–68). Hillsdale, NJ: Erlbaum.

Katz, J. H. (1975). *White awareness: Handbook for anti-racism training*. Norman, OK: University of Oklahoma Press.

Kohlberg, L. (1969). Stage and sequence: The cognitive developmental approach to socialization. In D.

A. Goslin (eds.), *Handbook of socialization theory and research* (pp. 347–480). Chicago: Rand McNally.

Kohlberg, L. (1981). *Essays on moral development*. New York: Harper and Row.

Lam, J. A. (1989). *The impact of conflict resolution programs on schools: A review and synthesis of the evidence*. Amherst, MA: National Association for Mediation in Education.

Landis, D., Day, H. R., McGrew, P. L., Thomas, J. A., & Miller, A. B. (1976). Can a "Black" cultural assimilator increase racial understanding. *Journal of Social Issues, 32,* 169–83.

Lieberman, M. (1981). Facing History and Ourselves: A project evaluation. *Moral Education Forum, 6,* 36–41.

Lopez, G., Gurin, P., & Nagda, B. R. (1998). Education and understanding structural causes of group inequalities. *Political Psychology, 19,* 305–29.

Martin, P. & Widgren, J. (2002). International migration: Facing the challenge. *Population Bulletin, 57,* 3–40.

Nagda, B. A. & Zuniga, X. (2003). Fostering meaningful racial engagement through intergroup dialogues. *Group Processes and Intergroup Relations, 6,* 111–28.

Oser, F. K. (1985). Moral education and values education: The discourse perspective. In M. C. Wittrock (ed.), *Handbook of research on teaching* (3rd ed.). New York: Macmillan.

Phillips, K. P. (2002). *Wealth and democracy: A political history of the American rich*. New York: Broadway Books.

Power, F. C., Higgins, A., & Kohlberg, L. (1989). *Lawrence Kohlberg's approach to moral education*. New York: Columbia University Press.

Rynes, S. & Rosen, B. (1995). A field survey of factors affecting the adoption and perceived success of diversity training. *Personnel Psychology, 48,* 247–70.

Schultz, L. H., Barr, D. J., & Selman, R. L. (2001). The value of a developmental approach to evaluating character development programs: An outcome study of Facing History and Ourselves. *Journal of Moral Education, 30,* 3–27.

Slavin, R. E. (1995). *Cooperative learning: Theory, research, and practice* (2nd ed.). Boston: Allyn & Bacon.

Stephan, C. W., Renfro, L., & Stephan, W. G. (2004). The evaluation of intergroup relations programs: Techniques and a meta-analysis. In W. G. Stephan & W. P. Vogt (eds.), *Learning together: Intergroup relations programs*. New York: Teachers College Press.

Stephan, W. G. & Stephan, C. W. (2001). *Improving intergroup relations*. Thousand Oaks, CA: Sage.

Stephan, C. W. & Stephan, W. G. (2004). Intergroup relations in multicultural education programs. In J. A. Banks and C. McGee-Banks (eds.), *Handbook of research on multicultural education* (2nd ed.). New York: Jossey-Bass.

Tansik, D. A. & Driskill, J. D. (1977). Temporal persistence of attitudes induced through required training. *Group and Organization Studies, 2,* 310–23.

Weigel, R. H., Wiser, P. L., & Cook, S. W. (1975). The impact of cooperative learning experiences on cross-ethnic relations and helping. *Journal of Social Issues, 31,* 219–44.

Author Index

Subject Index